Remedies

Remedies

Basic Principles, Authorities, and Problems

Nicholas Emanuel
<small>SANTA CLARA UNIVERSITY SCHOOL OF LAW</small>

CAROLINA ACADEMIC PRESS
Durham, North Carolina

ISBN 978-1-5310-2182-5
eISBN 978-1-5310-2183-2
LCCN 2021947135

Carolina Academic Press, LLC
700 Kent Street
Durham, North Carolina 27701
(919) 489-7486
www.cap-press.com

Printed in the United States of America

For Nicole; and for Grayson and Everly.

Contents

Table of Cases

Preface

This is a casebook for a course on judicial remedies, designed for the modern law school curriculum. It covers the remedies concepts most likely to be tested on bar exams and encountered by lawyers in practice. It leans toward the practical more than the theoretical; the aim is to provide students with a firm grasp of the basic principles and illustrate how those principles operate in different situations.

Organization of the book tracks the way a remedies issue is approached analytically. Compensatory damages are discussed first, followed by injunctions and other specific relief awarded in situations where damages are not adequate. Tort and contract damages are handled separately, as are equitable remedies particular to contracts. After the major remedies are covered, later topics zoom out for a broader perspective. A chapter on selecting remedies looks at considerations for practitioners in deciding between remedies when multiple options are available. A chapter on remedies for civil rights violations explores how remedies can be an instrument of social justice.

The length of the text is intended to allow for cover-to-cover teaching. Instructors should be able to assign manageable readings and still finish most, if not all, of the chapters in a standard three-unit course.

The book presents the material in an approachable way. Concise, understandable explanations of legal rules are followed by edited cases involving those principles. All cases are preceded by introductory notes that set the stage with a description of the litigation and an overview of the issues.

The cases were chosen not only for their clear statements of the relevant rules along with thoughtful analysis but also for their overall readability. Though edited liberally for brevity, the opinions contain everything necessary to understand the issues and the reasoning behind the decision. (Omitted text is indicated by ellipses; footnotes have been omitted without notation.) Citations within opinions are mostly preserved to provide a reference point for further study if desired.

Contemporary authorities are presented whenever possible so students can see how courts use remedies to resolve disputes arising from today's challenges—for example, devastating wildfires, the COVID-19 pandemic, and racial injustice. But the staples of any remedies course—*Hadley v. Baxendale* and *Winter v. Natural Resources Defense Council*, for example—are here, too.

Instead of extensive notes following the cases, immediately before the cases in each section are several "things to think about," or questions to consider while reading. This positioning provides context and allows students to read cases as lawyers do: not aimlessly but searching for an answer to a specific question. Having the questions in mind while reading the cases enhances comprehension and focuses attention on the relevant issues.

Problems are included throughout the text to use as independent study aids or for classroom discussion. The problems present brief, easily digestible factual scenarios that allow the rules discussed in each section to be applied in a new setting.

The ultimate goal is to leave readers with an understanding of the different remedies available to litigants and an appreciation of how those remedies work as part of a system to resolve disputes.

Online Materials

Additional content for *Remedies: Basic Principles, Authorities, and Problems* is available on Carolina Academic Press's *Core Knowledge for Lawyers* (CKL) website.

Core Knowledge for Lawyers is an online teaching and testing platform that hosts practice questions and additional content for both instructors and students.

To learn more, please visit:

coreknowledgeforlawyers.com

Instructors may request complimentary access through the "Faculty & Instructors" link.

Remedies

Chapter 1

Judicial Remedies: An Introduction and Historical Perspective

Introduction to Remedies

A remedy is a device to resolve a problem. In medicine, a remedy cures an illness. In the law, a remedy provides justice to someone who has been legally wronged. Remedies provided by a court are judicial remedies. (Remedies can come from other sources, too — administrative tribunals and private dispute resolution processes like arbitration are common alternatives.)

One way to think about judicial remedies is as the benefit a plaintiff can obtain through a lawsuit. A person can sue for any number of legally recognized harms; having done so, what can the plaintiff expect to achieve through that lawsuit? Another way to view remedies is as the different tools a court has available to resolve a dispute. Civil litigation always involves a dispute of some kind. The court's role is to resolve it. Remedies are the ways a court can do that.

The study of judicial remedies encompasses a variety of procedural mechanisms and rules of law. The basic idea behind remedial jurisprudence is that for every recognized legal wrong there is a corresponding and appropriate remedy.

Some remedies are substitutionary, intended to replace what a plaintiff has lost. An example of substitutionary relief is monetary damages.

Other remedies are specific, intended to reverse or eliminate a harm. An example of specific relief is an order requiring that the terms of a contract be performed (specific performance).

The different remedies available to a plaintiff are further categorized as either legal or equitable. The primary difference between legal and equitable remedies is in the way the remedy is enforced. Legal remedies are enforced by a court issuing a judgment, which can then be executed by attaching or recording a lien on the defendant's property. Equitable remedies are effectuated by a court issuing an order requiring a person to do something. A violation of the order can result in the violator being punished for contempt of court.

For the civil practitioner, it is essential to be aware of the remedies available for torts, breaches of contract, and unjust enrichment. One remedy may be more beneficial than another, depending on the situation. And some remedies are available only for certain kinds of wrongs.

It is also important to understand the policy decisions reflected by the availability of certain remedies. Allowing or precluding a remedy for a particular wrong is not accidental. It is a considered legislative or judicial choice designed to achieve a specific policy goal.

Historical Perspective

A brief look at the history underlying our current remedial system is helpful not only because it puts things in context but also because there are historical reasons for some aspects of it — meaning certain things are the way they are because that is how they used to be.

The American legal system is modeled on England's, which existed long before the United States'. Indeed, the English system can be traced back more than 1,000 years, to a time when justice was administered by a combination of local government officials and the monarchy.

Early English justice bore little resemblance to the courts of today. Remarkably (at least to modern sensibilities), trial by combat was the usual method of resolving property ownership disputes. The process called for litigants to physically fight, with the winner deemed the rightful owner of the property at issue.

By the 12th century, the system had evolved to a more formal process. The king began designating local knights or persons of nobility to resolve disputes regarding title to land that arose within their jurisdiction. One might think of those knights as the first federal district judges.

The judges appointed by the king made decisions based on the common law and were therefore said to preside over a court of law. Courts of law had authority to issue judgments requiring a defendant to pay money. While surely an improvement over trial by combat, the procedural rules governing courts of law were rigid. Petitioners who did not strictly comply with the rules — by failing to plead their claim for relief in the precise language required, for instance — were denied recovery altogether.

Worse still, courts of law fell into widespread corruption. Petitioners who were poor or of lower status often found they were not treated fairly, particularly when the defendant was wealthy and powerful. Those who won a judgment against a politically powerful defendant sometimes discovered the courts simply would not enforce it.

Eventually, those who felt the common law court had not adequately resolved their dispute, whether due to noncompliance with technical requirements or to corruption, started petitioning directly to the king for redress of their grievances. Facing a deluge of these petitions for equitable relief, the king appointed a chancellor to rule on them. The result was the creation of the court of equity. In the equity courts, the chancellor could not issue monetary judgments like a court of law but instead could order a person to perform a particular act. And — in contrast to the rule-bound courts of law — the chancellor had broad authority to make whatever orders were necessary to achieve a fair outcome.

Not every dispute could be brought to the court of equity, however. A petitioner was entitled to seek equitable relief from the chancellor only by first showing that no adequate remedy could be obtained from the court of law.

The court of equity and court of law employed different procedures to resolve cases. For instance, courts of law used juries comprised of local community members to decide which party should prevail. In the court of equity, the chancellor alone made the decision. And when a court of law ruled in favor of a party, it issued a judgment — a proclamation of how much the prevailing party was entitled to collect from the defendant. In a court of equity, the chancellor issued an order directly compelling a party to do something.

Colonial settlements imported this dual court structure to America. When the United States became an independent country, the founders retained some of the traditional distinction between law and equity (Article III of the Constitution refers to "all cases, in law and equity"), but Congress fashioned the judiciary without creating separate legal and equitable courts. With the adoption of the Federal Rules of Civil Procedure in 1938, federal judges were expressly empowered to hear suits arising both in law and in equity.

The individual states initially had separate law and equity courts, but that began to change in the mid-19th century. In 1848, New York adopted procedures to unify law and equity. Other states soon followed suit, and today only Delaware, Mississippi, Tennessee, New Jersey, Arkansas, and South Carolina maintain any meaningful distinction between law and equity courts.

Procedural differences between legal and equitable claims generally persist, however. Jury trials are allowed for claims seeking legal relief but not for equitable claims. Equitable relief can be denied unless the legal remedy of damages is inadequate. Equitable remedies are still enforced by way of an *in personam* order; legal remedies are enforced by judgments that operate *in rem*.

And, at least in theory if not practice, judges deciding equitable claims have flexibility to rule in a way that is fair under the circumstances and less constrained by procedural rules — a remnant of a time when chancellors of equity were appointed by the king to ensure complete justice was done where none could be found in a court of law.

Introductory Note — *Clark v. Teeven Holding Co.*

Clark is a real estate nondisclosure case from Delaware, a jurisdiction that has retained separate law and equity courts. The plaintiff filed the lawsuit in the equity branch; the defendant moved to dismiss for lack of subject matter jurisdiction. In ruling on the motion, the court must decide if the claims alleged in the complaint are the kind that can properly be brought in a court of equity.

THINGS TO THINK ABOUT while reading *Clark v. Teeven Holding Co*:

1. How does the historical separation of law and equity courts affect modern litigation?

2. What does the term "jurisdiction" mean in the context of a court's jurisdiction over either legal or equitable claims?

Clark v. Teeven Holding Co.

Delaware Court of Chancery
625 A.2d 869 (1992)

HARTNETT, Vice Chancellor.

This controversy arose because the purchaser of a parcel of real estate, Teeven Holding Company, Inc. ("Teeven"), discovered that the lands it purchased were contaminated by seepage from an underground storage tank. . . .

Teeven joined in this suit certain third-party defendants, and sought to assert money damages against them arising from the contamination.

The third-party defendants have now moved to dismiss this action as to them alleging that this Court does not have jurisdiction to hear the claims asserted by the plaintiff (Teeven) because the complaint essentially alleges a claim for money damages for which there is an adequate remedy at law.

The motion to dismiss must be granted because there is an adequate remedy at law for all the claims.

On August 15, 1988, defendant/third-party plaintiff Teeven Holding Company, Inc. (Teeven) purchased property located on E. Main Street in Newark, Delaware from third-party defendant, the Estate of Grace W. McCambridge.

Prior to the purchase of the property by Teeven, the other third-party defendants allegedly had owned the property or had conducted a dry cleaning business on the property. After taking title to the property, Teeven discovered underground storage tanks and notified the Delaware Department of Natural Resources and Environmental Control ("the Department") of its intent to remove the tanks. During the course of removing the tanks, soil samples were taken that revealed that the subsurface soils had been contaminated by petroleum products and tetrachlorethane. Teeven and the Department then agreed to a remedial plan to reduce the contaminants in the subsurface soils and groundwater. . . .

I

On October 19, 1990, Teeven filed a complaint against the third-party defendants alleging that they were liable to Teeven for any remediation costs incurred by it pursuant to the Consent Order. In the complaint it was alleged that the defendants were liable to Teeven under several legal theories and Teeven prayed for a declaratory judgment and money damages. On May 26, 1992, this Court granted Teeven leave to amend its complaint to join additional third-party defendants and to add an additional claim under the provisions of the Delaware Hazardous Substance Cleanup Act ("Hazardous Substance Act"), 7 *Del.C.* Ch. 91, seeking relief similar to that sought in the original third-party complaint.

On December 27, 1991, one of the third-party defendants M & M Cleaners, Inc. filed a motion to dismiss the complaint for lack of subject matter jurisdiction pursuant to Chancery Court Rule 12(b)(1) on the grounds that this Court lacked subject matter jurisdiction over the underlying action filed by the Department against Teeven and that, in any case, Teeven has an adequate remedy at law for its claims.

II

This Court as a court of limited jurisdiction exercises jurisdiction only "over all matters and causes in equity". 10 *Del.C.* § 341. It has the same jurisdiction as the English High Court of Chancery had in 1776. *Glanding v. Industrial Trust Co.*, Del. Supr., 45 A.2d 553, 555–56 (1945). This Court thus has jurisdiction to hear such traditional, equitable matters as trusts and fiduciary relations. It also has jurisdiction to hear claims where the law courts cannot afford an adequate remedy. Thus, this Court exercises jurisdiction over matters where an injunction is sought. 1 POMEROY, *Equity Jurisprudence* § 139 (5th ed. 1951).

This Court may also exercise jurisdiction in matters that were unknown in 1776 but where there is today no adequate remedy in any other court. *Severns v. Wilmington Medical Center, Inc.*, Del.Supr., 421 A.2d 1334 (1980).

The General Assembly may also expand the jurisdiction of the Court of Chancery beyond the bounds of the jurisdiction of the English High Court of Chancery as it existed in 1776 by adding jurisdiction by statute. *See, e.g.,* 8 *Del.C.* § 225 (granting authority to Court of Chancery to adjudicate results of corporate elections).

10 *Del.C.* § 342 provides:

> The Court of Chancery shall not have jurisdiction to determine any matter wherein sufficient remedy may be had by common law, or statute, before any other court or jurisdiction of this State.

The Delaware Supreme Court in *Glanding v. Industrial Trust Co.*, Del.Supr., 45 A.2d 553 (1945), held that the predecessor to 10 *Del.C.* § 342 merely represented a legislative declaration of a traditional maxim by which equity courts defined their jurisdiction and that the statute "did not operate as a restriction or limitation of the exercise of equitable jurisdiction. *Id.* at 557. Therefore, the Court held that if the subject matter of a claim was within the jurisdiction of the English High Court of Chancery in 1776, this Court's jurisdiction over that subject matter would not be divested by the General Assembly granting jurisdiction over it to another court of this State unless it was clear the General Assembly intended to abrogate the jurisdiction of the Court of Chancery. *Id.* at 559–60. Absent a manifestation of such intent, the Court held that a person could elect to proceed either in the Court of Chancery or the other court in which the General Assembly had granted jurisdiction. *Id.* at 560.

Similar reasoning applies in situations in which the law courts assume jurisdiction over a right or remedy that was traditionally equitable. As Judge Rodney observed:

> [Chancery] will not allow itself to be ousted of any part of its original jurisdiction because a court of law happens to fall in love with the same or a similar jurisdiction.

Glanding v. Industrial Trust Co., Del.Supr., 45 A.2d at 565 (1945) (Rodney, J., dissenting) (quoting *Fox v. Wharton,* 5 Del.Ch. 200 (1878).

While a court of equity may not be deprived of its jurisdiction simply because a court of law has expanded its jurisdiction into a particular area, equitable jurisdiction may be abandoned. 1 POMEROY, *Equity Jurisprudence* § 281a (5th ed. 1941). For example, a court of equity will no longer entertain a suit simply because it is brought by the assignee of a debt or of a chose in action. *Id., Illinois Finance Co. v. Interstate Rural Credit Ass'n,* Del.Ch., 101 A. 870 (1917). Similarly, while courts of equity may originally have had jurisdiction over all instances of fraud, equity today will assume jurisdiction over fraud only when other equitable relief — such as equitable rescission — is sought. *Hegarty v. American Commonwealths Power Corp.,* Del.Ch., 163 A. 616 (1932); McCLINTOCK, *Equity* § 84 (1948).

Equity may also, at its discretion, exercise concurrent jurisdiction over a purely legal claim for which there is an adequate remedy at law in the course of deciding other claims for which equity jurisdiction exists. *Getty Ref. & Marketing Co. v. Park Oil, Inc.,* Del.Ch., 385 A.2d 147 (1978).

The term "equity jurisdiction" is often misunderstood. The term "jurisdiction of a court" usually is used to mean the power conferred upon a court by the sovereign authority to consider and determine controversies and to enforce its decisions. The term "equity jurisdiction", however, correctly means something else, i.e., the aggregate of the controversies in which the Court of Chancery may properly exercise its power to grant equitable relief. McCLINTOCK, *Equity* § 40 (West Pub. Co. 2d ed. 1948).

III

To determine whether this Court should entertain Teeven's third-party complaint, each claim in it must be considered *seriatim* to determine if an adequate remedy for it exists at law.

Teeven first alleges, in its third-party complaint, that the third-party defendants are strictly liable to it because they conducted an ultrahazardous activity. This claim is clearly a claim for money damages and the law courts afford an adequate remedy for it.

IV

Teeven next alleges that certain third-party defendants committed fraud. Whether a claim for fraud asserted by an alleged defrauded purchaser may be brought as a legal or equitable claim depends upon the relief sought. A defrauded party may elect to affirm the challenged contract and seek money damages. He then has an action at law for the tort of deceit. *Hegarty v. American Commonwealths Power Corp.*, Del.Ch., 163 A. 616, 619 (1932). On the other hand, a defrauded purchaser may elect to disaffirm the contract and be restored to the status quo ante. In such a case, he would have an equitable action for rescission. *Hegarty, supra,* 163 A. at 618. Teeven, however, does not seek to rescind the contract to purchase the property but instead seeks money damages for the alleged fraud on it by the sellers. Teeven, therefore, has an adequate remedy at law for its claim for damages arising from fraudulent conduct. . . .

V

For the reasons stated above, Teeven has an adequate remedy at law for all its claims and there is no reason why this Court should entertain them. While the motion to dismiss was brought by certain third-party defendants only and did not address Teeven's Hazardous Substance Act claim, the third-party action must be dismissed as to all claims. This Court has the power to dismiss an action for lack of equity jurisdiction *sua sponte.* Therefore, the motion of certain third-party defendants to dismiss will be granted and the amended third-party complaint will be dismissed in its entirety, subject to an election of transfer of these claims to the Superior Court pursuant to 10 *Del.C.* §1902.

IT IS SO ORDERED.

* * *

Problem 1

To obtain equitable relief, a plaintiff traditionally had to show that damages were not an adequate remedy. Are damages adequate in the following situation? Why or why not?

A grocer agreed to purchase $5,000 worth of apples from an apple grower. The grocer changes his mind and refuses to buy the apples after finding them for a lower price. The apple grower is unable to procure a new buyer, so the apples rot and become worthless. The apple grower sues the grocer for breaching the agreement.

Introductory Note — *Thomerson v. DeVito*

Thomerson comes from South Carolina, another state that maintains distinct legal and equitable branches of the court. But the issue presented is not whether the plaintiff can bring his lawsuit in a particular branch; rather, it is whether he can pursue the suit at all — if the statute of limitations for legal claims applies to the cause of action for promissory estoppel, the suit is time barred. The result hinges on the distinction between legal and equitable remedies. A dissenting justice eschews any continued procedural distinction between the two.

THINGS TO THINK ABOUT while reading *Thomerson v. DeVito*:

1. How does a court determine whether the plaintiff is seeking legal or equitable relief?

2. What is the justification for not applying the statute of limitations to an equitable claim?

3. What reasons might there be for continuing to distinguish between legal and equitable claims?

Thomerson v. DeVito

South Carolina Supreme Court

844 S.E.2d 378 (2020)

CHIEF JUSTICE BEATTY:

. . . .

Facts

Plaintiff alleges Defendants, the former owners of Lenco Marine (a manufacturer of boat products), failed to give him a three-percent ownership interest in Lenco that was promised to him as part of his compensation package. Plaintiff was hired by Lenco no later than May 2007. Defendant Samuel Mullinax was the CEO of Lenco and Defendant Richard DeVito was its president. Lenco was sold in December 2016 to Power Products, LLC.

In his complaint, Plaintiff asserted claims against Defendants for (1) breach of contract and the covenant of good faith and fair dealing, (2) promissory estoppel, (3) *quantum meruit* and unjust enrichment, (4) negligent misrepresentation, (5) constructive fraud, and (6) amounts due under the South Carolina Payment of Wages Act. Defendants moved for summary judgment, arguing the claims were time-barred. . . .

The district court granted summary judgment to Defendants on all of Plaintiff's claims — except promissory estoppel — on the basis they were time-barred by the three-year statute of limitations contained in S.C. Code Ann. §15-3-530 (2005). The district court found Plaintiff should have known he potentially had a claim against Defendants in 2013 (after the litigation concluded with Bennett Marine and the equity shares were not distributed). The parties disagreed on whether the claim for promissory estoppel was subject to the three-year statute of limitations. The district court certified this question to the Court after finding it presented a question of law that could be outcome determinative and there appeared to be no controlling state precedent.

Discussion

Plaintiff contends this Court has held promissory estoppel is an equitable claim and has expressly stated in long-standing precedent that the statute of limitations is not applicable to equitable claims. As a result, the statute of limitations in S.C. Code Ann. §15-3-530 (2005) is not directly applicable to a claim for promissory estoppel. Defendants, in contrast, assert Plaintiff is seeking monetary damages, which they contend is legal, not equitable, relief. Defendants note promissory estoppel has been described in our case law as a quasi-contractual equitable remedy and that the statute of limitations has been applied to claims for *quantum meruit*, which has also been characterized as a quasi-contract, so application of the statute of limitations should be extended to claims for promissory estoppel, either under the subsection governing contracts, obligations, or liabilities (express or implied) in S.C. Code Ann. §15-3-530(1), or the subsection applicable to injuries to the rights of others not arising on contract or enumerated by law, contained in S.C. Code Ann. §15-3-530(5). We agree with Plaintiff that the statute of limitations is not applicable to a claim of promissory estoppel. Our decision rests on (A) an examination of our statute of limitations, and (B) the determination whether a claim for promissory estoppel is properly characterized as legal or equitable in nature.

A. The Statute of Limitations

This Court has long recognized that the statute of limitations now codified in section 15-3-530 applies to actions at law, while the doctrine of laches applies to suits in equity. Although the statute of limitations may be applied by analogy in a court of equity, the court has the authority to extend that period if it believes a longer period is warranted under the circumstances. This distinction logically flows from the fact that equity transcends the direct application of legal restrictions such as the statute of limitations to provide relief to wronged parties where the law otherwise affords no relief:

> This Court has held that the statute of limitations does not apply to actions in equity. *See Anderson v. Purvis*, 211 S.C. 255, 44 S.E.2d 611 (1947); *Anderson v. Purvis*, 220 S.C. 259, 67 S.E.2d 80 (1951) (holding that the Court's power to do equity transcends the limitations of the statute of limitations).

Dixon v. Dixon, 362 S.C. 388, 400, 608 S.E.2d 849, 855 (2005)[.]

[I]f "obligation" is read as broadly as urged by Defendants, it could potentially envelope a multitude of claims, whether at law or in equity, erasing the historic distinctions between the two. In our view, this interpretation would extend the statute's reach much further than was ever intended by the General Assembly. . . . Thus, whether the statute of limitations applies to a claim for promissory estoppel turns on the characterization of the claim as legal or equitable.

B. Development and Characterization of Promissory Estoppel

. . . This Court has stated the basis of the doctrine lies not so much in contract, but rather, it is an application of the equitable principle of estoppel[.]

South Carolina courts have consistently characterized promissory estoppel as an equitable claim. . . . It has also been observed that "[p]romissory estoppel is a quasi-contract remedy." *See, e.g., N. Am. Rescue Prods., Inc. v. Richardson*, 411 S.C. 371, 379 (2015) (citing *Higgins*). A "quasi-contract" has been defined as "an obligation imposed by law because of some special relationship between the parties or because one of them would otherwise be unjustly enriched"; it "is not actually a contract *but instead a remedy* that allows the plaintiff to recover a benefit conferred on the defendant." *Quasi-Contract*, Black's Law Dictionary (11th ed. 2019) (emphasis added). It is also termed an "implied-in-law contract." *Id.* . . .

Defendants assert Plaintiff's claim is subject to section 15-3-530 because it "is an equitable quasi-contractual remedy when it seeks money damages." . . . Describing promissory estoppel as quasi-contractual is not dispositive of the issue before us. . . . A request for monetary relief should not be viewed in isolation to convert what is otherwise an equitable claim to a legal claim. . . . Monetary relief is not available at law for an unenforceable promise. Thus, monetary relief is not properly characterized as legal if the source for its recovery lies solely in a principle of equity. The claim — and the remedy — are still equitable because the recovery does not exist at law but is provided solely to avoid injustice in a court of equity. In this case, if Defendants had not sold the company, Plaintiff would be seeking transfer of the promised equity shares. The relief awarded is ultimately an equitable matter for the court to determine, not a jury. The fact that a court might have to fashion some other equitable relief for the unmet promise (assuming Plaintiff is able to establish his claim), does not lessen its overall nature as equitable. *See generally* 28 Am. Jur. 2d *Estoppel and Waiver* § 51 (2011) (stating "[a] trial court retains broad discretion under promissory estoppel to fashion whatever remedies or damages justice requires"). As a result, equitable defenses such as laches, not the statute of limitations, apply. . . .

Conclusion

Based on the foregoing, we answer the certified question in the negative. The statute of limitations in S.C. Code Ann. § 15-3-530 does not apply to a claim for promissory estoppel.

KITTREDGE, HEARN and JAMES, JJ., concur. FEW, J., dissenting in a separate opinion.

Justice Few

I would apply the statute of limitations to all actions for money damages. For this reason, I respectfully dissent.

The procedural differences between actions at law and suits in equity arose centuries ago for accidental reasons hardly known to any modern South Carolina lawyer or judge. Not long after the already outdated distinctions arrived in the new world, states began refusing to recognize them. In New York in 1848, for example, the legislature provided in the new "Field Code,"

> The distinction between actions at law and suits in equity, and the forms of all such actions and suits heretofore existing, are abolished; and there shall be in this state, hereafter, but one form of action, for the enforcement or protection of private rights and the redress or prevention of private wrongs, which shall be denominated a civil action.

Charles E. Clark, *The Union of Law and Equity*, 25 Colum. L. Rev. 1, 1 (1925) (quoting N.Y. Laws 1848, c. 379 § 62).

The movement to do away with meaningless differences between actions at law and suits in equity continued into the twentieth century. *See* Edward R. Taylor, *The Fusion of Law and Equity*, 66 U. Pa. L. Rev. 17 (1917). Discussing his view of how an "organized, civilized society" should approach a meaningful unity of the divergent systems, this author wrote, "Until we have taken steps to achieve that [unity] we are simply walking round and round like one lost." *Id.* at 17; *see also* Charles T. McCormick, *The Fusion of Law and Equity in United States Courts*, 6 N.C. L. Rev. 283, 285 (1927) ("Any separation of the stream of equity from the main channel of legal administration is today seen to be unjustifiable as an administrative device and explainable only as a historical survival from an era of multitudinous separate courts.").

The unification of the two systems — particularly the elimination of their silly distinctions — hit its full stride in 1938 with Rule 2 of the Federal Rules of Civil Procedure. Rule 2 then provided, "There shall be one form of action to be known as 'civil action.'" Rule 2 now provides, "There is one form of action — the civil action." Fed. R. Civ. P. 2. South Carolina adopted Rule 2 in 1985. "There shall be one form of action to be known as 'civil action.'" Rule 2, SCRCP.

There remain substantive differences between law and equity, but the differences remain because the differences make sense. As Professors Wright, Miller, and Steinman stated, "The Rules have not abrogated the distinction between equitable and legal remedies," but "the procedural distinctions have been abolished." 4 Charles Alan Wright, Arthur R. Miller & Adam N. Steinman, FEDERAL PRACTICE AND PROCEDURE §1043 n.1 (4th ed. 2015). These procedural distinctions were abolished because there was no reason to have the distinctions in the first place.

There is likewise no reason to draw the distinction the majority makes in this case. Whether labeled an action for promissory estoppel in equity or breach of contract in law, Thomerson's action is one action in which he must prove the promise, a breach, and his resulting damages. The consideration he must prove in the law action is no different from the reliance he must prove in the equity action. There is simply no substantive difference arising from the label he puts on the claim. . . .

I would not answer the certified question by merely reciting the answer we used to give in different cases based on procedural distinctions that should no longer exist.

> How absurd for us to go on until the year [2020] obliging judges and lawyers to climb over a barrier which was put up by historical accident in 14th century England. . . .

T. Leigh Anenson, *Treating Equity Like Law: A Post-Merger Justification of Unclean Hands*, 45 Am. Bus. L.J. 455, 455 (2008) (quoting Zechariah Chafee Jr., *Foreword to Selected Essays on Equity* iii, iv (Edward D. Re ed., 1955)).

I respectfully dissent.

* * *

Problem 2

A key distinction between legal and equitable remedies is the manner of enforcement. Would the relief described below be considered a legal or equitable remedy?

A business owner discovers her bookkeeper has embezzled $1,000,000. The bookkeeper transferred that sum from the company's bank account to a personal account labeled "Embezzlement Proceeds." In the business owner's lawsuit against the bookkeeper, the court finds in favor of the business owner and orders: "Defendant shall immediately return to the plaintiff the $1,000,000 in the Embezzlement Proceeds account."

---

equitable
- constructive trust

Chapter 2

Compensatory Damages

Damages are the default remedy in the American civil law system. The system is designed to compensate an injured party with money, which the law assumes to be an adequate replacement for whatever has been lost. When a plaintiff comes to court and claims to have suffered harm, an award of money, payable by the defendant, is usually considered the appropriate remedy. That monetary award is called damages.

Damages are a legal remedy, effectuated by a judgment entered against the defendant that memorializes the sum owed. If the defendant does not voluntarily pay the amount of the judgment, the plaintiff has various options to enforce it. Typical methods of enforcing a judgment are recording a lien against real property owned by the defendant, attaching the defendant's bank account, or garnishing the defendant's wages. So an award of damages is really a conferral of the right to collect a sum from the defendant through various enforcement procedures.

Damages provide substitutionary relief because an award of money does not reverse the harm that has occurred but may instead make up for it. Another way to think about the concept is that damages make a plaintiff whole after an injury or loss — they are intended to put plaintiffs in as favorable a position as they would have been in had the harm not occurred. Damages are meant to be compensatory; they compensate for a loss. That means a central component of a damages award will be the proper calculation of the amount of the plaintiff's loss. The calculation can be fairly straightforward in some cases (breach of a contract to pay a sum of money, for instance) and more complicated in others (years of lost future income for an injured plaintiff unable to work).

Contract and Tort Distinction

One does not have a right to recover damages for every conceivable harm. To be entitled to an award of damages, a plaintiff must prove that the harm resulted from the defendant's invasion of some legally protected interest. Broadly speaking, the law recognizes protected interests in two categories: contract and tort.

When two people make an agreement supported by consideration, the law recognizes a right to performance of that agreement. An invasion of that legally protected interest — the right to receive the other party's performance as agreed — results in an entitlement to damages for breach of contract.

Contract damages promote predictability and stability in economic relationships. In a sense, the availability of contract damages functions as an insurance policy for contracting parties: upon entering into a contract, they can be assured either the other party will do what the contract requires, or, in the event of nonperformance, they will be reimbursed for any resulting financial loss.

Invasions of legally protected interests outside contractual relationships are called torts. For example, the law recognizes a right to be free from exposure to danger because someone else did not act carefully enough. (Stated another way, everyone has a duty to act with reasonable care.) If a person is injured because another person failed to act with reasonable care, that is the tort of negligence.

Tort damages serve a different, and broader, purpose than contract damages. They are intended to compensate for harm caused to the plaintiff but also to protect society's interest in holding wrongdoers responsible for the effects of conduct deemed undesirable. Tort damages additionally create a deterrent to future misconduct.

Cognizable Harm Requirement

A prerequisite to recovering compensatory damages, whether in contract or tort, is some type of injury. The plaintiff must show that the defendant's conduct caused a cognizable harm, the kind for which the law allows monetary recovery. If the defendant's conduct breached a legal obligation but caused no appreciable harm, that may result in an award of nominal damages: a purely symbolic award of no more than $1, recognizing that defendant's conduct was wrongful but the plaintiff was not damaged by it and therefore is not entitled to compensatory damages.

To be entitled to compensatory damages, a plaintiff must precisely articulate the harm for which compensation is requested.

Introductory Note — *Ustrak v. Fairman* and *Gulf, C. & S.F. Railway Co. v. Shepard*

Ustrak is an appeal in a suit against a prison warden by a former inmate (or, as Judge Posner puts it, "an alumnus of the Illinois state prison"). The plaintiff claimed reverse discrimination — less favorable treatment because he is white — and unlawful retaliation for complaining about it. A skeptical Seventh Circuit finds no merit to the discrimination claim. The key issue regarding the retaliation claim, however, is whether the plaintiff demonstrated any harm sufficient to allow for compensatory damages.

Gulf Railway Co. presents a variation on the question of whether a tree falling in the forest makes a sound if no one is around to hear it: if a plaintiff is too intoxicated to remember a harm, did the harm actually occur? The plaintiff was awarded damages for emotional distress after being forcibly removed from a passenger train. On appeal, the defendant train company argued the plaintiff had not suffered any such damages because he was too drunk at the time of the incident to know what was happening.

———————

THINGS TO THINK ABOUT while reading *Ustrak v. Fairman* and *Gulf, C. & S.F. Railway Co. v. Shepard*:

1. Can damages be recovered without proof of liability?

2. Can liability be imposed without proof of damages?

3. What is the fundamental purpose of compensatory damages?

Ustrak v. Fairman

United States Court of Appeals, Seventh Circuit
781 F.2d 573 (1986)

POSNER, Circuit Judge.

Stephen Ustrak, an alumnus of the Illinois state prison at Pontiac, where he served time for burglary and related offenses and for bail jumping, won a verdict of almost $50,000 in compensatory and punitive damages for violations of his civil rights by the warden. 42 U.S.C. §1983. The warden appeals. Ustrak cross-appeals from the grant of summary judgment in the warden's favor on one count in the complaint.

Ustrak is white, as were all the members of the jury; 80 to 90 percent of the prisoners in Pontiac are black, as is the warden, Fairman, although 80 to 90 percent of the prison staff is white. Two of the three claims on which Ustrak prevailed are claims of racial discrimination. The first arises from an incident in which Ustrak was penalized by withdrawal of commissary privileges for one month for having contraband in his cell. Ustrak's cellmate, who was black, was not disciplined, even though there apparently was a practice of punishing both cellmates for possessing contraband in the cell unless it was crystal clear that only one was guilty. Here it was not crystal clear, although the contraband was found on Ustrak's side of the cell. The guard who found the contraband and lodged charges against Ustrak but not his cellmate was white.

Although the warden approved the punishment of Ustrak, there is no evidence that he did so for racial reasons. This ought to end the matter, for no doctrine of superiors' liability is recognized in section 1983 cases. *McKinnon v. City of Berwyn*, 750 F.2d 1383, 1390 (7th Cir.1984); *Duckworth v. Franzen*, 780 F.2d 645, 650 (7th Cir.1985). But the warden waived this ground for challenging the verdict, by failing to object to instructions under which the jury had only to find that he had "purposefully and intentionally concurred in and acquiesced in the discriminatory proceedings brought against Mr. Ustrak." Although the meaning of this instruction is far from clear, we read it as allowing the jury to find against Fairman if it determined that he had been aware of and had approved of Ustrak's being punished even though Ustrak's cellmate was not punished; and of this awareness and approval there was some evidence.

But we do not think a rational trier of fact could have found that Ustrak was a victim of racial discrimination. The contraband was found on Ustrak's side of the cell, so it was natural that he rather than his cellmate was disciplined. There may have been a practice of disciplining both cellmates in a situation such as presented in this case; but in no area of life is discipline meted out with perfect consistency. "Selective, incomplete enforcement of the law is the norm in this country." *Hameetman v. City of Chicago,* 776 F.2d 636, 641 (7th Cir.1985). This is not only because some violations are not detected, but also because the resources for law enforcement are often radically inadequate to the number of violations. The authorities must pick and choose; and given the well-known disciplinary problems of American prisons it is not to be believed that prison authorities never overlook known violations of disciplinary regulations. Moreover, Ustrak's charge of incomplete enforcement focuses on the failure to enforce not a written regulation but an unwritten policy by no means in keeping with the best American traditions: collective guilt. Although the evidence pointed to Ustrak's having brought the contraband into his cell, that policy required punishment of his cellmate as well, even though the cellmate probably was innocent. Failure to enforce consistently a rule of collective guilt is one of the less insidious examples of the selective enforcement of law, provided the inconsistency is not racially motivated. . . .

If the jury verdict stands, Pontiac's guards and officials are exposing themselves to potential liability for racial discrimination every time they fail to attain the unattainable — perfect consistency in enforcing the prison's rules, written and unwritten.

A prima facie case, whether under the equal protection clause of the Fourteenth Amendment or Title VII of the Civil Rights Act of 1964 or any other antidiscrimination principle that we are familiar with, requires proof of a state of facts that makes it more likely than not that there has been discrimination. See, e.g., *Cooper v. Federal Reserve Bank,* 467 U.S. 867 (1984). Since Ustrak had a cellmate of a different race, no significance can be assigned to the bare fact of a departure from consistent enforcement that favored the cellmate. Any departure had to injure one cellmate at the expense of another of a different race yet most inconsistencies in enforcement are unrelated to racial discrimination, being the result merely of imperfections in law enforcement. It would be insulting and unfair to Warden Fairman to presume that because he is black any unequal enforcement of prison regulations that hurts a white prisoner is the product of racial prejudice; and remember that it was a white guard who failed to charge Ustrak's black cellmate and that most of the prison staff is white.

Since the charge of discriminatory punishment must be dismissed, we have no occasion to consider whether, if it were proved, an award of damages would be a suitable remedy. Ustrak does not complain that it was wrong to punish him. He complains only that it was wrong not to punish his black cellmate also. . . .

Ustrak's [next] complaint is more substantial. He claims and the jury found that he was refused a transfer to the "farm," a medium security facility within the prison (Ustrak was in the maximum security part of the prison), because the warden was annoyed by the ten or so letters that Ustrak had written him over a two-year period complaining about racial discrimination in disciplinary sanctions and about earlier denials of Ustrak's request for transfer to the farm. The prison's assignment committee had eventually recommended the transfer but the warden had turned it down on the ground that Ustrak had once jumped bail and was therefore a poor risk for the farm, which is easier to escape from than the maximum security part of the prison. Although the warden argues that bail jumpers were not eligible for the farm, the evidence on whether bail jumping was an absolute bar was conflicting and the jury could have found that it was not; the prison's assignment committee, as we have said, did not think it an absolute bar to transferring Ustrak. A rational jury could have found that the real reason for the warden's overruling the committee was that he was annoyed by Ustrak's letters. cause of action

retaliation claim

As an original matter one might doubt whether convicted criminals should have much if any freedom of speech within prison walls; prison inmates are fractious enough as it is without having a right enforceable by damage suits against their keepers to complain continually about conditions for which their own conduct is largely responsible. But this seems not to be the Supreme Court's view. We say "seems not" rather than "is not" because all of the Court's cases dealing with free speech in prisons have involved communications with persons outside of the prison, a point stressed in *Procunier v. Martinez,* 416 U.S. 396 (1974), but dropped in later cases, such as *Jones v. North Carolina Prisoners' Labor Union, Inc.,* 433 U.S. 119 (1977), which involved communications among prisoners rather than with outsiders — but prisoners in different prisons. The lower courts have extended the right of free speech to internal prison communications, as in *Wolfel v. Bates,* 707 F.2d 932 (6th Cir.1983) (per curiam), which held that punishing a prisoner for complaining violates the First Amendment. Whatever the merits of this extension, Warden Fairman makes no issue of it in this court. His only and insufficient argument is that the jury was unreasonable in inferring that he was acting in retaliation when he overruled his committee's recommendation (his opening brief states, with inexcusable inaccuracy, that he was following rather than overruling the recommendation). That is a purely factual question on which the jury's answer, being in fact reasonable, is conclusive on us.

But we agree with Fairman that the jury's damage award — $3,000 in compensatory damages and $15,000 in punitive damages — cannot stand. With regard to the award of compensatory damages, there is a complete failure of proof on the extent of the injury sustained by Ustrak. There is no credible evidence that his transfer to the "farm" was delayed by more than two months, and his only claim of actual damages is based on the loss during that period of the superior amenities of the "farm." He does not claim that he was deterred from his letter-writing campaign or that he was beaten or starved or otherwise savaged in the prison; only that it would have been nicer to have those extra two months at the "farm." How much nicer? On this question the record is barren of probative evidence. Do not be deceived by the bucolic title; the "farm" is not a farm; it is not even a minimum security prison; it is a medium security prison. Ustrak testified that the difference between medium and maximum security at Pontiac "is better food, better accommodations, less attention put on you daily," and that his living conditions would have been "100 percent better." This is the entire evidence regarding the difference between living conditions in the two sections of the prison. Even though Ustrak had lived in the "farm" after his request for a transfer was finally granted, he did not testify about the living conditions there. He offered merely a conclusion.

evidence offered by π [handwritten marginal note]

The lack of evidence cannot be ascribed to Ustrak's being unrepresented by counsel at trial. He was represented by counsel at trial. Besides testifying to his own experiences in greater detail than he did Ustrak could have called witnesses from the prison staff to describe differences, if there were any, in cell sizes, prisoners' daily routines, diet, or incidents of violence, to bolster his conclusory observation about the difference in living conditions. The loss of amenities within prison is a recoverable item of damages, true, but it must be proved; it cannot be assumed; yet so far as the evidence of record in this case is concerned the difference in living conditions between the maximum and medium security sections of Pontiac is insignificant. Evidence in another recent case suggests that in fact inmates in the "farm" "enjoyed substantially greater freedom of movement than residents of the maximum security unit." *Mathews v. Fairman,* 779 F.2d 409, 410 (7th Cir.1985). No such evidence was introduced in this case. And no effort to attach a dollar value to the difference between living conditions in the two parts of the prison was made.

In the general run of tort cases, if only the fact and not the extent of injury is proved only nominal damages may be awarded. This principle has been applied to constitutional torts, notably in *Carey v. Piphus,* 435 U.S. 247, 264–67 (1978). In some areas of the law, of course, such as defamation, "general damages" are recoverable without proof of specific loss; and this principle may have some application in cases of constitutional tort. Sometimes damages for loss of a constitutional right are impossible to monetize; and then it is general damages or nothing. That might be true where a person was prevented from exercising his rights of free speech. But that is not Ustrak's case. He claims that he was retaliated against for exercising those rights — not that he was ever prevented or deterred from exercising them. Hence all he can recover by way of damages is the cost that the retaliation imposed on him. And he failed to prove any such cost. . . .

We have been at pains to emphasize in recent cases that damages, like every other contested element of a plaintiff's case, must be proved in order to be recovered; a plaintiff who wants substantial damages can't just ask for them. *Douglass v. Hustler Magazine, Inc.,* 769 F.2d 1128, 1144 (7th Cir.1985). Ustrak's brief does not bother even to discuss the compensatory damages awarded for the delay in transferring him to the farm.

We do not mean to erect insurmountable barriers to proof of damages in cases of intangible harm. If Ustrak for example had put in evidence on the difference (if any) in the size of cells between the maximum security part of Pontiac prison and the farm, he would have given the jury some basis for estimating the dollar value of the disamenity of being in the smaller cell two months longer. Instead the jury was asked to speculate in a void.

The failure of proof on extent of loss does not invalidate the award of punitive damages for the refusal to transfer Ustrak to the "farm," since the object of punitive damages is to deter rather than to compensate. But we think that the award of punitive damages for the transfer, $15,000, was grossly excessive (and again Ustrak's brief contains no separate discussion of those damages). Any violation of constitutional rights is reprehensible, but this one was at the bottom of the scale of gravity. Faced with having to decide whether to transfer a convicted bail jumper to a part of the prison that is easier to escape from (oddly, in describing the "farm," Ustrak's brief emphasizes that it has only one fence around it), the warden allowed annoyance with a pest — Ustrak's own counsel describes Ustrak as "a chronic complainer" — to color his judgment. We have been forced to assume that this violated the First Amendment, but it subjected Ustrak to what appears to have been at worst a trivial deprivation of amenities. Any award of punitive damages in excess of $1,000 would be unconscionable.

The damages awarded by the jury . . . were so extraordinary as to suggest that not only the jury's assessment of damages but also its assessment of liability may have been tainted by "passion and prejudice," thereby requiring that the entire verdict, and not merely the damages part of it, be set aside. *Douglass v. Hustler Magazine, Inc., supra,* 769 F.2d at 1143; *Edwards v. Sears, Roebuck & Co.,* 512 F.2d 276, 282–83 (5th Cir.1975). But the warden has not asked for a new trial on this ground. So far as the jury's damage award is concerned, all he wants is a reduction in damages; so that is all he can get. . . .

could have requested
new trial

AFFIRMED IN PART, REVERSED IN PART, AND REMANDED.

* * *

Gulf, C. & S.F. Railway Co. v. Shepard
Texas Court of Civil Appeals
63 Tex.Civ.App. 102 (1910)

RICE, J.

This suit was brought by appellee against appellant to recover damages on account of being unlawfully ejected from its cars while riding as a passenger thereon. The facts show that the appellee, on the 19th of December, 1907, purchased from appellant's agent at Ballinger, a ticket entitling him to passage over its railway from said point to Brenham, Tex.; that prior to the purchase of the ticket appellee had been drinking with some friends whom he had met, and, after boarding the train, the car being warm, it appears that he fell into a stupor, but that his ticket was taken up by the conductor before reaching Brownwood; that, after passing Brownwood, the conductor, while going through the train and taking up tickets, again demanded of appellee his ticket, and upon appellee's being unable to find it, after searching some time, he was forced to disembark in the night from said train at Zepher, a station below Brownwood, at the instance of the conductor, who, together with the brakeman, assisted him off.

At this time it appears from all the evidence that appellee was in a helpless condition, had been orderly and quiet, and seemed not to know what he was doing; that his overcoat and baggage were left on the train, and that, after wandering about in the dark for some time, he was taken by some boys to the hotel, where he spent the night; that he became sick during the night, and was treated by a physician, but was all right the next morning. The conductor admitted that he had made a mistake in reading the ticket from Ballinger to Brownwood, whereas it was, in fact, from Ballinger to Brenham, and that at the time of putting the appellee off the train he had a portion of his ticket in his pocket; that he did not discover this until the next morning when he was looking through his tickets, whereupon he wired the conductor on the south-bound morning train to bring appellee to Temple.

Appellee testified that he did not know anything about his being put off the train until he "came to" that night at the hotel at Zepher; that he was very much humiliated on account of it; that if he had not been put off he would have arrived at home at 4 o'clock the morning of that night, but, on account of this delay, he did not arrive there until about 6 o'clock the next evening; that he was a drummer and had been a traveling man for the past 25 years. Upon the conclusion of the evidence the court charged the jury that, under the undisputed testimony, the plaintiff was entitled to recover, and instructed them to find for the plaintiff such actual damages as they might find he had sustained by reason of being put off said train; and, in assessing the same, they might take into consideration the mental anguish caused by humiliation, if any, occasioned the plaintiff by reason of being so put off. There was a verdict in behalf of plaintiff for the sum of $250, and judgment accordingly, from which this appeal is prosecuted.

Appellant complains of the giving of said charge, and insists that the verdict is excessive; and also contends that the plaintiff was not entitled to recover, for the reason that the evidence showed that when he was put off of the train he was too drunk to understand or comprehend what was being done, and therefore could not have been humiliated thereby, as claimed by him.

We think, since the evidence showed that appellee was ejected from the train without any legal justification, that the court was correct in charging the jury that the only question for their determination was the amount of damages to which appellee was entitled under the facts; and therefore overrule the assignment complaining of this question. It is true that it appears that at the very time that plaintiff was ejected he was too drunk to know that he was in fact being expelled from the train, but it also appears from the evidence that as soon as he came to himself he was mortified and humiliated on account of what had occurred; that he had occasion frequently to explain to his friends how he came to be ejected from the train, which caused him chagrin and mortification. These facts, in our judgment, entitled him to a recovery. It is wholly immaterial whether he experienced the humiliation at the very time of his ejection or not, if he was prevented from so doing by his inebriated condition. To hold otherwise would be equivalent to saying that one committing an indignity upon another might escape liability, if it were shown that at the time of the commission the person, from any cause, was unconscious of or insensible to such indignity, notwithstanding the fact that upon regaining consciousness he might intensely suffer by reason thereof, which doctrine would not only be inhumane but repulsive to our sense of justice and right, for which reason we overrule this assignment.

We do not think that the verdict was excessive. The plaintiff, it seems, was a drummer, had been a traveling salesman for many years; and we must suppose, in the absence of evidence to the contrary, that he was a man possessed of at least ordinary intelligence, pride of character, and refined feeling, and that his unlawful ejection, under the circumstances indicated in the record would necessarily have the tendency to greatly humiliate and mortify him. We therefore cannot say that the verdict for $250, as matter of law, was excessive compensation for his unlawful ejection. See Ry. Co. v. Hood, 122 S.W. 569, where a judgment of $500 was affirmed for ejecting the plaintiff from the train. In Railway Co. v. Patterson, 46 S.W. 848, a judgment of $250 actual and $500 exemplary damages was sustained, where a plaintiff was unlawfully, though courteously, put off the train. In Southern Railway Co. v. Wood, 114 Ga. 144, 39 S.E. 896, 55 L.R.A. 538, Justice Cobb said, in passing upon a similar question: "When it appears to us that one who has the legal right to ride upon a train has been wrongfully expelled therefrom, and held up by such expulsion before the passengers on the train as one who is trying to ride thereon without lawful right or authority, and subjected to the mortification that such conduct on the part of the company's agent would necessarily bring about in the case of a young man of sensibility and pride, we cannot say, as a matter of law, that $450 is too much to pay him as compensation for the outrage thus committed upon him." Believing that the verdict is not excessive, we overrule this assignment; and, finding no error in the record, the judgment of the court below is affirmed.

Affirmed.

* * *

Problem 3

Damages compensate for harm, so to recover damages a plaintiff must be able to articulate a harm that has been suffered. What is the harm in the following situation — if any?

Paul's neighbor builds a fence that encroaches by two inches onto Paul's property. Paul consults a real estate appraiser who reports that since the fence crosses over the property line only a minimal distance, it will not affect the market value of Paul's property. Still, Paul is displeased that the area he owns is now smaller, even slightly. He asks his neighbor to remove the fence and the neighbor refuses.

Introductory Note — *Reardon v. Allegheny College*

The plaintiff in *Reardon* is a college student who believed she was unfairly disciplined for plagiarizing a paper. The unfairness she alleged was that the school did not follow the procedures outlined in the student handbook. Failure to follow those procedures is the basis for the lawsuit's breach of contract claim. But the student also brought tort claims, including for negligence. The trial court dismissed all causes of action for failure to state a claim. On appeal, the reviewing court analyzes the merits of the breach of contract claim and then decides whether a separate negligence cause of action should be allowed on these facts.

THINGS TO THINK ABOUT while reading *Reardon v. Allegheny College*:

1. Why is it necessary to categorize a plaintiff's claim as one in contract or tort?

2. How does a court decide if a cause of action is based in contract or tort?

3. Can a plaintiff in a breach of contract lawsuit ever bring a tort claim against the defendant?

Reardon v. Allegheny College

Pennsylvania Superior Court
926 A.2d 477 (2007)

OPINION BY TAMILIA, J.:

Laura Reardon appeals from the Order dismissing her complaint with prejudice and sustaining appellees' preliminary objections in the nature of a demurrer.

The trial court found the following facts. Appellant was a student at Allegheny College (Allegheny) majoring in music with a minor in biology, having since graduated. During the spring semester of 2004, appellant, as part of her biology curriculum, enrolled in an investigative laboratory biology course taught by appellee Margaret Nelson. Professor Nelson assigned appellant, appellee Stacy Miller, and appellee Megan Reilly to work on a lab experiment as a group. Each student was required to submit an individual paper analyzing the results of the experiment upon completion.

When Professor Nelson viewed the class paper submissions, she immediately suspected plagiarism as appellant and Reilly's papers contained identical sections. Upon further reflection, Professor Nelson's suspicions pointed to appellant as the plagiarizer. Shortly thereafter, Allegheny's administration was notified of appellant's indiscretion.

The trial court concluded Allegheny faithfully adhered to its internal procedure in adjudicating the plagiarism charge. First, a panel of the Honors Committee was convened and it determined there was a reasonable likelihood that appellant had violated the Honor Code, thereby warranting further action. Next, the College Judicial Board (CJB) conducted a lengthy adjudicatory hearing wherein appellant was given the opportunity to present evidence and confront the witnesses offered against her. The CJB found appellant guilty of plagiarism and imposed a failing grade for the biology lab course; stripped appellant of her Latin Honors; ordered appellant to complete community service; and placed appellant on academic probation for the duration of her academic career at Allegheny. Appellant then was afforded the opportunity, as of right, to appeal to the school's President who affirmed the findings and disposition of the CJB.

Appellant filed a written complaint raising claims for breach of contract against Allegheny and, in a separate count, against Professor Nelson; claims for defamation against Allegheny and Professor Nelson and, in a separate count, defamation claims against both Miller and Reilly. She also pursued a claim for the intentional infliction of emotional distress against Allegheny, Professor Nelson, Miller, and Reilly. After appellees filed preliminary objections that were sustained, appellant filed an amended complaint raising, with more specificity, the claims that had been raised in the first complaint along with a newly pled negligence claim against both Allegheny and Professor Nelson. Appellee responded by demurring to all six counts contained in the amended complaint. Following dismissal of the amended complaint, appellant perfected a timely appeal with this Court. . . .

Appellant contends Allegheny breached its contract with her by failing to follow its promised internal procedure for disposing of academic misconduct claims. She further contends Allegheny breached the contract by conducting the process in a "flawed, biased, and unfair" manner.

The relationship between a privately funded college and a student has traditionally been defined in this Commonwealth as strictly contractual in nature. *Barker v. Trustees of Bryn Mawr College,* 278 Pa. 121, 122 (1923). As such, we review the agreement between the parties concerning disciplinary procedures, contained within a portion of the student handbook known as *The Compass,* as we would any other agreement between two private parties. *See Murphy v. Duquesne Univ. of the Holy Ghost,* 565 Pa. 571 (2001). "When a contract so specifies, generally applicable principles of contract law will suffice to insulate the institution's internal, private decisions from judicial review." *Id.* at 429.

Appellant does not contend the language of *The Compass* is ambiguous. *See generally, Murphy, supra* at 429 ("When a writing is clear and unequivocal, its meaning must be determined by its contents alone."). Rather, she contends Allegheny breached its promised procedure by failing to notify her of a preliminary hearing held by the Honors Committee panel.

A thorough review of *The Compass* reveals the Honors Committee had an express obligation to inform appellant of the hearing that was held to determine whether there was a reasonable likelihood that she committed an Honors Code violation. Appellant avers she was not notified of an Honors Committee hearing held on September 1, 2004. Appellee contends appellant was given notice of, and indeed did attend, an Honors Committee hearing held on May 1, 2004. Appellee further states the September 1, 2004, hearing pertained to the plagiarism allegations leveled against Miller and Reilly and, as such, appellant was not entitled to attend that meeting.

A thorough review of appellant's amended complaint reveals appellant acknowledges a hearing did take place on May 1, 2004. In a not so creative attempt at subterfuge, appellant contends over and over again that she was not informed of the September 1, 2004, hearing, *yet she never once states she did not receive notice of the May 1, 2004 hearing.* The terms of *The Compass* do not give an accused student the right to attend a preliminary hearing held by the Honors Committee pertaining to charges leveled at a *co-defendant,* irrespective of the nature of the testimony and evidence to be offered at such a hearing. Furthermore, there is nothing in *The Compass* stating that a defendant is entitled to more than one preliminary hearing — the pertinent provisions unambiguously states the Honors Committee is required to hold "a" hearing. . . .

Assuming, as we must, that all of these contentions, as laid out in appellant's amended complaint, are true, we still conclude appellant is not entitled to relief. . . . Our review of the record indicates appellant was afforded the rights promised to her in *The Compass*. That is all that was required.

Appellant also alleges the lower court erred when it determined her negligence claim was barred by the "gist of the action doctrine" and that no other duties or obligations existed between the parties.

In her amended complaint at count VI, appellant contends Allegheny and Professor Nelson were negligent in conducting the disciplinary process and failing to obtain allegedly exculpatory computer data in their control.

The trial court dismissed appellant's negligence claim by relying on the "gist of the action doctrine," which allows a court to dismiss a negligence claim that is nothing more than a re-characterized contract claim. Appellant asserts our Supreme Court has not yet adopted this doctrine and, therefore, sufficient doubt exists as to the validity of her negligence claim to allow the claim to proceed. We disagree.

While an intensive research effort does indicate that our Supreme Court has not explicitly reviewed the concept under the appellation "gist of the action," dicta from the Court indicates it recognizes that allowing plaintiffs to forward both tortious and contractual theories of recovery arising out of damages allegedly incurred in the context of a contractual relationship is problematic. Over 40 years ago the Court stated:

> To permit a promisee to sue his promissor in tort for breaches of contract *inter se* would erode the usual rules of contractual recovery and inject confusion into our well-settled forms of actions. Most courts have been cautious about permitting tort recovery for contractual breaches and we are in full accord with this policy. *See* Developments in the Law — Competitive Torts, 77 Harv.L.Rev. 888, 968 (1964). The methods of proof and the damages recoverable in actions for breach of contract are well established and need not be embellished by new procedures or new concepts which might tend to confuse both the bar and litigants.

Glazer v. Chandler, 414 Pa. 304 (1964). Thereafter, both this Court and various federal courts have operated under the assumption that the gist of the action doctrine is a viable doctrine that will eventually be explicitly adopted by our state's High Court. The Supreme Court is clearly aware of the frequent use of this doctrine by both the lower and federal courts of this state, but has declined at least three opportunities to put an end to its use. As a consequence, we consider the gist of the action doctrine to be viable.

The gist of the action doctrine acts to foreclose tort claims: 1) arising solely from the contractual relationship between the parties; 2) when the alleged duties breached were grounded in the contract itself; 3) where any liability stems from the contract;

and 4) when the tort claim essentially duplicates the breach of contract claim or where the success of the tort claim is dependent on the success of the breach of contract claim. *Hart v. Arnold*, 884 A.2d 316, 340 (Pa.Super.2005), *citing eToll, Inc. v. Elias/Savion Advertising, Inc.*, 811 A.2d 10, 19 (Pa.Super.2002). The critical conceptual distinction between a breach of contract claim and a tort claim is that the former arises out of "breaches of duties imposed by mutual consensus agreements between particular individuals," while the latter arises out of "breaches of duties imposed by law as a matter of social policy." *Hart* at 339.

It is axiomatic that a plaintiff must establish he or she was owed a duty of care by the defendant, the defendant breached this duty, and this breach resulted in injury and actual loss in order to successfully prove negligence. *McCandless v. Edwards*, 908 A.2d 900, 903 (Pa.Super.2006).

Appellant's charges of negligence are premised on the concept that Allegheny and Professor Nelson owed appellant, "as a member of the college community," duties that are "in addition to and apart from any contractual obligation raised."

The problem with this concept is that appellant fails to plead from where this duty arises or what this duty entails. The only duties owed by Allegheny and Professor Nelson we can discern are rooted in *The Compass*— not some external and undefined general duty of care. Indeed, *The Compass* represents the sole basis for the relationship between the parties — appellant promises to adhere to the Honor Code in exchange for an education at Allegheny, while Allegheny, and to a lesser degree Professor Nelson, promises to adhere to the terms of *The Compass* in giving this education in exchange for monetary compensation. If this context were stripped away, there would be no relationship between the parties. Any potential liability Allegheny and Professor Nelson could incur, therefore, would arise out of their breach of the terms set forth in *The Compass*. Furthermore, if appellant is unable to demonstrate *The Compass* was breached, it is impossible to discern any other source from which liability could flow.

We find that the trial court correctly applied the gist of the action doctrine in dismissing appellant's negligence claim as legally defective. . . .

As appellant's amended complaint did not furnish any legally cognizable grounds for recovery, we conclude the trial court properly dismissed appellant's claims.

Order affirmed.

* * *

Problem 4

It can be difficult to distinguish between contract and tort when there is an existing contract and one of the parties does something that violates the contract *and* constitutes a tort. Under the facts that follow, can the plaintiff bring a tort claim for negligence? Why or why not?

A homeowner contracts with a landscaper for lawnmowing services. According to the contract, the landscaper is required to mow the homeowner's lawn once per week, "with all requisite care and according to industry standards for quality." While mowing the lawn one day, the landscaper is using his cellphone and not paying attention. He runs the mower into an antique garden gnome statue, shattering the statute to pieces. The homeowner sues the landscaper for the damage to the gnome.

[handwritten margin note: look to terms of the contract]

General and Special Damages

Compensatory damages are categorized as either "general" or "special." What those terms mean depends on whether the case is one in tort or in contract. General damages in a tort case refer to compensation for a harm that would be expected to occur in every case of that type. General damages in a contract case are similarly defined, as compensation for harm that is the natural and probable consequence of the breach.

Special damages in a tort case are compensation for harm that would not necessarily be incurred in every case of that type but rather might or might not be incurred depending on who the plaintiff is and that plaintiff's particular experience.

Special damages in a contract case refer to compensation for harm that does not flow directly from the breach but is more attenuated. The general versus special distinction is particularly important in contract cases because there are rules limiting the recovery of special damages — they can be recovered only if the harm was foreseeable at the time the contract was formed. There is no such limitation in tort cases, however. This reflects a policy decision to promote predictability in contractual relationships, even at the expense of not fully compensating a plaintiff for a loss caused by a breach.

The terminology and different categories of compensatory damages are further explored in the upcoming chapters discussing tort and contract damages. For now, what is important is becoming comfortable with damages terminology and understanding how the distinction between general and special damages can matter in litigation.

Introductory Note — *Cohn v. J.C. Penney Co.*

The question for the Utah Supreme Court in *Cohn* is whether the jury verdict in a personal injury case is defective because it is internally inconsistent. (If it is, a new trial would be required.) The trial judge did not think the verdict defective and denied the plaintiff's motion for a new trial. The propriety of that ruling comes down to the definition of general and special damages. The judgment is ultimately affirmed — though not because the trial judge's decision was correct.

THINGS TO THINK ABOUT while reading *Cohn v. J.C. Penney Co.*:

1. Why is it necessary to distinguish between general and special damages for a tort claim?

2. In a tort case, what kind of harm is compensated by general damages? By special damages?

Cohn v. J.C. Penney Co.

Utah Supreme Court
537 P.2d 306 (1975)

ELLETT, Justice:

This is an appeal from the refusal of the district court to grant a new trial.

The plaintiff fell on premises occupied by defendants and claimed damages. Counsel stipulated that she incurred medical expenses in the sum of $352.25 and lost wages amounting to $656.

The case was tried to a jury and submitted on a special verdict. The jury found negligence on the part of the defendants but no contributory negligence. It found damages as follows:

Medical expenses	$352.25
Loss of income	656.00
General Damages	0

Judgment was entered in accordance with the answers contained in the special verdict. The plaintiff duly moved for a new trial, claiming inadequacy of general damages. The trial court overruled the motion, apparently thinking that lost wages were an element of general damages. He instructed the jury regarding damages for the injury which plaintiff claimed she sustained and specifically mentioned suffering, both mental and physical, and the extent which she had been prevented from pursuing the ordinary affairs of life, and the disability or loss of earning capacity resulting from the injury. He also instructed that the jury could not allow more than $656 for lost earnings. He further instructed in regard to special damages to include, inter alia, expenses paid for doctors, medicines, nurses, and x-rays, in the amount of $352.25.

His Honor noticed the inconsistency of the answers to the interrogatories in that hospital and doctor bills and lost wages were awarded but nothing was found for pain or suffering. A bench conference was called, and the court indicated to counsel that he thought the verdict was proper since lost wages were a part of general damages. He undoubtedly would not have accepted the verdict had he thought that lost wages were special damages.

There should be a consensus of opinion amongst the bench and bar of this state as to the distinction between various categories of general and special damages. We, therefore, set forth what we consider to be the proper distinction between the two. The difference between the two types of damages is of importance because special damages must ordinarily be pleaded in order to be recovered.

General damages are those which naturally and necessarily result from the harm done. They are damages which everybody knows are likely to result from the harm described and so are said to be implied in law. Special damages are those which occur as a natural consequence of the harm done but are not so certain to flow therefrom as to be implied in law. One claiming them must plead them so as to let his adversary know what will be involved. An illustration will show the difference:

Plaintiff sues defendant for blowing up his dam in the river and claims damages in the amount of $5,000. His proof shows the cost of repairs to the dam to be $1,000. He offers evidence to the effect that he had a water mill which had to be shut down for two months during the rebuilding of the dam and that he lost profits in the amount of $4,000 as a result thereof. The rebuilding of the dam is an item of general damages, but the loss of profits due to inoperation of the mill is an item of special damage because it is peculiar to his case. Another man might have his dam blown up and might not even own a mill, or it might not be operative. Still another man might have special damages because he could not irrigate his farm as a result of the destruction of the dam which he owned and the lowering of the water below the bottom of his lateral ditch. Each dam owner would need to set forth his particular special damages because such special damages do not of necessity follow as a result of the tort.

The text material in 22 Am.Jur.2d, Damages s 15, states the law as follows:

> Compensatory damages are classified as either 'general' or 'special.' General damages are those which are the natural and necessary result of the wrongful act or omission asserted as the foundation of liability, and include those which follow as a conclusion of law from the statement of the facts of the injury. In other words, general damages are those which are traceable to, and the probable and necessary result of, the injury, or which are presumed by, or implied in, law to have resulted therefrom. The statement that general damages are those necessarily resulting from the wrong does not mean that

they are such only as must, a priori, inevitably and always result therefrom. It is enough if, in the particular instance, they do in fact result from the wrong, directly and proximately, and without reference to the special character, condition, or circumstances of the person wronged. The law then, as a matter of course, implies or presumes them as the effect which in the particular instance necessarily results from the wrong.

The term 'special damages' denotes such damages as arise from the special circumstances of the case, which, if properly pleaded, may be added to the general damages which the law presumes or implies from the mere invasion of the plaintiff's rights. Special damages are the natural, but not the necessary, result of an injury. In other words, special damages actually, but not necessarily, result from the injury, and thus are not implied by law. . . .

The distinctions between general and special damages are principally important with regard to the pleadings in damage actions. General damages, which necessarily result from the injury complained of, may be recovered under a general allegation of damage, whereas special damages must be specially pleaded. . . .

McCormick on Damages (Hornbook Series) makes the following statement at pages 37 and 38:

In personal injury suits, the following are usually treated as matters to be specially pleaded: Loss of time and earnings; impairment of future earning capacity; expenses of drugs, nursing, and medical care; aggravation by the injury of a pre-existing disease; and insanity resulting from the injury. Almost any of these, however, might be results so usually accompanying the particular injury alleged as that they would be regarded as sufficiently pleaded by the statement of the injury.

. . . Where the injuries alleged are of such a character as to give notice to all the world of the damages which would of necessity follow, then, of course, items usually classified as special damages could be proved without pleading them. A typist or a pianist who alleges the loss of a hand should be able to prove loss of earning capacity without specially alleging it because all the world knows that two hands are necessary to either occupation. . . .

In the instant case the plaintiff did plead that he would

'forever * * * be prevented from attending to and transacting his business or from performing any labor for the remainder of his lifetime to his damage in the sum of Twenty Thousand Dollars * * *.'

It is also alleged that the plaintiff was confined to the hospital and incurred an obligation amounting to over $600 for services rendered by the hospital. Under the holding of the Littledike case, supra, this is a sufficient allegation, when taken with the allegations concerning the nature of his injuries, to warrant the introduction of evidence relative to impairment of earning capacity. In the absence of special demurrer it is also probably sufficient to permit evidence as to loss of earnings although it would have been better if specifically pleaded.

In Utah there does not seem to be an inflexible rule regarding the pleading of special damages. It is a question of whether or not the pleadings contain such information as will apprise the defendant of such damages as must of necessity flow from that which is alleged.

In the instant matter the plaintiff made no objection to the verdict at the bench conference, and the defendants now claim that her failure to object constituted a waiver of the right to request a new trial or to appeal from the verdict. In the instant matter there was not merely an inadequate award of general damages — there was no award at all. The verdict was deficient in form, and counsel had an opportunity to have the jury sent back for further deliberations. This he did not do, perhaps fearing that the jury might either award some nominal amount or even change the verdict and award nothing to the plaintiff. It would be a smart trial tactic if he could have had a new trial on damages only before a jury which would not be acquainted with the weakness of plaintiff's cause of action.

. . . The judgment is, therefore, affirmed. Costs are awarded to the respondents.

* * *

Problem 5

Special damages must be specifically pleaded in the complaint to put the defendant on notice of the extent of potential liability. How should the court rule on a post verdict motion to vacate the following award of damages because of failure to plead them in the complaint?

At trial, the plaintiff proves that a slip and fall in a grocery store caused him to suffer a broken tailbone. Among other items of damages, the jury awards a large amount to compensate the plaintiff for emotional distress — $900,000. The defendant never anticipated such an award, partly because the plaintiff never asked for emotional distress damages in the complaint (it merely requested "all damages proximately caused by defendant's conduct"). The defendant moves to vacate the jury's award of emotional distress damages because the failure to plead them in the complaint did not provide adequate notice of the damages sought.

Yes emotional distress is a part of damage

* if it the type of damages you must be put on notice of

Introductory Note — *National Hispanic Circus, Inc. v. Rex Trucking, Inc.*

National Hispanic Circus, Inc., is another appeal from a jury trial where damages were awarded to the plaintiff. It is essentially a breach of contract case; it is in federal court because the plaintiff sued under a federal statute regulating interstate shipping. As is often the case in an appeal after a trial, the appellant raises numerous issues. Central to the resolution of several of the issues is whether the harm for which damages were awarded to the plaintiff was foreseeable at the time of contracting.

THINGS TO THINK ABOUT while reading *National Hispanic Circus, Inc. v. Rex Trucking, Inc.*:

1. In a contract case, what kind of harm is compensated by general damages? By special damages?

2. What are the special damages in this case?

3. Why might the special damages here have been foreseeable?

National Hispanic Circus, Inc. v. Rex Trucking, Inc.

United States Court of Appeals, Fifth Circuit
414 F.3d 546 (2005)

WIENER, Circuit Judge:

Defendant — Counter Claimant — Appellant Mason & Dixon Lines, Inc. ("Mason") challenges a jury verdict and damages awarded in favor of Plaintiff-Counter Defendant-Appellee the National Hispanic Circus (the "Circus"). We affirm.

This dispute arises out of a missing set of circus bleachers, lost somewhere between Texas and Chicago while in the care of Mason. The Circus regularly employed Mason's trucks and drivers to transport its equipment from one show to the next. On this occasion, however, one of seven trailers — the one carrying half of the Circus's bleachers — never made it to the Chicago show. Consequently, the Circus was forced to rent replacement bleachers which provided approximately 600–700 fewer seats than its own bleachers. Several weeks later, the Circus ordered replacement bleachers, which had to be custom-made in Italy to fit its tent. The cost of the replacement bleachers was $87,500.00, which the Circus was forced to pay in advance. The shipping cost was $36,104.00. (Approximately three months after its disappearance, the Circus's trailer containing its original bleachers was discovered in Arkansas.)

The Circus brought suit under the Carmack Amendment to the Interstate Commerce Act, 49 U.S.C. § 14706 *et seq.,* against Mason and Rex Trucking for damages it suffered as a result of the lost trailer. Mason asserted a counterclaim for the balance of the Circus's freight charges for the trailers Mason did deliver timely to Chicago.

At the completion of the trial, the jury awarded the Circus damages of $9,000 for rental of replacement bleachers, $123,000 for the purchase and shipping of the new bleachers, and $16,500 for lost ticket sales. It awarded Mason $15,600 on its counterclaim for payment for timely delivery of the six other trailers. Mason then renewed an earlier motion for judgment as a matter of law and moved alternatively for a new trial. The district court struck the award for lost ticket sales as too speculative and offset the rest of the Circus's award by the amount of Mason's award, thus granting total damages to the Circus of $116,400, including pre- and post-judgment interest, but upheld all other aspects of the jury's verdict and its own rulings. Mason appeals the district court's denial of its motions for judgment as a matter of law and for a new trial, as well as one of the district court's evidentiary rulings and its calculation of damages.

1. General v. Special Damages

We review *de novo* a district court's denial of a Federal Rule of Civil Procedure 50 motion for judgment as a matter of law. . . .

The Carmack Amendment allows a shipper to recover damages from a carrier for "actual loss or injury to the property" resulting from the transportation of cargo in interstate commerce. A carrier's liability under the Carmack Amendment includes all reasonably foreseeable damages resulting from the breach of its contract of carriage, "including those resulting from nondelivery of the shipped goods as provided by the bill of lading."

Both general and special damages may be recovered under the Carmack Amendment. General damages are those that are foreseeable at the time of contracting. Special damages are those that result from a party's breach of contract but are not reasonably foreseeable. Special damages generally are not recoverable in a breach of contract action absent actual notice to the defendant of special circumstances from which such damages might arise.

Mason argues that the district court erred by submitting the foreseeability of the Circus's damages to the jury rather than deciding as a matter of law that the Circus's damages were special rather than general. But, "[t]he question whether or not the defendant did in fact foresee, or had reason to foresee, the injury that the plaintiff has suffered is a question of fact for the jury."

The jury heard evidence that Mason (actually Rex) had previously shipped the Circus's equipment, that Mason employees filled out the bills of lading without listing the trailer's contents, and that Mason knew that it was shipping a "wide variety" of the Circus's equipment. This evidence was sufficient to support the jury's finding that Mason should have foreseen the injury to the Circus.

2. Jury Instructions; Denial of New Trial

As Mason objected to the district court's jury instructions at trial, our review is for abuse of discretion. A district court does not abuse its discretion if its instructions, as a whole, state the law correctly and instruct the jury properly on the legal principles to be applied to the facts that they will decide. Mason also appeals the district court's denial of its motion for a new trial based on what it terms inconsistent answers to the jury's interrogatories, a decision we review for abuse of discretion.

Mason asserts that the district court improperly refused to craft an interrogatory that requested the jury to determine whether the damages being sought by the Circus were foreseeable *in the absence of actual notice*. Instead, the district court separated the inquiry into two interrogatories, asking the jury, first, to determine whether the listed injuries were reasonably foreseeable to Mason at the time of contracting. The jury was instructed that, if it answered in the negative, it should then determine whether Mason had *actual notice* of circumstances that could give rise to the Circus's injuries. Posing this inquiry as two separate questions neither misstated the law nor made it impossible to tell whether the jury awarded general or special damages.

Mason goes on to argue that the jury's verdict was inconsistent. Rather than awarding money damages after determining that the Circus's damages were reasonably foreseeable, the jury instead determined that Mason also had actual notice of the Circus's potential damages. Mason contends that this mistake requires a new trial, as the Circus presented no evidence showing that Mason had actual notice of the possibility of special damages; thus, it asserts, the jury's verdict may have rested on a theory that lacked adequate support in the record.

Even if the jury's answers were inconsistent, — a highly implausible contention — a new trial still was not required if the verdict can be explained by assuming that the jury misunderstood the question. If the jury's answer to a question that was supposed to pretermit further inquiry is clear and disposes of the legal issues, we must ignore the jury's conflicting answers to any other questions, as they are irrelevant. As the jury's answer to the second question was superfluous to its finding that Mason could reasonably have foreseen the damages to the Circus, Mason is not entitled to a new trial or a judgment as a matter of law. . . .

3. Calculation of Damages

Mason insists that the district court erred in awarding the Circus the cost of its new bleachers. As it did not actually lose the bleachers but only misplaced them for several months, Mason argues, it should be liable only for damages resulting from the rental of temporary bleachers and any diminution in the bleachers' value during the time that Mason possessed them. . . .

Under particular circumstances, replacement cost can be a legitimate measure of Carmack Amendment damages. Here, the district court was required to determine the Circus's actual loss, using the most appropriate method. This case presents a circumstance in which awarding "market value" diminution or rental price of substitute equipment would not be appropriate, because the award would not fairly compensate the plaintiff for its actual loss.

The Circus requires custom-made bleachers to fit its tent. Although its bleachers were eventually found, the Circus had already fully paid for its new bleachers by that time, and the jury implicitly rejected Mason's argument that the Circus should have mitigated its damages by selling the old bleachers once they were recovered. The Circus had no reason to believe that the bleachers would be found or returned and, under these circumstances, made a reasonable decision to purchase new ones. The Circus was properly compensated for its actual loss, the cost of the new bleachers.

For these reasons, the district court's judgment is, in all respects,

AFFIRMED.

* * *

Problem 6

Distinguishing between general and special damages promotes predictability in contractual relationships. Are the below described damages general or special?

A woman contracts with a charter jet company to transport her across the country to interview for a job as chief executive of a major corporation. When she agrees to pay for the travel, she tells the jet company, "It's imperative that I arrive on time." A mechanical problem grounds the jet, forcing the woman to find a commercial flight that arrives three hours past her interview time. Because of her tardiness, she does not get the job. She sues the charter jet company for breach of contract and seeks damages for the salary she would have received from the chief executive job.

Chapter 3

Tort Damages

A tort is sometimes described as what it is not: a breach of an obligation not arising from contract. It is true that a tort is a legal wrong committed outside a contractual relationship. The reason torts are legal wrongs, though, is because they represent conduct society wants to deter. To achieve deterrence, liability is imposed. When a defendant commits a tort, a person harmed by that conduct can recover damages.

The goal of tort damages is to put plaintiffs in as favorable a position as they were in before the tort occurred. To measure damages in a tort case, it is necessary to first identify how the plaintiff was harmed — and there will often be more than one kind of harm — and then determine how much money it will take to compensate for the harm.

Importantly, tort damages are not limited by foreseeability (in contrast to contract damages, discussed in the next chapter). That means the defendant in a tort case will be liable for all harm caused to the plaintiff, even if the type of harm or the extent of harm could not have been anticipated. The only limitation is the concept of proximate cause, which allows defendants to avoid liability for harm they played such a minor role in causing that it would be unjust to hold them responsible for it.

By requiring tortfeasors to bear financial responsibility for all harm they inflict, others will be more motivated to avoid engaging in tortious conduct than they would be if no such responsibility were imposed. In addition to that deterrent effect, recovery of damages in tort promotes justice by providing compensation for injured victims. That makes for sound public policy because the cost of the harm inflicted is borne by the wrongdoer rather than being passed on to society.

This chapter explores tort damages in three settings: physical injury, harm to real property, and harm to personal property.

Physical Injury

A common scenario for an award of tort damages is when a tort causes physical injury to a person. The injury might be the result of unintentional conduct (the tort of negligence) or intentional conduct (for example, battery).

Physical injury cases present a variety of harms, reflective of the significant disruption to the plaintiff's life, especially in the case of a serious injury. Each harm must be identified and the appropriate amount of compensation calculated. That can be challenging since monetary damages are not a perfect fit when it comes to compensating for physical harm. No one would reasonably suggest money can make up for a severe, life altering bodily injury. It is simply the best we can do.

So physical injury is an example of a situation where damages are not *truly* an adequate remedy. But it is important to remember the law nonetheless presumes compensatory damages are adequate to make a physically injured plaintiff whole — the same presumption that applies to other kinds of harm.

Introductory Note — *Burgard v. Allstate Insurance Co.* and *Westphal v. Wal-Mart Stores, Inc.*

Burgard is a car accident case where the parties stipulated to liability, meaning the defendant did not dispute having negligently caused the accident. The only issue at trial was the appropriate amount of compensatory damages. The jury awarded damages in a variety of different categories. The plaintiff appealed, however, contending the award was "grossly inadequate in light of the evidence." The appellate court must determine whether there is sufficient evidence to support the jury's decision.

In *Westphal*, it is the defendant who is appealing a jury award to an injured plaintiff, arguing it is more than the plaintiff should get. On appeal, the task is again to determine if there is sufficient evidence to support the amount of damages awarded. The California Court of Appeal determines there is — and then some.

THINGS TO THINK ABOUT while reading *Burgard v. Allstate Insurance, Co.* and *Westphal v. Wal-Mart Stores, Inc.*:

1. What categories of damages are available in a personal injury action?

2. How are the damages in each category proven?

3. Which damages would be the easiest to prove? The most difficult?

injured [handwritten annotation]

Burgard v. Allstate Insurance Co.

Louisiana Court of Appeal

904 So.2d 867 (2005)

compensatory damages [handwritten annotation]

π brought appeal [handwritten annotation]

MARION F. EDWARDS, Judge.

Plaintiff/appellant, Donna Triay, appeals a jury verdict against defendants/appellants, Allstate Insurance Company, Louisiana Farm Bureau Insurance Company, Earl Robby Brock, and Bobby and Romona Brock.

Triay filed suit, alleging that on July 22, 2000, she was injured when her Ford Explorer was struck by a Mazda truck operated by Robby Brock. The matter was tried before a jury. Prior to trial, the parties entered into a stipulation that the accident was the result of the fault and negligence of Brock; that at the time of the accident, Brock was underinsured and that Louisiana Farm Bureau had in effect a UM policy issued to Triay with a primary limit of $300,000 and an excess of $1,000,000. The only issue left to the jury was the amount of damages due each plaintiff with certain qualifications. . . .

Following trial, the jury returned a verdict in favor of Triay in the total amount of $268,405 for her damages; $35,416 to her husband, Jimmy; and $9,583 to each of her children. In the resulting judgment, Triay's claims were dismissed in accordance with the above stipulation. Triay alleges that, due to errors made during the course of the trial, the verdict is grossly inadequate in light of the evidence.

Diane Hickman, Triay's sister, was in the Explorer with Triay on the day of the accident, along with their mother, and Triay's daughter, Candace. Hickman was pregnant at the time. The Ford was hit very forcefully from the rear, causing it to hit the guardrail, spin, and flip three times. Each time the truck turned over, the roof of the vehicle crushed in more, and they were very frightened. When the vehicle came to rest, it was upside down, and Hickman managed to unbuckle her seatbelt and get her niece out. They exited the SUV from the rear, but Donna was later extracted by medical personnel. Donna looked frightened and very bloody. Hickman herself had a broken collar bone and temporarily went into labor. Hickman saw her sister the next day, in the ICU unit at the hospital, where she looked "horrible."

Before the accident, Donna was the life of the party, very outgoing. She was organized and never forgot anything. After the accident, Donna became distant and has problems with her short-term memory. Her personality has changed, and she has lost a great deal of her patience. She only hears pieces of conversations. Donna does not complain. Before the accident, Donna did not have marital or psychiatric problems, or problems with memory or mathematics. However, Hickman did not know much about their finances or business arrangements.

Mary Burgard, Triay's mother, testified that after the impact, when the Explorer hit the guardrail, it looked as though they would go over into the water, then the car flipped and bounced three times. Since the accident, Donna has a short-term memory problem, and her personality has changed. Before, she was genuinely happy, but now she worries a lot, tires easily, and gets headaches. Her loving personality has not changed.

Triay and her husband owned a printing business, Printers Wholesale Group Inc., where Triay managed the day-to-day finances and was the bookkeeper. Triay also had another business, Crescent Graphics and Printing. Darlene Billiot, who was employed by the Triays' business accountant, Reginald Bresette, testified that before the accident, Triay would timely bring her financial information, but afterwards, she needed to be reminded to do so. She also became forgetful about bills, sometimes not paying them at all and sometimes paying them twice. Triay would forget to place and process orders. She was formerly very sharp and upbeat, but now her forgetfulness gets her down. . . .

Donna Triay testified that, prior to the accident, she handled all the accounting work for Printers, and she and her husband ran the business together. She enjoyed the work, working eight hours at the office and then at home in the evenings. She also handled sales calls, customer service, and whatever else had to be done. She was good at math and reading and enjoyed activities such as biking and boating.

. . . Jimmy Triay testified that he has been married to Donna Triay for seventeen years. For the first few months after the accident, she stayed home. Her head was swollen and she had headaches constantly. Triay does underestimate her discomfort and often worked when not feeling well. Prior to the accident, he would sell the printing and Triay would do the paperwork and bookkeeping. Triay was totally together, full of life, and loved to go on trips. They worked long hours. She wrote most of the checks, was good in math, and had good concentration. Since the accident, Triay is at the office only two to five hours a week. She does not pay attention anymore, does not transmit messages, and does not concentrate. She makes mistakes in check writing, overpaying bills on many occasions. After stopping the sales portion of the day, Mr. Triay has to go to the office to do bookkeeping and paperwork.

According to her husband, Triay is a "scared person," and has many phobias. If they drive over a bridge, she shakes. She does not play with the children anymore, she does not respond to him, and she rarely finishes books she is reading. She is easily annoyed and gets angry at herself when she forgets things. She is no longer interested in a physical relationship, and they argue about this. Triay did go on several trips to Florida with her husband after the accident, and clips from home videos showed Triay's activities on vacation, and on family outings. Triay continued to enjoy watching her sons play baseball and perform musically. . . .

Dr. Grant Butterbaugh was qualified as an expert in neuropsychology and psychology. He testified that Triay was referred to him by Dr. Howard Osofsky for evaluation. The purpose of his evaluation was to determine whether Triay had a brain injury and whether she had other problems such as learning disabilities. Dr. Butterbaugh spent sixteen hours with Triay over a period of two days, administering standardized tests as well as taking a personal history. Dr. Butterbaugh found no evidence that she was exaggerating symptoms, but was rather more likely to minimize them. The physician was particularly interested in her emotional functioning, as she had reported insomnia, nightmares, and fear when in an automobile. As a result of the tests, it was determined that her cognitive function in math decreased since the accident, and that her ability to continue her bookkeeping functions was impaired. . . .

At the time of the exam, Triay still had intermittent problems with dizziness and headaches, as well as with balance. She is at risk for a more serious head injury if she has another head accident. Dr. Butterbaugh determined that Triay had suffered a mild traumatic brain injury and that she suffers from post-traumatic stress disorder, anxiety disorder, and cognitive disorder. In the doctor's opinion, Triay would probably remain this way.

Dr. Josè Calderon testified as an expert in the field of psychiatry. Dr. Osofsky referred Triay to his care and he saw her initially in January 2003. Dr. Calderon found that, after the accident, Triay began to struggle with depression, anxieties, panic attacks, and phobias. She had cognitive difficulties and was no longer able to multi-task. She tended to minimize her symptoms. Dr. Calderon diagnosed her with post-concussion syndrome. . . .

Dr. Stuart Wood, an associate professor of economics and finance at Loyola, was qualified as an expert in the calculation of lost wages. He reviewed the personal tax returns of the Triays as well as the corporation tax returns of Crescent and Printing, Inc. for 1997–2002. He also had the financial statements for the companies for 2003. Dr. Wood calculated that Triay lost $15,871.97 in wages in the year 2000. The future lost income calculations were made using her 1999 wages as a base, and assumed a three percent growth in income from her 1999 wages to the present. Dr. Wood further assumed that she could work full time at minimum wage, and subtracted the minimum wage amount from those figures. The present value of her future lost income, based on a working life expectancy of 13.17 years, was between $203,668.19 and $237,113.36. . . .

In the jury verdict, the $268,405 award to Triay was divided as follows:

Past Physical Injuries, Pain and Suffering → general	$47,916.00
Future Physical Pain and Suffering	$47,916.00
Past Mental Pain, Psychological Injury and Suffering	$42,500.00
Future Mental Pain, Psychological Injury and Suffering	$42,500.00
Past Loss of Income	$14,166.00
Future Loss of Income	$4,250.00
Past Medical Expenses	$25,407.00
Future Medical Expenses	$10,000.00
Loss of Enjoyment of Life, Love, Affection, Companionship, and Society (general)	$33,750.00

On appeal, Triay contends that several legal errors occurred that mandate this Court to make a *de novo* review. Triay urges the court erroneously admitted irrelevant evidence concerning Jimmy Triay's earnings and irrelevant evidence relating to income made by Printers, which evidence unduly prejudiced the jury in awarding general damages as well as damages for loss of income. Triay contends that the issue before the jury was simply whether or not her injury rendered her unable to work and that introduction of the family income was not relevant to the wage she was capable of earning after the accident. According to Triay, drawing profits from a successful business is not analogous to her ability to earn a wage, and that while the evidence indicates the business makes a considerable amount of money, such evidence prejudiced the jury by showing that she makes large sums of money whether or not she works.

Generally, a district court is afforded great discretion concerning the admission of evidence at trial, and its decision to admit or exclude evidence may not be reversed on appeal in the absence of an abuse of that discretion.

To support a claim for loss of earning capacity, a plaintiff need not show a loss of income as compared to his pre-accident income. However, he must show, by a preponderance of the evidence, that his ability to earn a living is impaired. We recognize that loss of earning capacity may be awarded to a plaintiff if the injury has deprived him of a capacity he would have been entitled to enjoy even though he never profited from it monetarily.

Before a plaintiff can recover for loss of future earning capacity, he must prove the loss, not with mathematical certainty, but with reasonable certainty. Future loss of earnings is inherently speculative, and must be proved with a reasonable degree of certainty; purely conjectural or uncertain future loss earnings will not be allowed.

Although on appeal Triay characterizes Printers as her husband's business, and the now-defunct Crescent as hers, it is clear from the tax returns that these are family-owned businesses in which Triay is not simply a wage earner, but from which she derives income. Jimmy Triay testified that his wife is still part of the business. We find, therefore, that the trial court properly admitted the economic evidence. We further find that, although Triay showed a decline in the amount of time that she spends in the business, she failed to prove, by a preponderance of the evidence, that she was not able to perform the bookkeeping, and did in fact continue to write most of the checks.

. . . Finally, Triay urges that the damage award is inadequate in light of the evidence presented. The assessment of "quantum," or the appropriate amount of damages, by a jury is a determination of fact that is entitled to great deference on review.

> [I]t is only after articulated analysis of the facts discloses an abuse of discretion, that the award may on appellate review be considered either excessive or insufficient. Appellate courts review the evidence in the light which most favorably supports the judgment to determine whether the trier of fact was

clearly wrong in its conclusions. Before an appellate court can disturb the quantum of an award, the record must clearly reveal that the jury abused its discretion. In order to make this determination, the reviewing court looks first to the individual circumstances of the injured plaintiff.

General damages do not have a common denominator and must be decided on a case-by-case basis. General damages include physical pain and suffering, inconvenience, loss of physical enjoyment, and other factors that affect the victim's life. Factors to be considered when assessing quantum for pain and suffering are severity and duration.

In the present case, before the accident Triay apparently had a vibrant lifestyle and was successful in her business dealings. In the accident, she suffered a basilar skull fracture and a mild to moderate concussion. Following her initial hospitalization, Triay suffered headaches, dizziness, and loss of balance, partial loss of peripheral vision, and partial hearing loss. She also experiences intermittent shoulder and neck pain. She suffers from post-concussion syndrome, and post-traumatic stress disorder.

The mental and emotional components of the injury have clearly affected Triay. The medical testimony established several cognitive deficits related to the subject accident, including short-term memory loss. There was uncontradicted testimony that her personality had changed, that she is subject to anxiety and panic attacks, nightmares, and most significantly, depression. She has lost interest in a physical relationship with her husband and the testimony establishes that the level of interaction with her family has markedly decreased.

All physicians testified that Triay was not malingering, and that she tended to minimize her problems. . . .

On the other hand, evidence showed that, while Triay has difficulty doing her former bookkeeping, she is still able to perform the vast majority of that work. She is still capable of enjoying life with her family, as evidenced by the video clips viewed by the jury. Further, there is testimony that most of her psychological symptoms may be alleviated by treatment for depression and proper medication.

An appellate court should increase or decrease an award only when the amount is beyond that which a reasonable trier of fact could assess for a particular injury upon the particular plaintiff under the circumstances of the case. Although we find the award to be rather low, we cannot say that it is abusively so, that is, below that which a reasonable trier of fact could have assessed in these circumstances. A reviewing court might well disagree with the amount of the award fixed by the jury, but it is not entitled to substitute its opinion for that of the trier of fact.

For these reasons, the verdict and judgment are affirmed.

* * *

△ appeals

Westphal v. Wal-Mart Stores, Inc.

California Court of Appeal
68 Cal.App.4th 1071 (1998)

SCOTLAND, J.

Wal-Mart Stores, Inc. (defendant) appeals from the judgment in favor of Betty Westphal (plaintiff) in this personal injury action arising out of a slip and fall accident that occurred on defendant's property. Defendant contends the judgment must be reversed because the amount of damages awarded is excessive. Plaintiff retorts that the appeal is frivolous and asks for sanctions.

We shall affirm the judgment and grant plaintiff's request for sanctions. As we will explain, this appeal is frivolous because it indisputably has no merit.

The case was tried fairly in the superior court. Presented with evidence that defendant's negligence caused plaintiff to suffer severe pain in her back and foot (requiring her to use crutches and other devices for several months) and develop a recognized, chronic pain syndrome of headaches and constant discomfort of varying intensity in her neck, back, leg and foot (which has altered her lifestyle), the jury found that plaintiff had suffered special damages of $8,000 and general damages of $150,000. Finding the award generous but not outrageous, the trial court denied defendant's motion for a new trial on the ground of excessive damages.

Summarizing the evidence in the light most favorable to its position in the trial court, defendant asks us to be an "independent voice of conscience" and find the general damages award is excessive. Defendant fails to appreciate that, as a reviewing court, we view the evidence through a different lens than does the trier of fact. The judgment comes to us cloaked with the presumption that it is correct. In assessing a claim that the jury's award of damages is excessive, we do not reassess the credibility of witnesses or reweigh the evidence. To the contrary, we consider the evidence in the light most favorable to the judgment, accepting every reasonable inference and resolving all conflicts in its favor. We may interfere with an award of damages only when it is so large that it shocks the conscience and suggests passion, prejudice or corruption on the part of the jury.

Application of these well-established rules of appellate review to the evidence in this case leads to but one conclusion: defendant's appeal is utterly without merit, and plaintiff wrongly has been compelled to defend against it. Accordingly, we shall direct defendant to pay sanctions to plaintiff and to this court to compensate each for the expense of addressing plaintiff's frivolous appeal.

Facts

In December 1994, while working as a product demonstrator in premises owned by defendant, the 55-year-old plaintiff slipped and fell on a wet concrete floor. According to a witness, it was a "fast slip-fall" and plaintiff landed with a "pretty hard thump" on her back.

Plaintiff immediately felt pain in her whole left side, tailbone and left foot, and she could barely walk. After she rested and iced her leg, plaintiff was helped to her car. The drive home was difficult. Upon arriving, she crawled into the house and went to bed.

The next morning, plaintiff went to the hospital for X-rays and examination. She was diagnosed with lumbar, coccyx and ankle sprains, outfitted with a walking cast and crutches, and given a prescription for Motrin. For several months following the accident, she had to use assistive devices, such as crutches, a chair with rollers, and a walker, to help her ambulate due to the pain in her low back and left foot.

Between December 1994 and July 1995, Donald Davis, D.C., treated plaintiff for headaches, lower and upper back pain, neck pain, and foot/ankle pain. Davis conducted a "Sotohaul" test, a left-shoulder "Dressor" test, a compression test, a leg-raising test, and "Yoeman's" test, all of which indicated that plaintiff was injured and in pain. Plaintiff also had diminished reflexes of the left triceps. Davis diagnosed plaintiff's condition primarily as cervical strain syndrome, cephalgia and thoracolumbar strain/sprain, lumbosacral strain/sprain, and left ankle sprain.

The first time that Davis saw plaintiff, she rated her pain as 10 on a scale of 10. Plaintiff was sore and aching all over her body and felt like she had been beaten up. During her last few visits, her pain was staying around four and five on a 10-point scale, with higher pain ratings during the times when there were longer gaps between treatments. Davis found plaintiff to be a credible person and her complaints of symptoms were consistent with the fall.

Davis assessed plaintiff as being able to return to work on a limited basis in February 1995, but only for four hours per day, with no lifting over 15 pounds and no prolonged standing. Her job description at that time did not conform to these limitations. In April, Davis judged plaintiff to be permanent and stationary, with symptoms that would continue indefinitely, consisting of pain and stiffness in lumbar spine and difficulty rotating her head and neck to the left. Because plaintiff was suffering from chronic pain and had permanent residual disability, Davis did not expect her to get better.

Plaintiff saw Robert Fugitt, D.C., one time on November 28, 1995, for a qualified medical examination at the request of the workers' compensation carrier. At that time, plaintiff's primary complaint was pain in her left hip and low back pain, as well as pain radiating down her left leg, left heel and foot pain, neck pain, and shoulder pain. Ninety percent of her pain was attributed to the low back and left hip; it was constant and slight in the morning, increasing through the day.

Fugitt performed various orthopedic strength tests which indicated decreased strength, hypertonicity or muscle spasms, and pain. Fugitt's impression was that plaintiff was suffering from myofascial pain syndrome from injuries sustained in her accident. Fugitt stated plaintiff was as well as she was going to get and no longer could do what was required to work as a product demonstrator.

Eugene Abravanel, M.D., examined plaintiff in December 1995, a year after the accident. Plaintiff's history indicated she could not do any normal activities due to constant pain of the ankle, coccyx, left trochanter and buttocks area, as well as pain in the neck and shoulder muscles, and headaches. Plaintiff had tenderness in the intertrochanteric line, pain in the sacroiliac joint, a malrotation of the hips with an unweighting of the left hip, a tender coccyx upon just moderate palpation, and the possibility of coccygeal bursitis. She also had subtalar and subcalcaneus pain in her left foot, and ankle pain that was so severe plaintiff did not want to be touched for a range of motion test.

Abravanel opined plaintiff was suffering from Piriformis syndrome, a specific example of myofascial pain syndrome, which refers to an inflamed muscle or post-traumatic tear without a cure. He testified this could result in a tremendous amount of problems and plaintiff's condition was chronic. Furthermore, he noted, the postural changes created by plaintiff's rotated hip and her compensation for her pain would, in and of themselves, cause further pain. Abravanel noticed deconditioning, with a loss of muscle in the rhomboid trapezius area, which could have been caused by myofascial syndrome or fibromyalgia. According to Abravanel, soft tissue injuries do not show up on X-rays and sometimes are very serious, do not heal well, and can be much worse than fractures.

Plaintiff, who stopped seeing Dr. Davis when she moved to Wisconsin in July 1995, testified concerning the manner in which the accident changed her life. She saw a chiropractor for several months after moving to Wisconsin. Although the treatments were beneficial, she had to stop seeing him because she no longer could afford his services. She wakes up every day hurting all over and has constant headaches. Prior to the accident, she never had headaches. She still suffers from a dull ache and pain in her left hip and tailbone while sitting, rating the pain level at six to seven on a 10-point scale. She suffers from constant upper back pain of varying intensity, upper leg pain, shoulder and neck pain, as well as pain in the left foot. She has had to give up bicycling, roller skating with her sister, walking on the beach with her daughter in Oregon, and going on long drives. When she danced at her high school reunion, she "paid dearly for it" the next day, "aching all over" and hurting in her left side. She has had difficulty in finding and maintaining employment that is within her physical capabilities.

Corinne Hagan, plaintiff's former supervisor, verified that plaintiff no longer can walk quickly. Hagan has noticed a change in plaintiff following the accident; plaintiff looks a lot older and is in a lot of pain, which is obvious from the way she looks, sits, and moves.

Yolanda Herr, plaintiff's daughter, testified that her mother "worked alot," was in great health and was very physically active between 1991 and 1994. Following the accident, Herr had to assist plaintiff on a daily basis for three months. Plaintiff was not able to walk on her own, her head would shake uncontrollably, and she could not hold her infant grandchild, as she was very weak. As of the time of trial, plaintiff no longer could keep up on walks like she had been able to do, and she could not lift her grandchildren. Plaintiff is in chronic pain and is constantly suffering from headaches.

The jury returned a special verdict finding defendant's negligence was a cause of plaintiff's injuries. The jury found plaintiff had suffered economic damages in the amount of $8,000 and noneconomic damages in the amount of $150,000. The jury further found plaintiff was five percent contributorily negligent. Accordingly, judgment was entered against defendant in the amount of $150,100. . . .

Discussion

I

Defendant attacks the jury verdict on the ground of excessive damages, . . . We must uphold an award of damages whenever possible (*Seffert v. Los Angeles Transit Lines, supra,* 56 Cal.2d at p. 508) and "can interfere on the ground that the judgment is excessive only on the ground that the verdict is so large that, at first blush, it shocks the conscience and suggests passion, prejudice or corruption on the part of the jury." (*Id.,* at p. 507.) . . .

[margin note: excessive damages]

Defendant claims the award of $158,000 is excessive because it is several times the amount of plaintiff's out-of-pocket expenses for medical bills and lost income.

However, defendant cites to no authority establishing limits upon a general damage award based upon a small amount of special damages. In fact, there is no specific requirement that any special damages be awarded before general damages may be awarded. (*Hilliard v. A.H. Robins Co.* (1983) 148 Cal.App.3d 374, 412.) For example, *Sommer v. GABOR, SUPRA,* 40 Cal.App.4th 1455, upheld a $2,000,000 general damages award despite the absence of special damages.

According to defendant, "[plaintiff] suffered little more than a bruised tail bone and was diagnosed with the catch-all myofascial and Piriformis syndromes. The diagnoses were essentially made on reflections of plaintiff's subjective complaints. Plaintiff does not have anything objectively wrong with her and did not sustain any fractures, broken bones and did not require any surgery."

[margin note: Δ argues]

It appears that defendant questions the validity of myofascial pain syndrome and believes plaintiff is exaggerating her injuries. However, defendant presented no evidence, expert testimony, or authority casting doubt on the existence of this syndrome or the severity of the pain associated with it.

Myofascial pain syndrome, also known as fibromyalgia, is a syndrome characterized by persistent pain, which may arise following a traumatic injury and for which there is no cure. (*The Merck Manual of Diagnosis and Therapy* (15th ed.1987) p. 1271; *Sarchet v. Chater* (7th Cir.1996) 78 F.3d 305, 307; *Opgenorth v. Shalala* (E.D.Wis.1995) 897 F.Supp. 1199, 1202.) It engenders no positive objective test results, is not associated with any neurological or bony evidence of disease, and seems to arise from poorly understood changes in the muscle and fascia. (*Stedman's Medical Dict.* (5th Unabr.Lawyers' Ed.1982) p. 1391; *Sarchet v. Chater, supra,* at p. 306.) The only indication of its existence is the plaintiff's subjective description of pain.

The amount of pain and incapacity associated with myofascial pain syndrome or fibromyalgia can lead sufferers to become disabled occupationally, although this is not the usual result. (*Cline v. Sullivan* (8th Cir.1991) 939 F.2d 560, 567; *Opgenorth v. Shalala, supra*, 897 F.Supp. 1199.) When a treating physician has diagnosed a patient as suffering from this syndrome, the mere lack of objective medical evidence to substantiate the patient's symptoms or functional limitations is not a ground to reject a finding of disability.

Similarly, where a treating physician has diagnosed a plaintiff as suffering from myofascial pain syndrome, no objective medical evidence is needed to substantiate the plaintiff's pain and suffering. In fact, the absence of medical bills or medical testimony will not foreclose a recovery for pain and suffering. (*Hilliard v. A.H. Robins Co., supra*, 148 Cal.App.3d at p. 413.)

The law does not prescribe a definite standard or method to calculate compensation for pain and suffering; the jury merely is required to award an amount it finds reasonable in light of the evidence. (*Damele v. Mack Trucks, Inc.* (1990) 219 Cal. App.3d 29, 38.) It was for the jury to assess the various witnesses' credibility concerning the injuries suffered by plaintiff and the degree of her pain.

Here, health care professionals testified that plaintiff was afflicted with cervical strain syndrome, cephalgia thoracolumbar strain/sprain, lumbosacral strain/ sprain, left ankle sprain, myofascial pain syndrome, and Piriformis syndrome, a specific example of myofascial pain syndrome in the area of the Piriformis musculature. All of the health care professionals testified that plaintiff would be afflicted with pain, discomfort, and limitations for the rest of her life. In the month following the accident, she was not ambulatory without assistive devices. She required the assistance of friends and relatives for transportation, to cook her meals, and to help her with chores. Plaintiff was in treatment for her injuries for nearly a year and ceased treatment only because she no longer could afford it, although it was still beneficial to her. The amount of pain she suffers prevents her from participating in activities she used to enjoy and makes it difficult for her to find employment.

In short, evidence accepted by the jury disclosed that plaintiff suffered severe pain following the accident, presently suffers from pain on a daily basis which creates functional lifestyle limitations, and will have chronic pain for the rest of her life.

In light of this evidence, the jury verdict does not shock the conscience and it cannot be said that the verdict was the result of passion, prejudice or corruption. Thus, the trial court correctly denied defendant's motion for new trial on the ground of excessive damages.

II

Asserting that defendant's appeal is frivolous and was undertaken for the purpose of delay, plaintiff asks us to impose sanctions against defendant for the prosecution of a frivolous appeal.

Code of Civil Procedure section 907 states: "When it appears to the reviewing court that the appeal was frivolous or taken solely for delay, it may add to the costs on appeal such damages as may be just."

standard for sanctions to be given

... Given the stringent standard of appellate review for claims of excessive damages, the evidence in support of the judgment, and the absence of meaningful analysis by defendant, we conclude this appeal "indisputably has no merit." There are no unique issues, no facts that are not amenable to easy analysis in terms of existing law, and no reasoned argument by defendant for the extension of existing law. There is no arguable basis for reversing the judgment.

... Defendant simply asserts the damages are excessive solely because "plaintiff suffered nothing more than soft-tissue injuries." Yet, defendant cites no legal authority for the proposition that soft-tissue injuries never merit an award of $150,000 for pain and suffering even where the evidence establishes that plaintiff will suffer for the rest of her life with chronic pain which places functional limitations on her lifestyle.

Defendant attempts to minimize plaintiff's injuries by noting that, after she was treated at the hospital, "she never again saw a medical doctor and instead went to a chiropractor." Defendant points out that Dr. Abravanel was "the only licensed physician who examined plaintiff." Other than casting aspersions on the qualifications of a chiropractor to provide an adequate medical diagnosis, opinion and course of treatment, defendant presents no legal basis for casting doubt on, or rejecting the medical opinions of, chiropractors. This kind of unsubstantiated potshot indicates defendant does not have a substantive basis for attacking the verdict....

Defendant lists injuries which plaintiff did not suffer and medical tests which were not administered, rather than discussing fully the evidence of plaintiff's pain and injuries. Defendant points out that plaintiff did not lose consciousness and did not have any fractures, but does not explain how this undermines the evidence that plaintiff suffers from chronic pain as a result of the accident. Defendant ignores the testimony of Dr. Abravanel, indicating that soft-tissue injuries can be very serious, not heal well, and be much worse than fractures.

At trial, defendant presented no expert testimony casting doubt on the existence of myofascial pain syndrome or the degree of impairment it can cause. Furthermore, defendant did not provide any evidence that plaintiff was malingering. Although such evidence would not provide a basis to reverse the judgment in light of the substantial evidence standard of review on appeal, it would at least demonstrate a basis for defendant's decision to pursue an appellate claim of excessive damages. Without such evidence, there is no arguable basis for finding the damages excessive, and sanctions are appropriate.

additional sanctions

... Defendant is assessed sanctions in the amount of $11,000, payable to plaintiff within 15 days after issuance of the remittitur, to compensate her for the expense consumed in defending against this frivolous appeal. We further assess defendant sanctions in the amount of $2,500, payable to the clerk of this court within 15 days after issuance of the remittitur, to compensate the court for the expense of processing, reviewing, and deciding a frivolous appeal. . . .

Disposition

The judgment is affirmed. Sanctions in the amount $13,500, to be paid as directed in this opinion, are imposed against defendant for prosecuting a frivolous appeal. In addition, defendant shall pay plaintiff's costs on appeal. (Cal.Rules of Court, rule 26(a).)

* * *

Problem 7

Given that the law provides no fixed standard for measuring pain and suffering, what arguments might counsel for the plaintiff in the case below make to persuade the jury an award of at least $100,000 is appropriate?

The 26-year-old plaintiff was injured by a defective piece of machinery that crushed his foot. The injury was surgically repaired but will have lasting effects. Plaintiff will experience minor pain — similar to what a bruise feels like — whenever he walks, for the rest of his life.

Introductory Note — *Potter v. Firestone Tire & Rubber Co.*

Potter involves a relatively narrow issue: whether a plaintiff can recover damages for fear of developing cancer after toxic exposure. But the policy implications of the question are broad. Deciding if recovery should be allowed in that situation requires a careful consideration of the kind of harm that should be compensable by damages. The California Supreme Court weighs the competing policy considerations to decide whether the significant damage award to the plaintiffs should stand.

THINGS TO THINK ABOUT while reading *Potter v. Firestone Tire & Rubber Co.*:

1. How is physical harm defined?

2. What is the justification for the rule that emotional distress damages cannot be recovered absent physical impact?

3. Why was recovery of emotional distress damages allowed here?

Potter v. Firestone Tire & Rubber Co.

California Supreme Court
6 Cal.4th 965 (1993)

BAXTER, Justice.

. . . .

Factual and Procedural Background

This is a toxic exposure case brought by four landowners living adjacent to a landfill. As a result of defendant Firestone's practice of disposing of its toxic wastes at the landfill, the landowners were subjected to prolonged exposure to certain carcinogens. While none of the landowners currently suffers from any cancerous or precancerous condition, each faces an enhanced but unquantified risk of developing cancer in the future due to the exposure. . . .

[The trial court found] that although plaintiffs testified to a constellation of physical symptoms which they attributed to the toxic chemicals, it was "not possible to demonstrate with sufficient certainty a causal connection between these symptoms and the well water contamination. Nevertheless, plaintiffs will always fear, and reasonably so, that physical impairments they experience are the result of the well water and are the precursers [sic] of life threatening disease. Their fears are not merely subjective but are corroborated by substantial medical and scientific opinion." Based on these findings, plaintiffs were awarded damages totalling $800,000 for their lifelong fear of cancer and resultant emotional distress.

The court further concluded that since plaintiffs now live with an increased vulnerability to serious disease, it was axiomatic that they should receive periodic medical monitoring to detect the onset of disease at the earliest possible time and that early diagnosis was unquestionably important to increase the chances of effective treatment. Accordingly, the court awarded damages totalling $142,975 as the present value of the costs of such monitoring, based on plaintiffs' life expectancies.

The court also awarded plaintiffs damages totalling $269,500 for psychiatric illness and the cost of treating such illness, as well as damages totalling $108,100 for the general disruption of their lives and the invasion of their privacy. Finally, the court awarded punitive damages totalling $2.6 million based on Firestone's conscious disregard for the rights and safety of others in dumping its toxic wastes at the landfill after 1977. [Defendant appeals.]

Discussion

. . . .

A. Negligence: Fear of Cancer

"Fear of cancer" is a term generally used to describe a present anxiety over developing cancer in the future. Claims for fear of cancer have been increasingly asserted in toxic tort cases as more and more substances have been linked with cancer. Typically, a person's likelihood of developing cancer as a result of a toxic exposure is difficult to predict because many forms of cancer are characterized by long latency periods (anywhere from 20 to 30 years), and presentation is dependent upon the interrelation of myriad factors.

The availability of damages for fear of cancer as a result of exposure to carcinogens or other toxins in negligence actions is a relatively novel issue for California courts. Other jurisdictions, however, have considered such claims and the appropriate limits on recovery. Factors deemed important to the compensability of such fear have included proof of a discernible physical injury, proof of a physical impact or physical invasion, or objective proof of mental distress.

We must now consider whether, pursuant to California precedent, emotional distress engendered by the fear of developing cancer in the future as a result of a toxic exposure is a recoverable item of damages in a negligence action.

1. Parasitic Recovery: Immune System Impairment and/or Cellular Damage as Physical Injury

Because it initially appeared plaintiffs might have suffered damage to their immune systems, we solicited the views of the parties on whether such damage constitutes physical injury. We did so because it is settled in California that in ordinary negligence actions for physical injury, recovery for emotional distress caused by that injury is available as an item of parasitic damages. (Crisci v. Security Insurance Co. (1967) 66 Cal.2d 425, 433.) Where a plaintiff can demonstrate a physical injury caused by the defendant's negligence, anxiety specifically due to a reasonable fear of a future harm attributable to the injury may also constitute a proper element of damages.

Although the availability of parasitic damages for emotional distress engendered by a fear of developing cancer in the future appears to be an issue of first impression in California, other jurisdictions have concluded that such damages are recoverable when they are derivative of a claim for serious physical injuries. For example, the court in Ferrara v. Galluchio (1958) 5 N.Y.2d 16, 21–22 upheld an award of emotional distress damages based on the plaintiff's fear of cancer where she had been negligently burned in X-ray treatments and later advised by a dermatologist to have her tissue examined every six months as cancer might develop. (Accord, Dempsey v. Hartley (E.D.Pa.1951) 94 F.Supp. 918, 920–921 [fear of breast cancer due to traumatic breast injury]; Alley v. Charlotte Pipe & Foundry Co. (1912) 159 N.C. 327 [fear stemming from sarcoma liable to ensue from burn wound].) In these cases, the existence of a present physical injury, rather than the degree of probability that the disease may actually develop, is determinative.

No California cases address whether impairment of the immune system response and cellular damage constitute "physical injury" sufficient to allow recovery for parasitic emotional distress damages. Courts in other jurisdictions that have considered this issue recently have come to differing conclusions. . . .

It is not clear from the record in this case, however, that these plaintiffs' emotional distress is parasitic to this type of supposed injury. The statement of decision by the trial court does not include an express finding that plaintiffs' exposure to the contaminated well water resulted in physical injury, cellular damage or immune system impairment. The court made no mention of plaintiffs' immune system response, cellular systems or cells, and made no specific determination of damage or impairment thereto. While the trial court concluded that plaintiffs do have an enhanced "susceptibility" or "risk" for developing cancer and other maladies, it characterized this as a "presently existing physical condition," not as a physical injury. We conclude, therefore, that we lack an appropriate factual record for resolving whether impairment to the immune response system or cellular damage constitutes a physical injury for which parasitic damages for emotional distress ought to be available.

2. Nonparasitic Fear of Cancer Recovery

We next determine whether the absence of a present physical injury precludes recovery for emotional distress engendered by fear of cancer. Firestone argues that California should not recognize a duty to avoid negligently causing emotional distress to another, but, if such a duty is recognized, recovery should be permitted in the absence of physical injury only on proof that the plaintiff's emotional distress or fear is caused by knowledge that future physical injury or illness is more likely than not to occur as a direct result of the defendant's conduct. Amici curiae, many of whom represent organizations of manufacturers and their insurers, would preclude all recovery for emotional distress in the absence of physical injury.

a. Independent Duty

Firestone first asks the court to expressly adopt the rule recently applied by the Supreme Court of Texas in Boyles v. Kerr (1993) 855 S.W.2d 593. There the court held that there is no duty to avoid negligently causing emotional distress to another, and that damages for emotional distress are recoverable only if the defendant has breached some other duty to the plaintiff.

That is already the law in California. Indeed, the Texas court relied on recent decisions of this court in which we recognized that there is no independent tort of negligent infliction of emotional distress. The tort is negligence, a cause of action in which a duty to the plaintiff is an essential element. That duty may be imposed by law, be assumed by the defendant, or exist by virtue of a special relationship.

The lesson of these decisions is: unless the defendant has assumed a duty to plaintiff in which the emotional condition of the plaintiff is an object, recovery is available only if the emotional distress arises out of the defendant's breach of some other legal duty and the emotional distress is proximately caused by that breach of duty. Even then, with rare exceptions, a breach of the duty must threaten physical injury, not simply damage to property or financial interests. (See Cooper v. Superior Court (1984) 153 Cal.App.3d 1008, 1012–1013; Quezada v. Hart (1977) 67 Cal.App.3d 754.)

Those limits on recovery for emotional distress caused by the negligent conduct of another do not aid Firestone here, however. Firestone did violate a duty imposed on it by law and regulation to dispose of toxic waste only in a class I landfill and to avoid contamination of underground water. The violation led directly to plaintiffs' ingestion of various known and suspected carcinogens, and thus to their fear of suffering the very harm which the Legislature sought by statute to avoid. Their fear of cancer was proximately caused by Firestone's unlawful conduct which threatened serious physical injury.

This is not a case in which a negligence cause of action is predicated only on a claim that the defendant breached a duty to avoid causing emotional distress.

b. Absence of Physical Injury

Amici curiae argue that no recovery for emotional distress arising from fear of cancer should be allowed in any case unless the plaintiff can establish a present physical injury such as a clinically verifiable cancerous or precancerous condition. Amici curiae advance several legal and policy arguments to support this position. None is persuasive.

Amici curiae first assert that under California case law, the existence of a physical injury is a predicate to recovering damages for emotional distress in a negligence action unless the action involves "bystander" recovery (e.g., Thing v. La Chusa (1989) 48 Cal.3d 644) or there is a "preexisting relationship" between the plaintiff and defendant which creates a duty to the plaintiff, neither of which is implicated here. This assertion is plainly without merit.

Significantly, we recently reaffirmed the principle that in California, "damages for negligently inflicted emotional distress may be recovered in the absence of physical injury or impact. . . ." (Burgess, supra, 2 Cal.4th at p. 1074.) We held that "physical injury is not a prerequisite for recovering damages for serious emotional distress," especially where "there exists a 'guarantee of genuineness in the circumstances of the case." (Id., at p. 1079.)

Contrary to amici curiae's assertions, this principle has never been restricted to cases involving bystanders or preexisting relationships. Notably, amici curiae cite no authority even suggesting such a limitation. Nor is there any question but that Firestone had a duty to any person who might foreseeably come in contact with its hazardous waste to use care in the disposal of that material, care which includes compliance with all government regulations governing the location and manner of disposal.

Amici curiae next contend that substantial policy reasons nevertheless support a physical injury requirement for recovery of fear of cancer damages where no preexisting relationship exists. They suggest that allowing recovery in the absence of a physical injury would create limitless liability and would result in a flood of litigation which thereby would impose onerous burdens on courts, corporations, insurers and society in general. Allowing such recovery would promote fraud and artful pleading, and would also encourage plaintiffs to seek damages based on a subjective fear of cancer. In amici curiae's view, a physical injury requirement is thus essential to provide meaningful limits on the class of potential plaintiffs and clear guidelines for resolving disputes over liability without the necessity for trial.

This argument overlooks the reasons for our decision to discard the requirement of physical injury. As we observed more than a decade ago, "[t]he primary justification for the requirement of physical injury appears to be that it serves as a screening device to minimize a presumed risk of feigned injuries and false claims. [Citations.]" (Molien v. Kaiser Foundation Hospitals (1980) 27 Cal.3d 916, 925–926.) Such harm was "believed to be susceptible of objective ascertainment and hence to corroborate the authenticity of the claim." (Molien, supra, 27 Cal.3d at p. 926.)

In Molien, supra, 27 Cal.3d 916, we perceived two significant difficulties with the physical injury requirement. First, "the classification is both overinclusive and underinclusive when viewed in the light of its purported purpose of screening false claims." It is overinclusive in that it permits recovery whenever the suffering accompanies or results in physical injury, no matter how trivial, yet underinclusive in that it mechanically denies court access to potentially valid claims that could be proved if the plaintiffs were permitted to go to trial.

Second, we observed that the physical injury requirement "encourages extravagant pleading and distorted testimony." (Molien, supra, 27 Cal.3d at p. 929.) We concluded that the retention of the requirement ought to be reconsidered because of the tendency of victims to exaggerate sick headaches, nausea, insomnia and other symptoms in order to make out a technical basis of bodily injury upon which to predicate a parasitic recovery for the more grievous disturbance, consisting of the mental and emotional distress endured.

Therefore, rather than adhere to what we perceived as an artificial and often arbitrary means of guarding against fraudulent claims, we acknowledged that "[t]he essential question is one of proof[.]" (Molien, supra, 27 Cal.3d at pp. 929–930.) Thus, "'[i]n cases other than where proof of mental distress is of a medically significant nature, [citations] the general standard of proof required to support a claim of mental distress is some guarantee of genuineness in the circumstances of the case." (Id., at p. 930.)

Our reasons for discarding the physical injury requirement in Molien, supra, 27 Cal.3d 916, remain valid today and are equally applicable in a toxic exposure case. That is, the physical injury requirement is a hopelessly imprecise screening device — it would allow recovery for fear of cancer whenever such distress accompanies or results in any physical injury, no matter how trivial, yet would disallow recovery in all cases where the fear is both serious and genuine but no physical injury has yet manifested itself. While we agree with amici curiae that meaningful limits on the class of potential plaintiffs and clear guidelines for resolving disputes in advance of trial are necessary, imposing a physical injury requirement represents an inherently flawed and inferior means of attempting to achieve these goals. . . .

To summarize, we hold with respect to negligent infliction of emotional distress claims arising out of exposure to carcinogens and/or other toxic substances: Unless an express exception to this general rule is recognized: in the absence of a present *rule*

physical injury or illness, damages for fear of cancer may be recovered only if the plaintiff pleads and proves that (1) as a result of the defendant's negligent breach of a duty owed to the plaintiff, the plaintiff is exposed to a toxic substance which threatens cancer; and (2) the plaintiff's fear stems from a knowledge, corroborated by reliable medical or scientific opinion, that it is more likely than not that the plaintiff will develop the cancer in the future due to the toxic exposure. Under this rule, a plaintiff must do more than simply establish knowledge of a toxic ingestion or exposure and a significant increased risk of cancer. The plaintiff must further show that based upon reliable medical or scientific opinion, the plaintiff harbors a serious fear that the toxic ingestion or exposure was of such magnitude and proportion as to likely result in the feared cancer. . . .

Disposition

The judgment of the Court of Appeal is reversed insofar as it affirms the award of punitive damages and the award of damages for plaintiffs' fear of cancer, and reverses the award for future medical monitoring. The cause is remanded to the Court of Appeal for further proceedings consistent with this opinion, that may include, if appropriate, a remand to the trial court for a retrial on the above damages, a remand for a retrial on the issue of Firestone's liability for intentional infliction of emotional distress, and/or consideration of issues that were not heretofore reached by the Court of Appeal.

* * *

Problem 8

Emotional distress damages are not always recoverable even when the plaintiff has in fact experienced emotional harm. What are the best arguments for allowing recovery of emotional distress damages by the following plaintiffs? What are the best arguments against doing so?

A husband and wife are out for a walk when a driver carelessly drives too close to the sidewalk. The car hits the wife, injuring her severely. The husband is unharmed but extremely upset after seeing his wife injured in front of him. He later calls his daughter on the phone to tell her what happened; she too becomes extremely upset upon hearing the news about her mother.

The husband and the daughter both sue the driver for negligence and seek damages for emotional distress.

Introductory Note — *Benn v. Thomas*

Benn is a wrongful death case where the defendants' negligence would not have resulted in death for most people but did in this situation because the victim had a particular vulnerability. At trial, the jury found the defendants did not cause the death. On appeal, the plaintiff contends the jury would have found differently had it been properly instructed on the law.

THINGS TO THINK ABOUT while reading *Benn v. Thomas*:

1. What is the justification for the eggshell plaintiff rule?

2. Is it unfair that the same conduct can result in dramatically different amounts of liability merely because of who the victim is?

Benn v. Thomas

Iowa Supreme Court
512 N.W.2d 537 (1994)

McGIVERIN, Chief Justice.

The main question here is whether the trial court erred in refusing to instruct the jury on the "eggshell plaintiff" rule in view of the fact that plaintiff's decedent, who had a history of coronary disease, died of a heart attack six days after suffering a bruised chest and fractured ankle in a motor vehicle accident caused by defendant's negligence. The court of appeals concluded that the trial court's refusal constituted reversible error. We agree with the court of appeals and reverse the judgment of the trial court and remand for a new trial.

I. Background Facts and Proceedings

On February 15, 1989, on an icy road in Missouri, a semi-tractor and trailer rear-ended a van in which Loras J. Benn was a passenger. In the accident, Loras suffered a bruised chest and a fractured ankle. Six days later he died of a heart attack.

Subsequently, Carol A. Benn, as executor of Loras's estate, filed suit against defendants Leland R. Thomas, the driver of the semi-tractor, K-G Ltd., the owner of the semi-tractor and trailer, and Heartland Express, the permanent lessee of the semi-tractor and trailer. The plaintiff estate sought damages for Loras's injuries and death.

At trial, the estate's medical expert, Dr. James E. Davia, testified that Loras had a history of coronary disease and insulin-dependent diabetes. Loras had a heart attack in 1985 and was at risk of having another. Dr. Davia testified that he viewed "the accident that [Loras] was in and the attendant problems that it cause[d] in the body as the straw that broke the camel's back" and the cause of Loras's death. . . .

Based on Dr. Davia's testimony, the estate requested an instruction to the jury based on the "eggshell plaintiff" rule, which requires the defendant to take his plaintiff as he finds him, even if that means that the defendant must compensate the plaintiff for harm an ordinary person would not have suffered. *See Becker v. D & E Distrib. Co.*, 247 N.W.2d 727, 730 (Iowa 1976). The district court denied this request.

The jury returned a verdict for the estate in the amount of $17,000 for Loras's injuries but nothing for his death. In the special verdict, the jury determined the defendant's negligence in connection with the accident did not proximately cause Loras's death.

The estate filed a motion for new trial claiming the court erred in refusing to instruct the jury on the "eggshell plaintiff" rule. The court denied the motion, concluding that the instructions given to the jury appropriately informed them of the applicable law.

The plaintiff estate appealed. The court of appeals reversed the trial court, concluding that the plaintiff's evidence required a specific instruction on the eggshell plaintiff rule. . . .

II. Jury Instructions and the "eggshell plaintiff" Rule

The estate claims that the court erred in failing to include, in addition to its proximate cause instruction to the jury, a requested instruction on the eggshell plaintiff rule. Such an instruction would advise the jury that it could find that the accident aggravated Loras's heart condition and caused his fatal heart attack. . . .

A tortfeasor whose act, superimposed upon a prior latent condition, results in an injury may be liable in damages for the full disability. This rule deems the injury, and not the dormant condition, the proximate cause of the plaintiff's harm. This precept is often referred to as the "eggshell plaintiff" rule, which has its roots in cases such as *Dulieu v. White & Sons*, [1901] 2 K.B. 669, 679, where the court observed:

> If a man is negligently run over or otherwise negligently injured in his body, it is no answer to the sufferer's claim for damages that he would have suffered less injury, or no injury at all, if he had not had an unusually thin skull or an unusually weak heart.

See generally 4 Fowler V. Harper et al., *The Law of Torts* § 20.3, at 123 & n. 25 (2d ed. 1986); W. Page Keeton et al., *Prosser and Keeton on The Law of Torts* § 43, at 292 (5th ed. 1984) [hereinafter *Prosser & Keeton*].

The proposed instruction here stated:

> If Loras Benn had a prior heart condition making him more susceptible to injury than a person in normal health, then the Defendant is responsible for all injuries and damages which are experienced by Loras Benn, proximately caused by the Defendant's actions, even though the injuries claimed produced a greater injury than those which might have been experienced by a normal person under the same circumstances.

... Defendant claims that the instructions that the court gave sufficiently conveyed the applicable law.

The proximate cause instruction in this case provided:

> The conduct of a party is a proximate cause of damage when it is a substantial factor in producing damage and when the damage would not have happened except for the conduct.

> "Substantial" means the party's conduct has such an effect in producing damage as to lead a reasonable person to regard it as a cause.

See Iowa Uniform Jury Instruction 700.3. Special Verdict Number 4 asked the jury: "Was the negligence of Leland Thomas a proximate cause of Loras Benn's death?" The jury answered this question, "No."

We agree that the jury might have found the defendant liable for Loras's death as well as his injuries under the instructions as given. But the proximate cause instruction failed to adequately convey the existing law that the jury should have applied to this case. The eggshell plaintiff rule rejects the limit of foreseeability that courts ordinarily require in the determination of proximate cause. *Prosser & Keeton* § 43, at 291 ("The defendant is held liable for unusual results of personal injuries which are regarded as unforeseeable. . . ."). Once the plaintiff establishes that the defendant caused some injury to the plaintiff, the rule imposes liability for the full extent of those injuries, not merely those that were foreseeable to the defendant. Restatement (Second) of Torts § 461 (1965) ("The negligent actor is subject to liability for harm to another although a physical condition of the other . . . makes the injury greater than that which the actor as a reasonable man should have foreseen as a probable result of his conduct.").

The instruction given by the court was appropriate as to the question of whether defendant caused Lora's initial personal injuries, namely, the fractured ankle and the bruised chest. This instruction alone, however, failed to adequately convey to the jury the eggshell plaintiff rule, which the jury reasonably could have applied to the cause of Loras's death. . . .

III. Disposition

. . . The record in this case warranted an instruction on the eggshell plaintiff rule. We therefore affirm the decision of the court of appeals. We reverse the judgment of the district court and remand the cause to the district court for a new trial consistent with this opinion.

* * *

Problem 9

Lack of foreseeability does not limit tort damages; the doctrine of proximate cause does, however. In the following situation, will the defendant be liable for the plaintiff's lost wages? Why or why not?

In the glare of bright sunlight, a driver does not see a pedestrian in the crosswalk until the last second. The driver slams on the brakes. As the car comes to a stop, it lightly bumps the pedestrian. Though the driver could not have realized it, the pedestrian is a professional basketball player who has just signed a $20 million contract. Most people would have walked away unharmed, but the player has a preexisting medical condition which causes the nudge from the car to result in a broken leg. The broken leg would have healed before the upcoming basketball season, except for the fact that a doctor improperly sets the break when placing it in a cast. As a result, the leg does not heal correctly, and the player is unable to play professional basketball again. His contract is cancelled.

The player sues the driver to recover the $20 million he has lost.

Real Property

An owner of real property has a right to exclusive, undisturbed possession of it. When that right is violated, the owner can recover damages for resulting harm. Damages are also available to compensate for physical harm to the property.

Several theories of recovery are available to plaintiffs who allege a violation of rights related to possessing real property. There is trespass, which is an intentional tort, and nuisance, which encompasses both negligent and intentional conduct. Or a defendant might cause physical damage to property through negligence.

A plaintiff who sues for trespass alleges that the defendant either wrongfully entered the property or intentionally damaged it. For a nuisance cause of action, the plaintiff alleges the defendant interfered with the use and enjoyment of the property. Under a negligence theory, the plaintiff asserts the defendant damaged the property by not acting carefully enough.

As in other contexts, the purpose of damages for real property harm is to restore plaintiffs to their rightful position — to put them where they were before the tort was committed. The measure of damages for real property torts will always be aimed toward accomplishing that objective, regardless of the cause of action. Properly calculating damages involves considering the nature of the harm to the property as well as the owner's reason for possessing it. The harm from an entry without consent is different than the harm from physical damage to the property. And an owner of an investment property might be harmed by an interference with possession in different ways than an owner who possesses property for personal use.

Introductory Note — *Jacque v. Steenberg Homes*

A trespass is always intentional, but the trespass in this case is *really* intentional. Yet the jury awards nominal damages of $1, tantamount to a finding that the property owners did not show they suffered any actual harm. The Wisconsin Supreme Court must decide if the jury's additional award of $100,000 in punitive damages can stand in that situation. The broader question is how courts can effectively protect property ownership rights when a violation of those rights does not result in tangible harm.

THINGS TO THINK ABOUT while reading *Jacque v. Steenberg Homes*:

1. What legally protected interest is violated by a trespass to real property?

2. What is the purpose of nominal damages?

3. How were the property owners harmed here?

Jacque v. Steenberg Homes, Inc.

Wisconsin Supreme Court
563 N.W.2d 154 (1997)

WILLIAM A. BABLITCH, Justice.

Steenberg Homes had a mobile home to deliver. Unfortunately for Harvey and Lois Jacque (the Jacques), the easiest route of delivery was across their land. Despite adamant protests by the Jacques, Steenberg plowed a path through the Jacques' snow-covered field and via that path, delivered the mobile home. Consequently, the Jacques sued Steenberg Homes for intentional trespass. At trial, Steenberg Homes conceded the intentional trespass, but argued that no compensatory damages had been proved, and that punitive damages could not be awarded without compensatory damages. Although the jury awarded the Jacques $1 in nominal damages and $100,000 in punitive damages, the circuit court set aside the jury's award of $100,000. The court of appeals affirmed, reluctantly concluding that it could not reinstate the punitive damages because it was bound by precedent establishing that an award of nominal damages will not sustain a punitive damage award. We conclude that when nominal damages are awarded for an intentional trespass to land, punitive damages may, in the discretion of the jury, be awarded. We further conclude that the $100,000 awarded by the jury is not excessive. Accordingly, we reverse and remand for reinstatement of the punitive damage award.

I.

Plaintiffs, Lois and Harvey Jacques, are an elderly couple, now retired from farming, who own roughly 170 acres near Wilke's Lake in the town of Schleswig. The defendant, Steenberg Homes, Inc. (Steenberg), is in the business of selling mobile homes. In the fall of 1993, a neighbor of the Jacques purchased a mobile home from Steenberg. Delivery of the mobile home was included in the sales price.

Steenberg determined that the easiest route to deliver the mobile home was across the Jacques' land. Steenberg preferred transporting the home across the Jacques' land because the only alternative was a private road which was covered in up to seven feet of snow and contained a sharp curve which would require sets of "rollers" to be used when maneuvering the home around the curve. Steenberg asked the Jacques on several separate occasions whether it could move the home across the Jacques' farm field. The Jacques refused. The Jacques were sensitive about allowing others on their land because they had lost property valued at over $10,000 to other neighbors in an adverse possession action in the mid-1980's. Despite repeated refusals from the Jacques, Steenberg decided to sell the mobile home, which was to be used as a summer cottage, and delivered it on February 15, 1994.

On the morning of delivery, Mr. Jacque observed the mobile home parked on the corner of the town road adjacent to his property. He decided to find out where the movers planned to take the home. The movers, who were Steenberg employees, showed Mr. Jacque the path they planned to take with the mobile home to reach the neighbor's lot. The path cut across the Jacques' land. Mr. Jacque informed the movers that it was the Jacques' land they were planning to cross and that Steenberg did not have permission to cross their land. He told them that Steenberg had been refused permission to cross the Jacques' land. . . .

The employees, after beginning down the private road, ultimately used a "bobcat" to cut a path through the Jacques' snow-covered field and hauled the home across the Jacques' land to the neighbor's lot. . . .

II.

Steenberg argues that, as a matter of law, punitive damages could not be awarded by the jury because punitive damages must be supported by an award of compensatory damages and here the jury awarded only nominal and punitive damages. The Jacques contend that the rationale supporting the compensatory damage award requirement is inapposite when the wrongful act is an intentional trespass to land. We agree with the Jacques.

Our analysis begins with a statement of the rule and the rationale supporting the rule. First, we consider the individual and societal interests implicated when an intentional trespass to land occurs. Then, we analyze the rationale supporting the rule in light of these interests.

The general rule was stated in *Barnard v. Cohen*, 165 Wis. 417, 162 N.W. 480 (1917), where the question presented was: "In an action for libel, can there be a recovery of punitory damages if only nominal compensatory damages are found?" With the bare assertion that authority and better reason supported its conclusion, the *Barnard* court said no. *Id.* at. 418. *Barnard* continues to state the general rule of punitive damages in Wisconsin. The rationale for the compensatory damage requirement is that if the individual cannot show actual harm, he or she has but a nominal interest, hence, society has little interest in having the unlawful, but otherwise harmless, conduct deterred, therefore, punitive damages are inappropriate. *Jacque v. Steenberg Homes, Inc.,* 201 Wis.2d 22, 548 N.W.2d 80 (Ct.App.1996).

However, whether nominal damages can support a punitive damage award in the case of an intentional trespass to land has never been squarely addressed by this court. Nonetheless, Wisconsin law is not without reference to this situation. In 1854 the court established punitive damages, allowing the assessment of "damages as a punishment to the defendant for the purpose of making an example." *McWilliams v. Bragg,* 3 Wis. 424, 425 (1854). . . .

We turn first to the individual landowner's interest in protecting his or her land from trespass. The United States Supreme Court has recognized that the private landowner's right to exclude others from his or her land is "one of the most essential sticks in the bundle of rights that are commonly characterized as property." *Dolan v. City of Tigard,* 512 U.S. 374, 384 (1994).

Yet a right is hollow if the legal system provides insufficient means to protect it. Felix Cohen offers the following analysis summarizing the relationship between the individual and the state regarding property rights:

> [T]hat is property to which the following label can be attached:
>
> To the world:
>
> Keep off X unless you have my permission, which I may grant or withhold.
>
> > Signed: Private Citizen
> >
> > Endorsed: The state

Felix S. Cohen, *Dialogue on Private Property,* IX Rutgers Law Review 357, 374 (1954). Harvey and Lois Jacque have the right to tell Steenberg Homes and any other trespasser, "No, you cannot cross our land." But that right has no practical meaning unless protected by the State.

The nature of the nominal damage award in an intentional trespass to land case further supports an exception to *Barnard.* Because a legal right is involved, the law recognizes that actual harm occurs in every trespass. The action for intentional trespass to land is directed at vindication of the legal right. W. Page Keeton, *Prosser and Keeton on Torts,* § 13 (5th ed.1984). The law infers some damage from every direct entry upon the land of another. *Id.* The law recognizes actual harm in every trespass to land whether or not compensatory damages are awarded. *Id.* Thus, in the case of intentional trespass to land, the nominal damage award represents the recognition that, although immeasurable in mere dollars, actual harm has occurred.

. . . In sum, the individual has a strong interest in excluding trespassers from his or her land. Although only nominal damages were awarded to the Jacques, Steenberg's intentional trespass caused actual harm. . . .

Accordingly, we reverse and remand to the circuit court for reinstatement of the punitive damage award.

Reversed and remanded with directions.

* * *

Problem 10

Articulating the nature of the harm in a trespass case that does not involve physical damage to the property can be challenging. Has the plaintiff been appreciably harmed in the situation described below?

Dan lives on land next to Peter. Peter's parcel of land is large, several acres. For Dan to get to his house from the main road, he has to drive around to a rear access road. It is much quicker for him to cut across the front corner of Peter's property. Dan starts taking that shortcut daily. Peter has no idea — he never sees Dan doing it and Dan leaves no trace behind.

After taking the shortcut for weeks, Dan's conscience begins to bother him, so he stops and never does it again. Several months later, during a conversation with a (gossipy) neighbor, Peter is informed how Dan used to regularly drive across his property. Peter sues Dan for trespass.

Introductory Note — *Orndorff v. Christiana Community Builders*

Orndorff is a construction defect case. The defendants did not dispute the construction of the plaintiffs' home was faulty. But they did dispute how much it would cost to fix it, and how much the home would be worth after the repairs were done. The trial court awarded damages for the amount it would cost to fix the house. The appellate court must decide if cost to repair is the correct amount to make the plaintiffs whole.

THINGS TO THINK ABOUT while reading *Orndorff v. Christiana Community Builders*:

1. What theories of recovery did the plaintiffs pursue?

2. What is the measure of damages for physical harm to real property?

3. In calculating damages for harm to real property, why does the reason the owner possesses the property matter?

Orndorff v. Christiana Community Builders

California Court of Appeal
217 Cal.App.3d 683 (1990)

BENKE, Acting Presiding Justice.

Introduction

Plaintiffs have lived in their home since 1977. They have no plans to leave it. Unfortunately their home was built on defectively compacted soil. The plaintiffs presented evidence, and the trial court found, it will cost $243,539.95 to repair the defects and relocate the plaintiffs while the necessary repairs are being completed. Their appraiser testified that after their home is repaired it will be worth $238,500. The trial court awarded the plaintiffs their repair and relocation expenses as compensation for the damage caused by the defective soil.

On appeal the defendants, who stipulated the home was built on defectively compacted soil, argue the trial court should have awarded the plaintiffs only the amount by which the defects had diminished the value of the home. . . .

Summary of the Case

On November 14, 1985, plaintiffs Gerald Q. Orndorff and Roberta G. Orndorff filed a complaint against defendants Christiana Community Builders (Christiana) and Ponderosa Homes (Ponderosa). They alleged claims for breach of implied warranty, strict liability, negligence, fraud and violation of building codes. The defendants answered the complaint, denying its material allegations.

Cause of action

Trial without a jury commenced on April 25, 1988. At trial the parties stipulated "The subject property including lots, structures and improvements thereon exhibit distress as a result of fill settlement. As such, the lots, structures and improvements are defective." While agreeing the house was suffering the effects of fill settlement, the parties disputed whether further settlement was likely to occur and what method of repair was needed.

The Orndorffs presented evidence that further settlement was likely and that, in light of future settlement, a pier or caisson and beam system was necessary to repair their house. The Orndorffs' expert estimated it would cost $221,792.68 to install such a system. In addition to the cost of repair, the Orndorffs presented evidence they would be required to incur $21,747 in additional engineering costs, permit fees and relocation expenses while the repairs were completed.

The defendants presented evidence that no future settlement was likely and that, accordingly, a reinforced mat repair system would be sufficient. The cost of such a system would be $118,355.

The parties also disagreed about the value of the Orndorffs' home before and after any repair. The Orndorffs' appraiser testified that without repairs the home was worth $67,500 and that with repairs it would be worth $238,500. On the other hand the defendants' appraiser testified that without repairs the home was worth $160,500 and that with repairs it would be worth only $225,500.

Finally, the Orndorffs testified they had lived in the house for 11 years and had no desire to leave it. Gerald testified that when he and his wife bought the house they paid a premium because the house was located immediately adjacent to an open space easement. Gerald and Roberta each testified that if awarded the repair costs they would in fact repair their home. According to Roberta "I really like the house, I really hadn't planned on moving."

After considering the evidence presented by the parties and inspecting the Orndorffs' home, the trial judge issued a statement of decision. He found the measure of damages for construction defects was either the diminution in value or the likely repair costs and that in this case an award of repair costs, plus relocation expenses, was appropriate. He found fill settlement was likely to continue and that a pier or caisson and grade system was the most efficient method of repair. Thus he awarded the Orndorffs the $243,539.95 needed to install a pier and grade system and pay the Orndorffs' relocation expenses while the repairs were performed.

Issue Presented

On appeal the defendants argue the measure of damages in construction defect cases is the lesser of the diminution in value caused by the defect or the cost of repair. Since the Orndorffs' appraiser testified their home was worth $67,500 without repair and would be worth $238,500 following repairs, the defendants claim the trial court had no power to award more than the $171,000 diminution in value established by the Orndorffs' appraiser.

Discussion

I

Measure of Damages

We do not find the law as rigid as the defendants suggest. Where, as here, the plaintiffs have a personal reason to repair and the costs of repair are not unreasonable in light of the damage to the property and the value after repair, costs of repair which exceed the diminution in value may be awarded. (See *Heninger v. Dunn* (1980) 101 Cal.App.3d 858, 863–866.) In *Heninger* the defendants bulldozed a road over the plaintiffs' land. The road damaged or killed 225 of plaintiffs' trees and destroyed much vegetative undergrowth. However because of improved access the trial court found the road actually increased the value of the land from $179,000 to $184,000. The trial court also found it would cost $221,647 to replace the dead or dying trees and that the undergrowth could be restored for $19,610. Because the value of the property had been increased, the trial court denied the plaintiffs any award of damages.

The Court of Appeal reversed and remanded. In rejecting the trial court's rigid approach to damage calculation, the Court of Appeal stated: "The rule precluding recovery of restoration costs in excess of diminution in value is, however, not of invariable application. Restoration costs may be awarded even though they exceed the decrease in market value if 'there is a reason personal to the owner for restoring the original condition' (Rest.2d Torts, § 929, com. b, at pp. 545–546), or 'where there is reason to believe that the plaintiff will, in fact, make the repairs' (22 Am.Jur.2d, Damages, § 132, at p. 192)." (*Heninger, supra,* 101 Cal.App.3d at p. 863; see also *Raven's Cove Townhomes, Inc. v. Knuppe Development Co.* (1981) 114 Cal.App.3d 783.) After analyzing two California cases which had involved closely related damages disputes and noting that no California case had rejected the "personal reason" exception, the *Heninger* court concluded "the exception is viable in California." (*Heninger, supra,* 101 Cal.App.3d at p. 864.) . . .

Although the Court of Appeal in *Heninger* found that it would not be reasonable to award the plaintiffs the $221,647 needed to entirely restore the land, "On retrial, the court's determination whether a reasonable restoration is possible should focus on the question whether an award of the cost of restoring the vegetative undergrowth (or some other method of covering the scar on the land and preventing further erosion) would achieve compensation within the overall limits of what the court determines to be just and reasonable." (*Heninger, supra,* 101 Cal.App.3d at p. 866.)

[handwritten margin note: reasonable rule]

Here the "personal reason" exception adopted in *Heninger* supports the trial court's award. Contrary to the defendants' argument, the "personal reason" exception does not require that the Orndorffs own a "unique" home. Rather all that is required is some personal use by them and a bona fide desire to repair or restore. For instance in *Heninger* the court relied on the plaintiff's simple statement that "'I think the land is beautiful, the natural forest beautiful, and I would like to see it that way.'" (*Heninger, supra,* 101 Cal.App.3d at p. 866.) According to the commentators to the Restatement, "if a building such as homestead *is used for a purpose personal to the owner,* the damages ordinarily include an amount for repairs, even though this might be greater than the entire value of the building. So, when a garden has been maintained in a city in connection with a dwelling house, the owner is entitled to recover the expense of putting the garden in its original condition even though the market value of the premises has not been decreased by the defendant's invasion." (Rest.2d., Torts § 929, com. b, p. 546, italics added.) There is no dispute the Orndorffs enjoy the home they have occupied for 11 years and intend to repair it. To obtain reasonable repair costs they were not required to make any further showing. . . .

[handwritten margin note: π meets the burden of proof]

Neither a consumer's reliance upon a builder's expertise nor the builder's ability to spread his risks over a large number of his products suggests that a home, once purchased, can be readily replaced. Indeed the record in this case suggests quite the contrary. The Orndorffs purchased a house which abuts an open space easement and thus is free of neighbors on one side; they have also made substantial improvements to their home in the 11 years they have occupied it. Accordingly, we find no inconsistency in the Orndorffs' reliance on the doctrine of strict liability and their desire to repair their home rather than abandon it. . . .

By requiring that repair costs bear a reasonable relationship to value before harm and to the level of harm actually suffered, the *Heninger* case prevents the unusual or bizarre results the defendants in this case contend would occur should we stray in any manner from a diminution in value measure of damages. Contrary to the defendants' argument, application of the personal reason exception does not permit a plaintiff to insist on reconstruction of a unique product where the cost of repair will far exceed either the value of the product or the damage the defendant has caused. As we interpret *Heninger,* the owner of a unique home or automobile cannot insist on its reconstruction where the cost to do so far exceeds the value of the home or automobile. Nor are repair costs appropriate where only slight damage has occurred and the cost of repair is far in excess of the loss in value.

Here the damages awarded are well within the limitations imposed by *Heninger.* The record establishes that the Orndorffs' home was worth $238,500 in an undamaged condition. A total award — $243,539.95 — which is 2.5 percent greater than the undamaged value of the realty, is in our view, well within reason.

However, it bears emphasis that even where the repair costs are reasonable in relation to the value of the property, those costs must also be reasonable in relation to the harm caused. Here the trial court's finding that fill settlement was likely to continue and the Orndorffs' appraiser's opinion the home was worth only $67,500 in its present condition, suggest the damage sustained was indeed significant. Plainly this is not a case where the tortfeasors' conduct improved the value of the real property or only diminished it slightly. Rather we believe where, as here, the damage to a home has deprived it of most of its value, an award of substantial repair costs is appropriate.

In sum then we find the trial court had the power to award repair costs in this case. . . .

Judgment affirmed; respondents to recover their costs on appeal.

* * *

Problem 11

Property owners can generally recover the cost to repair damage to their property if they have a personal reason for wanting it repaired. Limits based on reasonableness may apply, however. In the following situation, how might a court rule on the plaintiff's request for cost to repair damages?

Cheryl lives near the coast on heavily wooded property. She enjoys the privacy and shade afforded by the three largest trees in her front yard. A contractor doing roadwork accidentally bulldozes the three trees. Removing them *increases* the market value of Cheryl's property because there is now an unobstructed ocean view from the living room window. But Cheryl loved the trees and is indifferent about the view. The trees can be replaced: it will cost $45,000 to procure and plant mature trees of comparable size. Cheryl sues the contractor to recover the cost of the new trees.

Introductory Note — *City of Gainesville v. Waters*

The nuisance experienced by the homeowner plaintiffs in *City of Gainesville* was flooding, including from their septic tank. The flooding had a single cause—damaged water lines—but it happened on multiple occasions. The primary question on appeal has to do with whether the nuisance was temporary (and therefore fixable), or permanent.

THINGS TO THINK ABOUT while reading *City of Gainesville v. Waters*:

1. What legally protected interest is implicated by a nuisance claim?

2. What is the measure of damages for nuisance?

3. Why is it necessary to distinguish between a temporary nuisance and a permanent one?

City of Gainesville v. Waters

Georgia Court of Appeals
258 Ga.App. 555 (2002)

BARNES, Judge.

Patsy and Gina Waters sued the City of Gainesville (the City) for damages and injunctive relief, claiming that the City failed to properly maintain the drainage system that serves their property. Following a jury trial, Patsy Waters was awarded $122,000 in damages attributable to the nuisance, and both women were awarded $50,000 in attorney fees. The trial court also entered an order for injunctive relief directing the City to abate the nuisance.

Viewed in the light most supportive of the jury's verdict, the evidence shows that Patsy and Gina Waters are mother and daughter and jointly own a home located on Sunset Boulevard. Patsy Waters and her ex-husband purchased the house in 1964 and remodeled the basement in 1983 to add a bathroom and kitchen so that their daughter Gina could live there. They also added a second septic tank at that time. The Waterses divorced in 1986, and title was transferred to Patsy. Gina was later added as a joint title holder. Gina Waters testified that she never experienced any water-related problems with the property until 1992 when the City fire department repressurized the water lines. She testified that several water lines were broken at that time, which resulted in the first basement flooding incident, and that although the City sent someone out to repair the damaged water lines, she still experienced problems with flooding.

She testified that in October 1995, the septic tank backed up into the basement and she went home to help her mother deal with the damage. She further testified that when she arrived, Patsy Waters was "in a bad way, is the best way to describe it, emotionally, physically. She was about to drop." She stated that her mother was soaking wet and appeared swollen, and that she was concerned for her mother's health. Gina Waters described an occasion when she and her mother observed that water flowing from a neighbor's draining pool flooded their front yard when it entered a "weir inlet," or catch basin, across the street from their home. She testified that the water was "spewing out of the bank" into their front yard. She further testified that as a result of the water problems, in addition to the flooding, they have numerous sinkholes in their yard caused by underground soil erosion.

The City finally placed a "riser" pipe in the septic tank to keep it from backing up into the house. Even though the Waterses have not experienced any flooding since the pipe was placed in the septic tank, the plumbing in the basement cannot be used because the contents of the septic tank would flow directly into the front yard. The basement is no longer usable as a separate residence.

... The City contends that the trial court erred in denying the directed verdict and j.n.o.v., arguing first that insufficient evidence supports a finding that the City had maintained a nuisance on the Waterses' property. ...

We will deal jointly with the trial court's denial of both the City's motion for directed verdict and its motion for j.n.o.v. because both arise from the same issues of law and fact and are governed by the same standards of appellate review. We apply the "any evidence" test to our review of the trial court's denial of a j.n.o.v. and affirm the trial court's ruling as long as there is some evidence to support the verdict. The City, therefore, must show "that there was no conflict in the evidence as to any material issue and that the evidence introduced, with all reasonable deductions therefrom, *demanded* a verdict in [its] favor. [Cit.]" *Alternative Health Care Systems v. McCown*, 237 Ga.App. 355–356 (1999).

The City argues that the evidence showed only one incident of flooding in the Waterses' house and was therefore insufficient to support a nuisance claim. We do not agree.

"[W]here a municipality negligently constructs or undertakes to maintain a sewer or drainage system which causes the *repeated* flooding of property, a continuing, abatable nuisance is established, for which the municipality is liable." *Hibbs v. City of Riverdale*, 267 Ga. 337, 338, (1996). The exercise of dominion or control over the property causing the harm is sufficient to establish nuisance liability.

While it is undisputed that there were no incidents of flooding after October 17, 1995, Gina Waters testified about several incidents of flooding in the basement and on the property's grounds that occurred prior to October 17. A former co-worker of Patsy Waters testified that she either missed work or was late for work frequently between 1994 and 1996, especially during the rainy periods, because of flooding in her home.

The City does not dispute that it exercised dominion and control over the pipe or drainage system. Accordingly, because the Waterses presented evidence of repeated incidents of flooding to the Waterses' property sufficient to establish an abatable nuisance, the trial court did not err in denying the motion for directed verdict or j.n.o.v. on these grounds.

The City also argues that the Waterses did not put forth evidence of property damages resulting from an abatable nuisance, but only of the diminished market value of their home, which it maintains is evidence of permanent nuisance damage. It contends that the only evidence of property damages came from a real estate appraiser who testified that, as a result of the water damage, the Waterses' home had depreciated in fair market value approximately $8,500. The City maintains that because of the Waterses' failure to present evidence of diminished rental value to establish abatable nuisance damages, the trial court erred in instructing the jury on abatable nuisances, and denying its motions for directed verdict and j.n.o.v. on this ground.

Although the diminution of fair market value is the measure of property damages for permanent nuisance and lost rental value is the measure of property damages for abatable nuisance, *City of Warner Robins v. Holt*, 220 Ga.App. 794, 796 (1996), property damages are not the only kind of damages available in a nuisance action. A plaintiff may also recover for damages to the person.

> In a continuing, abatable nuisance case, the plaintiff is not limited to a recovery of rental value or market value; rather, he may recover any special damages whether the injury is of a temporary or a permanent nature. Unlawful interference with the right of the owner to enjoy possession of his property may be an element of damages. The measure of damages for " discomfort, loss of peace of mind, unhappiness and annoyance" of the plaintiff caused by the maintenance of a nuisance is for the enlightened conscience of the jury.

(Citations omitted.) *City of Columbus v. Myszka,* 246 Ga. 571, 573 (1980).

In this case, the jury awarded Patsy Waters $122,000 in general damages. Because it was authorized to award Waters damages unrelated to the loss in rental value, we cannot go behind the jury's verdict to determine how the damages were apportioned. The City appears to argue that the existence of a claim for an abatable nuisance is *proved* by the diminished rental value, maintaining that "by offering only evidence of diminished market value, Appellees chose only to pursue a claim for a permanent nuisance." This argument confuses the issue of causation with the issue of damages and is simply not the law. . . .

Following a hearing, the trial court entered an abatement order instructing the City to "abate the nuisance of the flow of storm water onto [the Waterses'] property from Sunset Boulevard" by filling the pipe and inlet with grout or concrete and constructing a curb and gutter along the front of the Waterses' property. The City contends the trial court's grant of an injunction was an abuse of discretion. To support this contention, the City argues that, because the nuisance was permanent, injunctive relief is not a remedy. It also argues that the evidence is insufficient to support the finding of a nuisance.

These enumerations are meritless. In Division 1 we found that the evidence sufficiently supported the jury's determination that the City maintained an abatable nuisance. When a continuing nuisance is found, a property owner may obtain both damages and an injunction. *Dept. of Transp. v. Edwards,* 267 Ga. 733, 738 (1997). The granting of an injunction is within the sound discretion of the trial court and should be tailored to the improper taking.

We ascertain no abuse of discretion. . . .

Judgment affirmed.

* * *

Problem 12

The tort of nuisance protects a property owner's right to use and enjoyment of land. Does the property owner in the following situation have a cognizable nuisance claim?

A manufacturer of a very spicy chili sauce opens a plant next to a suburban neighborhood. The manufacturing process involves flash-drying chili peppers over flames which causes a strong odor to drift throughout the nearby neighborhood every weekday afternoon. Perry, one of the residents there, hadn't noticed anything because of a medical problem that left him without a sense of smell. He learns about the odor when he reads complaints posted on a neighborhood internet message board, and he then sues the plant for nuisance.

Personal Property

Just as ownership of real property comes with certain legally enforceable rights, so does ownership of personal property. The defining characteristic of personal property is that it is movable. That means personal property can be taken from its owner, an obvious interference with possessory rights.

When the owner of personal property is completely deprived of its possession — because the item was taken — that is the tort of conversion. If the owner maintains possession of the item but the defendant interferes with the owner's ability to use it, that is a trespass to personal property (often referred to by the antiquated term "trespass to chattels"). Damaging property interferes with the owner's use and is considered a trespass. Using an item without consent would qualify as well.

The causes of action that can be alleged for interference with personal property interests are conversion and trespass to chattels. Thinking about the rights these causes of action protect is helpful in determining how damages should be measured to return a plaintiff to the rightful position. What right has been interfered with by the defendant's conduct — the right to possess the property in the first place? The right to exclusive use of it? Or has the property itself been damaged? As always, determining the nature of the harm suffered is essential to calculating an appropriate award of damages.

Introductory Note — *Mackey v. Goslee*

Mackey is a conversion case. Plaintiff sued for theft of his trailer. The trial court found for the plaintiff and awarded compensatory and punitive damages. The issue on appeal is whether there is sufficient evidence to support the damage award. Deciding that question requires a review of the method of calculating damages for conversion and application of that method to the evidence presented by the plaintiff.

THINGS TO THINK ABOUT while reading *Mackey v. Goslee*:

1. What is the measure of damages for conversion?

2. How are conversion damages measured when there is no market for the property?

3. Why was the evidence insufficient to prove damages here?

Mackey v. Goslee

Missouri Court of Appeals
244 S.W.3d 261 (2008)

NANCY STEFFEN RAHMEYER, Judge.

Alvin Mackey ("Respondent") brought suit against Steven G. Goslee ("Appellant") for conversion of a trailer and personal property on or about January 27, 2003, in Wright County, Missouri. After a bench trial, a judgment was entered in favor of Respondent for actual damages of $14,000 and punitive damages of $2,500. Appellant challenges the sufficiency of the evidence to support a finding of conversion and claims a misapplication of the law in determining actual and punitive damages. We find that though the trial court properly determined that Appellant is responsible for the conversion of Respondent's property, the trial court did err in their determination of actual damages and, thus, both the actual and punitive damage awards must be reversed.

The record indicates that in January of 2003, Appellant and Respondent had a conversation regarding a bill that Respondent owed Appellant and had not paid; however, Respondent was on his way to an appointment and did not have time to discuss the matter thoroughly. According to Respondent's testimony, Appellant then made a threatening statement that "I [Appellant] will do whatever I have to do to protect my interest." Respondent then left his home and when he returned a few hours later, a trailer he owned was missing from his property along with the items that were on the trailer. On the day the trailer was taken, Respondent filed a police report that included information about the trailer and the additional personal property taken along with the trailer.

At trial, the trailer was described as a twenty-seven foot trailer with twenty feet of bed space. The trailer was a custom-built, heavy duty, all metal, twelve-ton trailer built for hauling industrial equipment such as backhoes, dozers, etc. Respondent built the trailer himself and testified that it was patterned after one designed by Bruce Kaylor, who testified at trial. The trailer was approximately twenty years old and had been used by Respondent in the course of his business.

The trailer, which had the tongue severed with a cutting torch, was discovered by law enforcement in July of 2004 at a business owned by Appellant and his wife. The items that were on the trailer when it was taken were not recovered. Respondent, on the day the trailer was taken, contacted local suppliers and priced the items that had been on the trailer. Those values, quoted by the suppliers of the items, were given in trial as "the replacement value" on or about the date of conversion. Two months prior to trial, in April of 2006, Respondent priced steel trailers; he found one for sale in Texas for over $13,000 that would be suitable.

In a court-tried case, the reviewing court affirms the trial court's decision unless there is no substantial evidence to support it, unless it is against the weight of the evidence, or unless it erroneously declares or applies the law. This Court gives due regard to the opportunity of the trial court to have judged the credibility of the witnesses as the trial court is free to believe or disbelieve all, part, or none of the testimony of any witness. When determining the sufficiency of the evidence, an appellate court will accept as true the evidence, and inferences from the evidence, that are favorable to the trial court's judgment and disregard all contrary evidence.

Appellant initially challenges the sufficiency of the evidence supporting a finding of conversion. Conversion is the unauthorized assumption of the right of ownership over another's personal property to the exclusion of the owner's rights. *Bell v. Lafont Auto Sales,* 85 S.W.3d 50, 54 (Mo.App. E.D.2002). Conversion requires an intentional exercise of dominion or control over property that so seriously interferes with the owner's right of control that the interferer may justly be required to pay the owner the full value of the property. *Weicht v. Suburban Newspapers of Greater St. Louis, Inc.,* 32 S.W.3d 592, 597 (Mo.App. E.D.2000). Conversion can be proven by establishing:

(1) a tortious taking; (2) any use or appropriation to the use of the person in possession, indicating a claim of right in opposition to the true owner's rights; or (3) by a refusal to give up possession to the owner on demand, even though the defendant's original possession of the property was proper.

R.J.S. Sec., Inc. v. Command Sec. Services, Inc., 101 S.W.3d 1, 15 (Mo.App. W.D.2003).

Conversion has also been found to require the following three elements: (1) plaintiff was the owner of the property or entitled to its possession; (2) defendant took possession of the property with the intent to exercise some control over it; and (3) defendant thereby deprived plaintiff of the right to possession.

Id. at 15 n. 6 (*citing JEP Enterprises, Inc. v. Wehrenberg, Inc.,* 42 S.W.3d 773, 776 (Mo. App. E.D.2001)).

The evidence presented in this case is that (1) Appellant spoke with Respondent on the day the trailer went missing about some outstanding debt, (2) the conversation ended when Appellant made "threatening" remarks, (3) the trailer was eventually recovered at Appellant's place of business, and (4) the trailer was returned damaged and unusable. A review of the transcript reveals that Appellant and Respondent had an ongoing business relationship and it is a reasonable inference, in light of the judgment, that Appellant knew the trailer was necessary to Respondent's livelihood. It is further a reasonable inference that the trial court could have found that Appellant intended to convert the trailer and equipment in order to pressure Respondent to pay his debt. Although there was no direct evidence that Appellant was responsible for the conversion of Respondent's property, the circumstantial evidence is clear; therefore, reviewing the record and all reasonable inferences therefrom in light of the judgment of the trial court, we find that there was sufficient evidence to support a finding of conversion. On the issue of conversion liability, the judgment of the trial court is affirmed.

Appellant next challenges the evidence supporting the award of damages for conversion. The measure of damages for the conversion of personal property is the fair market value at the time and place of the conversion. *Coffman v. Powell,* 929 S.W.2d 309, 312 (Mo.App. S.D.1996).

> "Fair market value" is defined as "the price which property will bring when it is offered for sale by an owner who is willing but under no compulsion to sell and is bought by a buyer who is willing or desires to purchase but is not compelled to do so."

Id. (*quoting Bridgeforth v. Proffitt,* 490 S.W.2d 416, 425 (Mo.App. 1973)). When property that is detained by the defendant for a period of time is subsequently recovered by the plaintiff, the measure of damages is the difference between the value of the property at the time of conversion and the value at the time of return, plus reasonable value for the loss of use during the period of detention. *Lacks v. R. Rowland & Co. Inc.,* 718 S.W.2d 513, 520 (Mo.App. E.D.1986).

The only evidence as to the value of the trailer came from Respondent's testimony that he priced trailers two months before the trial and found a trailer, which was suitable for his needs, in Texas, which would have cost approximately $13,000. Respondent did not present any evidence as to the age or condition of the trailer in Texas, or any other trailer he may have found, that might have helped the trial court ascertain the fair market value of the converted trailer at the time of the conversion. There simply was not any evidence as to the condition of the converted, twenty-year-old trailer at the time of conversion and there was no comparison made at trial between the Texas trailer and the converted trailer. It is clear that replacement value alone was insufficient for the court to determine the measure of damages for conversion of the trailer at the time of the conversion. The trial court was required to determine the fair market value of the converted property at the time of the conversion or within a reasonable time of the conversion. *Bell,* 85 S.W.3d at 55.

Although this Court must view the evidence in the light most favorable to the judgment and disregard all contrary evidence, this Court finds that there is simply not enough evidence on the record to adequately determine whether the trial court could infer the fair market value of the converted trailer at the time of conversion from the "replacement value" testimony at trial. The trial court erred in relying on the replacement value of the converted trailer two months before trial, which was almost three years after the conversion. To be clear, we are not saying that the owner could not have testified that the trailer in Texas was comparable in age, function, make, model or value to the converted trailer. He simply did not do so at trial.

Additionally, when the converted item is recovered by the true owner, the measurement of value is the difference between the value of the property at the time of conversion and the value at the time of return, plus reasonable value for the loss of use during the period of detention. *Lacks,* 718 S.W.2d at 520. As there was not evidence of the value of the returned trailer, which may have had scrap value, it cannot be said that the trial court considered the value of the trailer at the time of its return when determining the amount of damages. Furthermore, the trial court did not allow evidence to be presented on the possibility of financial loss of use due to the loss of the trailer, thus, there was no evidence concerning the loss of use during the period of detention.

Respondent argues that, even if a case had not been made as to the traditional damages, the trailer could have been classified as "unique" property under Missouri law. Damages for "unique" property most often contemplates the value of sentimental items such as family heirlooms and pictures, or property that served a special purpose such as churches and school yards. *See Ladeas v. Carter,* 845 S.W.2d 45, 53–54 (Mo.App. W.D.1992); *Leonard Missionary Baptist Church v. Sears Roebuck and Co.,* 42 S.W.3d 833, 836–37 (Mo.App. E.D.2001). Unique personal property cannot be valued in the same manner as common personal property because there may not be a market for such items, and often the items have more value to the owner than anyone else.

Although the record indicates that Respondent did craft much of the trailer by hand, there was also evidence that there were trailers, other than the trailer in Texas, that would have suited Respondent's business needs and that those trailers were for sale "up and down the road." This evidence indicates there is a market for the type of trailer converted in this case; therefore, it does not meet the definition of unique property. The proper measurement of damages for the trailer was that of fair market value for personal property.

Likewise, Appellant failed to provide adequate evidence of the fair market value of the items on the trailer. The only evidence presented at trial as to the value of the personal property located on the trailer was Respondent's testimony that, in January, near the time when the property was converted, he made many phone calls to determine how much it would cost to "replace" the items. These values were recorded and admitted as Plaintiff's Exhibit 1. No evidence was elicited as to the condition of each of the items except to say that they were all items that were replaced on a routine basis "because they wear out." Had Respondent testified more specifically as to the condition of each item on the trailer at the time of conversion, it would have been enough for the trial court to make an accurate finding as to fair market value. The record is clear that the values listed on Exhibit 1 represent the amount it would cost to replace each of the items. As with the trailer, replacement value does not suffice. Therefore, the judgment is reversed and the case is remanded with directions to have a new trial on damages only. . . .

In conclusion, the portion of the judgment regarding liability for the conversion of the trailer and the items on that trailer is affirmed; the case is further reversed and remanded with directions for a new trial on damages only.

LYNCH, C.J., BATES, J., concur.

* * *

Problem 13

Conversion damages are intended to compensate a property owner for the value of the property taken. How should damages be measured in the scenario described below?

Sharon buys a painting at a gallery because she likes it and thinks it will look nice in her living room. She pays $200 for it. Several years later, the artist who created the painting becomes famous, and his work is in very high demand. He then tragically passes away. All of his art, Sharon's painting included, dramatically increases in value. Though Sharon could sell her painting for $25,000, she chooses not to because she loves how it looks in her house. Sharon has a dinner party one night and an unscrupulous guest makes off with the painting while Sharon is doing the dishes.

Sharon sues the guest for conversion. At trial, Sharon admits she would never have sold the painting because she liked it so much.

Introductory Note — *Glidden v. Szybiak* and *Intel Corp. v. Hamidi*

Glidden is an old trespass to chattels case. Trespass is raised not as a cause of action by the plaintiff but rather as a defense to the plaintiff's claim. (Under the statute which plaintiff sued, no recovery can be had if the plaintiff engaged in trespass.) The personal property at issue is a dog. The alleged trespass by the plaintiff is pulling the dog's ears. So the court must decide: is pulling the dog's ears a trespass?

Intel Corp. is a new trespass to chattels case. Trespass is raised as a cause of action, asserted by an employer against its employee. The personal property at issue is an email system. The alleged trespass is sending unauthorized emails. So the court must decide: is sending unauthorized emails a trespass?

THINGS TO THINK ABOUT while reading *Glidden v. Szybiak* and *Intel Corp. v. Hamidi*:

1. What right is protected by the tort of trespass to chattels?

2. How is the measure of damages for trespass to chattels different than that for conversion?

3. Are any of the legal principles relied on by the *Glidden* court used to decide *Intel Corp. v. Hamidi*?

Glidden v. Szybiak

New Hampshire Supreme Court
63 A.2d 233 (1949)

BRANCH, Chief Justice.

Judgment on the verdicts against defendant Jane Szybiak and judgment for defendant Louis Szybiak.

Actions at law under the provisions of R.L. c. 180, §§ 23, 24, to recover for a dog bite sustained by the plaintiff Elaine Glidden upon September 29, 1946, and for medical expenses incurred by her father, Harold Glidden. Trial by the Court, with verdicts for the plaintiffs. The plaintiff Elaine Glidden, who was four years old at the time of the occurrence here involved, left her home about noon on the day of her injury, to go to a neighborhood store for candy. On the porch of the store Elaine encountered a dog named Toby and engaged in play with him. She eventually climbed on his back and pulled his ears. The dog snapped at her and bit her nose, inflicting wounds for which a recovery is sought. She was treated by two physicians and a successful result obtained. Such scars as were left are 'in no way disfiguring but discernible on close view.' The dog Toby was owned by the defendant Jane Szybiak, an unmarried daughter of the other two defendants, 26 years of age at the time of the trial, living with her parents.

The Court found that the defendant Louise Szybiak, although she exercised some care for the dog Toby, 'was not the owner or keeper of the dog.' The defendant Louis Szybiak, was found to be the head of the family at the time of the injury to Elaine Glidden. 'He tolerated and permitted the dog to be in his household and to roam at will throughout the house', and it was further found 'that Toby was in possession of the defendant Louis within the meaning of the statute.' To this finding the defendant excepted as being contrary to the evidence and unsupported by the evidence. The defendants also excepted to the denial of their motions for judgment at the close of the evidence. The Court also made the following finding: 'Elaine is found to have been of such tender years as to be incapable of being guilty of contributory negligence in her conduct toward the dog Toby. If she was too young to be guilty of negligence, she cannot be found to have been guilty of a trespass or a tort at the time she received her injury.' To this finding the defendants duly excepted.

The statute under which these actions were brought reads as follows: '23. Liability of owner. Any person to whom or to whose property damage may be occasioned by a dog not owned or kept by him shall be entitled to recover such damage of the person who owns or keeps the dog, or has it in possession, unless the damage was occasioned to him while he was engaged in the commission of a trespass or other tort.'

It is the contention of the defendants that the plaintiff Elaine was engaged in the commission of a trespass at the time of her injury and is, therefore, barred from recovery under the statute. The law in regard to a trespass to chattels is thus summarized in the Restatement of the Law of Torts, s. 218: 'One who without consensual or other privilege to do so, uses or otherwise intentionally intermeddles with a chattel which is in possession of another is liable for a trespass to such person if, (a) the chattel is impaired as to its condition, quality or value, or (b) the possessor is deprived of the use of the chattel for a substantial time, or (c) bodily harm is thereby caused to the possessor or harm is caused to some person or thing in which the possessor has a legally protected interest.' In comment (f) to clauses (a) and (b), it is pointed out that 'the interest of a possessor of a chattel in its inviolability, unlike the similar interest of a possessor of land, is not given legal protection by an action for nominal damages for harmless intermeddlings with the chattel. * * * Sufficient legal protection of the possessor's interest in the mere inviolability of his chattel is afforded by his privilege to use reasonable force to protect his possession against even harmless interference.'

No claim was advanced at the trial that the dog Toby was in any way injured by the conduct of the plaintiff Elaine. Consequently she could not be held liable for a trespass to the dog. Consequently her conduct did not constitute a trespass which will prevent her recovery under the statute here invoked.

The finding that 'Toby was in possession of the defendant Louis within the meaning of the statute' must be set aside. The evidence was uncontradicted that the dog belonged to the defendant Jane, who testified as follows:

'Q. Did your father object to having Toby in the house? A. Yes, he did.

'Q. Could he have thrown Toby out of the house? A. I suppose so.

'Q. Did he do it? A. No, he didn't.

'Q. So he allowed Toby to live there? A. He told me I would be fully responsible for the dog, take care of him.'

The evidence was also uncontradicted that Jane took care of the dog when she left for work in the morning and that thereafter he was in the care of her mother and that defendant Louis had nothing whatever to do with the care of the dog. Under these circumstances it must be held that the defendant Louis was not the possessor of the dog Toby and therefore as to him the motion for judgment at the close of the evidence should have been granted. Possessor as used in the statute implies the exercise of care, custody or control of the dog by one who though not the owner assumes to act in his stead. Here the actual care, custody and control of the dog was in the owner Jane Szybiak, who was of adult age, and she alone was responsible for the conduct of the animal. The statute furnishes no justification for imposing liability on the defendant Louis.

Judgment on the verdict against the defendant Jane.

Judgment for the defendant Louis.

* * *

Intel Corp. v. Hamidi

California Supreme Court
30 Cal.4th 1432 (2003)

WERDEGAR, J.

Intel Corporation (Intel) maintains an electronic mail system, connected to the Internet, through which messages between employees and those outside the company can be sent and received, and permits its employees to make reasonable nonbusiness use of this system. On six occasions over almost two years, Kourosh Kenneth Hamidi, a former Intel employee, sent e-mails criticizing Intel's employment practices to numerous current employees on Intel's electronic mail system. Hamidi breached no computer security barriers in order to communicate with Intel employees. He offered to, and did, remove from his mailing list any recipient who so wished. Hamidi's communications to individual Intel employees caused neither physical damage nor functional disruption to the company's computers, nor did they at any time deprive Intel of the use of its computers. The contents of the messages, however, caused discussion among employees and managers.

On these facts, Intel brought suit, claiming that by communicating with its employees over the company's e-mail system Hamidi committed the tort of trespass to chattels. The trial court granted Intel's motion for summary judgment and enjoined Hamidi from any further mailings. A divided Court of Appeal affirmed.

After reviewing the decisions analyzing unauthorized electronic contact with computer systems as potential trespasses to chattels, we conclude that under California law the tort does not encompass, and should not be extended to encompass, an electronic communication that neither damages the recipient computer system nor impairs its functioning. Such an electronic communication does not constitute an actionable trespass to personal property, i.e., the computer system, because it does not interfere with the possessor's use or possession of, or any other legally protected interest in, the personal property itself. (See *Zaslow v. Kroenert* (1946) 29 Cal.2d 541, 551; *Ticketmaster Corp. v. Tickets.com, Inc.* (C.D.Cal., Aug. 10, 2000, No. 99CV7654) 2000 WL 1887522, p. *4; Rest.2d Torts, § 218.) The consequential economic damage Intel claims to have suffered, i.e., loss of productivity caused by employees reading and reacting to Hamidi's messages and company efforts to block the messages, is not an injury to the company's interest in its computers — which worked as intended and were unharmed by the communications — any more than the personal distress caused by reading an unpleasant letter would be an injury to the recipient's mailbox, or the loss of privacy caused by an intrusive telephone call would be an injury to the recipient's telephone equipment.

. . . Intel's claim fails not because e-mail transmitted through the Internet enjoys unique immunity, but because the trespass to chattels tort — unlike the causes of action just mentioned — may not, in California, be proved without evidence of an injury to the plaintiff's personal property or legal interest therein.

Factual and Procedural Background

Hamidi, a former Intel engineer, together with others, formed an organization named Former and Current Employees of Intel (FACE-Intel) to disseminate information and views critical of Intel's employment and personnel policies and practices. FACE-Intel maintained a Web site (which identified Hamidi as Webmaster and as the organization's spokesperson) containing such material. In addition, over a 21-month period Hamidi, on behalf of FACE-Intel, sent six mass e-mails to employee addresses on Intel's electronic mail system. The messages criticized Intel's employment practices, warned employees of the dangers those practices posed to their careers, suggested employees consider moving to other companies, solicited employees' participation in FACE-Intel, and urged employees to inform themselves further by visiting FACE-Intel's Web site. The messages stated that recipients could, by notifying the sender of their wishes, be removed from FACE-Intel's mailing list; Hamidi did not subsequently send messages to anyone who requested removal.

Each message was sent to thousands of addresses (as many as 35,000 according to FACE-Intel's Web site), though some messages were blocked by Intel before reaching employees. Intel's attempt to block internal transmission of the messages succeeded only in part; Hamidi later admitted he evaded blocking efforts by using different sending computers. When Intel, in March 1998, demanded in writing that Hamidi and FACE-Intel stop sending e-mails to Intel's computer system, Hamidi asserted the organization had a right to communicate with willing Intel employees; he sent a new mass mailing in September 1998. . . .

Intel sued Hamidi and FACE-Intel, pleading causes of action for trespass to chattels and nuisance, and seeking both actual damages and an injunction against further e-mail messages. . . .

Discussion

I. Current California Tort Law

Dubbed by Prosser the "little brother of conversion," the tort of trespass to chattels allows recovery for interferences with possession of personal property "not sufficiently important to be classed as conversion, and so to compel the defendant to pay the full value of the thing with which he has interfered." (Prosser & Keeton, Torts (5th ed.1984) § 14, pp. 85–86.)

Though not amounting to conversion, the defendant's interference must, to be actionable, have caused some injury to the chattel or to the plaintiff's rights in it. Under California law, trespass to chattels "lies where an intentional interference with the possession of personal property *has proximately caused injury.*" (*Thrifty-Tel, Inc. v. Bezenek* (1996) 46 Cal.App.4th 1559, 1566.) In cases of interference with possession of personal property not amounting to conversion, "the owner has a cause of action for trespass or case, *and may recover only the actual damages suffered by reason of the impairment of the property or the loss of its use.*" (*Zaslow v. Kroenert, supra,* 29 Cal.2d at p. 551; accord, *Jordan v. Talbot* (1961) 55 Cal.2d 597, 610.) In modern American law generally, "[t]respass remains as an occasional remedy for minor interferences, *resulting in some damage,* but not sufficiently serious or sufficiently important to amount to the greater tort" of conversion. (Prosser & Keeton, Torts, *supra,* § 15, p. 90, italics added.)

The Restatement, too, makes clear that some actual injury must have occurred in order for a trespass to chattels to be actionable. Under section 218 of the Restatement Second of Torts, dispossession alone, without further damages, is actionable (see *id.,* par. (a) & com. d, pp. 420–421), but other forms of interference require some additional harm to the personal property or the possessor's interests in it. (*Id.,* pars. (b)-(d).) "The interest of a possessor of a chattel in its inviolability, unlike the similar interest of a possessor of land, is not given legal protection by an action for nominal damages for harmless intermeddlings with the chattel. In order that an actor who interferes with another's chattel may be liable, his conduct must affect some other and more important interest of the possessor. *Therefore, one who intentionally intermeddles with another's chattel is subject to liability only if his intermeddling is harmful to the possessor's materially valuable interest in the physical condition, quality, or value of the chattel, or if the possessor is deprived of the use of the chattel for a substantial time, or some other legally protected interest of the possessor is affected as stated in Clause (c).* Sufficient legal protection of the possessor's interest in the mere inviolability of his chattel is afforded by his privilege to use reasonable force to protect his possession against even harmless interference." (*Id.,* com. e, pp. 421–422, italics added.) . . .

In this respect, as Prosser explains, modern day trespass to chattels differs both from the original English writ and from the action for trespass to land: "Another departure from the original rule of the old writ of trespass concerns the necessity of some actual damage to the chattel before the action can be maintained. Where the defendant merely interferes without doing any harm — as where, for example, he merely lays hands upon the plaintiff's horse, or sits in his car — there has been a division of opinion among the writers, and a surprising dearth of authority. *By analogy to trespass to land there might be a technical tort in such a case. . . . Such scanty authority as there is, however, has considered that the dignitary interest in the inviolability of chattels, unlike that as to land, is not sufficiently important to require any greater defense than the privilege of using reasonable force when necessary to protect them. Accordingly it has been held that nominal damages will not be awarded, and that in the absence of any actual damage the action will not lie.*" (Prosser & Keeton, Torts, *supra,* § 14, p. 87, italics added, fns. omitted.)

. . . The dispositive issue in this case, therefore, is whether the undisputed facts demonstrate Hamidi's actions caused or threatened to cause damage to Intel's computer system, or injury to its rights in that personal property, such as to entitle Intel to judgment as a matter of law. To review, the undisputed evidence revealed no actual or threatened damage to Intel's computer hardware or software and no interference with its ordinary and intended operation. Intel was not dispossessed of its computers, nor did Hamidi's messages prevent Intel from using its computers for any measurable length of time. Intel presented no evidence its system was slowed or otherwise impaired by the burden of delivering Hamidi's electronic messages. Nor was there any evidence transmission of the messages imposed any marginal cost on the operation of Intel's computers. In sum, no evidence suggested that in sending messages through Intel's Internet connections and internal computer system Hamidi used the system in any manner in which it was not intended to function or impaired the system in any way. Nor does the evidence show the request of any employee to be removed from FACE-Intel's mailing list was not honored. The evidence did show, however, that some employees who found the messages unwelcome asked management to stop them and that Intel technical staff spent time and effort attempting to block the messages. A statement on the FACE-Intel Web site, moreover, could be taken as an admission that the messages had caused "[e]xcited and nervous managers" to discuss the matter with Intel's human resources department.

. . . Nor may Intel appropriately assert a *property* interest in its employees' time. "The Restatement test clearly speaks in the first instance to the impairment of the chattel. . . . But employees are not chattels (at least not in the legal sense of the term)." (Burk, *The Trouble with Trespass, supra,* 4 J. Small & Emerging Bus.L. at p. 36.) Whatever interest Intel may have in preventing its employees from receiving disruptive communications, it is not an interest in personal property, and trespass to chattels is therefore not an action that will lie to protect it. Nor, finally, can the fact Intel staff spent time attempting to block Hamidi's messages be bootstrapped into an injury to Intel's possessory interest in its computers. To quote, again, from the dissenting opinion in the Court of Appeal: "[I]t is circular to premise the damage element of a tort solely upon the steps taken to prevent the damage. Injury can only be established by the completed tort's consequences, not by the cost of the steps taken to avoid the injury and prevent the tort; otherwise, we can create injury for every supposed tort."

Intel connected its e-mail system to the Internet and permitted its employees to make use of this connection both for business and, to a reasonable extent, for their own purposes. In doing so, the company necessarily contemplated the employees' receipt of unsolicited as well as solicited communications from other companies and individuals. That some communications would, because of their contents, be unwelcome to Intel management was virtually inevitable. Hamidi did nothing but use the e-mail system for its intended purpose — to communicate with employees. The system worked as designed, delivering the messages without any physical or functional harm or disruption. These occasional transmissions cannot reasonably be viewed as impairing the quality or value of Intel's computer system. We conclude, therefore, that Intel has not presented undisputed facts demonstrating an injury to its personal property, or to its legal interest in that property, that support, under California tort law, an action for trespass to chattels. . . .

Disposition

The judgment of the Court of Appeal is reversed.

Concurring Opinion by KENNARD, J.

I concur.

Does a person commit the tort of trespass to chattels by making occasional personal calls to a mobile phone despite the stated objection of the person who owns the mobile phone and pays for the mobile phone service? Does it matter that the calls are not made to the mobile phone's owner, but to another person who ordinarily uses that phone? Does it matter that the person to whom the calls are made has not objected to them? Does it matter that the calls do not damage the mobile phone or reduce in any significant way its availability or usefulness?

The majority concludes, and I agree, that using another's equipment to communicate with a third person who is an authorized user of the equipment and who does not object to the communication is trespass to chattels only if the communications damage the equipment or in some significant way impair its usefulness or availability.

— argument

Intel has my sympathy. Unsolicited and unwanted bulk e-mail, most of it commercial, is a serious annoyance and inconvenience for persons who communicate electronically through the Internet, and bulk e-mail that distracts employees in the workplace can adversely affect overall productivity. But, as the majority persuasively explains, to establish the tort of trespass to chattels in California, the plaintiff must prove either damage to the plaintiff's personal property or actual or threatened impairment of the plaintiff's ability to use that property. Because plaintiff Intel has not shown that defendant Hamidi's occasional bulk e-mail messages to Intel's employees have damaged Intel's computer system or impaired its functioning in any significant way, Intel has not established the tort of trespass to chattels.

This is not to say that Intel is helpless either practically or legally. As a practical matter, Intel need only instruct its employees to delete messages from Hamidi without reading them and to notify Hamidi to remove their workplace e-mail addresses from his mailing lists. Hamidi's messages promised to remove recipients from the mailing list on request, and there is no evidence that Hamidi has ever failed to do so. From a legal perspective, a tort theory other than trespass to chattels may provide Intel with an effective remedy if Hamidi's messages are defamatory or wrongfully interfere with Intel's economic interests. Additionally, the Legislature continues to study the problems caused by bulk e-mails and other dubious uses of modern communication technologies and may craft legislation that accommodates the competing concerns in these sensitive and highly complex areas.

Accordingly, I join the majority in reversing the Court of Appeal's judgment.

Dissenting Opinion of BROWN, J.

Candidate A finds the vehicles that candidate B has provided for his campaign workers, and A spray paints the water soluble message, "Fight corruption, vote for A" on the bumpers. The majority's reasoning would find that notwithstanding the time it takes the workers to remove the paint and the expense they incur in altering the bumpers to prevent further unwanted messages, candidate B does not deserve an injunction unless the paint is so heavy that it reduces the cars' gas mileage or otherwise depreciates the cars' market value. Furthermore, candidate B has an obligation to permit the paint's display, because the cars are driven by workers and not B personally, because B allows his workers to use the cars to pick up their lunch or retrieve their children from school, or because the bumpers display B's own slogans. I disagree.

Intel has invested millions of dollars to develop and maintain a computer system. It did this not to act as a public forum but to enhance the productivity of its employees. Kourosh Kenneth Hamidi sent as many as 200,000 e-mail messages to Intel employees. The time required to review and delete Hamidi's messages diverted employees from productive tasks and undermined the utility of the computer system. "There may . . . be situations in which the value to the owner of a particular type of chattel may be impaired by dealing with it in a manner that does not affect its physical condition." (Rest.2d Torts, § 218, com. h, p. 422.) This is such a case. . . .

Because I do not share the majority's antipathy toward property rights and believe the proper balance between expressive activity and property protection can be achieved without distorting the law of trespass, I respectfully dissent.

Dissenting Opinion by MOSK, J.

The majority hold that the California tort of trespass to chattels does not encompass the use of expressly unwanted electronic mail that causes no physical damage or impairment to the recipient's computer system. They also conclude that because a computer system is not like real property, the rules of trespass to real property are also inapplicable to the circumstances in this case. Finally, they suggest that an injunction to preclude mass, noncommercial, unwelcome e-mails may offend the interests of free communication.

I respectfully disagree and would affirm the trial court's decision. In my view, the repeated transmission of bulk e-mails by appellant Kourosh Kenneth Hamidi (Hamidi) to the employees of Intel Corporation (Intel) on its proprietary confidential e-mail lists, despite Intel's demand that he cease such activities, constituted an actionable trespass to chattels. The majority fail to distinguish open communication in the public "commons" of the Internet from unauthorized intermeddling on a private, proprietary intranet. Hamidi is not communicating in the equivalent of a town square or of an unsolicited "junk" mailing through the United States Postal Service. His action, in crossing from the public Internet into a private intranet, is more like intruding into a private office mailroom, commandeering the mail cart, and dropping off unwanted broadsides on 30,000 desks. Because Intel's security measures have been circumvented by Hamidi, the majority leave Intel, which has exercised all reasonable self-help efforts, with no recourse unless he causes a malfunction or systems "crash." Hamidi's repeated intrusions did more than merely "prompt . . . discussions between '[e]xcited and nervous managers' and the company's human resource department" (maj. opn., *ante*); they also constituted a misappropriation of Intel's private computer system contrary to its intended use and against Intel's wishes.

The law of trespass to chattels has not universally been limited to physical damage. I believe it is entirely consistent to apply that legal theory to these circumstances — that is, when a proprietary computer system is being used contrary to its owner's purposes and expressed desires, and self-help has been ineffective. Intel correctly expects protection from an intruder who misuses its proprietary system, its nonpublic directories, and its supposedly controlled connection to the Internet to achieve his bulk mailing objectives — incidentally, without even having to pay postage.

. . . For these reasons, I respectfully dissent.

* * *

Problem 14

Harm can result from a trespass to personal property either because the property was damaged or because the owner's rights in possessing that property were interfered with. Should the following situation be considered a trespass? If so, how would damages be measured?

Martha lives in a walkable neighborhood and doesn't drive much. She owns a car that she parks in her garage and uses a few times a year. Dan's car breaks down, and without asking Martha, he takes her car and drives it to and from work during the week his car is being repaired. He drives over 500 miles in Martha's car before returning it. Martha did not need to use her car that week and did not notice it was gone.

trespass to chattels
- you would need
some actual damages
- wear/tear on the
vehicle

damages
. pre tort - post-tort
. loss of use - rental value?

Chapter 4

Contract Damages

A contract is a legally binding agreement. It is legally binding because if there is a breach — that is, if a party to the agreement violates its terms — the breaching party must pay damages. The appropriate amount of damages is the amount required to put the other party in as good of a position as he or she would have been in had the breach not occurred. (In some cases, a court can instead order that the contract actually be performed. That remedy — specific performance — is discussed in connection with specific remedies in Chapter 10.) The existence of contracts and remedies to enforce contractual obligations allows for a stable and predictable economic marketplace. Parties who enter into a business transaction can be assured they will get what they bargained for — either through performance of the contract or through compensation for any financial loss caused by nonperformance.

In measuring damages for breach of contract, courts are guided by fundamental principles of contract law. Prominent among those is the concept of "efficient breach," the idea that sometimes it is an overall benefit to society when a contract is breached (perhaps the breaching party's resources are better used elsewhere), so breaching a contract is a morally neutral act that should not necessarily be deterred. The damages allowed under contract law are carefully crafted to allow a party to obtain the benefit of the bargain struck but at the same time avoid unduly punishing the breacher for making the decision to breach.

As Judge Posner puts it, a contract is just "an option to perform or pay," which means a breach is not a wrongful act but merely one that triggers the duty to pay damages. (Richard A. Posner, *Let Us Never Blame a Contract Breaker*, 107 Mich. L. Rev. 1349 (2009).)

Limited to Economic Loss

Contract damages compensate a plaintiff for an economic loss incurred as a result of the defendant's failure to honor a contract. They go no further than that.

As seen in the previous chapter, tort damages look to compensate a plaintiff for every harm the defendant caused: not only out-of-pocket financial losses, but also pain, loss of enjoyment of life, and emotional distress. Contract damages are different, intended to compensate solely for financial harm, even when the plaintiff has experienced other kinds of harm as well. There are two main reasons for that limitation: (1) avoidance of a deterrent effect and (2) predictability. Limiting contract damages to economic loss helps prevent them from being overly punitive to the contract breacher while also enhancing the ability of parties to assess the risk of a transaction (they can better predict the financial downside should the deal not work out).

The policy of limiting contract damages to financial harm birthed a principle referred to as the economic loss rule. The economic loss "rule" is perhaps better thought of not as a single rule but instead as a group of principles designed to preserve the limitation that a plaintiff may recover only for financial harm when a contract is breached. If damages for other kinds of harm are to be recovered, it must be through a tort action. But the economic loss rule also ensures an ordinary breach of contract cannot be transformed into a tort claim. If a defendant's conduct causes financial harm only—no bodily injury, no property damage—a plaintiff cannot recover damages in tort.

The idea behind that limitation is to preserve a meaningful distinction between contract law, which is focused on predictability and compensation for economic harm; and tort law, which is focused on deterrence and complete compensation for the victim.

Introductory Note — *Patton v. Mid-Continent Systems, Inc.,* and *E.I. Du Pont de Nemours Co. v. Pressman*

The contract breached in *Patton* is a franchise agreement. The jury awarded the franchisee plaintiff compensatory damages for breach of contract along with punitive damages. One of the issues on appeal is whether the punitive damages award should stand, given that the applicable law allows punitive damages for breach of contract only for a breach that is fraudulent or malicious. The Seventh Circuit must determine if the breach was in bad faith (which would support a punitive damages award) or if it was an efficient breach (which would not).

E.I. Du Pont de Nemours Co. is an employment case. The jury awarded compensatory and punitive damages to an employee for being terminated by his employer in violation of his contract. The issue on appeal is essentially the same as in *Patton*: whether the breach is the opportunistic kind that allows for punitive damages or the efficient kind that does not.

THINGS TO THINK ABOUT while reading *Patton v. Mid-Continent Systems, Inc.,* and *E.I. Du Pont de Nemours Co. v. Pressman*:

1. What are the defining characteristics of an efficient breach of contract?

2. What is so efficient about an efficient breach?

3. What is an opportunistic breach, and how does it differ from an efficient breach?

Patton v. Mid-Continent Systems, Inc.

United States Court of Appeals, Seventh Circuit
841 F.2d 742 (1988)

POSNER, Circuit Judge.

The defendant, Mid-Continent Systems, appeals from a damages judgment entered upon a verdict for the plaintiffs (James Patton and R.L. Hildebrand, and their corporations) in a diversity breach of contract action. The jury awarded Patton and his company $592,000 in compensatory damages, and Hildebrand and his company $186,000. The jury also awarded the plaintiffs $2,250,000 in punitive damages, but the judge reduced this award to $100,000. Mid-Continent argues that it was entitled to a directed verdict on liability, that there was error in the jury instructions, that the compensatory damages were excessive, and that there was no legal basis for an award of punitive damages.

Mid-Continent provides a credit card that enables truck drivers to charge fuel and related expenses incurred at truck stops. In 1971 Patton, who operated a truck stop on Interstate Route 94 in Burns Harbor, Indiana, and Hildebrand, who operated a truck stop a few miles east on I-94 at New Buffalo, Michigan, entered into a franchise agreement with Mid-Continent. The agreement gave Patton and Hildebrand a specified territory, and authorized Mid-Continent to franchise additional truck stops in that territory only if the franchisees, upon being informed by Mid-Continent that additional coverage was required and upon being given the "first opportunity" to meet the requirement, failed to obtain the additional facilities needed.

In 1974 Mid-Continent franchised Truck-O-Mat, a truck stop located on I-94 west of the Patton and Hildebrand stops and just across the Illinois border; and beginning no later than 1976, Patton and Hildebrand complained to Mid-Continent that Truck-O-Mat's stop was in their territory, in breach of their franchise agreement. That is one of the alleged breaches; here is the other. In 1980 Mid-Continent decided it needed additional coverage in the territory occupied by Patton and Hildebrand, and so informed Patton in a letter that concluded, "We feel that a response within fifteen (15) days and a plan of action within thirty (30) days is reasonable." Two months later Patton replied, "We are working with a real estate broker to establish the coverage that you think is not covered," but added, "Before we invest much more money into this project, I would like to know what you are going to do with the other fuel stop in our franchise area. Mr. Hildebrand and I complained to you, in your office, about this over three (3) years ago. At that time you agreed that it was indeed in our area. To our knowledge there still has been nothing done." Mid-Continent replied by acknowledging that Truck-O-Mat was in the plaintiffs' area and by offering to cancel Truck-O-Mat's franchise if and when the plaintiffs gave Mid-Continent the additional coverage that it desired. There was no immediate response; and seven weeks later (November 1980) Mid-Continent mailed Patton its "notification that you have been given 'right of first refusal' [and] ... that I am now taking steps to fill this requirement." The "taking steps" involved Truckstops of America, which had opened a stop in Gary, Indiana (near Burns Harbor, the site of Patton's stop) in May 1980. Even before then, in April, the plaintiffs had seen a Mid-Continent sign lying on the ground at the Gary site and had complained to Mid-Continent, which had ordered Truckstops of America to get rid of the sign, and it did. No Mid-Continent credit cards were accepted at Truckstops' Gary stop until November 1980 — when Mid-Continent franchised that stop in order to obtain the additional coverage that it wanted.

We begin our analysis with the franchising, allegedly in breach of the plaintiffs' franchise agreement with Mid-Continent, of Truck-O-Mat. The description of the plaintiffs' territory in their franchise agreement is ambiguous. Mid-Continent concedes that it was a question for the jury whether Truck-O-Mat's stop was in that territory, in which event the franchising of the stop violated the agreement, but argues that Patton's truck stop, at Burns Harbor, was not a franchised location. If this is right, Patton has no standing to complain about the invasion of his territory — he has no territory — even though the negotiating history makes perfectly clear that Mid-Continent thought it was franchising two truck stops in the same territory, Patton's at Burns Harbor and Hildebrand's at New Buffalo.

. . . The other question on liability is whether Mid-Continent broke its contract with Patton and Hildebrand by failing to give them enough time to provide additional coverage in their territory. The contract does not say how long a franchisee has to comply with a notification that additional facilities are needed — how long its "first opportunity" lasts — but no options are forever, and a reasonable time can be assumed. *Barco Urban Renewal Corp. v. Housing Authority of City of Atlantic City,* 674 F.2d 1001, 1007 (3d Cir.1982); *Schmidt v. McKay,* 555 F.2d 30, 35 (2d Cir.1977); cf. *Holbrook v. Pitt,* 643 F.2d 1261, 1274 (7th Cir.1981). The jury was entitled to believe the plaintiffs' evidence that a year to acquire a suitable site and another year to complete the truck stop on the site — two years in all — were not an unreasonable amount of time for compliance. Mid-Continent tacitly concedes that the question how long the plaintiffs should have to comply with its demand was a jury question by arguing that all it demanded was a "plan" (the word it used in its first letter) for compliance and that the plaintiffs plainly were unwilling to come up with a plan.

There is no doubt that the plaintiffs were being coy; Patton virtually told Mid-Continent that he would drag his feet until Mid-Continent cured the long-standing violation created by the franchising of Truck-O-Mat in the plaintiffs' territory. The coyness was understandable, however, with the Truck-O-Mat issue unresolved. Patton was naturally hesitant to provide additional coverage when he reasonably believed that Mid-Continent was franchising additional truck stops within the exclusive territory that he shared with Hildebrand — not only Truck-O-Mat but perhaps also Truckstops of America (remember the sign discovered back in April, months before the demand for additional coverage). This conduct by Mid-Continent created a danger that Patton might be unable to recoup his investment in the additional facilities that Mid-Continent wanted him to acquire. . . .

It was within the jury's discretion to conclude that Mid-Continent's action in announcing the forfeiture of the right of first refusal seven weeks after Patton wrote Mid-Continent that he was working with a real estate broker but wanted a resolution of the Truck-O-Mat violation was too peremptory in the circumstances to be consistent with the elastic terms of the franchise agreement.

That brings us to the damages questions. . . .

The question regarding punitive damages is not the amount after the judge cut down the jury's verdict, but whether the plaintiffs were entitled to any punitive damages at all. The franchise agreement states that Arkansas law shall govern any dispute arising out of the agreement but the district judge ruled that, because the case had been brought in Indiana, the law of Indiana governed all substantive issues.

CoL

The law to be applied in a diversity case is the law that would be applied by the state courts in the state where the suit is brought; thus one starts with the forum state's rule on choice of law and ends with whatever law that rule makes applicable to the case at hand. *Casio, Inc. v. S.M. & R. Co., Inc.*, 755 F.2d 528, 530–31 (7th Cir.1985). . . . And since parties to contracts are permitted to specify the remedies that shall be available to them in the event of a breach, see, e.g., UCC § 2-719(1)(b); *Consolidated Data Terminals v. Applied Digital Data Systems, Inc.*, 708 F.2d 385, 392 (9th Cir.1983), since punitive damages were sought and awarded here as a remedy for a breach of contract rather than for a tort, and since the effect of stipulating which state's law would apply was, if not to specify, then at least to constrain, the available remedies, an argument could be made that Arkansas law should have determined the plaintiffs' entitlement to punitive damages. . . .

Mid-Continent acquiesced in the judge's ruling that Indiana law applied, and the question is therefore waived on appeal. Although under Arkansas law the victim of a breach of contract cannot obtain punitive damages without proving that the breach was tortious, see *L.L. Cole & Son, Inc. v. Hickman*, 282 Ark. 6, 665 S.W.2d 278 (1984); *Delta Rice Mill, Inc. v. General Foods Corp.*, 763 F.2d 1001, 1006 (8th Cir.1985); *McLeroy v. Waller*, 21 Ark.App. 292, 731 S.W.2d 789 (1987), there is no such requirement under Indiana law, but under that law he must demonstrate his entitlement to punitive damages by clear and convincing evidence, see *Travelers Indemnity Co. v. Armstrong*, 442 N.E.2d 349, 358–65 (Ind.1982); *Rose Acre Farms, Inc. v. Cone*, 492 N.E.2d 61, 69 (Ind.App.1986). Mid-Continent was eager to place this burden on the plaintiffs, and that is apparently why on balance it preferred to have the issue of punitive damages decided under Indiana law, and therefore acquiesced in the judge's ruling.

Indiana law

Indiana allows punitive damages to be awarded in suits for breach of contract if, "mingled" with the breach, are "elements of fraud, malice, gross negligence or oppression." *Travelers Indemnity Co. v. Armstrong, supra,* 442 N.E.2d at 359; see also *Rose Acre Farms, Inc. v. Cone, supra,* 492 N.E.2d at 70; *Indiana & Michigan Electric Co. v. Terre Haute Industries, Inc., supra,* 507 N.E.2d at 610–12; *Canada Dry Corp. v. Nehi Beverage Co.*, 723 F.2d 512, 524–26 (7th Cir.1983). In trying to give concrete meaning to these terms (especially "oppression"), it is important to bear in mind certain fundamentals of contractual liability. First, liability for breach of contract is, prima facie, strict liability. That is, if the promisor fails to perform as agreed, he has broken his contract even though the failure may have been beyond his power to prevent and therefore in no way blameworthy. The reason is that contracts often contain an insurance component. The promisor promises in effect either to perform or to compensate the promisee for the cost of nonperformance; and one who voluntarily assumes a risk will not be relieved of the consequences if the risk materializes. See *Field Container Corp. v. ICC,* 712 F.2d 250, 257 (7th Cir.1983); *Fidelity & Deposit Co. v. City of Sheboygan Falls,* 713 F.2d 1261, 1269–70 (7th Cir.1983).

Even if the breach is deliberate, it is not necessarily blameworthy. The promisor may simply have discovered that his performance is worth more to someone else. If so, efficiency is promoted by allowing him to break his promise, provided he makes good the promisee's actual losses. If he is forced to pay more than that, an efficient breach may be deterred, and the law doesn't want to bring about such a result. See *J. Yanan & Associates, Inc. v. Integrity Ins. Co.,* 771 F.2d 1025, 1034 (7th Cir.1985). Suppose that by franchising Truck-O-Mat in the plaintiffs' territory, Mid-Continent increased its own profits by $150,000 and inflicted damages of $75,000 on the plaintiffs. That would be an efficient breach. But if Mid-Continent had known that it would have to pay in addition to compensatory damages $100,000 in punitive damages, the breach would not have been worthwhile to it and efficiency would have suffered because the difference between Mid-Continent's profits of $150,000 and the plaintiffs' losses of $75,000 would (certainly after the plaintiffs were compensated) represent a net social gain.

Not all breaches of contract are involuntary or otherwise efficient. Some are opportunistic; the promisor wants the benefit of the bargain without bearing the agreed-upon cost, and exploits the inadequacies of purely compensatory remedies (the major inadequacies being that pre- and post-judgment interest rates are frequently below market levels when the risk of nonpayment is taken into account and that the winning party cannot recover his attorney's fees). This seems the common element in most of the Indiana cases that have allowed punitive damages to be awarded in breach of contract cases; see the discussion of cases in *Travelers Indemnity Co. v. Armstrong, supra,* 441 N.E.2d at 359. Granted, this is not how the legal test is phrased; in particular the category of "gross negligence" seems unrelated to opportunistic breach. We may have captured the core of the Indiana rule but missed the periphery. But whatever the exact dimensions of the rule, the facts of the present case are pretty clearly outside it. . . .

We find no evidence at all that Mid-Continent's action in franchising Truckstops of America after terminating the plaintiffs' right of first refusal was willful, considering that the franchise agreement with the plaintiffs failed to specify the period for which the right must be extended. There is little enough evidence that Mid-Continent was in breach of the agreement; there is none that the breach was wrongful in the strong sense required for an award of punitive damages under Indiana law.

efficiency policy arguments encourage K and non-b party is put back into position that K

The award of punitive damages must be vacated. The finding of breach of contract is affirmed and the case remanded for a new trial limited to compensatory damages.

AFFIRMED IN PART, VACATED IN PART, REMANDED.

* * *

E.I. DuPont de Nemours & Co. v. Pressman

Delaware Supreme Court
679 A.2d 436 (1996)

VEASEY, Chief Justice:

. . . .

I. Procedural Posture

E.I. DuPont de Nemours and Company ("DuPont"), defendant below, appeals from a judgment entered upon a jury verdict in favor of Norman J. Pressman ("Pressman"). The jury verdict for Pressman, which was based on his claim that DuPont breached the Covenant, awarded Pressman $422,700 in compensatory damages for lost wages. The jury also awarded Pressman $25,000 for emotional distress and interest, and $75,000 in punitive damages on the breach of the Covenant claim.

The jury rendered a verdict for DuPont on a claim for breach of an implied-in-fact contract requiring good cause for a termination of employment and for David Pensak ("Pensak"), Pressman's former supervisor, on a claim for defamation. Claims against DuPont for defamation and negligent evaluation were dismissed prior to trial. . . .

II. Facts

We view the evidence in the light most favorable to Pressman. Pressman presented evidence that his immediate supervisor, Pensak, engaged in a retaliatory campaign to persuade Pensak's superiors that Pressman should be fired. The campaign began after Pressman confronted Pensak with evidence that Pensak may have had a conflict of interest. DuPont presented evidence that Pressman was hired as a high level scientist and simply failed to meet the high expectations inherent in the position. The jury apparently credited Pressman's version of events and did not credit DuPont's.

Pressman, a Ph.D. graduate of the University of Pennsylvania in Biomedical Engineering, was hired away by DuPont from the Johns Hopkins School of Medicine in December 1986. DuPont sought Pressman's skills to develop the company's medical imaging technology. From the time he began work in early 1987 until April 1988, Pressman worked at various projects, receiving raises and positive evaluations from his superiors, including Pensak.

In January 1988, Pressman met with Pensak to discuss a possible conflict of interest created by Pensak's involvement as a technical advisor with a medical imaging technology company, Genesis. Pensak was paid $2,000 by Genesis to provide the company with information about and evaluations of new imaging technologies and to assist the company in identifying new business opportunities. Pressman raised his concerns with Pensak after Pensak arranged for representatives of Genesis to meet with Pressman about Genesis equipment and Pressman's knowledge of medical imaging technology.

When Pressman expressed his concerns about Pensak's relationship with Genesis, Pensak became livid and told Pressman to mind his own business. Shortly thereafter, on January 26, 1988, Pensak ordered Pressman "grounded." As a result, Pressman was not allowed to "travel off site . . . even to other DuPont locations." Pensak also told Pressman that he could have "no visitors without my [Pensak's] permission." In the first half of 1988, Pensak also began to express to Charles Ginnard, the personnel representative for Pressman's division, purported concerns regarding Pressman's performance. Pensak placed an "anonymous unsigned" negative evaluation in Pressman's file. Pressman's performance rating was lowered to satisfactory in October 1988. In February 1989 his status was lowered to marginal. He was informed by Pensak of his termination on April 12, 1989. He left DuPont in June 1989.

Evidence was admitted at trial from which a rational jury could conclude that Pensak: (1) misrepresented Pressman's responsibilities to superiors so that it would appear that Pressman was not completing assigned tasks; (2) edited a progress report to superiors which would have had the effect of understating Pressman's accomplishments; and (3) failed to pass along the progress report showing some of Pressman's significant accomplishments during the critical time period in which Pressman's termination was decided. . . .

III. Availability of Damages for Emotional Distress and Punitive Damages

. . . The jury was instructed that it could award emotional distress and punitive damages to Pressman if it found that "DuPont acted maliciously to terminate plaintiff's employment or breached its duty of good faith and fair dealing. . . ." . . .

A. Damages for Emotional Distress

Damages for emotional distress are not available for breach of contract in the absence of physical injury or intentional infliction of emotional distress. *Pierce v. International Ins. Co. of Ill.*, Del.Supr., 671 A.2d 1361, 1367 (1996). Pressman has not suffered physical injury, and he did not establish the elements of intentional infliction of emotional distress. The instruction with respect to emotional distress damages, therefore, was error.

B. Punitive Damages for Breach of Contract

The question of punitive damages is more difficult. The nature of the conduct which gives rise to a breach of the Covenant in the context of at-will employment requires consideration of the broader question of punitive damages as a remedy for breach of contract.

Historically, damages for breach of contract have been limited to the non-breaching parties' expectation interest. *See Restatement (Second) of Contracts* § 347. Also, punitive damages are not recoverable for breach of contract unless the conduct also amounts independently to a tort. *Id.* § 355. *See also* Farnsworth, *Contracts* § 12.8 ("[N]o matter how reprehensible the breach, damages that are punitive, in the sense of being in excess of those required to compensate the injured party for lost expectation, are not ordinarily awarded for breach of contract) (citing *J.J. White, Inc. v. Metropolitan Merchandise Mart, Inc.,* Del.Super., 107 A.2d 892, 894 (1954)). As the introductory note to the remedies portion of the *Restatement (Second) of Contracts* states:

The traditional goal of the law of contract remedies has not been compulsion of the promisor to perform but compensation of the promisee for the loss resulting from the breach. "Willful" breaches have not been distinguished from other breaches, punitive damages have not been awarded for breach of contract, and specific performance has not been granted where compensation in damages is an adequate substitute for the injured party. . . .

Traditional contract doctrine is also supported by the more recent theory of efficient breach. The theory holds that properly calculated expectation damages increase economic efficiency by giving "the other party an incentive to break the contract if, but only if, he gains enough from the breach that he can compensate the injured party for his losses and still retain some of the benefits from the breach." *Restatement (Second) of Contracts,* Reporter's Note to Introductory Note to ch. 16, Remedies; *see also* Barton, *The Economic Basis of Damages for Breach of Contract,* 1 J.Legal Studies 277 (1972). The notion of efficient breach "accords remarkably with the traditional assumptions of the law of contract remedies." Farnsworth, *Contracts* § 12.3 at 155. Punitive damages would increase the amount of damages in excess of the promisee's expectation interest and lead to inefficient results. . . .

Whether to expand punitive damages beyond the traditional applications is a question that occurs frequently. Some commentators have argued for greater availability of punitive damages for breach of contract. While these arguments have some force, we are reluctant to depart markedly from the well-established body of law.

. . . Parties would be more reluctant to join in contractual relationships, or would expend more effort explicitly defining such relationships, if they faced the prospect of damages which could be out of proportion to the amounts involved in the contract. Contracting is a bargained-for exchange. It is the primary mechanism for the allocation of goods, labor and other resources "in a socially desirable manner." *Restatement (Second) of Contracts,* Introductory Note to ch. 16. We recognize the need for caution in fashioning common-law remedies which might inhibit such activity. *See Harris v. Atlantic Richfield Co.,* 14 Cal.App.4th 70 (1993) (restrictions on contract remedies "promote contract formation by limiting liability to the value of the promise"); *Miller Brewing Co. v. Best Beers of Bloomington, Inc.,* Ind.Supr., 608 N.E.2d 975, 981 (1993) ("well-defined parameters . . . lend a needed measure of stability and predictability"). . . .

. . . The economic theory supporting the notion of efficient breach assumes a world without transaction costs. In some cases, particularly those involving relatively large proportionate transaction costs such as lawsuits involving small amounts, the theory may have less application. "Insurance is far from the market ideals of complete information and no transaction costs." Pennington, *Punitive Damages for Breach of Contract: A Core Sample From the Decisions of the Last Ten Years,* 42 Ark.L.Rev. 31, 54 (1989). The assumption of no transaction costs "is a particularly significant defect if the amount in controversy is small." Farnsworth, *Contracts* §12.3 at 157. Punitive damages or other supercompensatory remedies may be appropriate where a party "exploits the inadequacies of purely compensatory remedies. . . ." *Patton v. Mid-Continent Sys., Inc.,* 7th Cir., 841 F.2d 742, 751 (1988) (Posner, J.); *see also* Posner, *Economic Analysis of Law* 104–106 (3d ed. 1986); Kronman & Posner, *The Economics of Contract Law* (1979).

Accordingly, we hold that punitive damages are not available for any breach of the employment contract which may be found by the jury upon retrial of Pressman's claim. . . .

VIII. Conclusion

. . . The judgment of the Superior Court is REVERSED and REMANDED for proceedings consistent with this opinion. We AFFIRM the evidentiary rulings of the Superior Court.

* * *

Problem 15

An efficient breach is considered a net benefit to society because everybody wins, so to speak. Is the following breach of contract an efficient breach? Why or why not?

An engaged couple hires a caterer for their wedding. The contract price for the caterer's services is $5,000, which the couple pays up front. Three days before the wedding, the caterer gets an offer to cater another wedding on the same day, for $10,000. The caterer accepts that offer, notifies the original couple he will be unable to cater their wedding, and returns their $5,000.

Introductory Note — *Erlich v. Menezes*

The Erlichs hired Menezes to build their dream house, and he apparently did a poor job of it. The Erlichs sued for breach of the construction contract but also for the tort of negligence (as well as other torts). They prevailed at trial on the breach of contract and negligence claims. The damages awarded included a sum for emotional distress, something not typically allowed for a breach of contract claim. The fundamental question on appeal: what kind of case is it when a contractor negligently breaches a contract to build a home — breach of contract? Or negligence? The answer dictates what categories of damages can be awarded.

THINGS TO THINK ABOUT while reading *Erlich v. Menezes*:

1. What kind of damages are available for breach of contract?

2. Can a plaintiff ever recover damages in tort if the tortious conduct is also a breach of contract?

3. What are the tort damages in this case, and what are the contract damages?

Erlich v. Menezes

California Supreme Court
21 Cal.4th 543 (1999)

BROWN, J.

We granted review in this case to determine whether emotional distress damages are recoverable for the negligent breach of a contract to construct a house. A jury awarded the homeowners the full cost necessary to repair their home as well as damages for emotional distress caused by the contractor's negligent performance. Since the contractor's negligence directly caused only economic injury and property damage, and breached no duty independent of the contract, we conclude the homeowners may not recover damages for emotional distress based upon breach of a contract to build a house.

I. Factual and Procedural Background

Both parties agree with the facts as ascertained by the Court of Appeal. Barry and Sandra Erlich contracted with John Menezes, a licensed general contractor, to build a "dreamhouse" on their ocean-view lot. The Erlichs moved into their house in December 1990. In February 1991, the rains came. "[T]he house leaked from every conceivable location. Walls were saturated in [an upstairs bedroom], two bedrooms downstairs, and the pool room. Nearly every window in the house leaked. The living room filled with three inches of standing water. In several locations water 'poured in ... streams' from the ceilings and walls. The ceiling in the garage became so saturated ... the plaster liquefied and fell in chunks to the floor." ...

Both of the Erlichs testified that they suffered emotional distress as a result of the defective condition of the house and Menezes's invasive and unsuccessful repair attempts. Barry Erlich testified he felt "absolutely sick" and had to be "carted away in an ambulance" when he learned the full extent of the structural problems. He has a permanent heart condition, known as superventricular tachyarrhythmia, attributable, in part, to excessive stress. Although the condition can be controlled with medication, it has forced him to resign his positions as athletic director, department head and track coach.

Sandra Erlich feared the house would collapse in an earthquake and feared for her daughter's safety. Stickers were placed on her bedroom windows, and alarms and emergency lights installed so rescue crews would find her room first in an emergency.

Plaintiffs sought recovery on several theories, including breach of contract, fraud, negligent misrepresentation, and negligent construction. Both the breach of contract claim and the negligence claim alleged numerous construction defects.

Menezes prevailed on the fraud and negligent misrepresentation claims. The jury found he breached his contract with the Erlichs by negligently constructing their home and awarded $406,700 as the cost of repairs. Each spouse was awarded $50,000 for emotional distress, and Barry Erlich received an additional $50,000 for physical pain and suffering and $15,000 for lost earnings.

By a two-to-one majority, the Court of Appeal affirmed the judgment, including the emotional distress award. The majority noted the breach of a contractual duty may support an action in tort. The jury found Menezes was negligent. Since his negligence exposed the Erlichs to "intolerable living conditions and a constant, justifiable fear about the safety of their home," the majority decided the Erlichs were properly compensated for their emotional distress.

The dissent pointed out that no reported California case has upheld an award of emotional distress damages based upon simple breach of a contract to build a house. Since Menezes's negligence directly caused only economic injury and property damage, the Erlichs were not entitled to recover damages for their emotional distress.

We granted review to resolve the question.

II. Discussion

A.

In an action for breach of contract, the measure of damages is "the amount which will compensate the party aggrieved for all the detriment proximately caused thereby, or which, in the ordinary course of things, would be likely to result therefrom" (Civ.Code, § 3300), provided the damages are "clearly ascertainable in both their nature and origin" (Civ.Code, § 3301). In an action not arising from contract, the measure of damages is "the amount which will compensate for all the detriment proximately caused thereby, whether it could have been anticipated or not" (Civ.Code, § 3333).

"Contract damages are generally limited to those within the contemplation of the parties when the contract was entered into or at least reasonably foreseeable by them at that time; consequential damages beyond the expectation of the parties are not recoverable. [Citations.] This limitation on available damages serves to encourage contractual relations and commercial activity by enabling parties to estimate in advance the financial risks of their enterprise." (*Applied Equipment Corp. v. Litton Saudi Arabia Ltd.* (1994) 7 Cal.4th 503, 515.) "In contrast, tort damages are awarded to [fully] compensate the victim for [all] injury suffered. [Citation.]" (*Id.* at p. 516.)

"'[T]he distinction between tort and contract is well grounded in common law, and divergent objectives underlie the remedies created in the two areas. Whereas contract actions are created to enforce the intentions of the parties to the agreement, tort law is primarily designed to vindicate "social policy." [Citation.]'" (*Hunter v. Up-Right, Inc.* (1993) 6 Cal.4th 1174, 1180.) While the purposes behind contract and tort law are distinct, the boundary line between them is not (*Freeman & Mills, Inc. v. Belcher Oil Co.* (1995) 11 Cal.4th 85, 106 (conc. and dis. opn. of Mosk, J.) (*Freeman & Mills*)) and the distinction between the remedies for each is not "'found ready made.'" (*Ibid.,* quoting Holmes, The Common Law (1881) p. 13.) These uncertain boundaries and the apparent breadth of the recovery available for tort actions create pressure to obliterate the distinction between contracts and torts—an expansion of tort law at the expense of contract principles which Grant Gilmore aptly dubbed "con*torts*." In this case we consider whether a negligent breach of a contract will support an award of damages for emotional distress—either as tort damages for negligence or as consequential or special contract damages.

B.

In concluding emotional distress damages were properly awarded, the Court of Appeal correctly observed that "the same wrongful act may constitute both a breach of contract and an invasion of an interest protected by the law of torts." (*North American Chemical Co. v. Superior Court* (1997) 59 Cal.App.4th 764, 774, citing 3 Witkin, Cal. Procedure (4th ed. 1996) Actions, § 139, pp. 203–204.) Here, the court permitted plaintiffs to recover both full repair costs as normal contract damages and emotional distress damages as a tort remedy.

The Court of Appeal also noted that "[a] contractual obligation may create a legal duty and the breach of that duty may support an action in tort." This is true; however, conduct amounting to a breach of contract becomes tortious only when it also violates a duty independent of the contract arising from principles of tort law. (*Applied Equipment, supra,* 7 Cal.4th at p. 515.) "An omission to perform a contract obligation is never a tort, unless that omission is also an omission of a legal duty." (*Ibid.,* quoting *Jones v. Kelly* (1929) 208 Cal. 251, 255.)

Tort damages have been permitted in contract cases where a breach of duty directly causes physical injury (*Fuentes v. Perez* (1977) 66 Cal.App.3d 163, 168, fn. 2); for breach of the covenant of good faith and fair dealing in insurance contracts (*Crisci v. Security Ins. Co.* (1967) 66 Cal.2d 425, 433–434); for wrongful discharge in violation of fundamental public policy (*Tameny v. Atlantic Richfield Co.* (1980) 27 Cal.3d 167, 175–176); or where the contract was fraudulently induced. (*Las Palmas Associates v. Las Palmas Center Associates* (1991) 235 Cal.App.3d 1220, 1238–1239.) In each of these cases, the duty that gives rise to tort liability is either completely independent of the contract or arises from conduct which is both intentional and intended to harm. (See, e.g., *Christensen v. Superior Court* (1991) 54 Cal.3d 868, 885–886.)

Plaintiff's theory of tort recovery is that mental distress is a foreseeable consequence of negligent breaches of standard commercial contracts. However, foreseeability alone is not sufficient to create an independent tort duty. "'Whether a defendant owes a duty of care is a question of law. Its existence depends upon the foreseeability of the risk and a weighing of policy considerations for and against imposition of liability.' [Citation.]" (*Burgess v. Superior Court* (1992) 2 Cal.4th 1064, 1072.) Because the consequences of a negligent act must be limited to avoid an intolerable burden on society (*Elden v. Sheldon* (1988) 46 Cal.3d 267, 274), the determination of duty "recognizes that policy considerations may dictate a cause of action should not be sanctioned no matter how foreseeable the risk." (*Ibid.*) "[T]here are clear judicial days on which a court can foresee forever and thus determine liability but none on which that foresight alone provides a socially and judicially acceptable limit on recovery of damages for [an] injury." (*Thing v. La Chusa* (1989) 48 Cal.3d 644, 668.) In short, foreseeability is not synonymous with duty; nor is it a substitute.

The question thus remains: is the mere negligent breach of a contract sufficient? The answer is no. It may admittedly be difficult to categorize the cases, but to state the rule succinctly: "[C]ourts will generally enforce the breach of a contractual promise through contract law, except when the actions that constitute the breach violate a social policy that merits the imposition of tort remedies." (*Freeman & Mills, supra,* 11 Cal.4th at p. 107 (conc. and dis. opn. of Mosk, J.).) The familiar paradigm of tortious breach of contract in this state is the insurance contract. There we relied on the covenant of good faith and fair dealing, implied in every contract, to justify tort liability. (*Foley, supra,* 47 Cal.3d at pp. 689–690.) In holding that a tort action is available for breach of the covenant in an insurance contract, we have "emphasized the 'special relationship' between insurer and insured, characterized by elements of public interest, adhesion, and fiduciary responsibility." (*Freeman & Mills, supra,* 11 Cal.4th at p. 91, 44 Cal.Rptr.2d 420, 900 P.2d 669; see Louderback & Jurika, *Standards for Limiting the Tort of Bad Faith Breach of Contract* (1982) 16 U.S.F. L.Rev. 187, 227.)

The special relationship test, which has been criticized as illusory and not sufficiently precise (Putz & Klippen, *Commercial Bad Faith: Attorneys Fees — Not Tort Liability — Is the Remedy for "Stonewalling"* (1987) 21 U.S.F. L.Rev. 419, 478–479), has little relevance to the question before us. Menezes is in the business of building single-family homes. He is one among thousands of contractors who provide the same service, and the Erlichs could take their choice among any contractors willing to accept work in the area where their home would be constructed. Although they undoubtedly relied on his claimed expertise, they were in a position to view, inspect, and criticize his work, or to hire someone who could. Most significantly, there is no indication Menezes sought to frustrate the Erlichs' enjoyment of contracted-for benefits. He did build a house. His ineptitude led to numerous problems which he attempted to correct. And he remains ultimately responsible for reimbursing the cost of doing the job properly. . . .

In this case, the jury concluded Menezes did not act intentionally; nor was he guilty of fraud or misrepresentation. This is a claim for negligent breach of a contract, which is not sufficient to support tortious damages for violation of an independent tort duty. . . .

Here, the breach — the negligent construction of the Erlichs' house — did not cause physical injury. No one was hit by a falling beam. Although the Erlichs state they feared the house was structurally unsafe and might collapse in an earthquake, they lived in it for five years. The only physical injury alleged is Barry Erlich's heart disease, which flowed from the emotional distress and not directly from the negligent construction.

The Erlichs may have hoped to build their dream home and live happily ever after, but there is a reason that tag line belongs only in fairy tales. Building a house may turn out to be a stress-free project; it is much more likely to be the stuff of urban legends — the cause of bankruptcy, marital dissolution, hypertension and fleeting fantasies ranging from homicide to suicide. As Justice Yegan noted below, "No reasonable homeowner can embark on a building project with certainty that the project will be completed to perfection. Indeed, errors are so likely to occur that few if any homeowners would be justified in resting their peace of mind on [its] timely or correct completion. . . ." The connection between the service sought and the aggravation and distress resulting from incompetence may be somewhat less tenuous than in a malpractice case, but the emotional suffering still derives from an inherently economic concern.

. . . The available damages for defective construction are limited to the cost of repairing the home, including lost use or relocation expenses, or the diminution in value. (*Orndorff v. Christiana Community Builders* (1990) 217 Cal.App.3d 683.) The Erlichs received more than $400,000 in traditional contract damages to correct the defects in their home. While their distress was undoubtedly real and serious, we conclude the balance of policy considerations — the potential for significant increases in liability in amounts disproportionate to culpability, the court's inability to formulate appropriate limits on the availability of claims, and the magnitude of the impact on stability and predictability in commercial affairs — counsel against expanding contract damages to include mental distress claims in negligent construction cases.

Disposition

The judgment of the Court of Appeal is reversed and the matter is remanded for further proceedings consistent with this opinion.

* * *

Problem 16

When parties enter into a contract, they will normally be limited to contract damages for any harm that occurs in connection with the transaction covered by the contract. In the scenario described below, how should the court rule on the defendant's request for a jury instruction limiting the plaintiff's damages?

A bus company sues an engine manufacturer on a negligent design products liability theory after an engine the company purchased and installed on one of its buses exploded. As a result of the explosion, the bus in which the engine had been installed was completely destroyed. At trial, the defendant manufacturer argues that the plaintiff is limited to contract damages under the purchase contract for the engine. It requests a jury instruction that the plaintiff can recover no more than the purchase price of the defective engine.

Introductory Note — *Indianapolis-Marion County Public Library v. Charlier Clark & Linard*

Indianapolis-Marion County Public Library is another defective construction case. The plaintiff sued for breach of contract and negligence, with both causes of action based on the failure of the defendants to build the structure in conformity with industry standards for quality. The trial court granted summary judgment for the defendants on the negligence claim; the plaintiff appealed. In deciding whether summary judgment was properly granted, the Indiana Supreme Court reviews the history and purpose of the economic loss rule.

THINGS TO THINK ABOUT while reading *Indianapolis-Marion County Public Library v. Charlier Clark & Linard*:

1. What is the economic loss rule?

2. What is the effect of the economic loss rule?

3. What policy does the economic loss rule promote?

Indianapolis-Marion County Public Library v. Charlier Clark & Linard

Indiana Supreme Court
929 N.E.2d 722 (2010)

SULLIVAN, Justice.

The Indianapolis-Marion County Public Library ("Library") seeks to hold two subcontractors and an engineer responsible for negligence in rendering their respective services during the renovation and expansion of its downtown Indianapolis library facility. In accord with the analysis of the trial court and Court of Appeals, we affirm the trial court's dismissal of the Library's claims of negligence against the defendants. Primarily because the Library is connected with the defendants through a network or chain of contracts in which the parties allocated their respective risks, duties, and remedies, those contracts, and not negligence law, govern the outcome of the Library's claims.

Background

The Library hired Woollen Molzan and Partners, Inc. ("WMP") to serve as the architect for the renovation and expansion of many structures contained in the Library's downtown Indianapolis facility, including its parking garage. WMP then subcontracted with Thornton Tomasetti Engineers ("TTE") and Charlier Clark and Linard, P.C. ("CCL") to perform architectural and engineering services. Joseph G. Burns ("Burns"), a managing principal of TTE, served as "engineer of record" for the library project. Specifically, TTE performed structural engineering services and CCL administered various services for the project including reviewing and inspecting the construction plans and construction progress to determine if construction was in general compliance with the construction documents. The Library never contracted directly with TTE, CCL, or Burns for any services during the renovation and expansion project, but each was a party to one or more contracts with WMP or other entities involved in the project.

According to the Library, after construction of the project had progressed significantly, it became concerned about the structural integrity of the accompanying parking garage, which was to serve as the foundation for the rest of the library structure. The Library hired an expert who confirmed that there were several construction and design defects in the Library parking garage. . . .

The Library brought a lawsuit against WMP, TTE, Burns, CCL, and Shook, LLC (the general contractor), an insurance company, and other contractors working on the project alleging negligent failure to perform engineering, administrative, and design work in a skillful, careful, workmanlike manner along with breach of contract claims with the parties with whom the Library had a contractual relationship. The Library sought to recover damages for repair costs, project delay settlements, expert fees, utilities, rental fees, increased insurance premiums, and costs associated with seeking additional public funding.

The Defendants then moved for partial summary judgment, arguing that the negligence claims against them were barred by the so-called "economic loss rule." The trial court agreed and granted the Defendants' motions for partial summary judgment.

Discussion

Under long-standing Indiana law, a defendant is liable to a plaintiff for the tort of negligence if (1) the defendant has a duty to conform its conduct to a standard of care arising from its relationship with the plaintiff, (2) the defendant failed to conform its conduct to that standard of care, and (3) an injury to the plaintiff was proximately caused by the breach. *Estate of Heck ex rel. Heck v. Stoffer,* 786 N.E.2d 265, 268 (Ind.2003). Consistent with this principle, where the injury to the plaintiff is from a defective product or service (as the Library alleges here), the defendant is liable under a tort theory if the defect causes personal injury or damage to property other than the product or service itself. *Gunkel v. Renovations, Inc.,* 822 N.E.2d 150, 153 (Ind.2005). However, Indiana cases go on to hold that the defendant is not liable under a tort theory for any purely economic loss caused by its negligence (including, in the case of a defective product or service, damage to the product or service itself). *Id.* This rule precluding tort liability for purely economic loss — that is, pecuniary loss unaccompanied by any property damage or personal injury (other than damage to the product or service itself) — has become known as the "economic loss rule" and its applicability is the central issue in this appeal.

A

A recent project of the American Law Institute ("ALI") focusing on the economic loss rule has produced some detailed and highly illuminating materials on this subject. In discussing the history of the rule, Professor Mark P. Gergen of the University of Texas School of Law, the project's reporter, wrote that the "economic loss rule emerged alongside the modern negligence action" as courts wrestled with whether plaintiffs could bring "negligence claims for solely pecuniary harm." *Restatement (Third) of Economic Torts and Related Wrongs* § 8, Reporter's Note a (Council Draft No. 2, 2007) [hereinafter *Gergen Restatement Draft*]. . . .

A review of the case law and ALI materials suggests several principal justifications for the economic loss rule.

First, the economic loss rule reflects that the resolution of liability for purely economic loss caused by negligence is more appropriately determined by commercial rather than tort law. As noted at the very outset of this *Discussion supra,* the economic loss rule provides that a defendant is not liable under a tort theory for any purely economic loss caused by its negligence (including, in the case of a defective product or service, damage to the product or service itself) — but that a defendant is liable under a tort theory for a plaintiff's losses if a defective product or service causes personal injury or damage to property other than the product or service itself. The Seventh Circuit has written that

[i]t would be better to call ["an economic loss"] a "commercial loss," not only because personal injuries and especially property losses are economic losses, too—they destroy values which can be and are monetized—but also, and more important, because tort law is a superfluous and inapt tool for resolving purely commercial disputes. We have a body of law designed for such disputes. It is called contract law. Products liability law has evolved into a specialized branch of tort law for use in cases in which a defective product caused, not the usual commercial loss, but a personal injury to a consumer or bystander.

Miller v. U.S. Steel Corp., 902 F.2d 573, 574 (7th Cir.1990) (Posner, J.).

. . . This justification for the economic loss rule is clearly implicated by the case before us. From the outset of the project, the Library looked to a series of contracts to establish the relative expectations of the parties. . . .

A second justification for the economic loss rule is that "[l]iability should not be imposed when it creates a potential for liability that is so uncertain in time, class, or amount that [a defendant should not] fairly or practically be expected to account for the potential liability when undertaking the conduct that gives rise to" it. *Gergen Restatement Draft* § 8, cmt. d(2). This justification is implicated "when an accident causing physical harm has significant far-flung economic consequences." *Id.* § 8, cmt. b. It is also the focus of attention in claims of accountant liability and, more generally, negligent misstatement, "because of the ease of transmitting information that appears to invite a recipient's reliance." *Id.* § 8, cmt. d(2).

The rationale for this justification is that tort law ought not expose a defendant guilty of mere negligence "to a liability in an indeterminate amount for an indeterminate time to an indeterminate class." *Ultramares Corp. v. Touche*, 255 N.Y. 170 (1931) (Cardozo, C.J.). Chief Judge Cardozo's aphorism has been relied upon by the Court of Appeals on a number of occasions. *See, e.g., Thomas v. Lewis Eng'g, Inc.*, 848 N.E.2d 758, 761 (Ind.Ct.App.2006) (no claim for negligent misrepresentation against surveyor not in privity of contract with plaintiff); *Essex v. Ryan*, 446 N.E.2d 368, 373 (Ind.Ct.App.1983) (no claim for negligence against surveyor not in privity of contract with plaintiff). *Cf. First Cmty. Bank & Trust v. Kelley, Hardesty, Smith & Co.*, 663 N.E.2d 218, 224 (Ind.Ct.App.1996) (limiting *Ultramares* to cases where "non-contractual, non-assignee parties seek redress").

This second justification for the economic loss rule is not directly implicated by the case before us. While the damages are large, they are by no means indeterminate. Nor is there any exposure to the Defendants for an indeterminate time or to an indeterminate number of plaintiffs.

The discussion *supra* clearly demonstrates that the economic loss rule is well established in Indiana and that there are sound legal and economic justifications for it. But we emphasize before going further that the economic loss rule has limits, that while it operates as a *general* rule to preclude recovery in tort for economic loss, it does so only for *purely* economic loss—pecuniary loss unaccompanied by any property damage or personal injury (other than damage to the product or service provided by the defendant) — and even when there is purely economic loss, there are exceptions to the general rule. . . .

II

The Library's principal contention is that its loss is not "pure" economic loss and thus that its tort claims against the Defendants are not precluded by the economic loss rule. Specifically, the Library maintains that the damages it suffered were (A) to "other property" and (B) physical, not commercial, and even if not physical, should be treated as such because they created an imminent risk of personal injury.

A

The economic loss rule is only implicated where a plaintiff has suffered "pure economic loss." As we have already discussed, "pure economic loss" means pecuniary harm not resulting from an injury to the plaintiff's person or property. The Library contends that the nature of its losses take this case outside the economic loss rule. . . .

Here the Library purchased a complete refurbishing of its library facility from multiple parties. The Library did not purchase a blueprint from the Defendants, concrete from the materials supplier, and inspection services to ensure the safety of the construction project in isolation; it purchased a complete renovation and expansion of all the components of its facility as part of a single, highly-integrated transaction. Thus, irrespective of whether Defendants' negligence was the proximate cause of defects in the design of the library facility, for purposes of the other property rule, the product or service that the Library purchased was the renovated and expanded library facility itself.

B

The Library also argues that its claims are not governed by the economic loss rule because the damages it suffered were physical, not commercial, and even if not physical, should be treated as such because they presented the imminent risk of personal injury.

Contending that having to repair and reconstruct a substantial portion of the project was tantamount to suffering property damage, the Library argues that it suffered damages distinct from commercial losses such that the economic loss rule is not applicable. Had the Library suffered property damage to "other property," the economic loss rule would not apply and the Library would be entitled to recover in tort for the pecuniary harm attributable thereto. But our resolution of the Library's contention on "other property" in subpart A *supra* disposes of this contention as well. As the Court of Appeals correctly stated, "[a]lthough the repairs have a component of physical destruction, the repair and reconstruction of the garage and other portions of the project are economic losses that arose from the Library's complaint that it did not receive the benefit of its bargain." *Indianapolis-Marion County Pub. Library*, 900 N.E.2d at 812. This is also the view of many of our sister jurisdictions.

The Library further argues for a narrow construction of the economic loss rule where an imminent risk of danger implicates safety concerns for the public. Specifically, the Library argues that safety is more the concern of tort rather than breach of contract, and the proper redress for negligent design is tort. We acknowledge that in some cases, including the Library's situation, the absence of personal harm is a matter of fortune and future events could have resulted in personal injury had the Library not acted first to remedy the hazards posed by the faulty design and construction of the library facility. However,

> [t]he distinction that the law has drawn between tort recovery for physical injuries and warranty recovery for economic loss is not arbitrary and does not rest on the 'luck' of one plaintiff in having an accident causing physical injury. The distinction rests, rather, on an understanding of the nature of the responsibility a manufacturer must undertake in distributing his products. He can appropriately be held liable for physical injuries caused by defects by requiring his goods to match a standard of safety defined in terms of conditions that create unreasonable risks of harm. He cannot be held for the level of performance of his products in the consumer's business unless he agrees that the product was designed to meet the consumers' demands. A consumer should not be charged at the will of the manufacturer with bearing the risk of physical injury when he buys a product on the market. He can, however, be fairly charged with the risk that the product will not match his economic expectations unless the manufacturer agrees that it will.

Seely v. White Motor Co., 45 Cal.Rptr. 17. . . .

Conclusion

We affirm the judgment of the trial court.

* * *

Problem 17

The economic loss rule bars recovery in tort for a negligent act that causes purely financial harm. What result under the economic loss rule in the following case?

A train derails and slams into a warehouse next to the tracks. The collision causes significant damage to the building that takes several months to repair. During the repairs, the 150 people that work in the warehouse cannot go to work and they lose 12 weeks of pay as a result. The workers sue the train operator for negligence and seek to recover their lost wages.

Measure of Damages: Expectation and Reliance

Contract damages compensate a plaintiff for financial harm that results from a breach of contract. But how should that harm be measured? More to the point from a remedies perspective, how do we calculate the correct amount of damages for breach of contract?

The process starts with the underlying goal for all compensatory damages: to make up for a loss the plaintiff suffered as the result of a legal wrong. In this context, the legal wrong is a breach of contract. So the correct measure of damages will place the plaintiff in as good of a position as he or she would have been in had the contract not been breached.

Accomplishing that requires considering two concepts: expectation and reliance. The plaintiff can be put in the same position as though the contract were not breached by doing one of two things: by, at least financially speaking, making it as though the contract was fully performed, or by making it as though the contract never existed.

One way to make a plaintiff whole after the contract has been breached is to determine what the plaintiff expected to get, financially, had the contract been performed. The plaintiff should receive from the defendant an amount equal to the financial benefit that would have been realized had full performance occurred. That measurement is called expectation damages. It is sometimes also referred to as benefit of the bargain damages.

In many cases, the plaintiff might have made expenditures in reliance on the belief the contract was going to be performed. If so, the plaintiff can elect to measure damages by the amount of those expenditures instead of by the amount of gain expected from the contract. In that way, reliance damages make plaintiffs whole by putting them in the same position as if the contract had never been entered into in the first place.

Introductory Note — *Northrop Grumman Computing Systems v. United States* and *Paul v. Deloitte & Touche, LLP*

Northrop Grumman is a contract dispute between the federal government and a company it retained to supply surveillance equipment. *Paul* is a dispute between an accountant and his former firm. The plaintiffs in both cases seek expectation damages, arguing they were denied the benefit of the bargain they struck. But in both cases, the evidence is ultimately deemed insufficient to support an award of expectation damages.

THINGS TO THINK ABOUT while reading *Northrop Grumman Computing Systems v. United States* and *Paul v. Deloitte & Touche, LLP*:

1. When is a party to a contract entitled to expectation damages?

2. What is the measure of expectation damages in this case?

3. Why was the evidence insufficient to support an award of expectation damages here?

Northrop Grumman Computing Systems v. United States

United States Court of Federal Claims
120 Fed.Cl. 460 (2015)

ALLEGRA, Judge:

Plaintiff, Northrop Grumman Computing Systems, Inc. (Northrop), brings this action seeking damages for the alleged breach of an agreement with the Department of Homeland Security (DHS), Bureau of Immigration and Customs Enforcement (ICE). Under that agreement, Northrop leased surveillance software to ICE to be used in intercepting the internet communications of the targets of criminal investigations arising under Title III of the Omnibus Crime Control and Safe Streets Act of 1968, 18 U.S.C. § 2510, *et seq*. This case is pending before the court on defendant's motion for summary judgment on damages. In its motion, defendant asseverates that Northrop has received all the compensation to which it is entitled under the contract at issue. Having carefully reviewed the parties' briefs on this motion, the court holds that defendant is correct and it hereby GRANTS defendant's motion.

I. Background

Sometime in 2003, ICE's Technical Operations' National Program Manager for Internet Intercept identified the agency's need for Internet intercept software. Tech Ops' mission is to provide field agents with the most innovative cutting edge electronic surveillance equipment and support in furtherance of ICE investigations and national security operations. Prior to entering into the lease agreement below, DHS/ICE used other software to gather evidence, during a criminal investigation, of a subject's internet usage. This software, however, [had limits on its data capturing ability]. In 2004, DHS/ICE decided that it needed software that could overcome this limitation. After conducting market research, it chose Northrop's Internet Observer software, also known as the Oakley software (the Oakley software).

On September 24, 2004, ICE awarded Delivery Order COW-4-D-1025 (Delivery Order) to Northrop pursuant to a preexisting contract between ICE and plaintiff — Contract No. NAS5-01143. According to the Delivery Order, plaintiff was to lease the Oakley software to ICE and perform specific support services for a one-year base period in return for payment of $900,000, with three one-year options at $899,186 per option year — for a total contract price of $3,597,558 if all three options were exercised. On September 28, 2004, ICE provided plaintiff with an "essential use statement" that described the intended use of the Oakley software and was designed to facilitate third-party funding for the Oakley software. From September 30, 2004, to October 18, 2004, ICE executed three modifications to the Delivery Order, adding, *inter alia,* a first priority clause, a best efforts clause, and a nonsubstitution clause. On October 13, 2004, plaintiff delivered the Oakley software to defendant and was paid $900,000.

To finance the agreement, Northrop relied on ESCgov, with whom Northrop had a preexisting Purchase and Assignment Agreement. The Purchase and Assignment Agreement stated that if Northrop assigned its interest in a government contract to ESCgov and that contract was "discontinued because of non-appropriation of funds, failure of the Government to exercise a renewal option under the Government Contract or termination for convenience" Northrop would "not be liable to ESCgov for any costs, expenses or lost profits, whatsoever," as long as Northrop complied with Provision 19(a) of the agreement. Provision 19(a) provided, in relevant part: "[i]f ESCgov has substantial grounds for concluding that the actions taken by the U.S. Government constitute a sound basis for filing a claim with the Government, [Northrop] will use its best efforts to obtain the maximum recovery from the Government." Northrop agreed to "diligently pursue such recovery" in cooperation with ESCgov. If a claim or any subsequent litigation were successful, Provision 19(a) provided that ESCgov would have the first right to any damages awarded to Northrop. But, if no money was recovered, Northrop would not have to repay ESCgov any amount.

Consistent with the Purchase and Assignment Agreement, on October 22, 2004, ESCgov entered into Equipment Schedule No. 1, in which it agreed to pay Northrop $3,296,093 in exchange for Northrop's assignment to ESCgov of any payments it received under the Delivery Order. Of this amount, ESCgov paid $2,899,710 directly to Oakley Networks for, *inter alia,* the purchase of the Oakley software licenses, "operational support hours," and "annual maintenance." Also included in the total payment under Equipment Schedule No. 1 was a payment of $191,571 from ESCgov to Northrop, which represented Northrop's anticipated profit for its performance under the Delivery Order.

On October 22, 2004, Northrop also executed and delivered to Citizens Leasing Corporation, n/k/a RBS Citizens, N.A. (Citizens) a Consent to Assignment agreeing to ESCgov's plan to assign its rights under Equipment Schedule No. 1 to Citizens. On October 25, 2004, Northrop executed an Instrument of Assignment assigning its rights and interests to any payments from the United States under the Delivery Order to Citizens. On November 19, 2004, ESCgov executed an Assignment Agreement assigning its rights under Equipment Schedule No. 1 to Citizens in exchange for $3,325,252.16.

On September 30, 2005, ICE informed plaintiff that it would not exercise the first one-year option due to a lack of funds. On September 21, 2006, Northrop filed a claim with the contracting officer pursuant to the Contract Disputes Act of 1978 (the CDA), 41 U.S.C. § 601, *et seq.* (current version at 41 U.S.C. § 7101, *et seq.*):

to recover damages resulting from the Government's breach of the provisions of the [Delivery Order] by failing to use best efforts to seek and utilize available funding from all sources, by failing to reserve funds from the annual budget on a first priority designation, and by replacing the software with another system performing similar or comparable functions.

The claim requested damages of $2,697,558, because defendant's breach of contract entitled "a contractor to be placed in as good a position as it would have had the breach not been committed by the Government." Alternatively, Northrop asserted that "if the Government's breaches of the Contract are found to constitute a Termination for Convenience, the amount of . . . damages owed by the Government would be $2,674,032.80." . . .

On August 20, 2007, Northrop filed a complaint in this court, asserting that defendant breached the Delivery Order by failing to seek funding and exercise the options. The complaint averred that, as a result of this breach, "Northrop Grumman is entitled to recover its damages as described in the contract, including the payments not made under the Contract in the amount of $2,697,558.00, plus interest." . . .

On October 1, 2013, defendant filed a motion for summary judgment. Subsequent briefing on this motion has been completed. Oral argument was held on May 7, 2014.

II. Discussion

We begin with common ground. Summary judgment is appropriate when there is no genuine dispute as to any material fact and the moving party is entitled to judgment as a matter of law. *See* RCFC 56; *Anderson v. Liberty Lobby, Inc.,* 477 U.S. 242, 247–48 (1986); *Biery v. United States,* 753 F.3d 1279, 1286 (Fed.Cir.2014). Disputes over facts that are not outcome-determinative will not preclude the entry of summary judgment. However, summary judgment will not be granted if "the dispute about a material fact is 'genuine,' that is, if the evidence is such that a reasonable [trier of fact] could return a verdict for the nonmoving party." *Id..*

When making a summary judgment determination, the court is not to weigh the evidence, but to "determine whether there is a genuine issue for trial." *Anderson,* 477 U.S. at 249; *see also Agosto v. INS,* 436 U.S. 748, 756 (1978). . . .

This leads us to defendant's banner claim — that plaintiff has not proven that any damages are owed. Defendant asserts that the undisputed facts show that Northrop has received all the compensation to which it is owed pursuant to the Delivery Order — that plaintiff is not entitled to any further expectancy damages based on its claim. Defendant is correct.

Expectation damages give the injured party "the benefits [it] expected to receive had the breach not occurred." *Glendale Fed. Bank, FSB v. United States,* 239 F.3d 1374, 1380 (Fed.Cir.2001); *see also Fifth Third Bank v. United States,* 518 F.3d 1368, 1374 (Fed.Cir.2008). Conversely, "[i]t is . . . axiomatic that 'the non-breaching party should not be placed in a better position through the award of expectancy damages than if there had been no breach.'" *Cuyahoga Metro. Hous. Auth. v. United States,* 65

Fed.Cl. 534, 543 (2005). The Federal Circuit has further elucidated — "[t]he benefits that were expected from the contract, 'expectancy damages,' are often equated with lost profits, although they can include other damage elements as well." *Glendale,* 239 F.3d at 1380 (citing Restatement (Second) of Contracts, § 347). As such, "[e]xpectation damages are recoverable provided they are 'actually foreseen or reasonably foreseeable, are caused by the breach of the promisor, and are proved with reasonable certainty.'" *Nat. Australia Bank v. United States,* 63 Fed.Cl. 352, 355 (2004).

The goal of contract damages thus is "to put the injured party in as good a position as that party would have been in if performance had been rendered as promised." 11 Corbin on Contracts § 55.3 (rev. ed. 2009).). It is not to provide the contracting party with a windfall. Plaintiff seeks the latter — it seeks expectation damages that exceed the amount that defendant was obliged to pay under the contract. ESCgov expressly agreed to pay Northrop $3,296,093 for which Northrop agreed to assign the rights of all payments it received from ICE under the Delivery Order. There is no dispute that this amount was, in fact, paid to Northrop by ESCgov. The contract between ESCgov and Northrop further makes clear that if defendant were to terminate the contract for convenience or declined to exercise a renewal option, Northrop was not liable for costs, expenses, lost profits or other damages incurred or suffered by ESCgov. Northrop was paid the amount it expected to be paid for its performance under the Delivery Order. It is unable to identify any way that it, as opposed to ESCgov or Citizens, was harmed by defendant's actions.

Plaintiff, however, argues that defendant is seeking a windfall — that plaintiff was harmed because defendant did not make payments for the three unexercised option years under the Delivery Order. But, there is no indication that, under the contract terms, plaintiff was entitled to receive those payments. Contrary to plaintiff's claims, ICE paid in full for the one year it had the license for the software in question, and did not use the software thereafter. Had ICE exercised all three options, Northrop would not have received any further payments — those payments had been assigned to ESCgov. ESCgov's payment of $191,571 represented Northrop's anticipated profit for its anticipated performance under the Delivery Order. And Northrop, indeed, received that payment from its finance company, ESCgov. Northrop reaped the benefit of the bargain it negotiated — it is entitled to nothing more from defendant. *See Int'l Data Prods. Corp. v. United States,* 492 F.3d 1317, 1324 (Fed.Cir.2007).

Likewise, plaintiff is not entitled to any damages associated with software and server maintenance beyond that which the Delivery Order required for the base year. Fundamentally, Northrop cannot recover damages for any software and server maintenance work that was not performed under the Delivery Order — software and server maintenance that was unnecessary in the out-years based on ICE's decision not to exercise the first option. "The contractor may not recover for work not performed." *H.B. Nelson Constr. Co. v. United States,* 87 Ct.Cl. 375, 385 (1938). This court cannot permit otherwise.

III. Conclusion

The court will not gild the lily. The court concludes, as a matter of law on essentially undisputed facts, that defendant has demonstrated that plaintiff is not entitled to any damages under the Delivery Order in question or otherwise. Accordingly, the court GRANTS defendant's motion for summary judgment. The Clerk shall dismiss plaintiff's complaint.

* * *

Paul v. Deloitte & Touche, LLP

Delaware Supreme Court
974 A.2d 140 (2009)

RIDGELY, Justice:

This appeal arises out of a contractual dispute between Plaintiff-Appellant Alan D. Paul and Defendants-Appellees Deloitte & Touche LLP ("D & T"), and Deloitte & Touche, USA, LLP ("D & T USA") (collectively, "Deloitte"), in which Paul was severed from the Deloitte partnerships. . . .

Paul appeals from the court's grant of summary judgment in favor of Deloitte on grounds that Paul suffered no damages from Deloitte's breach of his employment contract. Paul raises two arguments on appeal. First, he contends that the court erred by misconstruing his reasonable expectations as of the date of the making of the contract. Second, he contends that he is entitled to recover damages reasonably foreseeable for the breach of his employment contract. We find no merit to Paul's arguments. Accordingly, we affirm the Superior Court's grant of summary judgment in favor of Deloitte.

I. Facts and Procedural History

Deloitte has several subsidiaries that provide professional accounting, auditing, and related services to public and private clients. Paul was a partner in the Lead Tax Services ("LTS") section of Deloitte's Boston, Massachusetts office. Paul had previously been a partner with Arthur Andersen LLP ("Andersen"), but joined Deloitte in May 2002, along with numerous other former Andersen partners.

A. Paul's Admission as a Partner

On April 2, 2002, D & T USA and Andersen entered into a "Memorandum of Understanding" (the "MOU"), with respect to the possible offer by Deloitte of partnerships to certain Andersen tax partners. On April 19, Deloitte extended a written offer to Paul to join as a tax partner. Paul accepted and Deloitte sent him a document confirming the terms of his admission as a partner (the "Admission Agreement"). He would serve in the LTS section of Deloitte's Boston office; he would be credited with 780 units of ownership; he would receive an initial biweekly draw in the amount of $10,770; and his required capital investment would be $741,000. Paul executed the Admission Agreement on May 4, 2002.

The Admission Agreement provided that Paul's admission was contingent on several events, including the finalization of the transaction between D & T USA and Andersen and Paul's acceptance and execution of two Memoranda of Agreement (each an "MOA" and collectively with the Admission Agreement, the "Partnership Agreements"). On May 7, 2002 D & T USA and Andersen executed the definitive agreement contemplated by the MOU and Paul's Admission Agreement (the "Andersen Agreement"). The Andersen Agreement stated that Deloitte had offered certain Andersen partners, including Paul, admission to the Deloitte partnership. Paul signed the MOAs the next day. . . .

The Admission Agreement added a "cause-based" termination section in §5(a) and provided for an additional method of involuntary termination without cause in §5(b). This provision was unique to the partners who, like Paul, joined Deloitte in connection with the Andersen Agreement. During the first two years of their partnerships, the former Andersen partners could be involuntarily severed by vote of an appointed six-person committee rather than the Board and a majority of the partners. Specifically, §5(b) of the Admission Agreement provided:

> In addition to those circumstances set forth in the second sentence of Section 7.03 of the Memorandum of Agreement of each Firm, you shall be deemed to have severed your association with each Firm . . . (b) as of the date specified within two years after the Effective Date by a committee . . . , which shall consist of three tax partners and principals of D & T USA who had been partners of [Andersen] and three tax partners and principals of D & T USA who had not been partners of [Andersen], with the leader of D & T's tax practice able to cast the deciding vote if such committee is deadlocked.

This more streamlined method of involuntary severance, unique to the former Andersen partners, placed the severance decision in the hands of what became known as the "Committee of 6" for a two year period, the last day of which was May 6, 2004. This system was a logistical necessity because of the virtually simultaneous admission of more than 160 new partners. Bradley Seltzer, a member of the Committee of 6, explained that with such a large influx of new partners arriving at almost the same time, Deloitte could not engage in the due diligence process it normally employed when considering the admission of a lateral partner. Mark Berkowitz, a former Andersen partner who joined Deloitte's Boston office with Paul, described the two-year period as a "probation period."

Deloitte understood the applicable language to mean that within two years, the Committee of 6 was required to conduct any vote to sever a partner, and to notify the partner to be severed of the date his severance would occur. Since the language did not say a person had to be severed by "a date within two years," but rather "a date specified within two years," Deloitte believed the actual severance could occur after the two year window as long as the partner was notified of the date of the severance within two years. This was consistent with the language used in the other severance sections of the Partnership Agreements.

B. Paul's severance as a partner

On March 25, 2004, Vincent DeGutis, the "Partner in Charge" of Paul's office, and Frank Marcos, the "Partner in Charge" of Deloitte's tax practice in the Northeast Region, decided to recommend that Paul be severed from the partnerships. DeGutis and Marcos prepared a draft severance recommendation, which they refined with the help of Steven Severin, one of the partners responsible for addressing Deloitte partners' performance throughout the country. The final recommendation was then submitted to the Committee of 6. On April 8, Marcos and DeGutis informed Paul of their recommendation. On April 12, the Committee of 6 met to consider the recommendation and voted unanimously to sever Paul from the Deloitte partnerships.

Marcos promptly informed Paul orally of the Committee's decision and offered Paul an additional severance payment of $50,000 based upon a notice date of April 12, 2004 (and corresponding last day of May 12, 2004) in exchange for his resignation and a general release. Paul initially accepted. Time passed while Paul and Marcos discussed the terms of Paul's resignation. Because of the delay, Paul received an additional two weeks' compensation (approximately $30,000), so Marcos reduced the additional severance offer to approximately $20,000. Paul ultimately declined the offer.

By letter dated April 22, 2004, within the two year window provided for in Paul's Admission Agreement, Deloitte informed Paul that the Committee of 6 had voted to sever him, gave him the required one month's notice "of such severance," and specified that his partnership was terminated effective May 27, 2004. It is undisputed that Paul received the sums and accommodations to which he was entitled by his Admission Agreement, including about $215,000 in severance payments and a return of his capital, which was then $665,000. On May 11, 2004, Paul was offered a partnership in another Boston accounting firm, Vitale, Caturano & Company and, on June 14, less than three weeks after he was severed from Deloitte, Paul joined Vitale Caturano as a partner. . . .

II. Discussion

We review the Superior Court's decision on a motion for summary judgment *de novo,* applying the same standard as the trial court. We must determine "whether the record shows that there is no genuine material issue of fact and the moving party is entitled to judgment as a matter of law." When the evidence shows no genuine issues of material fact in dispute, the burden shifts to the nonmoving party to demonstrate that there are genuine issues of material fact that must be resolved at trial. If there are material facts in dispute, it is inappropriate to grant summary judgment and the case should be submitted to the fact finder to determine the disposition of the matter. Questions concerning the interpretation of contracts are questions of law, which we review *de novo.* . . .

The Superior Court did not err in granting summary judgment in favor of Deloitte because Paul is not entitled to damages for breach of contract.

Paul contends that the Superior Court erred in concluding that he was not entitled to damages for breach of contract. Paul argues that the court misconstrued his reasonable expectations as of the date of the making of the Partnership Agreements. Paul also argues that he is entitled to recover the income he would have earned until his mandatory retirement at the age of sixty-two, less any income that he has and will earn in mitigation of those damages.

Assuming *arguendo* that Deloitte was in breach of the Partnership Agreements, in assessing the damages of such a breach, the non-breaching party is entitled to recover "damages that arise naturally from the breach or that were reasonably foreseeable at the time the contract was made." Contract damages "are designed to place the injured party in an action for breach of contract in the same place as he would have been if the contract had been performed. Such damages should not act as a windfall." "Expectation damages are measured by the losses caused and gains prevented by defendant's breach."

Paul argues that at the time of entering the Partnership Agreements, he had a clear and distinct reasonable expectation that he would remain a partner in Deloitte until he reached the mandatory retirement age of sixty-two and was therefore an employee for a defined period. Of course, as Deloitte points out, that was not the whole of Paul's expectations, he also had a reasonable expectation that he could be severed without cause (a) within the first two years by vote of the Committee of 6; and (b) at any time by vote of the Board and approved by vote of a majority of all active parties. Thus, even after the two-year period elapsed, Paul remained subject to termination without cause — the only thing that changed was the identity of the decisive body. In addition, Paul had a reasonable expectation that he could be severed for cause at any time by vote of the Board for certain enumerated conduct. Therefore, Paul's status with Deloitte was indefinite and not, as Paul claims, for any definable or fixed term. Accordingly, Paul is not entitled to recover the income he would have earned until his mandatory retirement at the age of sixty-two less any income that he has and will earn in mitigation of those damages.

Even assuming Deloitte breached the employment contract, Paul's expectations regarding the Admission Agreement were satisfied. Paul was notified on April 8, 2004 that the Committee of 6 was considering a recommendation that he be severed. He was then informed of the committee's decision to sever him orally on April 12, and in writing on April 22. Therefore, Paul's expectation of continuing as a partner with Deloitte was extinguished during the two year period. As the Superior Court noted, if Deloitte had used different language and said "effective April 22nd is the date of your severance but your last day of work will be May 27, 2004," the outcome would be the same.

Moreover, Paul lost nothing as a result of the three week delay. He knew within two years that he would be severed and was compensated fully until the actual date of severance. Paul received an additional three weeks of compensation as a result of

Deloitte's breach. In addition, there is no evidence that the three week delay caused Paul any disadvantage in obtaining another position. Paul was offered a partnership at another accounting firm on May 11, 2004 — even before his effective severance from the Deloitte partnerships — and began work less than three weeks later. Paul sustained no damages as a result of the delay in the effective date of his severance. Accordingly, the Superior Court did not err in granting summary judgment in favor of Deloitte.

III. Conclusion

The judgment of the Superior Court is **AFFIRMED**.

* * *

Problem 18

Expectation damages give plaintiffs the benefit of the bargain they struck. How should expectation damages be measured in the following situation?

Perry deals in rare books. He has a wealthy client looking for a recipe book from the early American colonial period that was last printed in the 1600s. The client tells Perry he will pay $2,500 for it. That is well over the book's market value (which is around $1,000), so Perry begins searching for it.

One of Perry's wholesalers is selling a copy of the book. Perry negotiates with the wholesaler and they reach an agreement for Perry to purchase it for $800. After Perry pays, the wholesaler breaches the agreement and refuses to deliver the book. No other copies of the book are currently available for sale anywhere else. Perry sues the wholesaler for breach of contract.

Introductory Note — *World of Boxing, LLC v. King*

A lot goes into putting together a professional boxing match. What happens if one of the fighters fails to show? That is the situation confronted by the federal district court in *World of Boxing, LLC v. King*. The lawsuit is for breach of contract (the company that put on the fight is suing the no-show boxer's representative). The trial judge, having already found there was a breach of contract, must now determine the amount that will adequately compensate for the breach. Since the plaintiff is seeking reliance damages, making that decision requires predicting the future to some degree: the court must evaluate not only the expenditures made in reliance on the contract but also what gains — or losses — the plaintiff would have seen had the fight gone off as planned.

THINGS TO THINK ABOUT while reading *World of Boxing, LLC v. King*:

1. In what situations would a plaintiff ask for reliance damages instead of expectation damages?

2. What is the measure of reliance damages in this case?

3. Can a plaintiff use reliance damages to avoid a bad bargain (a contract that would have been a losing proposition had it been performed)?

World of Boxing, LLC v. King

United States District Court, S.D. of New York
107 F.Supp.3d 265 (2015)

SHIRA A. SCHEINDLIN, District Judge:

I. Introduction

On October 1, 2014, I ruled that Don King, doing business as Don King Productions, breached his agreement with Vladimir Hrunov and Andrey Ryabinskiy, who do business as World of Boxing (collectively "WOB"), when he failed to "cause Guillermo Jones to participate in [a] bout" against Denis Lebedev ("the bout"). The remaining question — addressed in this Opinion — is the amount that King owes to WOB. After my merits ruling, WOB moved for summary judgment on a reliance theory of contract damages. For the reasons set forth below, the motion is GRANTED in part and DENIED in part.

II. Background

Because WOB's "lost profits" — *i.e.,* its expectation damages — "cannot be reasonably quantified," it seeks instead to recover the costs it incurred in anticipation of the bout. These costs are divided into two categories. *First,* per the terms of the parties' agreement, WOB paid $800,000 into an escrow account, of which "$250,000 [was] immediately payable to King." *Second,* WOB expended approximately one million dollars in preparation for the bout. These expenses include, *inter alia,* transportation, lodging, facilities, and promotion. WOB has moved to recover both categories of costs, for a total of approximately $1.8 million. Of this, King concedes that $536,000 — which represents the portion of the escrow account not immediately payable to King ($550,000), minus legal fees, plus interest — is due to WOB per the terms of the parties' escrow agreement ("Agreement"). The parties' dispute therefore concerns (1) the remaining $250,000 from the escrow account, and (2) the one million dollars of preparatory costs.

King has raised two arguments. *First,* he maintains that WOB should not be able to recover the $250,000 that was immediately payable to him upon execution of the Agreement. According to King, the disposition of that sum is governed by the terms of the Agreement, which earmarks the $250,000 as a "non-refundable" payment to

King, to be retained "whether or not the bout occur[s]." *Second,* King argues that although WOB is correct that "New York law provides for recovery of reasonable, foreseeable, reliance damages," those damages must be offset by "any loss that . . . the injured party would have suffered had the contract been performed." And in this case — according to King — WOB would have incurred significant losses even if the bout had gone forward. Therefore, its reliance damages should be capped at the amount of revenue that WOB could reasonably have expected from the bout, which, if measured in terms of the ticket sales that WOB was forced to refund, is just shy of $100,000. In light of this, King asks this Court either (1) to enter judgment for WOB in that amount, plus return of the $536,000 currently being held in escrow, or (2) to deny WOB's motion on the grounds that parties have a material dispute of fact regarding whether, and to what extent, WOB would have suffered losses if the bout had occurred.

III. Standard of Review

Summary judgment is appropriate "only where, construing all the evidence in the light most favorable to the [non-moving party] and drawing all reasonable inferences in that party's favor, there is no genuine issue as to any material fact and . . . the movant is entitled to judgment as a matter of law."

IV. Applicable Law

New York courts have long distinguished between two different forms of redress in breach of contract suits: "expectation damages" and "reliance damages." Expectation damages provide the injured party with the benefit she would have enjoyed had no breach occurred — *i.e.,* they aim to fulfill the injured party's *expectations* from the contract. Reliance damages, by contrast, seek to restore the injured party to the position she was in before the contract was formed. They allow for recovery of "expenditures [the injured party] made in reliance on defendant's representations and that he otherwise would not have made." Under New York law, when expectation damages defy precise calculation, reliance damages are the appropriate remedy. That is what WOB seeks.

To calculate reliance damages, courts must assess the costs that "a plaintiff [incurred from] . . . 'expenditures made in preparation for performance or in performance, less any loss that . . . the injured party would have suffered had the contract been performed.'" The purpose of offsetting reliance damages against anticipated losses is to ensure that contract damages do no more than make an injured party whole — *i.e.,* to ensure that damages do not "put the plaintiff [ ] in a better position than he would have occupied had the contract been fully performed." Thus, "[i]f the breaching party establishes that the plaintiff's losses upon full performance would have equaled or exceeded its reliance expenditures, the plaintiff will recover nothing under a reliance theory."

Typically, the party who moves for summary judgment bears the burden of demonstrating that no material dispute of fact exists. In this context, however, it is the party *in breach* — in this case, King — that bears the burden of "prov[ing] with

burden on the breaching party

reasonable certainty" what losses the "injured party would have suffered" in the event that all contractual obligations had been properly discharged.

V. Discussion

A. The Escrow Account

King's position — which WOB makes no effort to contest — is that under the terms of the Agreement, $250,000 of the $800,000 deposit was intended as an "immediately payable," non-refundable signing bonus. I agree. The Agreement explicitly contemplates the possibility of the bout "fail[ing] to take place." And in that case, King has the right — under the Agreement — to retain the $250,000. If WOB sought a refund of King's signing bonus in the event of a breach, it could have bargained for a provision to that effect. It did not. The money belongs to King.

B. The Preparatory Expenditures

King does not argue that WOB's preparatory expenditures are improperly calculated. Nor does he claim that any of WOB's preparatory expenditures were not reasonable or foreseeable. Instead, King invokes the principle that reliance damages should be offset against losses that WOB "reasonabl[y] certain[ly]" would have incurred, and he argues that WOB's damages should therefore be capped at $98,607 — the value of the tickets that WOB had to refund as a consequence of the bout's cancellation.

King's argument rests on the premise that WOB stood to derive only one type of benefit from the bout, had the bout gone forward — revenue already realized from ticket sales prior to the breach. This premise is erroneous. In fact, there are (at least) two other types of benefits that WOB might have enjoyed in connection with the bout.

First, WOB might well have realized revenue during and after the bout. Maxim Kopylkov, custodian of financial records for the WOB, testified that WOB "expected to receive an undetermined amount of revenue from the television broadcast of [the bout] and from business generated by promotional and advertising activity during [the bout]." King complains — correctly — that WOB has not provided a rigorous accounting of the post-bout revenue it expected to receive. But that is not surprising. The whole reason that WOB is seeking reliance damages rather than expectation damages is that its projected profits (and losses) from the bout are a matter of speculation. To fault WOB for failing to offer concrete projections of post-bout profit would reverse the burden of proof. It is not WOB's burden to prove how much profit it stood to gain. Rather, because King seeks to reduce the amount of preparatory costs that WOB can recover — costs that King admits WOB would not have incurred had no agreement existed — King has the burden to prove with certainty that WOB would *not* have made further revenue.

King has not sustained his burden. He has offered no theory — much less any factual material — to suggest that WOB would have seen no financial upside from the television broadcasting of such a hotly anticipated match. The lack of supporting evidence is not surprising, because King's economic analysis makes little sense. If King is right, WOB's revenue from the bout would have been less than the amount it pledged to King as a signing bonus, even putting *every other preparatory cost* to one side. That hypothesis is implausible. This was no small-time bout; it was the Cruiser-weight World Title match. Furthermore, WOB and King are both sophisticated parties, with proven track records in the boxing world. Although it is certainly *possible* that WOB agreed to underwrite a bout of this import without realizing how drastically its costs would outstrip its gains, that explanation seems very unlikely. And King has given the Court no reason to think it more likely on the specific facts of this case.

Second, WOB might have expected to derive future benefits from the bout — benefits that would not be manifest in immediate revenue, but that would nevertheless make the bout a worthwhile investment for WOB. Indeed, this possibility underscores the conceptual error at the heart of King's position. It disregards the fact that businesses can — and often do — engage in rational loss-leading. There are numerous ways that WOB might have derived value from the bout after the fact. Post-event gains might have included, for example, profit from future re-broadcasting; the benefit of a continued business relationship with Lebedev (the boxer whom WOB was promoting); or simply the creation of a positive track-record within the boxing world.

By way of analogy, imagine if a young art dealer, eager to promote her first gallery, entered into the following arrangement with a famous artist — she will pay him $5,000, and he will visit the gallery to give a lecture about this work. Having scheduled the event, the gallery owner sends out invitations, and she hires caterers, a live band, and security personnel — all of which costs her (a non-refundable) $10,000. The night before he is supposed to speak, the artist backs out, forcing the gallery owner to cancel the event. She sues him for breach of contract, seeking $10,000 in reliance damages. In response, the artist argues that the gallery owner stood to derive no profit from the event — indeed, she stood to lose $15,000 — so any reliance damages should be offset to zero.

The artist's logic, which is also King's logic, is flawed. It misses the point — even if it is accurate — to say that the gallery owner was not going to derive an immediate financial benefit from the event. That was not the event's purpose. Rather, the event was a capital investment, which the gallery owner thought would pay off in the future. In the real world, many investments are made without a guarantee of return, and some are even made with the explicit *intention* of losing money — at least in the short-term. A theory of contract damages that fails to account for this reality cannot be right.

Indeed, this is exactly why a breaching party bears the burden of "prov[ing] with reasonable certainty" that losses would have occurred absent a breach. To cap reliance damages, a breaching party must show, in effect, that losses were inevitable. In *St. Lawrence Factory Stores v. Ogdensburg Bridge & Port Authority,* for example, the Third Department held that an offset was appropriate when a construction project was simply "not feasible," because plaintiff was bound by covenant to build a retail factory outlet but was not able to secure adequate financing for the project. In

light of this, the court reasoned that plaintiff should not be able to recover preparatory expenditures — because the project was doomed. Here, it is far from clear that
WOB's investment in the bout was fated to be a losing proposition. Kopylkov's testimony suggests otherwise. As does common sense.

Ultimately, King has extrapolated the wrong principle from the case law. In his
view, if a breached contract was not going to yield an immediate and direct financial
benefit, no reliance damages should be awarded. But the correct principle is nar-
rower, and — as one might expect — more favorable to injured parties. Plaintiffs who
prevail on breach of contract claims may recover full reliance damages *unless* there
is evidence that completion of the contract could not possibly have resulted in gain.
Here, that is plainly not the case. WOB is entitled to recover its preparatory costs.

C. Offsetting Reliance Damages Against Retained Revenue

Putting the foregoing analysis to one side, King is certainly right about one thing.
Reliance damages are about restoration. They strive to "place [injured parties] in
the same position as they were prior to the execution of the contract," not to work a
"windfall" for injured parties. In this case, WOB retained approximately $75,000 in
revenue from ticket sales, notwithstanding the breach. This amount should be
deducted from the final judgment. Otherwise, WOB would recover its preparatory
costs *and* see the upside of ticket sales that never would have been earned absent the
contract.

VI. Conclusion

For the reasons set forth above, WOB is entitled to two remedies. *First,* the money
currently in the escrow account must be returned to WOB. *Second,* King must pay
WOB an amount equal to the costs enumerated in WOB's moving papers, minus:

(1) The $800,000 initially paid to King (which accounts for the money cur-
rently in escrow, plus the $250,000 non-refundable portion distributed to
King);

(2) The revenue that WOB has retained from non-refunded ticket sales.

WOB is also entitled to prejudgment interest on the resulting sum, to be calculated
from the date of the breach — April 25, 2014.

SO ORDERED.

* * *

Problem 19

Reliance damages reimburse plaintiffs for expenses incurred in connection with performing their end of the bargain. The goal is to put the plaintiff in as good of a position as if the contract had not been breached. How should reliance damages be measured in the following situation?

Karen believes a parcel of land for sale in west Texas has oil under the surface that will be worth several million dollars upon extraction. She enters into a contract to purchase the land for $200,000, with escrow scheduled to close in a month. She then spends $500,000 on equipment that she will need to drill for oil. The seller breaches the contract and sells the land to someone else. As it turns out, there is no oil on the property; to the contrary, the soil is contaminated with a toxic substance that renders the property worthless. Karen sues the seller for breach of the purchase contract.

Recovery of Special Damages

The distinction between general and special damages is particularly important in the contract setting. Recall that in a contract action, general damages are those damages which are the natural and probable consequence of a breach. That means they are objectively foreseeable: anyone who looks at the deal would know a breach is going to lead to that kind of harm.

Special damages in a contract action, on the other hand, are damages that were caused by the breach but are *not* the natural and probable consequence of it. (Special damages in contract cases are also referred to as consequential damages.) So while the typical person who enters into the contract in question would not experience that kind of harm from a breach, this particular plaintiff did. In that way, special damages are objectively unforeseeable.

The distinction between general and special damages is important in contract cases because special damages ordinarily cannot be recovered. Rather, special damages can be recovered only under specific circumstances: when the defendant knew or should have known, at the time the contract was formed, that the plaintiff would incur those damages in the event of a breach. So special damages are allowed only when the harm they compensate for was anticipated by the parties at the time of contracting.

This limitation on recovering special damages is unique to contract law. Why is there a foreseeability requirement for damages in contract damages but not in tort? Because of the interest in promoting predictability for parties who enter into contracts. Permitting recovery of only those damages that are foreseeable at the time of contracting allows parties to assess the financial risk of a deal before making it.

The wider the universe of damages that can be recovered, the riskier the deal. The riskier the deal, the more a party will charge to enter into it. Enhancing predictability therefore lowers the cost of contracting, at least in theory.

Introductory Note — *Hadley v. Baxendale* and *Kenford Co. v. County of Erie*

Hadley v. Baxendale is a classic case that presents a classic example of special damages in a breach of contract suit. The trial court awarded the plaintiff lost profits for the defendant's failure to timely deliver a replacement part the plaintiff needed to operate his mill. The lost profits resulted from the mill being out of commission while awaiting the part. The appellate court must determine whether the lost profits were foreseeable at the time the delivery contract was formed.

Kenford Co. v. County of Erie was decided 135 years after *Hadley*. But the appellate court relies heavily on *Hadley* in deciding whether the plaintiff was properly awarded special damages in a breach of contract case involving a contract to build a domed sports stadium.

THINGS TO THINK ABOUT while reading *Hadley v. Baxendale* and *Kenford Co. v. County of Erie*:

1. What is the policy reason for limiting the recovery of special damages in contract cases?

2. Why are the damages at issue here considered special damages? What are the plaintiff's general damages?

3. What made the damages sought by the plaintiff unforeseeable at the time of contracting? Under what circumstances would they have been foreseeable?

Hadley v. Baxendale

Court of Exchequer
9 Exch. 341, 156 Eng.Rep. 145 (1854)

At the trial before Crompton, J., at the last Gloucester Assizes, it appeared that the plaintiffs carried on an extensive business as millers at Gloucester; and that on the 11th on May, their mill was stopped by a breakage of the crank shaft by which the mill was worked.

The steam-engine was manufactured by Messrs. Joyce & Co., the engineers, at Greenwich, and it became necessary to send the shaft as a pattern for a new one to Greenwich. The fracture was discovered on the 12th, and on the 13th the plaintiffs sent one of their servants to the office of the defendants, who are the well-known carriers trading under the name of Pickford & Co., for the purpose of having the shaft carried to Greenwich.

The plaintiffs' servant told the clerk that the mill was stopped, and that the shaft must be sent immediately; and in answer to the inquiry when the shaft would be taken, the answer was, that if it was sent up by twelve o'clock any day, it would be delivered at Greenwich on the following day. On the following day the shaft was taken by the defendants, before noon, for the purpose of being conveyed to Greenwich, and the sum of 2l. 4s. was paid for its carriage for the whole distance; at the same time the defendants' clerk was told that a special entry, if required, should be made to hasten its delivery. The delivery of the shaft at Greenwich was delayed by some neglect; and the consequence was, that the plaintiffs did not receive the new shaft for several days after they would otherwise have done, and the working of their mill was thereby delayed, and they thereby lost the profits they would otherwise have received.

On the part of the defendants, it was objected that these damages were too remote, and that the defendants were not liable with respect to them. . . .

We think that there ought to be a new trial in this case; but, in so doing, we deem it to be expedient and necessary to state explicitly the rule which the Judge, at the next trial, ought, in our opinion, to direct the jury to be governed by when they estimate the damages. . . . Now we think the proper rule in such a case as the present is this: Where two parties have made a contract which one of them has broken, the damages which the other party ought to receive in respect of such breach of contract should be such as may fairly and reasonably be considered either arising naturally, i.e., according to the usual course of things, from such breach of contract itself, or such as may reasonably be supposed to have been in the contemplation of both parties, at the time they made the contract, as the probable result of the breach of it. Now, if the special circumstances under which the contract was actually made were communicated by the plaintiffs to the defendants, and thus known to both parties, the damages resulting from the breach of such a contract, which they would reasonably contemplate, would be the amount of injury which would ordinarily follow from a breach of contract under these special circumstances so known and communicated. But, on the other hand, if these special circumstances were wholly unknown to the party breaking the contract, he, at the most, could only be supposed to have had in his contemplation the amount of injury which would arise generally, and in the great multitude of cases not affected by any special circumstances, from such a breach of contract. For, had the special circumstances been known, the parties might have specially provided for the breach of contract by special terms as to the damages in that case; and of this advantage it would be very unjust to deprive them. Now the above principles are those by which we think the jury ought to be guided in estimating the damages arising out of any breach of contract. It is said, that other cases such as breaches of contract in the nonpayment of money, or in the not making a good title of land, are to be treated as exceptions from this, and as governed by a conventional rule. . . .

Now, in the present case, if we are to apply the principles above laid down, we find that the only circumstances here communicated by the plaintiffs to the defendants at the time of the contract was made, were, that the article to be carried was the broken shaft of a mill, and that the plaintiffs were the millers of the mill. But how do these circumstances shew reasonably that the profits of the mill must be stopped by an unreasonable delay in the delivery of the broken shaft by the carrier to the third person? Suppose the plaintiffs had another shaft in their possession put up or putting up at the time, and that they only wished to send back the broken shaft to the engineer who made it; it is clear that this would be quite consistent with the above circumstances, and yet the unreasonable delay in the delivery would have no effect upon the intermediate profits of the mill. . . . But it is obvious that, in the great multitude of cases of millers sending off broken shafts to third persons by a carrier under ordinary circumstances, such consequences would not, in all probability, have occurred; and these special circumstances were here never communicated by the plaintiffs to the defendants.

It follows therefore, that the loss of profits here cannot reasonably be considered such a consequence of the breach of contract as could have been fairly and reasonably contemplated by both the parties when they made this contract. For such loss would neither have flowed naturally from the breach of this contract in the great multitude of such cases occurring under ordinary circumstances, nor were the special circumstances, which, perhaps, would have made it a reasonable and natural consequence of such breach of contract, communicated to or known by the defendants. The Judge ought, therefore, to have told the jury that upon the facts then before them they ought not to take the loss of profits into consideration at all in estimating the damages.

There must therefore be a new trial in this case.

* * *

Kenford Co. v. County of Erie
New York Court of Appeals
73 N.Y.2d 312 (1989)

MOLLEN, Judge.

This appeal arises out of breach of contract litigation spanning 18 years and involving the proposed construction and operation of a domed stadium facility in the County of Erie. The issue is whether the plaintiff Kenford Company, Inc. (Kenford) is entitled to recover damages against the defendant County of Erie (County) for the loss of anticipated appreciation in the value of the land which Kenford owned in the periphery of the proposed stadium site. Under the circumstances of this case, we conclude that Kenford is not entitled to recovery on this claim since there is no evidence to support a determination that the parties contemplated, prior to or at the time of the contract, assumption by the County of liability for these damages.

By way of background, the County of Erie adopted enabling legislation in May 1968 authorizing it to finance and construct a domed sports stadium in the vicinity of the City of Buffalo. The County, simultaneously, adopted a resolution authorizing a $50 million bond resolution for the purpose of financing the construction of the proposed stadium. In December 1968, Kenford, through its president and sole shareholder, Edward H. Cottrell, submitted an offer to the County with regard to the stadium project. By its terms, Kenford, which had acquired options on various parcels of land located in the Town of Lancaster in Erie County, proposed to sell a portion of that land to the County as a site for the stadium facility. Although the County initially expressed interest in Kenford's proposal, it eventually declined the offer. Kenford, however, pursued the matter and thereafter engaged the services of Judge Roy Hofheinz, who had been instrumental in the development of the Houston Astrodome. Kenford then approached the County with a new offer. By its terms, Kenford was to donate to the County the land upon which the stadium was to be built, in exchange for which the County was to permit Hofheinz and Cottrell, who had formed the management company of Dome Stadium, Inc. (DSI), to lease or manage the proposed stadium facility.

In June 1969, the County adopted a resolution accepting Kenford's new offer, after which the parties engaged in contract negotiations. During this period of time, Cottrell, as agent for Kenford, exercised his options on several parcels of land located in the Town of Lancaster. On August 8, 1969, the County, Kenford and DSI executed a contract which provided, in pertinent part, that Kenford would donate 178 acres of land located in the Town of Lancaster to the County for use in construction of the stadium and necessary access roadways. In consideration therefor, the County agreed to commence construction of the stadium within 12 months. . . .

Following execution of the contract, the County solicited construction bids for the proposed stadium. The bids received by the County indicated that the proposed project would cost approximately $72 million which was $22 million in excess of the County's prior bond resolution. Although efforts were made to seek an increase in the appropriation for the stadium, those efforts were unsuccessful and, in January 1971, the County adopted a resolution terminating the contract with Kenford and DSI. Kenford's subsequent attempts to procure alternate financing for the proposed stadium facility proved futile.

In June 1971, Kenford and DSI instituted the instant breach of contract action and sought specific performance thereof, or, in the alternative, damages in the amount of $90 million. Following the award of summary judgment in favor of the plaintiffs on the issue of liability (*see, Kenford Co. v. County of Erie*, 88 A.D.2d 758), the matter was set down for a trial on the issue of damages. The damage trial lasted approximately nine months and resulted in a jury award to Kenford in the sum of $18 million for its lost appreciation in the value on its property located on the periphery of the proposed stadium site and an award of over $6 million in out-of-pocket expenses. DSI was awarded $25.6 million in lost profits under the parties' 20-year management contract. [This appeal followed.]

It is well established that in actions for breach of contract, the nonbreaching party may recover general damages which are the natural and probable consequence of the breach. "[I]n order to impose on the defaulting party a further liability than for damages [which] naturally and directly [flow from the breach], i.e., in the ordinary course of things, arising from a breach of contract, such unusual or extraordinary damages must have been brought within the contemplation of the parties as the probable result of a breach at the time of or prior to contracting" (*Chapman v. Fargo,* 223 N.Y. 32, 36; *see also*; *Hadley v. Baxendale,* 9 Exch 341, 156 Eng.Rep. 145). In determining the reasonable contemplation of the parties, the nature, purpose and particular circumstances of the contract known by the parties should be considered (*see, Mortimer v. Otto,* 206 N.Y. 89, 91, 99 N.E. 189; 36 NY Jur 2d, Damages, §40), as well as "what liability the defendant fairly may be supposed to have assumed consciously, or to have warranted the plaintiff reasonably to suppose that it assumed, when the contract was made" (*Globe Ref. Co. v. Landa Cotton Oil Co.,* 190 U.S. 540, 544 [Holmes, J.]; *see also, Kenford Co. v. County of Erie,* 67 N.Y.2d 257, 262).

In the case before us, it is beyond dispute that at the time the contract was executed, all parties thereto harbored an expectation and anticipation that the proposed domed stadium facility would bring about an economic boom in the County and would result in increased land values and increased property taxes. This expectation is evidenced by the terms of the provision of the parties' contract requiring the County and DSI to undertake negotiations of a lease which would provide for specified revenues to be derived from, *inter alia,* the increased taxes on the peripheral lands. We cannot conclude, however, that this hope or expectation of increased property values and taxes necessarily or logically leads to the conclusion that the parties contemplated that the County would assume liability for Kenford's loss of anticipated appreciation in the value of its peripheral lands if the stadium were not built. On this point, our decision in the prior appeal regarding DSI's right to recover damages for lost profits under the 20-year management contract is particularly instructive: "Initially, the proof does not satisfy the requirement that liability for loss of profits over a 20-year period was in the contemplation of the parties at the time of the execution of the basic contract or at the time of its breach (*see, Chapman v. Fargo,* 223 N.Y. 32; 36 N.Y.Jur.2d, Damages, §§ 39, 40, at 66–70). Indeed, the provisions in the contract providing remedy for a default do not suggest or provide for such a heavy responsibility on the part of the County. In the absence of any provision for such an eventuality, *the commonsense rule to apply is to consider what the parties would have concluded had they considered the subject.* The evidence here fails to demonstrate that liability for loss of profits over the length of the contract would have been in the contemplation of the parties at the relevant time" (67 N.Y.2d 257, 262, *supra* [emphasis added]).

Similarly, there is no provision in the contract between Kenford and the County, nor is there any evidence in the record to demonstrate that the parties, at any relevant time, reasonably contemplated or would have contemplated that the County was undertaking a contractual responsibility for the lack of appreciation in the value of Kenford's peripheral lands in the event the stadium was not built. This conclusion is buttressed by the fact that Kenford was under no contractual obligation to the County to acquire or maintain ownership of any land surrounding the 178 acres it was required to donate to the County. Although the County was aware that Kenford had acquired and intended to further acquire peripheral lands, this knowledge, in and of itself, is insufficient, as a matter of law, to impose liability on the County for the loss of anticipated appreciation in the value of those lands since the County never contemplated at the time of the contract's execution that it assumed legal responsibility for these damages upon a breach of the contract. As this court noted in *Booth v. Spuyten Duyvil Rolling Mill Co.,* 60 N.Y. 487, 494, *supra)* "bare notice of special consequences which might result from a breach of contract, unless under such circumstances as to imply that it formed the basis of the agreement, would not be sufficient [to impose liability for special damages]" (*see also, Czarnikow-Rionda Co. v. Federal Sugar Ref. Co.,* 255 N.Y. 33, *supra* [the defendant supplier of sugar was not made aware at the time of the contract that the plaintiff purchaser could not acquire sugar on the open market and, therefore, was not liable for the plaintiff's special damages arising out of the breach of contract]; *Baldwin v. United States Tel. Co.,* 45 N.Y. 744, *supra* [the defendant telegraph company was not liable for special damages caused by delay in delivery of message since it was without notice or information indicating that extraordinary care or speed of delivery was necessary]; *Hadley v. Baxendale,* 9 Exch. 341, 156 Eng.Rep. 145, *supra* [the common carrier was not liable for the loss of profits at the plaintiffs' flour mill since the carrier, who knew that the mill was closed, was not aware that the mill's continued operation was dependent solely on prompt delivery of the mill's broken shaft]).

Undoubtedly, Kenford purchased the peripheral lands in question with the hope of benefiting from the expected appreciation in the value of those lands once the stadium was completed and became operational. In doing so, Kenford voluntarily and knowingly assumed the risk that, if the stadium were not built, its expectations of financial gain would be unrealized. There is no indication that either Kenford or the County reasonably contemplated at the time of the contract that this risk was assumed, either wholly or partially, by the County. To hold otherwise would lead to the irrational conclusion that the County, in addition to promising to build the domed stadium, provided a guarantee that if for any reason the stadium were not built, Kenford would still receive all the hoped for financial benefits from the peripheral lands it anticipated to receive upon the completion of the stadium. According to Kenford's version of the facts, Kenford was to realize all of its anticipated gains with or without the stadium. Clearly, such a result is illogical and without any basis whatsoever in the record.

Thus, the constant refrain which flows throughout the legion of breach of contract cases dating back to the leading case of *Hadley v. Baxendale* (9 Exch. 341, 156 Eng.Rep. 145, *supra*) provides that damages which may be recovered by a party for breach of contract are restricted to those damages which were reasonably foreseen or contemplated by the parties during their negotiations or at the time the contract was executed. The evident purpose of this well-accepted principle of contract law is to limit the liability for unassumed risks of one entering into a contract and, thus, diminish the risk of business enterprise (*see,* McCormick, Damages § 138, at 566, *supra*). In the case before us, although Kenford obviously anticipated and expected that it would reap financial benefits from an anticipated dramatic increase in the value of its peripheral lands upon the completion of the proposed domed stadium facility, these expectations did not ripen or translate into cognizable breach of contract damages since there is no indication whatsoever that the County reasonably contemplated at any relevant time that it was to assume liability for Kenford's unfulfilled land appreciation expectations in the event that the stadium was not built. Thus, under the principles set forth in *Hadley v. Baxendale (supra)* and its progeny of cases in this State (*see, e.g., Kenford Co. v. County of Erie,* 67 N.Y.2d 257, *supra; Czarnikow-Rionda Co. v. Federal Sugar Ref. Co.,* 255 N.Y. 33; *Kerr S.S. Co. v. Radio Corp.,* 245 N.Y. 284, *supra; Chapman v. Fargo,* 223 N.Y. 32, *supra*), Kenford is not entitled to recovery, as a matter of law, for its lost appreciation in the value of its peripheral lands caused by the County's breach of the parties' contract.

Accordingly, the March 4, 1988 order of the Appellate Division insofar as appealed from and the April 12, 1985 order of the same court insofar as brought up for review should be reversed, with costs, and the award for loss of anticipated profits from appreciation in the value of peripheral lands stricken.

     * * *

Problem 20   [w/in the K of parties - existing customers]

The rule limiting recovery of special damages promotes predictability by limiting the extent to which a breaching party can be liable for the losses caused by a breach of contract. How should the lawyer in the below-described scenario advise her client?

Peter is in the ice cream business. He produces it and delivers it to local grocery stores. He contracts with a freezer manufacturer to install a new freezer on one of his trucks. The manufacturer installs the freezer incorrectly, causing it to abruptly shut off during a delivery run. The ice cream melts, and Peter is unable to fill that month's orders. Two of his biggest customers are upset and refuse to do business with Peter any longer. As a result, Peter loses $100,000 in profits that year.

Peter consults an attorney and asks whether a breach of contract suit against the freezer manufacturer would allow him to recover his lost profits.

[Handwritten margin notes:]

base K damages
K price - FMV
as delivered
$ = COR (usually)

Cause of action: breach of contract
goods or services?
- goods

you may only get
cost of installation
if freezer is not
broken

+incidental damages - new freezer
+ conseq. damages - lost profits. deal w/ 3rd parties

Liquidated Damages

If parties to a contract are allowed to agree to most anything (so long as it isn't illegal), why can't they agree on the amount of damages to be awarded in the event of a breach? The answer is they can, at least sometimes. An agreement in a contract about the precise amount of damages a party will pay for a breach is called a liquidated damages provision.

Liquidated damages promote an important policy goal of contract law. They provide supreme predictability for the parties to the transaction. With a liquidated damages provision, a party can assess *exactly* how much risk is involved before agreeing to a deal. In that respect, liquidated damages are very desirable from a contract law standpoint.

Left unchecked, though, liquidated damages could undermine another important principle of contract law: the idea that a breach of contract is sometimes beneficial to society and should not be deterred. If parties were allowed to choose any amount of liquidated damages, they might be tempted to set the amount so high it would severely penalize a breach. That kind of penalty runs contrary to the idea that breach should be encouraged if a party decides breaching is the most efficient use of resources.

To eliminate the temptation for a party to use liquidated damages as a deterrent to breach, a liquidated damages provision will be enforceable only where reasonably necessary. To decide if it is necessary, courts look at two aspects of the circumstances. The first is whether the amount of damages for a breach were difficult to anticipate at the time of contracting. If they were, liquidated damages are necessary to enhance predictability. The second factor is whether, after the breach has occurred, the amount of liquidated damages is reasonably close to the amount of harm the plaintiff actually incurred. If a liquidated damages provision requires payment of significantly more damages than the harm incurred, it might be considered too punitive to be enforceable.

Introductory Note — *B-Sharp Musical Productions v. Haber* and *Burzee v. Park Avenue Insurance Agency*

B-Sharp Musical Productions and *Burzee* both involve defendants in breach of contract cases challenging an award of liquidated damages. The liquidated damages provision at issue in *B-Sharp* is deemed enforceable; the one in *Burzee* is deemed unenforceable. Key to both decisions is the actual effect the provision has under the circumstances presented (as opposed to how it could potentially operate under other circumstances).

THINGS TO THINK ABOUT while reading *B-Sharp Musical Productions v. Haber* and *Burzee v. Park Avenue Insurance Agency*:

1. Why was the liquidated damages provision in each case deemed enforceable or unenforceable?

2. Would it be a reasonable policy choice to enforce all liquidated damages provisions? Why or why not?

B-Sharp Musical Productions v. Haber

New York Supreme Court
27 Misc.3d 41 (2010)

PER CURIAM.

James Haber entered into a contract pursuant to which plaintiff agreed to provide a designated 16-piece band on a specified date to perform at Mr. Haber's son's bar mitzvah. Mr. Haber was to pay approximately $30,000 for the band's services. The contract contained a liquidated damages clause stating, in pertinent part, "If [the contract] is terminated in writing by [Mr. Haber] for any reason within ninety (90) days prior to the engagement, the remaining balance of the contract will be immediately due and payable. If [the contract] is terminated in writing by [Mr. Haber] for any reason before the ninety (90) days period, 50% of the balance will be immediately due and payable."

Less than 90 days prior to the date of the bar mitzvah, Mr. Haber sent a letter to plaintiff notifying it that he was cancelling the contract. After Mr. Haber refused plaintiff's demand that he pay the remaining amount due under the contract—approximately $25,000—plaintiff commenced this action against Mr. Haber and his wife, defendant Jill Haber. Civil Court granted plaintiff's motion for summary judgment on its cause of action to enforce the liquidated damages clause and denied defendants' cross motion for partial summary judgment dismissing that cause of action and the complaint as against Mrs. Haber.

Given the nature of the contract and the particular circumstances underlying this case (*see JMD Holding Corp. v. Congress Fin. Corp.*, 4 N.Y.3d 373, 379 [2005]), Civil Court correctly determined that the subject provision of the contract is an enforceable liquidated damages clause, not an unenforceable penalty (*see Truck Rent-A-Ctr. v. Puritan Farms 2nd*, 41 N.Y.2d 420 [1977]). "The clause, which in effect uses an estimate of [plaintiff's] chances of re-booking the [band] as the measure of [its] probable loss in the event of a cancellation, reflects an understanding that although the expense and possibility of re-booking a canceled [performance] could not be ascertained with certainty, as a practical matter the expense would become greater, and the possibility would become less, the closer to the [performance] the cancellation was made, until a point was reached, [90] days before [the performance], that any effort to re-book could not be reasonably expected" (*Turner-Schraeter v. Brighton Travel Bureau, Inc.,* 258 A.D.2d 393, 393–394 [1999]).

Defendants' argument that the cause of action to enforce the liquidated damages clause must be dismissed because the clause does not comply with the type size requirement of CPLR 4544 is without merit. In an effort to demonstrate that the clause did not comply with the statutory type size requirement, defendants submitted a copy of the contract with the image of a ruler imprinted in the margin. However, defendants failed to establish that the type size of the copy they submitted is identical to that of the original contract, a critical failure given the precision with which type size must be measured and calculated. Therefore, defendants failed to raise a triable issue as to whether the clause violated the statutory type size requirement. . . .

THIS CONSTITUTES THE DECISION AND ORDER OF THE COURT.

* * *

Burzee v. Park Avenue Insurance Agency, Inc.

Florida Court of Appeal, Fifth District
946 So.2d 1200 (2006)

MONACO, J.

Jane Marie Burzee appeals the Final Judgment on Plaintiff's Motion For Entry of Final Judgment on Damages that held her liable for damages for breach of a non-compete agreement with her former employer, Park Avenue Insurance Agency, Inc. . . . We affirm the conclusion of the trial court in the Final Judgment that Ms. Burzee violated the non-compete provisions in the agreement. . . . Because we conclude that the consequence of the breach of the non-compete agreement amounted to a penalty, rather than liquidated damages, however, we reverse that part of the Final Judgment awarding damages.

Ms. Burzee and Park entered into an oral employment contract, but executed a written covenant-not-to-compete agreement in which she agreed that:

[F]or a period of two (2) years after leaving the employ of the Company she will not call upon or communicate with or endeavor by any means whatsoever, either directly or indirectly, to sell or to solicit to sell, any of the present customers of the Company or any customers of the Company who she shall have secured as customers for the Company or shall have become customers of the company during the entire period of her employment by it, or any other customers of the Company.

In the event of the violation of the non-competition provision by Ms. Burzee, the parties agreed that the measure of damages would be as follows:

[margin note: measure of damages]

Employee further agrees that in the event that she shall violate or break this covenant, which she hereby acknowledges would cause great loss and irreparable damage to the Company, which could not be ascertainable, she shall be and become liable for and be obligated to pay the Company *a sum as liquidated damages equal in amount to $10000 PLUS the entire commissions earned by the Company on the accounts sold and/or serviced by Employee during the TWENTY-FOUR (24) months prior to the month in which her employment with the Company is terminated,* and in addition to any and all other remedies available to it, the Company shall be entitled to both a temporary and permanent injunction restraining and enjoining Employee from any violations or breaches of this agreement. (emphasis added).

Park terminated Ms. Burzee in 2002, and a short time later she began to work for another competing insurance agency. The trial court concluded that while so employed, she violated the non-compete agreement and awarded damages of $161,572.88 to Park, in accordance with the damages provision. As specified in the agreement, the award was calculated by totalling all of the commissions earned by Park on the accounts either sold or serviced by Ms. Burzee during the two years prior to her termination, plus the $10,000 kicker. Ms. Burzee argues that this amounts to a penalty, while Park urges that it was properly determined to be liquidated damages. We think it was a penalty.

[margin note: Burzee argues this amounts to penalty]

We review the legal effect of a contractual provision *de novo* as an issue of law. *See Cox v. CSX Intermodal, Inc.,* 732 So.2d 1092 (Fla. 1st DCA) (1999). A reviewing court may, therefore, independently reassess the meaning of the non-compete provision and reach a conclusion different from that of the trial court. *See Coleman v. B.R. Chamberlain & Sons, Inc.,* 766 So.2d 427 (Fla. 5th DCA 2000). We begin our independent review by a consideration of the general principles underpinning the subject of liquidated damages.

The parties to a contract may stipulate in advance to an amount to be paid as liquidated damages in the event of a breach, provided that the damages resulting from the breach are not readily ascertainable, and provided that the sum stipulated as damages is not so grossly disproportionate to any damages that might reasonably be expected to follow from a breach that the parties could only have intended to induce full performance, rather than to liquidate their damages. *See Lefemine v. Baron,* 573 So.2d 326, 328 (Fla.1991); *RKR Motors.* If, however, a penalty provision is disguised as a liquidated damages provision, it is unenforceable. *See Hyman v. Cohen,* 73 So.2d 393, 399 (Fla.1954). The theory is simply that we do not allow one party to hold a penalty provision over the head of the other party "*in terrorem*" to deter that party from breaching a promise. *See Crosby Forrest Products, Inc. v. Byers,* 623 So.2d 565, 567 (Fla. 5th DCA 1993).

In the present case there is virtually no relationship between the gravity of the loss to Park that would result from a violation of the non-compete agreement and the amount specified as damages. The amount consists of all of the premiums earned by *Park* from any account "sold and/or serviced" by Ms. Burzee for two years, regardless of the extent of that servicing, and undiminished by her share of the commissions or by any other expenses that Park might have incurred in connection with those commissions. That is, the provision requires her to pay the gross amount of the commission earned by her employer from the identified accounts during the two-year calculation period. To that, the contract requires yet another $10,000 be lumped on top.

While it might be true that Park's damages could not have been calculated with particularity at the commencement of Ms. Burzee's employment, these numbers are grossly disproportionate to any damages that Park could have anticipated by a breach and, therefore, constitute a penalty. Our conclusion in this regard is validated to some extent by a review of some similar cases. In *Coleman* we held that a provision that required the employee upon breach to pay 200% of one year's gross revenue for each client that actually switched to the employee's new employer was a penalty and unenforceable. Similarly, in *Cherry, Bekaert & Holland v. LaSalle*, 413 So.2d 436 (Fla. 3d DCA 1982), the Third District also held that a covenant that required the departing employee to pay 200% of the fees charged to any former client of the firm served by the employee during the preceding year to be a penalty. In Ms. Burzee's case she would be compelled to pay as damages 100% of the commissions earned by her employer from any client she dealt with while employed for two years, regardless of whether any of the clients actually followed her to her new employer. The damage calculation is the same whether she breached with only one client or a hundred. The absence of proportionality is patent.

Finally, we note that our Supreme Court has held that even as against a properly conceived liquidated damages clause, equity may "relieve against the forfeiture if it appears unconscionable in light of the circumstances existing at the time of the breach." *Hutchison v. Tompkins*, 259 So.2d 129, 132 (Fla.1972). Here, we are convinced that even if the clause might ordinarily be enforceable, it is not enforceable in light of the present breach.

Accordingly, we reverse that part of the judgment finding the subject provision to be a valid liquidated damages clause, and remand for further consideration in light of this opinion. We otherwise affirm the final judgment.

REVERSED in part, AFFIRMED in part, and REMANDED.

* * *

1. damages at time of K?
2. proportional to

[handwritten margin note: no · grossly disproportionate + in terrorem]

Problem 21

The line between a valid liquidated damages provision and an unenforceable penalty can be a fine one. Is the below liquidated damages provision likely to be enforceable?

A clause in a residential lease reads:

"**Late Fee:** Rent is due on the first day of every month during the lease term. If the full amount of rent is not received by the first day of the month, liquidated damages of 25% of the monthly rent shall be added to the payment owed."

Special Rules for Sales of Goods Under the Uniform Commercial Code

This chapter has so far discussed common law rules for contract remedies. But different rules apply to certain commercial transactions. Contracts for the sale of goods are governed by Article 2 of the Uniform Commercial Code, a model statutory scheme intended to "simplify, clarify, and modernize the law governing commercial transactions." (UCC § 1-103.) All 50 states have adopted at least some version of the Uniform Commercial Code, commonly referred to as the UCC.

The UCC governs all aspects of the contractual relationship. It defines what constitutes an offer in particular situations, what constitutes acceptance, and whether the terms of a contract include an implied warranty. The UCC also provides the remedies available to an aggrieved party in the event of a breach, including the type of damages that can be recovered and how they should be measured.

For example, under the UCC, a seller's damages for a buyer's failure to honor a purchase contract are "any commercially reasonable charges," such as expenses incurred in stopping delivery of the goods, transporting them, or reselling them. (UCC § 2-710.) An aggrieved buyer's damages include the cost of procuring substitute goods to replace the ones the seller failed to deliver as promised — so called "cover" damages. (UCC § 2-712.)

Those are just some examples of UCC remedies; the statutory scheme is detailed and comprehensive. The comprehensive nature of the UCC means it requires its own course of study to fully understand. But a civil practitioner will at least need to know when the UCC rules apply instead of common law contract rules.

The UCC applies to "transactions in goods." (UCC § 2-102.) And goods are defined as all things "which are movable at the time of identification to the contract for sale." (UCC § 2-105(1).) So the UCC will generally apply to all contracts for the purchase of movable things. That is usually a straightforward enough determination. But not always. The question of whether the contract is a "transaction in goods" becomes more difficult when a contract involves both goods and services, a not uncommon scenario. (Think of the auto mechanic who installs a car battery, the window covering company who puts up shutters in a home, or the construction contractor that provides the heating and cooling equipment for a new office building.)

To decide whether the UCC applies to a contract that is mixed — that is, one that involves both goods and services — courts use the predominant purpose test: What was the consumer's predominant purpose in entering into the contract — to obtain goods or a service? In other words, what was the consumer *really* paying for — the movable thing or the seller's skill and expertise?

Making that determination is always fact intensive, and often a close call.

Introductory Note — *Fairchild v. Swearingen* and *Duro Bag Manufacturing, Inc. v. Printing Services Company*

The issue in both *Fairchild* and *Duro Bag Manufacturing* is whether the transaction in question is a sale of goods such that the UCC will apply. *Fairchild* involves a familiar situation, a contract to install a new roof. The contract in *Duro Bag Manufacturing* is more specialized: a custom printing on paper bags to be used in a retail store. Both courts apply the predominant purpose test to resolve the UCC issue.

THINGS TO THINK ABOUT while reading *Fairchild v. Swearingen* and *Duro Bag Manufacturing, Inc. v. Printing Services Company*:

1. To decide the purpose of the contract, is the court limited to looking only at the language of the contract itself?

2. What facts does each court consider most important in deciding what the predominant purpose of the contract is?

3. Is the analysis employed in *Fairchild* generally the same as in *Duro Bag Manufacturing*? Or do the courts approach the question differently?

Fairchild v. Swearingen

Court of Civil Appeals of Oklahoma
377 P.3d 1262 (2013)

JOHN F. FISCHER, Presiding Judge.

Dennis M. Fairchild filed this small claims action against his roofing contractor Swearingen Remodeling, Inc., who admittedly installed shingles of a lesser value than required by the parties' contract. After the case was tried to the district court, Judgment was entered in Fairchild's favor. The Judgment provided alternative forms of relief and permitted Swearingen to choose which form of relief to provide: (1) replace the non-conforming shingles with the shingles specified in the contract, (2) return Fairchild's partial payment. Swearingen elected the former and Fairchild appealed. We find no error by the district court and affirm.

Background

After storms damaged the roofs of two houses, Fairchild contracted with Swearingen to remove the damaged roofs and replace the roofs with new shingles. The roof on the first house was replaced to Fairchild's satisfaction and according to the parties' contract by July 22, 2011. It is not an issue in this case. The second house is Fairchild's personal residence. The contract for the roof on this house was signed on July 7, 2011. With respect to that contract, Fairchild specified impact resistant shingles, in part, to obtain a discount on his homeowner's insurance premium. After work began on the second house, Fairchild paid $6,000 of the $12,036.12 contract price. Swearingen completed reroofing that house in late July 2011. On August 6, 2011, Swearingen discovered that thirty-year laminated shingles had been installed rather than the impact resistant shingles required by the contract. Swearingen notified Fairchild of this mistake on August 11, 2011. The parties, with the involvement of Fairchild's insurance company, attempted to resolve the dispute but were ultimately unsuccessful. Fairchild filed this small claims action on November 11, 2011. Swearingen filed a counterclaim for the unpaid balance of the contract price.

At the conclusion of the trial, the district court entered judgment in favor of Fairchild on his breach of contract claim and on Swearingen's counterclaim. The judgment provided as follows:

> Judgment should be granted in favor of Plaintiff as follows (the option of Defendant):
>
> a. The Defendant be afforded to install the correct roof in a workman like manner and in accordance with installation standards, i.e. weather etc. within a reasonable time, weather permitting, or
>
> b. to refund the amount of $5,484.09 to Plaintiff.

Swearingen elected the first option and notified Fairchild that he would install the impact resistant shingles in March of 2012. Fairchild appealed, contending he should have been placed in the position he was in before the contract breach occurred and refunded the $6,000 he paid minus the amount attributable to replacement of the window screens and guttering.

Analysis

. . . The first issue raised by Fairchild concerns the applicability of the Oklahoma Uniform Commercial Code (UCC). 12A O.S.2011 §§ 1-101 to 15-121. Fairchild contends that Swearingen does not have the right to now install the correct shingles because he cannot do so "seasonably." Swearingen points to section 2-508(1) of the UCC: "Where any tender or delivery by the seller is rejected because nonconforming and the time for performance has not yet expired, the seller may seasonably notify the buyer of his intention to cure and may then within the contract time make a conforming delivery." The validity of this argument depends on whether the UCC is applicable to this transaction.

As relevant to this appeal, the UCC applies to "transactions in goods." 12A O.S.2011 § 2-102. It does not apply to contracts for labor and services. *Moore v. Vanderloo,* 386 N.W.2d 108 (Iowa 1986). The high impact shingles involved in this case satisfy the UCC's definition of goods. "'Goods' means all things (including specially manufactured goods) which are movable at the time of identification to the contract for sale. . . ." 12A O.S.2011 § 2-105(1). The determinative question, however, is whether the parties' contract which also called for the removal of the old shingles, installation of the new shingles and other items necessary to the installation of a new roof, is a transaction in goods. This issue has not been previously decided in Oklahoma.

In those jurisdictions that have addressed the issue, the court considers the transaction in its entirety and determines whether the goods or services aspect of the contract predominates. To determine that question: "[C]ourts look to the language and circumstances surrounding the contract, the relationship between the goods and services, the compensation structure and the intrinsic worth of the goods provided." *Integrity Material Handling Sys., Inc. v. Deluxe Corp.,* 317 N.J.Super. 406 (N.J.Super.Ct.App.Div.1999)). We are persuaded that this is the correct analytical framework for determining the applicability of the UCC in this case and will apply it here.

However, the record in this small claims action is not well developed. There is no transcript of the trial nor was a narrative statement of the trial proceedings prepared. . . . The district court's judgment does contain findings of fact, two of which are helpful: ¶ 2: "[T]he parties entered into an agreement for the tear off and replacement of Plaintiff's roof's [sic] among other repairs and services;" ¶ 3: "'[I]mpact resistant' shingles . . . are considered to be an upgrade from regular shingles and Plaintiff had agreed to pay the additional amount to have the 'impact resistant' shingles installed." However, these facts are insufficient to determine whether the "goods" aspect of the parties' contract predominates over the services aspect.

From the exhibits introduced at trial, it can be established that the total contract price for reroofing Fairchild's residence was $12,036.12. There are nine "specifications" included in that contract describing the scope of work to be done for the contract price. For example, in addition to removing and hauling off the old shingles and installing the new ones, the contract called for the installation of 30-weight felt to the entire roof, the installation of ice and water shield around "stacks," and the installation of various vents and gutters and six window screens. However, there is no segregation of the cost for the materials, including the shingles, from the cost of the labor to complete the work required by the contract. Consequently, the cost of the shingles as a percentage of the total contract price cannot be determined. Swearingen contends in his appellate brief that the cost of upgrading to impact resistant shingles was $1,000. And, his counterclaim was for $1,000 less than the remaining balance due on the contract. In his appellate briefs, Fairchild does not dispute that the difference in the cost of the two kinds of shingles was $1,000. . . .

Even considering the relatively minimal price differential between the shingles installed and the shingles bargained for as that might reflect on the cost of the shingles, we are unable to determine with certainty the value of the shingles as a percentage of the entire contract. Consequently, the main purpose of this contract cannot be determined from a cost comparison of the price of the goods to the total price of the contract. It is clear, however, from the scope of work described in the contract that much of this contract required labor and services to remove the old shingles and install the new ones and provide the various other services to install the new roof on Fairchild's residence. And, we are guided by the principle announced by one court: "Construction contracts are not governed by the UCC." *Urban Dev., Inc. v. Evergreen Bldg. Prod., LLC,* 114 Wash.App. 639, 59 P.3d 112, 116, (2002). We conclude that the primary purpose of the parties' contract was to provide the services required to install a new roof and the shingles, although an important term of the contract, were incidental to the main purpose of the contract. Consequently, this contract is not a transaction in goods and the UCC does not apply. Fairchild's arguments based on the UCC fail to show any error by the district court in granting the Judgment. . . .

Conclusion

In this breach of contract action, the predominant purpose of the contract was the labor and services required to remove a damaged roof and install a new roof and items related thereto. The shingles used on the new roof were incidental to the main purpose of the contract. Consequently, the contract did not involve a transaction in goods and the Oklahoma Uniform Commercial Code does not apply. The alternative forms of relief provided in the Judgment are reasonable and within the power and discretion of the district court to order. . . . The Judgment of the district court is affirmed.

* * *

Duro Bag Manufacturing, Inc. v.
Printing Services Company

United States District Court, Southern District of Ohio
No. 1:08-cv-842-TSH, 2010 WL 3586855 (Sep. 9, 2010)

TIMOTHY S. HOGAN, United States Magistrate Judge.

This matter is before the Court on the parties' cross-motions for summary judgment and their responsive memoranda.

Procedural History

... Pursuant to the Court's discussions with counsel at the status conference, the parties agree that the Court may determine as a matter of law whether the parties' contract is governed by the Uniform Commercial Code (UCC).... If the transaction at issue is one for the sale of goods, then the UCC governs and plaintiffs may proceed on their breach of warranty claims. If, however, the Court finds that the parties' transaction involved services, not goods, the UCC does not apply and plaintiffs' breach of warranty claims must be dismissed.

Background & Undisputed Facts

... Duro is the world's largest manufacturer of paper bags. In October 2007, Duro contracted with its customer, Abercrombie & Fitch, (A & F), to produce a medium sized paper shopping bag printed with A & F's artwork. Duro did not have the requisite printing capability to print the artwork with the color and image specifications for the bags as ordered by A & F. Duro contracted with defendant PSC to print sheets for Duro bearing A & F's artwork that Duro intended to and did convert into shopping bags for A & F. After the sheets were printed and shipped to Duro, and converted into shopping bags, A & F allegedly rejected the bags and refused to pay Duro the amounts owed under the separate agreement between Duro and A & F. Subsequently, Duro refused to pay PSC $169,946.00 due under the terms of the parties' agreement.

The parties's [sic] initial communications regarding the printing job were by electronic mail in October 2007. PSC then issued a Purchase Order reflecting the parties' agreed terms on November 14, 2007. The parties continued to negotiate and amend the terms of their agreement and the corresponding Purchase Order until November 30, 2007, when the third change order became the final Purchase Order governing the transaction. The terms of the agreement are likewise reflected in the January 8, 2008 Invoice sent to plaintiffs by PSC, following shipment of the order to Duro in Progresso, TX, on December 1, 2007. The invoice reflects a total amount due of $169,946.00, including: 1,364,000 printed sheets priced at $0.11 each, for a total of $160,952.00; $1,320.00 for "Prep Alterations New Files"; $824.00 for "Additional Skids" and $1,650.00 for "Solid Wood Tops" for shipping the sheets; $4,200.00 for "Press Proof"; and $1,000.00 for overtime adjusted pay.

PSC performed the printing job using sheets of paper and artwork specified by A & F and supplied to PSC by Duro. The color and image specifications, as required by A & F, were also set forth by Duro.

Applicable Law

... This Court's jurisdiction over this action is based on diversity of citizenship pursuant to 28 U.S.C. §1332. A federal court exercising diversity jurisdiction over state law claims must apply state substantive law to those claims. Accordingly, this Court, sitting in Ohio, will apply Ohio law. ...

Ohio has adopted the applicable provisions of the UCC. Article 2 of the UCC, as adopted by Ohio Rev.Code §§1302.01–1302.98, applies to "transactions in goods." The term "Goods" is defined as follows:

> "Goods" means all things (including specially manufactured goods) which are movable at the time of identification to the contract for sale other than the money in which the price is to be paid, investment securities, and things in action. ...

While the Ohio Supreme Court has not addressed the matter yet, all Ohio appellate courts to have considered the applicability of the UCC to hybrid or "mixed" contracts for the sale of goods and services, have applied the "predominant purpose" test. Federal courts applying Ohio law have likewise adopted the predominant purpose test.

The "predominant purpose" test was first set forth in *Allied Industrial Services Corp. v. Kasle Iron & Metals, Inc.,* 62 Ohio App.2d 144 (Ohio Ct.App.1977). The *Allied* court held that the test to determine applicability of the UCC to mixed contacts for goods and services is "whether the predominant factor and purpose of the contract is the rendition of service, with goods incidentally involved, or whether the contract is for the sale of goods, with labor incidentally involved." 405 N.E.2d at 310. In mixed contract cases, the burden of proof lies with the party who asserts that the contract is governed by the UCC. Thus, in the instant case, plaintiffs have the burden of proving that the primary purpose of the printing contract is the sale of goods. ...

Opinion

Plaintiff argues that the parties' contract is one for the sale of goods and clearly governed by the UCC. Plaintiff contends that the printed sheets ordered by Duro fall squarely within the UCC's definition of "goods" and that the contract language itself, as reflected in the November 30, 2007, Purchase Order evinces an agreement for the sale of a certain number of print sheets, not services. Plaintiff further argues that even if the Court finds that the transaction involved a mixed or hybrid contract for goods and services, under the predominant purpose test, the factors weigh clearly in favor of a finding that the parties agreed to a sale of goods.

Defendant counters that the agreement was one for services, work and labor, not for the sale of goods. PSC points to the fact that the printing was done using artwork and paper supplied by Duro and returned to Duro for fabrication in to shopping bags. PSC relies on several cases involving publishing, which hold that a contract in which a printer prints, binds, and completes a book is a contract for the work, labor, and services necessary to fabricate the book, and not one for the sale of the books from the printer to the publisher.

The parties agree that if the Court finds the contract to be one involving both goods and services that the "predominant purpose" test governs the Court's determination as to whether the UCC applies to the contract. In applying the predominant purpose test, Ohio federal and state appellate courts have considered several factors, including but not limited to the following: 1) the nature and language of the contract; 2) the nature of the business of the supplier or seller; 3) the price or value allocation in the contract between goods and services to be provided; and 4) the issues involved in the dispute.

Admittedly, this case involves a close call on the question of whether the UCC applies to the agreement between the parties. . . . At first blush, it appears that the contract at issue could be considered an agreement for the sale of goods. The contract itself contains per piece pricing language for each sheet printed and is based on a Purchase Order which implies the sale of goods. However, as the contract necessarily involved both goods, such as palates and wood tops for shipping, and services, namely the impressions re-producing A & F's artwork on the individual sheets, the contract is necessarily "mixed." As noted above, the Court must consider the ultimate issue of whether the predominant purpose of the contract was the rendition of service, with goods incidentally involved, or whether the contract was for the sale of goods, with labor incidentally involved. Upon consideration of the purpose of the contract, the nature of defendant's business, and the underlying issues involved in the dispute, this Court concludes that the better view is that the transaction was one for printing services, not the sale of individual printed sheets.

. . . In this case, Duro provided the sheets and the A & F artwork to PSC as well as the specifications for ink color and image specifications. PSC agreed to provide the work, labor, and services necessary to re-produce the artwork to specifications on sheets supplied by Duro and then to ship the sheets back to Duro for further processing into shopping bags. Duro has in-house printing facilities but lacked the capability to reproduce the images to the required A & F specifications. Accordingly, it sought a service from PSC — namely, imprinting on the sheets to the specification of Duro's customer A & F. The fact that the pricing was calculated per sheet bespeaks of the need to ensure that the correct number of impressions were made per Duro's specifications so that Duro could obtain the requisite number of sheets for production of the bags ordered by its customer, A & F. PSC was not selling sheets it produced for buyers to make shopping bags, rather, it was rendering the service of printing images on Duro's sheets so that Duro could fulfill its obligations to its own client.

. . . The only material supplied by PSC was the ink used to make the impression to A & F's specification. Under the totality of the circumstances, the Court finds that the transaction between the parties was predominantly for work, labor, and services such that the UCC is inapplicable.

IT IS THEREFORE ORDERED THAT: Defendant's motion for summary judgment is GRANTED IN PART and DENIED IN PART, SUBJECT TO RENEWAL such that plaintiff's breach of warranty claims arising under the UCC are DISMISSED pursuant to the terms of this Order. . . .

* * *

Problem 22

The predominant purpose test asks what the consumer values most about the transaction: the service or the good. What is the predominant purpose of the below transaction?

A water delivery company provides 5-gallon jugs of filtered water to its customers each month. As an alternative, the company begins to offer a home water filtration system. The system consists of a large cylindrical filter that fits underneath the sink and is hooked directly into the plumbing so filtered water flows from the tap. Installation is relatively complicated and takes a full day to complete.

A customer purchases one of the filtration systems. The cost is $2,000. Included in the price is an under-sink filter and the installation services necessary to connect it to the existing plumbing. The company will also deliver and install replacement filters as needed (usually about once a year), for no extra charge.

Chapter 5

Calculating Damages

Calculating damages requires first measuring, in monetary terms, the amount of harm a defendant has inflicted. Once that is accomplished, it must be determined whether any fairness or policy concerns dictate that an offset or adjustment should be made.

Discussed first in this chapter is the rule of certainty, which comes into play when calculating the amount of harm inflicted. Following that are sections on the collateral source rule, prejudgment interest, and reduction to present cash value — all concepts relevant to post-calculation adjustments to damages.

Certainty

Compensatory damages reimburse a plaintiff for a financial loss or compensate for other kinds of harm. To allow for accurate calculation of those damages, plaintiffs must demonstrate the amount that will adequately reimburse or compensate for the loss. That amount must be proven to a reasonable degree of certainty. The trier of fact has wide latitude to decide whether the reasonable certainty standard has been met, but there must be some evidentiary foundation to support the calculation. The amount awarded cannot be the product of speculation.

Both the fact of damages and the amount must be proven with certainty. That is, a plaintiff must prove, with reasonable certainty, that a harm has been incurred in the first place (fact of damages) and also must prove, with reasonable certainty, how much is necessary to compensate for that harm (amount of damages).

The concept of certainty becomes particularly important when a plaintiff seeks future damages: compensation for harm that has not yet occurred at the time of trial but is likely to occur in the future. Future damages are allowable — and desirable — because defendants should not escape liability merely because the harm they caused has not yet been fully realized by the time of trial. The problem that must be acknowledged, however, is that future damages are inherently uncertain, since there is no crystal ball to gaze into that can predict exactly what will happen in the months or years to come. Plaintiffs who claim future damages therefore face the unenviable task of proving inherently uncertain damages to a reasonable degree of certainty.

The reasonable certainty requirement applies to both tort and contract damages. But it can be more demanding in the contract setting because contract damages are economic — compensation for a financial harm — and therefore capable of a relatively precise calculation. Tort damages, on the other hand, sometimes compensate for a noneconomic harm: pain and suffering, emotional distress, or loss of enjoyment of life. Those kinds of damages are never capable of precise calculation; the amount awarded is essentially entirely within the discretion of the jury. So for noneconomic tort damages, once the fact of damage is established with reasonable certainty, the amount will be difficult to dispute. Economic damages are a different story — the issue of amount is often vigorously litigated.

Introductory Note — *TAS Distributing Co. v. Cummins Engine Co.*

TAS Distributing is a breach of contract case. The breach is a failure by the defendant distributor to adequately market the plaintiff's product, a component used in truck engines. The trial court granted the defendant summary judgment on the ground there was insufficient evidence to prove damages. The question on appeal is whether there is enough evidence to show how much the plaintiff would have made had the product been adequately marketed.

THINGS TO THINK ABOUT while reading *TAS Distributing Co. v. Cummins Engine Co.*:

1. Is the certainty issue in this case about the fact of damages or the amount?

2. How can damages that have not yet occurred ever be proven with reasonable certainty?

3. How high is the bar set by the reasonable certainty standard?

TAS Distributing Co. v. Cummins Engine Co.

United States Court of Appeals, Seventh Circuit
491 F.3d 625 (2007)

RIPPLE, Circuit Judge.

This case arises out of an agreement between TAS Distributing Company, Inc. ("TAS") and Cummins Engine Company, Inc. ("Cummins"). In that agreement, TAS granted Cummins a co-exclusive license to use its idle-control technology for heavy-duty truck engines. The agreements required Cummins to "make all reasonable efforts to market and sell" the licensed products in an effort to maximize royalties payable to TAS. TAS, believing that Cummins was not making "all reasonable efforts," filed this action in the Central District of Illinois. The complaint set forth twelve counts, including claims for breach of contract and for specific performance. At the close of discovery, Cummins moved for summary judgment, and

TAS cross-moved for partial summary judgment (relating specifically to Cummins' failure to market one particular product, the "Temp-A-Stop" Product). The district court granted Cummins' motion for summary judgment and denied in part and granted in part TAS' cross-motion. For the reasons set forth in this opinion, we affirm the judgment of the district court.

I

Background

A. Facts

TAS is an Illinois corporation with its principal place of business and corporate headquarters in Peoria, Illinois. It invents, develops, engineers, markets and licenses patented, proprietary technology. This technology automatically turns an engine on under certain circumstances ("Temp-A-Start") and off during other circumstances ("Temp-A-Stop"). Cummins is an Indiana corporation with its principal place of business in Columbus, Indiana. Cummins manufactures engines for use in trucks and has approximately thirty percent of the market share of the United States truck engine market.

1.

In order to permit a clear understanding of the litigation before us, we must provide some background pertaining to the underlying contractual arrangement between the parties.

a.

TAS has four technologies relevant to this dispute. Two of these technologies are used to manufacture "Temp-A-Start" Products; they perform functions that automatically turn on an engine. The other two involve "Temp-A-Stop" Products; they function to power down automatically an engine when it is not in use. Each of these products comes in two different varieties — an "ECM" or "One-Box" Product which is installed into the engine itself and a "Retrofit" or "Two-Box" Product which can be added to an existing engine or vehicle. . . .

b.

In February 1997, TAS and Cummins entered into a Master Agreement regarding the TAS technology. . . . The two companies also entered into a License Agreement. The License Agreement granted Cummins a license to utilize the TAS technology and set forth royalty and payment terms. The License Agreement also included the following clause:

> Licensee shall make all reasonable efforts to market and sell ECM Products and Retrofit Products so as to maximize the payment of royalties to Licensor under this License Agreement. . . .

clause

c.

Cummins integrated both the Temp-A-Start and the Temp-A-Stop technology into its "ICON Product." It developed a brochure for this product and featured it at trade shows and in product presentations. Despite these efforts, Cummins averaged sales of fewer than 200 ICON Products on an annual basis. Cummins developed and sold a "Two-Box" or "Retrofit" Product incorporating both the Temp-A-Start and Temp-A-Stop technology, and similarly developed and sold a "One-Box" or "ECM" Product.

The sales performance of Cummins' products was substantially below the expectations of the parties. Prior to entering into any contracts with TAS and during negotiations, Cummins made certain projections regarding its likely sales of engines incorporating the TAS technology. These projections ranged from likely sales of 4,000 products during the first year, and 10,000 each subsequent year, to the projection that Cummins would eventually attain 12,000 a year. Indeed, Cummins' competitor, DDC, allegedly sold significantly more TAS Products than did Cummins. Nevertheless, Cummins consistently made the minimum royalty payments as required by the License Agreement. It has fulfilled its contractual obligation to pay at least $1,000,000 in royalties.

TAS submitted an affidavit of its president, Harvey Slepian, in support of its motion for partial summary judgment. Slepian's testimony attempted to quantify damages owed to TAS through comparisons to sales of similar products by DDC. . . .

II

Discussion

A.

. . . In Illinois, "[i]n order to plead a cause of action for breach of contract, a plaintiff must allege: (1) the existence of a valid and enforceable contract; (2) substantial performance by the plaintiff; (3) a breach by the defendant; and (4) resultant damages. Only a duty imposed by the terms of a contract can give rise to a breach." *W.W. Vincent & Co. v. First Colony Life Ins. Co.,* 351 Ill.App.3d 752, 286 Ill.Dec. 734, 814 N.E.2d 960, 967 (2004). Therefore, under Illinois law, it is necessary to show damages — not the specific amount, but rather that the plaintiff did, in fact, suffer some damages. *See Transp. & Transit Assocs., Inc. v. Morrison Knudsen Corp.,* 255 F.3d 397, 401 (7th Cir.2001). Merely showing that a contract has been breached without demonstrating actual damage does not suffice, under Illinois law, to state a claim for breach of contract. *Id.*

Because the district court granted summary judgment to Cummins on the ground that TAS had failed to demonstrate that it could prove damages, we pause at this point to set forth the basic principles that govern that issue. TAS essentially is seeking the profits it allegedly had lost because Cummins had breached the "all reasonable efforts" requirement of the parties' agreement. We therefore must focus on the requirements to prove and receive lost profit damages.

As a general principle, when seeking the recovery of lost profits, a claimant must establish these lost profits with "reasonable certainty." *See,* Note, *The Requirement of Certainty in the Proof of Lost Profits,* 64 Harv. L.Rev. 317, 317 (1950). This "reasonable certainty" rule was formerly a rule of "absolute certainty," but this requirement has fallen into disuse. The absolute certainty requirement was reformed some time ago to the less demanding requirement of "reasonable certainty." *See* J. Mayne & H. McGregor, *Mayne & McGregor on Damages* §174, at 163 (12th ed.1961); *see also* C. McCormick, *Handbook on the Law of Damages* §26, at 99–100 (1935) ("[T]he certainty rule in its most important aspect, is a standard requiring a reasonable degree of persuasiveness in the proof of the fact and the amount of damages. . . . [I]t appears that the epithet certainty is overstrong, and that the standard is a qualified one, of 'reasonable certainty' merely, or, in other words, of 'probability.'"). The Restatement (Second) of Contracts likewise expresses the requirement of proof of the precise amount of loss as one of "reasonable certainty." Restatement (Second) of Contracts §352. Today, all United States jurisdictions enforce the requirement of "certainty" in damage award amount, but limit this requirement to "reasonable certainty."

In Illinois, in order to recover for breach of contract, a plaintiff must establish both "that he sustained damages . . . [and] he must also establish a reasonable basis for computation of those damages." *Ellens v. Chicago Area Office Fed. Credit Union,* 216 Ill.App.3d 101, 159 (1991). Dating back to the start of the 20th Century, Illinois courts have stated that, for lost profits to be an element of damages, they must be established with certainty, *see Trout Auto Livery Co. v. People's Gas Light & Coke Co.,* 168 Ill.App. 56 (Ill.App.Ct.1912), capable of definite proof, *see Mugge v. Erkman,* 161 Ill.App. 180 (Ill.App.Ct.1911), or capable of tangible proof, *see Favar v. Riverview Park,* 144 Ill.App. 86 (Ill.App.Ct.1908).

The party claiming damage bears the burden of proving those damages to a reasonable degree of certainty. However, when a party establishes that it is entitled to damages but fails to prove the amount of those damages to a reasonable degree of certainty, only nominal damages are recoverable at the discretion of the trial judge.

More recently, in the specific context of lost profits damages, Illinois courts have stated that "[l]ost profits will be allowed only if: their loss is proved with a reasonable degree of certainty; the court is satisfied that the wrongful act of the defendant caused the lost profits; and the profits were reasonably within the contemplation of the defaulting party at the time the contract was entered into." *Milex Prods., Inc. v. Alra Labs., Inc.,* 237 Ill.App.3d 177 (1992); *see also Royal's Reconditioning Corp. v. Royal,* 293 Ill.App.3d 1019 (1997). When the profits arise out of a breached contract, those profits are considered an element of the contract and thus, within the contemplation of the parties at the time the contract was established; these damages are recoverable if proved to a reasonable degree of certainty.

Certainly, because damages for lost profits are prospective, these damages will be inherently uncertain and incapable of calculation with mathematical precision. *Royal's Reconditioning,* 228 Ill.Dec. 365. Nevertheless, the evidence presented must afford a reasonable basis for the computation of damages. Indeed, the Supreme Court of Illinois has stated expressly that "the law does not require that lost profits be proven with absolute certainty. Rather, the evidence need only afford a reasonable basis for the computation of damages which, with a reasonable degree of certainty, can be traced to defendant's wrongful conduct." *Belleville Toyota, Inc. v. Toyota Motor Sales, U.S.A., Inc.,* 199 Ill.2d 325 (2002).

Illinois courts consistently have rejected "the use of speculative, inaccurate or false projections of income in the valuation of a business" and reviewing courts will reverse damage awards "based on speculation or conjecture." *SK Hand Tool Corp. v. Dresser Indus.,* 284 Ill.App.3d 417 (1996). Moreover, the party requesting damages must show causation, that is that the alleged breach is the cause of those damages, with reasonable certainty.

. . . Although many cases addressing damages for lost profits have included expert testimony, *see, e.g., Milex Products,* 177 Ill.Dec. 852, Illinois law does not require expressly expert testimony to prove lost profits damages. Illinois courts likewise have highlighted that "mathematical certainty is not required" in the proof of lost profits. *Drs. Sellke & Conlon, Ltd. v. Twin Oaks Realty, Inc.,* 143 Ill.App.3d 168 (1986).

With these principles in mind, we now turn to the question of whether TAS has shown that it has suffered damages through Cummins' alleged failure to market engines with TAS' technology. . . .

TAS submits first that it was damaged beyond the minimum royalty payments because Cummins' competitor, DDC, sold many more products than did Cummins. Relevant to this analysis is Illinois' "new business rule" which states that the reasonable certainty requirement for recovery of lost profits damages may be satisfied by comparable "past profits in an established business, but that the lost profits of a new business would be too speculative" on which to base recovery. *Malatesta v. Leichter,* 186 Ill.App.3d 602 (1989). The general rule under Illinois law is that a new business has no right to recover lost profits. *See, e.g., Stuart Park Assoc. Ltd. P'ship v. Ameritech Pension Trust,* 51 F.3d 1319, 1328 (7th Cir.1995) (interpreting Illinois law). Illinois courts have upheld damage awards based on comparable businesses where the "profits [are] of a person other than plaintiff, who operated the same established business at the identical location for the period of time which plaintiff seeks damages." *Id.* In situations where the plaintiff operated an established business at an identical location during the same time period as a party for whom profit information is available, Illinois courts have held these comparisons to be "not of such a speculative nature to require a finding that plaintiff's lost profits may not be proved to a reasonable certainty." *Id.* The reasoning behind the rule is simply that a new business has not demonstrated yet what its profits will be. *See Milex Prods.,* 177 Ill. Dec. 852.

We have recognized that Illinois' new business rule can apply when an entity, while established in the field, markets a new product. In *Stuart Park Associates Ltd. Partnership v. Ameritech Pension Trust,* 51 F.3d 1319, 1328 (7th Cir.1995), one party argued that its successes with other apartment complexes should dictate its likely profits regarding the disputed complex. However, we stated in that case that, because the complexes were different pieces of real estate from different markets, they did not provide a self-evident mode from which to generalize any lost profits incurred. . . .

Other courts also have stated that past successes with similar products or businesses do not provide sufficient information from which to calculate lost profits on a new product or new business. *See Kinesoft,* 139 F.Supp.2d at 909. . . .

In this case, the Illinois "new business rule" provides significant guidance for our decision. It appears that Cummins manufactured two different products incorporating the TAS technology, a One-Box ECM ICON Product and a Two-Box Retrofit ICON Product. Each of these products incorporated both the Temp-A-Start and Temp-A-Stop technologies. Although DDC did manufacture and market TAS technology, it is undisputed, on this record, that only Cummins manufactured the ICON Product that incorporated both the Temp-A-Start and Temp-A-Stop technologies. Because a product containing both technologies is inherently different from one that contains only one type of TAS' proprietary technologies, the Illinois "new business rule" renders a comparison to DDC's sales of engines somewhat speculative, and, consequently, counsels extreme caution in relying on this comparison as a measure of TAS' lost profits.

Moreover, Illinois law, even without reference to the new business rule, clearly requires that damages be proved to a reasonable certainty. TAS submits first that it was damaged beyond the minimum royalty payments because Cummins' competitor, DDC, sold many more products than did Cummins. TAS has failed, however, to produce any evidence that proves its lost profits to a reasonable certainty, and therefore TAS' claim must fail. We note that "Illinois courts have not hesitated to reverse damage awards based on false assumptions or data as speculative." *SK Hand Tool,* 219 Ill.Dec. 833; *Reynolds v. Coleman,* 173 Ill.App.3d 585 (1988); *F.L. Walz, Inc. v. Hobart Corp.,* 157 Ill.App.3d 334 (1987). Illinois courts also have stated that "[i]t is perhaps true that absolute certainty as to the amount of loss or damage in such cases involving lost profits is unattainable, but that is not required to justify a recovery. All the law requires is that it be approximated by competent proof." *Curt Bullock Builders, Inc. v. H.S.S. Dev., Inc.,* 261 Ill.App.3d 178 (1994) (internal citations and quotation marks omitted). The evidence before us on summary judgment simply does not establish a basis upon which damages can be calculated to a reasonable degree of certainty.

TAS submits that Cummins should have sold as many products incorporating the subject technology as did DDC. There is scant evidence in the record pertaining to the DDC's sales of engines with the TAS technology. Slepian, TAS' president, asserted in an affidavit that DDC sold approximately 15,000 such engines per year. TAS concedes that the exact number of units incorporating the TAS technology is a matter of proof for trial. However, TAS must still face the principle that, to survive a motion for summary judgment on a breach of contract claim, the plaintiff must provide a basis upon which lost profits may be calculated to a reasonable certainty. *E.J. McKernan Co.,* 191 Ill.Dec. 391.

There is no evidence in the record, aside from TAS' assertions, suggesting that DDC's product sales provide a reasonable basis upon which to calculate damages. TAS submits that DDC is a chief competitor of Cummins, and, therefore, that DDC's sales numbers likewise should have been attained by Cummins. Merely stating that Cummins *should have* sold as many engines incorporating the TAS technology as did DDC, without more, does not warrant reversal of the district court's judgment. There is nothing in the record tending to suggest that Cummins could have sold as many products as DDC; the record is devoid of information relating to DDC's precise role in the engine market. The record also does not contain facts, beyond unsupported contentions, tending to establish that DDC and Cummins are sufficiently comparable companies to warrant imputing DDC's engine sales to Cummins. . . .

TAS has failed to present, on this record, a reasonable basis for the calculation of any damages and likewise TAS has failed to show it was damaged beyond the minimum royalty payments paid by Cummins. . . .

Conclusion

For the foregoing reasons, the judgment of the district court is affirmed.

Introductory Note — *Sargon Enterprises, Inc. v. University of Southern California* and *Felder v. Physiotherapy Associates*

Both *Sargon* and *Felder* involve a high degree of difficulty in proving damages. The plaintiff in *Sargon* seeks up to $1 billion for future lost profits that would have been realized had it become the industry leader in dental implants. In *Felder*, the plaintiff asks for millions of dollars he would have been paid had he become a professional baseball player. The damages in *Sargon* are found to lack certainty; the damage award in *Felder* is upheld.

THINGS TO THINK ABOUT while reading *Sargon Enterprises, Inc. v. University of Southern California* and *Felder v. Physiotherapy Associates*:

1. What is the practical significance of the distinction between the fact of damages and the amount?

2. Is the evidence of damages less persuasive in *Sargon* than the evidence in *Felder*? Why?

Sargon Enterprises, Inc. v. University of Southern California

California Supreme Court
55 Cal.4th 747 (2012)

CHIN, J.

A small dental implant company that had net profits of $101,000 in 1998 has sued a university for breach of a contract for the university to clinically test a new implant the company had patented. The company seeks damages for lost profits beginning in 1998, ranging from $200 million to over $1 billion. It claims that, but for the university's breach of the contract, the company would have become a worldwide leader in the dental implant industry and made many millions of dollars a year in profit. Following an evidentiary hearing, the trial court excluded as speculative the proffered testimony of an expert to this effect. We must determine whether the court erred in doing so.

We conclude that the trial court has the duty to act as a "gatekeeper" to exclude speculative expert testimony. Lost profits need not be proven with mathematical precision, but they must also not be unduly speculative. Here, the court acted within its discretion when it excluded opinion testimony that the company would have become extraordinarily successful had the university completed the clinical testing.

We reverse the judgment of the Court of Appeal, which had held the trial court erred in excluding the testimony.

I. Factual and Procedural History

. . . In 1991, plaintiff Sargon Enterprises, Inc. (Sargon) patented a dental implant that its president and chief executive officer, Dr. Sargon Lazarof, had developed. The United States Food and Drug Administration approved the implant, which meant it could be sold and used in the United States. As the Court of Appeal opinion described it, Sargon's implant "could be implanted immediately following an extraction and contained both the implant and full restoration. In the 1980's, the standard implant was the Branemark implant developed at the University of Gothenburg in Sweden. The Branemark implant required several steps. First, surgery would place the implant in a healed extraction socket in the patient's mouth; a second surgery would inspect the implant to see if it had properly integrated with the bone (a process known as 'osseointegration'); last, a crown would be placed on the implant. Sargon's implant was a one stage implant: it expanded immediately into the bone socket with an expanding screw; this mechanism permitted the implant to be 'loaded' with a crown the same day."

In 1996, Sargon contracted with defendant University of Southern California (USC) for the USC School of Dentistry to conduct a five-year clinical study of the implant. In May 1999, Sargon sued USC and faculty members of its dental school involved in the study, alleging breach of contract and other causes of action. . . .

USC moved to exclude as speculative the proffered opinion testimony of one of Sargon's experts, James Skorheim. The court presided over an eight-day evidentiary hearing at which Skorheim was the primary witness. . . .

In Skorheim's opinion, three key "market drivers" operate in the dental implant industry: (1) innovation, (2) clinical studies, and (3) outreach to general practitioners. A company must have all three to be successful. Skorheim had testified, the Court of Appeal stated, that "[t]he value of a clinical study to an implant maker is two-fold: It establishes the efficacy of the device and permits entry into the universities where students can be taught to use the device, with the expectation that, upon graduation, they will use the product in their practices." He believed that clinical success of the Sargon implant would likely lead to commercial success. Skorheim also had testified that because virtually every dental implant company employed clinical studies and general practitioner outreach, innovation really determined market success and what market share a company would achieve. He had explained, "The greater the technological achievement in the product mix, the greater the likelihood for revenues." In Skorheim's opinion, innovation was a necessary prerequisite to achieving market success. "[F]irst and foremost, you have to have the technological innovation and the efficacy."

As the Court of Appeal observed, "Skorheim's 'market share' approach was based upon a comparison of Sargon to six other large, multinational dental implant companies that were the dominant market leaders in the industry, and which controlled in excess of 80 percent of global sales (Big Six): Nobel Biocare, Straumann, [Biomet 3i], Zimmer, Dentsply, and Astra Tech. Although there are approximately 96 companies worldwide that make dental implants, Skorheim believed the Big Six were the top innovators based upon his analysis of the [Millennium] report and market intelligence." . . .

Skorheim believed that Sargon was innovative, like the "Big Six," and not a "copycat" or "price cutter," like the other small companies. He acknowledged that Sargon was a very small company whose annual profits peaked in 1998 at around $101,000 and, unlike the big companies, it had no meaningful marketing or research and development organization and no parent company to assist it. But he believed these factors were merely "incidental" to innovation and played little role in achieving market share. Accordingly, and because innovation is the key factor driving market success, Skorheim had compared Sargon to the "Big Six" rather than to the smaller companies in computing lost profits. He considered the "Big Six" and Sargon to be "comparable companies."

. . . For the reasons he gave, Skorheim believed that Sargon, unlike any of the other smaller companies, would, over time, have become a market leader, one of the "Big Six". In calculating Sargon's lost profits, he had not considered profits Sargon had ever actually realized, but instead considered the market leaders' profits. He believed that Sargon's profits would have increased over time until they reached the level of one of the market leaders. . . .

Thus, Skorheim had projected total lost profits of $220 million if the jury found Sargon's innovation was comparable to that of the least innovative market leaders, making what he described as a "meaningful contribution to innovation"; of $315 million if the jury found Sargon's innovation was somewhat greater; of $600 million if the jury found Sargon's innovation was somewhat greater yet; and of $1.2 billion if the jury found Sargon's innovation was comparable to that of the market leaders, making what he described as "revolutionary industry changing technology." . . .

The [trial] court concluded "that Mr. Skorheim's opinions are not based upon matters upon which a reasonable expert would rely, and do not show the nature and occurrence of lost profits with evidence of reasonable reliability, because his opinion is not based on any historical data from Plaintiff or a comparison to similar businesses. The court also finds his 'market drivers' meaningless for comparison purposes. Additionally, his opinion rests on speculation and unreasonable assumptions."

Accordingly, the court granted USC's motion to exclude Skorheim's testimony. . . .

II. Discussion

Lost Profits

Lost profits may be recoverable as damages for breach of a contract. "[T]he general principle [is] that damages for the loss of prospective profits are recoverable where the evidence makes reasonably certain their occurrence and extent." (*Grupe v. Glick* (1945) 26 Cal.2d 680, 693.) Such damages must "be proven to be certain both as to their occurrence and their extent, albeit not with 'mathematical precision.'" (*Lewis Jorge Construction Management, Inc. v. Pomona Unified School Dist.* (2004) 34 Cal.4th 960, 975.) The rule that lost profits must be reasonably certain is a specific application of a more general statutory rule. "No damages can be recovered for a breach of contract which are not clearly ascertainable in both their nature and origin." (Civ.Code, § 3301; see *Greenwich S.F., LLC v. Wong* (2010) 190 Cal. App.4th 739, 760.)

Regarding lost business profits, the cases have generally distinguished between established and unestablished businesses. "[W]here the operation of an established business is prevented or interrupted, as by a . . . breach of contract . . . , damages for the loss of prospective profits that otherwise might have been made from its operation are generally recoverable for the reason that their occurrence and extent may be ascertained with reasonable certainty from the past volume of business and other provable data relevant to the probable future sales." (*Grupe v. Glick, supra,* 26 Cal.2d at p. 692.) "Lost profits to an established business may be recovered if their extent and occurrence can be ascertained with reasonable certainty; once their existence has been so established, recovery will not be denied because the amount cannot be shown with mathematical precision. Historical data, such as past business volume, supply an acceptable basis for ascertaining lost future profits. In some instances, lost profits may be recovered where plaintiff introduces evidence of the profits lost by similar businesses operating under similar conditions." (*Berge v. International Harvester Co.* (1983) 142 Cal.App.3d 152, 161–162.)

"On the other hand, where the operation of an unestablished business is prevented or interrupted, damages for prospective profits that might otherwise have been made from its operation are not recoverable for the reason that their occurrence is uncertain, contingent and speculative. [Citations] . . . But although generally objectionable for the reason that their estimation is conjectural and speculative, anticipated profits dependent upon future events are allowed where their nature and occurrence can be shown by evidence of reasonable reliability." (*Grupe v. Glick, supra,* 26 Cal.2d at pp. 692–693.)

"Where the *fact* of damages is certain, the amount of damages need not be calculated with absolute certainty. The law requires only that some reasonable basis of computation of damages be used, and the damages may be computed even if the result reached is an approximation. This is especially true where . . . it is the wrongful acts of the defendant that have created the difficulty in proving the amount of loss of profits or where it is the wrongful acts of the defendant that have caused the other party to not realize a profit to which that party is entitled." (*GHK Associates v. Mayer Group, Inc.* (1990) 224 Cal.App.3d 856, 873–874 [permitting an award of profits calculated from a project's "*actual* income"].)

. . . Once again, we add a cautionary note. The lost profit inquiry is always speculative to some degree. Inevitably, there will always be an element of uncertainty. Courts must not be too quick to exclude expert evidence as speculative merely because the expert cannot say with absolute certainty what the profits would have been. Courts must not eviscerate the possibility of recovering lost profits by too broadly defining what is too speculative. A reasonable certainty only is required, not absolute certainty.

Application to This Case

We now apply these principles to this case. The issue before us is whether the court abused its discretion in excluding the expert testimony, not whether substantial evidence supports a lost profits award. But the substantive law regarding lost profits is relevant to help define the type of matter on which an expert may reasonably rely. For example, as the trial court explained, "While lost profits can be established with the aid of expert testimony, economic and financial data, market surveys and analysis, business records of similar enterprises and the like, the underlying requirement for each is '"a substantial similarity between the facts forming the basis of the profit projections and the business opportunity that was destroyed."'" (Quoting *Kids' Universe v. In2Labs, supra,* 95 Cal.App.4th at p. 886.) But, as the trial court further found, Skorheim's analysis relied "on data that in no way is analogous to Plaintiff."

To the extent that the expert relied on data that is not relevant to the measure of lost profit damages, the trial court acted within its discretion to exclude the testimony because it was not "[b]ased on matter . . . that is of a type that reasonably may be relied upon by an expert in forming an opinion upon the subject to which his testimony relates. . . ." (Evid.Code, § 801, subd. (b); see *Westrec Marina Management, Inc. v. Jardine Ins. Brokers Orange County, Inc.* (2000) 85 Cal.App.4th 1042, 1050–105 [upholding the exclusion of expert testimony due in part to substantive law of lost profits].) Accordingly, although the issue is the admissibility of expert testimony, we will also consider the law of lost profits to the extent it is relevant to that issue.

The trial court did not abuse its discretion in the sense of making a ruling that was irrational or arbitrary. It presided over a lengthy evidentiary hearing and provided a detailed ruling. The Court of Appeal majority identified no specific error in that ruling. As the dissenter in the Court of Appeal stated, "Nothing in the trial judge's reasonable, straightforward and clearly articulated evidentiary ruling bears even a smidgeon of arbitrariness or capriciousness." Indeed, the court could hardly have exercised its discretion more carefully.

The trial court also excluded the expert testimony for proper reasons. It properly found the expert's methodology was too speculative for the evidence to be admissible. The court assumed that Skorheim's market share approach would be appropriate in a proper case. We will do so also. An expert might be able to make reasonably certain lost profit estimates based on a company's share of the overall market. But Skorheim did not base his lost profit estimates on a market share Sargon had ever actually achieved. Instead, he opined that Sargon's market share would have increased spectacularly over time to levels far above anything it had ever reached. He based his lost profit estimates on that hypothetical increased share. . . .

Skorheim gave the opinion that, to a "reasonable certainty," Sargon would have become a market leader within 10 years. The quoted term derives from the law of lost profits. We stated in *Grupe v. Glick, supra,* 26 Cal.2d at page 693, that lost profits must be "reasonably certain" to be recoverable. But, as the trial court found, this testimony was inherently speculative. It "involved numerous variables that made any calculation of lost profits inherently uncertain." (*Greenwich S.F., LLC v. Wong, supra,* 190 Cal.App.4th at p. 766.) Skorheim's attempt to predict the future was in no way grounded in the past.

If a professional football team claims lost profits because a certain defensive lineman did not play for it the previous season, could an expert testify that in his opinion the key driver for success in the National Football League is quarterback sacks and, because the player was the best in the league in sacking the quarterback, the team would have won the Super Bowl had he played? Could another expert counter that testimony by expressing her opinion that the key to success is turnovers, and, because the player was not particularly adept at forcing turnovers, the team would not even have made the playoffs with that player? Should the court ask the jury to choose between the two experts? Or could the jury choose something in between and conclude the team would have reached, but lost, the Super Bowl? Or lost in the conference title game?

Similarly, if a first-time author sues a publisher for breach of a contract to publish a novel, could a witness who was an expert on the publishing business, literature, and popular culture testify that the novel, if published, would have become a national bestseller, won the Pulitzer Prize, and spawned a megahit movie with several blockbuster sequels? Could a jury award lost profits based on that scenario? Or could it compromise by finding the book would have been a bestseller but would not have won the Pulitzer Prize, and would have spawned a moderately successful movie but no sequel?

World history is replete with fascinating "what ifs." What if Alexander the Great had been killed early in his career at the Battle of the Granicus River, as he nearly was? What if the Saxon King Harold had prevailed at Hastings, and William, later called the Conqueror, had died in that battle rather than Harold? What if the series of Chinese overseas discovery expeditions that two Ming Dynasty emperors sponsored, and that reached at least the east coast of Africa by 1432, had continued rather than stopped? Many serious, and not-so-serious, historians have enjoyed speculating about these what ifs. But few, if any, claim they are considering what *would* have happened rather than what *might* have happened. Because it is inherently difficult to accurately predict the future or to accurately reconstruct a counterfactual past, it is appropriate that trial courts vigilantly exercise their gatekeeping function when deciding whether to admit testimony that purports to prove such claims.

An accountant might be able to determine with reasonable precision what Sargon's profits would have been *if* it had achieved a market share comparable to one of the "Big Six." The problem here, however, is that the expert's testimony provided no logical basis to infer that Sargon *would* have achieved that market share. The lack of sound methodology in the expert's testimony for determining what the future would have brought supported the trial court's ruling. . . .

The trial court properly acted as a gatekeeper to exclude speculative expert testimony. Its ruling came within its discretion. The majority in the Court of Appeal erred in concluding otherwise.

III. Conclusion

We reverse the judgment of the Court of Appeal and remand the matter to that court for further proceedings consistent with this opinion.

* * *

Felder v. Physiotherapy Associates

Arizona Court of Appeals
158 P.3d 877 (2007)

IRVINE, Presiding Judge.

Physiotherapy Associates appeals from the trial court's rulings, judgment, and award of damages to Appellee Kenneth Felder. We find that the trial court properly allowed the jury to determine Felder's lost earning capacity as a professional baseball player. Therefore, we affirm.

Facts and Procedural History

In 1992, the Milwaukee Brewers drafted Felder in the first round of the Major League draft. He signed a contract to play in the Brewers' minor league system. From 1992 through 1996, Felder progressed in his career as the Brewers promoted him from the rookie league to the Class A level, AA level, and up to the AAA level.

In 1996, Felder injured his elbow. Although the injury affected his throwing and hitting, he was twice named Player of the Week when he played in the AAA level in New Orleans. He healed during the off-season, but tore an elbow ligament during spring training in 1997.

Felder had surgery to repair the ligament and recuperated for the rest of the 1997 season. The Brewers sent Felder to Physiotherapy for physical rehabilitation and paid his rehabilitation costs. Physiotherapy is a national physical rehabilitation company with a number of major and minor league baseball players among its clientele.

About seven-and-a-half months into his rehabilitation, Felder's elbow was improving. He passed a Brewers' physical administered at Physiotherapy in January 1998. In February 1998, shortly before the accident at issue here, the Brewers signed Felder to a salary addendum contract for the 1998 minor league season.

After conferring with the Brewers and Felder's surgeon, one of Physiotherapy's physical therapists, Keith Kocher, decided that it was time for Felder to begin hitting. Eventually, at Physiotherapy's Tempe location, Felder began hitting balls in the batting cage.

On February 25, 1998 Felder arrived at Physiotherapy for his scheduled rehabilitation. He warmed up, stretched and practiced throwing. Kocher then told Felder to take some batting practice.

Felder hit a ball that ricocheted off of a concrete lip in the batter's box, bounced back up at him, and struck his left eye. His eye bled. He felt nauseous, dizzy and was in pain. For the next two days, he coughed up blood.

Dr. Alan Gordon, Felder's ophthalmologist and retina specialist, testified that Felder sustained a fracture of the orbital bone below his eye, a rupture of his cornea, subretinal hemorrhaging, and bleeding into his sinus cavity. Irremediable retinal damage left him with a blind spot in the middle of his vision. He also suffers from blurry vision that worsens in bright light, and he has constant headaches.

The injury initially left Felder with 20/400 vision in his left eye, but it eventually improved to 20/40 plus. Felder has less than a 1% risk of completely losing his vision in that eye due to subretinal neovascularization, the growth of new blood vessels that can leak fluid under the retina.

About a week after he injured his eye, Felder reported to the Brewers' spring training camp. He failed his physical because of his eye injury and the team sent him away. He returned to the Brewers' training facility two more times. Each time, they told him to leave. The Brewers subsequently released him from his contract. Felder filed suit against Physiotherapy in August 1998.

. . . Al Goldis testified as an expert witness for Felder about whether Felder would have played in the major leagues and the expected length of his career. At the time of trial, Goldis was the special assistant to the general manager of the New York Mets and had previously worked for several major league teams. He had twenty-seven years of experience in drafting, scouting and developing players for major league baseball teams. Goldis stated that he was not paid to testify.

Goldis reviewed the Brewers' pre-draft scouting reports and minor league coaching reports about Felder. He noted that the Brewers had promoted Felder all the way up from the rookie league to the AAA level, and that his next step would have been the major leagues. Despite some conflicting reports from the minor league coaches regarding Felder's ability, Goldis testified to a reasonable degree of certainty that not only would Felder have made it to the major leagues, but that he would have been an impact player.

Goldis also compared Felder to major league players who hit fifteen home runs or more per season from 1981–1990. Goldis opined that Felder had more power than Frank Thomas, a player that Goldis had drafted. Goldis stated that he could make comparisons between Felder and Thomas to a reasonable degree of certainty. Given that Thomas had been playing for approximately seventeen years as of the date of trial, Goldis testified that Felder's career would have lasted between twelve and fifteen years.

. . . Felder also had Mead testify again about economic damages and the range of player salaries. Mead testified that he knew who Felder was even though he was not Felder's agent, because as a first-round draft choice, Felder was a "very high-profile baseball player back when . . . he was being drafted and coming out of [Florida State University]."

In calculating Felder's expected earnings, Mead selected two comparable minor league players, Jeremy Burnitz and Geoff Jenkins, who moved on to the major leagues. Like Felder, Burnitz and Jenkins were college outfielders, first-round draft picks, power hitters, and played for the Brewers. Mead also presented evidence of how Felder's minor league performance differed from Burnitz and Jenkins. Mead valued a seven year career for Felder at $27,790,440.

In response, Physiotherapy presented two experts who testified that Felder did not have a bright future in baseball. Eddie Epstein worked for several teams in major league baseball and evaluates players' performance by statistical calculation. Steve Phillips was formerly General Manager of the New York Mets. Both testified that Felder's chances of making the major leagues were slim.

. . . The court concluded that there was sufficient evidence presented by the close of Felder's case that would allow reasonable jurors to differ about whether Felder would have made it into the major leagues, the length of his major league career and the range of his compensation. Regarding the unique role of the jury, the court remarked, "juries are allowed to find in the middle and to look at all of the evidence and don't have to go with either the plaintiff or the defendants or with management or the player." The court declined to substitute its judgment for the jury's, and added "[t]here is sufficient evidence to allow the jury to consider [Felder] as a potential Major League baseball player."

. . . The jury found $7,000,000 in damages, with Felder 30% at fault, resulting in an award of $4,900,000. Physiotherapy timely filed its motion for a new trial or remittitur. The court denied that motion. Physiotherapy timely appealed.

Discussion

. . . .

Lost Earnings Claim

Physiotherapy contends that the trial court erred by denying its motion for judgment as a matter of law regarding Felder's lost earnings claim. Physiotherapy asserts that the evidence of whether Felder would have reached the major leagues, the length of his career and the calculation of his earnings was just as speculative as the evidence Felder had presented in the first trial.

Felder rejects Physiotherapy's characterization that his evidence was speculative and argues that the expert testimony he presented at the second trial was sufficient to prove his damages to a reasonable certainty.

. . . Physiotherapy argues that the evidence fails to provide a sufficient evidentiary basis for a jury to find that Felder has a claim for lost earnings. Specifically, Physiotherapy contends that the trial court erred as a matter of law by failing to find that the evidence was speculative and therefore insufficient to support a claim for lost earnings as a matter of law.

"Past and future lost wages are an appropriate measure of damages." "Once the right to damages is established, uncertainty as to the amount of damages does not preclude recovery." *Lewis,* 170 Ariz. at 397.

> This is simply a recognition that doubts as to the extent of the injury should be resolved in favor of the innocent plaintiff and against the wrongdoer. But it cannot dispel the requirement that the plaintiff's evidence provide some basis for estimating his loss. This court stated in *McNutt Oil & Refining Co. v. D'Ascoli,* 79 Ariz. 28 (1955), that "conjecture or speculation" cannot provide the basis for an award of damages, and said in *Martin v. LaFon,*

[55 Ariz. 196, 100 P.2d 182 (1940)] that the evidence must make "an approximately accurate estimate" possible.

Gilmore v. Cohen, 95 Ariz. 34, 36 (1963). The evidence required will depend "on the individual circumstances of each case and, although absolute certainty is not required, the jury must be guided by some rational standard." *Short v. Riley*, 150 Ariz. 583, 586 (App.1986).

Arizona law on this point is consistent with the rule set out in the Restatement. The comment to the Restatement of Torts (Second) § 912 (1979) provides:

> It is desirable that responsibility for harm should not be imposed until it has been proved with reasonable certainty that the harm resulted from the wrongful conduct of the person charged. It is desirable, also, that there be definiteness of proof of the amount of damage as far as is reasonably possible. It is even more desirable, however, that an injured person not be deprived of substantial compensation merely because he cannot prove with complete certainty the extent of harm he has suffered.

Id. at cmt. a. Thus, fairly compensating the injured person in a personal injury case may require trusting the jury to fairly evaluate evidence that is inherently uncertain but is the best evidence available.

This trust in the jury is consistent with our supreme court's recognition that a central task for juries is resolving disputes over difficult and conflicting evidence. Uncertainty alone does not justify taking away a party's right to have evidence heard by a jury. With regard to damages, the court has stated:

> The difficult problem of quantifying general damages should not have prevented the courts from awarding such damages *if* in fact an injury had occurred. It is the genius of the common law that difficult damage questions are left to juries. *See Meyer v. Ricklick*, 99 Ariz. 355, 357–58 (1965) (damage amount in personal injury action is peculiarly within jury's province, and the "law does not fix precise rules for the measure of damages but leaves their assessment to a jury's good sense and unbiased judgment"). . . .

Walker v. Mart, 164 Ariz. 37, 41 (1990); *see also Logerquist v. McVey*, 196 Ariz. 470, 491 (2000) (retaining *Frye* rule because "evidentiary testing should come from the adversary system and be decided by the jury"). The basic issue in this case is whether the trial court properly relied on the "good sense and unbiased judgment" of the jury to evaluate Felder's claim for damages related to his loss of earning capacity as a professional baseball player. *Meyer*, 99 Ariz. at 358, 409 P.2d at 282.

The jury found Physiotherapy liable for Felder's injury. Moreover, the evidence plainly showed that Felder's career as a professional baseball player ended as a direct result of the injury. Consequently, the *fact* of damage was proven. Physiotherapy argues that Felder must prove he would have been promoted to the major leagues, in effect arguing that the fact of damage is damage to his major league career. We disagree with this characterization. Felder was a professional baseball player at the time he was injured. The injury to his eye ended his playing career. Being promoted to the major leagues would not have been a different career, but simply a significant advancement in his existing career.

We recognize that simply dreaming of a career as a professional athlete is not enough to create an issue of fact appropriate for a jury. *See Sheppard v. Crow-Barker-Paul No. 1 Ltd. P'ship,* 192 Ariz. 539, 548–49 (App.1998) (affirming jury instruction that refused to let jury speculate on star high school basketball player's possible earnings during a professional career). As the comment to the Restatement recognized, however, it is desirable that "an injured person not be deprived of substantial compensation merely because he cannot prove with complete certainty the extent of harm he has suffered." Restatement (Second) of Torts, § 912, cmt. a. In analyzing where to draw the line between certainty and speculation, the Tennessee Court of Appeals stated:

> Impairment of earning capacity is not necessarily measured by an injured person's employment or salary at the time of the injury. It is not uncommon for an injured person to assert that an injury has caused him or her to abandon plans to change employment, to obtain additional education or training, or to otherwise advance a career. In the face of such an assertion, the trier of fact must distinguish between persons with only vague hopes of entering a new profession and those with the demonstrated ability and intent to do so.

Overstreet v. Shoney's, Inc., 4 S.W.3d 694, 704–05 (Tenn.App.1999) (internal citation omitted) (affirming damage award to nurse relating to future career advancements).

Felder had more than a vague hope of a successful career as a professional baseball player. Although the parties disagree as to his major league prospects, it is undisputed that Felder had advanced within professional baseball and at the time of his injury he had been signed to another AAA contract. He had demonstrated his ability to be a professional baseball player. His injury plainly took away his chance to continue and advance as a player.

The issue, therefore, becomes what degree of reasonable certainty is required to set the amount of Felder's damages. As noted, the degree of certainty that is reasonably required varies depending on the circumstances of each case, and, indeed, on the cause of action asserted. "In an action for personal injuries, the law does not fix precise rules for the measure of damages but leaves their assessment to a jury's good sense and unbiased judgment." *Meyer,* 99 Ariz. at 358. This rule includes claims for loss of earnings resulting from personal injuries.

In contrast, "[d]amages for diminution in future earning power or capacity are not recoverable in an action for breach of an employment contract." *Lindsey v. Univ. of Ariz.,* 157 Ariz. 48, 54 (App.1987). Our courts have decided that "[i]n an action for breach of contract, the employee is not permitted recovery for injury to his reputation because the computation of damages is too speculative and the damage cannot reasonably be presumed to be within the contemplation of the parties when they entered into the contract." *Id.* In effect, our courts have decided that in breach of employment contract cases it is reasonable to require almost complete certainty as reflected in the actual terms of the contract and the expectations of the parties to the contract.

In breach of contract cases in which lost profits are claimed as damages the issue becomes more complicated. Indeed, the line between the fact of damage and the amount of damage may be blurred when lost profits are at issue. Although discussed in terms of *amount* of lost profits, many cases actually focus on whether a plaintiff has presented sufficient proof of the *fact* of lost profits. . . .

Once the fact of lost profits is established in a breach of contract action, our courts have not been as strict about the amount. As quoted above, where it can be proven that profits were lost, "doubts as to the extent of the injury should be resolved in favor of the innocent plaintiff and against the wrongdoer." *Gilmore,* 95 Ariz. at 36. That being said, "[t]he requirement of 'reasonable certainty' in establishing the amount of damages applies with added force where a loss of future profits is alleged. This is so because such loss is capable of proof more closely approximating 'mathematical precision.'" *Id.* at 36, 386 P.2d at 82–83 (internal citation omitted). Reasonable certainty as to the amount of lost profits can be shown by books of account, records of previous transactions or tax returns, or the "profit history from a similar business operated by the plaintiff at a different location." *Rancho Pescado,* 140 Ariz. at 184. Disagreements as to the evidence used to establish the amount of damages will go to the "weight of the evidence." *Short,* 150 Ariz. at 586.

From these authorities we conclude that when determining what constitutes "reasonable certainty" as to the amount of damages in a personal injury action, the key consideration must be what is "reasonable" under the circumstances of the particular case. Some cases will simply not be conducive to a high degree of certainty because the future itself is uncertain. This does not, however, deprive an injured plaintiff of a remedy. A plaintiff may still claim damages in an amount supported by the best evidence available and the essential consideration is that "the jury must be guided by some rational standard." *Short,* 150 Ariz. at 586.

Applying this standard, we do not believe it would be reasonable in a personal injury action to require a professional athlete to prove with complete certainty how successful he will be at his chosen profession. There will always be uncertainty concerning the athlete's physical performance and success in competition. For damage to a sports career, the evidence reasonably available will generally be what was presented at trial in this case — qualified expert testimony concerning the athlete's prospects, statistics showing past performance, and comparative data concerning other athletes. We need not detail all of the evidence concerning Felder's career. Suffice it to say that the jury learned in detail about his batting averages, fielding performances, and injuries between 1992 and 1998. The jury was provided with evaluations from minor league coaches and opinions from several experts with major league player development experience. The jury also heard about the economics of baseball compensation, including how long a professional's career might be and what similar players were being paid.

In ruling on whether the lost earning capacity issue should go to the jury, the trial court found that reasonable people could disagree about Felder's prospects and therefore allowed the issue to go to the jury. We agree with that conclusion. No one can say with complete certainty whether Felder would, or would not, have been promoted to the major leagues or how long he might have played there. We can say, however, as the jury did, that his eye injury prevented him from having that chance. Under these circumstances, the amount of his damages for being deprived of that chance was for the jury to decide. . . .

Conclusion

For the reasons discussed above, we affirm the judgment.

* * *

Problem 23

Causation + Certainty issue

There is no bright line to establish what constitutes reasonable certainty when it comes to calculating damages. Has the plaintiff in the following case proven damages with enough certainty?

A retail storeowner sues her landlord for failing to properly maintain the common areas of the shopping center where her store is located. The storeowner alleges that the center's shabby appearance and leaky roof have caused customers to avoid coming to her store, and she has lost sales as a result. At trial, the storeowner presents evidence that she consistently made at least $100,000 in profits annually for the first five years she was in business. The previous year (when the landlord failed to maintain the property) she made only $60,000. In response, the landlord presents expert testimony that there was a general economic downturn that year, and retail sales were down 25 to 40 percent nationwide.

Adjustments

To calculate the appropriate amount of damages, it is necessary to ascertain the amount of harm the defendant caused. But the inquiry does not end there. A court must then decide whether any policy reasons dictate that an adjustment—either upward or downward—should be made to the amount the plaintiff is ultimately awarded.

Discussed below are two situations where adjustments affecting the calculation of damages are made: when a plaintiff receives compensation from a third party, and when trial happens either before, or long after, the plaintiff experiences the harm in question.

Collateral Source Rule

Sometimes a plaintiff receives compensation for harm caused by a defendant from someone other than the defendant. That compensation from a third party is called a collateral source payment.

The most common example of a collateral source payment is medical insurance. Consider a defendant who drives negligently and causes a car accident that injures the plaintiff, who then requires medical treatment at a hospital. If the plaintiff has medical insurance, it is the insurer who pays the hospital for the medical treatment. The plaintiff has received a benefit from a collateral source.

Under the collateral source rule, the payment by the insurer is not deducted from the amount of damages the plaintiff can recover in a lawsuit against the driver. The collateral source rule says that a benefit received from a source wholly independent of the tortfeasor does not reduce the damages owed by the tortfeasor.

Thinking in terms of adjustments, the effect is that the plaintiff's damages are adjusted upward: the damage award is calculated to include the entire amount of the medical treatment cost even though the plaintiff has already been compensated for that loss. There are several policy reasons for the collateral source rule, but chief among them is the deterrence of tortious conduct. Allowing a defendant to pay less than the total amount of harm caused by the tortious conduct would be less effective from a deterrence standpoint. The collateral source rule ensures defendants are held responsible for the entire loss they cause, even if someone else made a payment to offset that loss.

Introductory Note — *Mitchell v. Haldar*

In *Mitchell*, the plaintiff was injured by medical malpractice and required further medical treatment. The cost of that additional medical treatment was paid by the plaintiff's insurer. As is typical, the insurer had an agreement with the hospital to pay a significantly reduced rate. The issue on appeal is how to measure the plaintiff's damages for medical expenses — by the amount the hospital billed for the treatment, or by the reduced amount actually paid by the insurer?

THINGS TO THINK ABOUT while reading *Mitchell v. Haldar*:

1. Does application of the collateral source rule result in a windfall for the plaintiff? If so, is that problematic?

2. When a hospital discounts the amount owed by a plaintiff's health insurance carrier, is that a benefit received by the plaintiff from a third party?

Mitchell v. Haldar

Delaware Supreme Court
883 A.2d 32 (2005)

HOLLAND, Justice:

This is an appeal by the plaintiffs-appellants, John Mitchell, Sr. and Donna Mitchell, following a jury trial in the Superior Court in an action for alleged medical malpractice against the defendant-appellee, Dr. Joydeep Haldar. The jury returned a verdict in favor of the plaintiffs in the total amount of $15,000. The plaintiffs filed a motion for a new trial, arguing that the damage award was inadequate, because it was substantially less than the medical expenses of $37,997.27. That motion was denied. . . .

Facts

Mr. Mitchell underwent abdominal surgery for a ruptured appendix. That procedure was performed by Anis Saliba, M.D., a general surgeon at the Beebe Medical Center on the afternoon of July 19, 2001. This litigation concerns the alleged medical negligence of Dr. Haldar, an emergency physician. Dr. Haldar was involved in Mr. Mitchell's evaluation and care during a presentation to the Beebe Medical Center Emergency Department on July 17, 2001. The appellants contend that Mr. Mitchell had appendicitis at the time of that presentation and that Dr. Haldar negligently failed to diagnose it and to arrange for surgery to be performed that evening.

Mr. Mitchell had been sent to the Beebe Emergency Department on July 17, 2001 from another facility to have an abdominal CT scan performed to evaluate the cause of his complaint of abdominal pain. Dr. Haldar's first involvement with Mr. Mitchell was after the completion of the CT scan, which was reported back by the radiologist as normal. Dr. Haldar testified that he also performed a physical abdominal examination which was normal. Because of Mr. Mitchell's negative CT scan, reduced pain level and normal abdominal examination, Dr. Haldar testified that he felt the probability of appendicitis or another immediate surgical emergency was very low and that Mr. Mitchell could be discharged with appropriate instructions.

The parties agree that if Dr. Haldar felt Mr. Mitchell had appendicitis on July 17, his course of action would have been to consult a general surgeon, who would have been the individual to make the decision whether Mr. Mitchell required admission and surgery. . . .

The discharge instructions given to Mr. Mitchell by Dr. Haldar on July 17 advised Mr. Mitchell that his condition could be consistent with "a serious problem requiring surgery (such as appendicitis) or something innocent which would resolve on its own." . . .

The record reflects that on July 18, the day after he left the Emergency Department, Mr. Mitchell developed persistent vomiting, chills and fever, increased pain and failed to improve. Nevertheless, Mr. Mitchell did not return to the Emergency Department or see a doctor on July 18. When Mr. Mitchell sought medical assistance on July 19, his appendix was found to be ruptured. The record reflects that Mr. Mitchell's appendix was not ruptured on July 17. . . .

The appellants sought to recover the expenses associated with all of the medical treatment that Mr. Mitchell received from July 17, 2001 to the time of trial. This included visits with his family doctor, treatments with his pulmonologist for emphysema which was diagnosed on July, 2003, cardiology consultations, and the February, 2004 hernia surgery. The appellants proffered copies of medical bills to prove that the total reasonable cost of Mr. Mitchell's necessary medical treatment was $58,997.27. The trial judge, however, ruled that the appellants could recover only those expenses that were actually paid by Mr. Mitchell's private insurance carrier, Blue Cross, as opposed to those amounts that were billed by Mr. Mitchell's health care providers. After that evidentiary ruling, the parties stipulated that the total medical expenses actually paid by Mr. Mitchell's private insurance coverage with Blue Cross were $37,997.27.

The jury concluded that Dr. Haldar was negligent. The jury awarded damages to Mr. Mitchell in the amount of $13,000.00. The jury awarded $2,000.00 in damages to his wife for loss of consortium. The appellants moved for a new trial on the grounds that the jury's verdicts were inadequate, especially since the total award of damages was less than one-third of their evidence of Mr. Mitchell's medical expenses. The trial judge denied that motion.

Collateral Source Rule

When it is alleged that a tortfeasor is responsible for medical services, the plaintiff bears the burden of proof on two distinct issues. First, the plaintiff must demonstrate that value claimed for those medical services was reasonable. Second, the plaintiff must establish that the need for those medical services was proximately caused by the negligence of the alleged tortfeasor.

Prior to trial, the plaintiffs proffered an exhibit of bills from health care providers which itemized Mr. Mitchell's medical expenses and totaled $58,997.27. Dr. Haldar objected to the admission of the medical bills on the grounds that the plaintiffs could only recover the expenses actually paid by his private health care insurer and not the total amounts billed by the health care providers.

The trial judge sustained Dr. Haldar's objection. Thereafter, the parties entered into a stipulation to submit a revised exhibit which contained a listing of the health care providers' services without any itemization of the actual individual costs that were paid by Blue Cross and a total in the amount of $37,997.27.

The appellants contend that the trial judge's evidentiary decision to exclude the full amount of Mr. Mitchell's medical bills was erroneous because it violated the collateral source rule. The first application of the collateral source rule in American jurisprudence was apparently more than one hundred and fifty years ago in a case ultimately decided by the United States Supreme Court. Although its operation had raised questions for over a century, more than four decades ago, the collateral source rule was recognized by this Court as already "firmly embedded" in Delaware law.

The collateral source rule is "predicated on the theory that a tortfeasor has no interest in, and therefore no right to benefit from monies received by the injured person from sources unconnected with the defendant." According to the collateral source rule, "a tortfeasor has no right to any mitigation of damages because of payments or compensation received by the injured person from an independent source." The rationale for the collateral source rule is based upon the quasi-punitive nature of tort law liability. It has been explained as follows:

> The collateral source rule is designed to strike a balance between two competing principles of tort law: (1) a plaintiff is entitled to compensation sufficient to make him whole, but no more; and (2) a defendant is liable for all damages that proximately result from his wrong. A plaintiff who receives a double recovery for a single tort enjoys a windfall; a defendant who escapes, in whole or in part, liability for his wrong enjoys a windfall. Because the law must sanction one windfall and deny the other, it favors the victim of the wrong rather than the wrongdoer.

Thus, the tortfeasor is required to bear the cost for the full value of his or her negligent conduct even if it results in a windfall for the innocent plaintiff.

Under the collateral source rule, a plaintiff may recover damages from a tortfeasor for the reasonable value of medical services, even if the plaintiff has received complete recompense for those services from a source other than the tortfeasor. The collateral source rule requires the injured party to be made whole exclusively by the tortfeasor and not by a combination of compensation from the tortfeasor and collateral sources. The benefit conferred on the injured person from the collateral source is not credited against the tortfeasor's liability, even if the plaintiff has received partial or even complete value. Thus, under the collateral source rule, a plaintiff could recover from a tortfeasor for the reasonable value of medical services provided even if those services were provided gratuitously.

The vast majority of courts have held that the collateral source rule prohibits the tortfeasor from reaping the benefit of a health insurance contract for which the tortfeasor paid no compensation. Therefore, when an injured person has insurance which pays for the cost of treatment and hospitalization, in whole or in part, those payments inure to the benefit of the insured rather than the tortfeasor. Accordingly, the general rule is that the plaintiff's damages may not be reduced because of payments for treatment paid for by medical insurance to which the tortfeasor did not contribute. Conversely, this Court and other courts have recognized that there is no reason why a risk adverse insured may not contract for a double recovery.

In this case, Dr. Haldar acknowledges that the collateral source rule applies and permits Mr. Mitchell to recover the actual payments made by Mr. Mitchell's private health insurance carrier. Dr. Haldar contends, however, that the Superior Court correctly ruled Mr. Mitchell could not recover the full amounts of his medical bills unless those amounts were actually paid by Blue Cross. Dr. Haldar's argument reflects a fundamental misunderstanding of the proper application of the collateral source rule to a tortfeasor's responsibility to pay the full reasonable value of the necessary medical treatment caused by the negligent conduct.

The collateral source rule provides that "it is the tortfeasor's responsibility to compensate for the reasonable value of all harm that he [or she] causes [and that responsibility] is not confined to the net loss that the injured party receives."

In this case, each of Mr. Mitchell's health care providers contracted to accept reduced payments from his *private* medical insurance carrier, Blue Cross, as payment in full. As we recently held in *Onusko v. Kerr,* the portions of medical expenses that health care providers write off constitute "compensation or indemnity received by a tort victim from a source collateral to the tortfeasor." The result is the same whether the write off is generated by a cash payment such as Kerr's or, as in this case, because of a reduction attributable to a health insurance contract for which the tortfeasor paid no compensation. Consequently, Mr. Mitchell was entitled to present evidence of the full amount of his medical expenses without any reduction for the amounts written off by his health care providers because of their contracts with Mr. Mitchell's health insurance carrier, Blue Cross.

We hold that the trial judge erred by excluding the full amount of the medical bills as evidence of the total amount of Mr. Mitchell's reasonable medical expenses.... The trial judge's evidentiary ruling erroneously reduced the appellants' damage claim for medical treatment by $20,000 to approximately $38,000 instead of approximately $58,000.

Conclusion

[The court found the evidentiary error did not affect the verdict and affirmed the judgment.]

* * *

Problem 24

The collateral source rule prevents a tortfeasor from benefiting when someone else steps in to compensate a plaintiff for harm the tortfeasor caused. Would the collateral source rule apply in the following scenario, or should the plaintiff be precluded from recovering damages for lost wages?

Larry works for his older brother, Harry. Larry gets paid hourly and typically works 40 hours per week. One day Larry is injured when he is hit by a car while walking to work. He misses two months of work while he recovers. Harry feels bad for his brother, so he continues to pay him at his usual rate and for 40 hours per week for the entire time Larry is out. Larry sues the driver of the car and seeks damages including lost wages.

Introductory Note — *Helfend v. Southern California Rapid Transit District* and *Howell v. Hamilton Meats & Provisions, Inc.*

Helfend and *Howell* were both decided by the California Supreme Court (*Helfend* in 1970 and *Howell* about 40 years later). Both cases purportedly apply the collateral source rule to decide whether damages for medical expenses were properly calculated. But the plaintiff in *Helfend* is awarded the full amount of the medical bills, while the *Howell* plaintiff is awarded far less than the amount the hospital billed for the treatment. The difference in result is driven by a fact that was not present in *Helfend* (or at least not discussed): a discounted rate provided by the hospital to the medical insurer.

THINGS TO THINK ABOUT while reading *Helfend v. Southern California Rapid Transit District* and *Howell v. Hamilton Meats & Provisions, Inc.*:

1. What are the policy objectives of the collateral source rule?

2. Compare the California Supreme Court's decision in *Helfend* with its decision in *Howell*. Is the reasoning consistent?

3. Does the holding in *Howell* undermine any of the policy objectives identified in *Helfend*?

Helfend v. Southern California Rapid Transit District

California Supreme Court
2 Cal.3d 1 (1970)

TOBRINER, Acting Chief Justice.

Defendants appeal from a judgment of the Los Angeles Superior Court entered on a verdict in favor of plaintiff, Julius J. Helfend, for $16,400 in general and special damages for injuries sustained in a bus-auto collision that occurred on July 19, 1965, in the City of Los Angeles.

We have concluded that the judgment for plaintiff in this tort action against the defendant governmental entity should be affirmed. The trial court properly followed the collateral source rule in excluding evidence that a portion of plaintiff's medical bills had been paid through a medical insurance plan that requires the refund of benefits from tort recoveries.

1. The facts

Shortly before noon on July 19, 1965, plaintiff drove his car in central Los Angeles east on Third Street approaching Grandview. At this point Third Street has six lanes, four for traffic and one parking lane on each side of the thoroughfare. While traveling in the second lane from the curb, plaintiff observed an automobile driven by Glen A. Raney, Jr., stopping in his lane and preparing to back into a parking space. Plaintiff put out his left arm to signal the traffic behind him that he intended to stop; he then brought his vehicle to a halt so that the other driver could park.

At about this time Kenneth A. Mitchell, a bus driver for the Southern California Rapid Transit District, pulled out of a bus stop at the curb of Third Street and headed in the same direction as plaintiff. Approaching plaintiff's and Raney's cars which were stopped in the second lane from the curb, Mitchell pulled out into the lane closest to the center of the street in order to pass. The right rear of the bus sideswiped plaintiff's vehicle, knocking off the rearview mirror and crushing plaintiff's arm, which had been hanging down at the side of his car in the stopping signal position. . . .

Plaintiff filed a tort action against the Southern California Rapid Transit District, a public entity, and Mitchell, an employee of the transit district. At trial plaintiff claimed slightly more than $2,700 in special damages, including $921 in doctor's bills, a $336.99 hospital bill, and about $45 for medicines. Defendant requested permission to show that about 80 percent of the plaintiff's hospital bill had been paid by plaintiff's Blue Cross insurance carrier and that some of his other medical expenses may have been paid by other insurance. . . . The court ruled that defendants should not be permitted to show that plaintiff had received medical coverage from any collateral source. . . .

2. The collateral source rule

The Supreme Court of California has long adhered to the doctrine that if an injured party receives some compensation for his injuries from a source wholly independent of the tortfeasor, such payment should not be deducted from the damages which the plaintiff would otherwise collect from the tortfeasor. (See, e.g., Peri v. Los Angeles Junction Ry. Co. (1943) 22 Cal.2d 111, 131.) As recently as August 1968 we unanimously reaffirmed our adherence to this doctrine, which is known as the 'collateral source rule.' (De Cruz v. Reid (1968) 69 Cal.2d 217, 223–227; see City of Salinas v. Souza & McCue Construction Co., supra, 66 Cal.2d 217, 226.)

Although the collateral source rule remains generally accepted in the United States, nevertheless many other jurisdictions have restricted or repealed it. In this country most commentators have criticized the rule and called for its early demise. . . .

The collateral source rule as applied here embodies the venerable concept that a person who has invested years of insurance premiums to assure his medical care should receive the benefits of his thrift. The tortfeasor should not garner the benefits of his victim's providence.

The collateral source rule expresses a policy judgment in favor of encouraging citizens to purchase and maintain insurance for personal injuries and for other eventualities. Courts consider insurance a form of investment, the benefits of which become payable without respect to any other possible source of funds. If we were to permit a tortfeasor to mitigate damages with payments from plaintiff's insurance, plaintiff would be in a position inferior to that of having bought no insurance, because his payment of premiums would have earned no benefit. Defendant should not be able to avoid payment of full compensation for the injury inflicted merely because the victim has had the foresight to provide himself with insurance. . . .

Furthermore, insurance policies increasingly provide for either subrogation or refund of benefits upon a tort recovery, and such refund is indeed called for in the present case. (See Fleming, The Collateral Source Rule and Loss Allocation in Tort Law, supra, 54 Cal.L.Rev. 1478, 1479.) Hence, the plaintiff receives no double recovery; the collateral source rule simply serves as a means of by-passing the antiquated doctrine of non-assignment of tortious actions and permits a proper transfer of risk from the plaintiff's insurer to the tortfeasor by way of the victim's tort recovery. The double shift from the tortfeasor to the victim and then from the victim to his insurance carrier can normally occur with little cost in that the insurance carrier is often intimately involved in the initial litigation and quite automatically receives its part of the tort settlement or verdict.

Even in cases in which the contract or the law precludes subrogation or refund of benefits, or in situations in which the collateral source waives such subrogation or refund, the rule performs entirely necessary functions in the computation of damages. For example, the cost of medical care often provides both attorneys and juries in tort cases with an important measure for assessing the plaintiff's general damages. (Cf., e.g., Rose v. Melody Lane (1952) 39 Cal.2d 481, 489.) To permit the defendant to tell the jury that the plaintiff has been recompensed by a collateral source for his medical costs might irretrievably upset the complex, delicate, and somewhat indefinable calculations which result in the normal jury verdict. (See Hoffman v. Brandt (1966) 65 Cal.2d 549, 554–555.)

We also note that generally the jury is not informed that plaintiff's attorney will receive a large portion of the plaintiff's recovery in contingent fees or that personal injury damages are not taxable to the plaintiff and are normally deductible by the defendant. Hence, the plaintiff rarely actually receives full compensation for his injuries as computed by the jury. The collateral source rule partially serves to compensate for the attorney's share and does not actually render 'double recovery' for the plaintiff. Indeed, many jurisdictions that have abolished or limited the collateral source rule have also established a means for assessing the plaintiff's costs for counsel directly against the defendant rather than imposing the contingent fee system. In sum, the plaintiff's recovery for his medical expenses from both the tortfeasor and his medical insurance program will not usually give him 'double recovery,' but partially provides a somewhat closer approximation to full compensation for his injuries.

If we consider the collateral source rule as applied here in the context of the entire American approach to the law of torts and damages, we find that the rule presently performs a number of legitimate and even indispensable functions. Without a thorough revolution in the American approach to torts and the consequent damages, the rule at least with respect to medical insurance benefits has become so integrated within our present system that its precipitous judicial nullification would work hardship. In this case the collateral source rule lies between two systems for the compensation of accident victims: the traditional tort recovery based on fault and the increasingly prevalent coverage based on non-fault insurance. Neither system possesses such universality of coverage or completeness of compensation that we can easily dispense with the collateral source rule's approach to meshing the two systems. (Cf., e.g., Bilyeu v. State Employees' Retirement System (1962) 58 Cal.2d 618, 629 (concurring opn. of Peters, J.).) . . .

Hence, we concluded that in a case in which a tort victim has received partial compensation from medical insurance coverage entirely independent of the tortfeasor the trial court properly followed the collateral source rule and foreclosed defendant from mitigating damages by means of the collateral payments. . . .

The judgment is affirmed.

* * *

Howell v. Hamilton Meats & Provisions, Inc.

California Supreme Court
52 Cal.4th 541 (2011)

WERDEGAR, J.

When a tortiously injured person receives medical care for his or her injuries, the provider of that care often accepts as full payment, pursuant to a preexisting contract with the injured person's health insurer, an amount less than that stated in the provider's bill. In that circumstance, may the injured person recover from the tortfeasor, as economic damages for past medical expenses, the undiscounted sum stated in the provider's bill but never paid by or on behalf of the injured person? We hold no such recovery is allowed, for the simple reason that the injured plaintiff did not suffer any economic loss in that amount. (See Civ.Code, §§ 3281 [damages are awarded to compensate for detriment suffered], 3282 [detriment is a loss or harm to person or property].)

The collateral source rule, which precludes deduction of compensation the plaintiff has received from sources independent of the tortfeasor from damages the plaintiff "would otherwise collect from the tortfeasor" (*Helfend v. Southern Cal. Rapid Transit Dist.* (1970) 2 Cal.3d 1, 6 (*Helfend*)), ensures that plaintiff here may recover in damages the amounts her insurer paid for her medical care. The rule, however, has no bearing on amounts that were included in a provider's bill but for which the plaintiff never incurred liability because the provider, by prior agreement, accepted a lesser amount as full payment. Such sums are not damages the plaintiff would otherwise have collected from the defendant. They are neither paid to the providers on the plaintiff's behalf nor paid to the plaintiff in indemnity of his or her expenses.

Because they do not represent an economic loss for the plaintiff, they are not recoverable in the first instance. The collateral source rule precludes certain deductions against otherwise recoverable damages, but does not expand the scope of economic damages to include expenses the plaintiff never incurred.

Factual and Procedural Background

Plaintiff Rebecca Howell was seriously injured in an automobile accident negligently caused by a driver for defendant Hamilton Meats & Provisions, Inc. (Hamilton). At trial, Hamilton conceded liability and the necessity of the medical treatment plaintiff had received, contesting only the amounts of plaintiff's economic and non-economic damages.

Hamilton moved in limine to exclude evidence of medical bills that neither plaintiff nor her health insurer, PacifiCare, had paid. Hamilton asserted that PacifiCare payment records indicated significant amounts of the bills from plaintiff's health care providers (the physicians who treated her and Scripps Memorial Hospital Encinitas, where she was treated) had been adjusted downward before payment pursuant to agreements between those providers and PacifiCare and that, under plaintiff's preferred provider organization (PPO) policy with PacifiCare, plaintiff could not be billed for the balance of the original bills (beyond the amounts of agreed patient copayments). . . .

Plaintiff's surgeon and her husband each testified that the total amount billed for her medical care up to the time of trial was $189,978.63, and the jury returned a verdict awarding that same amount as damages for plaintiff's past medical expenses.

Hamilton then made a "post-trial motion to reduce past medical specials . . . ," seeking a reduction of $130,286.90, the amount assertedly "written off" by plaintiff's medical care providers, Scripps Memorial Hospital Encinitas (Scripps) and CORE Orthopaedic Medical Center (CORE). In support of the motion, Hamilton submitted billing and payment records from the providers and two declarations, the first by Scripps's collections supervisor, the second by an employee of CORE's billing contractor. The Scripps declaration stated that of the $122,841 billed for plaintiff's surgeries, PacifiCare paid $24,380, plaintiff paid $3,566, and the remaining $94,894 was "'written off' or waived by [Scripps] pursuant to the agreement between [Scripps] and the patient's private healthcare insurer, in this case Pacificare PPO." The CORE declaration stated that of the surgeon's bill for $52,915, PacifiCare paid $9,665, and $35,392 was waived or written off pursuant to CORE's agreement with PacifiCare. Both declarants stated the providers had not filed liens for, and would not pursue collection of, the written-off amounts.

In opposition, plaintiff argued reduction of the medical damages would violate the collateral source rule. . . .

The trial court granted Hamilton's motion, reducing the past medical damages award "to reflect the amount the medical providers accepted as payment in full." Accordingly, the court reduced the judgment by $130,286.90.

The Court of Appeal reversed the reduction order, holding it violated the collateral source rule. Because it viewed the reduction of the award as substantively improper, the Court of Appeal did not resolve plaintiff's additional contentions that the procedures used in the trial court were statutorily unauthorized and the evidence Hamilton presented was insufficient.

We granted Hamilton's petition for review.

Discussion

Compensatory damages are moneys paid to compensate a person who "suffers detriment from the unlawful act or omission of another" (Civ.Code, § 3281), and the measure of damages generally recoverable in tort is "the amount which will compensate for all the detriment proximately caused" by the tort (*id.,* § 3333). Civil Code section 3282, in turn, defines "detriment" as "a loss or harm suffered in person or property." A person who undergoes necessary medical treatment for tortiously caused injuries suffers an economic loss by taking on liability for the costs of treatment. Hence, any reasonable charges for treatment the injured person has paid or, having incurred, still owes the medical provider are recoverable as economic damages. (See *Melone v. Sierra Railway Co.* (1907) 151 Cal. 113, 115 [plaintiff is entitled to "[s]uch reasonable sum . . . as has been necessarily expended or incurred in treating the injury"].)

When, as here, the costs of medical treatment are paid in whole or in part by a third party unconnected to the defendant, the collateral source rule is implicated. The collateral source rule states that "if an injured party receives some compensation for his injuries from a source wholly independent of the tortfeasor, such payment should not be deducted from the damages which the plaintiff would otherwise collect from the tortfeasor." (*Helfend, supra,* 2 Cal.3d at p. 6.) Put another way, "Payments made to or benefits conferred on the injured party from other sources [i.e., those unconnected to the defendant] are not credited against the tortfeasor's liability, although they cover all or a part of the harm for which the tortfeasor is liable." (Rest.2d Torts, § 920A, subd. (2).) The rule thus dictates that an injured plaintiff may recover from the tortfeasor money an insurer has paid to medical providers on his or her behalf.

Helfend, like the present case, involved a health insurer's payments to medical providers on the plaintiff's behalf. In these circumstances, we explained, the collateral source rule ensures plaintiffs will receive the benefits of their decision to carry insurance and thereby encourages them to do so. (*Helfend, supra,* 2 Cal.3d at pp. 9–10.) Since insurance policies frequently allow the insurer to reclaim the benefits paid out of a tort recovery by refund or subrogation, the rule, without providing the plaintiff a double recovery, ensures the tortfeasor cannot "avoid payment of full compensation for the injury inflicted. . . ." (*Id.* at p. 10.)

In *Helfend,* we addressed a challenge to the continued acceptance of the collateral source rule. After considering the rule's operation and consequences, we rejected that challenge, concluding that "in the context of the entire American approach to the law of torts and damages, . . . the rule presently performs a number of legitimate and even indispensable functions." (*Helfend, supra,* 2 Cal.3d at p. 13.) *Helfend* did not, however, call on this court to consider *how* the collateral source rule would apply to damages for past medical expenses when the amount billed for medical services substantially exceeds the amount accepted in full payment. While *Helfend* unequivocally reaffirmed California's acceptance of the rule, it did not explain how the rule would operate in the circumstances of the present case. . . .

Hanif and the Measure of Damages for Past Medical Expenses

We agree with the *Hanif* court that a plaintiff may recover as economic damages *no more* than the reasonable value of the medical services received and is not entitled to recover the reasonable value if his or her actual loss was less. California decisions have focused on "reasonable value" in the context of *limiting* recovery to reasonable expenditures, not expanding recovery beyond the plaintiff's actual loss or liability. To be recoverable, a medical expense must be both incurred *and* reasonable. (See *Melone v. Sierra Railway Co., supra,* 151 Cal. at p. 115 [proper measure of damages for medical expenses is "[s]uch reasonable sum . . . *as has been necessarily expended or incurred* in treating the injury" (italics added).)

The rule that a plaintiff's expenses, to be recoverable, must be both incurred *and* reasonable accords, as well, with our damages statutes. "Damages must, in all cases, be reasonable. . . ." (Civ.Code, § 3359.) But if the plaintiff negotiates a discount and thereby receives services for less than might reasonably be charged, the plaintiff has not suffered a pecuniary loss or other detriment in the greater amount and therefore cannot recover damages for that amount. The same rule applies when a collateral source, such as the plaintiff's health insurer, has obtained a discount for its payments on the plaintiff's behalf. . . .

Where a plaintiff has incurred liability for the billed cost of services and the provider later "writes off" part of the bill because, for example, the plaintiff is unable to pay the full charge, one might argue that the amount of the write-off constitutes a gratuitous benefit the plaintiff is entitled to recover under the collateral source rule. But in cases like that at bench, the medical provider has agreed, before treating the plaintiff, to accept a certain amount in exchange for its services. That amount constitutes the provider's price, which the plaintiff and health insurer are obligated to pay without any write-off. There is no need to determine a reasonable value of the services, as there is in the case of services gratuitously provided. "[W]here, as here, the exact amount of expenses has been established by contract and those expenses have been satisfied, there is no longer any issue as to the amount of expenses for which the plaintiff will be liable. In the latter case, the injured party should be limited to recovering the amount paid for the medical services." (*Moorhead v. Crozer Chester Medical Center* (2001) 564 Pa. 156.)

Nor does the tortfeasor obtain a "windfall" (*Arambula v. Wells, supra,* 72 Cal. App.4th at p. 1013) merely because the injured person's health insurer has negotiated a favorable rate of payment with the person's medical provider. When an injured plaintiff has received collateral compensation or benefits as a gift, allowing a deduction from damages in that amount would result in a windfall for the tortfeasor and underpayment for the injury. Because the tortfeasor would not pay the full cost of his or her negligence or wrongdoing, the deduction would distort the deterrent function of tort law. (See Katz, *Too Much of a Good Thing: When Charitable Gifts Augment Victim Compensation* (2003) 53 DePaul L.Rev. 547, 564 [if a charitable gift to the plaintiff reduces the tort recovery, the defendant "pays less than the full social costs of his conduct and is underdeterred"].) Analogously, if it were established a medical provider's full bill generally represents the value of the services provided, and the discounted price negotiated with the insurer is an artificially low fraction of that true value, one could make a parallel argument that relieving the defendant of paying the full bill would result in underdeterrence. The complexities of contemporary pricing and reimbursement patterns for medical providers, however, do not support such a generalization. We briefly explore those complexities below.

A 2005 study of hospital cost setting conducted for the Medicare Payment Advisory Commission concluded: "Hospital charge setting practices are complex and varied. Hospitals are generally faced with competing objectives of balancing budgets, remaining competitive, complying with health care and regulatory standards, and continuing to offer needed services to the community. . . . [¶] Disparities between charges and costs [have] been growing over time as many existing charges were set before hospitals had a good idea of their costs and/or were set in response to budgetary and competitive considerations rather than resource consumption. Hospital charges are set within the context of hospitals' broader communities, including their competitors, payers, regulators, and customers. . . . These competing influences and hospitals' efforts to address them often produce charges which may not relate systematically to costs." (Dobson et al., A Study of Hospital Charge Setting Practices (2005) p. v, < http://www.medpac.gov/documents/Dec05_Charge_ setting. pdf> (as of Aug. 18, 2011).)

The rise of managed care organizations, which typically restrict payments for services to their members, has reportedly led to increases in the prices charged to uninsured patients, who do not benefit from providers' contracts with the plans. As one article explains: "Before managed care, hospitals billed insured and uninsured patients similarly. In 1960, 'there were no discounts; everyone paid the same rates' — usually cost plus ten percent. But as some insurers demanded deep discounting, hospitals vigorously shifted costs to patients with less clout." (Hall & Schneider, *Patients as Consumers: Courts, Contracts, and the New Medical Marketplace* (2008) 106 Mich. L.Rev. 643, 663, fns. omitted (hereafter *Patients as Consumers*).) As a consequence, "only uninsured, self-paying U.S. patients have been billed the full charges listed in hospitals' inflated chargemasters," so that a family might find itself "paying off over many years a hospital bill of, say, $30,000 for a procedure that Medicaid would have reimbursed at only $6,000 and commercial insurers somewhere in between." (Reinhardt, *The Pricing of U.S. Hospital Services: Chaos Behind a Veil of Secrecy* (2006) 25 Health Affairs 57, 62 (hereafter *The Pricing of U.S. Hospital Services*).) Some physicians, too, have reportedly shifted costs to the uninsured, resulting in significant disparities between charges to uninsured patients and those with private insurance or public medical benefits. (*Patients as Consumers,* at pp. 661–663.)

Nor do the chargemaster rates necessarily represent the amount an uninsured patient will pay. In California, medical providers are expressly authorized to offer the uninsured discounts, and hospitals in particular are required to maintain a discounted payment policy for patients with high medical costs who are at or below 350 percent of the federal poverty level. (Bus. & Prof.Code, § 657, subd. (c); Health & Saf.Code, § 127405, subd. (a)(1)(A).) . . .

We do not suggest hospital bills always exceed the reasonable value of the services provided. Chargemaster prices for a given service can vary tremendously, sometimes by a factor of five or more, from hospital to hospital in California. (See *The Pricing of U.S. Hospital Services, supra,* 25 Health Affairs at p. 58, exhibit No. 1 [prices for a chest x-ray at selected California hospitals, showing low of around $200 and high of around $1,500].) With so much variation, making any broad generalization about the relationship between the value or cost of medical services and the amounts providers bill for them — other than that the relationship is not always a close one — would be perilous. . . .

If the negotiated rate differential is not a gratuitous payment by the provider to the injured plaintiff (recoverable, at least in the Restatement's view, under the collateral source rule), nor an arbitrary reduction (arguably recoverable to prevent a defense windfall and underdeterrence), is it, as plaintiff contends and the Court of Appeal held, recoverable as a benefit provided to the insured plaintiff under her policy? Plaintiff contends the negotiated rate differential represents the monetary value of the administrative and marketing advantages a provider obtains through its agreement with the insurer. Having incurred liability for the full price of her medical care, plaintiff maintains, she then received the benefit of having her insurer extinguish that obligation through a combination of cash payments and noncash consideration in the amount of the negotiated rate differential. Both parts of this consideration being benefits accruing to her under her policy, for which she paid premiums, both parts should assertedly be recoverable under the collateral source rule.

We disagree. As previously discussed, plaintiff did not incur liability for her providers' full bills, because at the time the charges were incurred the providers had already agreed on a different price schedule for PacifiCare's PPO members. (See *Parnell v. Adventist Health System/West, supra,* 35 Cal.4th at p. 609, 26 Cal.Rptr.3d 569, 109 P.3d 69.) Having never incurred the full bill, plaintiff could not recover it in damages for economic loss. For this reason alone, the collateral source rule would be inapplicable. The rule provides that "if an injured party receives some compensation for his injuries from a source wholly independent of the tortfeasor, such payment should not be deducted from the *damages which the plaintiff would otherwise collect from the tortfeasor.*" (*Helfend, supra,* 2 Cal.3d at p. 6, 84 Cal.Rptr. 173, 465

P.2d 61, italics added.) The rule does not speak to losses or liabilities the plaintiff did not incur and would not otherwise be entitled to recover. . . .

We conclude the negotiated rate differential is not a collateral payment or benefit subject to the collateral source rule. We emphasize, however, that the rule applies with full force here and in similar cases. Plaintiff here recovers the amounts paid on her behalf by her health insurer as well as her own out-of-pocket expenses. No "credit against the tortfeasor's liability" (Rest.2d Torts, § 920A, subd. (2)) and no deduction from the "damages which the plaintiff would otherwise collect from the tortfeasor" (*Helfend, supra,* 2 Cal.3d at p. 6, 84 Cal.Rptr. 173, 465 P.2d 61) is allowed for the amount paid through insurance. Plaintiff thus receives the benefits of the health insurance for which she paid premiums: her medical expenses have been paid per the policy, and those payments are not deducted from her tort recovery. . . .

In holding plaintiff may not recover as past medical damages the amount of a negotiated rate differential, then, we do not alter the collateral source rule as articulated in *Helfend* and the Restatement. Rather, we conclude that because the plaintiff does not incur liability in the amount of the negotiated rate differential, which also is not paid to or on behalf of the plaintiff to cover the expenses of the plaintiff's injuries, it simply does not come within the rule. "[A] rule limiting the measure of recovery to paid charges (where the provider is prohibited from balance billing the patient) . . . provides certainty without violating the principles protected by the collateral source rule. Even with a limit of recovery to the net loss there is no lessening of the deterrent force of tort law, the defendant does not gain the benefit of the plaintiff's bargain, and the plaintiff receives full compensation for the amount of the expense he was obligated to pay." (Beard, *The Impact of Changes in Health Care Provider Reimbursement Systems on the Recovery of Damages for Medical Expenses in Personal Injury Suits, supra,* 21 Am. J. Trial Advoc., at p. 489.) . . .

We hold, therefore, that an injured plaintiff whose medical expenses are paid through private insurance may recover as economic damages no more than the amounts paid by the plaintiff or his or her insurer for the medical services received or still owing at the time of trial. In so holding, we in no way abrogate or modify the collateral source rule as it has been recognized in California; we merely conclude the negotiated rate differential — the discount medical providers offer the insurer — is not a benefit provided to the plaintiff in compensation for his or her injuries and therefore does not come within the rule. . . .

It follows from our holding that when a medical care provider has, by agreement with the plaintiff's private health insurer, accepted as full payment for the plaintiff's care an amount less than the provider's full bill, evidence of that amount is relevant to prove the plaintiff's damages for past medical expenses and, assuming it satisfies other rules of evidence, is admissible at trial. . . .

In the case at bench, the trial court correctly ruled plaintiff could recover as damages for her past medical expenses no more than her medical providers had accepted as payment in full from plaintiff and PacifiCare, her insurer. . . .

Disposition

The judgment of the Court of Appeal is reversed. The matter is remanded to that court for further proceedings consistent with our opinion.

* * *

Problem 25

Application of the collateral source rule can lead to some tricky evidentiary issues. How should the trial court rule on the defendant's motion to exclude evidence in the following case?

An injured plaintiff was treated at a hospital. The bill for the treatment was $500,000, but under a standing agreement with the plaintiff's medical insurance carrier, the hospital discounted the bill to just $75,000. At trial, the defendant moves to exclude evidence of medical treatment cost beyond $75,000, on the ground that such evidence is not relevant. Plaintiff's counsel concedes that based on the jurisdiction's interpretation of the collateral source rule, the full $500,000 bill is not relevant as evidence of medical expenses. But she argues the $500,000 bill is relevant and admissible as evidence of plaintiff's general damages — emotional distress and pain and suffering — to demonstrate the full extent of the treatment that was needed for the injuries.

Adjustments for Time

Damages awarded to a plaintiff will often need to be adjusted for time, meaning either increased or decreased to account for the time value of money. The time value of money is a principle better suited for a course in economics, but a basic understanding of it is enough to grasp the implications for an award of damages.

Because the passage of time affects its ultimate value, money in hand now is worth more than an identical sum in the future. That is because money can earn interest. If a person has the money now, it can be invested and earn a return. If a person does not have the money until later, it obviously cannot be invested now. The implications for an award of monetary damages are as follows: damages received for a loss that already occurred do not make a plaintiff completely whole unless they are *increased*, to account for the return that could have been earned during the time between when the loss occurred and when the damages are awarded. And damages awarded for harm that has not yet occurred must be *decreased*, so the plaintiff will not receive an undue benefit from having the money now instead of later.

Increasing an award of damages for past harm to reflect the time value of money is called adding prejudgment interest. A certain amount of interest (the rate is set by statute) is added to the amount of the damages. The interest runs from the date the loss was incurred until the date the damages are awarded, which occurs upon entry of judgment.

Not all damages awarded for past harm need to be adjusted. Since the time value concept assumes there was a debt owed at a certain point in the past, prejudgment interest is added only to damages that are capable of calculation at the time the harm was incurred. If the amount of damages could not accurately be ascertained until entry of judgment, it cannot fairly be said that a debt was previously owed.

Decreasing damages awarded for future harm to reflect the time value of money is called reducing the damages to present cash value. To avoid giving the plaintiff a windfall, the amount awarded for the future harm is reduced by an appropriate amount, which is calculated by taking into account a reasonable rate of return if the money were invested during the relevant timeframe. (This fairly complex calculation typically requires an expert, probably an economist.)

Not all damages for future harm are subject to reduction to present cash value. Noneconomic damages, such as for emotional distress, need not be reduced to present cash value even when some of the emotional harm contemplated by the damage award is in the future. Reduction to present cash value applies only to economic damages.

Introductory Note — *Wickham Contracting Co. v. Local Union No. 3*

A jury awarded the plaintiff, an electrical contractor, damages against an electricians' union for conducting an unlawful strike. Because of a procedural perfect storm, that damage award was not issued until more than *15* years after the strike. That meant, in something of an anomaly, the prejudgment interest on the damages exceeded the damage award itself. Unsurprisingly, the defendant contends on appeal that the prejudgment interest should not be allowed.

THINGS TO THINK ABOUT while reading *Wickham Contracting Co. v. Local Union No. 3*:

1. What considerations are relevant to determine whether prejudgment interest should be awarded?

2. Of those considerations, which are most important?

3. Why was prejudgment interest appropriately awarded here?

Wickham Contracting Co. v. Local Union No. 3

United States Court of Appeals, Second Circuit

955 F.2d 831 (1992)

MINER, Circuit Judge:

Defendant-appellant Local No. 3 of the International Brotherhood of Electrical Workers ("union") appeals from a judgment of the United States District Court for the Southern District of New York (Mukasey, J.) awarding prejudgment interest on damages recovered by plaintiffs-appellees Wickham Contracting Co. and Ralph Perone (collectively, "Wickham"), as employers and former joint-venture partners. The damages were awarded under Section 303(b) of the Labor Management Relations Act ("LMRA"), 29 U.S.C. §§ 141–197, which provides a civil remedy to employers sustaining damages from secondary strike activity by a labor organization.

The union contends that prejudgment interest is inappropriate in Section 303 cases because the LMRA, being silent on the subject of prejudgment interest, provides no "statutory authority" for such awards, and because the damages involved are unliquidated, or difficult to ascertain prior to judgment. The union further contends that, even if prejudgment interest may be awarded under Section 303, the district court erred in awarding interest in this particular case. We have not previously addressed the question of prejudgment interest under this provision of the LMRA. For the reasons that follow, we hold that an award of prejudgment interest under Section 303 is within the sound discretion of a district court, and that Judge Mukasey did not abuse his discretion in awarding interest in this case.

Background

The union represents electricians who are employed by contractors to perform electrical construction work. Wickham was an electrical contractor. In early 1974, Wickham entered into contracts with the Board of Education of the City of New York under which Wickham was to perform electrical modernization and construction work at three New York City public schools, P.S. 8, P.S. 41, and the Tremont Early Childhood Center. Wickham's electricians were represented by Teamsters Local 363.

During the week of July 8, 1974, while Wickham's work on the schools was under way, the union caused its members to strike against all electrical contractors performing work for the Board of Education. The immediate goal of the strike was to force the Board of Education to cease doing business with Wickham. The ultimate goal of the strike was to oust the Teamsters from their position as representative of Wickham's electricians.

On July 22, 1974, the Board of Education issued stop work orders to every electrical contractor that did not have a collective bargaining agreement with the union, including Wickham. Wickham's work on the schools came to an immediate halt. Wickham commenced this civil suit against the union under Section 303(b) of the

LMRA on July 29, 1974. At the same time, Wickham filed unfair labor practice charges with the NLRB.

. . . On September 26, 1975, the NLRB found that the union had engaged in an unfair labor practice under Section 8(b)(4) of the National Labor Relations Act ("NLRA"), and issued a cease and desist order. The NLRB's determination and order were upheld by this Court the following year. *See NLRB v. Local 3, Int'l Bhd. of Elect. Workers,* 542 F.2d 860 (2d Cir.1976) (*"Wickham I "*). In the civil suit commenced by Wickham, a jury eventually found the union liable in 1982, and awarded $959,000 in damages under Section 303. We affirmed the jury's finding of liability, but remanded the case for a new trial on the amount of damages. *See Wickham Contracting Co. v. Board of Educ.,* 715 F.2d 21 (2d Cir.1983) (*"Wickham II"*).

The new damages trial was not held until April 1991. The jury returned an award of $41,000. At Wickham's request, Judge Mukasey awarded prejudgment interest on this amount accruing from September 1, 1975. The interest component amounted to $50,905, for a total award to Wickham of $91,905.

Discussion

Section 303(a) of the LMRA makes it unlawful for a labor organization to engage in conduct defined as an "unfair labor practice" in Section 8(b)(4) of the NLRA. *See* 29 U.S.C. § 187(a). Section 8(b)(4) of the NLRA makes it an "unfair labor practice" for a labor organization to engage in, or to induce any individual to engage in, a strike, where an object thereof is to force any person to cease doing business with any other person or to force an employer to recognize or bargain with a labor organization not certified as the representative of the employer's employees. *See* 29 U.S.C. § 158(b)(4) (i)(B). Section 303(b) of the LMRA provides that any person injured in "his business or property" by virtue of a Section 303(a) violation "shall recover the damages by him sustained and the cost of the suit." *See* 29 U.S.C. § 187(b). The LMRA is silent on the subject of prejudgment interest.

I. The Law of Prejudgment Interest

Since the early part of this century, the United States Supreme Court has stated repeatedly that discretionary awards of prejudgment interest are permissible under federal law in certain circumstances. Under the Court's analysis, the award should be a function of (i) the need to fully compensate the wronged party for actual damages suffered, (ii) considerations of fairness and the relative equities of the award, (iii) the remedial purpose of the statute involved, and/or (iv) such other general principles as are deemed relevant by the court. *See Loeffler v. Frank,* 486 U.S. 549, 557–58, 108 S.Ct. 1965, 1970–71, 100 L.Ed.2d 549 (1988); *Blau v. Lehman,* 368 U.S. 403, 414, 82 S.Ct. 451, 457, 7 L.Ed.2d 403 (1962); *Rodgers v. United States,* 332 U.S. 371, 373–74, 68 S.Ct. 5, 6–7, 92 L.Ed. 3 (1947); *Board of County Comm'rs of the County of Jackson v. United States,* 308 U.S. 343, 352, 60 S.Ct. 285, 289, 84 L.Ed. 313 (1939); *Miller v. Robertson,* 266 U.S. 243, 257–58, 45 S.Ct. 73, 78–79, 69 L.Ed. 265 (1924).

. . . The Court has, however, disallowed prejudgment interest awards in certain instances. Prejudgment interest may not be awarded, of course, when Congressional intent is to the contrary. Intent to deny recovery of prejudgment interest may be obvious from the language of the statute itself. *See United States v. Goltra,* 312 U.S. 203, 207, 211, 61 S.Ct. 487, 490, 492, 85 L.Ed. 776 (1941) (statute governing plaintiff's claim against the United States provided no interest until "rendition of judgment"). Even when the statute is silent, intent to deny recovery of interest may be inferable from (i) the state of the law on prejudgment interest, for the type of claim involved, at the time the statute was passed, and (ii) consistent denial by the courts of pre-judgment interest under the statute and failure by Congress, despite amendments to the statute, to address prejudgment interest awards. *See Monessen Southwestern Ry. Co. v. Morgan,* 486 U.S. 330, 336–39, 108 S.Ct. 1837, 1842–44, 100 L.Ed.2d 349 (1988) (denying prejudgment interest under Federal Employers' Liability Act).

[handwritten margin note: the statute did not say]

Awards of prejudgment interest must not result in over-compensation of the plaintiff. Accordingly, the Court has suggested disapproval of such awards where the statute itself fixes damages deemed fully compensatory as a matter of law. *See Brooklyn Sav. Bank v. O'Neil,* 324 U.S. 697, 699, 714–16, 65 S.Ct. 895, 898, 905–07, 89 L.Ed. 1296 (1945) (interest not recoverable on liquidated damages provided by Fair Labor Standards Act of 1938). Similarly, prejudgment interest should not be awarded if the statutory obligation on which interest is sought is punitive in nature. *See Rodgers,* 332 U.S. at 374–76, 68 S.Ct. at 7 (interest not recoverable on penalty imposed on farmer for exceeding quota under Agricultural Adjustment Act); *United States v. Childs,* 266 U.S. 304, 308–10, 45 S.Ct. 110, 111, 69 L.Ed. 299 (1924) (interest recoverable on back taxes due, but not on penalty assessed for nonpayment).

[handwritten margin note: question of relative equities of the parties]

The relative equities may make prejudgment interest inappropriate when the defendant acted innocently and had no reason to know of the wrongfulness of his actions, *see Jackson County,* 308 U.S. at 352–53, 60 S.Ct. at 289; when there is a good faith dispute between the parties as to the existence of any liability, *see St. Louis & O'Fallon Ry. Co. v. United States,* 279 U.S. 461, 478, 483, 49 S.Ct. 384, 385, 387, 73 L. Ed. 798 (1929) (suit under Interstate Commerce Act to recover excess income alleg-edly earned); or when the plaintiff himself is responsible for the delay in recovery, *see Redfield v. Bartels,* 139 U.S. 694, 695, 702–03, 11 S.Ct. 683, 686, 35 L.Ed. 310 (1891) (suit to recover duties wrongfully imposed; interest denied since plaintiff neglected bringing suit for years).

. . . The certainty of the damages due the plaintiff has been another factor in resolving prejudgment interest issues. The Supreme Court initially embraced the strict common law view that interest may not be recovered where damages are unliquidated, or difficult to ascertain with precision at the time of the alleged wrongdoing. *See, e.g., Mowry v. Whitney,* 81 U.S. (14 Wall.) 620, 653, 20 L.Ed. 860 (1872) (denying prejudgment interest in patent law infringement action). Accord-ingly, prejudgment interest originally was available only in contract actions, if at all. The reasoning of the common law was that interest would be unjust if the party committing the wrongdoing could not know exactly how much to tender to the wronged party to make the latter whole.

[handwritten margin note: reasons not giving prejudg. interest previously]

Even in the modern cases awarding prejudgment interest, damages have been ascertainable with precision, at least by the time of trial or judgment. For instance, the amount of back pay due an employee or the losses incurred in a fraudulent securities transaction could be calculated with certainty in many cases by the finder of fact, after consideration of the available information. However, the significant feature of these same cases was that no party could foresee, at the time of the wrongdoing, the full amount of damages that would result. The difficulty of computing a "make whole" amount frequently persisted until judgment itself. In an employment case, nobody knows on the date of the wrongful termination the amount of back pay that will be necessary to make the plaintiff whole. The quantity can only be determined at trial, on the date verdict is rendered, and is therefore not "liquidated" in the common law sense. *See Greenberg v. Paramount Pictures, Inc.,* 85 F.2d 42, 45 (2d Cir.1936) (L. Hand, J.). These problems of calculation also exist in cases in which the injury is more similar to Wickham's. In a securities fraud case, for example, no one knows on the date of the deception how much loss there will be in the value of the stock, or what the stock's price will be on the date suit is brought. Similarly, in a patent infringement case, it is impossible to determine at the time of infringement the profits that will be lost by one party or gained by the other. Yet, prejudgment interest awards have been upheld frequently in these and analogous cases, both by the Supreme Court and by this Court.

Accordingly, the old common law rule of liquidated damages no longer retains its full vitality. The Supreme Court has practically said as much, *see Miller,* 266 U.S. at 258, 45 S.Ct. at 78; *see also Funkhouser v. J.B. Preston Co.,* 290 U.S. 163, 168–69, 54 S. Ct. 134, 136, 78 L.Ed. 243 (1933), as have we, *see United Aircraft,* 534 F.2d at 447; *see also Greenberg,* 85 F.2d at 45, as has at least one other circuit, *see Eazor Express, Inc. v. International Bhd. of Teamsters,* 520 F.2d 951, 973 (3d Cir.1975) (citing *Miller,* 266 U.S. at 258, 45 S.Ct. at 79), *cert. denied,* 424 U.S. 935, 96 S.Ct. 1149, 47 L.Ed.2d 342 (1976). Moreover, the current "equitable" and discretionary rule, based on the need for full compensation and fairness under the circumstances, necessarily rejects much of the common law's approach to prejudgment interest.

The speculative nature of the damages in question will always be relevant to a sound decision on a consideration of whether prejudgment interest should be awarded. However, the proper inquiry must include the other factors we have identified: analysis of the pertinent statute and its purposes; the need to fully compensate the injured party; fairness and the relative equities; and the specific circumstances of the parties and of the case. The degree of speculation must then be considered in light of these other factors to determine the propriety of prejudgment interest. We recognize that in some Section 303 actions the fact finder's calculation of losses suffered by the employer will be so conjectural that prejudgment interest should not be awarded. Nonetheless, while the presence of "abstruse inquiries" and "difficult questions of proof" in the calculation of damages are factors to be considered carefully, these problems must be considered together with other factors that may favor prejudgment interest. *See Hughes,* 449 F.2d at 80.

For the foregoing reasons, we cannot agree with the union that the silence of the LMRA on the subject of interest, or the unliquidated nature of damages in a Section 303 case, are sufficient without more to bar the award made to Wickham.

II. The Award of Interest Against the Union

The factors generally justifying an award of interest are present in this case. Wickham clearly suffered actual damage to its business because of the secondary strike. . . . Hence, Wickham was deprived of money that it otherwise would have earned but for the secondary strike. As Judge Mukasey pointed out, the damage was incurred by Wickham on September 1, 1975, the date on which Wickham was to have received payment under the original schedule contemplated by the contracts. Therefore, Wickham has been deprived of a sum owed to it, under Section 303 of the LMRA, for over 16 years. It was not an abuse of discretion for the district court to determine that prejudgment interest was necessary to compensate Wickham fairly under the circumstances, especially in view of high inflation during several of those years. *See Rolf v. Blyth, Eastman Dillon & Co.,* 637 F.2d 77, 87 (2d Cir.1980). . . .

The availability of both injunctive and monetary relief under the labor laws for secondary strikes reflects a strong national policy against behavior Congress found quite objectionable. *See* Robert A. Gorman, *Basic Text on Labor Law, Unionization and Collective Bargaining* 291 (1976). The policy is rooted in the desire to protect innocent third parties from labor disputes. In this case, the union's unlawful activity led to the disruption of public schools. These observations are offered not to suggest in any way that the union deserves to be penalized by an award of prejudgment interest, but rather to emphasize that the award does not strike us as inequitable under the circumstances. . . .

Lastly, the damages suffered by Wickham in this case were not so conjectural that an award of prejudgment interest was an abuse of discretion under the circumstances. The total revenue to be earned by Wickham under the three contracts was known with certainty to be $502,000. Further, as an experienced contractor, Wickham probably had a good idea of the expected cost of labor and materials. . . .

We have carefully considered the union's remaining arguments, and find them to be without merit.

Conclusion

The judgment of the district court awarding prejudgment interest under Section 303(b) of the LMRA is affirmed.

* * *

Problem 26

Prejudgment interest is allowed only on damages that are capable of calculation before a factfinder (judge or jury) decides the case. Is the plaintiff in the following case entitled to prejudgment interest?

A toy designer licenses a design for a new toy to a manufacturer. The license agreement entitles the designer to a 40 percent royalty on all sales. When the royalty payments come due, the parties disagree about whether the 40 percent should be calculated based on gross sales (all amounts received by the manufacturer) or net sales (the profits after manufacturing and marketing expenses). The contract does not specify. The manufacturer refuses to pay the royalty on the gross sales, and the designer sues. A jury determines the designer's interpretation of the contract is the most reasonable and awards the designer damages equal to 40 percent of gross sales. The designer requests prejudgment interest on the damages award.

Introductory Note — *Howard v. Sanborn*

Howard is a physical injury case arising from a rear-end car accident. The jury found for the defendant and awarded no damages. But the case is reversed on appeal due to a defective jury instruction. Because there will be a retrial, the appellate court provides the trial court with some insight on the method for reducing damages to present cash value, in case damages are awarded the second time around.

THINGS TO THINK ABOUT while reading *Howard v. Sanborn*:

1. How does a jury decide the amount by which an award of future damages should be reduced to account for the time value of money?

2. Which types of damages are subject to reduction to present cash value, and which are not?

Howard v. Sanborn

South Dakota Supreme Court

483 N.W.2d 796 (1992)

MILLER, Chief Justice.

Jean and Jim Howard sued for damages sustained when their car was struck from the rear by a car driven by Robert Sanborn. Sanborn principally defended on grounds of contributory negligence and unavoidable accident. The jury returned a verdict for Sanborn. This is an appeal from the orders denying Howards' motions for directed verdict and judgment notwithstanding the verdict. We reverse and remand for a new trial.

Facts

On the evening of November 20, 1987, Howards were enroute to dinner at the Cattleman's Club, a steakhouse which is located approximately five miles east of Pierre, South Dakota, on Highway 34. Jean was driving and Jim was in the passenger's seat. Jean testified that as they approached the driveway of the Cattleman's Club, she turned on her left turn signal and slowed to a stop.

Traffic was heavy that night and she had to wait for several cars to go by before she could safely make the left turn. Before making the turn, Jean noticed a car was coming up fast behind them. She remarked to her husband that she thought this car might hit them. Her husband had also seen the car approaching in the side mirror. He told his wife that she better turn quickly. Jean had started the turn when the vehicle driven by Sanborn crashed into Howards' car.

Howards initiated this suit against Sanborn to recover for damages they incurred as a result of the collision. Jean sought recovery for her personal injuries and other damages, including lost income and medical expenses. Jim claimed damages for replacement labor costs and loss of consortium. As noted earlier, Sanborn asserted contributory negligence and unavoidable accident and the jury returned a verdict in his favor.

On appeal, Howards assert that the trial court erred in: (1) instructing the jury on contributory negligence; [and] (2) ... giving the instruction on adjusting the award of damages to present value.

I. Whether the Trial Court Erred in Instructing on Contributory Negligence

Howards contend that it was improper for the trial court to instruct on the issue of contributory negligence since there was no evidence in the record supporting it. Sanborn's defense of contributory negligence was based on two theories: (1) Jean, the driver, failed to signal; and (2) Jim, the passenger, failed to warn his wife of the approaching danger.

. . . Based on the record, it is clear there was no competent evidence indicating Jean failed to signal. Therefore, it was improper to instruct the jury on her alleged contributory negligence.

. . . The danger in this case (Sanborn's approaching vehicle) was obvious to both driver and passenger. In fact, Jean commented to her husband that she thought the car coming up behind them was going to hit them and he told her to turn quickly. These facts do not give rise to a duty on Jim's behalf to warn Jean of the danger. Accordingly, the trial court erred in instructing on Jim's alleged contributory negligence.

Under South Dakota law and the instructions as given, the plaintiff is totally barred from recovering if the jury finds the plaintiff to be contributorily negligent in an amount more than slight. Thus, this instruction was extremely prejudicial to Howards. We believe the jury's verdict may and probably would have been different if the jury had not been instructed on contributory negligence.

[II. Whether the Trial Court Erred in Approving an Instruction on Adjusting the Award of Damages to Present Value]

The jury did not ultimately reach this issue; however, because we remand for a new trial, we will address it.

Howards contend that the trial court erred in giving an instruction which generally expanded upon the pattern instruction by adding a section on how to calculate the present cash value and included a present worth table, when no evidence was offered to support such an instruction. The trial court's Instruction No. 26, which is nearly identical to the federal instruction from *Federal Jury Practice and Instructions,* Devitt, Blackmar and Wolff, Vol. 3, § 85.11 (1987), reads as follows:

> If you should find that plaintiff Jean Howard is entitled to a verdict, and further find that the evidence in the case establishes either: (1) a reasonable likelihood of future medical expense, or (2) a reasonable likelihood of loss of future earnings, or if you should find that plaintiff Jim Howard is entitled to a verdict, and you further find the evidence establishes a reasonable likelihood that he will be deprived of the services, aid, comfort, society, companionship and conjugal affections of his wife then it becomes your duty to ascertain the present worth in dollars of such future damage, since the award of future damages necessarily requires that payment be made now for a loss that will not actually be sustained until some future date.

> Under these circumstances, the result is that plaintiffs Jean and Jim Howard will in effect be reimbursed in advance of the loss, and so will have the use of money which they would not have received until some future date, but for the verdict.

> In order to make a reasonable adjustment for the present use, interest free, of money representing a lump-sum payment of anticipated future loss, the law requires that you discount, or reduce to its present worth, the amount

of the anticipated future loss, by taking (1) the interest rate or return which such plaintiffs could reasonably be expected to receive on an investment of the lump-sum payment together with (2) the period of time over which the future loss is reasonably certain to be sustained; and then reduce, or in effect deduct from, the total amount of anticipated future loss whatever that amount would be reasonably certain to earn or return, if invested at such rate of interest over such period of time; and include in the verdict an award for only the present-worth — the reduced amount — of anticipated future loss.

As already explained to you, this computation is made by using the so-called "present-worth" table (present worth of one per period), which the Court had judicially noticed and which are attached to this instruction for your use.

Bear in mind that your duty to discount to present value applies only to loss of future earnings, future medical expenses or loss of consortium and not to any other damages the plaintiffs may have sustained in this instance. Also bear in mind that the evidence of Jean Howard's claim for loss of future earnings as submitted by Dr. Brown has already been reduced to present value. It is, however, your duty to determine whether his adjustment for present value of that claim was reasonable, and if not, you should make your own adjustment for present value of any sum to which you determine Jean Howard is entitled, if any.

The federal instructions also include an alternative instruction entitled "Lost Wages and/or Earning Capacity — When Economic Experts Testify." *See* Devitt, Blackmar and Wolff, § 85.12.

South Dakota law "is silent on the issue of proper computation of the discount rate for estimating the present value of future income." *Robichaud v. Theis,* 858 F.2d 392, 396 (8th Cir.1988). Additionally, the South Dakota Pattern Jury Instruction does not tell the jury how to reduce the damages. As of yet, neither this court nor the United States Supreme Court has endorsed one particular method for determining present value. Some states have either statutorily or judicially endorsed a method. We determine that, at this time, we should clarify the meaning of our previous holdings on how to properly instruct the jury on reducing awards to present value.

We held in *Watkins v. Ebach,* 291 N.W.2d 765, 767 (S.D.1980): "Although it is true this court has never held that the trial court must give a present value instruction regarding loss of future earnings, we think that this requirement should now be imposed." In that case, we adopted the prevailing rule that damages for loss of future earnings should be reduced to present value. However, therein we went on to say that the record did not support the giving of such an instruction because the appellant/defendant "offered no *testimony* upon which the jury could have made an intelligent decision on reducing the award for loss of future earnings to present value." *Id.* (emphasis added). *See also Flagtwet v. Smith,* 367 N.W.2d 188 (S.D.1985).

We used language in *Watkins* that might suggest that expert testimony is required in every case where future earnings might be awarded. We now hold that expert testimony on the reduction of future earnings is *not required* in every case. However, if an expert testifies and reduces the damages to present value for the jury, an instruction (such as the one given in this case) which includes present worth tables must be carefully crafted to prevent confusion. We believe the instruction given by the trial court here was adequate and not confusing.

When there is no expert testimony on present value, as in *Watkins*, then the jury must have some direction to help it intelligently reduce the award to present value. In *Watkins*, we quoted with approval from *Brodie v. Philadelphia Transportation Co.*, 415 Pa. 296, 203 A.2d 657, 660 (1964), wherein it stated:

> The involved process of reducing future losses to their present worth has, undoubtedly, led to confusion and guesswork verdicts. *Reason, logic and fairness would, therefore, dictate that enlightenment is necessary.* Such can be provided, at least in part, by permitting the *use of accepted tables or the testimony of a qualified expert,* who can compose the proper computations.

This reflects our acceptance of the practice of *either* providing the jury with instructions including tables or some other helpful means to reduce to present value, *or* providing an expert to reduce the damages for the jury. We generally approve of the Devitt, Blackmar and Wolff instructions cited above.

Accordingly, we reverse and remand for a new trial consistent with the foregoing.

* * *

Problem 27

Reduction to present value is required for damages awarded for future economic harm. In the case below, which damages should be reduced to present value?

A plaintiff is permanently injured in a car accident and will be unable to work because of the injury. At trial, the jury awards him a total of $2,000,000 in damages, categorized as follows: $100,000 for medical expenses incurred; $50,000 for a surgery likely to be required next year; $100,000 in lost wages; $500,000 for lost future earning capacity; $1,000,000 for pain and suffering; and $250,000 for future pain and suffering.

Chapter 6

Punitive Damages

Despite the similarity in name, punitive damages are not like compensatory damages. Compensatory damages focus on reimbursing for a loss, that is, making the plaintiff whole. Punitive damages have a different purpose. They look to punish a wrongdoer and deter future wrongful conduct.

Given that purpose, punitive damages are available in only certain types of cases. Punitive damages cannot generally be recovered for breach of contract. Nor can they be recovered for unintentional harm. Punitive damages are traditionally available exclusively for intentional torts and gross negligence (engaging in dangerous conduct with an intentional disregard for its risk). The reason is because that sort of conduct is what society most wants to deter. It is conduct that carries a high risk of seriously harming others. And it has no redeeming value, or silver lining, so to speak, like the economic value society might derive from an efficient breach of contract.

Punitive damages are sometimes allowed for specific types of contract breaches, but that is an exception, not the rule. The most common example is a bad faith breach of an insurance contract by the insurer — a refusal to pay insurance benefits obviously owed under the policy. Allowing punitive damages is a policy judgment that the particular kind of breach ought to be deterred in all cases because the benefit society gains from deterring the breach outweighs any costs. If some contract breaches are considered *per se* undesirable, it is logical to carve them out as an exception from the general rule that there are no punitive damages for contract breaches.

Procedure

Punitive damages are available for the most undesirable misconduct. But even then, legislatures reserve them for only the most egregious examples. In California, for instance, punitive damages cannot be awarded unless a jury finds that the defendant committed an intentional wrong and then makes the additional finding that in doing so the defendant acted with "fraud, malice, or oppression." (Cal. Civil Code, section 3294.) Georgia requires that "the defendant's actions constitute willful misconduct, malice, fraud, wantonness, oppression, or that entire want of care which would raise the presumption of conscious indifference to consequences." (O.C.G.A., section 51-12-5.1.) Alaska allows punitive damages only on a showing that "the defendant's conduct was outrageous, including acts done with malice or bad motives, or reckless indifference to the interest of another person." (Alaska Statutes, 09.17.020.) Most other jurisdictions have similar statutory provisions.

And states typically want to be quite certain that the defendant has in fact engaged in the conduct for which the punishment is being administered. For that reason, a high standard of proof is imposed for punitive damages. Before a defendant can be held liable for punitive damages, the jury must find *by clear and convincing evidence* that the defendant acted with the requisite malice, oppression, or the like. (See, for example, the California, Georgia, and Alaska code sections cited above, which all impose that standard.) The clear and convincing standard of proof is significantly higher than the preponderance of the evidence standard by which other facts are proven in civil cases, which requires only that the jury believe something is more likely true than not (sometimes illustrated with the example of placing a feather on one side of evenly balanced scales).

Policy Issues

Punitive damages are a useful tool for deterring conduct lawmakers deem most harmful to society. But they have been criticized as providing a windfall to plaintiffs and exposing defendants to liability that is disproportionate to culpability. Many states have responded to such criticism by enacting legislation requiring a split recovery or by imposing caps on punitive damages. Split recovery statutes mandate that a punitive damages award be divided between the state and the plaintiff. Caps set a maximum amount of punitive damages that can be imposed against a defendant, often around $250,000.

One context in which punitive damages are viewed as a necessary safeguard in modern society is in preventing large corporations from putting business interests ahead of consumer safety — by knowingly marketing a dangerously defective product, for example. Imposing punitive damages on corporations creates its own set of issues, however. Corporations can act only through people, but it may be unfair to punish an entire company for the isolated misconduct of one bad actor. Punitive damages will therefore usually be imposed against a corporation only when the party that engaged in the misconduct is a managing agent, someone with significant control over company policy. There is also the matter of amount: even a punitive damages award that on its face seems quite large, even excessive, might be insufficient to effectively deter a large corporation that generates many millions of dollars in profit annually.

Whether in the case of corporate or individual defendants, punitive damages require courts to strike a careful balance that preserves the underlying purpose of punishment and deterrence while avoiding unfair and disproportionate liability.

Introductory Note — *Molenaar v. United Cattle Co.*

In *Molenaar*, a jury awarded the plaintiff compensatory and punitive damages for conversion, an intentional tort. The defendant moved for judgment notwithstanding the verdict, contending that punitive damages were not available because the only harm was to property. The trial judge agreed and vacated the punitive damages award. On appeal, the court considers whether punitive damages can be recovered under Minnesota law for an intentional tort that results in injury to property.

THINGS TO THINK ABOUT while reading *Molenaar v. United Cattle Co.*:

1. What sort of conduct should allow for an entitlement to punitive damages?

2. Why are punitive damages a necessary component of a civil remedial system? Or are they?

Molenaar v. United Cattle Co.

Minnesota Court of Appeals
553 N.W.2d 424 (1996)

LANSING, Judge.

On appeal from the denial of posttrial motions in a livestock conversion action, we revisit the issue of punitive damages for property injury and review the jury determinations on liability and compensatory damages. We reverse and remand the entry of JNOV on punitive damages and affirm the district court's denial of JNOV on liability and its denial of JNOV, a new trial, or remittitur on compensatory damages.

Facts

A jury found United Cattle Company liable for converting Orville Molenaar's sixty-five heifers. The verdict awarded both compensatory and punitive damages. Molenaar had purchased the heifers in Montana in 1994 and transported them to Minnesota for feeding, care, and breeding at Michael Frank's farm. Frank and Molenaar had similar arrangements in previous years. Molenaar's cattle were identified by the blue ear tags they wore at the farm.

Frank also kept, cared for, and bred cattle for United Cattle Company. White and yellow ear tags identified United's cattle. United and Frank's relationship deteriorated and United brought a replevin action against Frank, alleging breach of contract and conversion of its cattle. The district court granted United a replevin order on October 11, 1994, authorizing United to take immediate possession of its cattle including 306 heifers. The next day Dana Hansen, vice president of United, arrived at Frank's farm to take possession of the cattle. Frank explained to Hansen that sixty-five of the heifers on the farm belonged to Molenaar, but Hansen took all of the cattle, including Molenaar's heifers.

Frank told Molenaar on October 16 that United had taken Molenaar's heifers. The next day Molenaar contacted United's attorney to find the cattle. The attorney refused to tell him where the cattle were kept. Molenaar sent the attorney a photograph of his heifers and a copy of his original purchase invoice. Molenaar, still attempting to locate the cattle, then contacted Hansen. Hansen also refused to tell Molenaar where the cattle had been taken. Neither the attorney nor Hansen asked for any documentation of ownership. United sold Molenaar's heifers on November 18, 1994, and they cannot be traced.

Molenaar sued United for conversion, alleging that its actions caused severe financial injury, and moved to amend his complaint to add a claim for punitive damages. The district court permitted the amendment, and the jury awarded $400,000 in punitive damages in addition to $59,375 in compensatory damages for conversion.

United moved for JNOV on liability, compensatory damages, and punitive damages. The district court granted JNOV on punitive damages, holding that these damages could only be recovered for personal injury. . . .

Analysis

I

Punitive damages have been permitted in conversion actions since the formation of the state. *Huebsch v. Larson,* 291 Minn. 361, 364 (1971); *Matteson v. Munroe,* 80 Minn. 340, 342–43, (1900); *Lynd v. Picket,* 7 Minn. 184 (1862); *Minnesota Valley Country Club v. Gill,* 356 N.W.2d 356, 363 (Minn.App.1984). Permitting punitive damages in these actions demonstrates the state's strong policy against malicious, willful, or reckless disregard of another's property rights. *Huebsch,* 291 Minn. at 364.

Punitive damages "further a State's legitimate interests in punishing unlawful conduct and deterring its repetition." *BMW of N. Am. v. Gore,* 517 U.S. 559 (1996). A substantial body of this state's jurisprudence on intentional torts has recognized punitive damages as a proper remedy for intentional violations of the rights of others.

In addition to punitive damages as a remedy evolved through caselaw, the Minnesota legislature has specifically permitted punitive damages for misconduct that injures the rights of others. Some states, including Minnesota, have limited legislatively created punitive damages in amount. State legislatures have imposed other reforms, such as avoiding a windfall by requiring the punitive damages to be paid to the state rather than a litigant.

In 1980 the supreme court extended the scope of punitive damages in Minnesota
to include strict products-liability cases. *Gryc v. Dayton-Hudson Corp.,* 297 N.W.2d
727, 741 (Minn. 1980). This extension shifted the focus from a defendant's conduct
to the severity of a plaintiff's injuries and removed the requirement of clear and
convincing evidence of willful indifference to the rights or safety of others. In 1982
the court limited this expansion by prohibiting punitive damages in strict products-
liability cases absent personal injury. *Eisert v. Greenberg Roofing & Sheet Metal,*
314 N.W.2d 226, 229 (Minn.1982) (noting the "extraordinary measure of deterrence"
of punitive damages in strict liability cases).

The court subsequently applied this limitation to all products-liability claims
whether or not the cause of action was based on strict liability. *Independent Sch.
Dist. No. 622 v. Keene Corp.,* 511 N.W.2d 728, 732 (Minn.1994) (denying punitive
damages for asbestos cleanup). The court looked beyond the formal pleadings and
restricted punitive damages stemming from products liability to circumstances
involving personal injury.

This approach to punitive damages in products-liability claims mirrors the
supreme court's analysis of punitive damages for breach of contract. Traditionally,
punitive damages were not available for breach of contract. *Minnesota-Iowa T.V. Co.
v. Watonwan T.V. Improvement Ass'n,* 294 N.W.2d 297, 309 (Minn.1980). But when
an independent tort accompanies a breach of contract, a plaintiff may seek punitive
damages. The supreme court looks beyond the formal pleadings and limits punitive damages to those cases involving a willful independent tort, not merely willful
breach of contract. *Barr/Nelson, Inc. v. Tonto's, Inc.,* 336 N.W.2d 46, 52 (Minn.1983).
The focus falls on the underlying tort, rather than the nature of damages or the specific legal pleadings. *See Cherne Indus. v. Grounds & Assocs.,* 278 N.W.2d 81, 95–96
(Minn.1979) (assessing evidence of tortious interference with contract). . . .

In addition to authorizing punitive damages in civil actions, the statute specifically permits punitive damages for "deliberate disregard for the *rights* or safety of
others." Minn.Stat. § 549.20, subd. 1 (emphasis added). Violations of rights do not
necessarily involve personal injuries. Conversion, for instance, generally violates
property *rights* without personal harm to the owner. By including disregard of *rights*
as well as disregard of safety, the statute permits punitive damages for both property
damage and personal injury. Any court decision that abolished punitive damages
for disregarding the rights of others would eviscerate the statute.

Finally, this reading is consistent with the philosophy that underlies punitive
damages. The purpose of punitive damages is "to both punish and deter according
to the gravity of the act giving rise to a punitive damage award * * *." *Rosenbloom v.
Flygare,* 501 N.W.2d 597, 601 (Minn.1993). Punitive damages "are imposed to punish
the defendant and to deter him, and others like him, from intentional wrongs and

deliberate disregard of the safety or rights of others." *Id.* at 602. The focus lies on the defendant's wrongful conduct that must be deterred, not the specific outcome of the conduct.

Punitive damages implement this philosophy by economically deterring wrongful interference with the rights of others. Absent punitive damages, criminal prosecution and tainted goodwill remain the only sanctions moderating the conduct of individuals or companies that would seek to wrongfully deprive others of their property through fraud or trickery. *See Gore,* 517 U.S. at — —, 116 S.Ct. at 1599 ("exemplary damages imposed on a defendant should reflect 'the enormity of his offense.' *Day v. Woodworth,* 54 U.S. (13 How.) 363, 371, 14 L.Ed. 181 (1852). * * * '[T]rickery and deceit' are more reprehensible than negligence.") (quoting *TXO Prod. Corp. v. Alliance Resources,* 509 U.S. 443, 462 (1993)). Absent punitive damages, one who intentionally and wrongfully takes another's property has little to fear. The worst civil consequence is that the converted property must be returned to its proper owner. Even this remedy must be discounted by the possibility that the owner will not seek legal recovery or will not prevail. Universal abolition of punitive damages for property damage dramatically improves the profitability of theft and diminishes society's reenforcement of personal accountability. Some states have restricted or otherwise restructured punitive damages, but we are aware of no state that has abolished punitive damages for injuries to property while allowing punitive damages for personal injury. . . .

The facts, taken in the light most favorable to the jury's verdict, demonstrate an intentional violation of property rights. . . . We therefore reinstate the jury's determination that punitive damages are appropriate but remand to the district court to complete the statutory procedures. Punitive damages are an exceptional remedy and even when permitted must be reviewed by the district court. Minn.Stat. §549.20, subd. 5. The district court must make specific findings on the misconduct's severity, profitability, duration, concealment, the defendant's awareness, attitude, and financial condition, the number of employees involved, and the effect of punitive damages. Consequently, we remand to the district court for the findings required by section 549.20. . . .

Decision

. . . .

Affirmed in part, reversed in part, and remanded.

* * *

Problem 28

Punitive damages serve to deter intentional and egregious misconduct. Should punitive damages be available in the following scenario?

A fast food restaurant serves its coffee extremely hot, about 180 degrees Fahrenheit. A safety consultant warns the restaurant that such a high temperature presents an extreme risk of causing burns on contact with skin. The restaurant continues to serve the coffee at that temperature, however, and several customers are indeed burned when coffee spills on their hands. The management considers implementing a new policy requiring its restaurants to serve the coffee at a lower temperature but ultimately decides against it, believing the restaurants may lose business if customers find the coffee is lukewarm. The following month, a customer orders a coffee to go and is severely burned when she gets in her car and puts the cup between her legs while putting on her seatbelt. Her legs are burned so badly she requires skin grafts. She sues the restaurant and seeks compensatory and punitive damages.

CA-fraud, malice or oppression

Introductory Note — *Grimshaw v. Ford Motor Co.* and *Pacific Gas & Electric Co. v. Superior Court*

Grimshaw presents a classic example of egregious corporate misconduct: continuing to market a defective car (the infamous Pinto) even though management knew it posed a significant danger of causing death or serious injury to its occupants.

Pacific Gas & Electric Co. is a more recent case of corporate malfeasance, also with devastating effects: a utility company's failure to maintain its equipment resulted in wildfires that destroyed homes and killed people.

Punitive damages were allowed in *Grimshaw* but not in *Pacific Gas & Electric Co.* The different outcomes hinged on the role each corporation's managing agents played in causing the harm and how much culpability they should be assigned.

THINGS TO THINK ABOUT while reading *Grimshaw v. Ford Motor Co.* and *Pacific Gas & Electric Co. v. Superior Court*:

1. What is the test to determine whether a corporation can be liable for punitive damages?

2. Why was the evidence sufficient for corporate liability in *Grimshaw* but not in *Pacific Gas & Electric*?

Grimshaw v. Ford Motor Co.

California Court of Appeal
119 Cal.App.3d 757 (1981)

TAMURA, Acting Presiding Justice.

A 1972 Ford Pinto hatchback automobile unexpectedly stalled on a freeway, erupting into flames when it was rear ended by a car proceeding in the same direction. Mrs. Lilly Gray, the driver of the Pinto, suffered fatal burns and 13-year-old Richard Grimshaw, a passenger in the Pinto, suffered severe and permanently disfiguring burns on his face and entire body. Grimshaw and the heirs of Mrs. Gray (Grays) sued Ford Motor Company and others. Following a six-month jury trial, verdicts were returned in favor of plaintiffs against Ford Motor Company. Grimshaw was awarded $2,516,000 compensatory damages and $125 million punitive damages; the Grays were awarded $559,680 in compensatory damages. On Ford's motion for a new trial, Grimshaw was required to remit all but $3 ½ million of the punitive award as a condition of denial of the motion.

Ford appeals from the judgment and from an order denying its motion for a judgment notwithstanding the verdict as to punitive damages. . . .

Facts

. . . The Accident

In November 1971, the Grays purchased a new 1972 Pinto hatchback manufactured by Ford in October 1971. The Grays had trouble with the car from the outset. During the first few months of ownership, they had to return the car to the dealer for repairs a number of times. Their car problems included excessive gas and oil consumption, down shifting of the automatic transmission, lack of power, and occasional stalling. It was later learned that the stalling and excessive fuel consumption were caused by a heavy carburetor float.

On May 28, 1972, Mrs. Gray, accompanied by 13-year-old Richard Grimshaw, set out in the Pinto from Anaheim for Barstow to meet Mr. Gray. The Pinto was then six months old and had been driven approximately 3,000 miles. Mrs. Gray stopped in San Bernardino for gasoline, got back onto the freeway (Interstate 15) and proceeded toward her destination at 60–65 miles per hour. As she approached the Route 30 off-ramp where traffic was congested, she moved from the outer fast lane to the middle lane of the freeway. Shortly after this lane change, the Pinto suddenly stalled and coasted to a halt in the middle lane. It was later established that the carburetor float had become so saturated with gasoline that it suddenly sank, opening the float chamber and causing the engine to flood and stall. A car traveling immediately behind the Pinto was able to swerve and pass it but the driver of a 1962 Ford Galaxie was unable to avoid colliding with the Pinto. The Galaxie had been traveling from 50 to 55 miles per hour but before the impact had been braked to a speed of from 28 to 37 miles per hour.

At the moment of impact, the Pinto caught fire and its interior was engulfed in flames. According to plaintiffs' expert, the impact of the Galaxie had driven the Pinto's gas tank forward and caused it to be punctured by the flange or one of the bolts on the differential housing so that fuel sprayed from the punctured tank and entered the passenger compartment through gaps resulting from the separation of the rear wheel well sections from the floor pan. By the time the Pinto came to rest after the collision, both occupants had sustained serious burns. When they emerged from the vehicle, their clothing was almost completely burned off. Mrs. Gray died a few days later of congestive heart failure as a result of the burns. Grimshaw managed to survive but only through heroic medical measures. He has undergone numerous and extensive surgeries and skin grafts and must undergo additional surgeries over the next 10 years. He lost portions of several fingers on his left hand and portions of his left ear, while his face required many skin grafts from various portions of his body. Because Ford does not contest the amount of compensatory damages awarded to Grimshaw and the Grays, no purpose would be served by further description of the injuries suffered by Grimshaw or the damages sustained by the Grays.

Design of the Pinto Fuel System:

In 1968, Ford began designing a new subcompact automobile which ultimately became the Pinto. Mr. Iacocca, then a Ford Vice President, conceived the project and was its moving force. Ford's objective was to build a car at or below 2,000 pounds to sell for no more than $2,000.

Ordinarily marketing surveys and preliminary engineering studies precede the styling of a new automobile line. Pinto, however, was a rush project, so that styling preceded engineering and dictated engineering design to a greater degree than usual. Among the engineering decisions dictated by styling was the placement of the fuel tank. It was then the preferred practice in Europe and Japan to locate the gas tank over the rear axle in subcompacts because a small vehicle has less "crush space" between the rear axle and the bumper than larger cars. The Pinto's styling, however, required the tank to be placed behind the rear axle leaving only 9 or 10 inches of "crush space" far less than in any other American automobile or Ford overseas subcompact. In addition, the Pinto was designed so that its bumper was little more than a chrome strip, less substantial than the bumper of any other American car produced then or later. The Pinto's rear structure also lacked reinforcing members known as "hat sections" (2 longitudinal side members) and horizontal cross-members running between them such as were found in cars of larger unitized construction and in all automobiles produced by Ford's overseas operations. The absence of the reinforcing members rendered the Pinto less crush resistant than other vehicles. Finally, the differential housing selected for the Pinto had an exposed flange and a line of exposed bolt heads. These protrusions were sufficient to puncture a gas tank driven forward against the differential upon rear impact.

Crash Tests

During the development of the Pinto, prototypes were built and tested. Some were "mechanical prototypes" which duplicated mechanical features of the design but not its appearance while others, referred to as "engineering prototypes," were true duplicates of the design car. These prototypes as well as two production Pintos were crash tested by Ford to determine, among other things, the integrity of the fuel system in rear-end accidents. Ford also conducted the tests to see if the Pinto as designed would meet a proposed federal regulation requiring all automobiles manufactured in 1972 to be able to withstand a 20-mile-per-hour fixed barrier impact without significant fuel spillage and all automobiles manufactured after January 1, 1973, to withstand a 30-mile-per-hour fixed barrier impact without significant fuel spillage.

The crash tests revealed that the Pinto's fuel system as designed could not meet the 20-mile-per-hour proposed standard. Mechanical prototypes struck from the rear with a moving barrier at 21-miles-per-hour caused the fuel tank to be driven forward and to be punctured, causing fuel leakage in excess of the standard prescribed by the proposed regulation. A production Pinto crash tested at 21-miles-per-hour into a fixed barrier caused the fuel neck to be torn from the gas tank and the tank to be punctured by a bolt head on the differential housing. In at least one test, spilled fuel entered the driver's compartment through gaps resulting from the separation of the seams joining the real wheel wells to the floor pan. The seam separation was occasioned by the lack of reinforcement in the rear structure and insufficient welds of the wheel wells to the floor pan. . . .

The Cost To Remedy Design Deficiencies

When a prototype failed the fuel system integrity test, the standard of care for engineers in the industry was to redesign and retest it. The vulnerability of the production Pinto's fuel tank at speeds of 20 and 30-miles-per-hour fixed barrier tests could have been remedied by inexpensive "fixes," but Ford produced and sold the Pinto to the public without doing anything to remedy the defects. Design changes that would have enhanced the integrity of the fuel tank system at relatively little cost per car included the following: Longitudinal side members and cross members at $2.40 and $1.80, respectively; a single shock absorbent "flak suit" to protect the tank at $4; a tank within a tank and placement of the tank over the axle at $5.08 to.$5.79; a nylon bladder within the tank at $5.25 to $8; placement of the tank over the axle surrounded with a protective barrier at a cost of $9.95 per car; substitution of a rear axle with a smooth differential housing at a cost of $2.10; imposition of a protective shield between the differential housing and the tank at $2.35; improvement and reenforcement of the bumper at $2.60; addition of eight inches of crush space a cost of $6.40. Equipping the car with a reinforced rear structure, smooth axle, improved bumper and additional crush space at a total cost of $15.30 would have made the fuel tank safe in a 34 to 38-mile-per-hour rear end collision by a vehicle the size of the Ford Galaxie. If, in addition to the foregoing, a bladder or tank within a tank were used or if the tank were protected with a shield, it would have been safe in a 40 to 45-mile-per-hour rear impact. If the tank had been located over the rear axle, it would have been safe in a rear impact at 50 miles per hour or more.

Management's Decision To Go Forward With Knowledge Of Defects:

The idea for the Pinto, as has been noted, was conceived by Mr. Iacocca, then Executive Vice President of Ford. The feasibility study was conducted under the supervision of Mr. Robert Alexander, Vice President of Car Engineering. Ford's Product Planning Committee, whose members included Mr. Iacocca, Mr. Robert Alexander, and Mr. Harold MacDonald, Ford's Group Vice President of Car Engineering, approved the Pinto's concept and made the decision to go forward with the project. During the course of the project, regular product review meetings were held which were chaired by Mr. MacDonald and attended by Mr. Alexander. As the project approached actual production, the engineers responsible for the components of the project "signed off" to their immediate supervisors who in turn "signed off" to their superiors and so on up the chain of command until the entire project was approved for public release by Vice Presidents Alexander and MacDonald and ultimately by Mr. Iacocca. The Pinto crash tests results had been forwarded up the chain of command to the ultimate decision-makers and were known to the Ford officials who decided to go forward with production. . . .

Punitive Damages

Ford contends that it was entitled to a judgment notwithstanding the verdict on the issue of punitive damages[.]

(1) "Malice" Under Civil Code Section 3294

The concept of punitive damages is rooted in the English common law and is a settled principle of the common law of this country. (Owen, Punitive Damages in Products Liability Litigation, 74 Mich.L.Rev. 1258, 1262–1263 (hereafter Owen); Mallor & Roberts, Punitive Damages, Towards A Principled Approach, 31 Hastings L.J. 639, 642–643 (hereafter Mallor & Roberts); note, Exemplary Damages in the Law of Torts, 70 Harv.L.Rev. 517, 518–520.) The doctrine was a part of the common law of this state long before the Civil Code was adopted. When our laws were codified in 1872, the doctrine was incorporated in Civil Code section 3294, which at the time of trial read: "In an action for the breach of an obligation not arising from contract, where the defendant has been guilty of oppression, fraud, or malice, express or implied, the plaintiff, in addition to the actual damages, may recover damages for the sake of example and by way of punishing the defendant."

Ford argues that "malice" as used in section 3294 and as interpreted by our Supreme Court in Davis v. Hearst, 160 Cal. 143, requires animus malus or evil motive an intention to injure the person harmed and that the term is therefore conceptually incompatible with an unintentional tort such as the manufacture and marketing of a defectively designed product. This contention runs counter to our decisional law. As this court recently noted, numerous California cases after Davis v. Hearst, supra, have interpreted the term "malice" as used in section 3294 to include, not only a malicious intention to injure the specific person harmed, but conduct evincing "a conscious disregard of the probability that the actor's conduct will result in injury to others." (Dawes v. Superior Court, 111 Cal.App.3d 82, 88.)

In Taylor v. Superior Court, supra, 24 Cal.3d 890, our high court's most recent pronouncement on the subject of punitive damages, the court observed that the availability of punitive damages has not been limited to cases in which there is an actual intent to harm plaintiff or others. The court concurred with the Searle (G. D. Searle & Co. v. Superior Court, supra, 49 Cal.App.3d 22) court's suggestion that conscious disregard of the safety of others is an appropriate description of the animus malus required by Civil Code section 3294, adding: "In order to justify an award of punitive damages on this basis, the plaintiff must establish that the defendant was aware of the probable dangerous consequences of his conduct, and that he wilfully and deliberately failed to avoid those consequences." (Id., 24 Cal.3d at pp. 895–896.)

Ford attempts to minimize the precedential force of the foregoing decisions on the ground they failed to address the position now advanced by Ford that intent to harm a particular person or persons is required because that was what the lawmakers had in mind in 1872 when they adopted Civil Code section 3294. Ford argues that the Legislature was thinking in terms of traditional intentional torts, such as, libel, slander, assault and battery, malicious prosecution, trespass, etc., and could not have intended the statute to be applied to a products liability case arising out of a design defect in a mass produced automobile because neither strict products liability nor mass produced automobiles were known in 1872.

... The interpretation of the word "malice" as used in section 3294 to encompass conduct evincing callous and conscious disregard of public safety by those who manufacture and market mass produced articles is consonant with and furthers the objectives of punitive damages. The primary purposes of punitive damages are punishment and deterrence of like conduct by the wrongdoer and others. (Civ.Code, s 3294; Owen, supra, pp. 1277, 1279–1287; Mallor & Roberts, supra, pp. 648–650.) In the traditional noncommercial intentional tort, compensatory damages alone may serve as an effective deterrent against future wrongful conduct but in commerce related torts, the manufacturer may find it more profitable to treat compensatory damages as a part of the cost of doing business rather than to remedy the defect. (Owens, supra, p. 1291; Note, Mass Liability and Punitive Damages Overkill, 30 Hastings L.J. 1797, 1802.) Deterrence of such "objectionable corporate policies" serves one of the principal purposes of Civil Code section 3294. (Egan v. Mutual of Omaha Ins. Co., 24 Cal.3d 809, 820.) Governmental safety standards and the criminal law have failed to provide adequate consumer protection against the manufacture and distribution of defective products. (Owen, supra, pp. 1288–1289; Mallor & Roberts, supra, pp. 655–656; Developments in the Law: Corporate Crime, 92 Harvard L.Rev. 1227, 1369.) Punitive damages thus remain as the most effective remedy for consumer protection against defectively designed mass produced articles. They provide a motive for private individuals to enforce rules of law and enable them to recoup the expenses of doing so which can be considerable and not otherwise recoverable.

Sufficiency of the Evidence to Support the Finding of Malice and Corporate Responsibility

Ford contends that its motion for judgment notwithstanding the verdict should have been granted because the evidence was insufficient to support a finding of malice or corporate responsibility for such malice. The record fails to support the contention.

"The rules circumscribing the power of a trial judge to grant a motion for judgment notwithstanding the verdict are well established. The power to grant such a motion is identical to the power to grant a directed verdict; the judge cannot weigh the evidence or assess the credibility of witnesses; if the evidence is conflicting or if several reasonable inferences may be drawn, the motion should be denied; the motion may be granted ""only if it appears from the evidence, viewed in the light most favorable to the party securing the verdict, that there is no substantial evidence to support the verdict."" (Clemmer v. Hartford Insurance Co. (1978) 22 Cal.3d 865, 877–878.) There was ample evidence to support a finding of malice and Ford's responsibility for malice.

Through the results of the crash tests Ford knew that the Pinto's fuel tank and rear structure would expose consumers to serious injury or death in a 20 to 30 mile-per-hour collision. There was evidence that Ford could have corrected the hazardous design defects at minimal cost but decided to defer correction of the shortcomings by engaging in a cost-benefit analysis balancing human lives and limbs against corporate profits. Ford's institutional mentality was shown to be one of callous indifference to public safety. There was substantial evidence that Ford's conduct constituted "conscious disregard" of the probability of injury to members of the consuming public.

Ford's argument that there can be no liability for punitive damages because there was no evidence of corporate ratification of malicious misconduct is equally without merit. California follows the Restatement rule that punitive damages can be awarded against a principal because of an action of an agent if, but only if, "'(a) the principal authorized the doing and the manner of the act, or (b) the agent was unfit and the principal was reckless in employing him, or (c) the agent was employed in a managerial capacity and was acting in the scope of employment, or (d) the principal or a managerial agent of the principal ratified or approved the act.' (Rest.2d Torts (Tent. Draft No. 19, 1973) s 909.)" (Egan v. Mutual of Omaha Ins. Co., supra, 24 Cal.3d 809, 822.) The present case comes within one or both of the categories described in subdivisions (c) and (d).

There is substantial evidence that management was aware of the crash tests showing the vulnerability of the Pinto's fuel tank to rupture at low speed rear impacts with consequent significant risk of injury or death of the occupants by fire. There was testimony from several sources that the test results were forwarded up the chain of command; Vice President Robert Alexander admitted to Mr. Copp that he was aware of the test results; Vice President Harold MacDonald, who chaired the product review meetings, was present at one of those meetings at which a report on the crash tests was considered and a decision was made to defer corrective action; and it may be inferred that Mr. Alexander, a regular attender of the product review meetings, was also present at that meeting. MacDonald and Alexander were manifestly managerial employees possessing the discretion to make "decisions that will ultimately determine corporate policy."

There was also evidence that Harold Johnson, an Assistant Chief Engineer of Research, and Mr. Max Jurosek, Chief Chassis Engineer, were aware of the results of the crash tests and the defects in the Pinto's fuel tank system. Ford contends those two individuals did not occupy managerial positions because Mr. Copp testified that they admitted awareness of the defects but told him they were powerless to change the rear-end design of the Pinto. It may be inferred from the testimony, however, that the two engineers had approached management about redesigning the Pinto or that, being aware of management's attitude, they decided to do nothing. In either case the decision not to take corrective action was made by persons exercising managerial authority. Whether an employee acts in a "managerial capacity" does not necessarily depend on his "level" in the corporate hierarchy. (Id., at p. 822.) As the Egan court said: "'Defendant should not be allowed to insulate itself from liability by giving an employee a nonmanagerial title and relegating to him crucial policy decisions.'" (Id., at p. 823.)

While much of the evidence was necessarily circumstantial, there was substantial evidence from which the jury could reasonably find that Ford's management decided to proceed with the production of the Pinto with knowledge of test results revealing design defects which rendered the fuel tank extremely vulnerable on rear impact at low speeds and endangered the safety and lives of the occupants. Such conduct constitutes corporate malice. (See Toole v. Richardson-Merrell, Inc., supra, 251 Cal.App.2d 689, 713.) . . .

Disposition

The judgment in Carmen Gray, et al. v. Ford Motor Company is affirmed.

* * *

Pacific Gas & Electric Co. v. Superior Court
California Court of Appeal
24 Cal.App.5th 1150 (2018)

RENNER, J.

This coordinated proceeding arises out of the Butte Fire, a devastating wildfire that swept through Calaveras and Amador Counties in September 2015. The fire started when a tree came into contact with an overhead power line owned and operated by petitioners Pacific Gas and Electric Company and PG&E Corporation (together, PG&E or the company). Real parties in interest (plaintiffs) brought suit against PG&E, seeking punitive damages under Public Utilities Code section 2106 and Civil Code section 3294. PG&E sought summary adjudication of plaintiffs' request for punitive damages under section 3294 only. The trial court denied the motion.

PG&E seeks writ relief from the trial court's order. We conclude there are no triable issues of fact which, if resolved in plaintiffs' favor, could subject PG&E to punitive damages under section 3294. Accordingly, we grant the petition.

I. Background

A. The Butte Fire

The Butte Fire started on September 9, 2015, near Butte Mountain Road in Jackson, California. The fire spread rapidly through drought-stricken Amador and Calaveras counties. By the time the blaze was contained some three weeks later, the fire had consumed more than 70,868 acres, damaging hundreds of structures and claiming two lives. It is undisputed that the fire started when a gray pine (the subject tree) came into contact with one of PG&E's power lines.

B. The Litigation

More than 2,050 plaintiffs brought suit against PG&E and others. Plaintiffs' complaints were consolidated in a judicial council coordinated proceeding in Sacramento Superior Court. A master complaint was filed on behalf of plaintiffs (many of whom have been named as real parties in interest) who suffered personal injuries and losses to real and personal property as a result of the fire. The master complaint names PG&E, ACRT, Inc. (ACRT) and Trees, Inc. as defendants. According to the master complaint, ACRT and Trees, Inc. (together, contractors) provided vegetation management services to PG&E as independent contractors.

The master complaint alleges that PG&E and the contractors failed to properly maintain the power line and adjacent vegetation. According to the master complaint, the events leading to the Butte Fire were set into motion when two trees were removed from a stand near the power line, leaving the subject tree exposed and unsupported. The master complaint alleges that the removal of the two trees left the subject tree open and leaning to the south, towards the path of the sun and the nearby power line. The subject tree is alleged to have been approximately 44 feet tall and seven inches in diameter. Under the circumstances, the master complaint avers, it was foreseeable that the subject tree would fail and come into contact with the power line, producing sparks that could — and tragically, did — ignite a wildfire.

The master complaint asserts causes of action against PG&E for negligence, wrongful death and survival, inverse condemnation, public nuisance, private nuisance, premises liability, trespass, violation of Public Utilities Code section 2106 and violation of Health and Safety Code section 13007. The master complaint seeks punitive damages from PG&E under Public Utilities Code section 2106 and section 3294.

C. The Motion for Summary Adjudication

PG&E moved for summary adjudication of the request for punitive damages under section 3924, arguing that plaintiffs could not raise a triable issue of material fact to support the request under any theory. In support of the motion, PG&E presented evidence that contractors' employees visited the area near the subject tree several times over the course of the year preceding the fire, but did not identify the subject tree as a danger or report any compliance issue to PG&E. PG&E also presented evidence that the company has expended substantial resources to establish vegetation management programs intended to prevent or minimize the risk of wildfire. According to PG&E, the existence of such programs affirmatively disproves any inference that PG&E acted with conscious disregard for the safety of others, thereby negating a necessary element of plaintiffs' claim for punitive damages.

Plaintiffs opposed the motion, arguing that contractors' employees are unqualified and improperly trained, and PG&E's vegetation management programs are superficial and ineffective. According to plaintiffs, these programs are little more than window dressing, designed to create the appearance of an effective risk management program and attention to public safety. . . .

[T]he trial court denied PG&E's motion for summary adjudication.

II. Discussion

PG&E contends the trial court erred in denying the motion for summary adjudication of plaintiffs' request for punitive damages under section 3294. We agree.

Standard of Proof

Punitive damages may be recovered under section 3294 "where it is proven by *clear and convincing evidence* that the defendant has been guilty of oppression, fraud, or malice." (§ 3294, subd. (a), italics added.) . . .

Under the clear and convincing standard, the evidence must be "'so clear as to leave no substantial doubt' and 'sufficiently strong to command the unhesitating assent of every reasonable mind.'" (*Shade Foods, Inc. v. Innovative Products Sales & Marketing, Inc.* (2000) 78 Cal.App.4th 847, 891.) . . . Summary judgment or summary adjudication "on the issue of punitive damages is proper" only "when no reasonable jury could find the plaintiff's evidence to be clear and convincing proof of malice, fraud or oppression." (*Ibid.*)

Section 3294

As noted, section 3294 permits an award of punitive damages "where it is proven by clear and convincing evidence that the defendant has been guilty of oppression, fraud, or malice." (§ 3294, subd. (a).) Plaintiffs contend PG&E acted with malice.

Malice is defined by section 3294, subdivision (c)(1) as "conduct which is intended by the defendant to cause injury to the plaintiff or despicable conduct which is carried on by the defendant with a willful and conscious disregard of the rights or safety of others." "Despicable conduct" is conduct that is "'so vile, base, contemptible, miserable, wretched or loathsome that it would be looked down upon and despised by most ordinary decent people." (*Mock v. Michigan Millers Mutual Ins. Co.* (1992) 4 Cal.App.4th 306, 330.) Such conduct has been described as having the character of outrage frequently associated with crime. (*Tomaselli v. Transamerica Ins. Co.* (1994) 25 Cal.App.4th 1269, 1287.) "Conscious disregard" means "that the defendant was aware of the probable dangerous consequences of his conduct, and that he willfully and deliberately failed to avoid those consequences." (*Hoch v. Allied-Signal, Inc.*

(1994) 24 Cal.App.4th 48, 61.) Put another way, the defendant must "have *actual knowledge* of the risk of harm it is creating and, in the face of that knowledge, fail to take steps it knows will reduce or eliminate the risk of harm." (*Ehrhardt v. Brunswick, Inc.* (1986) 186 Cal.App.3d 734, 742.)

Section 3294's malice requirement has evolved over time. As another panel of this court explained in *Lackner v. North* (2006) 135 Cal.App.4th 1188, 1210–1211 (*Lackner*): "The definition of malice has not always included the requirement of willful and despicable conduct. Prior to 1980, section 3294 did not define malice. It was construed to mean malice in fact, which could be proven directly or by implication [citations] and could be established by conduct that was done only with 'a conscious disregard of the safety of others.'"

Our Supreme Court addressed the then existing malice requirement in *Taylor v. Superior Court* (1979) 24 Cal.3d 890 (*Taylor*). In that case, the court affirmed that a conscious disregard for the rights or safety of others may constitute malice within the meaning of section 3294, but clarified that, "In order to justify an award of punitive damages on this basis, the plaintiff must establish that the defendant was aware of the probable dangerous consequences of his conduct, and that he willfully and deliberately failed to avoid those consequences."

The Legislature amended section 3294 in 1980. Among other things, the Legislature added subdivision (b), which "limited the circumstances under which an employer could be held liable for punitive damages 'based upon acts of an employee.'" (*College Hospital Inc. v. Superior Court* (1994) 8 Cal.4th 704, 712–713 ["The drafters' goals [in amending section 3294 to add subdivision (b)] were to avoid imposing punitive damages on employers who were merely negligent or reckless and to distinguish ordinary respondeat superior liability from corporate liability for punitive damages"].) The Legislature also defined the terms "oppression," "fraud," and "malice," adopting the definition of malice set forth in *Taylor*.

The Legislature revisited section 3294 in 1987. As relevant here, the Legislature increased the plaintiffs' burden of proving punitive damages to "clear and convincing evidence." As previously discussed, the statute now "'requires a finding of high probability . . .''so clear as to leave no substantial doubt,' [and] 'sufficiently strong to command the unhesitating assent of every reasonable mind.'"" (*Lackner, supra,* 135 Cal.App.4th at p. 1211.) The Legislature also refined the definition of "malice" by adding the terms "despicable" and "willful."

Our Supreme Court considered the effect of the 1987 amendments in *College Hospital,* noting: "By adding the word 'willful' to the 'conscious-disregard' prong of malice, the Legislature has arguably conformed the literal words of the statute to existing case law formulations. (See [*Taylor*], *supra,* 24 Cal.3d 890, 895–896 [malice involves awareness of dangerous consequences and a willful and deliberate failure to avoid them].) However, the statute's reference to 'despicable' conduct seems to represent a new substantive limitation on punitive damage awards. Used in its ordinary sense, the adjective 'despicable' is a powerful term that refers to circumstances that are 'base,' 'vile,' or 'contemptible.' (4 Oxford English Dict. (2d ed. 1989) p. 529.) As amended to include this word, the statute plainly indicates that absent an intent to injure the plaintiff, 'malice' requires more than a 'willful and conscious' disregard of the plaintiffs' interests. The additional component of 'despicable conduct' must be found." (*College Hospital, supra*, 8 Cal.4th at p. 725.)

"Because punitive damages are imposed 'for the sake of example and by way of punishing the defendant' (§ 3294, subd. (a)), they are typically awarded for intentional torts such as assault and battery, false imprisonment, intentional infliction of emotional distress, defamation, nuisance intentionally maintained, fraud, trespass, conversion, civil rights violations, insurer's breach of covenant of good faith, wrongful termination and job discrimination, and products liability cases." (*Lackner, supra*, 135 Cal.App.4th at p. 1212.) By contrast, "cases involving unintentional torts are far fewer and the courts have had to consider various factors in determining whether the defendant's conduct was despicable. Thus, punitive damage awards have been reversed where the defendant's conduct was merely in bad faith and overzealous, or the defendant took action to protect or minimize the injury to the plaintiff." (*Ibid.*) We have found no case considering an award of punitive damages in circumstances similar to those presented here.

Analysis

The Master Complaint

The master complaint alleges that PG&E contracted with contractors to provide vegetation management services in Amador and Calaveras counties. According to the master complaint, "Those services include, but are not limited to, assessing, monitoring, inspecting, trimming, cutting, maintaining, managing, and/or replacing vegetation surrounding and in close proximity to the lines and facilities operated by PG&E to [e]nsure that those power lines operate safely and consistently with State and Federal regulations." . . .

The master complaint alleges that "defendants" inspected a stand of gray pines near the power line in October 2014. Two trees from the exterior of the stand were targeted for removal. The two trees were removed in January 2015, leaving the subject tree exposed and leaning towards the power line. According to the master complaint, "It is commonly known that when a stand is altered and interior trees previously captured are then exposed to open spaces, they are prone to failure. It is also well understood that trees have a physical orientation toward the path of the sun and this can have significant consequences for maintaining safety." Within less than a year, the subject tree made contact with the power line and ignited the Butte Fire.

. . . The master complaint seeks punitive damages from PG&E on the grounds that it "acted willfully, wantonly, with . . . malice, and/or with a knowing, conscious disregard for the rights and or safety of others." The master complaint avers that punitive damages are appropriate "for the sake of example" and seeks an award "sufficient to punish . . . PG&E . . . for [its] despicable conduct."

PG&E's Showing

In seeking summary adjudication, PG&E submitted evidence that the company devotes significant resources to vegetation management programs, which are intended to minimize the risk of wildfire. According to PG&E, the company spends more than $190 million per year on vegetation management operations, which target a roughly 70,000 square mile service area, with nearly 135,000 miles of overhead power lines.

PG&E's vegetation management operations encompass a variety of programs and initiatives, including routine annual patrols, quality assurance and quality control programs, a vegetation management improvement initiative, a vegetation management catastrophic event memorandum account (CEMA) program, and a public safety and reliability program. . . .

Plaintiffs' Showing

In opposing summary adjudication, plaintiffs submitted evidence that PG&E views wildfire as the single greatest threat to the company's business, and the gray pine as the species of tree posing the greatest risk of wildfire. According to plaintiffs, PG&E demonstrated conscious disregard for the rights and safety of others by failing to ensure the proper functioning of risk management controls and fire mitigation measures designed to protect the public from the known risk of wildfire.

Plaintiffs Failed to Raise a Triable Issue of Material Fact

"Punitive damages are appropriate if the defendant's acts are reprehensible, fraudulent or in blatant violation of law or policy. The mere carelessness or ignorance of the defendant does not justify the imposition of punitive damages. . . . Punitive damages are proper only when the tortious conduct rises to levels of extreme indifference to the plaintiff's rights, a level which decent citizens should not have to tolerate." (*American Airlines, supra,* 96 Cal.App.4th at p. 1051.)

Even viewing the evidence as favorably to plaintiffs as we can, plaintiffs fail to demonstrate the existence of a triable issue of material fact with respect to malice. Plaintiffs argue that PG&E evinces a cavalier attitude towards public safety, which justifies an award of punitive damages. They point to numerous potential shortcomings in PG&E's risk management controls and fire mitigation efforts, raising thought-provoking questions about the efficacy of the risk and compliance committee's reporting structure, the wisdom of the decision to extend the routine patrol cycle in 2013 and loosen hiring standards for seasonal CEMA inspectors, the soundness of the company's audit methodologies and incentives for reducing patrol workload, and the timeliness of Quantum Spatial's delivery of LiDAR data. But these criticisms, whatever their merits, do not amount to clear and convincing proof that PG&E acted with malice. At most, plaintiffs' evidence shows "mere carelessness or ignorance," which is insufficient to establish malice. (*American Airlines, supra,* 96 Cal.App.4th at p. 1051.) We therefore conclude, as the trial court did, that no reasonable jury could find plaintiffs' challenges to PG&E's risk management controls and fire mitigation efforts to be clear and convincing proof of malice.

company policy

. . . We have no quarrel with the notion that an inference of corporate malice can be based on the existence of a company policy that willfully, consciously, and despicably disregards the rights and safety of others. (*Romo I, supra,* 99 Cal.App.4th at pp. 1144 [substantial evidence supported an inference of corporate malice where policymakers decided to disregard safety standards to bring product to market]; see also *Neal v. Farmers Ins. Exchange* (1978) 21 Cal.3d 910, 923 [substantial evidence supported an inference of corporate malice where insurer's denial of coverage was "part of a conscious course of conduct, firmly grounded in established company policy"].) We likewise accept the premise that corporate malice can be shown, in the case of a large corporation, "by piecing together knowledge and acts of the corporation's multitude of managing agents." (*Romo I, supra,* at p. 1141.) But plaintiffs would have us go one step further and hold that a company policy that fails to protect against a known risk of harm necessarily raises an inference of corporate malice, since the existence of the policy establishes the company's state of mind with respect to the risk. Put another way, plaintiffs would have us conclude that an unsuccessful risk management policy necessarily reflects a conscious and willful company decision to ignore or disregard the risk. This we decline to do.

. . . We acknowledge that there may be circumstances in which a company policy of outsourcing essential corporate duties to independent contractors could contribute to an inference of malice. But we cannot agree with the trial court that PG&E's unstated policy or practice of deferring to contractors to properly train their own employees could lead a reasonable jury to find by clear and convincing evidence that PG&E acted with malice. As we have suggested, nothing in the record supports an inference that PG&E willfully or consciously disregarded the need for contractors to use properly trained employees. To the contrary, PG&E required that contractors hire qualified employees, train their employees on vegetation management programs and practices, and "diligently perform all [w]ork in a proper and professional manner . . . in accordance with the approved principles of modern Arboriculture." No reasonable jury could find by clear and convincing evidence that PG&E acted with malice in failing to ensure that contractors complied with these requirements. Contrary to plaintiffs' previously articulated theory, on this record there was nothing despicable in PG&E's assumption that contractors were training their employees as required.

"'Where there is no evidence that gives rise to an inference of actual malice or conduct sufficiently outrageous to be deemed equivalent to actual malice, the trial court need not, and indeed should not, submit the issue of punitive damages to the jury.'" (*Kolstad v. American Dental Association* (1999) 527 U.S. 526, 539.) Here, there is no evidence that PG&E acted maliciously in setting policies designed to minimize the risk of wildfire or engaging contractors to assist in the company's fire mitigation efforts. Accordingly, there are no triable issues as to whether PG&E is properly subject to punitive damages under section 3294, and PG&E is entitled to summary adjudication on that issue.

III. Disposition

Let a peremptory writ of mandate issue directing the respondent court to vacate its decision denying the motion for summary adjudication of petitioners Pacific Gas and Electric Company and PG&E Corporation, and to enter a new order granting summary adjudication in favor of those parties.

* * *

Problem 29

Corporate liability for punitive damages must be premised on bad acts by someone in a position to control corporate policy. Would punitive damages be properly imposed against the corporation in the following situation?

A multinational bank offers home mortgage loans. The bank has a policy, duly ratified by its board of directors, that encourages the denial of loans to applicants in certain zip codes, in violation of anti-discrimination laws. Under the policy, the ultimate discretion to issue a loan remains with individual loan agents, who are low level, non-managerial employees. Although the loan agents can deviate from the policy if they wish, in practice nearly every applicant from the zip codes in question is rejected. A class action lawsuit is brought against the bank for unlawful discrimination and the plaintiffs seek punitive damages.

[handwritten margin notes: discriminatory loan policy; CoH.; oppression, fraud or malice; clear and convincing evidence; corporate liability]

Constitutional Limitations

The phrase "punitive damages" does not appear in the United States Constitution. But that does not mean the Constitution has nothing to say about the manner in which punitive damages can be awarded in lawsuits. The Due Process Clause, which prohibits the government from arbitrarily taking property, places certain constraints on state law punitive damage awards. (Though not everyone agrees. See, e.g., *State Farm Mutual Auto Ins. Co. v. Campbell*, 538 U.S. 408 (2003), Scalia, J., dissenting; Thomas, J., dissenting.)

The reason state law punitive damages awards implicate the constitutional right to due process has to do with the core due process principle of notice. If there is no proportionality between a defendant's conduct and the amount of punitive damages a jury imposes, the thinking goes, then a defendant has no prior notice of the consequences of the misconduct. Further, the lack of a fixed standard for calculating punitive damages means a jury's decision regarding the amount of punitive damages runs the risk of being arbitrary: the same conduct could result in very different penalties merely because of what the jury deciding the case wants to do.

Given those constitutional concerns, the Supreme Court has endeavored to provide a standard—the Court refers to it as guidance—for calculating the appropriate amount of punitive damages. As with any standard, the goal is to provide consistency and therefore fairness. That is accomplished by requiring proportionality between the harm caused by the defendant and the punishment imposed. Proportionality is measured by comparing the amount of compensatory damages awarded (which presumably reflect the degree of harm the plaintiff suffered) with the amount of punitive damages. If the punitive damages exceed the compensatory damages by too much, the punitive damages award may be considered arbitrary, and unconstitutional.

An important procedural point: the standard for determining the constitutionality of punitive damages is not something applied by the jury in deciding the case. Rather, it is applied by the trial judge post-verdict and is subject to review on appeal. It comes into play only after the jury has imposed a punitive damages award so large it may be unconstitutional; if the trial court (or an appellate court) believes it is, the jury's award will be reduced or vacated.

Introductory Note — *BMW of North America v. Gore* and *State Farm Mutual Automobile Insurance Co. v. Campbell*

Several years before *BMW of North America*, the Supreme Court had decided that the Due Process Clause prohibits "grossly excessive punishment" in civil cases. *BMW* marks the Court's first foray into fashioning a standard for determining what is grossly excessive when it comes to punitive damages.

Seven years after *BMW*, in *State Farm Mutual Automobile Insurance Co. v. Campbell*, the Court provided even more — and much more specific — guidance on the point. The specific guidance is, according to the majority opinion, grounded in constitutional principles. But dissenting justices in both cases believe the Constitution has nothing whatsoever to say about state law punitive damage awards.

THINGS TO THINK ABOUT while reading *BMW of North America v. Gore* and *State Farm Mutual Automobile Insurance Co. v. Campbell*:

1. In what ways can an excessive state law punitive damages award violate the Due Process Clause?

2. What is necessary to ensure a punitive damages award is constitutional?

3. What is the test to gauge the constitutionality of a punitive damages award?

BMW of North America v. Gore

United States Supreme Court
517 U.S. 559 (1996)

Justice STEVENS delivered the opinion of the Court.

The Due Process Clause of the Fourteenth Amendment prohibits a State from imposing a "'grossly excessive'" punishment on a tortfeasor. *TXO Production Corp. v. Alliance Resources Corp.,* 509 U.S. 443, 454 (1993) (and cases cited). The wrongdoing involved in this case was the decision by a national distributor of automobiles not to advise its dealers, and hence their customers, of predelivery damage to new cars when the cost of repair amounted to less than 3 percent of the car's suggested retail price. The question presented is whether a $2 million punitive damages award to the purchaser of one of these cars exceeds the constitutional limit.

I

In January 1990, Dr. Ira Gore, Jr. (respondent), purchased a black BMW sports sedan for $40,750.88 from an authorized BMW dealer in Birmingham, Alabama. After driving the car for approximately nine months, and without noticing any flaws in its appearance, Dr. Gore took the car to "Slick Finish," an independent detailer, to make it look "'snazzier than it normally would appear.'" 646 So.2d 619, 621 (Ala.1994). Mr. Slick, the proprietor, detected evidence that the car had been repainted. Convinced that he had been cheated, Dr. Gore brought suit against petitioner BMW of North America (BMW), the American distributor of BMW automobiles. Dr. Gore alleged, *inter alia,* that the failure to disclose that the car had been repainted constituted suppression of a material fact. The complaint prayed for $500,000 in compensatory and punitive damages, and costs.

At trial, BMW acknowledged that it had adopted a nationwide policy in 1983 concerning cars that were damaged in the course of manufacture or transportation. If the cost of repairing the damage exceeded 3 percent of the car's suggested retail price, the car was placed in company service for a period of time and then sold as used. If the repair cost did not exceed 3 percent of the suggested retail price, however, the car was sold as new without advising the dealer that any repairs had been made. Because the $601.37 cost of repainting Dr. Gore's car was only about 1.5 percent of its suggested retail price, BMW did not disclose the damage or repair to the Birmingham dealer.

Dr. Gore asserted that his repainted car was worth less than a car that had not been refinished. To prove his actual damages of $4,000, he relied on the testimony of a former BMW dealer, who estimated that the value of a repainted BMW was approximately 10 percent less than the value of a new car that had not been damaged and repaired. To support his claim for punitive damages, Dr. Gore introduced evidence that since 1983 BMW had sold 983 refinished cars as new, including 14 in Alabama, without disclosing that the cars had been repainted before sale at a cost of more than $300 per vehicle. Using the actual damage estimate of $4,000 per vehicle, Dr. Gore argued that a punitive award of $4 million would provide an appropriate penalty for selling approximately 1,000 cars for more than they were worth.

. . . The jury returned a verdict finding BMW liable for compensatory damages of $4,000. In addition, the jury assessed $4 million in punitive damages, based on a determination that the nondisclosure policy constituted "gross, oppressive or malicious" fraud. See Ala.Code §§ 6-11-20, 6-11-21 (1993). . . .

II

Punitive damages may properly be imposed to further a State's legitimate interests in punishing unlawful conduct and deterring its repetition. *Gertz v. Robert Welch, Inc.,* 418 U.S. 323, 350 (1974). In our federal system, States necessarily have considerable flexibility in determining the level of punitive damages that they will allow in different classes of cases and in any particular case. Most States that authorize exemplary damages afford the jury similar latitude, requiring only that the damages awarded be reasonably necessary to vindicate the State's legitimate interests in punishment and deterrence. See *TXO,* 509 U.S., at 456; *Haslip,* 499 U.S., at 21, 22. Only when an award can fairly be categorized as "grossly excessive" in relation to these interests does it enter the zone of arbitrariness that violates the Due Process Clause of the Fourteenth Amendment. Cf. *TXO,* 509 U.S., at 456. For that reason, the federal excessiveness inquiry appropriately begins with an identification of the state interests that a punitive award is designed to serve. We therefore focus our attention first on the scope of Alabama's legitimate interests in punishing BMW and deterring it from future misconduct.

No one doubts that a State may protect its citizens by prohibiting deceptive trade practices and by requiring automobile distributors to disclose presale repairs that affect the value of a new car. But the States need not, and in fact do not, provide such protection in a uniform manner. Some States rely on the judicial process to formulate and enforce an appropriate disclosure requirement by applying principles of contract and tort law. Other States have enacted various forms of legislation that define the disclosure obligations of automobile manufacturers, distributors, and dealers. The result is a patchwork of rules representing the diverse policy judgments of lawmakers in 50 States.

That diversity demonstrates that reasonable people may disagree about the value of a full disclosure requirement. Some legislatures may conclude that affirmative disclosure requirements are unnecessary because the self-interest of those involved in the automobile trade in developing and maintaining the goodwill of their customers will motivate them to make voluntary disclosures or to refrain from selling cars that do not comply with self-imposed standards. Those legislatures that do adopt affirmative disclosure obligations may take into account the cost of government regulation, choosing to draw a line exempting minor repairs from such a requirement. In formulating a disclosure standard, States may also consider other goals, such as providing a "safe harbor" for automobile manufacturers, distributors, and dealers against lawsuits over minor repairs.

. . . We think it follows from these principles of state sovereignty and comity that a State may not impose economic sanctions on violators of its laws with the intent of changing the tortfeasors' lawful conduct in other States. Before this Court Dr. Gore argued that the large punitive damages award was necessary to induce BMW to change the nationwide policy that it adopted in 1983. But by attempting to alter BMW's nationwide policy, Alabama would be infringing on the policy choices of other States. To avoid such encroachment, the economic penalties that a State such as Alabama inflicts on those who transgress its laws, whether the penalties take the form of legislatively authorized fines or judicially imposed punitive damages, must be supported by the State's interest in protecting its own consumers and its own economy. Alabama may insist that BMW adhere to a particular disclosure policy in that State. Alabama does not have the power, however, to punish BMW for conduct that was lawful where it occurred and that had no impact on Alabama or its residents. Nor may Alabama impose sanctions on BMW in order to deter conduct that is lawful in other jurisdictions.

In this case, we accept the Alabama Supreme Court's interpretation of the jury verdict as reflecting a computation of the amount of punitive damages "based in large part on conduct that happened in other jurisdictions." 646 So.2d, at 627. As the Alabama Supreme Court noted, neither the jury nor the trial court was presented with evidence that any of BMW's out-of-state conduct was unlawful. "The only testimony touching the issue showed that approximately 60% of the vehicles that were refinished were sold in states where failure to disclose the repair was not an unfair trade practice." *Id.,* at 627, n. 6. The Alabama Supreme Court therefore properly eschewed reliance on BMW's out-of-state conduct, *id.,* at 628, and based its remitted award solely on conduct that occurred within Alabama. The award must be analyzed in the light of the same conduct, with consideration given only to the interests of Alabama consumers, rather than those of the entire Nation. When the scope of the interest in punishment and deterrence that an Alabama court may appropriately consider is properly limited, it is apparent — for reasons that we shall now address — that this award is grossly excessive.

III

Elementary notions of fairness enshrined in our constitutional jurisprudence dictate that a person receive fair notice not only of the conduct that will subject him to punishment, but also of the severity of the penalty that a State may impose. Three guideposts, each of which indicates that BMW did not receive adequate notice of the magnitude of the sanction that Alabama might impose for adhering to the nondisclosure policy adopted in 1983, lead us to the conclusion that the $2 million award against BMW is grossly excessive: the degree of reprehensibility of the nondisclosure; the disparity between the harm or potential harm suffered by Dr. Gore and his punitive damages award; and the difference between this remedy and the civil penalties authorized or imposed in comparable cases. We discuss these considerations in turn.

Degree of Reprehensibility

Perhaps the most important indicium of the reasonableness of a punitive damages award is the degree of reprehensibility of the defendant's conduct. As the Court stated nearly 150 years ago, exemplary damages imposed on a defendant should reflect "the enormity of his offense." *Day v. Woodworth,* 13 How. 363, 371 (1852). See also *St. Louis, I.M. & S.R. Co. v. Williams,* 251 U.S. 63, 66–67 (1919) (punitive award may not be "wholly disproportioned to the offense"); *Browning-Ferris Industries of Vt., Inc. v. Kelco Disposal, Inc.,* 492 U.S. 257, 301 (1989) (O'CONNOR, J., concurring in part and dissenting in part) (reviewing court "should examine the gravity of the defendant's conduct and the harshness of the award of punitive damages"). This principle reflects the accepted view that some wrongs are more blameworthy than others. Thus, we have said that "nonviolent crimes are less serious than crimes marked by violence or the threat of violence." *Solem v. Helm,* 463 U.S. 277, 292–293 (1983). Similarly, "trickery and deceit," *TXO,* 509 U.S., at 462, are more reprehensible than negligence. . . .

In this case, none of the aggravating factors associated with particularly reprehensible conduct is present. The harm BMW inflicted on Dr. Gore was purely economic in nature. The presale refinishing of the car had no effect on its performance or safety features, or even its appearance for at least nine months after his purchase. BMW's conduct evinced no indifference to or reckless disregard for the health and safety of others. To be sure, infliction of economic injury, especially when done intentionally through affirmative acts of misconduct, or when the target is financially vulnerable, can warrant a substantial penalty. But this observation does not convert all acts that cause economic harm into torts that are sufficiently reprehensible to justify a significant sanction in addition to compensatory damages. . . .

Ratio

The second and perhaps most commonly cited indicium of an unreasonable or excessive punitive damages award is its ratio to the actual harm inflicted on the plaintiff. See *TXO,* 509 U.S., at 459. The principle that exemplary damages must bear a "reasonable relationship" to compensatory damages has a long pedigree. Scholars have identified a number of early English statutes authorizing the award of multiple damages for particular wrongs. Some 65 different enactments during the period between 1275 and 1753 provided for double, treble, or quadruple damages. Our decisions in both *Haslip* and *TXO* endorsed the proposition that a comparison between the compensatory award and the punitive award is significant.

In *Haslip* we concluded that even though a punitive damages award of "more than 4 times the amount of compensatory damages" might be "close to the line," it did not "cross the line into the area of constitutional impropriety." 499 U.S., at 23–24. *TXO,* following dicta in *Haslip,* refined this analysis by confirming that the proper inquiry is "'whether there is a reasonable relationship between the punitive damages award and *the harm likely to result* from the defendant's conduct as well as the harm that actually has occurred.'" *TXO*, 509 U.S., at 460. Thus, in upholding the $10 million award in *TXO*, we relied on the difference between that figure and the harm to the victim that would have ensued if the tortious plan had succeeded. That difference suggested that the relevant ratio was not more than 10 to 1.

The $2 million in punitive damages awarded to Dr. Gore by the Alabama Supreme Court is 500 times the amount of his actual harm as determined by the jury. Moreover, there is no suggestion that Dr. Gore or any other BMW purchaser was threatened with any additional potential harm by BMW's nondisclosure policy. The disparity in this case is thus dramatically greater than those considered in *Haslip* and *TXO*.

Of course, we have consistently rejected the notion that the constitutional line is marked by a simple mathematical formula, even one that compares actual *and potential* damages to the punitive award. *TXO*, 509 U.S., at 458. Indeed, low awards of compensatory damages may properly support a higher ratio than high compensatory awards, if, for example, a particularly egregious act has resulted in only a small amount of economic damages. A higher ratio may also be justified in cases in which the injury is hard to detect or the monetary value of noneconomic harm might have been difficult to determine. It is appropriate, therefore, to reiterate our rejection of a categorical approach. Once again, "we return to what we said ... in *Haslip*: 'We need not, and indeed we cannot, draw a mathematical bright line between the constitutionally acceptable and the constitutionally unacceptable that would fit every case. We can say, however, that [a] general concer[n] of reasonableness ... properly enter[s] into the constitutional calculus.'" *Id.,* at 458. In most cases, the ratio will be within a constitutionally acceptable range, and remittitur will not be justified on this basis. When the ratio is a breathtaking 500 to 1, however, the award must surely "raise a suspicious judicial eyebrow." *TXO*, 509 U.S., at 481 (O'CONNOR, J., dissenting).

Sanctions for Comparable Misconduct

Comparing the punitive damages award and the civil or criminal penalties that could be imposed for comparable misconduct provides a third indicium of excessiveness. As Justice O'CONNOR has correctly observed, a reviewing court engaged in determining whether an award of punitive damages is excessive should "accord 'substantial deference' to legislative judgments concerning appropriate sanctions for the conduct at issue." *Browning-Ferris Industries of Vt., Inc. v. Kelco Disposal, Inc.,* 492 U.S., at 301. In *Haslip*, 499 U.S., at 23, the Court noted that although the exemplary award was "much in excess of the fine that could be imposed," imprisonment was also authorized in the criminal context. In this case the $2 million economic sanction imposed on BMW is substantially greater than the statutory fines available in Alabama and elsewhere for similar malfeasance. ...

IV

We assume, as the juries in this case and in the *Yates* case found, that the undisclosed damage to the new BMW's affected their actual value. Notwithstanding the evidence adduced by BMW in an effort to prove that the repainted cars conformed to the same quality standards as its other cars, we also assume that it knew, or should have known, that as time passed the repainted cars would lose their attractive appearance more rapidly than other BMW's. Moreover, we of course accept the Alabama courts' view that the state interest in protecting its citizens from deceptive trade practices justifies a sanction in addition to the recovery of compensatory damages. We cannot, however, accept the conclusion of the Alabama Supreme Court that BMW's conduct was sufficiently egregious to justify a punitive sanction that is tantamount to a severe criminal penalty.

The fact that BMW is a large corporation rather than an impecunious individual does not diminish its entitlement to fair notice of the demands that the several States impose on the conduct of its business. Indeed, its status as an active participant in the national economy implicates the federal interest in preventing individual States from imposing undue burdens on interstate commerce. While each State has ample power to protect its own consumers, none may use the punitive damages deterrent as a means of imposing its regulatory policies on the entire Nation.

As in *Haslip*, we are not prepared to draw a bright line marking the limits of a constitutionally acceptable punitive damages award. Unlike that case, however, we are fully convinced that the grossly excessive award imposed in this case transcends the constitutional limit. Whether the appropriate remedy requires a new trial or merely an independent determination by the Alabama Supreme Court of the award necessary to vindicate the economic interests of Alabama consumers is a matter that should be addressed by the state court in the first instance.

The judgment is reversed, and the case is remanded for further proceedings not inconsistent with this opinion.

It is so ordered.

Justice SCALIA, with whom Justice THOMAS joins, dissenting.

Today we see the latest manifestation of this Court's recent and increasingly insistent "concern about punitive damages that 'run wild.'" *Pacific Mut. Life Ins. Co. v. Haslip*, 499 U.S. 1, 18 (1991). Since the Constitution does not make that concern any of our business, the Court's activities in this area are an unjustified incursion into the province of state governments. . . .

Justice GINSBURG, with whom THE CHIEF JUSTICE joins, dissenting.

The Court, I am convinced, unnecessarily and unwisely ventures into territory traditionally within the States' domain, and does so in the face of reform measures recently adopted or currently under consideration in legislative arenas. . . .

For the reasons stated, I dissent from this Court's disturbance of the judgment the Alabama Supreme Court has made.

* * *

State Farm Mutual Automobile Insurance Co. v. Campbell
United States Supreme Court
538 U.S. 408 (2003)

Justice KENNEDY delivered the opinion of the Court.

We address once again the measure of punishment, by means of punitive damages, a State may impose upon a defendant in a civil case. The question is whether, in the circumstances we shall recount, an award of $145 million in punitive damages, where full compensatory damages are $1 million, is excessive and in violation of the Due Process Clause of the Fourteenth Amendment to the Constitution of the United States.

I

In 1981, Curtis Campbell (Campbell) was driving with his wife, Inez Preece Campbell, in Cache County, Utah. He decided to pass six vans traveling ahead of them on a two-lane highway. Todd Ospital was driving a small car approaching from the opposite direction. To avoid a head-on collision with Campbell, who by then was driving on the wrong side of the highway and toward oncoming traffic, Ospital swerved onto the shoulder, lost control of his automobile, and collided with a vehicle driven by Robert G. Slusher. Ospital was killed, and Slusher was rendered permanently disabled. The Campbells escaped unscathed.

In the ensuing wrongful death and tort action, Campbell insisted he was not at fault. Early investigations did support differing conclusions as to who caused the accident, but "a consensus was reached early on by the investigators and witnesses that Mr. Campbell's unsafe pass had indeed caused the crash." 65 P.3d 1134, 1141 (Utah 2001). Campbell's insurance company, petitioner State Farm Mutual Automobile Insurance Company (State Farm), nonetheless decided to contest liability and declined offers by Slusher and Ospital's estate (Ospital) to settle the claims for the policy limit of $50,000 ($25,000 per claimant). State Farm also ignored the advice of one of its own investigators and took the case to trial, assuring the Campbells that "their assets were safe, that they had no liability for the accident, that [State Farm] would represent their interests, and that they did not need to procure separate counsel." *Id.*, at 1142. To the contrary, a jury determined that Campbell was 100 percent at fault, and a judgment was returned for $185,849, far more than the amount offered in settlement.

At first State Farm refused to cover the $135,849 in excess liability. Its counsel made this clear to the Campbells: "'You may want to put for sale signs on your property to get things moving.'" *Ibid.* Nor was State Farm willing to post a supersedeas bond to allow Campbell to appeal the judgment against him. Campbell obtained his own counsel to appeal the verdict. During the pendency of the appeal, in late 1984, Slusher, Ospital, and the Campbells reached an agreement whereby Slusher and Ospital agreed not to seek satisfaction of their claims against the Campbells. In exchange the Campbells agreed to pursue a bad faith action against State Farm and to be represented by Slusher's and Ospital's attorneys. . . .

The jury awarded the Campbells $2.6 million in compensatory damages and $145 million in punitive damages, which the trial court reduced to $1 million and $25 million respectively. Both parties appealed.

The Utah Supreme Court sought to apply the three guideposts we identified in *Gore, supra,* at 574–575, and it reinstated the $145 million punitive damages award. . . .

II

We recognized in *Cooper Industries, Inc. v. Leatherman Tool Group, Inc.,* 532 U.S. 424 (2001), that in our judicial system compensatory and punitive damages, although usually awarded at the same time by the same decisionmaker, serve different purposes. Compensatory damages "are intended to redress the concrete loss that the plaintiff has suffered by reason of the defendant's wrongful conduct." *Ibid.* (citing Restatement (Second) of Torts § 903, pp. 453–454 (1979)). By contrast, punitive damages serve a broader function; they are aimed at deterrence and retribution. *Cooper Industries, supra,* at 432; see also *Gore, supra,* at 568 ("Punitive damages may properly be imposed to further a State's legitimate interests in punishing unlawful conduct and deterring its repetition"); *Pacific Mut. Life Ins. Co. v. Haslip,* 499 U.S. 1, 19 (1991) ("[P]unitive damages are imposed for purposes of retribution and deterrence").

While States possess discretion over the imposition of punitive damages, it is well established that there are procedural and substantive constitutional limitations on these awards. . . . The reason is that "[e]lementary notions of fairness enshrined in our constitutional jurisprudence dictate that a person receive fair notice not only of the conduct that will subject him to punishment, but also of the severity of the penalty that a State may impose." *Id.,* at 574.

Although these awards serve the same purposes as criminal penalties, defendants subjected to punitive damages in civil cases have not been accorded the protections applicable in a criminal proceeding. This increases our concerns over the imprecise manner in which punitive damages systems are administered. We have admonished that "[p]unitive damages pose an acute danger of arbitrary deprivation of property. Jury instructions typically leave the jury with wide discretion in choosing amounts, and the presentation of evidence of a defendant's net worth creates the potential that juries will use their verdicts to express biases against big businesses, particularly those without strong local presences." *Honda Motor, supra,* at 432; see also *Haslip, supra,* at 59 (O'CONNOR, J., dissenting) ("[T]he Due Process Clause does

DP-14th A.

not permit a State to classify arbitrariness as a virtue. Indeed, the point of due process — of the law in general — is to allow citizens to order their behavior. A State can have no legitimate interest in deliberately making the law so arbitrary that citizens will be unable to avoid punishment based solely upon bias or whim"). . . .

In light of these concerns, in *Gore, supra,* we instructed courts reviewing punitive damages to consider three guideposts: (1) the degree of reprehensibility of the defendant's misconduct; (2) the disparity between the actual or potential harm suffered by the plaintiff and the punitive damages award; and (3) the difference between the punitive damages awarded by the jury and the civil penalties authorized or imposed in comparable cases. *Id.,* at 575. . . .

III

Under the principles outlined in *BMW of North America, Inc. v. Gore,* this case is neither close nor difficult. It was error to reinstate the jury's $145 million punitive damages award.

A

"[T]he most important indicium of the reasonableness of a punitive damages award is the degree of reprehensibility of the defendant's conduct." *Gore,* 517 U.S., at 575. We have instructed courts to determine the reprehensibility of a defendant by considering whether: the harm caused was physical as opposed to economic; the tortious conduct evinced an indifference to or a reckless disregard of the health or safety of others; the target of the conduct had financial vulnerability; the conduct involved repeated actions or was an isolated incident; and the harm was the result of intentional malice, trickery, or deceit, or mere accident. The existence of any one of these factors weighing in favor of a plaintiff may not be sufficient to sustain a punitive damages award; and the absence of all of them renders any award suspect. It should be presumed a plaintiff has been made whole for his injuries by compensatory damages, so punitive damages should only be awarded if the defendant's culpability, after having paid compensatory damages, is so reprehensible as to warrant the imposition of further sanctions to achieve punishment or deterrence.

Applying these factors in the instant case, we must acknowledge that State Farm's handling of the claims against the Campbells merits no praise. The trial court found that State Farm's employees altered the company's records to make Campbell appear less culpable. State Farm disregarded the overwhelming likelihood of liability and the near-certain probability that, by taking the case to trial, a judgment in excess of the policy limits would be awarded. State Farm amplified the harm by at first assuring the Campbells their assets would be safe from any verdict and by later telling them, postjudgment, to put a for-sale sign on their house. While we do not suggest there was error in awarding punitive damages based upon State Farm's conduct toward the Campbells, a more modest punishment for this reprehensible conduct could have satisfied the State's legitimate objectives, and the Utah courts should have gone no further. . . .

The Campbells have identified scant evidence of repeated misconduct of the sort that injured them. Nor does our review of the Utah courts' decisions convince us that State Farm was only punished for its actions toward the Campbells. Although evidence of other acts need not be identical to have relevance in the calculation of punitive damages, the Utah court erred here because evidence pertaining to claims that had nothing to do with a third-party lawsuit was introduced at length. . . .

B

Turning to the second *Gore* guidepost, we have been reluctant to identify concrete constitutional limits on the ratio between harm, or potential harm, to the plaintiff and the punitive damages award. 517 U.S., at 582 ("[W]e have consistently rejected the notion that the constitutional line is marked by a simple mathematical formula, even one that compares actual *and potential* damages to the punitive award"); *TXO, supra,* at 458. We decline again to impose a bright-line ratio which a punitive damages award cannot exceed. Our jurisprudence and the principles it has now established demonstrate, however, that, in practice, few awards exceeding a single-digit ratio between punitive and compensatory damages, to a significant degree, will satisfy due process. . . .

Nonetheless, because there are no rigid benchmarks that a punitive damages award may not surpass, ratios greater than those we have previously upheld may comport with due process where "a particularly egregious act has resulted in only a small amount of economic damages." *Ibid.;* see also *ibid.* (positing that a higher ratio *might* be necessary where "the injury is hard to detect or the monetary value of noneconomic harm might have been difficult to determine"). The converse is also true, however. When compensatory damages are substantial, then a lesser ratio, perhaps only equal to compensatory damages, can reach the outermost limit of the due process guarantee. The precise award in any case, of course, must be based upon the facts and circumstances of the defendant's conduct and the harm to the plaintiff.

In sum, courts must ensure that the measure of punishment is both reasonable and proportionate to the amount of harm to the plaintiff and to the general damages recovered. In the context of this case, we have no doubt that there is a presumption against an award that has a 145-to-1 ratio. The compensatory award in this case was substantial; the Campbells were awarded $1 million for a year and a half of emotional distress. This was complete compensation. The harm arose from a transaction in the economic realm, not from some physical assault or trauma; there were no physical injuries; and State Farm paid the excess verdict before the complaint was filed, so the Campbells suffered only minor economic injuries for the 18-month period in which State Farm refused to resolve the claim against them. The compensatory damages for the injury suffered here, moreover, likely were based on a component which was duplicated in the punitive award. Much of the distress was caused by the outrage and humiliation the Campbells suffered at the actions of their insurer; and it is a major role of punitive damages to condemn such conduct. Compensatory damages, however, already contain this punitive element. See

Restatement (Second) of Torts §908, Comment *c*, p. 466 (1977) ("In many cases in which compensatory damages include an amount for emotional distress, such as humiliation or indignation aroused by the defendant's act, there is no clear line of demarcation between punishment and compensation and a verdict for a specified amount frequently includes elements of both")....

C

The third guidepost in *Gore* is the disparity between the punitive damages award and the "civil penalties authorized or imposed in comparable cases." *Id.*, at 575. We note that, in the past, we have also looked to criminal penalties that could be imposed. The existence of a criminal penalty does have bearing on the seriousness with which a State views the wrongful action. When used to determine the dollar amount of the award, however, the criminal penalty has less utility. Great care must be taken to avoid use of the civil process to assess criminal penalties that can be imposed only after the heightened protections of a criminal trial have been observed, including, of course, its higher standards of proof. Punitive damages are not a substitute for the criminal process, and the remote possibility of a criminal sanction does not automatically sustain a punitive damages award.

Here, we need not dwell long on this guidepost. The most relevant civil sanction under Utah state law for the wrong done to the Campbells appears to be a $10,000 fine for an act of fraud, 65 P.3d, at 1154, an amount dwarfed by the $145 million punitive damages award. The Supreme Court of Utah speculated about the loss of State Farm's business license, the disgorgement of profits, and possible imprisonment, but here again its references were to the broad fraudulent scheme drawn from evidence of out-of-state and dissimilar conduct. This analysis was insufficient to justify the award.

IV

An application of the *Gore* guideposts to the facts of this case, especially in light of the substantial compensatory damages awarded (a portion of which contained a punitive element), likely would justify a punitive damages award at or near the amount of compensatory damages. The punitive award of $145 million, therefore, was neither reasonable nor proportionate to the wrong committed, and it was an irrational and arbitrary deprivation of the property of the defendant. The proper calculation of punitive damages under the principles we have discussed should be resolved, in the first instance, by the Utah courts.

The judgment of the Utah Supreme Court is reversed, and the case is remanded for further proceedings not inconsistent with this opinion.

It is so ordered.

Justice SCALIA, dissenting.

I adhere to the view expressed in my dissenting opinion in *BMW of North America, Inc. v. Gore,* 517 U.S. 559, 598–99 (1996), that the Due Process Clause provides no substantive protections against "excessive" or "'unreasonable'" awards of punitive

230   6 · PUNITIVE DAMAGES

damages. I am also of the view that the punitive damages jurisprudence which has sprung forth from *BMW v. Gore* is insusceptible of principled application; accordingly, I do not feel justified in giving the case *stare decisis* effect. I would affirm the judgment of the Utah Supreme Court.

Justice THOMAS, dissenting.

I would affirm the judgment below because "I continue to believe that the Constitution does not constrain the size of punitive damages awards." *Cooper Industries, Inc. v. Leatherman Tool Group, Inc.*, 532 U.S. 424, 443 (2001) (THOMAS, J., concurring) (citing *BMW of North America, Inc. v. Gore*, 517 U.S. 559, 599 (1996) (SCALIA, J., joined by THOMAS, J., dissenting)). Accordingly, I respectfully dissent.

Justice GINSBURG, dissenting.

. . . I remain of the view that this Court has no warrant to reform state law governing awards of punitive damages. *Gore*, 517 U.S., at 607 (GINSBURG, J., dissenting). Even if I were prepared to accept the flexible guides prescribed in *Gore*, I would not join the Court's swift conversion of those guides into instructions that begin to resemble marching orders. For the reasons stated, I would leave the judgment of the Utah Supreme Court undisturbed.

* * *

Problem 30

A punitive damages award may violate the Constitution if it is disproportionate to the defendant's conduct. What are the best arguments that the following punitive damages award is unconstitutional? What are the best arguments that it does not violate the Constitution?

A hotel knowingly allows guests to check into rooms infested with bedbugs. Over a period of six months, 85 guests are bitten by bedbugs, causing red marks that are unsightly, itchy, and mildly painful. The bites heal in around three weeks. One of the guests sues the hotel. After trial, a jury awards $10,000 in damages for pain and suffering and emotional distress. The jury also awards the plaintiff $90,000 in punitive damages.

Introductory Note — *Phillip Morris USA v. Williams*

As a general proposition, it seems uncontroversial to say that a plaintiff should not be awarded damages for harm the defendant caused to someone else. But what about when the damages are punitive damages — which are measured by how egregious the defendant's conduct was — and the conduct in question is egregious precisely *because* it harmed many people? Should the jury then be allowed to consider that the bad conduct harmed more than just the plaintiff? That is the issue the Supreme Court wrestles with in *Phillip Morris*.

THINGS TO THINK ABOUT while reading *Phillip Morris USA v. Williams*:

1. How does it violate the Due Process Clause when a punitive damages award punishes a defendant based on harm to someone who is not before the court?

2. In calculating punitive damages, can a jury permissibly consider that the defendant's conduct harmed others besides the plaintiff? If so, how is the jury allowed to use that information?

Philip Morris USA v. Williams

United States Supreme Court
549 U.S. 346 (2007)

Justice BREYER delivered the opinion of the Court.

The question we address today concerns a large state-court punitive damages award. We are asked whether the Constitution's Due Process Clause permits a jury to base that award in part upon its desire to *punish* the defendant for harming persons who are not before the court (*e.g.,* victims whom the parties do not represent). We hold that such an award would amount to a taking of "property" from the defendant without due process.

I

This lawsuit arises out of the death of Jesse Williams, a heavy cigarette smoker. Respondent, Williams' widow, represents his estate in this state lawsuit for negligence and deceit against Philip Morris, the manufacturer of Marlboro, the brand that Williams favored. A jury found that Williams' death was caused by smoking; that Williams smoked in significant part because he thought it was safe to do so; and that Philip Morris knowingly and falsely led him to believe that this was so. The jury ultimately found that Philip Morris was negligent (as was Williams) and that Philip Morris had engaged in deceit. In respect to deceit, the claim at issue here, it awarded compensatory damages of about $821,000 (about $21,000 economic and $800,000 noneconomic) along with $79.5 million in punitive damages. . . .

II

This Court has long made clear that "[p]unitive damages may properly be imposed to further a State's legitimate interests in punishing unlawful conduct and deterring its repetition." *BMW, supra,* at 568. At the same time, we have emphasized the need to avoid an arbitrary determination of an award's amount. Unless a State insists upon proper standards that will cabin the jury's discretionary authority, its punitive damages system may deprive a defendant of "fair notice . . . of the severity of the penalty that a State may impose," *BMW, supra,* at 574; it may threaten "arbitrary punishments," *i.e.,* punishments that reflect not an "application of law" but "a decisionmaker's caprice," *State Farm, supra,* at 416, 418 (internal quotation marks omitted); and, where the amounts are sufficiently large, it may impose one State's (or one jury's) "policy choice," say, as to the conditions under which (or even whether) certain products can be sold, upon "neighboring States" with different public policies, *BMW, supra,* at 571–572.

For these and similar reasons, this Court has found that the Constitution imposes certain limits, in respect both to procedures for awarding punitive damages and to amounts forbidden as "grossly excessive." See *Honda Motor Co. v. Oberg,* 512 U.S. 415, 432 (1994) (requiring judicial review of the size of punitive awards); *Cooper Industries, Inc. v. Leatherman Tool Group, Inc.,* 532 U.S. 424, 443 (2001) (review must be *de novo*); *BMW, supra,* at 574–585 (excessiveness decision depends upon the reprehensibility of the defendant's conduct, whether the award bears a reasonable relationship to the actual and potential harm caused by the defendant to the plaintiff, and the difference between the award and sanctions "authorized or imposed in comparable cases"); *State Farm, supra,* at 425 (excessiveness more likely where ratio exceeds single digits). Because we shall not decide whether the award here at issue is "grossly excessive," we need now only consider the Constitution's procedural limitations.

III

In our view, the Constitution's Due Process Clause forbids a State to use a punitive damages award to punish a defendant for injury that it inflicts upon nonparties or those whom they directly represent, *i.e.,* injury that it inflicts upon those who are, essentially, strangers to the litigation. For one thing, the Due Process Clause prohibits a State from punishing an individual without first providing that individual with "an opportunity to present every available defense." *Lindsey v. Normet,* 405 U.S. 56, 66 (1972). Yet a defendant threatened with punishment for injuring a nonparty victim has no opportunity to defend against the charge, by showing, for example in a case such as this, that the other victim was not entitled to damages because he or she knew that smoking was dangerous or did not rely upon the defendant's statements to the contrary.

For another, to permit punishment for injuring a nonparty victim would add a near standardless dimension to the punitive damages equation. How many such victims are there? How seriously were they injured? Under what circumstances did injury occur? The trial will not likely answer such questions as to nonparty victims.

The jury will be left to speculate. And the fundamental due process concerns to which our punitive damages cases refer — risks of arbitrariness, uncertainty, and lack of notice — will be magnified. *State Farm,* 538 U.S., at 416, 418; *BMW,* 517 U.S., at 574.

Finally, we can find no authority supporting the use of punitive damages awards for the purpose of punishing a defendant for harming others. We have said that it may be appropriate to consider the reasonableness of a punitive damages award in light of the *potential* harm the defendant's conduct could have caused. But we have made clear that the potential harm at issue was harm potentially caused *the plaintiff.* See *State Farm, supra,* at 424 ("[W]e have been reluctant to identify concrete constitutional limits on the ratio between harm, or potential harm, *to the plaintiff* and the punitive damages award" (emphasis added). . . .

. . . Given the risks of unfairness that we have mentioned, it is constitutionally important for a court to provide assurance that the jury will ask the right question, not the wrong one. And given the risks of arbitrariness, the concern for adequate notice, and the risk that punitive damages awards can, in practice, impose one State's (or one jury's) policies (*e.g.,* banning cigarettes) upon other States — all of which accompany awards that, today, may be many times the size of such awards in the 18th and 19th centuries — it is particularly important that States avoid procedure that unnecessarily deprives juries of proper legal guidance. We therefore conclude that the Due Process Clause requires States to provide assurance that juries are not asking the wrong question, *i.e.,* seeking, not simply to determine reprehensibility, but also to punish for harm caused strangers. . . .

V

As the preceding discussion makes clear, we believe that the Oregon Supreme Court applied the wrong constitutional standard when considering Philip Morris' appeal. We remand this case so that the Oregon Supreme Court can apply the standard we have set forth. Because the application of this standard may lead to the need for a new trial, or a change in the level of the punitive damages award, we shall not consider whether the award is constitutionally "grossly excessive." We vacate the Oregon Supreme Court's judgment and remand the case for further proceedings not inconsistent with this opinion.

It is so ordered.

Justice STEVENS, dissenting.

The Due Process Clause of the Fourteenth Amendment imposes both substantive and procedural constraints on the power of the States to impose punitive damages on tortfeasors. See *State Farm Mut. Automobile Ins. Co. v. Campbell,* 538 U.S. 408 (2003); *Cooper Industries, Inc. v. Leatherman Tool Group, Inc.,* 532 U.S. 424 (2001); *BMW of North America, Inc. v. Gore,* 517 U.S. 559 (1996). I remain firmly convinced that the cases announcing those constraints were correctly decided. In my view the Oregon Supreme Court faithfully applied the reasoning in those opinions to the egregious facts disclosed by this record. . . .

Of greater importance to me, however, is the Court's imposition of a novel limit on the State's power to impose punishment in civil litigation. Unlike the Court, I see no reason why an interest in punishing a wrongdoer "for harming persons who are not before the court," should not be taken into consideration when assessing the appropriate sanction for reprehensible conduct.

Whereas compensatory damages are measured by the harm the defendant has caused the plaintiff, punitive damages are a sanction for the public harm the defendant's conduct has caused or threatened. There is little difference between the justification for a criminal sanction, such as a fine or a term of imprisonment, and an award of punitive damages. . . .

Essentially for the reasons stated in the opinion of the Supreme Court of Oregon, I would affirm its judgment.

Justice GINSBURG, with whom Justice SCALIA and Justice THOMAS join, dissenting.

The purpose of punitive damages, it can hardly be denied, is not to compensate, but to punish. Punish for what? Not for harm actually caused "strangers to the litigation," the Court states, but for the *reprehensibility* of defendant's conduct. "[C]onduct that risks harm to many," the Court observes, "is likely more reprehensible than conduct that risks harm to only a few." The Court thus conveys that, when punitive damages are at issue, a jury is properly instructed to consider the extent of harm suffered by others as a measure of reprehensibility, but not to mete out punishment for injuries in fact sustained by nonparties. The Oregon courts did not rule otherwise. They have endeavored to follow our decisions, most recently in *BMW of North America, Inc. v. Gore,* 517 U.S. 559 (1996), and *State Farm Mut. Automobile Ins. Co. v. Campbell,* 538 U.S. 408 (2003), and have "deprive[d] [no jury] of proper legal guidance," *ante.* Vacation of the Oregon Supreme Court's judgment, I am convinced, is unwarranted.

The right question regarding reprehensibility, the Court acknowledges, would train on "the harm that Philip Morris was prepared to inflict on the smoking public at large." (quoting 340 Or. 35, 51, 127 P.3d 1165, 1175 (2006)). See also *id.,* at 55, 127 P.3d, at 1177 ("[T]he jury, *in assessing the reprehensibility of Philip Morris's actions,* could consider evidence of similar harm to other Oregonians caused (or threatened) by the same conduct." (emphasis added)). The Court identifies no evidence introduced and no charge delivered inconsistent with that inquiry. . . .

For the reasons stated, and in light of the abundant evidence of "the potential harm [Philip Morris'] conduct could have caused," I would affirm the decision of the Oregon Supreme Court.

     * * *

Problem 31

When a plaintiff seeks punitive damages against a defendant who caused widespread harm, the trial court must decide whether the defendant's other acts of misconduct are admissible to show reprehensibility. How should the court rule on the below-described motion to exclude evidence of other misconduct?

A state law completely bans the sale of fireworks because of their potential to injure, making it one of the most restrictive firework regulations in the country. A nationwide retailer sells fireworks in that state in violation of the law, and Dave buys a package of them. Dave takes the fireworks home and sets them off in his front yard. One strikes and injures Dave's neighbor, Pam, who was watching nearby. Pam sues the retailer and seeks punitive damages for its intentional misconduct of selling fireworks in violation of the law.

Pam learns through discovery that fireworks sold by the retailer in several other states have resulted in thousands of injuries. At trial, she attempts to introduce evidence of those injuries to show that the retailer has an ongoing practice of selling fireworks that caused injuries, which is more reprehensible than a single such incident. The retailer moves to exclude the evidence on constitutional due process grounds.

Chapter 7

Injunctions

An injunction is an equitable remedy. It is a court order requiring its subject to either do something or refrain from doing something. Injunctions provide specific relief (as opposed to substitutionary) because they reverse the effect of a harm or prevent it from occurring in the first place.

Injunctions can be awarded as the sole remedy in a case, when a threatened harm has not yet occurred. Or they can be awarded in conjunction with damages or another substitutionary remedy: monetary compensation for harm that has already occurred, and injunctive relief to prevent more harm from occurring in the future. Because timing might be key to effective prevention — if the harm is imminent, preventive relief is needed right away — courts are authorized to award provisional injunctions. Provisional injunctions are temporary relief to prevent irreparable harm from happening during the time it takes to litigate a civil lawsuit.

This chapter first examines the criteria courts use to decide if injunctive relief is an appropriate remedy, then discusses the procedure for awarding a provisional injunction.

Standard for Granting Injunctive Relief

The defining characteristic of injunctions is that they prevent irreparable harm. Damages are the default remedy for a plaintiff who comes to court alleging a legally cognizable wrong. That default assumes money is an adequate substitute for whatever loss the plaintiff complains of. But not all harms are created equal, and not all are adequately remedied by money. In some cases, the plaintiff cannot be made whole by a judgment conferring the right to recover a sum of money from the defendant. The harm in such cases is called irreparable harm. Recall that traditionally, to get an equitable remedy like an injunction, a plaintiff had to show an inadequate remedy at law. A showing of irreparable harm — harm that cannot be repaired through monetary damages — would qualify.

Examples of injuries that courts have deemed irreparable are damage to the environment (destruction of the habitat for an endangered species, perhaps), violation of a constitutional right, and harm to one's reputation. The common thread is that money cannot fix the problem. In contrast, lost profits or a similar economic loss will not generally be considered irreparable because money can compensate for that harm. If the defendant is insolvent, however — unable to pay a damages judgment if one were rendered in plaintiff's favor — that might cause a court to view damages as an inadequate remedy, opening the door to injunctive relief.

Injunctions are perhaps most useful as a preventive remedy, when a potentially irreparable injury looks reasonably certain to occur in the future. To determine whether preventive injunctive relief is warranted, courts consider the following questions:

- Can the plaintiff be made whole by an award of damages?
- Has the harm already occurred? If so, is it likely to reoccur?
- If the harm has not already occurred, how likely is it that it will?
- Would granting an injunction impose a greater hardship on the defendant than what the plaintiff would experience if the injunction is denied?

Guided by the answers to those questions, a court will determine whether (as in most cases) a damages award is a sufficient remedy, or whether (in some extraordinary cases) an injunction is necessary.

Mandatory and Prohibitory Injunctions

Injunctions are characterized as either mandatory or prohibitory. A mandatory injunction requires its subject to affirmatively do something. A prohibitory injunction, on the other hand, requires the subject to not do something. Mandatory injunctions are usually more difficult to enforce; it can be hard to make someone do something they do not want to do. For that reason, mandatory injunctions are said to be disfavored, meaning a court may be more hesitant to grant one than it would be to grant a prohibitory injunction. Ensuring compliance with a mandatory injunction will often require a good deal of court supervision, and the court has to be careful about how it expends limited judicial resources. There are many cases competing for the court's attention at any given time; fairness dictates a judge cannot allow any one case to monopolize the courthouse.

In the end, any injunction — mandatory or prohibitory — requires at least some continuing court supervision to ensure compliance. So an injunctive order involves an expenditure of judicial resources that a damages judgment does not. That reality can factor into a court's decision about whether an injunction is the appropriate remedy.

Introductory Note — *eBay, Inc. v. MercExchange*

eBay involves injunctive relief in a specific context — a patent infringement suit — but it is decided based on generally applicable injunction principles. The plaintiff won at trial (the jury found eBay had infringed the patent), but the court denied the plaintiff's request for an injunction, believing damages to be the appropriate remedy. The court of appeals reversed, ruling that a plaintiff who proves patent infringement is automatically entitled to an injunction preventing further infringement. The Supreme Court must decide the appropriate standard for injunctive relief in patent cases.

THINGS TO THINK ABOUT while reading *eBay, Inc. v. MercExchange, LLC*:

1. What kind of harm constitutes an irreparable injury?

2. Is there a difference between irreparable injury and an inadequate remedy at law?

3. What justification would there be for a rule that says injunctive relief is always available in a patent infringement case?

---

eBay, Inc. v. MercExchange, LLC

United States Supreme Court
547 U.S. 388 (2006)

Patent infringement suit

permanent injunction

Justice THOMAS delivered the opinion of the Court.

Ordinarily, a federal court considering whether to award permanent injunctive relief to a prevailing plaintiff applies the four-factor test historically employed by courts of equity. Petitioners eBay Inc. and Half.com, Inc., argue that this traditional test applies to disputes arising under the Patent Act. We agree and, accordingly, vacate the judgment of the Court of Appeals.

I

Petitioner eBay operates a popular Internet Web site that allows private sellers to list goods they wish to sell, either through an auction or at a fixed price. Petitioner Half.com, now a wholly owned subsidiary of eBay, operates a similar Web site. Respondent MercExchange, L.L.C., holds a number of patents, including a business method patent for an electronic market designed to facilitate the sale of goods between private individuals by establishing a central authority to promote trust among participants. See U.S. Patent No. 5,845,265. MercExchange sought to license its patent to eBay and Half.com, as it had previously done with other companies, but the parties failed to reach an agreement. MercExchange subsequently filed a patent infringement suit against eBay and Half.com in the United States District Court for the Eastern District of Virginia. A jury found that MercExchange's patent was valid, that eBay and Half.com had infringed that patent, and that an award of damages was appropriate.

Following the jury verdict, the District Court denied MercExchange's motion for permanent injunctive relief. 275 F.Supp.2d 695 (2003). The Court of Appeals for the Federal Circuit reversed, applying its "general rule that courts will issue permanent injunctions against patent infringement absent exceptional circumstances."

401 F.3d 1323, 1339 (2005). We granted certiorari to determine the appropriateness of this general rule.

II

According to well-established principles of equity, a plaintiff seeking a permanent injunction must satisfy a four-factor test before a court may grant such relief. A plaintiff must demonstrate: (1) that it has suffered an irreparable injury; (2) that remedies available at law, such as monetary damages, are inadequate to compensate for that injury; (3) that, considering the balance of hardships between the plaintiff and defendant, a remedy in equity is warranted; and (4) that the public interest would not be disserved by a permanent injunction. See, *e.g., Weinberger v. Romero-Barcelo,* 456 U.S. 305, 311–313 (1982); *Amoco Production Co. v. Gambell,* 480 U.S. 531, 542 (1987). The decision to grant or deny permanent injunctive relief is an act of equitable discretion by the district court, reviewable on appeal for abuse of discretion.

These familiar principles apply with equal force to disputes arising under the Patent Act. As this Court has long recognized, "a major departure from the long tradition of equity practice should not be lightly implied." *Ibid.;* see also *Amoco, supra,* at 542. Nothing in the Patent Act indicates that Congress intended such a departure. To the contrary, the Patent Act expressly provides that injunctions "may" issue "in accordance with the principles of equity." 35 U.S.C. § 283.

To be sure, the Patent Act also declares that "patents shall have the attributes of personal property," § 261, including "the right to exclude others from making, using, offering for sale, or selling the invention," § 154(a)(1). According to the Court of Appeals, this statutory right to exclude alone justifies its general rule in favor of permanent injunctive relief. 401 F.3d, at 1338. But the creation of a right is distinct from the provision of remedies for violations of that right. Indeed, the Patent Act itself indicates that patents shall have the attributes of personal property "[s]ubject to the provisions of this title," 35 U.S.C. § 261, including, presumably, the provision that injunctive relief "may" issue only "in accordance with the principles of equity," § 283.

This approach is consistent with our treatment of injunctions under the Copyright Act. Like a patent owner, a copyright holder possesses "the right to exclude others from using his property." *Fox Film Corp. v. Doyal,* 286 U.S. 123 (1932); see also *id.,* at 127–128 ("A copyright, like a patent, is at once the equivalent given by the public for benefits bestowed by the genius and meditations and skill of individuals and the incentive to further efforts for the same important objects" (internal quotation marks omitted)). Like the Patent Act, the Copyright Act provides that courts "may" grant injunctive relief "on such terms as it may deem reasonable to prevent or restrain infringement of a copyright." 17 U.S.C. § 502(a). And as in our decision today, this Court has consistently rejected invitations to replace traditional equitable considerations with a rule that an injunction automatically follows a determination that a copyright has been infringed.

Neither the District Court nor the Court of Appeals below fairly applied these traditional equitable principles in deciding respondent's motion for a permanent injunction. Although the District Court recited the traditional four-factor test, 275 F.Supp.2d, at 711, it appeared to adopt certain expansive principles suggesting that injunctive relief could not issue in a broad swath of cases. Most notably, it concluded that a "plaintiff's willingness to license its patents" and "its lack of commercial activity in practicing the patents" would be sufficient to establish that the patent holder would not suffer irreparable harm if an injunction did not issue. *Id.*, at 712. But traditional equitable principles do not permit such broad classifications. For example, some patent holders, such as university researchers or self-made inventors, might reasonably prefer to license their patents, rather than undertake efforts to secure the financing necessary to bring their works to market themselves. Such patent holders may be able to satisfy the traditional four-factor test, and we see no basis for categorically denying them the opportunity to do so. To the extent that the District Court adopted such a categorical rule, then, its analysis cannot be squared with the principles of equity adopted by Congress. . . .

[handwritten margin note: t.c. error]

In reversing the District Court, the Court of Appeals departed in the opposite direction from the four-factor test. The court articulated a "general rule," unique to patent disputes, "that a permanent injunction will issue once infringement and validity have been adjudged." 401 F.3d, at 1338. The court further indicated that injunctions should be denied only in the "unusual" case, under "exceptional circumstances" and "'in rare instances . . . to protect the public interest.'" *Id.*, at 1338–1339. Just as the District Court erred in its categorical denial of injunctive relief, the Court of Appeals erred in its categorical grant of such relief. Cf. *Roche Products, Inc. v. Bolar Pharmaceutical Co.*, 733 F.2d 858, 865 (C.A.Fed.1984) (recognizing the "considerable discretion" district courts have "in determining whether the facts of a situation require it to issue an injunction").

[handwritten margin note: app. error]

Because we conclude that neither court below correctly applied the traditional four-factor framework that governs the award of injunctive relief, we vacate the judgment of the Court of Appeals, so that the District Court may apply that framework in the first instance. In doing so, we take no position on whether permanent injunctive relief should or should not issue in this particular case, or indeed in any number of other disputes arising under the Patent Act. We hold only that the decision whether to grant or deny injunctive relief rests within the equitable discretion of the district courts, and that such discretion must be exercised consistent with traditional principles of equity, in patent disputes no less than in other cases governed by such standards.

Accordingly, we vacate the judgment of the Court of Appeals and remand the case for further proceedings consistent with this opinion.

It is so ordered.

* * *

Problem 32

Convincing the court that the harm flowing from the defendant's conduct is irreparable is essential to obtaining injunctive relief. What is the irreparable harm in the following situation?

A landowner has a contract with a youth soccer league that allows the league to use the property every Saturday to play its soccer games. The league's players are children, ages eight to twelve. The landowner tells the soccer league it will no longer be able to use the field because a farmer's market has offered more money to hold its markets there on Saturdays. The league now has nowhere to play soccer games.

The league sues the landowner for breach of contract and asks for an injunction allowing it to continue to use the field.

Introductory Note — *Holubec v. Brandenberger*

The harm at issue in *Holubec* is the nuisance (noise, smell, and the like) experienced by neighbors of a sheep feedlot. What is the appropriate remedy for that kind of harm: Damages? An injunction? Both? That is the question posed to the Texas Court of Appeals.

———————

THINGS TO THINK ABOUT while reading *Holubec v. Brandenberger*:

1. In a case decided by a jury, who decides whether the plaintiff gets an injunction — the jury or the judge?

2. Can the same type of harm support an award of both damages and an injunction? How?

Holubec v. Brandenberger *nuisance*

Texas Court of Appeals

214 S.W.3d 650 (2006)

G. ALAN WALDROP, Justice.

Carl Brandenberger, individually and as next friend of Payton Brandenberger, Carson Brandenberger and McKenna Brandenberger; Kathy Brandenberger; and First Mason II, Ltd. sued David Holubec and Mary Holubec for nuisance, negligence, and trespass stemming from the Holubecs' operation of a sheep feedlot in close proximity to the Brandenbergers' home. After a jury found against the Holubecs on nuisance, trespass, and negligence, the trial court entered a final judgment awarding actual damages for past personal injuries to the Brandenbergers and punitive damages. The trial court also entered a permanent injunction that abates the existing nuisance and prohibits the Holubecs from relocating the feedlot to an alternate site on their property. The injunction also directs the Holubecs to remove all of their sheep ranching equipment from the feedlot despite evidence that there was an acceptable level of sheep feeding on the land prior to 1997, when the nuisance conditions began.

The questions presented on appeal concern the propriety of the permanent injunction and damage awards entered by the trial court. Specifically, the Holubecs contend that the appellees are not entitled to injunctive relief because they have an adequate remedy at law in the form of monetary damages. . . . We conclude that, although the appellees are entitled to equitable relief in the form of a permanent injunction, the injunction entered by the trial court was overly broad and not supported by the evidence in the record. . . . Accordingly, we affirm in part and reverse and remand in part.

injunction was overly broad

Factual and Procedural Background

The Holubecs own a 450-acre ranch in McCullough County, Texas. In 1994, the Lee family purchased a ranch to the south and west of the Holubecs' ranch. Also in 1994, the Lees' ranch foreman, Carl Brandenberger, moved with his family to a stone house near the common boundary between the Lees' and the Holubecs' properties. According to Carl Brandenberger, when he and his family moved to the stone house, there were "only a few sheep and a brushy pasture" on the Holubecs' adjacent property.

At the end of 1996, the Holubecs began clearing land near the Brandenbergers' house to construct a ten-acre feedlot for sheep. The feedlot's ten acres were partitioned from a twenty-acre area of fenced pasture the Holubecs had used since 1986 to wean lambs and fatten them for sale. Before being cleared, this pasture was thick with mesquite and brush, although lanes had been cut to permit the sheep to reach feeders placed on the property. Although it is undisputed that the Holubecs fed sheep on the twenty-acre tract beginning in 1986, the Holubecs kept no written records of how many sheep were kept on the twenty-acre tract between 1986 and

1997. When the ten-acre feedlot was constructed, it contained twenty sheep pens and other improvements to accommodate about 6000 sheep. David Holubec testified that he kept as many as 5800 sheep on the ten-acre feedlot at various times. The nearest sheep pen on the ten-acre feedlot was approximately 135 feet from the Brandenbergers' home.

Carl Brandenberger testified that the nuisance conditions began when thousands of sheep were confined in the newly constructed feedlot pens. Specifically, by August 1997, the Brandenbergers noticed foul odors, swarms of flies, increased dust, and noise from bleating lambs being weaned from their mothers. In February 1998, the Holubecs added elevated lights to the feedlot to permit night work. The Brandenbergers claimed that these lights illuminated their house and disturbed their sleep.

On July 31, 1998, the Brandenbergers and the Lees filed suit, complaining that the foul odors, flies, dust, noise, and light resulting from the construction and operation of the ten-acre feedlot constituted a nuisance. . . . The trial court's final judgment awarded actual damages for past personal injuries to the Brandenbergers and punitive damages to both the Brandenbergers and the Lees. Additionally, the trial court permanently enjoined the Holubecs from:

tc decision

> 1. Operating a feedlot or stabling, confining, feeding, weaning or maintaining any animals in confinement areas that do not sustain such animals on the crops, vegetation, forage growth, or post harvest residues produced in such areas in the normal growing season, on any of the Holubecs' land that is within 1000 feet of the boundary line between the Holubecs' land and the Lees' land, other than confinement in existing working pens for normal ranching activities such as medicating, sorting, and shipping.

> 2. Feeding hay or other feed on the ground within 1000 feet of the Rock House on the Lees' land in a manner which will encourage or result in the breeding or proliferation of fly larva and/or flies in the area.

> 3. Placing feed troughs or self-feeders within 1000 feet of the Rock House on the Lees' land in close proximity to the Rock House or in greater number that existed prior to November 1996 or at the time the Holubecs began construction on the pens which ultimately formed the feed lot operation in question, whichever came first.

> 4. Maintaining lights on the Holubecs' land that shine directly on the existing residence (Rock House) on the Lees' property.

> 5. Disposing of dead animals on Defendants' Land within one-half mile radius of the Rock House on Plaintiffs' Land or within 1,000 feet of the boundary line between Plaintiffs' Land and Defendants' Land.

In addition to this prohibitory injunctive relief, the trial court also granted mandatory injunctive relief ordering the Holubecs to take the following affirmative action:

> 1. Remove all feeders from the pens in the approximately 10 acre feedlot adjacent to Plaintiffs' Land;

2. Remove all sheds and water troughs from the pens in the approximately 10 acre feedlot adjacent to Plaintiffs' Land;

3. Remove the wire fencing and feedlot pens now existing in the approximately 10 acre feedlot adjacent to Plaintiffs' Land;

4. Remove Southernmost overhead lights pole now existing in the approximately 10 acre feedlot adjacent to Plaintiffs' Land;

5. Clean the feedlot area of manure, spilled feed and hay residue in such a manner that substantially all fly breeding areas are destroyed, feedlot odor is remediated and hay residue will not provide a breeding site for stable flies or produce mold.

In this appeal, the Holubecs do not dispute the jury's findings of nuisance, negligence, and trespass. Instead, they contend that the trial court abused its discretion by entering a permanent injunction because the appellees possess an adequate remedy at law in the form of monetary damages. . . .

Injunction

The Holubecs contend that the trial court abused its discretion by entering a permanent injunction because the appellees possess an adequate remedy at law in the form of monetary damages. In support of this position, they point to the jury's findings regarding the type and amount of damages for the trial court to award the Brandenbergers and the Lees for their injuries. The jury found that the Brandenbergers should be awarded $32,500 for past personal injuries and $20,000 in punitive damages, and that the Lees should be awarded $10,000 in punitive damages. The jury also found that the Brandenbergers were not entitled to damages for injuries "that in reasonable probability will be sustained in the future." Finally, the jury found that $82,500 would "fairly and reasonably compensate the owner of the Lee Ranch for the reduction in value, if any, of the entire ranch, including the rock house and the surrounding one acre of land, which was proximately caused by the nuisance, trespass, and/or negligence." The Holubecs assert that these jury findings amount to a conclusive determination that the appellees possess an adequate legal remedy that precludes equitable relief in the form of an injunction.

[The jury's findings] concerning the proper amount and type of damages to award the appellees do not have the conclusive effect of precluding an injunction. "The jury does not determine the expediency, necessity, or propriety of equitable relief." *Shields v. State*, 27 S.W.3d 267, 272 (Tex.App.-Austin 2000). Instead, "the determination whether to grant an injunction based on ultimate issues of fact found by the jury is for the trial court, exercising chancery powers, and not the jury." *Id.* Therefore, it was appropriate for the trial court to assess the need for or propriety of a permanent injunction to abate the feedlot nuisance as a potential remedy in addition to monetary damages.

The trial court was within its discretion to determine that injunctive relief is appropriate in this case because there was evidence that the nuisance is of a recurring nature. When the nuisance complained of is of a "recurring nature," an injunction "will lie irrespective of legal remedy at law." *Lamb v. Kinslow,* 256 S.W.2d 903, 905 (Tex.Civ.App.-Waco 1953). Monetary damages are not always an adequate remedy in situations where the nuisance is of a recurring nature because damages could be recovered only as of the time of the bringing of the action, and a multiplicity of suits would be necessary. In this case, Mr. Holubec testified that he would continue to operate the ten-acre feedlot in the manner at issue unless the court ordered him to do otherwise. He stated that he intended to keep the feedlot in its current location indefinitely, 135 feet from the Brandenbergers' house. The trial court could have reasonably concluded that the Holubecs are operating and will continue to operate the feedlot in a manner so as to create a recurring nuisance. The trial court's award of past damages and punitive damages will not prevent the Holubecs from operating their feedlot in this manner. Therefore, without injunctive relief, the Brandenbergers will continue to experience the nuisance caused by the Holubecs' operation of the feedlot. Under these circumstances, the trial court's award of injunctive relief affords the Brandenbergers and the Lees relief from a recurring nuisance. This relief is in addition to, rather than duplicative of, the award of monetary damages, and is designed to grant the appellees complete relief. Granting injunctive relief in addition to monetary damages awarded is not an abuse of discretion in these circumstances.

Not an abuse of discretion

[However,] the permanent injunction is overly broad because it directs the Holubecs to remove all feeders, sheds, water troughs, and wire fencing from the ten-acre feedlot site despite evidence in the record that some form of sheep farming existed on the site of the ten-acre feedlot, known as the "brushy trap," prior to November 1996 that did not constitute a nuisance. While the record is unclear as to exactly how many sheep were run on the "brushy trap" prior to November 1996, both David Holubec and Mary Holubec testified that they began feeding sheep there in 1986. According to David Holubec, there were approximately 27 feeders on the "brushy trap" between 1986 and 1997. Carl Brandenberger confirmed the Holubecs' testimony that sheep were fed on the "brushy trap" when he moved with his family to the stone house in 1994. He stated that the nuisance conditions did not begin until the ten-acre site was transformed into a feedlot after November 1996. Thus, some amount of sheep feeding or farming activity on the ten-acre site did not constitute a nuisance. From this record, we conclude that injunctive relief requiring the complete removal of the Holubecs' sheep farming equipment on the ten-acre feedlot site prohibits more sheep farming activity than the evidence supports and, as a result, is overly broad and constitutes an abuse of discretion. . . .

Conclusion

We hold that the trial court acted within its discretion to award injunctive relief in addition to the monetary damages awarded by the jury because the injunctive relief is designed to remedy a recurring nuisance. . . . Therefore, the judgment of the trial court awarding past damages as well as punitive damages is affirmed. Although we find that the trial court did not abuse its discretion by considering and awarding injunctive relief, we conclude that the permanent injunction entered by the trial court is overly broad[.] Therefore, the permanent injunction entered by the trial court is affirmed in part and reversed in part. This cause is remanded to the trial court for reformation by the court of the award of injunctive relief consistent with the evidence adduced at trial[.]

* * *

Introductory Note — *Walgreen Co. v. Sara Creek Property Co.*

The unanimous opinion in *Walgreen* was written by now-retired Judge Richard Posner, an expert on the intersection of law and economics. As he often did, Judge Posner brought his economic perspective on the law to the Seventh Circuit's decision in this contract dispute between a shopping center and one of its tenants. Note the separate concurring opinion, reproduced here in its entirety.

THINGS TO THINK ABOUT while reading *Walgreen Co. v. Sara Creek Property Co.*:

1. Can monetary loss ever justify an injunction? If so, under what circumstances?

2. What costs does an injunction impose on society?

3. In what situations would an injunction be less costly to society than a damages award?

Walgreen Co. v. Sara Creek Property Co.

United States Court of Appeals, Seventh Circuit
966 F.2d 273 (1992)

POSNER, Circuit Judge.

This appeal from the grant of a permanent injunction raises fundamental issues concerning the propriety of injunctive relief. The essential facts are simple. Walgreen has operated a pharmacy in the Southgate Mall in Milwaukee since its opening in 1951. Its current lease, signed in 1971 and carrying a 30-year, 6-month term, contains, as had the only previous lease, a clause in which the landlord, Sara Creek, promises not to lease space in the mall to anyone else who wants to operate a pharmacy or a store containing a pharmacy. Such an exclusivity clause, common in shopping-center leases, is occasionally challenged on antitrust grounds, Milton Handler & Daniel E. Lazaroff, "Restraint of Trade and the Restatement (Second) of Contracts," 57 *N.Y.U.L.Rev.* 669, 683–708 (1982); Note, "The Antitrust Implications of Restrictive Covenants in Shopping Center Leases," 86 *Harv.L.Rev.* 1201 (1973) — implausibly enough, given the competition among malls; but that is an issue for another day, since in this appeal Sara Creek does not press the objection it made below to the clause on antitrust grounds.

In 1990, fearful that its largest tenant — what in real estate parlance is called the "anchor tenant" — having gone broke was about to close its store, Sara Creek informed Walgreen that it intended to buy out the anchor tenant and install in its place a discount store operated by Phar-Mor Corporation, a "deep discount" chain, rather than, like Walgreen, just a "discount" chain. Phar-Mor's store would occupy 100,000 square feet, of which 12,000 would be occupied by a pharmacy the same size as Walgreen's. The entrances to the two stores would be within a couple of hundred feet of each other.

Walgreen filed this diversity suit for breach of contract against Sara Creek and Phar-Mor and asked for an injunction against Sara Creek's letting the anchor premises to Phar-Mor. After an evidentiary hearing, the judge found a breach of Walgreen's lease and entered a permanent injunction against Sara Creek's letting the anchor tenant premises to Phar-Mor until the expiration of Walgreen's lease. He did this over the defendants' objection that Walgreen had failed to show that its remedy at law — damages — for the breach of the exclusivity clause was inadequate. Sara Creek had put on an expert witness who testified that Walgreen's damages could be readily estimated, and Walgreen had countered with evidence from its employees that its damages would be very difficult to compute, among other reasons because they included intangibles such as loss of goodwill.

Sara Creek reminds us that damages are the norm in breach of contract as in other cases. Many breaches, it points out, are "efficient" in the sense that they allow resources to be moved into a more valuable use. *Patton v. Mid-Continent Systems, Inc.*, 841 F.2d 742, 750–51 (7th Cir.1988). Perhaps this is one — the value of Phar-Mor's occupancy of the anchor premises may exceed the cost to Walgreen of facing increased competition. If so, society will be better off if Walgreen is paid its damages, equal to that cost, and Phar-Mor is allowed to move in rather than being kept out by an injunction. That is why injunctions are not granted as a matter of course, but only when the plaintiff's damages remedy is inadequate. *Northern Indiana Public Service Co. v. Carbon County Coal Co.*, 799 F.2d 265, 279 (7th Cir.1986). Walgreen's is not, Sara Creek argues; the projection of business losses due to increased competition is a routine exercise in calculation. Damages representing either the present value of lost future profits or (what should be the equivalent, *Carusos v. Briarcliff, Inc.*, 76 Ga.App. 346, 351–52 (1947)) the diminution in the value of the leasehold have either been awarded or deemed the proper remedy in a number of reported cases for breach of an exclusivity clause in a shopping-center lease. Why, Sara Creek asks, should they not be adequate here?

Sara Creek makes a beguiling argument that contains much truth, but we do not think it should carry the day. For if, as just noted, damages have been awarded in some cases of breach of an exclusivity clause in a shopping-center lease, injunctions have been issued in others. The choice between remedies requires a balancing of the costs and benefits of the alternatives. The task of striking the balance is for the trial judge, subject to deferential appellate review in recognition of its particularistic, judgmental, fact-bound character. As we said in an appeal from a grant of a preliminary injunction — but the point is applicable to review of a permanent injunction as well — "The question for us [appellate judges] is whether the [district] judge exceeded the bounds of permissible choice in the circumstances, not what we would have done if we had been in his shoes." *Roland Machinery Co. v. Dresser Industries, Inc.,* 749 F.2d 380, 390 (7th Cir.1984).

The plaintiff who seeks an injunction has the burden of persuasion — damages are the norm, so the plaintiff must show why his case is abnormal. But when, as in this case, the issue is whether to grant a permanent injunction, not whether to grant a temporary one, the burden is to show that damages are inadequate, not that the denial of the injunction will work irreparable harm. "Irreparable" in the injunction context means not rectifiable by the entry of a final judgment. It has nothing to do with whether to grant a permanent injunction, which, in the usual case anyway, *is* the final judgment. The use of "irreparable harm" or "irreparable injury" as synonyms for inadequate remedy at law is a confusing usage. It should be avoided. Owen M. Fiss & Doug Rendleman, *Injunctions* 59 (2d ed. 1984).

[margin note: definition should be avoided]

The benefits of substituting an injunction for damages are twofold. First, it shifts the burden of determining the cost of the defendant's conduct from the court to the parties. If it is true that Walgreen's damages are smaller than the gain to Sara Creek from allowing a second pharmacy into the shopping mall, then there must be a price for dissolving the injunction that will make both parties better off. Thus, the effect of upholding the injunction would be to substitute for the costly processes of forensic fact determination the less costly processes of private negotiation. Second, a premise of our free-market system, and the lesson of experience here and abroad as well, is that prices and costs are more accurately determined by the market than by government. A battle of experts is a less reliable method of determining the actual cost to Walgreen of facing new competition than negotiations between Walgreen and Sara Creek over the price at which Walgreen would feel adequately compensated for having to face that competition.

[margin note: benefits of substituting an injunction]

That is the benefit side of injunctive relief but there is a cost side as well. Many injunctions require continuing supervision by the court, and that is costly. A request for specific performance (a form of mandatory injunction) of a franchise agreement was refused on this ground in *North American Financial Group, Ltd. v. S.M.R. Enterprises, Inc.,* 583 F.Supp. 691, 699 (N.D.Ill.1984); see Edward Yorio, *Contract Enforcement: Specific Performance and Injunctions* § 3.3.2 (1989). Some injunctions are problematic because they impose costs on third parties. A more subtle cost of injunctive relief arises from the situation that economists call "bilateral monopoly," in which two parties can deal only with each other: the situation that an injunction creates. The sole seller of widgets selling to the sole buyer of that product would be an example. But so will be the situation confronting Walgreen and Sara Creek if the injunction is upheld. Walgreen can "sell" its injunctive right only to Sara Creek, and Sara Creek can "buy" Walgreen's surrender of its right to enjoin the leasing of

[margin note: costs of an injunction]

the anchor tenant's space to Phar-Mor only from Walgreen. The lack of alternatives in bilateral monopoly creates a bargaining range, and the costs of negotiating to a point within that range may be high. Suppose the cost to Walgreen of facing the competition of Phar-Mor at the Southgate Mall would be $1 million, and the benefit to Sara Creek of leasing to Phar-Mor would be $2 million. Then at any price between those figures for a waiver of Walgreen's injunctive right both parties would be better off, and we expect parties to bargain around a judicial assignment of legal rights if the assignment is inefficient. R.H. Coase, "The Problem of Social Cost," 3 *J. Law & Econ.* 1 (1960). But each of the parties would like to engross as much of the bargaining range as possible — Walgreen to press the price toward $2 million, Sara Creek to depress it toward $1 million. With so much at stake, both parties will have an incentive to devote substantial resources of time and money to the negotiation process. The process may even break down, if one or both parties want to create for future use a reputation as a hard bargainer; and if it does break down, the injunction will have brought about an inefficient result. All these are in one form or another costs of the injunctive process that can be avoided by substituting damages.

The costs and benefits of the damages remedy are the mirror of those of the injunctive remedy. The damages remedy avoids the cost of continuing supervision and third-party effects, and the cost of bilateral monopoly as well. It imposes costs of its own, however, in the form of diminished accuracy in the determination of value, on the one hand, and of the parties' expenditures on preparing and presenting evidence of damages, and the time of the court in evaluating the evidence, on the other.

The weighing up of all these costs and benefits is the analytical procedure that is or at least should be employed by a judge asked to enter a permanent injunction, with the understanding that if the balance is even the injunction should be withheld. The judge is not required to explicate every detail of the analysis and he did not do so here, but as long we are satisfied that his approach is broadly consistent with a proper analysis we shall affirm; and we are satisfied here. The determination of Walgreen's damages would have been costly in forensic resources and inescapably inaccurate. The lease had ten years to run. So Walgreen would have had to project its sales revenues and costs over the next ten years, and then project the impact on those figures of Phar-Mor's competition, and then discount that impact to present value. All but the last step would have been fraught with uncertainty. . . .

Damages are not always costly to compute, or difficult to compute accurately. In the standard case of a seller's breach of a contract for the sale of goods where the buyer covers by purchasing the same product in the market, damages are readily calculable by subtracting the contract price from the market price and multiplying by the quantity specified in the contract. But this is not such a case and here damages would be a costly and inaccurate remedy; and on the other side of the balance some of the costs of an injunction are absent and the cost that is present seems low. The injunction here, like one enforcing a covenant not to compete (standardly enforced by injunction, Yorio, *supra*, 401–08), is a simple negative injunction — Sara

Creek is not to lease space in the Southgate Mall to Phar-Mor during the term of Walgreen's lease — and the costs of judicial supervision and enforcement should be negligible. There is no contention that the injunction will harm an *unrepresented* third party. It may harm Phar-Mor but that harm will be reflected in Sara Creek's offer to Walgreen to dissolve the injunction. (Anyway Phar-Mor *is* a party.) The injunction may also, it is true, harm potential customers of Phar-Mor — people who would prefer to shop at a deep-discount store than an ordinary discount store — but their preferences, too, are registered indirectly. The more business Phar-Mor would have, the more rent it will be willing to pay Sara Creek, and therefore the more Sara Creek will be willing to pay Walgreen to dissolve the injunction.

The only substantial cost of the injunction in this case is that it may set off a] *only substantial cost* round of negotiations between the parties. . . .

To summarize, the judge did not exceed the bounds of reasonable judgment in concluding that the costs (including forgone benefits) of the damages remedy would exceed the costs (including forgone benefits) of an injunction. We need not consider whether, as intimated by Walgreen, exclusivity clauses in shopping-center leases should be considered presumptively enforceable by injunctions. Although we have described the choice between legal and equitable remedies as one for case-by-case determination, the courts have sometimes picked out categories of case in which injunctive relief is made the norm. The best-known example is specific performance of contracts for the sale of real property. *Anderson v. Onsager,* 155 Wis.2d 504 (1990); *Okaw Drainage District v. National Distillers & Chemical Corp.,* 882 F.2d 1241, 1248 (7th Cir.1989); Anthony T. Kronman, "Specific Performance," 45 *U.Chi.L.Rev.* 351, 355 and n. 20 (1978). The rule that specific performance will be ordered in such cases as a matter of course is a generalization of the considerations discussed above. Because of the absence of a fully liquid market in real property and the frequent presence of subjective values (many a homeowner, for example, would not sell his house for its market value), the calculation of damages is difficult; and since an order of specific performance to convey a piece of property does not create a continuing relation between the parties, the costs of supervision and enforcement if specific performance is ordered are slight. The exclusivity clause in Walgreen's lease relates to real estate, but we hesitate to suggest that every contract involving real estate should be enforceable as a matter of course by injunctions. Suppose Sara Creek had covenanted to keep the entrance to Walgreen's store free of ice and snow, and breached the covenant. An injunction would require continuing supervision, and it would be easy enough if the injunction were denied for Walgreen to hire its own ice and snow remover and charge the cost to Sara Creek. On the other hand, injunctions to enforce exclusivity clauses are quite likely to be justifiable by just the considerations present here — damages are difficult to estimate with any accuracy and the injunction is a one-shot remedy requiring no continuing judicial involvement. So there is an argument for making injunctive relief presumptively appropriate in such cases, but we need not decide in this case how strong an argument.

AFFIRMED.

HARLINGTON WOOD, Jr., Senior Circuit Judge, concurring.

I gladly join in the affirmance reached in Judge Posner's expert analysis.

* * *

Problem 33

Courts can be hesitant to grant injunctive relief when there is difficulty in enforcement. In the following situation, how might an injunction be crafted to provide effective relief but minimize the court's role in enforcing it?

Prison inmates sue the warden in federal court, alleging there are three times as many inmates in the prison as it was designed to house and the overcrowded conditions subject them to cruel and unusual punishment in violation of their constitutional rights. The inmates request an injunction to remedy the constitutional violation. They prevail at trial. The court rules that to comply with the Constitution the prison population must be reduced by fifty percent.

[handwritten: conditional injunctions]

[handwritten margin notes: - inj. inquiry 1/2 satisfied; 3. hardship Δ cost; π C. right; policy: supervision economic efficiency?; - const. right is different, the court will deal w/ more]

Provisional Injunctive Relief

Injunctions are issued in cases of irreparable harm. An injunction is appropriate when a plaintiff prevails at trial by proving the defendant committed a legal wrong and further shows the harm caused by the defendant cannot be remedied by an award of damages. That type of injunction, issued after trial, is called a permanent injunction. The term is used even though the injunction may not actually be "permanent" — it could be a mandatory injunction requiring the defendant to perform a single act, or it could be a prohibitory injunction that lasts for a fixed period of time.

But what if, as in most cases involving injunctive relief, the irreparable harm the plaintiff is concerned about will occur before a trial can be conducted? (The reason that is true in most cases is because of the time it takes for a lawsuit to get to trial — in many jurisdictions, two years or more.) In those cases, assuming the harm is indeed irreparable, a victory for the plaintiff at trial will be hollow. The injury the plaintiff wanted to prevent by seeking an injunction has already happened.

Plaintiffs who find themselves in that situation need a stopgap that prevents the harm from occurring until the court determines who wins the lawsuit. This is often referred to as maintaining the status quo (existing state of affairs) until trial. A temporary injunction that maintains the status quo while the merits of a dispute are adjudicated is a provisional injunction, and it comes in two forms: a preliminary injunction and a temporary restraining order.

Preliminary Injunction

A preliminary injunction is an order preventing irreparable harm that lasts until a trial can be conducted. When a plaintiff requests such provisional relief, the court faces a dilemma. On the one hand, granting the plaintiff's request will amount to awarding a remedy — even if temporarily — to a party who has not yet proven they are entitled to one. That seems unfair to the defendant. On the other hand, denying the request could result in the court being unable to provide effective relief after the plaintiff proves its claims at trial because the irreparable harm already happened. That seems unfair to the plaintiff.

To mitigate the potential unfairness, the court must make a prediction about who will win the lawsuit. If it appears likely the plaintiff will be able to prove its claims and meet the standard for injunctive relief, that suggests the court should grant provisional relief, to preserve its ability to provide an effective remedy. If the plaintiff is likely to prevail, that lowers the risk of ordering a remedy that is ultimately undeserved. By the same reasoning, where a plaintiff appears *unlikely* to prevail at trial, a court should deny provisional relief.

But even where the plaintiff can show a likelihood of prevailing, a court may rightfully be hesitant about issuing a preliminary injunction if doing so will severely burden the defendant (who, after all, has not yet been proven to have done anything wrong). So the court will also consider the consequences that will be experienced by each party if injunctive relief is either granted or denied. This is called balancing the hardships. Even if a plaintiff is otherwise entitled to injunctive relief, if providing it will only be marginally beneficial to the plaintiff but will significantly harm the defendant, a court is justified in denying an injunction.

Given its predictive nature, ruling on a preliminary injunction request is inherently uncertain. Courts therefore often employ a flexible standard to reduce the risk that a plaintiff will suffer a severe and irreparable injury merely because of an inability at such an early stage of the case to marshal sufficient facts to show a likelihood of prevailing. Under the flexible approach, sometimes referred to as a sliding scale standard, a greater showing on one of the relevant considerations can make up for a lesser showing on another. A plaintiff who shows a virtual certainty of extreme hardship in the absence of provisional relief may not need to show as much of a likelihood of success. In that way, when a court is uncertain about who will prevail, it can still prevent irreparable harm during the time required to decide the merits of the case.

One way in which courts mitigate the risk that unfairness will occur from imposing interim provisional injunctive relief when, after the full facts are revealed, none was warranted, is by requiring the plaintiff to post a bond as a condition of obtaining the injunction. A bond is a sum of money (or other security, such as real property) posted with the clerk of the court to hold during the time the injunction is in effect. If it turns out the injunction should not have been issued — because the plaintiff does not prevail at trial, or new facts come to light before trial undermining the plaintiff's case — the defendant can be compensated by the bond for any harm caused by the wrongfully issued injunction. An example of that situation might be a retail store owner who is preliminarily enjoined from operating her business. If the injunction is later deemed improper, the store owner can be reimbursed with the bond for the sales lost during the time the injunction was in effect. The Federal Rules of Civil Procedure require a bond — the amount determined in the court's discretion — as a condition of obtaining a provisional injunction. (See Fed. Rules of Civil Proc. 65(c) ["Security. The court may issue a preliminary injunction or a temporary restraining order only if the movant gives security in an amount that the court considers proper to pay the costs and damages sustained by any party found to have been wrongfully enjoined or restrained."].)

Since a preliminary injunction substantially affects the rights of the enjoined party, due process requires that party be allowed the opportunity to present a defense at a hearing before a preliminary injunction can issue. This procedure is also required by statute — in federal court, Rule of Procedure 65(a) requires notice and a hearing before a court can grant a preliminary injunction.

Temporary Restraining Order

Sometimes the irreparable harm feared by the plaintiff will occur even before a hearing on a preliminary injunction can be held. In such a case, a plaintiff can request a temporary restraining order: an order preventing irreparable harm that lasts only until the hearing on a preliminary injunction. A temporary restraining order acts as a placeholder to preserve the status quo between the filing of the lawsuit and the hearing on a preliminary injunction request.

Because the essence of a temporary restraining order is that relief is needed immediately, the order can be issued without a hearing. There may not even be time to provide notice to the defendant that the plaintiff is seeking the relief. From a constitutional perspective, that is highly unusual. The right to due process requires notice and an opportunity to be heard before a court can make an order affecting a party's rights. So an *ex parte* temporary restraining order — one that is issued without the other side being heard — is an intrusion on the restrained party's constitutional rights. The court must balance that intrusion with the competing interest of preserving the plaintiff's right to effective relief against irreparable harm.

One way in which the proper balance is struck is by making the duration of a temporary restraining order very short. In federal court, an *ex parte* temporary restraining order can last no more than 14 days. Federal Rules of Civil Procedure, Rule 65(b) sets forth the procedural rules for temporary restraining orders and includes several other measures intended to protect the due process rights of the restrained party:

Rule 65. Injunctions and Restraining Orders.

[. . .]

(b) Temporary Restraining Order.

(1) *Issuing Without Notice.* The court may issue a temporary restraining order without written or oral notice to the adverse party or its attorney only if:

> (A) specific facts in an affidavit or a verified complaint clearly show that immediate and irreparable injury, loss, or damage will result to the movant before the adverse party can be heard in opposition; and

> (B) the movant's attorney certifies in writing any efforts made to give notice and the reasons why it should not be required.

(2) *Contents; Expiration.* Every temporary restraining order issued without notice must state the date and hour it was issued; describe the injury and state why it is irreparable; state why the order was issued without notice; and be promptly filed in the clerk's office and entered in the record. The order expires at the time after entry — not to exceed 14 days — that the court sets, unless before that time the court, for good cause, extends it for a like period or the adverse party consents to a longer extension. The reasons for an extension must be entered in the record.

(3) *Expediting the Preliminary-Injunction Hearing.* If the order is issued without notice, the motion for a preliminary injunction must be set for hearing at the earliest possible time, taking precedence over all other matters except hearings on older matters of the same character. At the hearing, the party who obtained the order must proceed with the motion; if the party does not, the court must dissolve the order.

(4) *Motion to Dissolve.* On 2 days' notice to the party who obtained the order without notice — or on shorter notice set by the court — the adverse party may appear and move to dissolve or modify the order. The court must then hear and decide the motion as promptly as justice requires.

In deciding whether to issue a temporary restraining order, the court employs the same standard as it does for a preliminary injunction. But the decision will often have to be made based on much less information and without the benefit of a full adversarial hearing.

Introductory Note — *Blazel v. Bradley*

Blazel presents an unfortunately common scenario for temporary restraining orders: an allegation of domestic abuse. The procedural posture of the case is more unusual — a lawsuit brought by the subject of the restraining order against the state court judge who issued it. The plaintiff contends the restraining order violates his constitutional right to due process. The federal court must decide whether the Wisconsin procedure for issuing *ex parte* restraining orders is constitutionally permissible.

THINGS TO THINK ABOUT while reading *Blazel v. Bradley*:

1. When is a temporary restraining order necessary?

2. What kind of circumstances justify issuance of an ex parte order?

3. How does the court balance the requesting party's need for a temporary restraining order and the responding party's due process rights?

Blazel v. Bradley

United States District Court, Northern District of Wisconsin
698 F.Supp. 756 (1988)

CRABB, Chief Judge

This is a civil action brought pursuant to 42 U.S.C. § 1983 in which plaintiffs ask the court to declare unconstitutional Wis.Stat. § 813.12(3)(b), which permits the issuance of *ex parte* temporary restraining orders in domestic abuse actions.

I conclude that Wis.Stat. § 813.12 provides the essential due process protections that are required before the state may constitutionally deprive plaintiffs of the protected liberty and property interests at stake when a temporary restraining order is issued in a domestic abuse action. It is explicit in the statute that judicial participation and a verified petition containing detailed allegations are required before an *ex parte* order may issue and that a prompt post-deprivation hearing must be provided. And in light of the statute's legislative history, it is implicit that *ex parte* orders are to be issued only upon an allegation of risk of imminent and irreparable harm based on personal knowledge.

Facts

Plaintiff Alvin Blazel is an adult resident of Wisconsin. Defendant Ann Walsh Bradley is the duly elected Circuit Court Judge of Branch III of the Marathon County Circuit Court in Wausau, Wisconsin.

On March 13, 1987, plaintiff's wife, Donna Blazel, filed a petition for a temporary restraining order and injunction in the Marathon County Circuit Court, Branch III. Pursuant to Wis.Stat. § 813.12(5)(b), she was provided with a simplified form on which to file her petition. The form states that the allegations are made "under oath" and has preprinted responses that the petitioner can check indicating the petitioner's relation to respondent, whether both are adults, and the petitioner's legal interest in his or her residence. The form provides a space for the petitioner to describe the necessity for the order. In this space the form states "The respondent engaged in or might engage in domestic abuse to me because: (The conduct must include an intentional infliction of or threat to inflict physical pain, physical injury or illness; impairment of physical condition; or sexual contact or sexual intercourse without consent, as set forth in s. 940.225(1)(2) or 3, [sic] Wis.Stats.)." The form has a space where the petitioner must describe "what happened, when, where, who did what to whom." The petition then lists the types of protection that may be ordered, including requiring respondent to avoid petitioner's residence or to avoid contacting her, and a line marked "Other." The petitioner is to mark any of the boxes which apply.

In the space provided for a description of abuse Donna Blazel alleged as follows: "2–28–87 he grabbed me by the back of my hair & tried to throw my neck out, which hurts my arthritis. Called Mara. Co. Sheriff's Dept. About Feb. 12, 1987, threw a loaf of bread at me & then hit me in the back of the head with his fist and tried to throw my neck out, called MCSD and signed an abuse complaint."

Donna Blazel marked with an "X" the lines on the pre-printed petition indicating she was requesting that the court immediately issue a temporary restraining order requiring the named respondent to avoid his residence and to avoid contacting petitioner or causing any other person to have contact with her, and directing the sheriff to place her in physical possession of her residence.

On March 13, 1987, the day Donna Blazel filed the petition, defendant issued a temporary restraining order on a pre-printed form, ordering Alvin Blazel to avoid the petitioner's residence, to avoid contacting petitioner or causing any person other than a party's attorney to contact petitioner, and to leave the children in the home. The first two requirements were preprinted and then marked by the judge. The last requirement was typed on a line marked "other." The order provided that it was in effect until the injunction hearing, which a handwritten entry indicated was scheduled for March 19, 1987.

The temporary restraining order was issued without any notice to Alvin Blazel. He first became aware of the matter on March 14, 1987, when he was served with the order. . . .

Opinion

Plaintiffs' challenge to Wis.Stat. § 813.12(3) is directed to what they contend is the statute's authorization of procedures that violate due process. They argue that it is unconstitutional for judges and family court commissioners to issue temporary restraining orders without notice to the respondent, ordering the respondent to avoid petitioner's home and not to contact the petitioner simply because the petitioner alleges sufficient facts for a judge or family court commissioner to find "reasonable grounds to believe that the respondent has engaged in, or based on prior conduct of the petitioner and the respondent[,] may engage in, domestic abuse of the petitioner." Plaintiffs contend that the statute is deficient on its face and as applied because it does not require notice or hearing before the order is issued and because it does not incorporate necessary safeguards that would render an *ex parte* order constitutional, such as sworn statements, evidence of a pattern of abuse, allegations of imminent danger, narrowly drawn definitions, and intensive review of specific allegations.

The statute at issue is a fairly recent response to the growing public understanding of the serious problem of domestic abuse. It was preceded by an earlier version of the statute, § 813.025, enacted in 1979, and repealed and replaced with the current statute, § 813.12, in 1983. Both contain essentially similar provisions concerning *ex parte* temporary restraining orders.

Wisconsin is not alone in having this type of legislation. Every state and the District of Columbia have enacted legislation intended to respond to the problem of domestic violence. *See Ex Parte Protection Orders: Is Due Process Locked Out?*, 58 Temple Law Quarterly 841, 841 n. 1 (1985). Thirty-seven of these statutes provide *ex parte* preliminary relief. *Id.* at 848 n. 37. No federal court has yet addressed the constitutionality of any of these statutes, although the Eastern District of Wisconsin considered the constitutionality of a similar statute in the divorce context. *See Geisinger v. Voss,* 352 F.Supp. 104 (E.D.Wis.1972). Four state courts, including the Wisconsin court of appeals, have considered due process challenges to state statutes permitting *ex parte* orders in domestic abuse cases and have upheld the statutes. *See Schramek v. Bohren,* 145 Wis.2d 695 (Ct.App.1988); *Marquette v. Marquette,* 686 P.2d 990 (Okla.App.1984); *State v. Marsh,* 626 S.W.2d 223, 231 (Mo.1982) (en banc); *Boyle v. Boyle,* 12 D. & C.3d 767, 775 (C.P.Alleg.1979).

Due Process Analysis

As a general rule, *ex parte* temporary restraining orders are available only rarely and only after petitioners have satisfied stringent requirements. *See, e.g., Granny Goose Foods, Inc. v. Brotherhood of Teamsters,* 415 U.S. 423, 439 (1974); *American Can Co. v. Mansukhani,* 742 F.2d 314, 321 (7th Cir.1984); Fed.R.Civ.P. 65(b). "Our entire jurisprudence runs counter to the notion of court action taken before reasonable notice and an opportunity to be heard has been granted both sides of a dispute." *Granny Goose,* 415 U.S. at 439. Under the federal rules an applicant for an *ex parte* temporary restraining order must provide specific facts in affidavits or in a verified complaint that show immediate and irreparable injury will occur before the adverse party can appear, must certify reasons why notice should not be required, and must post a bond for payment of costs and damages that may be incurred. Fed.R.Civ.P. 65(b). . . .

Some process is due before a Wisconsin judge or family court commissioner may issue an *ex parte* temporary restraining order under § 813.12 because the order can cause two distinct deprivations. First, by requiring that the alleged abuser avoid the petitioner's residence, in which the respondent may well have a cognizable property interest, the statute threatens a deprivation of property which triggers due process protections. *See, e.g., North Georgia Finishing, Inc. v. DiChem, Inc.,* 419 U.S. 601 (1975); *Fuentes v. Shevin,* 407 U.S. 67 (1972). Second, the order may implicate cognizable liberty interests if it deprives an alleged abuser of his relation with his children. The Supreme Court has found that the liberty interest protected by the

Fifth and Fourteenth Amendments includes the right to establish a home and bring up children. *Board of Regents v. Roth,* 408 U.S. 564, 572 (1972). Accordingly, the state may not terminate the parent-child relationship without a hearing. *Stanley v. Illinois,* 405 U.S. 645 (1972); *Lassiter v. Department of Social Services,* 452 U.S. 18 (1981).

It is true that when an *ex parte* temporary restraining order is issued, there is only a temporary expulsion from the home and interruption of the parent-child relationship and not a termination of rights. The short duration of the deprivation may affect the nature of the process that must be provided, but it does not eliminate the basic requirement of due process protections.

Because the Wisconsin order can deprive plaintiffs of protected liberty and property interests, it implicates due process protections. The question is the nature of the protections that must be provided. Since notice and opportunity to be heard are the cornerstone of due process, *id.* 407 U.S. at 80; *Granny Goose,* 415 U.S. at 439, a pre-deprivation hearing is required unless extraordinary circumstances necessitate prompt action without a hearing, *Fuentes,* 407 U.S. at 82, 90, or unless sufficient safeguards are provided. *See, e.g., North Georgia,* 419 U.S. 601.

Circumstances justifying the postponing of notice and hearing "must be truly unusual," *Fuentes,* 407 U.S. at 90, and must be shown to have met three criteria:

> First, in each case, the seizure has been directly necessary to secure an important governmental or general public interest. Second, there has been a special need for very prompt action. Third, the State has kept strict control over its monopoly of legitimate force: the person initiating the seizure has been a government official responsible for determining, under the standards of a narrowly drawn statute, that it was necessary and justified in the particular instance.

Id. at 91. One could argue that the circumstances of domestic abuse restraining orders fulfill these criteria, but the fit is not perfect. First, the threat of harm is less to the general public than to a private individual. Second, there is not necessarily a need for prompt action. In some cases immediate action may be imperative, but in others it may not be. Third, the deprivation is not initiated by the government but by a private petitioner. The circumstances are not comparable to those cases in which seizure or suspension without notice or hearing based on extraordinary circumstances has been permitted. . . .

As with domestic abuse restraining orders, repossession and garnishment involve conflicting interests of petitioner and respondent. Debtors have a protected ownership interest in their wages and property and creditors have strong competing interests since they are owed money and can claim at least partial ownership of the property. In addition, as with domestic abuse cases, providing prior notice involves substantial risks: once notified of the proceeding, the debtor in possession could sell or hide the property. Finally, where the state statutes do not require documentary proof or specific allegations, there is substantial risk of erroneous deprivation.

Although the cases are not entirely consistent, I can conclude that in creditor repossession cases the Supreme Court has established that the due process clause requires either a pre-deprivation hearing or at least four minimum procedural safeguards: participation by a judicial officer; a prompt post-deprivation hearing; verified petitions or affidavits containing detailed allegations based on personal knowledge; and risk of immediate and irreparable harm. *See North Georgia*, 419 U.S. at 607.

Both on its face and as it was applied to plaintiff, the Wisconsin statute satisfies three of these criteria explicitly. It allows only a judge or a family court commissioner to issue an *ex parte* temporary restraining order, Wis.Stat. § 813.12(3); it provides for a post-deprivation hearing within seven days, Wis.Stat. § 813.12(3)(c); and it requires a verified petition based on personal knowledge and containing specific allegations. The pre-printed form states that the petition is made under oath. As such it is a verified petition. The statute requires more than a conclusory claim that petitioner is entitled to a restraining order. A petitioner must allege facts sufficient to show "that the respondent engaged in, or based on prior conduct of the petitioner and the respondent may engage in, domestic abuse of the petitioner." The petitioner must "[s]tate what happened, when, where, and who did what to whom."

In this case, both orders against plaintiff were issued by a judge, both orders provided for a post-deprivation hearing within seven days, and neither issued on the basis of merely conclusory allegations. Donna Blazel alleged specific and detailed facts about alleged abuse: the date the alleged incidents occurred and specific physical actions by the respondent. . . .

The fourth procedural safeguard is a showing of risk of immediate and irreparable harm. It is only the risk of immediate harm that justifies the issuance of an *ex parte* temporary restraining order. Otherwise issuance of the restraining order could await notice to respondent and the holding of an adversarial hearing. Neither the Wisconsin statute nor the pre-printed petition form requires an allegation that there is immediate risk of abuse, and Donna Blazel did not make such an allegation in her petition.

. . . An examination of the legislative history of the Wisconsin statute reveals that although there is no explicit provision that petitioners must allege immediate and irreparable harm, the legislature intended that the statute permit the issuance of an *ex parte* temporary restraining order only on a showing of risk of immediate and irreparable harm. . . .

I conclude that when the legislature required a showing of physical violence in Wis.Stat. § 813.025, it intended that showing to be a showing of imminent danger. I base this conclusion on the evidence of the legislature's awareness of the requirement of immediate and irreparable harm, its obvious desire to avoid in § 813.025 the constitutional problems the federal district court had found with § 247.23, and its deliberate inclusion of a requirement that petitioners allege that physical violence has occurred or may occur in the future, coupled with the presumptions that courts should find a statute constitutional when its language and history lend themselves reasonable to that interpretation and that federal courts should defer to a state court's finding that its own state's statute is constitutional. Because of the lack of any significant differences between § 813.025 and the statute challenged in this case, I conclude that the legislature intended § 813.12 to include the same requirement that the complainant make a showing of imminent danger before an *ex parte* order may issue. It is unnecessary to find that the legislature also intended to require a showing that the harm be irreparable. Any allegation of bodily harm makes that showing.

Because the statute's requirement of a showing of physical violence encompasses a requirement that the violence be shown to be imminent, the statute provides all the procedural safeguards necessary to satisfy the due process clause. Accordingly, I hold that when § 813.12 is construed to require a showing of imminent harm, the statute is constitutional on its face.

A holding of facial validity does not necessitate a finding that the statute was applied constitutionally to Alvin Blazel or other plaintiffs in the class. Although Donna Blazel's petitions were the basis for the two orders entered against Alvin Blazel, they contain no allegation of a risk of immediate harm. In the first, she states only that Alvin Blazel has assaulted her some two weeks before. There is no allegation that she feared he would attack her again in the near future. In the second petition, she adds allegations of previous assaults, but again, there is no allegation of a risk of imminent harm. I conclude that the *ex parte* order that required Alvin Blazel to avoid his home and children for seven days deprived him of property and liberty interests without due process of law, and that plaintiff is entitled to a declaration that his constitutional rights were violated. Plaintiff has not sought money damages from defendant, and she is immune from them.

Whether any of the other plaintiffs were similarly deprived is something that cannot be determined from the present record. Plaintiffs have not filed copies of the petitions which were the basis for the orders issued against the other plaintiffs in the class, from which I might determine whether those petitions contained the requisite allegations of imminent harm.

Order

IT IS ORDERED THAT plaintiff's motion for summary judgment is GRANTED in part and DENIED in part. It is further ORDERED that defendant's motion for summary judgment is GRANTED in part and DENIED in part. Wis.Stat. § 813.12 is constitutional on its face if construed as it should be to require that the complainant allege that the risk of physical harm is imminent. However, the statute was applied unconstitutionally to plaintiff Alvin D. Blazel.

* * *

Problem 34

To comply with constitutional due process protections, a temporary restraining order can be issued *ex parte* only when necessary to achieve the purpose of the order. Under the following facts, what is the best argument for issuing a temporary restraining order without notice to the restrained party? What is the best argument against doing so?

A homeowner receives a notice from the bank stating that her home is being foreclosed on and will be sold at auction in 30 days. The day before the sale is to occur, the homeowner files a lawsuit against the bank alleging wrongful foreclosure. She asks for an ex parte temporary restraining order preventing the sale.

Introductory Note — *University of Texas v. Camenisch*

The plaintiff in *Camenisch* won a preliminary injunction requiring his college to provide him with a sign language interpreter. The college complied with the injunction but appealed the decision to issue it. By the time that appeal was resolved, the plaintiff had graduated. The Supreme Court took the case to resolve two important procedural questions: (1) Is the trial court's decision to issue the preliminary injunction moot? and, (2) If the preliminary injunction is moot, does there still need to be a trial on the merits of the case?

THINGS TO THINK ABOUT while reading *University of Texas v. Camenisch*:

1. How does the procedure for obtaining a preliminary injunction differ from that for a temporary restraining order?

2. What are the reasons for those procedural differences?

3. Why did the Court decide it was a moot question whether a preliminary injunction was properly issued?

University of Texas v. Camenisch

United States Supreme Court
451 U.S. 390 (1981)

Justice STEWART delivered the opinion of the Court.

On March 1, 1978, Walter Camenisch, a deaf graduate student at the University of Texas, filed a complaint alleging that the University had violated §504 of the Rehabilitation Act of 1973, 87 Stat. 394, as amended, 29 U.S.C. §794 (1976 ed., Supp. III), which provides that "[n]o otherwise qualified handicapped individual in the United States . . . shall, solely by reason of his handicap, be excluded from the participation in, be denied the benefits of, or be subjected to discrimination under any program or activity receiving Federal financial assistance." The complaint alleged that the University received federal funds and that the University had discriminatorily refused to pay for a sign-language interpreter for Camenisch. The complaint asked the United States District Court for the Western District of Texas to grant declaratory relief and to "[p]reliminarily and permanently order defendants to appoint an interpreter for the plaintiff while he is a student in good standing at the defendant University."

The District Court applied the "Fifth Circuit standard for temporary relief to see if the injunction sought is appropriate." That standard, which was enunciated in *Canal Authority of Florida v. Callaway*, 489 F.2d 567 (1974), requires that a federal district court consider four factors when deciding whether to grant a preliminary injunction: whether the plaintiff will be irreparably harmed if the injunction does not issue; whether the defendant will be harmed if the injunction does issue; whether the public interest will be served by the injunction; and whether the plaintiff is likely to prevail on the merits. Finding a possibility that Camenisch would be irreparably harmed in the absence of an injunction, and finding a substantial likelihood that Camenisch would prevail on the merits, the District Court granted a preliminary injunction requiring that the University pay for Camenisch's interpreter, but the court did so on the condition that Camenisch "post a security bond in the amount of *$3,000.00* pending the outcome of this litigation pursuant to Rule 65(c), F. R. C. P." The District Court also ordered that the action be stayed "pending a final administrative determination on the merits, and that as a condition of preliminary injunctive relief, Plaintiff be required to initiate a complaint with HEW requesting the relief sought herein."

The Court of Appeals for the Fifth Circuit likewise applied the *Canal Authority* test, and found that the balance of hardships weighed in favor of granting an injunction and that Camenisch's claim would be successful on the merits. The Court of Appeals therefore affirmed the grant of the preliminary injunction. 616 F.2d 127.

By the time the Court of Appeals had acted, the University had obeyed the injunction by paying for Camenisch's interpreter, and Camenisch had been graduated. The Court of Appeals, however, rejected a suggestion that the case was therefore moot. The court said: "[A] justiciable issue remains: whose responsibility is it to pay for this interpreter?" *Id.*, at 130–131. We granted certiorari, and Camenisch has now raised the mootness issue before this Court.

The Court of Appeals correctly held that the case as a whole is not moot, since, as that court noted, it remains to be decided who should ultimately bear the cost of the interpreter. However, the issue before the Court of Appeals was not who should pay for the interpreter, but rather whether the District Court had abused its discretion in issuing a preliminary injunction requiring the University to pay for him. *Brown v. Chote*, 411 U.S. 452, 457; *Alabama v. United States*, 279 U.S. 229. The two issues are significantly different, since whether the preliminary injunction should have issued depended on the balance of factors listed in *Canal Authority*, while whether the University should ultimately bear the cost of the interpreter depends on a final resolution of the merits of Camenisch's case.

This, then, is simply another instance in which one issue in a case has become moot, but the case as a whole remains alive because other issues have not become moot.... Because the only issue presently before us — the correctness of the decision to grant a preliminary injunction — is moot, the judgment of the Court of Appeals must be vacated and the case must be remanded to the District Court for trial on the merits. See *Brown v. Chote, supra.*

Since Camenisch's likelihood of success on the merits was one of the factors the District Court and the Court of Appeals considered in granting Camenisch a preliminary injunction, it might be suggested that their decisions were tantamount to decisions on the underlying merits and thus that the preliminary-injunction issue is not truly moot. It may be that this was the reasoning of the Court of Appeals when it described its conclusion that the case was not moot as "simply another way of stating the traditional rule that issues raised by an expired injunction are not moot if one party was required to post an injunction bond." 616 F.2d, at 131. This reasoning fails, however, because it improperly equates "likelihood of success" with "success," and what is more important, because it ignores the significant procedural differences between preliminary and permanent injunctions.

The purpose of a preliminary injunction is merely to preserve the relative positions of the parties until a trial on the merits can be held. Given this limited purpose, and given the haste that is often necessary if those positions are to be preserved, a preliminary injunction is customarily granted on the basis of procedures that are less formal and evidence that is less complete than in a trial on the merits. A party thus is not required to prove his case in full at a preliminary-injunction hearing. *Progress Development Corp. v. Mitchell*, 286 F.2d 222 (C.A.7 1961), and the findings of fact and conclusions of law made by a court granting a preliminary injunction are not binding at trial on the merits, *Industrial Bank of Washington v. Tobriner*, 132 U.S.App.D.C. 51, 54, 405 F.2d 1321, 1324 (1968); *Hamilton Watch Co. v. Benrus Watch Co.*, 206 F.2d 738, 742 (C.A.2 1953). In light of these considerations, it is generally inappropriate for a federal court at the preliminary-injunction stage to give a final judgment on the merits. *E. g., Brown v. Chote, supra; Gellman v. Maryland*, 538 F.2d 603 (C.A.4 1976); *Santiago v. Corporacion de Renovacion Urbana y Vivienda de Puerto Rico*, 453 F.2d 794 (C.A.1 1972).

Should an expedited decision on the merits be appropriate, Rule 65(a)(2) of the Federal Rules of Civil Procedure provides a means of securing one. That Rule permits a court to "order the trial of the action on the merits to be advanced and consolidated with the hearing of the application." Before such an order may issue, however, the courts have commonly required that "the parties should normally receive clear and unambiguous notice [of the court's intent to consolidate the trial and the hearing] either before the hearing commences or at a time which will still afford the parties a full opportunity to present their respective cases." *Pughsley v. 3750 Lake Shore Drive Cooperative Bldg.*, 463 F.2d 1055, 1057 (C.A.7 1972). This procedure was not followed here.

In short, where a federal district court has granted a preliminary injunction, the parties generally will have had the benefit neither of a full opportunity to present their cases nor of a final judicial decision based on the actual merits of the controversy. Thus when the injunctive aspects of a case become moot on appeal of a preliminary injunction, any issue preserved by an injunction bond can generally not be resolved on appeal, but must be resolved in a trial on the merits. Where, by contrast, a federal district court has granted a permanent injunction, the parties will already have had their trial on the merits, and, even if the case would otherwise be moot, a determination can be had on appeal of the correctness of the trial court's decision on the merits, since the case has been saved from mootness by the injunction bond. . . .

The present case is replete with circumstances indicating the necessity for a full trial on the merits in the *nisi prius* court, where a preliminary injunction has become moot and an injunction bond has been issued. The proceedings here bear the marks of the haste characteristic of a request for a preliminary injunction: the parties have relied on a short stipulation of facts, and even the legal theories on which the University has relied have seemed to change from one level of the proceeding to another. The District Court and the Court of Appeals both properly based their decisions not on the ultimate merits of Camenisch's case but rather on the balance of the *Canal Authority* factors. While it is true that some of the Court of Appeals' language suggests a conclusion that Camenisch would win on the merits, the court certainly did not hold that the standards for a summary judgment had been met.

In sum, the question whether a preliminary injunction should have been issued here is moot, because the terms of the injunction, as modified by the Court of Appeals, have been fully and irrevocably carried out. The question whether the University must pay for the interpreter remains for trial on the merits. Until such a trial has taken place, it would be inappropriate for this Court to intimate any view on the merits of the lawsuit.

The judgment of the Court of Appeals is therefore vacated, and the case is remanded to the District Court for further proceedings consistent with this opinion.

It is so ordered.

* * *

Problem 35

Injunctive relief is available to correct an existing condition or prevent irreparable harm. Would an injunction be an appropriate remedy in the following situation?

An employee's supervisor constantly makes offensive comments reflecting race and gender-based stereotypes. The employee complains to the human resources department, and after an investigation, the supervisor is fired. The employee sues the company for creating a hostile work environment and for violation of anti-discrimination laws. She requests an injunction preventing further harassment.

Introductory Note — *Winter v. Natural Resources Defense Council, Inc.* and *CitiGroup Global Markets, Inc. v. VCG Special Opportunities Master Fund*

Winter requires the Supreme Court to balance two important — and, under the circumstances, competing — interests: national security and harm to the environment. In deciding whether a preliminary injunction preventing the Navy from conducting sonar training exercises that harmed dolphins was properly issued, the Supreme Court determined the standard used by the lower court was too lenient because it allowed for injunctive relief based on the mere possibility of irreparable harm.

Post-*Winter*, federal courts were left to decide just how high the bar for obtaining provisional injunctive relief is. *CitiGroup Global Markets* provides an answer to that question.

THINGS TO THINK ABOUT while reading *Winter v. Natural Resources Defense Council, Inc.* and *CitiGroup Global Markets, Inc. v. VCG Special Opportunities Master Fund*:

1. What is the standard for deciding if preliminary injunctive relief is warranted?

2. What are the most important considerations in the preliminary injunction analysis?

3. Why might it be desirable to have some degree of flexibility in the standard for granting a preliminary injunction?

Winter v. Natural Resources Defense Council, Inc.

United States Supreme Court
555 U.S. 7 (2008)

Chief Justice ROBERTS delivered the opinion of the Court.

"To be prepared for war is one of the most effectual means of preserving peace." 1 Messages and Papers of the Presidents 57 (J. Richardson comp. 1897). So said George Washington in his first Annual Address to Congress, 218 years ago. One of the most important ways the Navy prepares for war is through integrated training exercises at sea. These exercises include training in the use of modern sonar to detect and track enemy submarines, something the Navy has done for the past 40 years. The plaintiffs, respondents here, complained that the Navy's sonar-training program harmed marine mammals, and that the Navy should have prepared an environmental impact statement before commencing its latest round of training exercises. The Court of Appeals upheld a preliminary injunction imposing restrictions on the Navy's sonar training, even though that court acknowledged that "the record contains no evidence that marine mammals have been harmed" by the Navy's exercises. 518 F.3d 658, 696 (C.A.9 2008).

The Court of Appeals was wrong, and its decision is reversed.

I

The Navy deploys its forces in "strike groups," which are groups of surface ships, submarines, and aircraft centered around either an aircraft carrier or an amphibious assault ship. Seamless coordination among strike-group assets is critical. Before deploying a strike group, the Navy requires extensive integrated training in analysis and prioritization of threats, execution of military missions, and maintenance of force protection.

Antisubmarine warfare is currently the Pacific Fleet's top war-fighting priority. Modern diesel-electric submarines pose a significant threat to Navy vessels because they can operate almost silently, making them extremely difficult to detect and track. Potential adversaries of the United States possess at least 300 of these submarines.

The most effective technology for identifying submerged diesel-electric submarines within their torpedo range is active sonar, which involves emitting pulses of sound underwater and then receiving the acoustic waves that echo off the target. . . . The Navy conducts regular training exercises under realistic conditions to ensure that sonar operators are thoroughly skilled in its use in a variety of situations.

The waters off the coast of southern California (SOCAL) are an ideal location for conducting integrated training exercises, as this is the only area on the west coast that is relatively close to land, air, and sea bases, as well as amphibious landing areas. . . . Sharing the waters in the SOCAL operating area are at least 37 species of marine mammals, including dolphins, whales, and sea lions. The parties strongly dispute the extent to which the Navy's training activities will harm those animals or disrupt their behavioral patterns. The Navy emphasizes that it has used MFA sonar during training exercises in SOCAL for 40 years, without a single documented sonar-related injury to any marine mammal. The Navy asserts that, at most, MFA sonar may cause temporary hearing loss or brief disruptions of marine mammals' behavioral patterns.

The plaintiffs are the Natural Resources Defense Council, Inc., Jean-Michael Cousteau (an environmental enthusiast and filmmaker), and several other groups devoted to the protection of marine mammals and ocean habitats. They contend that MFA sonar can cause much more serious injuries to marine mammals than the Navy acknowledges, including permanent hearing loss, decompression sickness, and major behavioral disruptions.

[T]he plaintiffs sued the Navy, seeking declaratory and injunctive relief on the grounds that the Navy's SOCAL training exercises violated NEPA, the Endangered Species Act of 1973(ESA), and the Coastal Zone Management Act of 1972 (CZMA). The District Court granted plaintiffs' motion for a preliminary injunction and prohibited the Navy from using MFA sonar during its remaining training exercises. The court held that plaintiffs had "demonstrated a probability of success" on their claims under NEPA and the CZMA. The court also determined that equitable relief was appropriate because, under Ninth Circuit precedent, plaintiffs had established at least a "'possibility'" of irreparable harm to the environment. Based on scientific studies, declarations from experts, and other evidence in the record, the District Court concluded that there was in fact a "near certainty" of irreparable injury to the environment, and that this injury outweighed any possible harm to the Navy.

The Navy filed an emergency appeal, and the Ninth Circuit stayed the injunction pending appeal. 502 F.3d 859, 865 (2007). After hearing oral argument, the Court of Appeals agreed with the District Court that preliminary injunctive relief was appropriate. . . .

We granted certiorari, and now reverse and vacate the injunction.

II

A

A plaintiff seeking a preliminary injunction must establish that he is likely to succeed on the merits, that he is likely to suffer irreparable harm in the absence of preliminary relief, that the balance of equities tips in his favor, and that an injunction is in the public interest. See *Munaf v. Geren*, 553 U.S. 674, 689–690 (2008).

The District Court and the Ninth Circuit concluded that plaintiffs have shown a likelihood of success on the merits of their NEPA claim. The Navy strongly disputes this determination, arguing that plaintiffs' likelihood of success is low because the CEQ reasonably concluded that "emergency circumstances" justified alternative arrangements to NEPA compliance. . . .

The District Court and the Ninth Circuit also held that when a plaintiff demonstrates a strong likelihood of prevailing on the merits, a preliminary injunction may be entered based only on a "possibility" of irreparable harm. *Id.*, at 696–697; 530 F. Supp.2d, at 1118. The lower courts held that plaintiffs had met this standard because the scientific studies, declarations, and other evidence in the record established to "a near certainty" that the Navy's training exercises would cause irreparable harm to the environment. 530 F.Supp.2d, at 1118.

The Navy challenges these holdings, arguing that plaintiffs must demonstrate a likelihood of irreparable injury — not just a possibility — in order to obtain preliminary relief. On the facts of this case, the Navy contends that plaintiffs' alleged injuries are too speculative to give rise to irreparable injury, given that ever since the Navy's training program began 40 years ago, there has been no documented case of sonar-related injury to marine mammals in SOCAL. And even if MFA sonar does cause a limited number of injuries to individual marine mammals, the Navy asserts that plaintiffs have failed to offer evidence of species-level harm that would adversely affect their scientific, recreational, and ecological interests. For their part, plaintiffs assert that they would prevail under any formulation of the irreparable injury standard, because the District Court found that they had established a "near certainty" of irreparable harm.

We agree with the Navy that the Ninth Circuit's "possibility" standard is too lenient. Our frequently reiterated standard requires plaintiffs seeking preliminary relief to demonstrate that irreparable injury is likely in the absence of an injunction. *Los Angeles v. Lyons*, 461 U.S. 95, 103 (1983). Issuing a preliminary injunction based only on a possibility of irreparable harm is inconsistent with our characterization of injunctive relief as an extraordinary remedy that may only be awarded upon a clear showing that the plaintiff is entitled to such relief. *Mazurek v. Armstrong*, 520 U.S. 968, 972 (1997).

It is not clear that articulating the incorrect standard affected the Ninth Circuit's analysis of irreparable harm. Although the court referred to the "possibility" standard, and cited Circuit precedent along the same lines, it affirmed the District Court's conclusion that plaintiffs had established a "'near certainty'" of irreparable harm. 518 F.3d, at 696–697. At the same time, however, the nature of the District Court's conclusion is itself unclear. The District Court originally found irreparable harm from sonar-training exercises generally. But by the time of the District Court's final decision, the Navy challenged only two of six restrictions imposed by the court. See supra, at 373–374. The District Court did not reconsider the likelihood of irreparable harm in light of the four restrictions not challenged by the Navy. This failure is significant in light of the District Court's own statement that the 12 nautical mile exclusion zone from the coastline — one of the unchallenged mitigation restrictions — "would bar the use of MFA sonar in a significant portion of important marine mammal habitat." 530 F.Supp.2d, at 1119. . . .

As explained in the next section, even if plaintiffs have shown irreparable injury from the Navy's training exercises, any such injury is outweighed by the public interest and the Navy's interest in effective, realistic training of its sailors. A proper consideration of these factors alone requires denial of the requested injunctive relief.

For the same reason, we do not address the lower courts' holding that plaintiffs have also established a likelihood of success on the merits.

B

A preliminary injunction is an extraordinary remedy never awarded as of right. *Munaf,* 553 U.S., at 689–690. In each case, courts "must balance the competing claims of injury and must consider the effect on each party of the granting or withholding of the requested relief." *Amoco Production Co.,* 480 U.S., at 542. "In exercising their sound discretion, courts of equity should pay particular regard for the public consequences in employing the extraordinary remedy of injunction." *Romero-Barcelo,* 456 U.S., at 312; see also *Railroad Comm'n of Tex. v. Pullman Co.,* 312 U.S. 496, 500 (1941). In this case, the District Court and the Ninth Circuit significantly understated the burden the preliminary injunction would impose on the Navy's ability to conduct realistic training exercises, and the injunction's consequent adverse impact on the public interest in national defense.

This case involves "complex, subtle, and professional decisions as to the composition, training, equipping, and control of a military force," which are "essentially professional military judgments." *Gilligan v. Morgan,* 413 U.S. 1, 10 (1973). We "give great deference to the professional judgment of military authorities concerning the relative importance of a particular military interest." *Goldman v. Weinberger,* 475 U.S. 503, 507 (1986). . . .

Here, the record contains declarations from some of the Navy's most senior officers, all of whom underscored the threat posed by enemy submarines and the need for extensive sonar training to counter this threat. . . .

These interests must be weighed against the possible harm to the ecological, scientific, and recreational interests that are legitimately before this Court. Plaintiffs have submitted declarations asserting that they take whale watching trips, observe marine mammals underwater, conduct scientific research on marine mammals, and photograph these animals in their natural habitats. Plaintiffs contend that the Navy's use of MFA sonar will injure marine mammals or alter their behavioral patterns, impairing plaintiffs' ability to study and observe the animals.

While we do not question the seriousness of these interests, we conclude that the balance of equities and consideration of the overall public interest in this case tip strongly in favor of the Navy. For the plaintiffs, the most serious possible injury would be harm to an unknown number of the marine mammals that they study and observe. In contrast, forcing the Navy to deploy an inadequately trained antisubmarine force jeopardizes the safety of the fleet. Active sonar is the only reliable technology for detecting and tracking enemy diesel-electric submarines, and the President—the Commander in Chief—has determined that training with active sonar is "essential to national security."

The public interest in conducting training exercises with active sonar under realistic conditions plainly outweighs the interests advanced by the plaintiffs. Of course, military interests do not always trump other considerations, and we have not held that they do. In this case, however, the proper determination of where the public interest lies does not strike us as a close question. . . .

The factors examined above — the balance of equities and consideration of the public interest — are pertinent in assessing the propriety of any injunctive relief, preliminary or permanent. See *Amoco Production Co.*, 480 U.S., at 546, n. 12 ("The standard for a preliminary injunction is essentially the same as for a permanent injunction with the exception that the plaintiff must show a likelihood of success on the merits rather than actual success"). Given that the ultimate legal claim is that the Navy must prepare an EIS, not that it must cease sonar training, there is no basis for enjoining such training in a manner credibly alleged to pose a serious threat to national security. This is particularly true in light of the fact that the training has been going on for 40 years with no documented episode of harm to a marine mammal. A court concluding that the Navy is required to prepare an EIS has many remedial tools at its disposal, including declaratory relief or an injunction tailored to the preparation of an EIS rather than the Navy's training in the interim. See, e.g., *Steffel v. Thompson*, 415 U.S. 452, 466 (1974) ("Congress plainly intended declaratory relief to act as an alternative to the strong medicine of the injunction"). In the meantime, we see no basis for jeopardizing national security, as the present injunction does. Plaintiffs confirmed at oral argument that the preliminary injunction was "the whole ball game," Tr. of Oral Arg. 33, and our analysis of the propriety of preliminary relief is applicable to any permanent injunction as well.

President Theodore Roosevelt explained that "the only way in which a navy can ever be made efficient is by practice at sea, under all the conditions which would have to be met if war existed." President's Annual Message, 42 Cong. Rec. 81 (1907). We do not discount the importance of plaintiffs' ecological, scientific, and recreational interests in marine mammals. Those interests, however, are plainly outweighed by the Navy's need to conduct realistic training exercises to ensure that it is able to neutralize the threat posed by enemy submarines. The District Court abused its discretion by imposing a 2,200-yard shutdown zone and by requiring the Navy to power down its MFA sonar during significant surface ducting conditions. The judgment of the Court of Appeals is reversed, and the preliminary injunction is vacated to the extent it has been challenged by the Navy.

It is so ordered.

Justice GINSBURG, with whom Justice SOUTER joins, dissenting.

Flexibility is a hallmark of equity jurisdiction. "The essence of equity jurisdiction has been the power of the Chancellor to do equity and to mould each decree to the necessities of the particular case. Flexibility rather than rigidity has distinguished it." *Weinberger v. Romero-Barcelo*, 456 U.S. 305, 312.). Consistent with equity's character, courts do not insist that litigants uniformly show a particular, predetermined quantum of probable success or injury before awarding equitable relief. Instead, courts have evaluated claims for equitable relief on a "sliding scale," sometimes awarding relief based on a lower likelihood of harm when the likelihood of success is very high. 11A C. Wright, A. Miller, & M. Kane, Federal Practice and Procedure § 2948.3, p. 195 (2d ed.1995). This Court has never rejected that formulation, and I do not believe it does so today.

... The Court is correct that relief is not warranted "simply to prevent the possibility of some remote future injury." (quoting Wright & Miller, supra, § 2948.1, at 155). "However, the injury need not have been inflicted when application is made or be certain to occur; a strong threat of irreparable injury before trial is an adequate basis." Wright & Miller, supra, § 2948.1, at 155–156 (footnote omitted). I agree with the District Court that NRDC made the required showing here.

For the reasons stated, I would affirm the judgment of the Ninth Circuit.

* * *

CitiGroup Global Markets, Inc. v. VCG Special Opportunities Master Fund

United States Court of Appeals, Second Circuit
598 F.3d 30 (2010)

JOHN M. WALKER, JR., Circuit Judge:

VCG Special Opportunities Master Fund Limited ("VCG") appeals from the November 12, 2008 order of the United States District Court for the Southern District of New York (Barbara S. Jones, *Judge*) granting the plaintiff-appellee Citigroup Global Markets, Inc.'s ("CGMI") motion for a preliminary injunction and enjoining VCG from proceeding with an arbitration initiated against CGMI before the Financial Industry Regulatory Authority ("FINRA"). VCG also appeals from the district court's May 29, 2009 order denying its motion for reconsideration of the preliminary injunction. Because we conclude that the "serious questions" standard for assessing a movant's likelihood of success on the merits remains valid in the wake of recent Supreme Court cases, and because neither the district court's assessment of the facts nor its application of the law supports a finding of abuse of discretion, we AFFIRM as to both orders.

Background

On July 17, 2006, VCG, a hedge fund based on the Isle of Jersey, entered into a brokerage services agreement with CGMI. Under the agreement, CGMI was obligated to provide prime brokerage services by clearing and settling trades in fixed income securities for VCG. VCG then entered into a credit default swap agreement with Citibank, N.A. (Citibank) (a sister-affiliate of appellee CGMI under the corporate umbrella of Citigroup, Inc.). VCG alleges that it was a "customer" of CGMI, which allegedly acted as the middleman with respect to the series of transactions culminating in the credit default swap agreement with Citibank. After entering into the swap, Citibank eventually declared a writedown of the assets covered in its credit default swap agreement with VCG, triggering VCG's obligation to pay Citibank a total of $10,000,000.

VCG sued Citibank, seeking a declaration that, by declaring the writedown, Citibank had violated the terms of the parties' credit default swap agreement. . . . In addition to litigating its claims against Citibank, VCG began arbitration proceedings against CGMI before the FINRA pursuant to FINRA Rule 12200. In response, CGMI filed a complaint in the district court to permanently enjoin the arbitration and for a declaration that CGMI had no obligation to arbitrate with VCG regarding the claims submitted to the FINRA arbitrators. On June 20, 2008, CGMI moved for a temporary restraining order and preliminary injunction against the FINRA arbitration pending a final resolution of CGMI's claims. CGMI asserted that it was not a party to, and did not broker, the VCGCitibank credit default swap. Specifically, CGMI argued that VCG was not a "customer" of CGMI for purposes of those transactions and, therefore, CGMI was under no obligation to arbitrate VCG's claims under the FINRA rules. . . .

On November 12, 2008, the district court granted CGMI's motion for a preliminary injunction. In granting the injunction, the district court applied this circuit's long-established standard for the entry of a preliminary injunction, under which the movant is required to show "'irreparable harm absent injunctive relief, and either a likelihood of success on the merits, or a serious question going to the merits to make them a fair ground for trial, with a balance of hardships tipping decidedly in plaintiff's favor.'" *Citigroup Global Mkts. Inc. v. VCG Special Opportunities Master Fund Ltd.*, No. 08-cv-5520, 2008 WL 4891229, at *2 (S.D.N.Y. Nov. 12, 2008). The district court held that CGMI had demonstrated a likelihood of irreparable harm, but had failed to make a showing of "probable success" on the merits based on its claim that there was no customer relationship between CGMI and VCG with respect to the credit default swap transactions. *Id.* at *2, *4. The district court found, however, that CGMI had provided evidence that raised "serious questions" as to whether VCG was in fact a customer of CGMI with respect to the swap transaction and granted the preliminary injunction on that basis. *Id.* at *5–*6. . . .

On May 29, 2009, the district court denied VCG's motion for reconsideration, rejecting VCG's argument that *Winter v. Natural Resources Defense Council, Inc.*, 555 U.S. 7 (2008), had eliminated the "serious questions" prong of this circuit's preliminary injunction standard.

This appeal followed.

Discussion

VCG first contends that the district court abused its discretion by applying the wrong legal standard to CGMI's request for a preliminary injunction. VCG argues that three recent decisions of the Supreme Court — *Munaf v. Geren,* 553 U.S. 674 (2008); *Winter,* 555 U.S. 7; and *Nken v. Holder,* 556 U.S. 418 (2009) — have eliminated this circuit's "serious questions" standard for the entry of a preliminary injunction, and that, in light of the district court's finding that CGMI failed to demonstrate its likelihood of success on the merits, the entry of a preliminary injunction in this case must be reversed. In the alternative, VCG argues that even if this circuit's standard for a preliminary injunction remains intact, the district court committed several legal errors in determining that CGMI had presented "serious questions" as to the arbitrability of VCG's claims.

Winter articulates the following standard for issuing a preliminary injunction:

> A plaintiff seeking a preliminary injunction must establish that he is likely to succeed on the merits, that he is likely to suffer irreparable harm in the absence of preliminary relief, that the balance of equities tips in his favor, and that an injunction is in the public interest.

Winter, 129 S.Ct. at 374; *see also Munaf,* 128 S.Ct. at 2219; *Nken,* 129 S.Ct. at 1761. Although not stated explicitly in its briefs, we take VCG's position to be that the standard articulated by these three Supreme Court cases requires a preliminary injunction movant to demonstrate that it is more likely than not to succeed on its underlying claims, or in other words, that a movant must show a greater than fifty percent probability of success on the merits. Thus, according to VCG, a showing of "serious questions" that are a fair ground for litigation will not suffice. *See* VCG Br. 23–25 (describing the required showing as a "probability" of success, as opposed to a "possibility").

The Continued Viability of the "Serious Questions" Standard

For the last five decades, this circuit has required a party seeking a preliminary injunction to show "(a) irreparable harm and (b) either (1) likelihood of success on the merits or (2) sufficiently serious questions going to the merits to make them a fair ground for litigation and a balance of hardships tipping decidedly toward the party requesting the preliminary relief." *Jackson Dairy, Inc. v. H.P. Hood & Sons, Inc.,* 596 F.2d 70, 72 (2d Cir.1979). The "serious questions" standard permits a district court to grant a preliminary injunction in situations where it cannot determine with certainty that the moving party is more likely than not to prevail on the merits of the underlying claims, but where the costs outweigh the benefits of not granting the injunction. *See, e.g., F. & M. Schaefer Corp. v. C. Schmidt & Sons, Inc.,* 597 F.2d 814, 815–19 (2d Cir.1979). Because the moving party must not only show that there are "serious questions" going to the merits, but must additionally establish that "the balance of hardships tips *decidedly* " in its favor, *Jackson Dairy,* 596 F.2d at 72 (emphasis added), its overall burden is no lighter than the one it bears under the "likelihood of success" standard.

The value of this circuit's approach to assessing the merits of a claim at the preliminary injunction stage lies in its flexibility in the face of varying factual scenarios and the greater uncertainties inherent at the outset of particularly complex litigation. Preliminary injunctions should not be mechanically confined to cases that are simple or easy. Requiring in every case a showing that ultimate success on the merits is more likely than not "is unacceptable as a general rule. The very purpose of an injunction . . . is to give temporary relief based on a preliminary estimate of the strength of plaintiff's suit, prior to the resolution at trial of the factual disputes and difficulties presented by the case. Limiting the preliminary injunction to cases that do not present significant difficulties would deprive the remedy of much of its utility." 11A Charles Alan Wright, Arthur R. Miller & Mary Kay Kane, *Federal Practice and Procedure* § 2948.3 (2d ed.2009); *see also Dataphase Sys., Inc. v. CL Sys., Inc.,* 640 F.2d 109, 113 (8th Cir.1981) (en banc) ("The very nature of the inquiry on petition for preliminary relief militates against a wooden application of the probability test. . . . The equitable nature of the proceeding mandates that the court's approach be flexible enough to encompass the particular circumstances of each case. Thus, an effort to apply the probability language to all cases with mathematical precision is misplaced.").

Indeed, the Supreme Court, prior to the trilogy of cases cited by VCG, has counseled in favor of a preliminary injunction standard that permits the entry of an injunction in cases where a factual dispute renders a fully reliable assessment of the merits impossible. In *Ohio Oil Co. v. Conway,* 279 U.S. 813 (1929), the Court dealt with a factual dispute, relating to the effect on the plaintiff of a state tax on oil revenues, which had to "be resolved before the constitutional validity of [a] statute [could] be determined." *Id.* at 814. Faced with this situation, the Court instructed that "[w]here the questions presented by an application for an interlocutory injunction are grave, and the injury to the moving party [in the absence of such an injunction] will be certain and irreparable . . . the injunction usually will be granted." *Id.; see also Mazurek v. Armstrong,* 520 U.S. 968, 975–76, (1997) (reversing the Ninth Circuit's finding that movants had shown a "fair chance of success on the merits," while recognizing the "fair chance" standard and its potential application in future cases).

The Supreme Court's recent opinions in *Munaf, Winter,* and *Nken* have not undermined its approval of the more flexible approach signaled in *Ohio Oil.* None of the three cases comments at all, much less negatively, upon the application of a preliminary injunction standard that softens a strict "likelihood" requirement in cases that warrant it.

Nor does *Winter* address the requisite probability of success of the movant's underlying claims. While *Winter* rejected the Ninth Circuit's conceptually separate "possibility of irreparable harm" standard, it expressly withheld any consideration of the merits of the parties' underlying claims. Rather, the Court decided the case upon the balance of the equities and the public interest. . . .

If the Supreme Court had meant for *Munaf, Winter,* or *Nken* to abrogate the more flexible standard for a preliminary injunction, one would expect some reference to the considerable history of the flexible standards applied in this circuit, seven of our sister circuits, and in the Supreme Court itself. . . . We have found no command from the Supreme Court that would foreclose the application of our established "serious questions" standard as a means of assessing a movant's likelihood of success on the merits. Our standard accommodates the needs of the district courts in confronting motions for preliminary injunctions in factual situations that vary widely in difficulty and complexity. Thus, we hold that our venerable standard for assessing a movant's probability of success on the merits remains valid and that the district court did not err in applying the "serious questions" standard to CGMI's motion.

. . . .

For the foregoing reasons, we AFFIRM the district court's orders granting CGMI's motion for a preliminary injunction and denying VCG's motion for reconsideration.

* * *

Problem 36

A request for provisional injunctive relief requires the court to predict the plaintiff's chances of success while at the same time balancing other important considerations. Under the following facts, what is the best argument for granting the preliminary injunction request? What is the best argument for denying it?

A developer is building a new housing development. To provide access to the new homes, the developer has to clear space for a road. Doing that will destroy a single old-growth coastal redwood tree, estimated to be over 1,000 years old. An environmental conservation group sues the developer for violation of a federal statute protecting redwood trees. It is unclear whether the statute applies in this case because its text refers only to trees located in "close proximity" to other redwoods, and that language has never been interpreted by any court.

The conservation group requests a preliminary injunction to enjoin construction of the road.

Introductory Note — *Illinois Republican Party v. Pritzker*

Illinois Republican Party v. Pritzker is one of many cases decided during the 2020 COVID-19 pandemic involving the collision between the government's authority to enact public health protection measures, on the one hand, and constitutionally guaranteed individual freedoms, on the other. The procedural posture is an appeal from the denial of a preliminary injunction to prevent enforcement of an executive order limiting attendance at indoor religious services to 10 people. The Seventh Circuit Court of Appeals thoughtfully applies the standard for provisional injunctive relief from *Winter v. Natural Resources Defense Council* to decide whether the plaintiff was correctly denied a preliminary injunction.

THINGS TO THINK ABOUT while reading *Illinois Republican Party v. Pritzker*:

THINGS TO THINK ABOUT while reading *Illinois Republican Party v. Pritzker*:

1. What is the irreparable harm that is alleged by the plaintiff?

2. Which factor in the preliminary injunction analysis does the court find dispositive: Success on the merits? Irreparable harm? Or something else?

Illinois Republican Party v. Pritzker

United States Court of Appeals, Seventh Circuit
973 F.3d 760 (2020)

Wood, Circuit Judge.

As the coronavirus SARS-CoV-2 has raged across the United States, public officials everywhere have sought to implement measures to protect the public health and welfare. Illinois is no exception: Governor J. B. Pritzker has issued a series of executive orders designed to limit the virus's opportunities to spread. In the absence of better options, these measures principally rely on preventing the transmission of viral particles (known as virions) from one person to the next.

Governor Pritzker's orders are similar to many others around the country. At one point or another, they have included stay-at-home directives; flat prohibitions of public gatherings; caps on the number of people who may congregate; masking requirements; and strict limitations on bars, restaurants, cultural venues, and the like. These orders, and comparable ones in other states, have been attacked on a variety of grounds. Our concern here is somewhat unusual. Governor Pritzker's Executive Order 2020-43 (EO43, issued June 26, 2020) exhibits special solitude for the free exercise of religion. It does so through the following exemption:

> a. *Free exercise of religion*. This Executive Order does not limit the free exercise of religion. To protect the health and safety of faith leaders, staff, congregants and visitors, religious organizations and houses of worship are encouraged to consult and follow the recommended practices and guidelines from the Illinois Department of Public Health. As set forth in the IDPH guidelines, the safest practices for religious organizations at this time are to provide services online, in a drive-in format, or outdoors (and consistent with social distancing requirements and guidance regarding wearing face coverings), and to limit indoor services to 10 people. Religious organizations are encouraged to take steps to ensure social distancing, the use of face coverings, and implementation of other public health measures.

Emergency and governmental functions enjoy the same exemption. Otherwise, EO43 imposes a mandatory 50-person cap on gatherings.

The Illinois Republican Party and some of its affiliates ("the Republicans") believe that the accommodation for free exercise contained in the executive order violates the Free Speech Clause of the First Amendment. In this action, they seek a permanent injunction against EO43. In so doing, they assume that such an injunction would permit them, too, to congregate in groups larger than 50, rather than reinstate the stricter ban for religion that some of the Governor's earlier executive orders included, though that is far from assured. . . . The district court denied the Republicans' request for preliminary injunctive relief against EO43. See *Illinois Republican Party v. Pritzker*, No. 20 C 3489, — F.Supp.3d —, 2020 WL 3604106 (N.D. Ill. July 2, 2020). The Republicans promptly sought interim relief from that ruling, but we declined to disturb the district court's order, and Justice Kavanaugh in turn refused to intervene. *Illinois Republican Party v. Pritzker*, No. 19A1068 (Kavanaugh, J., in chambers July 4, 2020).

We did, however, expedite the briefing and oral argument of the merits of the preliminary injunction, and we heard argument on August 11, 2020. Guided primarily by the Supreme Court's decision in *Winter v. Natural Resources Defense Council*, 555 U.S. 7 (2008), we conclude that the district court did not abuse its discretion in denying the requested preliminary injunction, and so we affirm its order.

I

Before we turn to the heart of our analysis, a word or two about the standard of review for preliminary injunctions is in order. The Supreme Court's last discussion of the subject occurred in *Winter*, where the Court reviewed a preliminary injunction against the U.S. Navy's use of a sonar-training program. It expressed the standard succinctly: "A plaintiff seeking a preliminary injunction must establish that he is likely to succeed on the merits, that he is likely to suffer irreparable harm in the absence of preliminary relief, that the balance of equities tips in his favor, and that an injunction is in the public interest." *Id*. at 20. The question in *Winter*, however, just as in our case, is one of degree: *how* likely must success on the merits be in order to satisfy this standard? We infer from *Winter* that a mere possibility of success is not enough. . . .

An applicant for preliminary relief bears a significant burden, even though the Court recognizes that, at such a preliminary stage, the applicant need not show that it definitely will win the case. A "strong" showing thus does not mean proof by a preponderance — once again, that would spill too far into the ultimate merits for something designed to protect both the parties and the process while the case is pending. But it normally includes a demonstration of how the applicant proposes to prove the key elements of its case. And it is worth recalling that the likelihood of success factor plays only one part in the analysis. The applicant must also demonstrate that "irreparable injury is likely in the absence of an injunction," see *Winter*, 555 U.S. at 22. In addition, the balance of equities must "tip[ ] in [the applicant's] favor," and the "injunction [must be] in the public interest." *Id*. at 20.

II

With this standard in mind, we are ready to turn to the case at hand. . . .

Normally, parties challenging a state measure that appears to advantage religion invoke the Establishment Clause of the First Amendment (assuming for the sake of discussion that the challengers can establish standing to sue). That is emphatically not the theory that the Republicans are pursuing. We eliminated any doubt on that score at oral argument, where counsel assured us that this was not their position. As we explain in more detail below, the Republicans argue instead that preferential treatment for religious exercise conflicts with the interpretation in *Reed v. Gilbert*, 576 U.S. 155 (2015), of the Free Speech Clause of the same amendment. A group of 100 people may gather in a church, a mosque, or a synagogue to worship, but the same sized group may not gather to discuss the upcoming presidential election. The Republicans urge that only the content of the speech distinguishes these two hypothetical groups, and as they see it, *Reed* prohibits such a line.

Our response is to say, "not so fast." A careful look at the Supreme Court's Religion Clause cases, coupled with the fact that EO43 is designed to give *greater* leeway to the exercise of religion, convinces us that the speech that accompanies religious exercise has a privileged position under the First Amendment, and that EO43 permissibly accommodates religious activities. . . .

III

Before concluding, we must also comment on the Republicans' alternative argument: that the Governor is allowing Black Lives Matter protestors to gather in groups of far more than 50, but he is not allowing the Republicans to do so. They concede that their argument depends on practice, not the text of the executive order. The text contains no such exemption, whether for Black Lives Matter, Americans for Trump, Save the Planet, or anyone else. Should the Governor begin picking and choosing among those groups, then we would have little trouble saying that *Reed* would come into play, and he would either have to impose the 50-person limit on all of them, or on none of them.

The fact that the Governor expressed sympathy for the people who were protesting police violence after the deaths of George Floyd and others, and even participated in one protest, does not change the text of the order. Nonetheless, the Republicans counter, there are *de facto* changes, even if not *de jure* changes. Essentially, they charge that the state should not be leaving enforcement up to the local authorities, and that they are aggrieved by the lax or even discriminatory levels of enforcement that they see. . . . Although we do not rule out the possibility that someone might be able to prove this type of favoritism in the enforcement of an otherwise valid response to the COVID-19 pandemic, the record in this case falls short. Indeed, the problems of late have centered on ordinary criminal mobs looting stores, not on peaceful protestors. . . .

IV

We conclude with some final thoughts. The entire premise of the Republicans' suit is that if the exemption from the 50-person cap on gatherings for free-exercise activities were found to be unconstitutional (or if it were to be struck down based on the allegedly ideologically driven enforcement strategy), they would then be free to gather in whatever numbers they wished. But when disparate treatment of two groups occurs, the state is free to erase that discrepancy in any way that it wishes. . . . In other words, the state is free to "equalize up" or to "equalize down." If there were a problem with the religious exercise carve-out (and we emphasize that we find no such problem), the state would be entitled to return to a regime in which even religious gatherings are subject to the mandatory cap. . . . This would leave the Republicans no better off than they are today.

We AFFIRM the district court's order denying preliminary injunctive relief to the appellants.

* * *

Problem 37

To obtain provisional injunctive relief, a plaintiff must show a likelihood of prevailing on the merits of the substantive claim for relief. The plaintiff need not actually prove the claim, however. Assuming the other requirements for injunctive relief are satisfied, has the plaintiff in the following scenario shown enough of a likelihood of success to be granted a preliminary injunction?

A man sues a local police department in federal court for excessive force in violation of the Fourth Amendment to the United States Constitution (which prohibits law enforcement from making an arrest using force disproportionate to the threat presented). Because he often encounters police officers in his small community, the plaintiff asks for a preliminary injunction preventing further acts of excessive force by the department. As evidence in support of his request for injunctive relief, the plaintiff submits video footage from an officer's body-worn camera that shows three officers slamming the plaintiff onto a car hood and tackling him to the ground — seemingly without any justification whatsoever. In opposition, the police department submits declarations under penalty of perjury from the three involved officers saying that just before the body camera started recording, the plaintiff yelled that he had a knife and reached into his front pants pocket.

Chapter 8

Declaratory Judgments

Declaratory judgments are similar to injunctions in the sense that both remedies are intended to prevent a problem from occurring in the first place. A declaratory judgment is a judicial decree informing the parties to a dispute what their respective legal rights and obligations are. Its purpose is to resolve disputes early by providing clarity about who is obligated to do what in a particular situation. Unlike injunctions, however, the potential for *any* legally cognizable harm allows for a declaratory judgment; there is no requirement that the harm be irreparable.

A common situation where a declaratory judgment can be useful is in the interpretation of a contract—if one party to the agreement wants to know whether certain conduct would constitute a breach, for example. Another example might involve determining the applicability of a statute—a person may want to know if the statute prohibits certain conduct before engaging in it.

Declaratory relief is not something that existed in the early English courts of law and equity (though English courts were by statute given power to issue declaratory judgments in the late 1800s). It is not a remedy fashioned through American common law, either. Rather, the declaratory judgment was legislatively created. For federal cases, Congress enacted the Declaratory Judgment Act in 1934, which provides:

> In a case of actual controversy within its jurisdiction, . . . any court of the United States, upon the filing of an appropriate pleading, may declare the rights and other legal relations of any interested party seeking such declaration, whether or not further relief is or could be sought. (28 U.S.C. § 2201.)

Similar statutes provide for declaratory judgments in cases under state law; nearly every state has enacted some version of the Uniform Declaratory Judgments Act. As described by the Uniform Law Commission, the Act "authorizes courts to adjudicate actual controversies concerning legal rights and duties even though traditional remedies for damages or equitable relief are not available. It thus provides a means for settling disputes by judgments which do no more than declare the legal rights of the parties, where otherwise the controversy would have to remain unsettled." (Uniform Declaratory Judgments Act; Description.)

A declaratory judgment is both a remedy and a substantive cause of action. While most remedies require that a plaintiff first identify a recognized legal wrong and prove it has occurred, there is no such requirement to obtain declaratory relief. A plaintiff can simply bring a lawsuit seeking a declaratory judgment without another substantive cause of action. The plaintiff need only show there is a current dispute regarding the parties' legal rights or obligations.

As a purely statutory creation, declaratory judgments are not considered legal or equitable. In practice, however, the remedy has equitable characteristics. Though it is called a declaratory *judgment* — terminology that brings to mind a legal remedy — it functions in an equitable fashion. The enforcement of the remedy is *in personam*. Once the court has issued a decree adjudging the obligations of the parties, the court may then issue further equitable orders requiring the parties to abide by the terms of the decree.

Standing Requirement

Although irreparable harm is not a prerequisite for declaratory relief, what *is* required is an existing and legitimate dispute. Since courts are in the business of resolving disputes and not giving legal advice, for a plaintiff to bring an action seeking a declaratory judgment there must be an actual disagreement based on existing facts. Indeed, without a real dispute, a court has no authority to act. (See Article III of the United States Constitution, giving federal courts jurisdiction only over "cases or controversies.")

Precisely what counts as an existing dispute can be a difficult determination to make. Courts have emphasized that the dispute must be based on existing, not hypothetical, facts. In other words, the question asked of the court cannot be "What *would* my legal rights be *if* this happened?" but rather "What *are* my legal rights in this *current* situation?" That presents an inherent tension, however. Recall that the whole purpose of declaratory judgments is to resolve a dispute early, before it results in harm. So in deciding whether a party has standing to bring a declaratory relief action, the court must take care to not construe the "existing controversy" requirement so strictly that it defeats the purpose of the remedy.

Introductory Note — *MedImmune, Inc. v. Genentech, Inc.* and *HSK, LLC v. United States Olympic Committee*

Medimmune is a patent case. Patent cases provide fertile ground for declaratory relief actions because of the consequences that follow from infringing on a patent. If a party is found liable for profiting from an infringing technology, that party may be prevented from any further use of the technology (through an injunction) and forced to pay monetary penalties up to three times the amount of harm caused. Given those significant consequences, it makes sense to find out up front if the technology in question infringes. In this case, the Supreme Court decides whether initial compliance with the patent holder's demands prevents an action seeking a declaratory judgment that the patent is invalid.

In *HSK, LLC v. United States Olympic Committee*, the dispute is over a trademark, specifically, whether a party can use it in social media postings without permission. The issue before the federal district court on the defendant's motion to dismiss is whether the plaintiff has standing to assert a claim for declaratory relief before actually having posted on social media any of the potentially problematic material.

THINGS TO THINK ABOUT while reading *MedImmune, Inc. v. Genentech, Inc.* and *HSK, LLC v. United States Olympic Committee*:

1. What are the elements of a declaratory judgment cause of action?

2. How does a court determine if a lawsuit seeking a declaratory judgment presents an actual controversy sufficient to give the court jurisdiction?

MedImmune, Inc. v. Genentech, Inc.

United States Supreme Court
549 U.S. 118 (2007)

Justice SCALIA delivered the opinion of the Court.

We must decide whether Article III's limitation of federal courts' jurisdiction to "Cases" and "Controversies," reflected in the "actual controversy" requirement of the Declaratory Judgment Act, 28 U.S.C. § 2201(a), requires a patent licensee to terminate or be in breach of its license agreement before it can seek a declaratory judgment that the underlying patent is invalid, unenforceable, or not infringed.

I

Petitioner MedImmune, Inc., manufactures Synagis, a drug used to prevent respiratory tract disease in infants and young children. In 1997, petitioner entered into a patent license agreement with respondent Genentech, Inc. (which acted on behalf of itself as patent assignee and on behalf of the coassignee, respondent City of Hope). The license covered an existing patent relating to the production of "chimeric antibodies" and a then-pending patent application relating to "the coexpression of immunoglobulin chains in recombinant host cells." Petitioner agreed to pay royalties on sales of "Licensed Products," and respondents granted petitioner the right to make, use, and sell them. The agreement defined "Licensed Products" as a specified antibody, "the manufacture, use or sale of which ... would, if not licensed under th[e] Agreement, infringe one or more claims of either or both of [the covered patents,] which have neither expired nor been held invalid by a court or other body of competent jurisdiction from which no appeal has been or may be taken." App. 399. The license agreement gave petitioner the right to terminate upon six months' written notice.

In December 2001, the "coexpression" application covered by the 1997 license agreement matured into the "Cabilly II" patent. Soon thereafter, respondent Genentech delivered petitioner a letter expressing its belief that Synagis was covered by the Cabilly II patent and its expectation that petitioner would pay royalties beginning March 1, 2002. Petitioner did not think royalties were owing, believing that the Cabilly II patent was invalid and unenforceable, and that its claims were in any event not infringed by Synagis. Nevertheless, petitioner considered the letter to be a clear threat to enforce the Cabilly II patent, terminate the 1997 license agreement, and sue for patent infringement if petitioner did not make royalty payments as demanded. If respondents were to prevail in a patent infringement action, petitioner could be ordered to pay treble damages and attorney's fees, and could be enjoined from selling Synagis, a product that has accounted for more than 80 percent of its revenue from sales since 1999. Unwilling to risk such serious consequences, petitioner paid the demanded royalties "under protest and with reservation of all of [its] rights." This declaratory-judgment action followed. . . .

II

. . . The Declaratory Judgment Act provides that, "[i]n a case of actual controversy within its jurisdiction . . . any court of the United States . . . may declare the rights and other legal relations of any interested party seeking such declaration, whether or not further relief is or could be sought." 28 U.S.C. §2201(a). There was a time when this Court harbored doubts about the compatibility of declaratory-judgment actions with Article III's case-or-controversy requirement. See *Willing v. Chicago Auditorium Assn.,* 277 U.S. 274, 289 (1928); *Liberty Warehouse Co. v. Grannis,* 273 U.S. 70 (1927); see also *Gordon v. United States,* 117 U.S. Appx. 697, 702 (1864) (the last opinion of Taney, C. J., published posthumously) ("The award of execution is . . . an essential part of every judgment passed by a court exercising judicial power"). We dispelled those doubts, however, in *Nashville, C. & St. L.R. Co. v. Wallace,* 288 U.S. 249 (1933), holding (in a case involving a declaratory judgment rendered in state court) that an appropriate action for declaratory relief *can* be a case or controversy under Article III. The federal Declaratory Judgment Act was signed into law the following year, and we upheld its constitutionality in *Aetna Life Ins. Co. v. Haworth,* 300 U.S. 227 (1937). Our opinion explained that the phrase "case of actual controversy" in the Act refers to the type of "Cases" and "Controversies" that are justiciable under Article III.

Aetna and the cases following it do not draw the brightest of lines between those declaratory-judgment actions that satisfy the case-or-controversy requirement and those that do not. Our decisions have required that the dispute be "definite and concrete, touching the legal relations of parties having adverse legal interests"; and that it be "real and substantial" and "admi[t] of specific relief through a decree of a conclusive character, as distinguished from an opinion advising what the law would be upon a hypothetical state of facts." *Id.,* at 240–24. In *Maryland Casualty Co. v. Pacific Coal & Oil Co.,* 312 U.S. 270 (1941), we summarized as follows: "Basically, the question in each case is whether the facts alleged, under all the circumstances, show that there is a substantial controversy, between parties having adverse legal interests, of sufficient immediacy and reality to warrant the issuance of a declaratory judgment."

There is no dispute that these standards would have been satisfied if petitioner had taken the final step of refusing to make royalty payments under the 1997 license agreement. Respondents claim a right to royalties under the licensing agreement. Petitioner asserts that no royalties are owing because the Cabilly II patent is invalid and not infringed; and alleges (without contradiction) a threat by respondents to enjoin sales if royalties are not forthcoming. The factual and legal dimensions of the dispute are well defined and, but for petitioner's continuing to make royalty payments, nothing about the dispute would render it unfit for judicial resolution. Assuming (without deciding) that respondents here could not claim an anticipatory breach and repudiate the license, the continuation of royalty payments makes what would otherwise be an imminent threat at least remote, if not nonexistent. As long as those payments are made, there is no risk that respondents will seek to enjoin petitioner's sales. Petitioner's own acts, in other words, eliminate the imminent threat of harm. The question before us is whether this causes the dispute no longer to be a case or controversy within the meaning of Article III.

Our analysis must begin with the recognition that, where threatened action by *government* is concerned, we do not require a plaintiff to expose himself to liability before bringing suit to challenge the basis for the threat — for example, the constitutionality of a law threatened to be enforced. The plaintiff's own action (or inaction) in failing to violate the law eliminates the imminent threat of prosecution, but nonetheless does not eliminate Article III jurisdiction. For example, in *Terrace v. Thompson,* 263 U.S. 197 (1923), the State threatened the plaintiff with forfeiture of his farm, fines, and penalties if he entered into a lease with an alien in violation of the State's anti-alien land law. Given this genuine threat of enforcement, we did not require, as a prerequisite to testing the validity of the law in a suit for injunction, that the plaintiff bet the farm, so to speak, by taking the violative action.

Likewise, in *Steffel v. Thompson,* 415 U.S. 452 (1974), we did not require the plaintiff to proceed to distribute handbills and risk actual prosecution before he could seek a declaratory judgment regarding the constitutionality of a state statute prohibiting such distribution. As then-Justice Rehnquist put it in his concurrence, "the declaratory judgment procedure is an alternative to pursuit of the arguably illegal activity." *Id.,* at 480. In each of these cases, the plaintiff had eliminated the imminent threat of harm by simply not doing what he claimed the right to do (enter into a lease, or distribute handbills at the shopping center). That did not preclude subject-matter jurisdiction because the threat-eliminating behavior was effectively coerced. See *Terrace, supra,* at 215–216; *Steffel, supra,* at 459. The dilemma posed by that coercion — putting the challenger to the choice between abandoning his rights or risking prosecution — is "a dilemma that it was the very purpose of the Declaratory Judgment Act to ameliorate." *Abbott Laboratories v. Gardner,* 387 U.S. 136 (1967).

Supreme Court jurisprudence is more rare regarding application of the Declaratory Judgment Act to situations in which the plaintiff's self-avoidance of imminent injury is coerced by threatened enforcement action of *a private party* rather than the government. Lower federal courts, however (and state courts interpreting declaratory-judgment acts requiring "actual controversy"), have long accepted jurisdiction in such cases.

The only Supreme Court decision in point is, fortuitously, close on its facts to the case before us. *Altvater v. Freeman,* 319 U.S. 359 (1943), held that a licensee's failure to cease its payment of royalties did not render nonjusticiable a dispute over the validity of the patent. In that litigation, several patentees had sued their licensees to enforce territorial restrictions in the license. The licensees filed a counterclaim for declaratory judgment that the underlying patents were invalid, in the meantime paying "under protest" royalties required by an injunction the patentees had obtained in an earlier case. The patentees argued that "so long as [licensees] continue to pay royalties, there is only an academic, not a real controversy, between the parties." *Id.,* at 364. We rejected that argument and held that the declaratory-judgment claim presented a justiciable case or controversy: "The fact that royalties were being paid did not make this a 'difference or dispute of a hypothetical or abstract character.'" *Ibid.* (quoting *Aetna,* 300 U.S., at 240). The royalties "were being paid under protest and under the compulsion of an injunction decree," and "[u]nless the injunction decree were modified, the only other course [of action] was to defy it, and to risk not only actual but treble damages in infringement suits." 319 U.S., at 365. We concluded that "the requirements of [a] case or controversy are met where payment of a claim is demanded as of right and where payment is made, but where the involuntary or coercive nature of the exaction preserves the right to recover the sums paid or to challenge the legality of the claim." *Ibid.*

. . . Respondents assert that the parties in effect settled this dispute when they entered into the 1997 license agreement. When a licensee enters such an agreement, they contend, it essentially purchases an insurance policy, immunizing it from suits for infringement so long as it continues to pay royalties and does not challenge the covered patents. Permitting it to challenge the validity of the patent without terminating or breaking the agreement alters the deal, allowing the licensee to continue enjoying its immunity while bringing a suit, the elimination of which was part of the patentee's *quid pro quo.* Of course even if it were valid, this argument would have no force with regard to petitioner's claim that the agreement does not call for royalties because their product does not infringe the patent. But even as to the patent invalidity claim, the point seems to us mistaken. To begin with, it is not clear where the prohibition against challenging the validity of the patents is to be found. It can hardly be implied from the mere promise to pay royalties on patents "which have neither expired nor been held invalid by a court or other body of competent jurisdiction from which no appeal has been or may be taken." Promising to pay royalties on patents that have not been held invalid does not amount to a promise *not to seek* a holding of their invalidity.

Lastly, respondents urge us to affirm the dismissal of the declaratory-judgment claims on discretionary grounds. The Declaratory Judgment Act provides that a court "*may* declare the rights and other legal relations of any interested party," 28 U.S.C. §2201(a) (emphasis added), not that it *must* do so. This text has long been understood "to confer on federal courts unique and substantial discretion in deciding whether to declare the rights of litigants." *Wilton v. Seven Falls Co.*, 515 U.S. 277, 286 (1995). We have found it "more consistent with the statute," however, "to vest district courts with discretion in the first instance, because facts bearing on the usefulness of the declaratory judgment remedy, and the fitness of the case for resolution, are peculiarly within their grasp." *Wilton, supra,* at 289. . . . Under these circumstances, it would be imprudent for us to decide whether the District Court should, or must, decline to issue the requested declaratory relief. We leave the equitable, prudential, and policy arguments in favor of such a discretionary dismissal for the lower courts' consideration on remand. Similarly available for consideration on remand are any merits-based arguments for denial of declaratory relief.

We hold that petitioner was not required, insofar as Article III is concerned, to break or terminate its 1997 license agreement before seeking a declaratory judgment in federal court that the underlying patent is invalid, unenforceable, or not infringed. The Court of Appeals erred in affirming the dismissal of this action for lack of subject-matter jurisdiction.

The judgment of the Court of Appeals is reversed, and the cause is remanded for proceedings consistent with this opinion.

It is so ordered.

* * *

HSK, LLC v. United States Olympic Committee

United States District Court, District of Minnesota
248 F.Supp.3d 938 (2017)

Wilhelmina M. Wright, United States District Judge

In this declaratory-judgment action against Defendant The United States Olympic Committee (USOC), Plaintiff HSK, LLC d/b/a Zerorez MN (Zerorez) seeks a declaration that it may use its corporate social media accounts to discuss the Olympic Games without violating USOC's trademark rights. USOC moves to dismiss for lack of subject-matter jurisdiction, asserting that a concrete dispute does not exist between the parties. . . .

Background

Zerorez initiated this lawsuit the day before the 2016 Olympic Games commenced in Rio de Janeiro, Brazil. Zerorez alleges that it had planned to discuss the 2016 Olympic Games through Zerorez's corporate social media accounts. But USOC's U.S. Olympic and Paralympic Brand Usage Guidelines provide that "commercial entities [other than official Team USA sponsors] may not post about the

Games on their corporate social media accounts. This includes the use of USOC trademarks in hashtags such as # RIO2016 or # TeamUSA." The Brand Usage Guidelines also state that "[f]ederal law . . . allows the USOC to file a lawsuit against any entity using USOC trademarks, imagery or terminology for commercial purposes without express written consent." Zerorez alleges that USOC warned other commercial entities against posting comments about the Olympics through their social media accounts in advance of the 2016 Olympic Games. And certain media outlets, including The Guardian and ESPN, reported in July 2016 that USOC was threatening to enforce its trademark rights against businesses that are not official Team USA sponsors. Rather than risking legal action from USOC, Zerorez, which is not an official sponsor of Team USA, refrained from discussing the Olympics through its corporate social media accounts and filed this declaratory-judgment action. Zerorez seeks a determination of its rights to discuss on social media the 2016 Olympic Games and future Olympic events.

Specifically, Zerorez seeks a ruling that its proposed social media posts about the Olympics would not violate USOC's trademark rights or USOC's rights under the Ted Stevens Olympic and Amateur Sports Act, 36 U.S.C. § 220506. Zerorez also seeks declarations that USOC cannot preclude businesses that are not official Team USA sponsors from discussing the Olympics on social media and that, among other actions, USOC has "exaggerated the strength of its legal rights."

In support of its motion to dismiss Zerorez's claims for lack of subject-matter jurisdiction, USOC argues that there is no concrete dispute between the parties because Zerorez has not alleged that USOC threatened to enforce its trademark rights against Zerorez. USOC also contends that the declaratory relief Zerorez seeks is not sufficiently specific to support the Court's exercise of declaratory-judgment jurisdiction.

Analysis

USOC's Motion to Dismiss for Lack of Subject-Matter Jurisdiction

USOC seeks dismissal of Zerorez's claims for lack of subject-matter jurisdiction on the ground that there is no case or controversy between the parties. Under Article III of the United States Constitution, the jurisdiction of federal courts extends only to actual cases and controversies. U.S. Const. art. III, § 2, cl. 1; *Neighborhood Transp. Network, Inc. v. Pena*, 42 F.3d 1169, 1172 (8th Cir. 1994). When deciding a motion to dismiss for lack of subject-matter jurisdiction under Federal Rule of Civil Procedure 12(b)(1), a district court "must distinguish between a 'facial attack' and a 'factual attack.'" *Osborn v. United States*, 918 F.2d 724, 729 n.6 (8th Cir. 1990). When a facial attack is asserted, the court looks only at the pleadings to determine whether the plaintiff's allegations provide a sufficient basis for subject-matter jurisdiction; the non-moving party receives the same protections as if the court were deciding a motion under Federal Rule of Civil Procedure 12(b)(6). *Id.*; *accord Branson Label, Inc. v. City of Branson, Mo.*, 793 F.3d 910, 914 (8th Cir. 2015). But when a factual attack is asserted, the court considers matters outside the pleadings, and the non-moving party does not benefit from Rule 12(b)(6) safeguards. *Osborn*, 918 F.2d at 729 n.6. Here, USOC asserts a facial challenge to the Court's subject-matter jurisdiction. Even if Zerorez's allegations are true, USOC argues, no controversy exists between the parties to satisfy the requirements of Article III or the Declaratory Judgment Act. Accordingly, when deciding this motion, the Court accepts the factual allegations in the complaint as true and draws all reasonable inferences in favor of Zerorez.

The Declaratory Judgment Act limits the issuance of declaratory judgments to cases involving an "actual controversy." 28 U.S.C. § 2201(a). This requirement "refers to the type of 'Cases' and 'Controversies' that are justiciable under Article III." *MedImmune, Inc. v. Genentech, Inc.*, 549 U.S. 118, 127 (2007). In this context, an actual controversy requires a concrete dispute between parties with adverse legal interests, and the plaintiff must seek "specific relief through a decree of a conclusive character, as distinguished from an opinion advising what the law would be upon a hypothetical state of facts." *Aetna Life Ins. Co. v. Haworth*, 300 U.S. 227, 241 (1937). The burden of establishing the existence of an actual controversy rests with the party seeking a declaratory judgment. *Cardinal Chem. Co. v. Morton Int'l, Inc.*, 508 U.S. 83, 95 (1993).

[margin annotations: actual controversy; burden of proof; test]

To determine whether an "actual controversy" exists in the declaratory-judgment context, district courts consider "whether the facts alleged, under all the circumstances, show that there is a substantial controversy, between parties having adverse legal interests, of sufficient immediacy and reality to warrant the issuance of a declaratory judgment." *MedImmune*, 549 U.S. at 127. Prior to *MedImmune*, the United States Court of Appeals for the Federal Circuit required a declaratory-judgment plaintiff seeking to establish jurisdiction in a patent case to demonstrate that it had a "reasonable apprehension" of an infringement lawsuit and that it was taking concrete steps to conduct activity that could constitute infringement. *See Benitec Austl., Ltd. v. Nucleonics, Inc.*, 495 F.3d 1340, 1343 (Fed. Cir. 2007). Although *MedImmune* now requires courts to examine all the circumstances when analyzing whether an actual controversy exists between the parties, a reasonable apprehension of suit remains one way for a declaratory-judgment plaintiff to demonstrate that a justiciable controversy exists. *U.S. Water Servs., Inc. v. ChemTreat, Inc.*, 794 F.3d 966, 973 (8th Cir. 2015); *accord Prasco, LLC v. Medicis Pharm. Corp.*, 537 F.3d 1329, 1336 (Fed. Cir. 2008). Whether the declaratory-judgment plaintiff has engaged in potentially infringing activity or meaningful preparation for potentially infringing activity also is "an important element in the totality of the circumstances [that] must be considered in determining whether a declaratory judgment is appropriate." *Prasco*, 537 F.3d at 1336 n.4. When analyzing whether an actual controversy exists between the parties, other relevant circumstances include prior litigious conduct and the defendant's refusal to give assurances that it will not enforce its intellectual property rights.

To assess whether a declaratory-judgment plaintiff had a reasonable apprehension of a patent- or trademark-infringement lawsuit, courts often consider the extent and nature of communications between the parties, including whether the patent or trademark holder indicated that it might resort to litigation. Typically, a patent or trademark holder's direct statement of intent to enforce its intellectual property rights is indicative of an actual controversy. *See, e.g., ABB Inc. v. Cooper Indus., LLC*, 635 F.3d 1345, 1348–49 (Fed. Cir. 2011) (finding patent holder's statement that it would "act vigorously to protect its rights" against the letter's recipient indicative of an actual controversy); *Green Edge Ents., LLC v. Rubber Mulch Etc., LLC*, 620 F.3d 1287, 1301 (Fed. Cir. 2010) (stating that "a threat of suit in the form of a cease and desist letter, in addition to other litigious conduct, is sufficient to confer declaratory judgment jurisdiction"). But when the tenor of the direct communications is not threatening, such communications between the parties do not necessarily establish an "actual controversy." *See, e.g., Purely Driven Prods., LLC v. Chillovino, LLC*, 171 F. Supp.3d 1016, 1019 (C.D. Cal. 2016) (concluding that no controversy existed when defendants opposed plaintiffs' application to register their trademark but had not threatened an infringement action against the declaratory-judgment plaintiffs). . . .

No actual controversy between Zerorez and USOC is established from the totality of circumstances presented here. Zerorez does not allege that USOC ever communicated directly with Zerorez regarding USOC's trademark rights; nor does Zerorez allege that there is a history of trademark litigation (or any litigation) between the parties. Instead, Zerorez contends that the combination of three elements — USOC's Brand Usage Guidelines, written communications notifying other businesses that their use of USOC's trademarks without permission is prohibited, and USOC's track record of commencing trademark litigation — creates an actual controversy between USOC and Zerorez. And Zerorez asserts that media reports published during the weeks prior to the Olympics demonstrate that USOC was threatening to take legal action against business owners that infringe its trademarks on social media. Those media reports do not create an actual controversy, even if they made Zerorez reluctant to post comments about the Olympics through its corporate social media accounts. Importantly, USOC never threatened litigation against Zerorez. As in *Edmunds*, Zerorez's concern that it might become the target of a trademark-infringement lawsuit is speculative and one-sided. It is not based on the existence of a concrete dispute between the parties.

Because the totality of the circumstances alleged does not establish that an actual controversy exists between Zerorez and USOC, the Court grants USOC's motion to dismiss for lack of subject-matter jurisdiction.

* * *

Problem 38

The only requirement to bring an action for a declaratory judgment is an actual and existing dispute. Is that requirement satisfied in the following scenario?

A law firm has a five-year lease for an office in a downtown high rise, with an option to extend it for another three years. To exercise the option, the lease requires written notice to the landlord that the firm intends to exercise it, delivered no later than the end of the fourth year of the lease. Two weeks before the end of the fourth year, the law firm mails notice to the landlord of intent to exercise the option. But the notice is temporarily misplaced by the post office and is not delivered for three weeks. When the law firm inquires about whether the landlord will accept the notice as a valid exercise of the option, the landlord says it has not decided yet. (The law firm suspects the landlord is waiting to see if it gets a better offer to rent the office.) The firm wants to know whether it will need to relocate next year or whether it has a three-year lease extension.

Applicability to Criminal Law

A declaratory judgment is a civil remedy—a tool to resolve disputes arising under civil law. It cannot be used to adjudicate criminal liability, that is, whether a person is guilty of committing a crime. The criminal law, and criminal procedure, is used for that. Even so, a declaratory judgment is available to test the *validity* of a criminal statute, either as applied to a particular situation or on its face. A person can bring an action for a declaratory judgment to determine whether certain conduct is prohibited by a criminal law.

The requirement of an actual and existing dispute still applies, however. A court will not issue a declaratory judgment to decree what someone's rights might be if certain things happen a certain way. There must be an existing, concrete set of facts for the court to evaluate. In the criminal context, this translates to a requirement that prosecution of the plaintiff must be imminent. The prosecution cannot actually have started, though—otherwise, a defendant in a criminal proceeding could launch a parallel proceeding to determine guilt or innocence as a plaintiff in a declaratory relief action. That would undermine, and potentially conflict with, the decision in the criminal case. So there is a fairly delicate balance in bringing a declaratory relief action testing the validity of a criminal statute. Prosecution of the plaintiff must not be in process but must be imminent.

When prosecution is imminent and there is a concrete set of facts for the court to evaluate, the declaratory judgment remedy can be used to determine whether a criminal law will apply to the plaintiff's conduct.

Introductory Note — *Bunis v. Conway* and *Malloy v. Cooper*

Both *Bunis* and *Malloy* are appeals from a trial court decision to dismiss a declaratory judgment lawsuit based on lack of jurisdiction. In both cases, the trial court thought it did not have the authority to issue a declaratory judgment because the plaintiff asked for a decree whether certain conduct violated a criminal law. And in both cases, the appellate court reverses, finding that the situation meets the requirements for a declaratory judgment.

THINGS TO THINK ABOUT while reading *Bunis v. Conway* and *Malloy v. Cooper*:

1. Why is a declaratory judgment particularly desirable when its subject is the validity of a criminal statute?

2. When deciding whether a criminal law can properly apply to certain conduct, is the court answering a factual question or a legal question?

3. How can one determine whether prosecution is imminent enough to bring a declaratory judgment action regarding a criminal law?

Bunis v. Conway

New York Supreme Court, Appellate Division
234 N.Y.S.2d 435 (1962)

HALPERN, Justice.

The plaintiff appeals from an order dismissing his complaint as insufficient, in an action for a declaratory judgment seeking an adjudication that the book 'Tropic of Cancer' by Henry Miller is not 'obscene' within the meaning of section 1141 of the Penal Law. The complaint alleged that the plaintiff conducted a book store in the City of Rochester and that he desired to sell the book but that the defendant, the District Attorney of Monroe County, had threatened to prosecute him for violation of section 1141 of the Penal Law if he sold it. The complaint alleged that the defendant 'has made similar statements to others and to the public at large to the effect that anyone who sold the book would be subject to prosecution under said section of the Penal Law'. The complaint further alleged that the plaintiff believed that the book was not obscene and that he 'desire[d] to sell it if it [was] legal to do so'. The complaint concluded with the statement that a prosecution would cause 'irreparable harm to the plaintiff personally and to his business [and that the] plaintiff has no adequate remedy at law'.

The Special Term dismissed the complaint upon motion upon the ground that an action for a declaratory judgment would not lie under the circumstances set forth in the complaint. In our opinion, the dismissal was erroneous.

An action for a declaratory judgment is the appropriate remedy for the determination of a justiciable controversy, where the plaintiff is in doubt as to his legal rights and wishes to avoid the hazard of taking action in advance of the determination of such rights (James v. Alderton Dock Yards, 256 N.Y. 298, 305).

It is the settled law that an action for a declaratory judgment will lie 'where a constitutional question is involved or the legality or meaning of a statute is in question and no question of fact is involved.' (Dun & Bradstreet v. City of New York, 276 N.Y. 198, 206). The remedy of declaratory judgment is available, not only where the validity of a statute is in question, but also where its construction or its application to an undisputed set of facts is in question (New York Foreign Trade Zone Operators, Inc. v. State Liquor Authority, 285 N.Y. 272).

However, as the Court of Appeals noted in the case last cited, the remedy 'is not available to restrain the enforcement of a criminal prosecution where the facts are in dispute, or open to different interpretation' (285 N.Y. at p. 276). The rationale seems to be that, if the facts upon which the propriety of a criminal prosecution would depend are in dispute, the dispute ought to be resolved by the trier of the facts in the criminal prosecution in accordance with the rules governing criminal cases and that the obtaining of a declaratory judgment as to the facts would improperly interfere with the administration of the criminal law. This reasoning, however, is inapplicable, if the crucial question is one of law, since the question of law will be decided by the court in any event and not by the trier of the facts. Therefore, it has been held that a determination of the question of law in a declaratory judgment action would not 'improperly interfere with criminal processes' (New York Foreign Trade Zone Operators, Inc. v. State Liquor Authority, supra, 285 N.Y. at p. 277). 'Resort to this remedy and also to that of an injunction may be had even with respect to penal statutes and against a public official or public agency whose duty it is to conduct appropriate prosecutions, if the purpose be to avoid irreparable injury and if the sole question is one of law' (De Veau v. Braisted, 5 A.D.2d 603, 606–607).

The question of whether a particular book is obscene within the meaning of section 1141 of the Penal Law is a question of law, appropriate for decision in a declaratory judgment action, under the rule laid down in the authorities cited. No question of fact is involved, in the sense of a question as to what had factually occurred or what is factually proposed to be done. The content of the book is fixed and immutable. There may be different views as to whether the book comes within the condemnation of section 1141 of the Penal Law but this presents a question of law for ultimate decision by the court, depending upon the court's determination of the meaning, scope and applicability of the statute.

The peculiar nature of the question to be decided in an obscenity case was eluci-dated by Judge Fuld in People v. Richmond County News, Inc., 9 N.Y.2d 578: '[T]he question whether a particular work is of that character [obscene] involves not really an issue of fact but a question of constitutional *judgment* of the most sensitive and delicate kind,' quoting from the concurring opinion of Mr. Justice Harlan in Roth v. United States, 354 U.S. 476, 497–498. 'It involves not a simple question of fact, but a mixed question of fact and constitutional law, calling upon the court to make an appraisal of a publication and its contents against the requirements embodied in both State and Federal Constitutions (N.Y.Const. art. I, § 8; U.S.Const., 1st and 14th Amdts.). Consequently, if an appellate court were to rely upon and be bound by the opinion of the trier of the facts as to the obscenity of a publication it would be abdicating its role as an arbiter of constitutional issues' (9 N.Y.2d pp. 580–581).

As this statement indicates, the question in an obscenity case is ultimately a ques-tion of constitutional law, in view of the limitations upon the power of the legisla-ture in this field, imposed by Article I, section 8, of the New York State Constitution and by the First and Fourteenth Amendments of the United States Constitution. If the book is held not to fall within the terms of the statute, that is the end of the matter but, if it is held that it comes within the terms of the statute, then the ques-tion must be faced whether the statute, as construed and applied, is a constitutional one. This question is ultimately one for decision, so far as the courts of this State are concerned, by the Court of Appeals (whose jurisdiction is of course limited, with exceptions not here relevant, to questions of law). Finally, the decision of the Court of Appeals may be reviewed by the United States Supreme Court. Each court is required 'to make an independent constitutional appraisal' of the book in con-troversy (People v. Richmond County News, supra, 9 N.Y.2d 578, 580). The remedy of an action for a declaratory judgment is particularly appropriate for the determi-nation of constitutional questions (Dun & Bradstreet v. City of New York, supra, 276 N.Y. 198, 206). . . .

If relief by way of a declaratory judgment were not available, the chief of police, the district attorney or other local law enforcement authorities could impose an informal censorship merely by announcing that anyone selling a particular book would be prosecuted. Booksellers are naturally reluctant to incur the risk of crimi-nal prosecution since that entails adverse publicity and physical and mental strain as well as expense, even though the prosecution should ultimately terminate in the dismissal of the charge. They may therefore refrain from selling the book denounced by the authorities and, in that event, no occasion for criminal prosecution ever arises. The mere threat of prosecution may thus have the effect of deterring or sup-pressing the sale of the book without any judicial determination ever being made as to whether the book is actually obscene. Such a system of informal censorship has been repeatedly condemned as a prior restraint by the action of governmental officials, in violation of the First and Fourteenth Amendments. It has been held that, if the public authorities promulgate a list of 'objectionable' books or magazines and threaten to prosecute any person who sells the listed books or magazines, an action for an injunction may be maintained against the publicizing of the list and the making of the threats of prosecution, on the ground that these acts of themselves are a violation of due process .

The use of declaratory judgment procedure is the most effective method of overcoming any attempt by local government officials to impose extralegal censorship. A bookseller, faced with a threat of prosecution if he sells a book condemned by the authorities, may escape from the dilemma by procuring, in an action for a declaratory judgment, a judicial determination as to the legality of the sale of the book, without first selling the book and incurring the risk of prosecution.

The entertaining of declaratory judgment actions in obscenity cases thus not only protect the legitimate interests of booksellers but also serves the public interest by preventing the creation of an extralegal system of censorship by the local police or prosecuting authorities.

We need hardly add that we are not concerned at this time with the question of whether the particular book here involved is or is not obscene within the meaning of section 1141 of the Penal Law. That question is to be determined by the court in its decision upon the merits. All that we hold at this time is that a declaratory judgment action will lie and that the dismissal of the complaint was erroneous.

The order appealed from should therefore be reversed and the motion to dismiss the complaint denied.

* * *

Malloy v. Cooper

North Carolina Supreme Court
356 N.C. 113 (2002)

PARKER, Justice.

On 3 March 1999 plaintiff instituted this action for declaratory judgment against defendants Roy Cooper, Attorney General for the State of North Carolina; David R. Waters, District Attorney for the Ninth Prosecutorial District; David S. Smith, Sheriff of Granville County; and the State of North Carolina. The issue before this Court is whether the Court of Appeals erred in holding that the trial court lacked jurisdiction and should have dismissed plaintiff's declaratory judgment action under North Carolina Rule of Civil Procedure 12(b)(1). The uncontroverted facts are as follows.

Plaintiff is a resident of Granville County, North Carolina, and owns an unincorporated business operating under the name "Dogwood Gun Club." Twice a year plaintiff sponsors a pigeon shoot, known as "The Dogwood Invitational," on his private land in Granville County. Plaintiff has sponsored, organized, and operated the pigeon shoots since 1987. Contestants participate by invitation only, and each contestant pays $275.00 per day to participate. According to plaintiff's response to interrogatories, the pigeon shoot is conducted as follows: "Each contestant faces a ring. Inside the ring are a number of boxes which are opened on cue. An individual ferel

[sic] pigeon flies from a particular box. The feral pigeon serves as a target at which the contestant shoots." The last two pigeon shoots conducted before institution of this action utilized approximately 40,000 pigeons each. Pigeons that are killed by the contestants are buried, whereas pigeons that are merely injured are "dispatched promptly" and buried. Plaintiff claims to have spent $500,000 in capital improvements to his land to further the pigeon shoots and further claims that the pigeon shoots provide approximately fifty percent of his net income.

In response to interrogatories, plaintiff answered that the District Attorney for the Ninth Prosecutorial District, which covers Granville County, "notified the Plaintiff, through counsel, that he considers the conduct at the Dogwood Invitational to be in violation of amended N.C.G.S. § 14–360 [entitled "Cruelty to animals; construction of section"] and that if given the opportunity, he will prosecute the Plaintiff." Thus, the District Attorney appears to have determined that the 1998 amendments to the statute, *see* Act of Oct. 30, 1998, ch. 212, sec. 17.16(c), 1997 N.C. Sess. Laws 937, 1192, brought plaintiff's pigeon shoots within the purview of the statute. After receiving this threat of prosecution, plaintiff filed the complaint for declaratory judgment praying the trial court to declare that plaintiff's pigeon shoots do not violate the statute; that the statute is unconstitutional as applied to plaintiff; that the statute is unconstitutionally vague; and that defendants be enjoined from enforcing the statute against plaintiff.

... The sole issue before this Court is whether jurisdiction exists to grant a declaratory judgment regarding the constitutionality of the statute in question. ... The Declaratory Judgment Act states that courts "shall have power to declare rights, status, and other legal relations, whether or not further relief is or could be claimed." N.C.G.S. § 1–253. Accordingly, any person "whose rights, status or other legal relations are affected by a statute . . . may have determined any question of construction or validity arising under the . . . statute . . . and obtain a declaration of rights, status, or other legal relations thereunder." N.C.G.S. § 1–254.

However, "the apparent broad terms of the [Declaratory Judgment Act] do not confer upon the court unlimited jurisdiction of a merely advisory nature to construe and declare the law." *State ex rel. Edmisten v. Tucker,* 312 N.C. 326, 338 (1984). Thus, "jurisdiction under the Declaratory Judgment Act may be invoked only in a case in which there is an actual or real existing controversy between parties having adverse interests in the matter in dispute." *Tucker,* 312 N.C. at 338.

> Persons directly and adversely affected by the decision may be expected to analyze and bring to the attention of the court all facets of a legal problem. Clear and sound judicial decisions may be expected when specific legal problems are tested by fire in the crucible of actual controversy. So-called friendly suits, where, regardless of form, all parties seek the same result, are "quicksands of the law."

City of Greensboro v. Wall, 247 N.C. 516, 520 (1958).

The case before us presents an actual existing controversy between parties with adverse interests. The uncontroverted evidence shows that plaintiff conducted the pigeon shoots in a substantially identical manner twice a year for twelve years before filing this action. No question is in dispute about the birds used—how they are gathered, how the actual shooting is conducted, how the birds are killed, and how the birds are disposed of. Nor is any other material fact in dispute. Given that the uncontroverted evidence shows that plaintiff has conducted the pigeon shoots in the same manner for such an extended period of time, and with such regularity and frequency, this controversy rises above mere speculation that he will conduct the pigeon shoots in the same manner in the future. Thus, this case presents a concrete and real controversy, as opposed to mere speculation as to future conduct; therefore, plaintiff is not seeking an advisory opinion from this Court.

Likewise, the record is clear that the parties have adverse interests. Plaintiff, given the amount of money he has invested in the pigeon shoots and the amount of income he derives therefrom, is situated to advocate strongly his position that the statute is unconstitutional. Likewise, defendants, who represent the State and are charged with enforcing its laws, are situated to advocate strongly that the statute is constitutional. Thus, the basic requirement of a real controversy between parties with adverse interests is satisfied in this case.

However, even when an actual controversy exists between adverse parties, declaratory judgment is not generally available to challenge the constitutionality of a criminal statute. *See, e.g., Tucker,* 312 N.C. at 349 ("It is widely held that a declaratory judgment is not available to restrain enforcement of a criminal prosecution," especially where a criminal action is already pending.); *Jernigan v. State,* 279 N.C. 556, 560 (1971) ("A declaratory judgment is a civil remedy which may not be resorted to try ordinary matters of guilt or innocence."); *Chadwick v. Salter,* 254 N.C. 389, 394,(1961) ("Ordinarily, the constitutionality of a statute . . . will not be determined in an action to enjoin its enforcement."). Nevertheless, a declaratory judgment action to determine the constitutionality of a criminal statute prior to prosecution is not completely barred. . . .

This Court has enunciated what a plaintiff must show in order to seek a declaratory judgment that a criminal statute is unconstitutional.

> The key to whether or not declaratory relief is available to determine the constitutionality of a criminal statute is whether the plaintiff can demonstrate that a criminal prosecution is imminent or threatened, and that he stands to suffer the loss of either fundamental human rights or property interests if the criminal prosecution is begun and the criminal statute is enforced.

Tucker, 312 N.C. at 350.

We agree with the Court of Appeals' holding that "the record does establish that the State has threatened plaintiff with prosecution under the statute if plaintiff hosts a subsequent pigeon shoot." Plaintiff stated in response to interrogatories that the District Attorney "notified the Plaintiff, through counsel, that he considers the conduct at the Dogwood Invitational to be in violation of amended N.C.G.S. §14–360 and that if given the opportunity, he will prosecute the Plaintiff." This unrefuted allegation clearly satisfies plaintiff's burden to allege imminent or threatened prosecution.

However, the Court of Appeals incorrectly held that plaintiff failed to show that he stands to suffer the loss of either fundamental human rights or property interests if the prosecution is begun and the criminal statute is enforced.

This Court has held that "[a]n Act will be declared unconstitutional and its enforcement will be enjoined when it clearly appears either that property or fundamental human rights are denied in violation of constitutional guarantees." *Roller v. Allen,* 245 N.C. 516, 518 (1957). . . . Thus, if plaintiff can show that the statute's enforcement, if unconstitutional, will deny him his fundamental right to conduct a lawful business or to earn a livelihood, this second criterion is satisfied.

Plaintiff alleges that he receives fifty percent of his income from conducting the pigeon shoots. Furthermore, he alleges that he has expended $500,000 in capital improvements to his land in furtherance of the pigeon shoots. Based on these facts, the pigeon shoots constitute a substantial portion of plaintiff's livelihood. If the statute is, indeed, unconstitutional, then its enforcement will deny plaintiff his fundamental right to conduct a lawful business. Thus, as to plaintiff's claims that the statute is unconstitutionally vague and overbroad, that the statute permits an unconstitutional delegation of legislative power, and that the unconstitutional portions of the statute are not severable from the remainder of the statute, plaintiff has sufficiently alleged facts to establish the second criterion. . . .

In summary, we hold that this case presents an actual controversy between parties with adverse interests. Furthermore, plaintiff has sufficiently alleged imminent prosecution and that he stands to lose fundamental human rights and property interests if the statute is enforced and is later determined to be unconstitutional. Accordingly, the trial court properly denied defendants' motion to dismiss. We, therefore, remand this case to the Court of Appeals for decision on the merits of the underlying action.

The judgment of the Court of Appeals is REVERSED.

* * *

Problem 39

Declaratory judgments cannot be used to determine whether someone is guilty of a criminal violation, but they can be used to determine whether a criminal law is valid, so long as prosecution is imminent. Is the plaintiff in the following situation entitled to a declaratory judgment?

David wants to start a marijuana sales business. The state where he intends to open the business allows the sale of marijuana to adults 21 years or older. But selling marijuana is prohibited by federal law, punishable as a felony. David believes the state law controls because the federal law is invalid as an unconstitutional infringement on state police power. Before investing the significant money that will be required to start his business, David wants to know whether the federal law criminalizing marijuana is valid as applied to him. He brings a lawsuit in federal court asking for a declaratory judgment regarding that question.

crim pros. is imminent or threatened

actual or existing controversy between the parties?

adverse interests?

- lawful right to conduct a business

- is it a lawful?

- lacking credible threat of enforcement

Chapter 9

Restitution

Restitution is a remedy to prevent unjust enrichment. It requires a defendant to return to the plaintiff a benefit that was wrongfully obtained.

Restitution functions as both a remedy and a theory of recovery. It can be asserted as a standalone cause of action. No independent legal wrong, aside from the defendant having unjustly received a benefit, is necessary to support a claim for restitution.

Though an award of restitution will be a sum of money, it is important to remember that restitution is not the same as damages. Damages compensate a plaintiff for a loss. Restitution prevents a defendant from unjustly benefiting. So while damages are measured by the amount of the plaintiff's loss, restitution is measured by the amount of the defendant's gain.

Not all cases of harm to a plaintiff result in a gain for the defendant. A common example of harm for which the law allows recovery is physical injury caused by negligence. A defendant who injures someone by not acting carefully enough has caused harm. But the defendant has not economically benefited. Restitution would therefore not be an appropriate remedy in that case.

Instead, restitution is appropriate where the harm inflicted creates an economic benefit for the defendant. Sometimes the amount of harm is equal to the defendant's gain. For example, if a defendant steals $100,000 cash from the plaintiff, the plaintiff has lost $100,000 and the defendant has gained $100,000. In that kind of situation, compensatory damages will usually be an adequate remedy. The remedy of restitution comes into play when the defendant's gain exceeds the amount of the plaintiff's loss, or when the loss is difficult to calculate while the gain is easier to measure. In those situations, restitution may be a more desirable remedy than damages.

Restitution as a Theory of Recovery

Since restitution is a theory of recovery, a plaintiff need not have a cause of action in tort or contract to obtain restitution. That means it is available to a plaintiff who has no other available theory of liability. For instance, sometimes a benefit is conferred on a defendant purely through mistake, so the plaintiff has no obvious avenue to recover in tort (because the defendant's conduct does not amount to one).

Consider the case of an art dealer that sells both original paintings and copies, and an inexperienced employee mistakenly gives an expensive original work of art to a customer who actually paid for a copy. Though the customer has not committed a tort, the art dealer may be able to recover in restitution for a benefit mistakenly conferred.

Similarly, a plaintiff who does not have an enforceable contract and cannot bring a breach of contract action may be able to recover through restitution. Restitution in this context is sometimes referred to as a contract implied by law, or a "quasi-contract." The idea is that although there is no enforceable agreement to compensate the plaintiff for the benefit provided to the defendant, the law will imply one where necessary to avoid unjust enrichment. A common example is quantum meruit (a Latin phrase meaning roughly "what has been earned"). Quantum meruit is the remedy of restitution in a specific context: where the plaintiff has provided a service to the defendant, there is no enforceable contract to compensate the plaintiff, and it would be unjust to allow the defendant to retain the benefit without paying for it. In that situation, the law will imply an obligation for the defendant to pay the reasonable value of the services provided — quantum meruit, what has been earned. Under quasi-contractual theories, the remedial goal is the same as it is for the plaintiff who was unable recover in tort: to prevent the defendant from retaining a wrongfully acquired benefit.

The availability of restitution as an independent theory of recovery has another implication, too. It means that a plaintiff who *can* bring a cause of action in tort or for breach of contract can choose restitution as an alternative. A plaintiff who has a tort cause of action might instead pursue restitution as a theory of recovery if the defendant has gained more than the plaintiff lost. (Thinking back to the example of the $100,000 cash theft, perhaps this time the defendant took not cash, but $100,000 in gold bars. Several months later, as sometimes happens, the price of gold rises dramatically, making the value of the stolen bars $150,000.) Restitution is a viable theory of recovery whenever a defendant has wrongfully acquired an economic benefit, whether or not the plaintiff has another potentially available cause of action.

Legal and Equitable Characteristics

Restitution can have either legal or equitable characteristics, depending on the nature of the award. An award of restitution takes one of two forms: a judgment entitling the plaintiff to collect the sum awarded from the defendant or an order requiring the defendant to turn the sum over to the plaintiff. If issued as a judgment, the remedy is legal — enforced *in rem*, by attaching or forcing a sale of the defendant's property. If an order, the remedy is equitable — enforced *in personam*, requiring that the defendant comply or face contempt sanctions.

Introductory Note — *Bank of America v. Gibbons*

The defendant in *Bank of America v. Gibbons* is an innocent spouse who unknowingly benefited, quite handsomely, from her husband's embezzlement. The bank sued for unjust enrichment and the trial court granted summary judgment for the defendant spouse. The bank appeals, requiring the appellate court to determine the elements for an unjust enrichment cause of action.

THINGS TO THINK ABOUT while reading *Bank of America v. Gibbons*:

1. What are the elements of a restitution cause of action?

2. Why might a traditional tort cause of action be inadequate as a remedy here?

3. Is it fair to impose liability on someone who did not knowingly engage in misconduct?

Bank of America v. Gibbons

Maryland Court of Special Appeals
173 Md. App. 261 (2007)

Opinion by ADKINS, J.

Over a six year period, Thomas Patrick Gibbons, the husband of appellee Lynne Margaret Gibbons (Mrs. Gibbons), pocketed proceeds from unauthorized sales of securities owned by several customers of his employer, appellant Bank of America Corporation (the Bank). The value of these misappropriated stocks allegedly exceeds $1.5 million.

Thomas Gibbons deposited ill-gotten funds into an account at Provident Bank of Maryland, held in the name of L & S Computer Consultants (LSSC). From this account, Mr. Gibbons regularly withdrew funds that he then deposited into a different Provident account he held jointly with Mrs. Gibbons, and thereafter into jointly held Bank of America accounts. The misappropriated monies were commingled with $502,331 in salary and bonus earnings that Mr. Gibbons also deposited into that joint Bank account over this period. Mrs. Gibbons wrote most of the checks drawn on this account, primarily for household and family purposes.

In an effort to recover some of the stolen funds allegedly deposited into and spent to fund a lavish lifestyle for Mrs. Gibbons and the Gibbons children, Bank of America filed suit against Mrs. Gibbons. During the litigation, it became clear that Mrs. Gibbons had no knowledge of her husband's theft, her belief being that the source of funds he deposited into the joint household account was her husband's legitimate earnings. The Bank pursued conversion and unjust enrichment claims against Mrs. Gibbons.

On cross-motions for summary judgment, the Circuit Court for Harford County held that Mrs. Gibbons is entitled to judgment on the Bank's conversion and unjust enrichment claims. The court explained its ruling in a written opinion that analyzed each element of unjust enrichment and concluded that the Bank "failed to meet [its] burden on all three prongs of the cause of action." The Bank argues that the motion court committed legal error by applying the wrong legal principles to each element. We agree.

Discussion

Unjust Enrichment

"One whose money or property is taken by fraud or embezzlement, or by conversion, is entitled to restitution[.]" 1 Dan B. Dobbs, *Law of Remedies* § 4.1(1), at 553 (2d ed.1993) (hereinafter cited as "*Dobbs*"). Under the restitutionary remedies of quasi-contract and constructive trust, "[t]he idea is that the plaintiff's property has been found in the hands of the defendant and must be restored to the plaintiff, even if legal title has passed, and even if the property has undergone a change in form by reason of an exchange or otherwise." 2 *Dobbs* § 6.1(3), at 11. "A person who receives a benefit by reason of an infringement of another person's interest, or of loss suffered by the other, owes restitution to him in the manner and amount necessary to prevent unjust enrichment." *Berry & Gould v. Berry,* 360 Md. 142, 151 (2000) (quoting *Restatement (Second) of Restitution* § 1 (Tentative Draft No. 1, 1983)).

"The restitutionary remedies and unjust enrichment are simply flip sides of the same coin." *Alternatives Unlimited, Inc. v. New Baltimore City Bd. of School Comm'rs,* 155 Md.App. 415, 454 (2004). Thus, "[r]estitution involves the disgorgement of unjust enrichment." *Consumer Protection Div. v. Morgan,* 387 Md. 125 (2005). "In explaining the law's reluctance to permit instances of unjust enrichment, John P. Dawson, 'The Self-Serving Intermeddler,' 87 Harv. L.Rev. 1409, 1411 (1974), traces back to the Book of Matthew the belief that men 'should not reap where they have not sown.'" *Alternatives Unltd.,* 155 Md.App. at 455. "The doctrine of unjust enrichment is applicable where 'the defendant, upon the circumstances of the case, is obliged by the ties of natural justice and equity to refund the money,' and gives rise to the policy of restitution as a remedy." *Hill v. Cross Country Settlements, LLC,* 172 Md.App. 350 (2007). The purpose of restitution, therefore, "is to prevent the defendant's unjust enrichment by recapturing the gains the defendant secured in a transaction." 1 *Dobbs* § 4.1(1), at 552.

"Restitution measures the remedy by the defendant's gain and seeks to force disgorgement of that gain." 1 *Dobbs* § 4.1(1), at 555. "'[A] constructive trust [may] be imposed to avoid unjust enrichment arising out of . . . the violation of any fiduciary duty or any other wrongdoing.'" *Bailiff v. Woolman,* 169 Md.App. 646, 654.

"In an action for unjust enrichment the burden is on the plaintiff to establish that the defendant holds plaintiff's money and that it would be unconscionable for him to retain it." *Plitt v. Greenberg,* 242 Md. 359, 364 (1966). Under Maryland law,

> [a] claim of unjust enrichment is established when: (1) the plaintiff confers a benefit upon the defendant; (2) the defendant knows or appreciates the benefit; and (3) the defendant's acceptance or retention of the benefit under the circumstances is such that it would be inequitable to allow the defendant to retain the benefit without the paying of value in return.

Benson v. State, 389 Md. 615, 651–52,(2005). As we discuss below, the motion court erred in concluding as a matter of law that Bank of America could not establish any of these three elements.

I.

First Element: Benefit Conferred

"A person confers a benefit upon another if he gives to the other possession of or some other interest in money[.]" *Restatement of Restitution* § 1 cmt. a (1937, updated through 2006). The Bank challenges the motion court's ruling that the Bank did not confer a benefit on Mrs. Gibbons. . . .

The Bank argues that the motion court committed several legal errors in concluding that the Bank cannot establish the threshold "benefit conferred" element of its unjust enrichment claim. In its view, the court's threshold error was to premise its benefit analysis on implied-in-fact contract principles, which require some evidence from which a mutual agreement can be inferred, rather than on quasi-contract (also known as implied-in-law contract) principles, which "involve[ ] no assent between the parties, no 'meeting of the minds.'" The Bank contends that the motion court then compounded this error by holding that the Bank had to directly deal with Mrs. Gibbons in order to warrant recovery under a theory of unjust enrichment. Finally, the Bank argues, the court erred in concluding that "there is not one scintilla of evidence . . . that any direct benefit was conferred on Ms. Gibbons," despite the obvious cash benefits conferred upon both Mr. and Mrs. Gibbons by the Bank. We agree with all three contentions.

A.

No Meeting Of The Minds Required

The motion court erroneously believed that, for an implied contract, there must be some "meeting of the minds" that creates the obligation to perform. The Court of Appeals has distinguished between contracts that are implied-in-fact, which require evidence of a "meeting of the minds," and contracts that are implied as a matter of law, for which a meeting of the minds is not required.

"An implied contract is an agreement which legitimately can be inferred from intention of the parties as evidenced by the circumstances and 'the ordinary course of dealing and the common understanding of men.'" . . . *Black's Law Dictionary* . . . defines [a *quasi*-contract] as a

[I]egal fiction invented by common law courts to permit recovery by contractual remedy in cases where, in fact, there is no contract, but where circumstances are such that justice warrants a recovery as though there had been a promise. It is not based on intention or consent of the parties, but is founded on considerations of justice and equity, and on doctrine of unjust enrichment. It is not in fact a contract, but an obligation which the law creates in absence of any agreement, when and because the acts of the parties or others have placed in the possession of one person money, or its equivalent, under such circumstances that in equity and good conscience he ought not to retain it.

See County Comm'rs of Caroline County v. J. Roland Dashiell & Sons, Inc., 358 Md. 83, 94–95 (2000) (citations omitted). *See also* Restatement (Second) of Contracts § 4 cmt. b (1981, updated through 2007) (contracts implied in law "are not based on the apparent intention of the parties to undertake the performances"; "[t]hey are obligations created by law for reasons of justice").

Because an "unjust enrichment claim is based on a quasi-contract or an implied-in-law contract[,]" *Alternatives Unltd.,* 155 Md.App. at 461, "it is simply a rule of law that requires restitution to the plaintiff of something that came into defendant's hands but belongs to the plaintiff in some sense.'" *Mass Transit Admin. v. Granite Constr. Co.,* 57 Md.App. 766, 775 (1984) (quoting 1 *Dobbs* § 4.2). The motion court erred in holding that the Bank's unjust enrichment claim fails for lack of evidence showing a meeting of the minds.

B.

No Dealings Directly Between The Parties Required

The court also erroneously required direct dealings between the Bank and Mrs. Gibbons. Contrary to the motion court's legal conclusion, a cause of action for unjust enrichment may lie against a transferee with whom the plaintiff had no contract, transaction, or dealing, either directly or indirectly.

[T]he dispositive question is whether Lynne Gibbons, as the defendant transferee, paid value for the funds transferred to her by Thomas Gibbons, the culpable third party. If the misappropriated Bank funds can be traced into her account, there was no consideration for such deposits, and there is no other defense to the Bank's claim for restitution, then the Bank could prevail on its unjust enrichment cause of action.

The motion court's emphasis on "direct dealings" between the Bank and Lynne Gibbons ignores the potential significance of evidence that Mrs. Gibbons did not pay value. In particular, the court erred in concluding, as a matter of law, that stolen funds traced into the Gibbons' joint accounts should be treated as if those funds had been used to purchase cars, gamble at casinos, or dine in fine restaurants. As Bank of America points out, if an innocent transferee may retain the benefit of stolen funds without paying value for them, not only would she receive a windfall, but so would the thief. He would benefit from his wrongdoing by being permitted to place the funds beyond reach of the victim simply by depositing them into a joint account with his spouse and shielding her from any knowledge of his wrongdoing.

C.

Benefit Conferred

Bank of America argues that the court's third error with respect to the first element of unjust enrichment was to conclude that there was no evidence "that any direct benefit was conferred on Mrs. Gibbons." The Bank points to Mrs. Gibbons' admission that proceeds from her husband's thefts were deposited into her joint checking account. Those funds belonged to the Bank and its customers.

Mrs. Gibbons responds that "there is no authority under Maryland law supporting th[e] proposition" that the benefit conferred element of an unjust enrichment cause of action may be satisfied by evidence that such benefit was conferred upon the defendant by the third-party wrongdoer, rather than by the plaintiff itself. . . .

In our view, *Plitt* illustrates that the benefit may be conferred by the wrongdoer *or* the plaintiff seeking restitution. *See also Restatement (First) of Restitution* § 123 (1937, updated through 2006) (innocent recipient of property that he could not lawfully acquire must account to true owner if he is not a purchaser for value). Many courts have held an innocent spouse accountable for a benefit conferred by the embezzling mate, rather than the unjust enrichment claimant. *See, e.g., In re Marriage of Allen,* 724 P.2d 651, 659 (Colo.1986) (ex-wife whose husband deposited embezzled funds into family account used to purchase family home and other property was subject to unjust enrichment claim); *Fed. Ins. Co. v. Smith,* 144 F.Supp.2d 507, 524–25 (E.D.Va.2001), *aff'd,* 63 Fed.Appx. 630, 634–35 (4th Cir.2003) (innocent spouse of embezzler who used stolen funds to satisfy spouse's personal and joint obligations and expenses held liable under conversion theory); *Bransom v. Std. Hardware, Inc.,* 874 S.W.2d 919, 927 (Tex.App.1994) (husband of embezzler who used stolen funds for household purposes held liable on unjust enrichment claim). Here, the motion court erred in concluding that lack of evidence that the Bank approved Mrs. Gibbons' receipt of the stolen money prevented the Bank from prevailing on its unjust enrichment claim.

II.

Second Element: Knowledge Of The Benefit

. . . Bank of America asserts that the erroneous "view taken by the trial court was that a defendant must have actual or constructive knowledge of the **source** of the benefit received in order to satisfy the second element [.]" (Emphasis added.) Citing *Plitt,* the Bank argues that a transferee's innocence as to the source of the deposited funds is not a bar to recovery for a claim based on unjust enrichment. Acknowledging that the good faith of Mrs. Gibbons is a factor that the court can consider when determining the third element of unjust enrichment, the Bank urges that her good faith is not the "determining factor" on this second element.

We agree that Bank of America is not required to prove Mrs. Gibbons knew of her husband's thefts. The *Restatement (First) of Restitution* section 123, as cited and applied in *Plitt,* explains that the knowledge necessary to establish the second element of an unjust enrichment claim is not necessarily knowledge that the funds were obtained by wrongful conduct against the plaintiff who seeks their return:

§ 123. Bona Fide Transferee Who Is Not A Purchaser For Value

A person who, **non-tortiously and without notice that another has the beneficial ownership of it,** acquires property which it would have been wrongful for him to acquire with notice of the facts and of which he is not a purchaser for value is, upon discovery of the facts, under a duty to account to the other for the direct product of the subject matter and the value of the use to him, if any, and in addition, to:

(a) return the subject matter in specie, if he has it;

(b) pay its value to him, if he has non-tortiously consumed it in beneficial use;

(c) pay its value or what he received therefore at his election, if he has disposed of it. (Emphasis added.)

This rule "is applicable to a person who, by gratuitous grant, by will or by descent, has received the title to property, either real or personal, in which another has a beneficial ownership **of which the transferee has no notice at the time of the receipt.**" *Id.,* cmt. a (emphasis added).

. . . Here, the motion court erred in granting summary judgment on the ground that Bank of America failed to establish that Mrs. Gibbons knew her husband was depositing the proceeds of his thefts from Bank clients into their joint bank accounts.

III.

Third Element: Unjust Retention Of The Benefit

"[W]hile 'a person is enriched if he has received a benefit,' the law does not consider him unjustly enriched unless 'the circumstances of the receipt of the benefit are such as between the two that to retain it would be unjust.'" *First Nat'l Bank v. Shpritz,* 63 Md.App. 623, 640). With respect to this final element, the motion court also determined that Bank of America failed to establish a dispute. . . .

The Bank argues that the motion court mistakenly relied on Lynne Gibbons' innocence regarding her husband's thefts in concluding that she should not be required to return the money he stole from the Bank. Citing *Plitt* and the *Restatement,* the Bank also contends that "consideration of the respective financial positions of the parties is . . . improper[.]" Although Mrs. Gibbons' good faith "is a factor that the court can consider when determining whether the circumstances are such that it would be inequitable for the defendant to retain the benefit without payment of its value, it is neither the exclusive nor determining factor."

We conclude that the motion court's almost exclusive focus on Lynne Gibbons' lack of knowledge undermined and unduly limited its analysis about whether, as a matter of law, it would be equitable to require her to pay money to the Bank as restitution. Although Mrs. Gibbon's good faith is a highly relevant factor, it does not, by itself, support a determination as a matter of law that "'the circumstances of the receipt of the benefit are such as between the [Bank and Mrs. Gibbons] that to retain it would be unjust.'" *See also Ammons v. Coffee County,* 716 So.2d 1227 (Ala.Civ. App.1998) (affirming verdict against innocent spouse when stolen funds were used to acquire boat and trailer.)

Courts often have required an innocent recipient benefitted by third party wrongdoing to establish a change of circumstances that makes it inequitable to order restitution. *See Fed. Ins. Co.,* 144 F.Supp.2d at 524–25; *Restatement Restitution* §142. Thus, when the recipient's change of circumstances was not caused by his or her wrongful conduct, "the primary rule is that if repayment will cause the recipient loss, restitution is barred to the extent that such loss would occur." *Hilliard v. Fox,* 735 F.Supp. 674, 677–78 (W.D.Va.1990). *See also Restatement Restitution* §142 cmt. b ("Any change of circumstances which would cause . . . the recipient entire or partial loss if the claimant were to obtain full restitution, is such a change as prevents full restitution"). This rule rests on the recognition that the innocent recipient's repayment of ill-gotten funds "will not normally cause the recipient any net loss—he will merely be returned to the *status quo ante.*" *Hilliard,* 735 F.Supp. at 678.

An innocent spouse could also avoid liability by proving that the money deposited in a joint account was used by the wrongdoing spouse for his (or her) own benefit, without any benefit to the family.

In sum, the motion court erred in granting summary judgment based on Mrs. Gibbons' lack of knowledge. The innocence of Mrs. Gibbons, by itself, does not preclude a claim for unjust enrichment. The motion court did not consider whether exclusive use of money by Mr. Gibbons (without benefiting the family), a change in Mrs. Gibbons' circumstances, or other equitable circumstances might warrant denial or reduction of the Bank's unjust enrichment claim. On remand, the parties may present evidence pertinent to these equitable considerations.

JUDGMENT VACATED. CASE REMANDED FOR FURTHER PROCEEDINGS NOT INCONSISTENT WITH THIS OPINION.

* * *

Problem 40

For a successful restitution cause of action, the plaintiff must prove a benefit was received by the defendant and injustice would result if that benefit were retained. Are those elements satisfied in the below scenario?

A husband and wife own a restaurant. They have one child, a daughter. Upon reaching adulthood, she starts paying for significant upgrades to the restaurant — new kitchen equipment, new dining tables, and the like. Over several years, the daughter spends more than $200,000 on improvements. She does so because she assumes (though they have never told her this) that her parents will give her the restaurant when they retire. Just before they get to retirement age, the parents sell the restaurant to someone else, without consulting their daughter. The daughter sues for unjust enrichment based on the value of the improvements she purchased.

Introductory Note — *Marking v. Marking* and *Mullens v. Hansel-Henderson*

These cases are both appeals from judgments for the defendant on the plaintiff's cause of action for restitution. That is, the lower court in both cases ruled the plaintiff did not prove there was unjust enrichment. The lower court determination in that regard is affirmed in *Marking*, but it is reversed in *Mullens*.

THINGS TO THINK ABOUT while reading *Marking v. Marking* and *Mullens v. Hansel-Henderson*:

1. What was the enrichment in this case?

2. Why would it be unjust — or not — to allow the defendant to retain the benefit in this situation?

Marking v. Marking
Minnesota Court of Appeals
366 N.W.2d 386 (1985)

NIERENGARTEN, Judge.

Appellants Roger and Nancy Marking appeal from summary judgment entered on August 2, 1984, in favor of respondents Lavern and Katherine Marking. We affirm.

Facts

In 1978, Roger and Nancy Marking moved a mobile home onto a farm in Wabasha County owned by Lavern and Katherine Marking, Roger's parents. Roger also constructed a basement under the mobile home and made several other improvements near the mobile home. Before the mobile home was placed on the farm, Lavern had indicated that some day Roger could purchase the farm.

Roger and Nancy lived in the mobile home from 1979 to October 1981. In September 1981, Lavern entered into a purchase agreement to sell the farm to Robert Evers. The sale included all improvements which were placed on the farm by Roger. Roger subsequently moved the mobile home off the farm and relocated in Lake City, Minnesota.

Roger and Nancy commenced this action against Lavern and Katherine Marking seeking the cost of labor and materials expended as a result of making certain improvements on the farm. On May 23, 1984, the trial court granted Lavern's and Katherine's motion from summary judgment. Judgment was entered on August 2, 1984. Roger and Nancy appealed.

Analysis

Summary judgment is appropriate if the record shows there is "no genuine issue as to any material fact." Minn.R.Civ.P. 56.03. On review, the court must view the evidence in the light most favorable to the party against whom summary judgment was granted. *Grondahl v. Bulluck,* 318 N.W.2d 240, 242 (Minn.1982).

Roger and Nancy argue the facts establish a cause of action in quasi contract or unjust enrichment since it would be unjust for Lavern and Katherine to retain the benefit of the improvements on the farm.

The Minnesota Supreme Court has recognized the theory of quasi contract for many years. A quasi contract is sometimes called a contract implied in law. However,

> [Q]uasi contracts are not, however, contracts at all, for "neither promise nor privity, real or imagined, is necessary." The quasi-contractual obligation is raised or imposed by law and is independent of any real or expressed intent of the parties. The obligation is called quasi-contractual because as a matter of legal history the remedy took the contract form just as if based on an actual contract or agreement. Under the theory of a quasi contract, the

obligation is defined in equity and good conscience and is imposed by law
to prevent unjust enrichment at the expense of another.

Dusenka v. Dusenka, 221 Minn. 234, 238 (1946). No recovery can be had in quasi
contract against one not shown to have been wrongfully enriched at the plaintiff's
expense. *Lamson v. Towle-Jamieson Investment Co.,* 187 Minn. 368, 372 (1932). When
dealing with investments to real property, a plaintiff must present evidence that the
investments added to the value of the land. *See generally Holste v. Baker,* 223 Minn.
321, 328 (1947).

Roger and Nancy Marking have not met their burden of showing that a benefit
was conferred on Lavern or Katherine. Roger and Nancy only submitted an accounting of their expenses in constructing the basement and making the improvements.
These figures do not reflect an added value to the farm. Lavern testified he was not
paid anything in addition to the expenditures for the basement and miscellaneous
improvements and there was no evidence whatsoever regarding an increase in value
to the farm as a result of the improvements. No appraisal evidence of any increase
in value was sought and there was no evidence from the purchaser, Robert Evers,
that the basement and improvements resulted in any increase in the purchase price.

Decision

Because there was no evidence regarding the value of the improvements to the
farm, summary judgment was properly granted.

Affirmed.

* * *

Mullens v. Hansel-Henderson

Colorado Supreme Court
65 P.3d 992 (2002)

Justice MARTINEZ delivered the Opinion of the Court.

I. Introduction

We granted certiorari to decide whether the court of appeals erred in holding
that an attorney must return fees received for legal services when the services were
successfully completed but the agreement was not in writing. The court of appeals
ordered attorney Steven Mullens to return fees earned during representation of Victoria Hansel-Henderson in claims against her former employer because the underlying contingent fee agreement did not comply with the requirements of Colorado
Rules of Civil Procedure Chapter 23.3, and was therefore unenforceable. We hold
that an attorney is entitled to fees under quantum meruit when the agreed upon services are successfully completed but the contingent fee agreement is not in writing.
Therefore, we reverse and remand the case to the court of appeals with directions to
decide any remaining issues in accordance with the views expressed in this opinion.

II. Facts and Procedural History

In 1990, respondent Victoria Hansel-Henderson entered into a written contingent fee agreement with petitioner Steven Mullens, a Colorado attorney with over twenty years experience in Workers' Compensation claims. Under the terms of this initial contract, Mullens agreed to represent Hansel in a Workers' Compensation claim against her employer Public Service Company for injuries sustained on the job. In exchange for representation, Mullens would receive twenty percent (20%) of any monies received by him on her behalf. Mullens agreed to carry all costs related to this litigation.

As Mullens worked on the Workers' Compensation claim over the next two years, he learned of attempts by Public Service Company to influence medical diagnoses being made for purposes of evaluating Hansel's injuries. Mullens recognized that these tactics supported a potential Bad Faith claim for the intentional mishandling and manipulation of the Workers' Compensation claim. Mullens discussed this potential claim with Hansel and the two agreed that he would also represent her in this Bad Faith claim for an additional fee. Although testimony regarding the precise fee to be paid under this new agreement varied somewhat, the trial court found that Mullens and Hansel had an agreement for a fee of forty percent (40%) of any monies received for this new claim. This separate agreement was never committed to writing.

In 1993, after three years of work, Mullens settled the two claims. The employer agreed to pay Hansel $37,560 to settle the Workers' Compensation claim and $262,440 to settle the Bad Faith claim for a total on the two claims of $300,000. From the settlement amounts Mullens retained thirty-three percent (33%) of the total settlement amount, instead of twenty percent (20%) of the Workers' Compensation claim and forty percent (40%) of the Bad Faith claim. This arrangement allowed Hansel to receive $12,488 more than she could have expected to receive under the terms of the oral contingent fee agreement. Hansel accepted the amounts and signed two documents, one for each claim, releasing the employer from further liability. The trial court found that at disbursement Hansel was very pleased with the outcome of the claims and did not object to the amounts of attorney's fees. Hansel negotiated the settlement checks.

In 1995, two years after Mullens received his attorney's fees and Hansel accepted the settlement money, Hansel initiated action against Mullens to recover all of the attorney's fees paid for the Bad Faith settlement. Hansel asserted in her complaint that Mullens was not entitled to attorney's fees from the Bad Faith settlement because the contingent fee agreement for the Bad Faith claim was not in writing as required by Colorado Rules of Civil Procedure Chapter 23.3, and was therefore not enforceable. Hansel argued that because Mullens was not entitled to payment under an oral contingent fee agreement, Mullens should be required to return to Hansel all of the attorney fees that she paid for the Bad Faith claim. . . .

III. Analysis

This case requires us to examine whether an attorney may keep attorney's fees paid for services performed pursuant to an unenforceable oral contingent fee agreement when the services were successfully completed. . . .

Rules Governing Contingent Fees

Whether or not the terms of a contingent fee agreement are enforceable is controlled by Chapter 23.3 of Colorado Rules of Civil Procedure. Rule 6 of Chapter 23.3 states that "no contingent fee agreement shall be enforceable by the involved attorney unless there has been substantial compliance with all of the provisions of this chapter." C.R.C.P. Ch. 23.3, Rule 6. Hence, if a contingent fee agreement fails to substantially comply with the rules of Chapter 23.3, it is unenforceable.

According to Rule 1, a contingent fee agreement must be in writing. C.R.C.P. Ch. 23.3, Rule 1; *Beeson v. Indus. Claim Appeals Office,* 942 P.2d 1314, 1316 (Colo.App.1997). Therefore, an oral contingent fee agreement is not enforceable and the attorney cannot recover the fee amount specified in the oral agreement. This, however, does not necessarily preclude the attorney from recovering fees altogether. Generally attorneys may recover on an unenforceable contract on the basis of quantum meruit. Restatement (Third) of the Law Governing Lawyers § 39 (2002) (If a client and lawyer have not made a valid contract providing for another measure of compensation, a client owes a lawyer who has performed legal services for the client the fair value of the lawyer's services); 7 Am.Jur.2d § 289 (attorneys may recover on a quantum meruit basis even where the parties have entered an unenforceable fee contract).

Although recovery under quantum meruit is generally allowed for unenforceable fee agreements, Chapter 23.3 limits such recovery. *Elliott v. Joyce,* 889 P.2d 43, 46 (Colo.1994). Chapter 23.3 limits compensation under quantum meruit through a notice requirement detailed in Rule 5(d). Rule 5(d) mandates that contingent fee agreements contain "a statement of the contingency upon which the client is to be liable to pay compensation otherwise than from amounts collected for him by the attorney." C.R.C.P. Ch. 23.3, Rule 5(d). I. . . .

Quantum Meruit When the Legal Services are Completed

We have never before examined whether the Rule 5(d) notice requirement applies to situations where the agreed upon legal services, such as a settlement or judgment, have been completed. . . .

In her complaint Hansel asserts a claim for "money had and received," under which she argues that all fees retained by Mullens should be returned to her. Under this principle, a party will not be allowed to keep money which in equity and good conscience should be returned to another. D. Dobbs, Handbook on the Law of Remedies, § 4.2 (1973). Under the claim "money had and received" the task of the court is not to determine whether something was taken away from the client but whether the attorney was unjustly enriched by wronging the client, such as accepting payment he was not entitled to. *Recovery Based on Tortfeasor's Profits in Action for Procuring Breach of Contract,* 5 A.L.R.4th 1276 (2002); D. Dobbs, Handbook on the Law of Remedies, § 4.2 (1973).

"Money had and received," like quantum meruit, exists to prevent unjust enrichment. In the circumstances before us, "money had and received" operates to return funds to a client from an attorney who has been unjustly enriched. Quantum meruit, on the other hand, assists the attorney in obtaining fees from the client to prevent unjust enrichment of the client. The difference between the two doctrines in the circumstances before us is merely whether the fees have been received by the attorney. Both doctrines seek to prevent unjust enrichment in the attorney-client relationship, and to determine the reasonable value of the legal services rendered. For this reason, our discussion of quantum meruit completely resolves the claim for "money had and received."

Neither the Rules Governing Contingency Fees under Chapter 23.3 nor our prior cases maintain that equity is unavailable to the attorney who completes the agreed upon legal services solely because the agreement was not in writing. Further, the client has notice that she must pay for legal services because she agreed to do so from the monies recovered by the attorney on her behalf. Here, Hansel agreed to pay for legal services from the monies her attorney recovered. Mullens completed the agreed upon legal services, thereby obtaining a substantial settlement for Hansel. While it is true that Mullens may not enforce the terms of the contingent fee agreement, we find that he may be compensated under quantum meruit for the reasonable worth of the legal services he provided to Hansel.

IV. Conclusion

We hold that Mullens earned reasonable attorney fees, despite an unenforceable contingency agreement, under quantum meruit. Thus, we reverse the judgment of the court of appeals and remand for the court to decide any remaining issues consistent with this opinion.

* * *

Problem 41

Quantum meruit is a quasi-contractual theory that allows recovery of a benefit conferred on the defendant even where no contract requires compensation to the plaintiff. Should quantum meruit apply to allow recovery in restitution in the following case?

A homeowner hires a builder to build an addition to her home. The contract calls for the builder to first obtain all required permits for the addition, then build it according to industry standards for quality. The builder is confident he will be able to get the necessary permits from the city, so he begins construction even before applying for them. Six months later, and after completing substantial construction work on the project, the builder applies for the permits and learns the property's zoning does not allow the addition. The permits are not issued; the homeowner will be required to demolish all the new construction. The parties' contract does not require payment because no permits were obtained. The builder files suit under a quantum meruit theory, seeking to recover for the costs he expended during the construction.

Introductory Note — *Olwell v. Nye & Nissen Co.* and *Pro-Pac, Inc. v. WOW Logistics Co.*

The asserted unjust enrichment in *Olwell* is straightforward: the defendant used machinery belonging to the plaintiff without permission. In *Pro-Pac*, it is more complicated: a consultant went behind the back of the company that hired him in order to seek personal gain. But both cases present the issue of how to properly measure the benefit obtained by the defendant.

THINGS TO THINK ABOUT while reading *Olwell v. Nye & Nissen Co.* and *Pro-Pac, Inc. v. WOW Logistics Co.*:

1. How was restitution measured in this case?

2. In what situations would restitution be a more favorable remedy for a plaintiff than tort damages?

Olwell v. Nye & Nissen Co.

Washington Supreme Court
26 Wash.2d 282 (1946)

MALLERY, Justice.

On May 6, 1940, plaintiff, E. L. Olwell, sold and transferred to the defendant corporation his one-half interest in Puget Sound Egg Packers, a Washington corporation having its principal place of business in Tacoma. By the terms of the agreement, the plaintiff was to retain full ownership in an 'Eggsact' egg-washing machine, formerly used by Puget Sound Egg Packers. The defendant promised to make it available for delivery to the plaintiff on or before June 15, 1940. It appears that the plaintiff arranged for and had the machine stored in a space adjacent to the premises occupied by the defendant but not covered by its lease. Due to the scarcity of labor immediately after the outbreak of the war, defendant's treasurer, without the knowledge or consent of the plaintiff, ordered the egg washer taken out of storage. The machine was put into operation by defendant on May 31, 1941, and thereafter for a period of three years was used approximately one day a week in the regular course of the defendant's business. Plaintiff first discovered this use in January or February of 1945 when he happened to be at the plant on business and heard the machine operating. Thereupon plaintiff offered to sell the machine to defendant for $600 or half of its original cost in 1929. A counter offer of $50 was refused and approximately one month later this action was commenced to recover the reasonable value of defendant's use of the machine, and praying for $25 per month from the commencement of the unauthorized use until the time of trial. A second cause of action was alleged but was not pressed and hence is not here involved. The court entered judgment for plaintiff in the amount of $10 per week for the period of 156 weeks covered by the statute of limitations, or $1,560, and gave the plaintiff his costs.

Defendant has appealed to this court assigning error upon the judgment, upon the trial of the cause on the theory of unjust enrichment, upon the amount of damages, and upon the court's refusal to make a finding as to the value of the machine and in refusing to consider such value in measuring damages.

The theory of the respondent was that the tort of conversion could be 'waived' and suit brought in quasi-contract, upon a contract implied in law, to recover, as restitution, the profits which inured to appellant as a result of its wrongful use of the machine. With this the trial court agreed and in its findings of facts found that the use of the machine 'resulted in a benefit to the users, in that said use saves the users approximately $1.43 per hour of use as against the expense which would be incurred were eggs to be washed by hand; that said machine was used by Puget Sound Egg Packers and defendant, on an average of one day per week from May of 1941, until February of 1945 at an average saving of $10.00 per each day of use.'

In substance, the argument presented by the assignments of error is that the principle of unjust enrichment, or quasi-contract, is not of universal application, but is imposed only in exceptional cases because of special facts and circumstances and in favor of particular persons; that respondent had an adequate remedy in an action at law for replevin or claim and delivery; that any damages awarded to the plaintiff should be based upon the use or rental value of the machine and should bear some reasonable relation to its market value. Appellant therefore contends that the amount of the judgment is excessive.

It is uniformly held that in cases where the defendant *tort feasor* has benefited by his wrong, the plaintiff may elect to 'waive the tort' and bring an action in assumpsit for restitution. Such an action arises out of a duty imposed by law devolving upon the defendant to repay an unjust and unmerited enrichment. Woodward, The Law of Quasi-Contracts, § 272(2), p. 439; Keener on Quasi-Contracts, p. 160.

It is clear that the saving in labor cost which appellant derived from its use of respondent's machine constituted a benefit.

According to the Restatement of Restitution, § 1(b), p. 12,

> 'A person confers a benefit upon another if he gives to the other possession of or some other interest in money, land, chattels, or choses in action, performs services beneficial to or at the request of the other, satisfies a debt or a duty of the other, or in any way adds to the other's security or advantage. *He confers a benefit not only where he adds to the propety of another, but also where he* saves the other from expense or loss. The word 'benefit', therefore denotes any form of advantage.' (Italics ours)

It is also necessary to show that while appellant benefited from its use of the egg-washing machine, respondent thereby incurred a loss. It is argued by appellant that since the machine was put into storage by respondent, who had no present use for it, and for a period of almost three years did not know that appellant was operating it and since it was not injured by its operation and the appellant never adversely claimed any title to it, nor contested respondent's right of repossession upon the latter's discovery of the wrongful operation, that the respondent was not damaged because he is as well off as if the machine had not been used by appellant.

The very essence of the nature of property is the right to its exclusive use. Without it, no beneficial right remains. However plausible, the appellant cannot be heard to say that his wrongful invasion of the respondent's property right to exclusive use is not a loss compensable in law. To hold otherwise would be subversive of all property rights since his use was admittedly wrongful and without claim of right. The theory of unjust enrichment is applicable in such a case.

We agree with appellant that respondent could have elected a 'common garden variety of action,' as he calls it, for the recovery of damages. It is also true that except where provided for by statute, punitive damages are not allowed, the basic measure for the recovery of damages in this state being compensation. If, then, respondent had been *limited* to redress *in tort* for damages, as appellant contends, the court below would be in error in refusing to make a finding as to the value of the machine. In such case the award of damages must bear a reasonable relation to the value of the property. Hoff v. Lester, Wash., 168 P.2d 409.

But respondent here had an election. He chose rather to waive his right of action *in tort* and to use *in assumpsit* on the implied contract. Having so elected, he is entitled to the measure of restoration which accompanies the remedy.

> 'Actions for restitution have for their primary purpose taking from the defendant and restoring to the plaintiff something to which the plaintiff is entitled, or if this is not done, causing the defendant to pay the plaintiff an amount which will restore the plaintiff to the position in which he was before the defendant received the benefit. If the value of what was received and what was lost were always equal, there would be no substantial problem as to the amount of recovery, since actions of restitution are not punitive. In fact, however, the plaintiff frequently had lost more than the defendant has gained, and sometimes the defendant has gained more than the plaintiff has lost.

> 'In such cases the measure of restitution is determined with reference to the tortiousness of the defendant's conduct or the negligence or other fault of one or both of the parties in creating the situation giving rise to the right to restitution. If the defendant was tortious in his acquisition of the benefit he is required to pay for what the other has lost although that is more than the recipient benefited. *If he was consciously tortious in acquiring the benefit, he is also deprived of any profit derived from his subsequent dealing with it.* If he was no more at fault than the claimant, he is not required to pay for losses in excess of benefit received by him and he is permitted to retain gains which result from his dealing with the property.' (Italics ours) Restatement of Restitution, pp. 595, 596.

Respondent may recover the profit derived by the appellant from the use of the machine.

Respondent has prayed 'on his first cause of action for the sum of $25.00 per month from the time defendant first commenced to use said machine subsequent to May 1940 (1941) until present time.'

In computing judgment, the court below computed recovery on the basis of $10 per week. This makes the judgment excessive since it cannot exceed the amount prayed for. . . .

We therefore direct the trial court to reduce the judgment, based upon the prayer of the complaint, to $25 per month for thirty-six months, or $900.

The judgment as modified is affirmed. Appellant will recover its costs.

* * *

Pro-Pac, Inc. v. WOW Logistics Co.

United States Court of Appeals, Seventh Circuit
721 F.3d 781 (2013)

PER CURIAM.

Pro-Pac, Inc. (Pro-Pac) was a packaging business that filed for Chapter 11 bankruptcy in 2006. Pro-Pac then filed an adversary proceeding against WOW Logistics Co. (WOW), a logistics service provider, for aiding and abetting a Pro-Pac employee's breach of fiduciary duty. The bankruptcy court found that WOW had indeed aided and abetted the Pro-Pac employee, for which tort the court attempted to calculate the damages. But the bankruptcy court instead thought that its award to Pro-Pac had to rest on an independent unjust enrichment claim. On appeal, the district court ordered the bankruptcy court to dismiss the case because the unjust-enrichment argument had been introduced too late in the proceeding. Pro-Pac appeals from the district court's ruling, arguing that the district court erred in dismissing the case and seeking reinstatement of the bankruptcy court's ruling. We agree that the district court erred in dismissing the case, but the bankruptcy court also erred in its approach to Pro-Pac's damages. Thus, we reverse the judgment of the district court with instructions to remand to the bankruptcy court. On remand, the bankruptcy court should reexamine the issues relating to a proper remedy for WOW's tort liability.

I. Facts

Pro-Pac decided to expand into the warehouse and transportation industry. To do so, Pro-Pac contacted George Chapes, an experienced and well-connected veteran of the warehouse industry, and hired him in June 2005 to be its vice president of sales. Chapes received a salary from Pro-Pac and a benefits package that was worth significantly more than the packages paid to other members of Pro-Pac's sales team.

In August 2005, Pro-Pac subleased a warehouse in East Troy, Wisconsin, from WOW, a logistics service provider that brokers transportation services nation-wide and operates public warehouses in Wisconsin, Illinois, and Idaho. Pro-Pac met with WOW in April 2006 to consider another business deal, and WOW asked Pro-Pac if it could use Chapes as a business consultant. Pro-Pac expressed surprise in learning that WOW had been talking to Chapes about being a consultant for WOW. Pro-Pac told Chapes that "from this point forward . . . if you're working with WOW or there's something going on, [Pro-Pac] need[s] to know what's happening. [WOW is] our landlord. This is too close to home."

Pro-Pac and WOW entered into negotiations that would permit WOW to use Chapes as a consultant. These negotiations began on July 17, 2006, when Pro-Pac sent an email to WOW proposing that Chapes could work for WOW in exchange for an extension of Pro-Pac's lease with WOW and a rebate of its rent for two months per year for five years. Pro-Pac and WOW engaged in a series of calls and emails in an attempt to work out the details of an agreement. Ultimately, as the bankruptcy court determined, WOW offered to give Pro-Pac free rent for two months per year for five years in exchange for Chapes's services, provided that Chapes actually secured a deal for WOW. On August 3, 2006, Pro-Pac sent WOW an email "touching base" regarding the negotiations, and on August 8, 2006, Pro-Pac sent an email indicating that the parties were unable to reach a deal. WOW responded on August 9, 2006, agreeing to "table the idea for now."

While Pro-Pac and WOW were engaged in these negotiations, Chapes and WOW were secretly in contact with each other about a business opportunity with Vangard Distribution, Inc. (Vangard). Vangard was a warehouse company, whose president had called Chapes on August 2, 2006, with information about a substantial business deal. Vangard had a customer who needed storage for an overflow of sugar, but Chapes had only 24 hours to commit to the deal. Even though Chapes was working for Pro-Pac to secure accounts with companies like Vangard, he informed WOW about the deal, allowing WOW to negotiate a short-term agreement with Vangard and secure the Vangard account.

Chapes and WOW remained in contact after the Vangard deal. Throughout August 2006, Chapes and WOW called each other numerous times and WOW began to issue checks to Chapes for his commission on the Vangard deal. In November 2006, Pro-Pac reminded WOW that Pro-Pac should be included in any communication between WOW and Chapes. WOW, however, had purchased a disposable cell phone for Chapes to use for its calls to him. WOW representative(s) also accompanied Chapes on a trip to Idaho to meet a substantial client at about the same time. WOW continued to pay Chapes for the Vangard deal in amounts totaling $6,490, and in early 2007, WOW hired Chapes.

Pro-Pac filed for Chapter 11 bankruptcy on November 20, 2006, and filed an adversary proceeding against WOW and Chapes on May 19, 2007. Among other allegations, Pro-Pac alleged that Chapes, aided and abetted by WOW, breached his fiduciary duty to Pro-Pac by diverting business to WOW. Pro-Pac remained unaware of the full extent of the ongoing relationship between WOW and Chapes until WOW released documents during discovery that revealed the amount of revenues from the Vangard account. Pro-Pac presented several claims in its initial complaint, on some of which the bankruptcy court granted partial summary judgment, and Pro-Pac abandoned others. Ultimately, Pro-Pac proceeded with a single claim: for breach of fiduciary duty based on Chapes's diversion of the Vangard deal to WOW, and for WOW's aiding and abetting of Chapes's breach of fiduciary duty. . . .

II. Discussion

. . . In its memorandum opinion, the bankruptcy court ruled that WOW was liable to Pro-Pac for aiding and abetting Chapes's breach of fiduciary duty. Chapes's breach of fiduciary duty is recognized as a tort under Wisconsin law. See *Zastrow v. Journal Commc'ns, Inc.*, 291 Wis.2d 426 (2006). WOW is also liable in tort for aiding and abetting Chapes's breach of fiduciary duty. Restatement (Second) of Torts § 874 cmt. c (1979) ("A person who knowingly assists a fiduciary in committing a breach of trust is himself guilty of tortious conduct. . . .").

Despite the bankruptcy court's liability determination against WOW, the district court instructed the bankruptcy court to dismiss those claims, thus vacating the basis for any damages in Pro-Pac's favor. We hold that Pro-Pac is entitled to damages, however. Given the bankruptcy court's improper calculation of damages, remand is appropriate.

On remand, the bankruptcy court has a variety of options under Wisconsin law in crafting a remedy based on WOW's liability. Restitution may be available as an equitable remedy in tort under Wisconsin law to offset WOW's unjust enrichment. *Puttkammer v. Minth,* 83 Wis.2d 686 (1978). While one recognized measure of damages is based on the harm inflicted on the plaintiff, restitution is another recognized option, which is measured by "the defendant's gain or benefit." *Ludyjan v. Cont'l Cas. Co.,* 308 Wis.2d 398 (Wis.Ct.App.2008) (quoting 1 Dan B. Dobbs, Dobbs Law of Remedies: Damages, Equity, Restitution § 3.1, at 280 (2d ed.1993)) (internal quotation marks omitted).

Wisconsin law does not limit restitution to merely unjust enrichment claims, but also allows plaintiffs to receive restitution as compensation for tort claims:

> In cases in which a tortfeasor has received from the commission of a tort against another person a benefit that constitutes unjust enrichment at the expense of the other, he is ordinarily liable to the other, at the latter's election, either for the damage done to the other's interests or for the value of the benefit received through the commission of the tort.

N. Air Servs., Inc. v. Link, No. 2008AP2897, 2012 WL 130531, at *4 (Wis.Ct.App. Jan. 18, 2012) (footnote omitted) (quoting Restatement (Second) of Torts § 903 cmt. b (1979)).

Wisconsin courts have also recognized restitution as an appropriate remedy for a tortious breach of fiduciary duty. In *Hartford Elevator, Inc. v. Lauer,* the Wisconsin Supreme Court ruled that restitution was an appropriate remedy for an employee who breached his fiduciary duty to his employer. 94 Wis.2d 571 (1980). Although the complaint alleged a cause of action based on the employee's contract, the court analyzed the issue in terms of the employee's breach of fiduciary duty. Regardless of whether a breach of a fiduciary duty is pled as a tort or contract claim, the same legal analysis applies to both types of claims when they overlap. See *Loehrke,* 445 N.W.2d at 720 ("If, however, a tort duty coincides with a contract obligation, either a contract or a tort action will lie for its breach. A tort duty coincides with a contractual obligation when the breaching party has a fiduciary duty to the other party."). . . .

Finally, the Restatement (Second) of Torts explains in detail the manner in which restitution for a <u>breach of fiduciary duty can be calculated:</u>

> In addition to or in substitution for . . . damages [for harm,] the beneficiary may be entitled to restitutionary recovery, since not only is he entitled to

recover for any harm done to his legally protected interests by the wrongful conduct of the fiduciary, but ordinarily he is entitled to profits that result to the fiduciary from his breach of duty and to be the beneficiary of a constructive trust in the profits. . . .

. . . The measure of . . . liability [for a defendant who assisted in the breach of a fiduciary duty], however, may be different from that of the fiduciary since he is responsible only for harm caused or profits that he himself has made from the transaction, and he is not necessarily liable for the profits that the fiduciary has made nor for those that he should have made.

Restatement (Second) of Torts § 874 cmt. b-c (1979); see also *Loehrke,* 445 N.W.2d at 721 (citing § 874).

To award restitution damages in favor of Pro-Pac requires an examination of WOW's profits from the Vangard deal. The bankruptcy court determined that by encouraging Chapes to breach his fiduciary duty, WOW helped direct the Vangard deal from Pro-Pac to itself, from which WOW presumably benefitted. The record is underdeveloped on this point, indicating only that WOW's revenues on the Vangard deal averaged $62,670 per month. Even if this number is accurate, it does not likely reflect profits, which would be based on a determination of revenues as well as costs. If the bankruptcy court pursues this remedy, unless the parties stipulate to WOW's profit from the Vangard deal, the bankruptcy court must direct the parties to properly develop these facts.

Alternatively, the "value of the benefit received through the commission of the tort" (*i.e.,* Chapes's consulting services) could be measured by examining what WOW was willing to exchange for those services immediately prior to its tortious conduct. During negotiations in the summer of 2006, WOW offered Pro-Pac free rent for two months per year for five years in exchange for Chapes's services, but following Chapes's referral of the Vangard deal to WOW, the negotiations between Pro-Pac and WOW ceased. As a result, WOW obtained access to Chapes's contacts without providing Pro-Pac any payment, including the free rent. Pro-Pac calculated the value of this free rent as $385,000. But this value does not reflect a present-value calculation, which would discount the rent amount over the five-year time period. It is also debatable whether $385,000, the value WOW placed on five years of Chapes's services, represents a fair approximation of the value of the (much briefer) services wrongfully obtained. On the other hand, we note that WOW initially offered Pro-Pac significant rent concessions over a shorter period of time for the privilege of speaking with Chapes, regardless of whether Chapes's contacts helped WOW to secure any new business opportunities; this suggests a "floor" on the value of the services wrongfully obtained. If the bankruptcy court wishes to pursue this remedy, unless the parties are able to stipulate to the value of services that WOW received when the negotiations fell apart, the bankruptcy court must require the parties to properly develop these facts.

The bankruptcy court could also choose to award compensatory damages that address the harm sustained by Pro-Pac. This compensatory measure of liability and restitution often overlap, such that "the benefit to the one and the loss to the other are co-extensive." Restatement (First) of Restitution § 1 cmt. d (1937). Under a compensatory damages theory, Pro-Pac would be entitled to receive the benefit of the free rent that it lost when WOW discontinued its negotiations for Chapes's services. As previously noted, the bankruptcy court estimated that these damages amount to $385,000, but again, this does not reflect a present-value calculation. Nor is it clear that this amount, which reflects five years' worth of losses, is an appropriate measure of the harm caused by WOW's single breach. If the bankruptcy court wishes to pursue this remedy, unless the parties stipulate to the value of the free rent that Pro-Pac lost, the bankruptcy court must require the parties to properly develop these facts.

Regardless of whether the bankruptcy court awards damages premised on gain to WOW (*i.e.,* restitutionary damages) or loss to Pro-Pac (*i.e.,* compensatory damages), punitive damages are also available, if otherwise appropriate. Wisconsin law allows awards of punitive damages when "compensatory damages" are imposed. *Groshek v. Trewin,* 325 Wis.2d 250 (2010). The Restatement (Second) of Torts defines "compensatory damages" as "the damages awarded to a person as compensation, indemnity or restitution for harm sustained by him," Restatement (Second) of Torts § 903 (1979), and Wisconsin has adopted this definition. Pro-Pac's reliance on any particular theory of tort damages does not foreclose an award of punitive damages to deter intentional wrongdoing, if such damages are deemed appropriate.....

III. Conclusion

The bankruptcy court erred in its determination that WOW must pay $385,000 in damages to Pro-Pac based on Pro-Pac's unjust-enrichment theory. The case is remanded to the district court and to the bankruptcy court to reformulate the award of damages based on WOW's aiding and abetting of Chapes's breach of fiduciary duty.....

MANION, Circuit Judge, concurring in part, dissenting in part.

I concur with the court's per curiam opinion with the exception of the court's final analysis holding that punitive damages could be available even when the court awards only restitution based on the defendant's gain (as opposed to the plaintiff's loss). As I see it, Wisconsin law does not permit punitive damages unless there has been an award of compensatory damages. *Groshek v. Trewin,* 325 Wis.2d 250 (2010) ("[W]here there is no award of compensatory damages, punitive damages are not available.").

Restitution based on the defendant's gain is not a form of compensatory damages under Wisconsin law. For starters, restitution and compensatory damages are not calculated in the same way; compensatory damages are based on the harm suffered by the plaintiff, while restitution is based on the defendant's gain. Because these remedies are calculated differently and do not always produce the same value of damages, restitution based on the defendant's gain is treated as an alternative remedy to compensatory damages. Furthermore, restitution is an equitable remedy, and Wisconsin still retains a distinction between law and equity for damages purposes. *See Groshek*, 784 N.W.2d at 175.

Therefore, restitution based on the benefit that WOW received would not be a sufficient basis for punitive damages. If the bankruptcy court wishes to award punitive damages, it must first award compensatory damages based on the harm Pro-Pac suffered.

* * *

Problem 42

Restitution is measured by the total amount of the gain realized by the defendant. What is the correct amount of restitution in the case described below?

The chief financial officer of a large investment banking corporation embezzles $20 million by paying himself several unauthorized bonuses. Because the bonuses were paid along with his regular salary, payroll taxes and income tax are withheld. His paychecks therefore reflect $14 million in unauthorized bonuses. Battling a guilty conscience, he donates a total of $4 million to charity that year. When the company discovers the embezzlement, it fires the CFO and sues him for restitution.

Constructive Trust

A trust is a legal relationship where one person agrees to hold property for the benefit of another. A *constructive* trust is a restitutionary remedy where the agreement to hold property for another does not actually exist but is implied by law. It is a quasi-contractual sort of restitution: to prevent unjust enrichment, the court imposes on the defendant an obligation to hold wrongfully acquired property in trust for the benefit of the plaintiff.

A constructive trust is useful when a defendant has unjustly benefited at the expense of the plaintiff but an award of damages would be inadequate; perhaps because the defendant is insolvent or the improperly acquired property is unique. The trust arrangement implied by law allows the plaintiff to obtain a specific item of property in the defendant's possession.

The remedy is available only where the property the plaintiff seeks to have held in trust is traceable from the wrongfully acquired property. Traceable means the wrongfully acquired property was used to obtain the property that is subject to the trust. A plaintiff who merely proves the defendant embezzled $85,000 cannot obtain a constructive trust on the defendant's luxury speedboat. But the plaintiff can be awarded a constructive trust on the boat if she also proves embezzled funds were used to purchase it. That additional showing is referred to as tracing.

A constructive trust is an equitable remedy because it is an *in personam* order requiring its subject to do something (hold certain property for the benefit of the plaintiff).

Introductory Note — *Estate of Cowling v. Estate of Cowling* and *Cruz v. McAneny*

Estate of Cowling is a woman's effort to recover from her stepchildren certain assets transferred to them by her now deceased husband. (It may be helpful in reading the case to draw a family tree showing the parties to the litigation and their relationship to one another.) One of the theories of recovery she pursues is constructive trust, which triggers some fairly complicated tracing issues.

Cruz is a dispute over a disbursement from the September 11 victim compensation fund. Because the decedent had a domestic partner, the disbursement was more than it would be for a single person. At issue is the proper distribution of the proceeds and whether they can appropriately be the subject of a constructive trust.

THINGS TO THINK ABOUT while reading *Estate of Cowling v. Estate of Cowling* and *Cruz v. McAneny*:

1. What is required for imposition of a constructive trust?

2. How is the remedy of constructive trust enforced?

3. Can money be the subject of a constructive trust? If so, under what circumstances?

Estate of Cowling v. Estate of Cowling
Ohio Supreme Court
847 N.E.2d 405 (2006)

PFEIFER, J.

Grace and Garnard Cowling married in 1967. It was a second marriage for both of them, and each of them had children from a previous marriage. Sandra Reddington and appellees Gary Cowling and Richard Cowling are Garnard's children from his previous marriage. Appellee Deanna Cowling is Gary's wife; appellee Dianne Cowling is Richard's wife. The appellees will be referred to collectively as the Cowlings. Grace and Garnard had no children together.

Grace and Garnard owned various brokerage accounts and stock investments jointly with rights of survivorship. On July 16, 1996, Grace signed irrevocable documents that transferred stocks to Garnard. This transaction gave Garnard exclusive possession and control over these stocks, which previously had been owned and controlled by both Grace and Garnard. Garnard placed the stocks in an account that he designated in December 1996 as a transfer-on-death ("TOD") account, with his children named as the beneficiaries. Garnard gave some of these stocks to Gary, Richard, and Sandra between December 1996 and February 1997. Garnard transferred additional assets from joint brokerage accounts into his own name sometime in 1996 or 1997. He then placed those assets in the TOD accounts. The assets in the TOD accounts passed to Gary, Richard, and Sandra upon Garnard's death on February 8, 1998. The total amount received by Garnard's children as a result of the gifts of stock ($142,363.00) and the proceeds of the TOD accounts ($182,995.69) was $325,358.69.

Grace filed an equitable claim against the Cowlings for a declaratory judgment to establish a constructive trust over the assets transferred by Garnard to the Cowlings. Grace's complaint also made claims against Garnard's estate for breach of contract, conversion, breach of fiduciary duty, negligent misrepresentation, and fraud.

. . . The court instructed the jury (1) to determine whether Garnard had withdrawn funds from the joint and survivorship accounts in excess of the contributions attributable to him and (2) to assess damages in the amount of assets that had been wrongfully transferred by Garnard. The court also instructed the jury to award only damages that were proven by Grace by a preponderance of the evidence. The jury found that Garnard had withdrawn funds from the accounts in excess of the contributions attributable to him and that the damages suffered by Grace were $255,354.

In its judgment, the trial court also declared a constructive trust in the total amount of $255,354, imposed on each of the Cowlings in proportion to the amount that each had individually received from Garnard. The trial court did not designate the specific property or assets over which the constructive trust was to be imposed. The Cowlings moved for a new trial and for judgment notwithstanding the verdict; the motion was denied. . . .

The court of appeals reversed the trial court's denial of the Cowlings' motions for directed verdict and judgment notwithstanding the verdict regarding the claim for the establishment of a constructive trust. The court of appeals thereby reversed the trial court's equitable order for the imposition of a constructive trust. Grace's estate appealed. . . .

[Discussion]

A constructive trust is a "'trust by operation of law which arises contrary to intention and in invitum, against one who, by fraud, actual or constructive, by duress or abuse of confidence, by commission of wrong, or by any form of unconscionable conduct, artifice, concealment, or questionable means, or who in any way against equity and good conscience, either has obtained or holds the legal right to property which he ought not, in equity and good conscience, hold and enjoy. It is raised by equity to satisfy the demands of justice.'" (Footnotes omitted.) *Ferguson v. Owens* (1984), 9 Ohio St.3d 223, 225, quoting 76 American Jurisprudence 2d (1975) 446, Trusts, Section 221. A constructive trust is considered a trust because "'[w]hen property has been acquired in such circumstances that the holder of the legal title may not in good conscience retain the beneficial interest, equity converts him into a trustee.'" Id. at 225, 9 OBR 565, 459 N.E.2d 1293.

A constructive trust is an <u>equitable remedy</u> that protects against unjust enrichment and is usually invoked when property has been obtained by fraud. *Ferguson,* 9 Ohio St.3d at 226; *Aetna Life Ins. Co. v. Hussey* (1992), 63 Ohio St.3d 640, 642. "[A] constructive trust may also be imposed where it is against the principles of equity that the property be retained by a certain person even though the property was acquired without fraud." *Ferguson,* 9 Ohio St.3d at 226. "In applying the theories of constructive trusts, courts also apply the well known equitable maxim, 'equity regards [as] done that which ought to be done.'" *Ferguson,* 9 Ohio St.3d at 226.

Although this court has never addressed the issue of tracing, various Ohio courts have held that a constructive trust cannot be imposed absent tracing by the claimant. See *Dixon v. Smith* (1997), 119 Ohio App.3d 308, 320; *State ex rel. Marietta v. Groves* (Aug. 9, 1985), 4th Dist. No. 84 X 7, 1985 WL 8297, at *2 ("Ohio follows the majority rule that there must be tracing"). The parties agree that tracing is a necessary predicate to the imposition of a constructive trust in Ohio. See Ashley S. Hohimer, Constructive Trusts in Bankruptcy: Is an Equitable Interest in Property More Than Just a "Claim"? (2003), 19 Bankr.Dev.J. 499, 510–511 ("Tracing is a process where the claimant basically must be able to point to the identifiable property or fund and say, 'This is mine.' If the funds or property are untraceable — meaning the claimant cannot determine where they were deposited or what the debtor has done with them — the equitable remedy is not available").

tracing

When they have addressed tracing, courts in Ohio have required the claimant to offer sufficient proof of tracing the property through any changes in form or possessor to the possessor of the property over whom the constructive trust should be placed. See *Dixon,* 119 Ohio App.3d at 320. We are in accord with these decisions and hold that before a constructive trust can be imposed, there must be adequate tracing from the time of the wrongful deprivation of the relevant assets to the specific property over which the constructive trust should be placed.

We have previously held that a party seeking the judicial imposition of a constructive trust "bears the burden of producing clear and convincing evidence justifying it." *Lynch,* 96 Ohio St.3d 118. *Lynch* specifically referred to the claimant's burden of proof and the evidentiary standard for proving the unjust-enrichment aspect of a constructive trust. We conclude that the same evidentiary burden should apply to tracing and that the burden of proof is on the claimant.

A claimant seeking the imposition of a constructive trust must specify the particular property over which the constructive trust is to be placed. If the form or possessor of the property over which the constructive trust should be placed changes during a lawsuit, the claimant should be given an opportunity to conduct discovery, if necessary, and present evidence of the new location or form of the property over which the trust should be placed.

A constructive trust is an equitable remedy that must be imposed on particular assets, not on a value. For example, if a party is inequitably deprived of 100 shares of stock that are valued at $10,000, a constructive trust should be imposed over 100 shares of stock, not $10,000. The value of the stock may decrease to $9,000 through no fault of the present possessor. In that instance, it would be inequitable to impose a constructive trust for a higher dollar amount than the stock's new value. Similarly, should the stock rise, the beneficiary of a constructive trust should not be deprived of that increase in value.

Constructive trusts should be placed over the property of the party who wrongfully obtained the property. When, as in this case, the property was subsequently transferred to third parties, a constructive trust can be imposed.

We must consider whether Grace's estate presented sufficient evidence regarding her claim for the imposition of a constructive trust to defeat a motion for directed verdict and a motion for judgment notwithstanding the verdict. We must consider whether Grace's estate presented clear and convincing evidence of the inequitable situation or unjust enrichment that would result if the Cowlings retain the assets and whether Grace's estate provided clear and convincing evidence tracing the assets from the joint and survivorship accounts in the name of Grace and Garnard to property held by the Cowlings.

Garnard withdrew all of the assets that he subsequently transferred to his children from joint and survivorship accounts that were in his and Grace's names. Grace's estate presented evidence indicating that these withdrawals exceeded Garnard's contributions. Garnard transferred all of the assets that he had withdrawn from the joint and survivorship accounts to his children. Construing this evidence most strongly in Grace's estate's favor, reasonable minds could only conclude that inequity had been proven by clear and convincing evidence. We conclude that Grace's estate presented sufficient evidence with respect to this element of a constructive-trust claim to survive motions for a directed verdict and judgment notwithstanding the verdict.

As to the tracing requirement, the parties stipulated that at the time of the trial, the assets that Garnard had transferred to his children were in the same form in which Garnard had received them. According to the stipulation, the Cowlings retained the assets throughout the trial and (with the exception of Reddington, who paid her share of the assets to Grace's estate) then sold the assets to post cash deposits for an appeal. We conclude that the evidence and stipulations on the record are sufficient to satisfy the tracing requirement.

. . . Despite the imprecision of some of the standards we apply in equity, we can only conclude, under any standard, that the Cowlings would unjustly benefit in the absence of a constructive trust. Accordingly, we reverse the decision of the court of appeals. The trial court's order for a constructive trust, however, cannot stand unmodified.

The trial court did not specify the particular assets over which the constructive trust was to be imposed. That was error, and we hereby order that the constructive trust be specifically imposed over the assets currently held by the Lorain County Clerk of Courts. The trial court ordered that the constructive trust be placed over a specific dollar amount, which now, given the conversion of assets into cash, is appropriate. At the time, however, the trust should have been placed over the proportion of the specific assets held by the Cowlings that equaled Grace's net contributions, as determined by the jury.

The total value of the assets on February 8, 1998, the day of Garnard's death, was $325,358.69. The jury determined damages of $255,354.00. The trial court order should be modified to place a constructive trust over 78.5 percent ($255,354.00 divided by $325,358.69) of the assets held by each appellee in their current form.

We hereby order the reinstatement of the trial court's order for the imposition of a constructive trust and modify the order to place the constructive trust over the assets currently held by the Lorain County Clerk of Courts.

So ordered.

* * *

Cruz v. McAneney

New York Supreme Court, Appellate Division, Second Department
31 A.D.3d 54 (2006)

FLORIO, J.P.

Patricia McAneney (hereinafter Patricia) died intestate on September 11, 2001, as a result of the terrorist attacks on the World Trade Center. Patricia's brother, the defendant James P. McAneney, as her personal representative, filed a claim on her behalf with the September 11th Victim Compensation Fund of 2001 (hereinafter the Fund). While the claim was pending, the plaintiff, Margaret Cruz, submitted a statement of financial interest with the Fund, stating that she was entitled to all or part of any award because she was Patricia's loving, domestic partner for more than 15 years. At that time, the Fund's Special Master allegedly told the plaintiff that an award had already been approved in the sum of $278,087.42. This amount allegedly reflected Patricia's pain and suffering, as well as the economic loss of Patricia's survivors analogous to the amount awarded in a traditional wrongful death suit.

On March 10, 2003, the Special Master allegedly explained to the plaintiff that the approved award of the sum of $278,087.42 had been calculated as if Patricia were single and lived in a one-person household. However, the Special Master also expressed a willingness to re-calculate the economic loss portion of the award and increase it by the sum of $253,454, to a total sum of $531,541.42, to account for the reality of the plaintiff's domestic partnership with Patricia. Allegedly, the Fund was willing to distribute the full award to the defendant, as personal representative for Patricia, provided he agreed in writing to distribute the increased portion ($253,454) to the plaintiff. However, the Fund was unwilling to mandate that the defendant, as personal representative, distribute the full award of the sum of $531,541.42 to the plaintiff as Patricia's sole survivor and beneficiary.

Additionally, some representatives of the Fund allegedly told the plaintiff that the Fund would not distribute the increased portion of the award to the defendant absent a settlement agreement regarding distribution of the increased portion to her. The parties then attempted to settle this matter. Unfortunately, they were unable to do so.

With negotiations at an impasse, representatives of the Fund allegedly informed the plaintiff on May 23, 2003, that it was in the process of distributing the award to the defendant, but assured her that only the smaller, original award of the sum of $278,087.42 would go to the defendant if a settlement could not be reached. While the plaintiff requested that the Fund mandate that the defendant distribute the increased portion of the award to her, the Fund refused to assist her.

Allegedly, the plaintiff continued her attempts to negotiate with the defendant, but he would not make any decision regarding a settlement before June 23, 2003, when his newly retained litigation counsel would be available for consultation. In the interim, on or about June 12, 2003, the Fund informed the plaintiff that it would soon distribute the larger award of the sum of $531,541.42, despite the absence of a settlement agreement. The alleged rationale for distributing the larger award under these circumstances was that the plaintiff could litigate the dispute in State court.

Ultimately, the defendant, as Patricia's personal representative, received an award of the sum of $531,541.42 from the Fund. He refused further negotiations with the plaintiff and declined to distribute any portion of the award to her. Instead, he distributed the entire award to himself, on the ground that he was Patricia's only surviving blood relative. The plaintiff, therefore, commenced the instant action to compel the defendant to disburse all or part of the award to her.

The complaint asserts three causes of action based on the factual allegations stated above. The first cause of action alleges, inter alia, that the plaintiff is entitled, as the surviving domestic partner of the decedent, to the full award or a portion of the award, and the defendant, as the personal representative of the decedent, is under a fiduciary duty to distribute same to her.

Alternatively, in the second and third causes of action, the plaintiff asserts claims under the equitable theories of constructive trust and unjust enrichment. Under these theories, the plaintiff alleges that she is entitled to at least the sum of $253,454 because the Fund intended that this portion be distributed to her. Since this amount was added on to the original award to account for the reality of her domestic partnership with Patricia, the plaintiff alleges that the defendant has an equitable duty to convey, at least, this amount to her.

The defendant moved to dismiss the complaint in its entirety alleging, inter alia, that it failed to state a cause of action. The Supreme Court, inter alia, in effect, denied the motion. The defendant appeals, and we affirm.

The Fund was created by the federal government as Title IV of the Air Transportation Safety and System Stabilization Act of 2001 (49 USC § 40101, as added by Pub. L. 107–42, 115 U.S. Stat. 230) (hereinafter the Act). The Fund's purpose is "to provide compensation to any individual (or relatives of a deceased individual) who was physically injured or killed as a result of the terrorist-related aircraft crashes of September 11, 2001" (Act § 403[49 USC § 40101]). Thereunder, a personal representative may file a claim with the Fund on behalf of a deceased victim of the terrorist attacks (see Act §§ 405[c][2][C], 406[a][49 USC § 40101]; 28 CFR 104.2[a][1], [3]).

A Special Master, appointed by the United States Attorney-General, administers the Fund (see Act § 404[a][49 USC § 40101]). The Special Master's tasks include determining the eligibility of claimants and the amount of compensation to be awarded (see Act §§ 404[a], 405[a][2], 405[b][49 USC § 40101]). Once the Special Master makes a determination regarding amount and eligibility, the Special Master authorizes payment of the full award to the claimant, who must be the personal representative in cases of deceased victims (see Act §§ 405[c] [2][C], 406[a][49 USC § 40101]; 28 CFR 104.2[a][1],[3]). Under the Act, the personal representative has the duty to "distribute the award in a manner consistent with the law of the decedent's domicile or any applicable rulings made by a court of competent jurisdiction" (28 CFR 104.52), which has been interpreted as not precluding an expansive definition of who is entitled to be compensated (see 67 Fed. Reg. 11233[2002], 11242–11243).

In the instant case, it is undisputed that Patricia's state of domicile was New York and, thus, the defendant, as her personal representative, has a duty to distribute the award "in a manner consistent with the law" of this State (28 CFR 104.52). In this instance, the New York State laws enacted for the purpose of providing relief to the victims of the September 11, 2001, terrorist attack evince an intent to compensate surviving domestic partners, as family members, for their losses from this tragedy (see September 11th Victims and Families Relief Act, chap. 73 Laws of New York,

2002, hereinafter the State September 11th Act). Based on the federal statutes and regulations regarding the Fund, a state's intestacy laws, while relevant, do not solely determine the identity of beneficiaries of the award (*see* 67 Fed. Reg., *supra*) and, notwithstanding the absence of a valid will, a partner in a longstanding domestic relationship may share in any award made by the Fund. Thus, the first cause of action, especially in light of allegations that the award was increased as a result of the plaintiff's application to the fund, stated a cause of action.

It is true that the plaintiff and Patricia were not married under the laws of any state at the time of Patricia's death and, thus, the plaintiff cannot be treated as the surviving "spouse" for purposes of the intestate distribution of the award from the Fund (*see Langan v. St. Vincent's Hosp. of N.Y.,* 25 A.D.3d 90, 802 N.Y.S.2d 476). Nevertheless, the plaintiff may be entitled to some unspecified portion of the award from the Fund, albeit not the entire sum of $531,541.42 (*see generally* Feinberg, What Is Life Worth?: The Unprecedented Effort to Compensate the Victims of 9/11 [2005], at 68–69).

Moreover, under principles of equity, the second and third causes of action also state viable claims for the imposition of a constructive trust and unjust enrichment. The ultimate purpose of a constructive trust is to prevent unjust enrichment and, thus, a constructive trust may be imposed "'[w]hen property has been acquired in such circumstances that the holder of the legal title may not in good conscience retain the beneficial interest'" (*Sharp v. Kosmalski,* 40 N.Y.2d 119. The usual elements of a constructive trust are "(1) a confidential or fiduciary relation [ship], (2) a promise, (3) a transfer in reliance thereon and (4) unjust enrichment" (*Sharp v. Kosmalski, supra* at 121. However, these factors should be applied flexibly. Thus, courts can and will impose constructive trusts "whenever necessary to satisfy the demands of justice" (*Simonds v. Simonds,* 45 N.Y.2d 233, 241.

Similarly, to prevail on a claim of unjust enrichment, "a party must show that (1) the other party was enriched, (2) at that party's expense, and (3) that 'it is against equity and good conscience to permit [the other party] to retain what is sought to be recovered'" (*Citibank, N.A. v. Walker,* 12 A.D.3d 480, 481. "Unjust enrichment, however, does not require the performance of any wrongful act by the one enriched" (*Ptachewich v. Ptachewich,* 96 A.D.2d 582). "Innocent parties may frequently be unjustly enriched" (*id.; see Simonds v. Simonds, supra* at 242).

Viewing the allegations in the light most favorable to the plaintiff, justice in the instant case could conceivably require the imposition of a constructive trust, and concomitantly show that the defendant, in his personal capacity, would be unjustly enriched if he was also allowed to retain the portion of the Fund's award that was allegedly increased after the plaintiff's application to the Fund and in recognition of the plaintiff's loss of her lifetime partner. . . .

ORDERED that the order is affirmed, with costs.

* * *

Problem 43

A constructive trust can be ordered over property that is traceable from wrongfully acquired funds. Is a constructive trust available for this plaintiff?

Wally defrauds his neighbor by soliciting a $100,000 donation to "Save the Seagulls," purportedly an organization "dedicated to the preservation and advancement of the humble seagull." In fact, the charity does not exist; Wally simply made it up. He takes the $100,000 and deposits it directly into his checking account, which already contained $50,000 Wally had earned from his job as a lifeguard. Six months later, he buys a parcel of land for $80,000. A year after that, he is able to sell the land for $90,000. With that $90,000, he buys a classic sports car.

When Wally's neighbor discovers there is no such thing as "Save the Seagulls," he sues Wally for fraud and asks the court to impose a constructive trust over the sportscar.

Introductory Note — *Mattel, Inc. v. MGA Entertainment, Inc.*

Mattel is an interesting constructive trust case for two reasons: (1) the wrongfully acquired property is intangible (an idea for a new toy), and (2) the property was not worth much when it was acquired, but by the time of the lawsuit its value had increased dramatically. The trial court ordered a constructive trust as a remedy, and the Ninth Circuit must determine whether that was appropriate. The reason for the property's increase in value plays a key role in the court's decision.

THINGS TO THINK ABOUT while reading *Mattel, Inc. v. MGA Entertainment, Inc.*:

1. When property subject to a constructive trust increases in value, is the plaintiff entitled to that benefit? Or would that give the plaintiff an undeserved windfall?

2. Why is the plaintiff not entitled to a constructive trust in this case?

Mattel, Inc. v. MGA Entertainment, Inc.

United States Court of Appeals, Ninth Circuit
616 F.3d 904 (2010)

KOZINSKI, Chief Judge:

Who owns Bratz?

I

Barbie was the unrivaled queen of the fashion-doll market throughout the latter half of the 20th Century. But 2001 saw the introduction of Bratz, "The Girls With a Passion for Fashion!" Unlike the relatively demure Barbie, the urban, multi-ethnic and trendy Bratz dolls have attitude. This spunk struck a chord, and Bratz became an overnight success. Mattel, which produces Barbie, didn't relish the competition. And it was particularly unhappy when it learned that the man behind Bratz was its own former employee, Carter Bryant.

Bryant worked in the "Barbie Collectibles" department, where he designed fashion and hair styles for high-end Barbie dolls intended more for accumulation than for play. In August 2000, while he was still employed by Mattel, Bryant pitched his idea for the Bratz line of dolls to two employees of MGA Entertainment, one of Mattel's competitors. Bryant was soon called back to see Isaac Larian, the CEO of MGA. Bryant brought some preliminary sketches, as well as a crude dummy constructed out of a doll head from a Mattel bin, a Barbie body and Ken (Barbie's ex) boots. The Zoe, Lupe, Hallidae and Jade dolls in Bryant's drawings eventually made it to market as Cloe, Yasmin, Sasha and Jade, the first generation of Bratz dolls.

Bryant signed a consulting agreement with MGA on October 4, 2000, though it was dated September 18. Bryant gave Mattel two weeks' notice on October 4 and continued working there until October 19. During this period, Bryant was also working with MGA to develop Bratz, even creating a preliminary Bratz sculpt. A sculpt is a mannequin-like plastic doll body without skin coloring, face paint, hair or clothing.

MGA kept Bryant's involvement with the Bratz project secret, but Mattel eventually found out. This led to a flurry of lawsuits, which were consolidated in federal district court. Proceedings below were divided into two phases. Phase 1 dealt with claims relating to the ownership of Bratz; Phase 2 is pending and will deal with the remaining claims. This is an interlocutory appeal from the equitable orders entered at the conclusion of Phase 1.

During Phase 1, Mattel argued that Bryant violated his employment agreement by going to MGA with his Bratz idea instead of disclosing and assigning it to Mattel. Mattel claimed it was the rightful owner of Bryant's preliminary sketches and sculpt, which it argued MGA's subsequent Bratz dolls infringed. And it asserted that

MGA wrongfully acquired the ideas for the names "Bratz" and "Jade," so the Bratz trademarks should be transferred from MGA to Mattel.

Mattel won virtually every point below. The jury found that Bryant thought of the "Bratz" and "Jade" names, and created the preliminary sketches and sculpt, while he was employed by Mattel. It found that MGA committed three state-law violations relating to Bryant's involvement with Bratz. And it issued a general verdict finding MGA liable for infringing Mattel's copyrights in Bryant's preliminary Bratz works. Mattel sought more than $1 billion in copyright damages but the jury awarded Mattel only $10 million, or about 1% of that amount, perhaps because it found only a small portion of the Bratz dolls infringing.

The district court entered equitable relief based on the jury's findings. As to the state-law violations, the district court imposed a constructive trust over all trademarks including the terms "Bratz" and "Jade," essentially transferring the Bratz trademark portfolio to Mattel. The transfer prohibited MGA from marketing any Bratz-branded product, such as Bratz dolls (Bratz, Bratz Boyz, Lil' Bratz, Bratz Lil' Angelz, Bratz Petz, Bratz Babyz, Itsy Bitsy Bratz, etc.), doll accessories (Bratz World House, Bratz Cowgirlz Stable, Bratz Spring Break Pool, Bratz Babyz Ponyz Buggy Blitz, etc.), video games ("Bratz: Girlz Really Rock," "Bratz: Forever Diamondz," "Bratz: Rock Angelz," etc.) and *Bratz* the movie.

As to the copyright claim, the district court issued an injunction prohibiting MGA from producing or marketing virtually every Bratz female fashion doll, as well as any future dolls substantially similar to Mattel's copyrighted Bratz works. The injunction covered not just the original four dolls, but also subsequent generations (e.g., "Bratz Slumber Party Sasha" and "Bratz Girlfriendz Nite Out Cloe") and other doll characters (e.g., "Bratz Play Sportz Lilee" and "Bratz Twins Phoebe and Roxxi").

In effect, Barbie captured the Bratz. The Bratz appeal.

II

A constructive trust is an equitable remedy that compels the transfer of wrongfully held property to its rightful owner. *Communist Party of U.S. v. 522 Valencia, Inc.,* 35 Cal.App.4th 980 (1995); *see also* Cal. Civ.Code § 2223 ("One who wrongfully detains a thing is an involuntary trustee thereof, for the benefit of the owner."). A plaintiff seeking imposition of a constructive trust must show: (1) the existence of a *res* (property or some interest in property); (2) the right to that *res;* and (3) the wrongful acquisition or detention of the *res* by another party who is not entitled to it. *Communist Party,* 41 Cal.Rptr.2d at 623–24.

Prior to trial, the district court held that Bryant's employment agreement assigned his ideas to Mattel, and so instructed the jury. What was left for the jury to decide was *which* ideas Bryant came up with during his time with Mattel. It found that Bryant thought of the names "Bratz" and "Jade" while he was employed by Mattel, and that MGA committed several state-law violations by interfering with Bryant's agreement as well as aiding and abetting its breach. After trial, the district court imposed a constructive trust over all Bratz-related trademarks. We review that decision for abuse of discretion. *See GHK Assocs. v. Mayer Group, Inc.,* 224 Cal.App.3d 856 (1990).

A.

A constructive trust would be appropriate only if Bryant assigned his ideas for "Bratz" and "Jade" to Mattel in the first place. Whether he did turns on the interpretation of Bryant's 1999 employment agreement, which provides: "I agree to communicate to the Company as promptly and fully as practicable all *inventions* (as defined below) conceived or reduced to practice by me (alone or jointly by others) at any time during my employment by the Company. I hereby assign to the Company . . . all my right, title and interest in such *inventions,* and all my right, title and interest in any patents, copyrights, patent applications or copyright applications based thereon." (Emphasis added.) The contract specifies that "the term 'inventions' includes, but is not limited to, all discoveries, improvements, processes, developments, designs, know-how, data computer programs and formulae, whether patentable or unpatentable." . . .

We conclude that the agreement could be interpreted to cover ideas, but the text doesn't compel that reading. The district court thus erred in holding that the agreement, by its terms, clearly covered ideas. . . . Because we must vacate the constructive trust in any event, for reasons explained below, this is a matter the district court can take up on remand.

B.

The very broad constructive trust the district court imposed must be vacated regardless of whether Bryant's employment agreement assigned his ideas to Mattel. Even assuming that it did, and that MGA therefore misappropriated the names "Bratz" and "Jade," the value of the trademarks the company eventually acquired for the entire Bratz line was significantly greater because of MGA's own development efforts, marketing and investment. The district court nonetheless transferred MGA's entire Bratz trademark portfolio to Mattel on the ground that the "enhancement of value [of the property held in trust] is given to the beneficiary of the constructive trust." As a result, Mattel acquired the fruit of MGA's hard work, and not just the appreciation in value of the ideas Mattel claims it owns.

In general, "[t]he beneficiary of the constructive trust is entitled to enhancement in value of the trust property." *Haskel Eng'g & Supply Co. v. Hartford Accident & Indem. Co.,* 78 Cal.App.3d 371 (1978). This is so "not because [the beneficiary] has a substantive right to [the enhancement] but rather to prevent unjust enrichment of the wrongdoer-constructive trustee." *Id.* Thus, a person who fraudulently acquired a house worth $100,000 in 2000 that appreciates to $200,000 by 2010 because of a strong real estate market can't complain when the rightful owner takes the benefit of the $100,000 increase. "[I]t is simple equity that a wrongdoer should disgorge his fraudulent enrichment." *Janigan v. Taylor,* 344 F.2d 781, 786 (1st Cir.1965).

This principle has the greatest force where the appreciation of the property is due to external factors rather than the efforts of the wrongful acquisitor. "When the defendant profits from the wrong, it is necessary to identify the profits and to recapture them without capturing the fruits of the defendant's own labors or legitimate efforts." Dan B. Dobbs, *Dobbs Law of Remedies: Damages–Equity–Restitution* § 6.6(3) (2d ed. 1993). This is because "the aim of restitution has been to avoid taking the defendant's blood along with the pound of flesh." *Id.* § 6.6(3) n. 4. A constructive trust is therefore "not appropriate to every case because it can overdo the job." *Id.* § 4.3(2).

When the value of the property held in trust increases significantly because of a defendant's efforts, a constructive trust that passes on the profit of the defendant's labor to the plaintiff usually goes too far. For example, "[i]f an artist acquired paints by fraud and used them in producing a valuable portrait we would not suggest that the defrauded party would be entitled to the portrait, or to the proceeds of its sale." *Janigan,* 344 F.2d at 787. Even assuming that MGA took some ideas wrongfully, it added tremendous value by turning the ideas into products and, eventually, a popular and highly profitable brand. The value added by MGA's hard work and creativity dwarfs the value of the original ideas Bryant brought with him, even recognizing the significance of those ideas. We infer that the jury made much the same judgment when it awarded Mattel only a small fraction of the more than $1 billion in interest-adjusted profit MGA made from the brand.

From the ideas for the names "Bratz" and "Jade," MGA created not only the first generation of Bratz dolls (Cloe, Yasmin, Sasha and Jade), but also many other Bratz characters (Ciara, Dana, Diona, Felicia, Fianna and so on), as well as subsequent generations of the original four dolls ("Bratz Flower Girlz Cloe," "Bratz on Ice Doll Yasmin," etc.). MGA also generated other doll lines, such as the Bratz Boyz, Bratz Petz and Bratz Babyz. And it made a variety of Bratz doll accessories, along with several Bratz video games and a movie. These efforts significantly raised the profile of the Bratz brand and increased the value of the Bratz trademarks.

It is not equitable to transfer this billion dollar brand — the value of which is overwhelmingly the result of MGA's legitimate efforts — because it may have started with two misappropriated names. The district court's imposition of a constructive trust forcing MGA to hand over its sweat equity was an abuse of discretion and must be vacated. . . .

America thrives on competition; Barbie, the all-American girl, will too.

EQUITABLE RELIEF VACATED. Each party shall bear its own costs.

* * *

Problem 44

The general rule is that a party entitled to a constructive trust is entitled to an increase in value of the property subject to the trust. There is an exception, though, when the increase is due solely to the efforts of the wrongdoer. Is the plaintiff in the below case entitled to the increase in value of the wrongfully acquired property?

Janelle is a diligent and talented financial advisor with a knack for investing in stocks at just the right time. She is also the caregiver for her grandmother and has joint access to her checking account. One day, without authorization, she transfers $5,000 from her grandmother's account to her own. Janelle uses that money to invest in a stock—an initial public offering that she has spent many hours researching and has identified as having significant upside. After Janelle invests, the value of the $5,000 in stock skyrockets to over $50,000. Her grandmother sues for a constructive trust on the $50,000 worth of stock.

Defenses to Restitution Claims

There are certain defenses uniquely applicable to claims for restitution. Since the key inquiry in a restitution case is whether it would be unjust to allow the defendant to retain the benefit in question, the defenses to restitution essentially amount to a showing that, under the circumstances, fairness dictates that the defendant should be allowed to keep the benefit. To put it another way, the enrichment is not unjust.

The defense of a volunteer or officious intermeddler applies when the plaintiff conferred a benefit on the defendant that the defendant did not want, or at least did not ask for. The underlying theory is that someone cannot willingly provide a benefit for free only to later have a change of heart and seek compensation. Courts will seldom find unjust enrichment where the benefit was not actively *acquired* by the defendant but rather was voluntarily *provided* by the plaintiff.

Similarly, the change of position defense applies where a benefit is mistakenly conferred on the defendant — think about a banking error resulting in an extra $1000 credited to an account — and the defendant relies on that benefit. Reliance means the defendant did something he or she would not have done had it not been for receiving the benefit. In most cases, the benefit is money and the reliance is that the defendant spent it. When there is that kind of change of position, it would be unfair to make the defendant come out of pocket to repay money long since spent. The defense only works where the defendant is unaware of the mistake that resulted in the benefit, however. It probably *is* fair to impose liability on defendants who know they received a benefit they are not entitled to and look to take advantage of the situation.

The central theme to restitution defenses is that rather than it being unjust for the defendant to retain the benefit, it would be unjust to require the defendant to return it.

Introductory Note — *Kenworth Sales Co. v. Skinner Trucking, Inc.*

Kenworth Sales Co. is a commercial dispute where the plaintiff contends the defendant was unjustly enriched by being relieved of a debt obligation. The trial court found for the defendant based on the officious intermeddler defense. On appeal, the Idaho Supreme Court decides both a procedural issue — whether the officious intermeddler defense is an affirmative defense — and a substantive one — whether the plaintiff in this case was in fact an officious intermeddler.

THINGS TO THINK ABOUT while reading *Kenworth Sales Co. v. Skinner Trucking, Inc.*:

1. What is the procedural difference between a defense and an affirmative defense?

2. Why is restitution unavailable in cases of volunteering and officious intermeddling?

3. Why did the court decide the plaintiff voluntarily conferred the benefit in this case?

Kenworth Sales Co. v. Skinner Trucking, Inc.

Idaho Supreme Court
454 P.3d 580 (2019)

BRODY, Justice.

This appeal concerns an unjust enrichment claim brought by Kenworth, a commercial truck dealer, against Skinner Trucking, one of its customers. Kenworth claims Skinner was unjustly enriched when Kenworth paid past due lease payments and the residual balance owed on Skinner's lease with GE Transportation Finance. The district court entered judgment for Skinner on the grounds that, as to the residual value of the trucks, Kenworth had not conferred a benefit on Skinner, and that as to both the residual value of the trucks and the past due lease payments, Kenworth was an "officious intermeddler" because it had voluntarily paid GE without request by Skinner and without a valid reason. . . .

I. Factual and Procedural Background

Kenworth Sales Company ("Kenworth") is a commercial truck dealer. In August of 2011, Kenworth sold three trucks to GE Transportation Finance ("GE"), a financing company, for lease to Skinner Trucking. Kenworth negotiated Skinner's lease with GE on Skinner's behalf, but the lease was signed only by Skinner and GE.

Skinner's lease with GE was known as a "TRAC" lease (terminal rental adjustment clause). In a TRAC lease, the vehicle's post-lease residual value is determined at the beginning of the lease. Once the lease ends, the lessee has three options: refinance the vehicle based on its residual value, buy the vehicle by paying an amount equal to the vehicle's residual value, or return the vehicle to the lessor to be sold. If the lessee chooses the third option, and the vehicle is sold for less than its residual amount, the lessee will owe the lessor the difference. If the vehicle is sold for more than the residual amount, the lessor will owe the lessee the difference. In this case, the lease provided that the residual value for each truck was $58,051.20 and that the monthly rental payment for each truck was $2,357.72.

Skinner turned in two of the trucks in October of 2015, and the third truck in December of 2015. The trucks were turned in to Kenworth, where Skinner typically turned in its trucks. (The lease provides that, at the end of the lease, Skinner would turn in the trucks at a location designated by GE.) Ultimately, Kenworth paid GE the total of the trucks' residual values ($174,153.60) as well as back rent that Skinner owed for one of the trucks ($7,073.17). As a result of the payments, Kenworth owned the trucks. Kenworth employees gave similar answers regarding why the decision was made to buy the trucks, stating that Kenworth had no profit motive; it merely hoped to break even. Kenworth employees testified, for example, that the Skinners "were long term customers," that they were "friends" and Kenworth "cared," and "[i]t had been a long relationship."

In January 2016, Kenworth appraised one of the trucks and determined that the trucks were each worth $42,000 at the time Skinner turned them in. Two days later, Kenworth invoiced Skinner for $55,226.77: the difference between the three trucks' combined residual value and what Kenworth estimated the trucks were worth ($174,153.60 — $126,000.00), plus the back rent owed on one of the trucks ($7,073.17). Neither party disputes that there is no writing showing an agreement between Skinner and Kenworth that Kenworth would pay Skinner's "obligation" to GE or that Skinner would pay Kenworth back.

About six months later, Kenworth filed a complaint in district court claiming that Skinner was unjustly enriched by Kenworth's payments to GE, and requested a judgment against Skinner in the amount of $55,226.77. After a bench trial, the district court entered judgment in favor of Skinner, denying Kenworth's unjust enrichment claim and dismissing it with prejudice. In its findings of fact, the district court found that Skinner owed approximately $7,000 in back rent and that Kenworth made the payments to GE because "Kenworth was sympathetic to Skinner's position and did not wish to see Skinner get into a worse financial position by having the trucks sold at auction." And that "[t]he most substantial evidence supporting the reason for [Kenworth's decision to make the payments to GE] was that Skinner was a good customer and they wanted to help them." Additionally, the district court found that there was no agreement between Skinner and Kenworth about what would happen if the trucks could not be sold for enough money to repay Kenworth. The court reasoned that while the trial record was not clear about the discussions between Skinner and Kenworth, Skinner had never asked Kenworth to pay off its debt. The most substantial evidence supporting Kenworth's decision to make the payments was that "Skinner was a good customer and they wanted to help them." ...

Analysis

A. The Officious Intermeddler Rule is Not An Affirmative Defense.

The district court found that Kenworth's unjust enrichment claim failed because the company was an "officious intermeddler." Kenworth argues that the officious intermeddler rule is an affirmative defense, and because Skinner never pled or argued it until post-trial briefing, the district court should not have considered it. We hold that the officious intermeddler rule is not an affirmative defense.

Rule 8(c) of the Idaho Rules of Civil Procedure provides that "[i]n responding to a pleading, a party must affirmatively state any avoidance or affirmative defense. . . ." Black's Law Dictionary defines an "affirmative defense" as "[a] defendant's assertion of facts and arguments that, if true, will defeat the plaintiff's or prosecution's claim, even if all the allegations in the complaint are true." *Affirmative Defense*, Black's Law Dictionary (11th ed. 2019). The purpose of the rule is to alert the parties to the issues of fact which will be tried and to afford them an opportunity to present evidence to meet those defenses. *Williams v. Paxton*, 98 Idaho 155, 164 (1976). The rule lists nineteen affirmative defenses. I.R.C.P. 8(c)(1). The officious intermeddler rule is not on the list. *See id.*

We have made it clear that Rule 8(c)'s list is not intended to be exhaustive. *See Garren v. Butigan*, 95 Idaho 355 (1973) (stating that Rule 8(c)'s listing of affirmative defenses "is not intended to be exhaustive or exclusive."). In fact, this Court has recognized a host of affirmative defenses that are not listed in the rule.

 To determine whether the officious intermeddler rule constitutes an affirmative defense, we have to begin with the doctrine of unjust enrichment. We have long held that a prima facie case for unjust enrichment exists where: "(1) there was a benefit conferred upon the defendant by the plaintiff; (2) appreciation by the defendant of such benefit; and (3) acceptance of the benefit under circumstances that would be *inequitable* for the defendant to retain the benefit without payment to the plaintiff for the value thereof." *Med. Recovery Servs., LLC v. Bonneville Billing & Collections, Inc.*, 157 Idaho 395, 398 (2014) (citations omitted) (emphasis added). It is well understood that "[u]njust enrichment will not apply in the instance of an officious intermeddler." *Teton Peaks Inv. Co., LLC v. Ohme*, 146 Idaho 394, 398 (2008). "The officious intermeddler rule essentially provides that a mere volunteer who, without request therefor, [sic] confers a benefit upon another is not entitled to restitution. This rule exists to protect persons who have had unsolicited 'benefits' thrust upon them." *Id.*

Kenworth acknowledges that Idaho courts have not explicitly held that the officious intermeddler rule constitutes an affirmative defense, but argues that they have treated it as such, citing to our decision in *Teton Peaks* and the Court of Appeals' decisions in *Curtis v. Becker*, 130 Idaho 378, 382 (Ct. App. 1997) and *Chinchurreta v. Evergreen Management, Inc.*, 117 Idaho 591 (Ct. App. 1989). Kenworth argues that the discussion of the officious intermeddler rule in these cases occurs separately from the list of elements that a plaintiff must satisfy in order to prevail on an unjust enrichment claim. Therefore, the rule must be a separate affirmative defense. We disagree.

The officious intermeddler rule will defeat a plaintiff's claim, but this is true not because the rule is an affirmative defense, but rather because the voluntary nature of the payment bears directly on whether it would be inequitable for the defendant to retain the benefit of the payment. Stated differently, Kenworth had the burden of proving at trial circumstances which would make it inequitable for Skinner to benefit from Kenworth's payments to GE. This would require more than evidence of a voluntary payment. *See, e.g., Chinchurreta*, 117 Idaho at 593 ("It is well settled that a person cannot — by way of set-off, counterclaim or direct action — recover money which he or she 'has voluntarily paid with full knowledge of all the facts, and without any fraud, duress or extortion, although no obligation to make such payment existed'") (quoting *McEnroe v. Morgan*, 106 Idaho 326, 335 (Ct.App. 1984)). A defendant who receives the benefit of a voluntary payment may be enriched, but he is not *unjustly* enriched. *See* Restatement (First) of Restitution § 2, cmt. a (1937). While Skinner did not invoke the officious intermeddler doctrine until its post-trial briefing, Kenworth understood that proving the equitable circumstances under which the purchase of the trucks was made was essential to its prima facie case. Kenworth's cry of trial by ambush is unjustified.

B. The District Court did not err when it Concluded that Kenworth was an Officious Intermeddler.

Kenworth asserts that even if this Court holds that the officious intermeddler rule is not an affirmative defense, the district court erred in applying it to the facts of this case. Kenworth argues that the district court incorrectly found that Kenworth had no valid reason for purchasing the trucks from GE because it ignored the reason that Kenworth gave: to keep Skinner, "a long-time customer," in business. Kenworth also disputes the district court's statement that there was "no indication that Skinner would continue to do business with [Kenworth]." Given the basis for the doctrine, we agree with the district court that merely keeping Skinner in business was not the kind of interest sufficient to avoid application of the officious intermeddler rule.

The term "officious intermeddler" first appeared in Idaho case law in the Court of Appeals' decision in *Chinchurreta v. Evergreen Management, Inc.*, 117 Idaho 59 (Ct. App. 1989). Explaining the basis for the rule, the Court of Appeals cited section 2 of the First Restatement of Restitution which states that:

> A person who officiously confers a benefit upon another is not entitled to restitution therefor.

Restatement (First) of Restitution § 2 (1937). Comment "a" to this provision describes "officiousness" as unjustified interference in the affairs of others and explains that there must be a "valid reason" for conferring a benefit in order to prevail on a claim for unjust enrichment:

> *Officiousness means interference in the affairs of others not justified by the circumstances under which the interference takes place.* Policy ordinarily requires that a person who has conferred a benefit either by way of giving another services or by adding to the value of his land or by paying his debt or even by transferring property to him should not be permitted to require the other to pay therefor, unless the one conferring the benefit had a *valid reason* for so doing. A person is not required to deal with another unless he so desires and, ordinarily, a person should not be required to become an obligor unless he so desires.
>
> The principle stated in this Section is not a limitation of the general principle stated in § 1; where a person has officiously conferred a benefit upon another, the other is enriched but is not considered to be unjustly enriched. The rule denying restitution to officious persons has the effect of penalizing those who thrust benefits upon others and protecting persons who have had benefits thrust upon them (see § 112).

Restatement (First) of Restitution § 2 (1937) (emphasis added). "Valid reasons" are found in comment "a" to section 112 and include mistake, fraud, coercion (caused by duress or the necessity of protecting the interest of the person who conferred the benefit), and an agreement with the person receiving the benefit. Restatement (First) of Restitution § 112, cmt. a (1937).

. . . Therefore, Kenworth's desire to keep Skinner in business was not an interest sufficient to relieve Kenworth of officious intermeddler status. . . .

IV. Conclusion

We affirm the district court's judgment in favor of Skinner.

* * *

Problem 45

The officious intermeddler defense applies when a benefit is voluntarily conferred on a defendant who did not ask for it. Would that defense be successful in the following case?

Tom has developed a new technology that accurately locates underground petroleum deposits. He approaches a large oil company and inquires if it wants to buy the technology. The company is interested but skeptical that Tom's product will work as well as he says it does. Tom offers to demonstrate its effectiveness by using it on a parcel of land the company owns, which the company suspects contains large petroleum deposits. None has yet been found there, however. Tom's technology quickly locates a large amount of petroleum on the property. The company offers to buy Tom's petroleum locator for $1 million. Tom insists it is worth $2 million. The parties walk away without reaching an agreement. But now that the company knows where the petroleum on its property is, it is able to extract it and sell it for $500,000. When Tom learns about that, he sues the company for restitution.

Introductory Note — *Hobbs v. St. Martin*

The lawsuit in *Hobbs* arises out of a Ponzi scheme — a fraudulent arrangement where the perpetrator induces victims to invest money with a promise it will earn a significant return, only to pocket that money and use funds obtained from new victims to pay off the original ones. When the scheme ends, the newer investors lose everything. In *Hobbs*, both parties are victims of a Ponzi scheme. The perpetrator induced the plaintiff to invest a large sum, then used it to pay off another victim. The plaintiff sues that victim to recover the money. The defendant asserts the plaintiff acted voluntarily and moves for summary judgment based on the volunteer defense.

THINGS TO THINK ABOUT while reading *Hobbs v. St. Martin*:

1. What must be shown to establish a volunteer/officious intermeddler defense?

2. Why is the plaintiff in this case not a volunteer?

Hobbs v. St. Martin

United States District Court, District of Maryland

320 F.Supp.3d 748 (2018)

James K. Bredar, Chief Judge

Gary Hobbs ("Plaintiff") brought an action against Sean St. Martin ("Defendant") for Money Had and Received (Count I) and Unjust Enrichment (Count II). Now pending before the Court is Defendant's Motion for Summary Judgment. For the reasons set forth below, Defendant's Motion will be DENIED.

Background

This case revolves around the conduct of an individual named Richard Hagen, a nonparty. Mr. Hagen operated a Ponzi scheme for years: He solicited money from individuals to "invest" in various endeavors and then used the money to support an extravagant lifestyle and pay off other "investors." Both Plaintiff and Defendant invested money with Mr. Hagen over the years. Although they both received returns on some of their investments, they now generally agree that Mr. Hagen likely never used any of their money for legitimate purposes. Unfortunately for Plaintiff, he was left holding the short straw when Mr. Hagen failed to pay back a $500,000 loan from Plaintiff that Mr. Hagen used to pay off a debt he owed to Defendant's company, Stag Mountain LLC. Mr. Hagen subsequently committed suicide.

Plaintiff met Mr. Hagen in 2002 or 2003 when they were working together at a company called Unisys. Beginning in 2003, Mr. Hagen started soliciting funds from Plaintiff, purportedly to invest in various companies and endeavors. Plaintiff first gave Mr. Hagen $20,000 to $50,000 to invest in a grocery store. A short time later, Mr. Hagen informed Plaintiff that he could get a better return on his investment by putting it towards an operation that involved purchasing land in New Jersey to build "cell towers" on and then leasing the land to the state "for highway maintenance stuff." Plaintiff contributed another $40,000 to the purported cell tower land project, and Mr. Hagen also rolled over Plaintiff's original investment into this new venture. (*Id.* at 41.) Plaintiff did not receive any documentation from Mr. Hagen regarding either of these "investments."

Mr. Hagen subsequently approached Plaintiff about investing money in a fund that was set up to contribute to a "classified operation" that was similar to "AirAmerica.") Plaintiff's original investment was purportedly rolled over into this fund. Plaintiff also contributed significantly more money to the fund in three tranches, ultimately bringing his total investment in the fund to approximately $495,000. Mr. Hagen told Plaintiff that he would receive regular interest payments from the fund and would eventually receive a payout of $3 million in anywhere from four to seven years. From June 2010 through May 2014, Plaintiff received a monthly check from Mr. Hagen in the amount of $5,500, which was purported to be an interest payment on his investment in the fund. Because the fund was investing in a classified operation, Plaintiff never received nor asked for any documentation that would verify its operations (or even its existence).

Defendant and Mr. Hagen first met in 2008 through a mutual acquaintance named Bill Cowan. Mr. Hagen approached Mr. Cowan and Defendant with a purported investment opportunity involving a contract to supply services to the Department of Homeland Security ("DHS") for a survey project at airports, ports, and other facilities. Mr. Hagen and Mr. Cowan formed a joint venture called Tamarack Systems, which they used to facilitate their investments in the purported DHS contract. Tamarack invested $1,478,471.71 in the DHS project through Mr. Hagen and received $2,023,322.71 in return between October 2008 and September 2011. Defendant and Mr. Cowan never received any documentation from Mr. Hagen about the DHS contract due to the purportedly sensitive and secure nature of the work.

In 2012, Mr. Hagen acquired a ten percent stake in Stag Mountain, LLC, ("Stag") a government contractor in the security field. Defendant is the managing (and only other) member of Stag. According to Defendant, Mr. Hagen "did not participate in the business of the company" and "was not an employee." However, Mr. Hagen told Plaintiff that he was the Chief Executive Officer of Stag Mountain and gave him a business card indicating as much. . . .

In February 2014, Mr. Hagen solicited a $500,000 "investment" from an individual named Bret Anderson. This investment triggered a cascading series of events ending with the instant lawsuit. Mr. Hagen told Mr. Anderson that his money would be invested in a company called In-Q-Tel, which Mr. Hagen described as a private arm of the CIA. Due to the nature of In-Q-Tel's work with the CIA, Mr. Anderson did not receive any documentation regarding his investment. Mr. Anderson's investment was for a forty-five day term with the opportunity to reinvest at the end of that time period. However, Mr. Anderson became nervous about his "strong leap of faith" and told Mr. Hagen he wanted to cash out at the end of the first forty-five day period.

. . . In early June 2014, Mr. Hagen approached Plaintiff and requested a loan of $500,000. Mr. Hagen claimed that the money would be used to buy out an investor in the purported fund that Plaintiff had already sunk roughly $495,000 into. Mr. Hagen led Plaintiff to believe that once the investor was bought out he would receive the substantial multi-million dollar return from the fund he had been promised. Of course, it now seems clear that there was no fund and Mr. Hagen simply needed the money to repay Stag. Mr. Hagen instructed Plaintiff to wire the money to Defendant, and Plaintiff then instructed his broker to wire $500,000 from his Individual Retirement Account ("IRA") directly to Defendant's bank account.

Upon receiving the money, Defendant retained $289,000 in his personal bank account. Defendant transferred an additional $70,000 to Affiliations Group, another entity owned by Defendant that Stag allegedly owed money for past loans. Finally, Defendant transferred the remaining $141,000 to Stag.

Analysis

As this Court has previously stated, Plaintiff's claims for unjust enrichment and money had and received are subject to a common analysis: "To recover under either theory, the plaintiff must demonstrate that the defendant received a benefit which equity requires the defendant to relinquish." (Mem. Op. on Mot. to Dismiss, ECF No. 18, at 4–5 (citing *Jennings v. Rapid Response Delivery, Inc.*, Civ. No. WDQ-11-0092, 2011 WL 2470483, at *6 (D. Md. June 16, 2011)).) Specifically, a claim for unjust enrichment requires the plaintiff to establish three elements: (1) the plaintiff conferred a benefit upon the defendant; (2) the defendant knew of or appreciated the benefit; and (3) the defendant accepted or retained the benefit under such circumstances that it would be inequitable to allow the defendant to retain the benefit without paying value in return. *Hill v. Cross Country Settlements, LLC*, 402 Md. 281 (2007). There is no dispute that Plaintiff conferred a benefit upon Defendant and that Defendant knew of or appreciated the benefit. Thus, the only issue is whether it would be inequitable for Defendant to retain the benefit conferred on him by Plaintiff.

Defendant has moved for summary judgment on one, and only one, ground: He contends that Plaintiff is not entitled to restitution because he "voluntarily and personally authorized $500,000.00 to be transferred from his investment account to Defendant." In other words, Plaintiff was a "voluntary payor" and cannot seek restitution from Defendant for money Plaintiff foisted on him. Plaintiff counters that he is not a voluntary payor, and therefore is entitled to restitution unless Defendant was a bona fide purchaser. Plaintiff argues that he is not a voluntary payor because he only transferred money to Defendant as a result of Mr. Hagen's fraud. Plaintiff also argues that Defendant was not a bona fide purchaser because (1) he was aware (or at least should have been aware) of Mr. Hagen's fraud in procuring the $500,000 transfer from Plaintiff to Defendant, and (2) he failed to give valuable consideration for the $500,000. For the reasons set forth below, the Court concludes that Defendant is not entitled to judgment as a matter of law. Accordingly, his Motion will be DENIED.

Plaintiff is Not a Voluntary Payor or Officious Intermeddler

Generally, "[a] person who receives a benefit by reason of an infringement of another person's interest . . . owes restitution to him in the manner and amount necessary to prevent unjust enrichment." *Berry & Gould, P.A. v. Berry*, 360 Md. 142 (2000) (quoting Restatement (Second) of Restitution § 1 (Tentative Draft No. 1, 1983)). However, a person "is not *unjustly* enriched, and therefore not required to make restitution where the benefit was conferred by a volunteer or intermeddler." *Hill*, 936 A.2d at 352 (emphasis added) (quoting *Dan B. Dobbs*, Handbook on the Law of Remedies § 4.9 (1973)). The principle behind this rule is that one should not be allowed to unilaterally insert himself into the affairs of another, for example, by paying the other's debt, and then demand restitution. *Id.*; *see* Restatement (First) of

Restitution § 2 cmt. (Am. Law Inst. 1937) (hereinafter "Restatement") ("Officiousness means interference in the affairs of others not justified by the circumstances under which the interference takes place."). A volunteer (also sometimes called an officious intermeddler) is "[a] person who *without mistake, coercion or request* has unconditionally conferred a benefit upon another." Restatement § 112 (emphasis added); *accord Diane Sales, Inc. v. Am. Express Centurion Bank*, No. CV GLR-14-1063, 2015 WL 10986308, at *3 (D. Md. Oct. 26, 2015). On the other hand, "a plaintiff is not officious when he . . . acts under a legal compulsion or duty, . . . acts to protect his or her own property interests, . . . or acts pursuant to a reasonable or justifiable mistake as to any of the aforementioned categories." *Hill*, 936 A.2d at 358.

Defendant argues that Plaintiff is a voluntary payor, and therefore not entitled to restitution, because Plaintiff personally authorized the wire transfer to Defendant. In fact, Defendant is so sure that this argument is a slam dunk he has filed a separate motion seeking sanctions against Plaintiff for filing a frivolous lawsuit. (ECF No. 56.) Defendant misunderstands the meaning of a voluntary payor. The fact that Plaintiff knew he was wiring $500,000 to Defendant does not mean that he intended to voluntarily, officiously, and unconditionally confer a benefit on Defendant. Indeed, Defendant himself repeatedly insists that he had no idea who Plaintiff was prior to the filing of this lawsuit. It would be odd, to say the least, for Plaintiff to unconditionally confer such a significant financial benefit on someone he does not know.

More importantly, however, Plaintiff cannot be a voluntary payor if he conferred a benefit on Defendant by mistake (i.e., fraud). Restatement § 112 cmt. (explaining that "a person is entitled to restitution for a benefit conferred as the result of mistake including fraud"). This rule applies with equal force whether the fraud is committed by the beneficiary (in this case, Defendant) or a third party (i.e., Mr. Hagen). Restatement § 17 cmt. ("[A] donee beneficiary who has acquired a benefit by the fraud of the third person, has the same duties of restitution as the third person would have had. . . ."). In arguing that Plaintiff is a voluntary payor, Defendant simply ignores the underlying fraud by Mr. Hagen that prompted Plaintiff to transfer $500,000 to Defendant. . . .

Accordingly, Defendant is not entitled to summary judgment on the ground that Plaintiff is a voluntary payor.

Finally, although Defendant is not entitled to summary judgment, the Court notes that Plaintiff's entitlement to restitution is far from a foregone conclusion. Indeed, Plaintiff is just as guilty as Defendant of taking an ostrichlike approach in his dealings with Mr. Hagen. Every accusation of bad faith Plaintiff makes against Defendant could just as easily be leveled against Plaintiff. . . .

Conclusion

For the foregoing reasons, an Order shall enter DENYING Defendant's Motion for Summary Judgment

* * *

Problem 46

A true volunteer willingly confers a benefit on someone who did not ask for it. Is the address painter described here a volunteer?

Cathy comes up with an idea to make some quick money: she will tape a flier to the door of every home in her neighborhood, notifying the homeowner she intends to repaint the address number on the curb in front of the house the following Monday. The flier further notifies each homeowner that the cost of this address painting service is $20, which she will collect upon completion of the painting. In tiny print, at the bottom of the flier, is written: "If you do not wish to have your address repainted, simply tape a piece of plastic over the curb before 9:00 a.m. on Monday." Come Monday, no one has taped plastic over the curb. Cathy repaints all the addresses in the neighborhood and expects to collect $20 from each homeowner.

Introductory Note — *Monroe Financial Corp. v. DiSilvestro*

Monroe Financial Corp. is a stock overpayment case. The plaintiff is a stockbroker seeking to recover funds mistakenly paid to an investor who sold stock that was actually worth far less than what the broker paid out. The defendant asserted the change of position defense — that no repayment should be required because the money had already been spent by the time of the lawsuit. The trial court found for the defendant, and the broker appealed. In a split decision, the Indiana Court of Appeals reverses, finding the circumstances insufficient to allow the defendant to escape liability.

THINGS TO THINK ABOUT while reading *Monroe Financial Corp. v. DiSilvestro*:

1. What kind of a change of position is sufficient to support the change of position defense?

2. What kind of behavior is the majority opinion seeking to deter?

Monroe Financial Corp. v. DiSilvestro

Indiana Court of Appeals
529 N.E.2d 379 (1988)

SULLIVAN, Judge.

Plaintiff-appellant, Monroe Financial Corporation (MFC), appeals the negative judgment of the Monroe Superior Court on its suit seeking to recover a sum of money paid in error to defendant-appellee, E. Ruth DiSilvestro (DiSilvestro). The money paid represented the market price for 62 shares of stock in Avery International Corporation. In fact DiSilvestro owned shares in Avery, Inc., the shares of which were trading at a substantially lower figure.

DiSilvestro owned 62 shares of Avery, Inc. stock. Having no special knowledge or expertise regarding stock transactions, DiSilvestro's husband, Frank, telephoned MFC on October 20, 1987 to determine at what price Avery, Inc. was trading. He spoke to Wayne Schuman (Schuman), a professional stockbroker and vice-president of MFC, who informed Frank that Avery, Inc. was trading at $38.50 per share. In fact, Avery, Inc. was not trading at that price. Schuman had made a mistake in researching the stock value. When consulting his list of stocks, Schuman saw only one Avery listed, Avery International Corporation. Schuman mistakenly assumed Ruth owned Avery International Corporation and quoted that price.

DiSilvestro brought the stock certificates to MFC that afternoon at which time Schuman informed her that the trading price of the stock had decreased 50 cents. This quote also represented the price at which Avery International Corporation was trading. DiSilvestro decided to sell her shares of Avery, Inc., and Schuman agreed that MFC would sell them as an agent for a commission. She left the stock certificates with Schuman, and he placed a sell order with the company in New York (the Company) that executes transactions entered into by MFC. On October 27, 1986, DiSilvestro returned to MFC and picked up a check in the amount of $2,304.97. The check represented the market price of 62 shares of Avery International Corporation at $38 per share less the commission retained by MFC for services rendered as agent for her in the transaction.

MFC, as it usually does in the course of its business, had advanced the proceeds of the stock sale to DiSilvestro prior to receiving the actual funds from the Company. Upon receiving the stock certificates from MFC, however, the Company detected the discrepancy in names. The Company informed Schuman of the mistake by telephone and returned the stock certificates directly to DiSilvestro. By the time MFC first notified her of Schuman's mistake on October 30, 1987, DiSilvestro had already spent a significant portion of the proceeds on home improvements. MFC requested that DiSilvestro return the money. She refused. Thereafter, MFC brought suit against her under the small claims procedures seeking to recover the $2,304.97. Following a hearing, the trial court issued a judgment permitting DiSilvestro to retain the proceeds of the transaction.

Recovery of Funds Mistakenly Paid

It must be kept in mind that this litigation involved a claim by MFC to recover moneys mistakenly paid to DiSilvestro. It does not encompass any claim by DiSilvestro that MFC failed to perform a contract to sell Avery, Inc. stock or that such contract was breached by MFC.

MFC contends DiSilvestro may not retain the money paid to her. It claims that to allow her to retain the money would constitute unjust enrichment. Under such circumstances, MFC argues it is entitled to restitution. DiSilvestro contends that a party making a unilateral mistake of fact is not entitled to restitution unless the mistake is basic to the contract and known to the other party, or circumstances are such that the other party should have known of the mistake. She claims she was unaware of the value of the stock and relied upon the expertise of MFC to value the stock. She claims further that recovery should be denied because she has expended the proceeds of the sale and substantially changed her position as a result.

Relatively few reported cases have been found which have considered whether the proceeds from a purported sale of stock other than that intended by the customer may be recovered. In fact, our research has failed to disclose any Indiana authority which has addressed the issue. However, other jurisdictions have had occasion to address the subject.

Almost identical fact patterns are presented in *Castock Corp. v. Bailey* (1985) 128 Misc.2d 1068, and *Donner v. Sackett* (1916) 251 Pa. 524. In *Castock,* the plaintiff-brokers sold 1,000 shares of Microbiological Sciences, Inc. stock for Bailey and delivered a check to her in the amount of $7,088.08. The stock certificate given by Bailey to the plaintiff-brokers, however, was for shares of Microbiological Research Corporation/Microbiological Sciences, Inc. This stock was worth between seven and ten cents a share, whereas the stock which was sold was worth approximately $7 per share. The mistake was solely the result of the conduct of the plaintiff-brokers. The trial court denied the plaintiff's complaint seeking to recover the overpayment of proceeds following the erroneous sale of stock. Upon appeal the *Castock* court reversed the trial court, holding that money paid under a mistake of fact may be recovered however careless the party paying it may have been. . . .

Also factually similar is *Smith v. Rubel* (1932) 140 Or. 422. A broker purported to sell shares of a company's Class A stock when the customer owned Class B stock in that company. A transaction for sale of Class A stock was completed, and the proceeds were forwarded to the customer in an amount twice the value of the Class B stock. The error was discovered and cancellation of the sale was secured. The customer's broker-agent requested return of the proceeds of the erroneous sale. The customer refused. Reversing a judgment for the customer, the Oregon Supreme Court stated the general rule applicable to actions for restitution based on a unilateral mistake:

"[P]ayment made under a mistake of fact which induces the belief that the other party is entitled to receive the payment when, in fact, the sum is neither legally nor morally due to him, may be recovered, provided the payment has not caused such a change in the position of the payee that it would be unjust to require the refund." 13 P.2d at 1079.

Under the facts stated, the court required the customer to return the proceeds.

... In the above cases the courts recognized that as a general rule money paid under a unilateral mistake of fact may be recovered when it would have not been otherwise paid, even though the party paying it may have been careless. This comports with the law of this state as enunciated in *Stotsenburg v. Fordice* (1895) 142 Ind. 490, wherein it was stated that money paid under a mistake of fact, which the payor is under no legal obligation to pay, may be recovered, notwithstanding a failure to employ the means of knowledge which would disclose the mistake.

... Accordingly, MFC was entitled to recover the proceeds paid to DiSilvestro following its erroneous sale of Avery International Corporation on her behalf.

Detrimental Reliance and Change of Position

The rule permitting a party to recover money paid under a unilateral mistake of fact is subject to a limitation. That is that the party receiving the money must not have so changed his position so as to make it inequitable to require him to make repayment. The result reached in each of the cases discussed above was based upon the court's determination that the money paid by reason of the mistaken sale had not caused the party receiving the money to change his position such that requiring repayment would be inequitable. Likewise, Indiana courts recognize that a payment made under a mistake of fact may not be recovered where the party receiving the money has changed his position to his prejudice in reliance upon the payment and cannot be restored to status quo. *Hullet v. Cadick Milling Co.* (1929) 90 Ind.App. 271.

DiSilvestro argues that upon receiving the payment of $2,304.97 and prior to learning of the mistake, she expended nearly $2,000 on redecorating and home improvement equipment, and that it would therefore be inequitable to require repayment. MFC argues DiSilvestro did not rely to her detriment upon receiving the payment. It contends that by purchasing furniture and appliances, DiSilvestro obtained value for value and therefore retained the benefit of the money paid to her.

As far as we can discern Indiana courts have not considered whether the application of money paid under a mistake of fact to purchase tangible property constitutes a detrimental change of position. In support of its argument that DiSilvestro has not detrimentally changed her position MFC cites *Ohio Co. v. Rosemeier* (1972) 32 Ohio App.2d 116. In *Rosemeier* a stockbroker mistakenly sold shares of a California corporation instead of the customer's unlisted stock of little value in a similarly named Colorado corporation. Before the mistake was discovered the customer had applied the proceeds of the sale to the payment of an existing mortgage on her home and other debts. In determining whether there had been a detrimental change of position, the Ohio Court of Appeals noted that the customer merely converted the cash into a paid mortgage and retained the value originally represented by the mistaken payment. The court held that such an expenditure did not constitute a detrimental change of position. *Rosemeier* cited with approval *Donner, supra,* 97 A. 89.

In *Donner,* the broker recovered although defendant had used the money to pay some of his debts. The court reasoned that it was defendant's duty "to pay his debts, whether he sold or kept the stock. It is not becoming that he asks to be relieved from paying back the money which he received by mistake for comparatively worthless stock, because he turned it over to a creditor." 97 A. at 90. Similarly, in *Castock, supra,* the broker was permitted to recover despite defendant's expenditure of the funds "to pay debts and purchase tangible property or benefits." 492 N.Y.S.2d at 922–23.

Even where the payee used the money mistakenly paid as downpayments on three parcels of investment real estate and in doing so incurred substantial debt obligations, the court held that this did not constitute a detrimental change of position sufficient to preclude the broker's recovery. In *Shearson/American Express, Inc., supra,* 814 F.2d at 306, the Court held:

> "While appellant assumed new debt obligations, the value of the mistaken payment has not been lost. We find this case, for analytical purposes, indistinguishable from *Rosemeier [supra]*."

If we were to hold that DiSilvestro has successfully circumvented the duty to repay the amount mistakenly paid by MFC due to her purchases and expenditures, we would be encouraging payees to hastily convert such receipts into tangible personal property in order to avoid a clear equitable duty. We should not adopt a principle of law which encourages a race to furniture and appliance stores.

MFC is entitled to recover the amount paid to DiSilvestro less any diminution in value of the Avery, Inc. stock which may have occurred as a result of MFC's failure to consummate the sale. *See Western Casualty & Surety Co. v. Kohm* (1982) Mo.App., 638 S.W.2d 798, in which the defendant used the money mistakenly paid to purchase a car. The court there stated:

> "Normally this type of change is *not* sufficient to bar restitution, since a purchaser generally receives something of value for his money." 638 S.W.2d at 801 (original emphasis). . . .

The trial court in ordering restitution may fashion the judgment so as to protect DiSilvestro from being unduly burdened. Among other possibilities available to the trial court is the possibility that a restitution judgment for $2,304.97 might be satisfied by delivery to MFC of those items purchased plus any cash amount as may represent the difference between the sum spent by DiSilvestro and the $2,304.97 paid by MFC.

Notwithstanding the flexibility with which the trial court might frame the judgment, the judgment upon appeal is in error and is hereby reversed with instructions to enter judgment for MFC.

NEAL, Judge, dissenting.

While conceding that MFC would not be entitled to recover if DiSilvestro had changed her position to her prejudice so that it would be inequitable to require her to make restitution, the majority opinion then proceeds to ignore, not merely reweigh, the evidence. Paraphrasing ancient legal bromides, the majority bases the rationale for its conclusion solely upon the extraordinary statements that "we would be encouraging payees to hastily convert such receipts into tangible personal property in order to avoid a clear equitable duty," and "we should not adopt a principle of law which encourages a race to furniture and appliance stores."

Indiana courts have not considered whether the application of money paid under a mistake of fact to purchase tangible property constitutes a detrimental change of position. . . . In each of the cases relied upon by MFC the courts held that the expenditure of money paid under a mistake of fact to discharge a debt did not constitute detrimental reliance. The underlying rationale of these cases is that an individual who receives money under a mistake of fact is not excused from repayment where he has expended the money in a way which he was otherwise required to. In each of the cases discussed above the defendant had applied the money received to the payment of an existing mortgage or to pay off other pre-existing debts.

In this case the evidence reveals that MFC is a professional stockbroker with connections of some sort in New York. In reliance upon MFC's professed expertise in stock matters, DiSilvestro sold her stock through MFC, upon MFC's terms, and upon MFC's dictated price. Without any knowledge of MFC's self-induced negligence she spent the money and it is gone. Under the majority's unfortunate ruling, DiSilvestro will now have a judgment lien upon her residence, and if she is unable to pay it she will lose her home upon an execution sale. Absent MFC's negligence, there would have been no sale, no purchase of improvements, and no judgment lien. It is to be emphasized that this is not the payment of an old debt, but the incurrence of new obligations in reliance upon a misplaced trust in MFC. If the facts of this case do not show a detrimental change of position, I am at a loss to know what facts would so qualify.

The majority has ignored the well established rule of appellate review that we do not reweigh the evidence or adjudge the credibility of the witnesses, such being the function of the trial court. In this case it was for the trial court, sitting without a jury, to decide whether or not DiSilvestro had changed position to her detriment. It decided that issue in the affirmative. The majority has now reweighed the evidence in clear violation of its appellate function.

I support the rule that would protect hapless citizens from the inexcusable mistake of professional brokers, and would affirm the decision of the trial court.

* * *

Problem 47

The change of position defense requires that the defendant show detrimental reliance on the benefit received. Would any of the following actions constitute a change of position?

Dan is retired and receives a pension from his former employer, paid monthly. One year, the pension administrator makes an error and pays Dan an extra $50,000. Thinking the excess payment is the result of a legitimate increase in his pension, Dan spends the entire $50,000, in this manner:

- $30,000 to pay that year's tuition for his daughter, who is a sophomore in college; *change in form*
- $10,000 to pay off the balance of the mortgage on his house; *form*
- $5,000 to pay off existing credit card debt; *form*
- $5,000 to invest in the stock market (an investment that becomes worthless when the company in which he bought shares goes out of business).

change in position
— you don't have any value
for what you did w/
the money

Chapter 10

Other Specific Relief

Equitable remedies — court orders that operate *in personam* and require the performance of a certain act — are available in lawsuits for breach of contract, harm to personal property, and harm to real property. These remedies are specific, not substitutionary; they aim to directly remediate the plaintiff's problem.

This chapter first discusses three equitable contract remedies: specific performance, rescission, and reformation. Following that is a discussion of replevin, a remedy for recovering personal property. The chapter concludes with ejectment, a remedy for recovering possession of real property.

Specific Performance

As with any other legal wrong, the default remedy for a breach of contract is damages. The law presumes the appropriate remedy when a contract is not honored is a monetary payment to cover what the nonbreaching party has lost. But sometimes a monetary award will not adequately deliver justice in a contract case.

A plaintiff for whom damages will not suffice might instead seek an order requiring the defendant to perform the contract. That remedy, specific performance, is available only when the plaintiff shows damages are inadequate. The same showing is required for the equitable remedy of an injunction, which makes sense — specific performance is, after all, a species of mandatory injunction. It is a court order requiring a party to perform the terms of a contract.

One reason why damages might be inadequate is that the subject matter of the contract is unique, like in the classic example of a contract to convey real property. Every parcel of land is considered by the law to be unique. So a buyer who has contracted to obtain a certain piece of property is not adequately compensated by money when title to that property is not delivered. Money would reimburse the plaintiff for out-of-pocket expenses and allow realization of any financial gain that would have come from owning the property. But the plaintiff would still not have title to that one-of-a-kind piece of property. The only way to fulfill the plaintiff's expectation interest in that scenario — to provide the true benefit of the bargain struck — is to award title to the property itself. Similar situations can be fairly easily imagined. Breach of a contract to sell an original work of art, for example, might involve the same considerations.

A plaintiff who demonstrates damages are inadequate to remedy the defendant's breach is *potentially* entitled to specific performance. But the inquiry does not end there — inadequacy of damages is a necessary but not sufficient condition for specific performance. Before ordering specific performance, a court will also pay close attention to the feasibility of such an order. After all, the defendant has already refused to perform voluntarily, and it can be difficult to make someone to do something they really do not want to do. The court will therefore want to ensure that the terms of the contract are sufficiently definite to allow for a clear order informing the defendant precisely what to do. A vague order will be too hard to enforce.

Further, the defendant must have the present ability to perform the contract, as a court will not order someone to do the impossible. For instance, what if, going back to the real property purchase example, the defendant no longer had title to the property because it had already been conveyed to someone else? An order requiring the defendant to deliver title to the plaintiff in that situation would not be helpful.

The party seeking performance must also itself be willing and able to perform its own obligations under the contract — it would not be fair to allow the plaintiff to benefit from the contract while at the same time shirking the responsibilities imposed by it.

Obtaining the remedy of specific performance involves the plaintiff not only showing that damages are inadequate but also satisfying the court that an order to perform the contract is feasible, fair, and will not prove problematic to enforce.

Introductory Note — *Keappler v. Miller* and *Oliver v. Ball*

The dispute in *Keappler* involves a contract to build a wall. The defendant demurred to the plaintiff's complaint on the ground that specific performance was not an available remedy because the terms of the contract were too vague. The trial court disagreed — the court thought it was feasible to order the contract performed. The defendant challenges that determination on appeal, leaving the Georgia Supreme Court to decide whether the trial judge was too optimistic about feasibility of enforcement.

Oliver is a real property sale case where the seller argues the rule that all real property is unique should not apply when the property is bought for investment purposes. The appellate court must decide whether damages are an adequate remedy or if the investor should be able to choose specific performance.

THINGS TO THINK ABOUT while reading *Keappler v. Miller* and *Oliver v. Ball*:

1. What test does the court use to determine whether specific performance is an appropriate remedy?

2. Why is specific performance not available in every case?

3. Why was specific performance available, or not, in this case?

Keappler v. Miller

Georgia Supreme Court

221 Ga.144 (1965)

MOBLEY, Justice.

Specific performance is not a remedy which either party can demand as a matter of absolute right, and will not in any given case be granted unless strictly equitable and just. Mere inadequacy of price may justify a court in refusing to decree a specific performance of a contract of bargain and sale; so also may any other fact the contract to be unfair, or unjust, or against good conscience. And, in order to authorize specific performance of a contract, its terms must be clear, distinct, and definite.

Applying the above stated principles of law to the allegations of facts of the petition in this case, the petition does not, as against general demurrer, state a cause of action for specific performance. The petition seeks specific performance by defendants of an oral contract to build a wall from the level of his property up a sloping embankment to the natural level of the ground on petitioners' property and afford lateral support to petitioners' land.

The petition alleges that the parties are adjoining property owners, that prior to petitioners' purchase of their land, defendants had excavated to the property of petitioners along the length of the property line from a depth of 3 to 25 feet; that the parties entered into an oral agreement that petitioners 'would permit defendants to slope approximately 200 feet of said vertical embankment by the excavation of an additional 5 feet westward into petitioners' property so that said embankment would be stabilized and more adaptable to a less expensive retaining wall so as to prevent cave ins and thereby give lateral support,' that '[I]n consideration of granting to defendant permission to slope said embankment back five feet into petitioners' property, the defendant agreed to erect a wall along 200 feet of said cut from the grade level of his property up said sloping embankment to the natural level of the ground on petitioners' property, and along the additional approximately 175 feet extending southward along said line the defendant agreed to fill and empack earth against said vertical embankment to furnish stability and lateral support'; that pursuant to the agreement defendants caused said vertical bank to be cut back and sloped five feet into petitioners' property, and that defendants failed and refused to build the wall as agreed upon.

Obviously the terms of the alleged agreement to build a wall are not certain, definite and clear. The dimensions of the wall agreed upon are not alleged-whether six inches or six feet in width, or what width it was to be, nor of what materials it was to be built-rock, brick, concrete or what.

If the court ordered specific performance of the agreement, what kind of wall would it order the defendants to build? The agreement does not provide the answer, thus there is no way for the court to require the building of the wall. While the petition prays 'that the defendant be required to specifically perform his part of the contract to build said wall and afford lateral support to petitioners' land,' the petition does not allege that the defendants had agreed to afford lateral support to petitioners' land. Plaintiff simply alleges that it agreed to build the wall but did not allege that he agreed to build a wall along the property line sufficient to furnish petitioners lateral support. The petition failing to set out a cause of action for any of the relief prayed, the trial court erred in overruling the general demurrer to the petition.

Judgment reversed.

* * *

Oliver v. Ball

Pennsylvania Superior Court
136 A.3d 162 (2016)

OPINION BY STABILE, J.:

The facts and procedural history underlying this case are undisputed. Appellant entered into a sale of real estate contract with Appellees Larry M. Ball, Danny R. Ball, Larry J. Ball and Mary H. Ball ("Balls") for the purchase of two tracts of land in Cranberry Township, Butler County, containing approximately 71.5 acres ("the Property"). Balls failed to convey the Property. Appellant filed suit against Balls for breach of contract, seeking specific performance and/or monetary damages. . . .

Appellant's claim for specific performance was severed from his claim for damages and proceeded to a non-jury trial. Following testimony on the liability phase, the trial court concluded that a valid and binding contract for the sale of the Property existed between the parties, which Balls breached. The case next proceeded to the damage phase, at which Appellant testified in support of specific performance. In particular, describing the Property, Appellant testified that "[i]t was wood[ed] property with some open fields, some old farm land, with a, like a wet weather stream running through it. It was hilly. Wasn't terribly hilly but it was sloping like all other property in Butler County." Appellant testified that he planned to purchase the Property for investment purposes. Specifically, he testified that "[m]y plans were to hold it for a long-term investment. At that time I was still in the timber business and there was some timber on [the Property] that I thought could be harvested." He also testified:

[a]s a real estate investor [the Property] had a lot of things I look for. It was big so it possibly could be subdivided in the future for, you know, further development. Of course, it had all the mineral rights coming with it so that was something that I hoped to put into my business in the future.

Appellant testified that the location of the Property was important to him because it "is only maybe five miles as the crow flies from my home so that is important, to try to keep my investments within a reasonable distance from my home and where I work." Explaining why the Property was important to him, Appellant testified:

It's basically the sum of the parts of this property are much more valuable than the whole. So, again, what I have learned through 26 years of business and what I have been able to do and have learned to do is to take a whole property like this that has valuable parts, subdivide those parts, if you will, and have it become very strong investment.

On cross-examination, Appellant acknowledged that he owns investment properties located as far away as Westmoreland and Crawford Counties.

Following Appellant's testimony, Balls moved for nonsuit, arguing that Appellant failed to establish that he lacked an adequate remedy at law. The trial court agreed, granting Balls' motion for nonsuit and denying Appellant's request for specific performance. [This appeal followed.]

. . . With respect to specific performance, our Supreme Court explained in *Payne v. Clark,* 409 Pa. 557 (1963):

From the moment an agreement of sale of real estate is executed and delivered it vests in the grantee [(purchaser)] what is known as an equitable title to the real estate. Thereupon the vendor [(seller)] is considered as a trustee of the real estate for the purchaser and the latter becomes a trustee of the balance of the purchase money for the seller. Hence, if the terms of the agreement are violated by the [seller], [the purchaser] may go into a court of equity seeking to enforce the contract and to compel specific performance.

Payne, 187 A.2d at 770–71. In other words, a request for specific performance is an appeal to the court's equitable powers. *See Lackner v. Glosser,* 892 A.2d 21, 31 (Pa.Super.2006). Specific performance generally is described as the surrender of a thing in itself, because that thing is unique and thus incapable — by its nature — of duplication. *See Cimina v. Bronich,* 517 Pa. 378 (1988). "A decree of specific performance is not a matter of right, but of grace." *Barnes v. McKellar,* 434 Pa.Super. 597 (1994) (citation omitted). Such a decree will be granted only if a plaintiff clearly is entitled to such relief, there is no adequate remedy at law, and the trial court believes that justice requires such a decree. *Id.* "Inequity or hardship may be a valid defense in an action for specific performance and such decree refused if in the exercise of a sound discretion it is determined that, under the facts, specific performance would be contrary to equity or justice." *Payne,* 187 A.2d at 771. Mere inadequacy of price, however, will not defeat specific performance, unless grossly disproportionate.

Courts in this Commonwealth consistently have determined that specific performance is an appropriate remedy to compel the conveyance of real estate where a seller violates a realty contract and specific enforcement of the contract would not be contrary to justice. *See Borie v. Satterthwaite,* 180 Pa. 542 (1897) (affirming specific performance for breach of real estate agreement); *see also Agnew v. Southern Ave. Land Co.,* 204 Pa. 192, 53 A. 752 (1902) (noting that a court may enforce specifically only an agreement for realty whose terms are definite); *Rusiski v. Pribonic,* 511 Pa. 383 (1986) (affirming only the award of specific performance for breach of a realty agreement); *Petry v. Tanglwood Lakes, Inc.,* 514 Pa. 51 (1987) (noting that real estate contracts "have been traditionally regarded as being specifically enforceable in equity by the buyer"). As explained in the second restatement:

> Contracts for the sale of land have traditionally been accorded a special place in the law of specific performance. A specific tract of land has long been regarded as unique and impossible of duplication by the use of any amount of money.

> Restatement (Second) of Contracts, § 360 cmt. e. As is obvious, specific performance for the sale of land is available because no two parcels of land are identical. An award of damages will not suffice to allow a plaintiff to acquire the same parcel of land anywhere else. Thus, in the context of realty agreements breached by a seller, "we can assume that [a buyer] has no adequate remedy at law." *Snyder v. Bowen,* 359 Pa.Super. 47 (1986) (citing 81 C.J.S. Specific Performance §76 (1977)); *cf. Petry,* 522 A.2d at 1055 ("[W]here Appellant is not claiming the right to have an *estate* in land conveyed to her, an automatic right to compel the remedy of specific performance cannot be successfully maintained.").

Instantly, we note that the parties do not dispute that a valid, enforceable contract for the Property existed and that Balls breached the same by failing to convey the Property. The parties also do not argue that hardship or injustice would ensue if Appellant's request for specific performance were granted. Rather, the issue on appeal concerns only the adequacy of a remedy at law, and as such, involves a question of law.

Appellant points out that the Property is unique because it had a wet weather stream running through it, was hilly, featured timber and other minerals, and provided opportunities to him for further development. It also was important that the Property was only five miles away from his home so that he could keep his investments within a reasonable distance from home and work. Appellant adequately testified to the unique aspects of the Property and to attributes that made the parcel valuable to him. The trial court dismissed this testimony upon the basis that Appellant did not demonstrate that these attributes could not be duplicated elsewhere. Given that all tracts of land long have been regarded as unique, and Appellant further testified to the Property's unique characteristics *vis-á-vis* his needs, we agree with Appellant that a remedy at law is inadequate. Accordingly, we reject the trial court's conclusion that Appellant was not entitled to specific performance because the Property did not have any unique characteristics that could not be found or purchased elsewhere. We conclude that, based on our review of pertinent case law, the trial court erred in denying Appellant's claim for specific performance and granting Balls' motion for nonsuit. As stated, courts in this Commonwealth must enforce specifically realty agreements breached by sellers, except in cases where hardship or injustice would result.

We reject Appellees' and the trial court's suggestion that *Boyd & Mahoney v. Chevron U.S.A.*, 419 Pa.Super. 24 (1992), stands for the proposition that land itself is not unique, and that specific performance is only available if some characteristic of or structure on the land, or the location of the land itself, is of such importance to a buyer that no other property can duplicate its value. . . . To the contrary, our law makes clear that the remedy of specific performance in realty contracts derives from the proposition that all land is unique. . . .

In sum, we conclude that the trial court erred in denying Appellant's post-trial motion for removal of nonsuit when the Appellant clearly established that his remedy at law was inadequate under the circumstances of this case.

Judgment reversed. Case remanded for proceedings consistent with this opinion.

* * *

Problem 48

Specific performance will not be ordered unless damages are inadequate. Is specific performance an available remedy in the case below?

Jan contracts with Dave to use 500 square feet of his car dealership as a store to sell her custom-made bumper stickers. The bumper sticker business is her sole source of income, and she has no other location from which to sell them as the building she was using has just been torn down. She makes around $80,000 annually from bumper sticker sales. But sales have increased every year, and she expects to have a long sticker-selling career. The day before Jan is scheduled to move her store into Dave's dealership, he gets a more lucrative offer for the space from a company that sells windshield wipers. Dave allows the windshield wiper company to move in and breaches his contract with Jan. With no other location from which to sell her bumper stickers, Jan will soon go out of business. She sues Dave for breach of contract and asks for specific performance: an order requiring Dave to allow her to use the space as originally agreed.

Introductory Note — *Bloch v. Hillel Torah North Suburban Day School*

Bloch is every school principal's nightmare. After the school expelled a student for excessive tardiness and absences, her parents sued for breach of contract. The issue on appeal is not the merits of the suit — whether the school breached its contract to educate the child, or legitimately exercised its authority to discipline — but rather the appropriate remedy: damages, or specific performance?

THINGS TO THINK ABOUT while reading *Bloch v. Hillel Torah North Suburban Day School*:

1. Why are contracts for personal services a poor fit for specific performance?

2. Why did the court feel specific performance was particularly inapt for this contract?

Bloch v. Hillel Torah North Suburban Day School

Illinois Appellate Court
426 N.E.2d 976 (1981)

McNAMARA, Justice:

Plaintiffs appeal from an order of the trial court granting summary judgment in favor of defendant Hillel Torah North Suburban Day School. Helen Bloch is a grade school child who was expelled from defendant, a private Jewish school, at mid-year in 1980. Her parents brought this action seeking to enjoin expulsion and for specific performance of defendant's contract to educate Helen.

The complaint alleged that defendant arbitrarily and in bad faith breached its contract, and that Helen's expulsion was motivated by defendant's disapproval of plaintiffs' leadership role in combatting an epidemic of head lice at the school. The complaint also alleged that the school uniquely corresponded exactly to the religious commitments desired by plaintiffs. Defendant's answer stated that Helen was expelled, pursuant to school regulations, for excessive tardiness and absences. The parties also disputed the duration of the contractual obligation to educate. Defendant contended that the contract was to endure only for a school year since tuition for only that period of time was accepted by it. Plaintiffs maintained that the contract, as implied by custom and usage, was to endure for eight years, the first year's tuition creating irrevocable option contracts for the subsequent school years, provided that Helen conformed to defendant's rules.

After the trial court denied plaintiffs' request for a preliminary injunction, both sides moved for summary judgment. The trial court denied plaintiffs' motion and granted the motion of defendant. In the same order, the trial court gave plaintiffs leave to file an amended complaint for money damages.

Whether a court will exercise its jurisdiction to order specific performance of a valid contract is a matter within the sound discretion of the court and dependent upon the facts of each case. (Williston on Contracts, s 1418, at 657–58 (3d ed. 1968); Fitzpatrick v. Allied Contracting Co. (1962), 24 Ill.2d 448.) Where the contract is one which establishes a personal relationship calling for the rendition of personal services, the proper remedy for a breach is generally not specific performance but rather an action for money damages. (Williston, s 1423, at 784–85; Zannis v. Lake Shore Radiologists, Ltd. (1979), 73 Ill.App.3d 901.) The reasons for denying specific performance in such a case are as follows: the remedy at law is adequate; enforcement and supervision of the order of specific performance may be problematic and could result in protracted litigation; and the concept of compelling the continuance of a personal relationship to which one of the parties is resistant is repugnant as a form of involuntary servitude. Williston, s 1423, at 786–87; Zannis v. Lake Shore Radiologists, Ltd.

Applying these principles to the present case, we believe that the trial court properly granted summary judgment in favor of defendant. It is beyond dispute that the relationship between a grade school and a student is one highly personal in nature. Similarly, it is apparent that performance of such a contract requires a rendition of a variety of personal services. Although we are cognizant of the difficulties in duplicating the personal services offered by one school, particularly one like defendant, we are even more aware of the difficulties pervasive in compelling the continuation of a relationship between a young child and a private school which openly resists that relationship. In such a case, we believe the trial court exercised sound judgment in ruling that plaintiffs are best left to their remedy for damages. (See Zannis v. Lake Shore Radiologists, Ltd.) ...

Plaintiffs' reliance on three Illinois cases is misplaced. In DeMarco v. University of Health Services (1976), 40 Ill.App.3d 474, a mandatory injunction was issued compelling a school to confer a degree on plaintiff. The order did not compel the continuance of a personal relationship, but instead provided for the performance of a solitary ministerial act which recognized the termination of the parties' relationship. Similarly, in Tanner v. Bd. of Trustees of Univ. of Illinois (1977), 48 Ill.App.3d 680, plaintiff sought to compel the issuance of a degree. In Steinberg v. Chicago Medical School (1977), 69 Ill.2d 320, the court held that the plaintiff stated a valid class action for an injunction against a medical school's misrepresentation of admission standards in its brochure and for restitution of application fees. In so holding, the court noted that plaintiff did not seek to compel the school to admit him. There was no issue concerning the enforcement of a personal relationship between adverse parties.

Illinois law recognizes the availability of a remedy for monetary damages for a private school's wrongful expulsion of a student in violation of its contract. (See Aronson v. North Park College (1981), 94 Ill.App.3d 211.) And especially, where, as here, the issue involves a personal relationship between a grade school and a young child, we believe plaintiffs are best left to a remedy for damages for breach of contract.

For the reasons stated, the judgment of the circuit court of Cook County is affirmed, and the cause is remanded for further proceedings permitting plaintiffs to file an amended complaint for money damages.

Affirmed and remanded.

* * *

Problem 49

Specific performance is generally not allowed in the case of a contract for personal services. Should specific performance be ordered in the following case?

A poultry farmer contracts with an egg distributor to sell the farmer's eggs. The contract requires the distributor to "use best efforts to market and sell" all eggs produced by the farmer. The term of the contract is for five years. After one year, having received a more lucrative offer from another egg producer, the distributor breaches the contract by informing the farmer it will no longer sell his eggs. The farmer sues the distributor for breach of contract and seeks specific performance.

Rescission and Reformation

Specific performance is helpful to a plaintiff who wants a contract enforced. But there is sometimes the opposite situation: a plaintiff might *not* want a contract to be enforced, or at least not enforced according to its terms — perhaps because he or she was fraudulently induced to enter the agreement, or because both parties to the transaction were mistaken about what the contract requires. Plaintiffs finding themselves in such a predicament can seek the remedy of rescission, an order that cancels the contract.

By seeking rescission, the plaintiff is said to disaffirm the bargain that was struck; meaning he or she wants it to be as though the contract never existed. That is fundamentally different from other breach of contract remedies like expectation damages and specific performance, which put a plaintiff in the position of the contract having been performed. Because of that difference, to obtain rescission a plaintiff must be willing and able to return any benefits already received under the contract. With specific performance, a plaintiff who seeks enforcement of the contract must also be willing to perform the obligations required by it. In the same way, a plaintiff who wants to rescind the contract must return the benefits already received. The concern in both scenarios is the same: fairness, by not letting the plaintiff have it both ways.

Rescission is appropriate where a contract should not be enforced because it does not reflect a true, voluntary agreement. Typical grounds for rescission are fraud and mutual mistake. Fraud is a basis for rescission because a party who was deliberately misled about what the contract requires cannot have voluntarily agreed to its terms. Similarly, mutual mistake is a basis for rescission because if both parties think the contract requires something other than what it does, there was no meeting of the minds as needed for a valid contract.

A party to a contract cannot invoke rescission simply as a way of avoiding what turns out to be a bad bargain, however. To prevent that from happening, the term the parties were mistaken about or that was misrepresented must be material to the deal as a whole. Plaintiffs cannot pick out some collateral term of little consequence, assert they were misled about it, and use that as a basis for avoiding the contractual obligations. Likewise, unilateral mistake — where only the plaintiff is mistaken about a term — will seldom provide a basis for rescission. If it did, any party who did not pay careful enough attention during negotiations would be able to nullify the agreement after the fact. But if one party is mistaken about a material term and the other party knows it and takes advantage by proceeding with the deal anyway, that might allow for rescission under the theory that consent was procured by fraud. The key inquiry for a rescission claim is whether fraud or mistake regarding a material point prevented the plaintiff from truly consenting to the terms of the contract.

A related remedy to rescission is reformation, an order that changes the terms of the contract to reflect the parties' true intentions, or at least to reflect the terms as they were understood by the plaintiff at the time of formation. Again, the goal is to achieve fairness by negating the effect of a mistake about what the contract requires or to prevent a defendant from benefiting from fraud in negotiations. Reformation is appropriate where the mistake or fraud is material enough to matter, but the alteration requested will not fundamentally change the nature of the contract. In other words, a court is unlikely to completely rewrite the agreement under the guise of reformation. But if keeping the agreement in place and changing a term or two will result in an accurate reflection of the parties' intent, reformation might be warranted.

Introductory Note — *Rancourt v. Verba* and *Wong v. Stoler*

Rancourt and *Stoler* are both cases involving the purchase of real property, and in both cases, it is ultimately determined that recission of the purchase contract is the appropriate remedy. The circumstances that lead each court to conclude rescission is warranted, however, are different. One case involves more blame-worthy conduct by the defendant than the other, yet the outcome is the same.

THINGS TO THINK ABOUT while reading *Rancourt v. Verba* and *Wong v. Stoler*:

1. What circumstances entitle a party to rescission of a contract?

2. What limits are placed on the remedy of rescission?

Rancourt v. Verba

Vermont Supreme Court

678 A.2d 886 (1996)

ALLEN, Chief Justice.

Defendants sold plaintiffs a parcel of land in North Hero, which the parties subsequently learned was unsuitable for lakeshore development. Plaintiffs sued to rescind, but the court allowed defendants to elect rescission or pay damages to plaintiffs for the diminished value of the property. It awarded plaintiffs attorney's fees, but denied plaintiffs' claim for prejudgment interest and consequential damages. Both parties appealed. We reverse.

In November 1989, defendants sold a ten-acre, lakeshore lot in North Hero to plaintiffs for $115,000. Defendants knew that plaintiffs intended to build a residence on the lot in close proximity to the lakeshore. Plaintiffs prepared the lakeshore building site by adding fill, but because this site preparation was done without permits, it violated state and federal wetland regulations. The trial court found that "[a]s a practical matter, a federal permit could not be obtained to place fill on or otherwise develop this wetland building site" and that the state permits were similarly "unavailable." Plaintiffs were later ordered to remove all fill placed on the building site, which included the fill placed by them after closing and by defendants prior to closing.

On learning that they could not build near the lake, plaintiffs demanded that defendants rescind the transaction, refund the purchase price, and pay consequential damages resulting from the purchase. After defendants refused, plaintiffs brought this rescission action, which is based on a claim of mutual mistake regarding the suitability of the lot for lakeshore development. In the alternative, plaintiffs requested compensatory damages.

The court found that the agreement was based upon a mutual mistake of fact resulting from "mutual, but innocent, misunderstanding." It concluded that defendants did not breach their contract with plaintiffs or their warranties of title, did not commit fraud, and did not violate Act 250. The court gave defendants the option of (1) paying plaintiffs $55,000 (the difference between the $60,000 fair market value of the lot at closing and the $115,000 purchase price), plus the cost of removing the fill which defendants had placed on the building site prior to closing, or (2) rescinding the transaction and refunding the purchase price of $115,000, less the cost of removing the fill which plaintiffs had placed on the building site after closing. . . .

Defendants advised the court of their election to pay the plaintiffs damages rather than rescind the transaction. Judgment was entered in plaintiffs' favor for $55,000, plus defendants' pro rated portion of the cost of removing the fill and attorney's fees.

The central issue in the case is when is rescission the proper remedy for mutual mistake. Plaintiffs argue that the trial court erred when it granted a remedy other than rescission. We agree.

The usual remedies applied to mutual mistake in contract formation are rescission and reformation. *Paradise Restaurant, Inc. v. Somerset Enterprises, Inc.*, 164 Vt. 405 (1995). "Where a contract has been entered into under a mutual mistake of the parties regarding a material fact affecting the subject matter thereof, it may be avoided . . . at the instance of the injured party, and an action lies to recover money paid under it." *Enequist v. Bemis,* 115 Vt. 209, 212 (1947); see also 13 Williston on Contracts § 1557, at 240 (3d ed. 1970) ("[W]here the error is in the substance of the bargain . . . rescission with restitution of whatever has been parted with is the only permissible relief. . . .").

In *Moonves v. Hill,* 134 Vt. 352 (1976), this Court addressed whether an abatement in the purchase price is a proper remedy for mutual mistake in a land contract. *Moonves* involved an in-gross sale of property where the trial court concluded that the buyer and seller were mutually mistaken as to the quantity of land conveyed. The trial court granted the buyer an abatement in the purchase price equal to the value of the disparity between the contract acreage and the actual acreage. This Court reversed, holding that the proper remedy for mutual mistake was rescission, not an abatement in the purchase price. In rejecting the contrary rule, which allowed a court to grant a pro tanto reduction in the purchase price, the Court said:

> In our view, this is substituting for the contract actually made by the parties a different one, which the court feels they would have made if they had known the correct quantities involved. Whatever the value of this rule when case law evolved largely from sales of rural acreage for farming purposes, or lumbering, its application loses much merit today, when access, *frontage,*

view, permitted uses, and other vastly different considerations often influence the purchase price.

Id. (emphasis added). Although *Moonves* involved mutual mistake as to the quantity of land, the rationale behind the Court's holding is equally, if not more, applicable to mutual mistake as to quality of the land.

Nevertheless, we have recognized limitations on the remedy of rescission, none of which is applicable here. First, a party seeking rescission of a contract entered into by mutual mistake is not entitled to retain favorable portions of the contract and disregard the rest. *Caledonia Sand & Gravel Co. v. Joseph A. Bass Co.,* 121 Vt. 161, 165 (1959). In essence, the injured party is given an all-or-nothing option in situations involving mutual mistake. See *Moonves,* 134 Vt. at 355, ("Rescission is, of course, an option of the plaintiffs on the facts as found. It is not relief they are compelled to take; they may prefer to keep the property in question and pay the stipulated price.").

Second, when a court finds that the party requesting rescission has assumed the risk of the mistake, rescission will be denied. See Restatement (Second) of Contracts §154, at 402–03 (1981); *Shavell v. Thurber,* 138 Vt. 217, 219–20 (1980) (even if court finds mutual mistake, no relief granted where buyer assumes risk of mistake by entering transaction knowingly); *Enequist,* 115 Vt. at 213 ("If it is shown that the hazard of gain or loss, whatever it may be, was accepted by the parties and entered into the contract, relief will be refused."). Here, the trial court made no finding that either party assumed the risk of mistake, and neither party has appealed the lack of such finding. Recently, this Court discussed the equitable circumstances where departure from the remedy of rescission is appropriate. *Paradise,* 164 Vt., 671 A.2d at 1263. We stated:

> "[R]escission is not the exclusive remedy for mutual mistake; a court may consider other equitable remedies in fashioning a just result. Indeed, the avoidance rule of *Restatement* §152 expressly recognizes that the materiality of the parties' mistake may be alleviated by other equitable relief. Correspondingly, §158(2) of the *Restatement* acknowledges the power of an equity court to eliminate the effect of mistake by supplying a new term or otherwise modifying the agreement as justice requires, thus protecting the parties' reliance interests."

Id. at 671 A.2d at 1263 (quoting *Thieme v. Worst,* 113 Idaho 455 (1987)). Both *Paradise* and *Thieme,* however, are distinguishable from this case. . . .

This case is more like *Renner v. Kehl,* 150 Ariz. 94 (1986), on the issue of intent. In *Renner,* buyer purchased land for the sole purpose of growing jojaba, and both buyer and seller were under the mistaken assumption that the land was suitable for that purpose. The *Renner* court held that buyer was "entitled" to rescission of the contract because the amount of water on the property was "a basic assumption on which both parties made the contract" and this mutual mistake "ha[d] such a material effect on the agreed exchange of performances as to upset the very bases of the contract." *Id.* at 265. In addition, the court noted that the "failure of the parties to make a thorough investigation of the water supply prior to signing the contract does not preclude rescission where the risk of mistake was not allocated among the parties." *Id.* at 265 n. 2.

Because the clear intent of plaintiffs was to purchase land suitable for lakeshore development, and because it is impossible to do so under state and federal wetland regulations, they are "entitled" to rescission. Also, as in *Renner,* the trial court did not find that the risk of mistake had been allocated to either party. In sum, although mutual mistake does not always require rescission, the facts of this case do not come within the limited circumstances where we have allowed a departure from rescission. . . .

Reversed and remanded.

* * *

Wong v. Stoler
California Court of Appeal
237 Cal.App.4th 1375

Humes, P.J.

I.

Introduction

Wayson and Susanna Wong bought a hillside home in San Carlos (City) for $2.35 million from Ira and Toby Stoler. Several months after they moved in, the Wongs discovered that they and 12 of their neighbors were connected to a private sewer system and were not directly serviced by the City's public system. Believing they had been deceived, they sued the Stolers and the real estate agents who brokered the sale alleging various causes of action, including rescission. After the Wongs settled their dispute with the real estate agents for $200,000, a court trial was held on the rescission claim only. Although the court found that the Stolers, with reckless disregard, made negligent misrepresentations to the Wongs, it declined to effectuate a rescission of the contract. Instead, it ordered the Stolers to be, for a limited time, indemnifiers to the Wongs for sewer maintenance and repair costs exceeding the $200,000 they obtained in their settlement with the agents.

On appeal, the Wongs contend that the trial court erred in denying rescission, ordering the alternative relief, and denying them attorney fees. . . .

We reverse. We conclude that the trial court declined to effectuate a rescission of the contract based on incorrect justifications and that its alternative remedy failed to provide the Wongs with the complete relief to which they were entitled.

II.

Background

A. The Property

The home is located on Sudan Lane, a privately maintained road on the west side of San Carlos in the Los Vientos Highlands area. When the developers built the house and 12 others, they installed a private system to carry sewage from these properties to a connecting point with the City's public sewer on a downhill street. Some of the homes on the private system are on a nearby street, Best Court. To meet the connecting point, the private system runs approximately 1,000 feet down a steep, unstable hillside through a public open-space and watershed area. At the time the 13 homes were built, the City required the developers to form a homeowners association to maintain, repair, and replace the private sewer lines. . . .

B. The Purchase and the Improvements

The Wongs bought the property from the Stolers in May 2008 for $2.35 million. Before the close of escrow, the Stolers provided the Wongs with a transfer disclosure statement completed in 2002 by the prior owners, an updated 2008 transfer disclosure statement, and a supplemental sellers' checklist. These combined documents represented to the Wongs that the property was connected to a public sewer system. . . .

In a roadside conversation, the parties directly discussed that Sudan Lane is a privately maintained road, and in a follow-up e-mail Mr. Wong specifically asked "is there any homeowners' association here?" Mr. Stoler replied, "no." . . .

C. Discovery of the Private Sewer System

The Wongs first learned of the private sewer system around November 6, 2008, when they received an e-mail from a neighbor discussing it. Unbeknownst to the Wongs, this neighbor had been the coordinator of an informal homeowners association since 2005. By this time, much of the home was down to the studs as a result of the demolition work.

The Wongs tried to resolve the problem without involving the Stolers. They and other neighbors met with the City and asked it to take possession of the sewer system. In April 2009, the City denied the request and instead proposed that the homeowners enter into a maintenance agreement. . . .

D. Commencement of Litigation and Trial

The Wongs sued the Stolers for negligence, negligent misrepresentation, fraudulent concealment, fraudulent misrepresentation, breach of contract, and breach of fiduciary duty. They also sought rescission of the purchase agreement. . . .

E. Statement of Decision

The court found that the Stolers acted with reckless disregard in negligently misrepresenting the material facts about the true nature of the sewer system and the existence of the informal association loosely established to maintain it. The court further found that the misrepresentations affected the property's value and that the Wongs would not have bought the property if they had known about the private sewer system and the informal association.

Nonetheless, the court denied rescission because of the "practicality of unwinding the transaction" and because of the undue burden it would place on the Stolers. The court reasoned that the Stolers had purchased a new home over four years ago and had spent $100,000 in improving it, and the Wongs had spent $300,000 improving the property and had removed a significant amount of the original landscaping. The court determined that, given the "burden that rescission would place on the Stolers," rescission was neither a fair nor appropriate remedy. . . .

III.

Discussion

a. Applicable Law and Standard of Review

A party to a contract has two different remedies when it has been injured by a breach of contract or fraud and lacks the ability or desire to keep the contract alive. (*Akin v. Certain Underwriters at Lloyd's London* (2006) 140 Cal.App.4th 291, 296.) The party may disaffirm the contract, treating it as rescinded, and recover damages resulting from the rescission. Alternatively, the party may affirm the contract, treating it as repudiated, and recover damages for breach of contract or fraud.

Rescission and damages are alternative remedies. A party may seek rescission or damages for breach of contract or fraud "in the event rescission cannot be obtained" in the same action. (*Williams v. Marshall* (1951) 37 Cal.2d 445, 457 [defrauded vendee], citing *Bancroft v. Woodward* (1920) 183 Cal. 99; *Walters v. Marler* (1978) 83 Cal.App.3d 1, 16 [breach of contract]. But "[t]he election of one remedy bars recovery under the other." (*Akin,* at p. 296, 44 Cal.Rptr.3d 284.)

. . . Rescission is intended to restore the parties as nearly as possible to their former positions and "to bring about substantial justice by adjusting the equities between the parties" despite the fact that "the status quo cannot be exactly reproduced." (*Sharabianlou, supra,* 181 Cal.App.4th at pp. 1144–1145.) "Rescission extinguishes the contract, terminates further liability, and restores the parties to their former positions by requiring them to return whatever consideration they have received. Thus, the '[r]elief given in rescission cases — restitution and in some cases consequential damages — puts the rescinding party in the *status quo ante,* returning him to his economic position before he entered the contract.'" (*Id.* at p. 1145.)

In rescission cases involving a real estate purchase, the seller must refund all payments received in connection with the sale. If the buyer has taken possession of the property, the buyer must restore possession to the seller. . . .

Whether to grant relief based on rescission "generally rests upon the sound discretion of the trial court exercised in accord with the facts and circumstances of the case [citations]." (*Hicks v. Clayton* (1977) 67 Cal.App.3d 251, 265; see also *Fairchild v. Raines* (1944) 24 Cal.2d 818, 826, ["the granting or withholding of equitable relief involves the exercise of judicial discretion"].) "However, that discretion is not an arbitrary one, but should be exercised in accord with the principles and precedents of equity jurisprudence." (*Hicks,* at p. 265.)

b. Analysis

. . . .

In deciding whether to effectuate the Wongs' rescission, the trial court's first task was to determine whether the Wongs' consent to the contract was given by mistake or obtained through fraud or undue influence. If it was, the court's duty was to effectuate the rescission and to otherwise award complete relief. The Wongs argue that the trial court was required as a matter of law to have found their rescission effective because it found that they were the victims of misrepresentations, and they contend the court erred in awarding the alternative equitable relief. . . .

We conclude that the trial court erred in declining to effectuate the Wongs' rescission and in basing its decision on the prejudice to the Stolers. . . .

We begin by rejecting the argument advanced by the Stolers that the Wongs' rescission could not have been effectuated by the trial court because the court did not find that the Stolers had engaged in actual fraud. Under California law, negligent misrepresentation is a species of actual fraud and a form of deceit. . . . Here, not only did the trial court find that the Stolers made misrepresentations, but it also found that these misrepresentations were made with reckless disregard. . . .

We also conclude that the trial court's determination was based on a flawed justification. The trial court declined to effectuate the rescission because of the prejudice *to the sellers* and the complications of unwinding the years-old real estate transaction. We conclude that the first reason — the Stolers' prejudice — was an improper consideration, and we are unconvinced that the second one — the complications of unwinding the deal — is supported by the record.

First, the trial court should not have so heavily relied on the potential harm rescission would cause the Stolers. "[W]here defendant has been guilty of fraudulent acts or conduct which have induced the agreement between him and the plaintiff, courts of equity are not so much concerned with decreeing that defendant receive back the identical property with which he parted in the transaction, as they are in declaring that his nefarious practices shall result in no damage to the plaintiff. Persons who attempt to secure profits by deceitful means may not confidently expect to receive special consideration from courts of equity. In such a case, as a result of the rescission by the court, *nothing is exacted from the plaintiff out of particular regard for the condition of the defendant.* If his fraudulent acts have resulted in disastrous financial consequences to himself, it is no one's fault but his own, and he must sustain the necessary inconveniences thereby entailed. Where it is possible to bring about substantial justice by adjusting the equities between the parties, the fact that the *status quo* cannot be exactly reproduced will not preclude the plaintiff from equitable relief. No matter what may be the complications or complexities, the powers of a court of equity are so broad as to adequately meet the exigencies of the case and render a decree which will justly determine the rights of the respective parties." (*Arthur v. Graham* (1923) 64 Cal.App. 608, 612, first italics added.)

Second, based on the record before us, the trial court appears to have been overly concerned with the complications of unwinding the transaction. We recognize that changes have been made to the property and years have transpired. But the changes in the property were commenced before the Wongs learned of the Stolers' misrepresentations, and much of the time that has elapsed has been due to the Stolers contesting the Wongs' rescission. As we discussed above, rescission involving a real estate purchase requires the seller to refund the payments received and requires the buyer to restore possession to the seller. (*Sharabianlou, supra,* 181 Cal.App.4th at pp. 1145–1146.) And consequential damages are allowed such as real estate commissions, escrow payments, interest on specific sums paid to the other party, and even the cost of improvements. Offsetting these amounts is the reasonable rental value of the property while the buyers possessed it. While untangling the deal may not be easy, we are unaware of any insurmountable obstacles.

Thus, we remand the case to the trial court to effectuate the Wongs' rescission and to consider additional relief as appropriate. . . .

IV.

Disposition

The judgment is reversed with directions for the trial court to take such action, including the taking of additional evidence if appropriate, and modify its findings, conclusions and judgment to conform to the views set forth in this opinion. The Wongs are entitled to their costs on appeal.

* * *

Problem 50

Rescission requires some basis for concluding that the contract in question does not reflect a true meeting of the minds and it would be unfair to enforce it. Would a court likely grant rescission in the case below?

Lauren inquires about purchasing a puppy from Darlene, a reputable breeder. Lauren tells Darlene that because she lives in an apartment, she needs a small breed puppy that will be no more than 10 pounds fully grown. Darlene says she has just the thing—a 12-week-old miniature "teacup" poodle, bred to be one of the smallest dogs around. Lauren agrees to buy the puppy, and the written contract states she is purchasing a teacup poodle for $2,500. As Lauren discovers a few months after bringing the dog home, however, it is not a miniature poodle at all—it is actually a full-size standard poodle, which will grow to 85 pounds. When Lauren informs Darlene about this, Darlene is shocked—she had mixed up the standard and miniature puppies when Lauren made her purchase and honestly believed she was sending Lauren home with a miniature. Darlene refuses to exchange the dog or refund the purchase price. Lauren sues to rescind the contract.

[handwritten margin notes: grounds -mutual mistake, notice/prej, offer to restore; recission is possible]

Introductory Note — *Hottinger v. Jensen*

In *Hottinger* it is the defendant who seeks reformation. The plaintiffs' deed indicates their property extends past the adjoining property's fence line; the adjoining property owners dispute that. The plaintiffs sued to quiet title and settle the boundary dispute. The defendant (the adjoining property owner) counter sued to reform the deed so the property description was consistent with what everyone had assumed for 20 years—that the boundary was the fence line. The basis for reformation asserted by the defendant is mutual mistake regarding where the property line falls.

THINGS TO THINK ABOUT while reading *Hottinger v. Jensen*:

1. What circumstances entitle a party to reformation of a contract?
2. Are the grounds for reformation different from those for rescission?
3. How did the court determine the intent of the parties in this case?

Hottinger v. Jensen

Utah Supreme Court
684 P.2d 1271 (1984)

HALL, Chief Justice:

Plaintiffs appeal the judgment of the district court that quieted title to the parcel of real property situated in Centerfield, Sanpete County, in defendant. No evidence was taken at trial, the parties having submitted the case for decision based upon stipulated facts.

In 1945 defendant and her late husband acquired approximately 15 acres of land. In 1958 they conveyed all of that land, except the parcel that comprised their home, yard and garden, to Ray and Georgia Jones with the mutual understanding and intent that the boundary line of the property to be conveyed was the existing fence and that it would divide their respective properties. However, as was determined 22 years later, the metes and bounds description in the deed of conveyance prepared by a third party did not follow the fence line but included a plot of approximately .78 acres to the north of the fence, which includes much of defendant's yard and garden spot. This acreage is the subject matter of this dispute.

A few years after the conveyance to the Joneses, they conveyed the property to N.E. Anglin, who in turn conveyed to D.A. Dove. All deeds used the same metes and bounds description as was contained in the original conveyance from defendant to the Joneses. However, it was stipulated that all of the parties understood and intended the fenceline to be the boundary between the two properties. In 1973 Dove conveyed the property to plaintiffs, utilizing the original metes and bounds description. The parties made clear on the record that there was no stipulation as to what representations Dove made to the plaintiffs concerning the boundary line. The plaintiffs, however, claim that no representations were made to them concerning the boundary line. In any event, plaintiffs treated the fenceline as the boundary until 1980. In 1980 plaintiffs had the property surveyed. The survey revealed that the deed description put the boundary some 90 feet north of the fence and within a few feet of defendant's house. Plaintiffs thereupon asserted ownership of the property as described by the deed, tore down the existing fence and erected a fence at the claimed boundary. Defendant objected, whereupon plaintiffs brought suit to quiet title in plaintiffs to the disputed property. Defendant counterclaimed asking reformation of the deed to conform to the previously understood boundary.

The trial court awarded the disputed property to defendant. The court found that plaintiffs' predecessors all understood the fenceline to be the boundary between the two properties and treated it as such, that defendant had been in continuous possession of the disputed land, using it for lawn and garden purposes since 1958, and that plaintiffs obtained their property recognizing the fenceline as the boundary. The court concluded that under those circumstances it would be inequitable to allow the plaintiffs to now claim the disputed property. On appeal, both parties argue boundary by acquiescence. The trial judge in his findings of fact and conclusions of law nowhere mentions boundary by acquiescence and does not address the elements of such. Rather, the trial judge recited that this proceeding was one in equity and, in effect, ordered reformation of the deed to quiet title to the disputed property in defendant.

Reformation of a deed is a proceeding in equity and is appropriate where the terms of the written instrument are mistaken in that they do not show the true intent of the agreement between the parties. There are two grounds for reformation of such an agreement: mutual mistake of the parties and ignorance or mistake by one party, coupled with fraud by the other party.

This case is a clear case of mutual mistake by the parties. The defendant and all subsequent purchasers except plaintiffs agreed that the understanding and the intent of the parties to the various deeds was that the fenceline be the boundary. It was only due to a mistake made by the drafter of the deed as to the metes and bounds description that the deed did not conform to the intent of the parties. Reformation is clearly appropriate where there is a variance between the written deed and the true agreement of the parties caused by a draftsman. However, the right of reformation of a deed can be cut off by purchase of the property by a bona fide purchaser for value without notice of the mistake.

There is no question that the plaintiffs were purchasers for value. Plaintiffs also contend that they took the deed without notice of any mistake. The trial judge, however, found that the plaintiffs purchased their property recognizing the fenceline as the boundary. Although this Court in equity cases can conduct its own review of the facts, we see no reason to disturb the findings of the court below.

The one fact that was not stipulated to below and was thus in dispute was what representations were made to plaintiffs upon purchase and what plaintiffs knew to be the boundary line. The remaining facts all indicate that plaintiffs recognized the fence as the boundary: they treated the fence as the boundary line for 7 years, and the defendant used the disputed property continuously for lawn and garden. It was only after a survey disclosed the mistake that plaintiffs asserted ownership. It could thus be contended that plaintiffs had actual notice of the intent of the original grantor and subsequent grantors. Furthermore, there is little doubt that the plaintiffs had constructive notice of that intent. It is a well-established principle of law that where circumstances are such that a reasonably prudent person should make inquiries, the law charges the person with notice of facts which a reasonably diligent inquiry would have disclosed. Possession and obvious use of the property by defendant prior to and subsequent to plaintiffs' purchase, coupled with the existing fence, should have put plaintiffs on notice of defendant's claim. A simple query to either defendant or to plaintiffs' grantor would have established the intent of the parties.

The judgment of the trial court is therefore affirmed.

* * *

Problem 51

Reformation is helpful to a plaintiff who wants a contract enforced but with modified terms; rescission will assist a plaintiff who does not want the contract enforced at all. Should the lawyer in the following situation advise her client to seek reformation or rescission?

Sandra is a business executive hired by a large corporation to be its Chief Operating Officer. Before she accepted the company's offer, Sandra received several other employment offers; she ultimately chose this one, however, because it included a grant of stock options at the end of each year and the others did not. Sandra and the company sign an employment contract that provides for a 5-year term and specifies her compensation during that period. Unfortunately, because of a drafting error, the written contract neglects to mention the stock option grants. Sandra does not notice the error until the end of her first year of employment. Since both parties intended for the agreement to include stock options, Sandra asks the company to sign an addendum to the contract providing for them. The company refuses. Sandra calls her lawyer.

reformation
- change to reflect the parties true intention
- terms understood by the π at the time of formation
- achieve fairness
- not fundamentally change the nature of the K

Replevin

Replevin is a form of specific relief available when a defendant is wrongfully in possession of personal property that belongs to the plaintiff. A plaintiff who wants the item of property back, rather than monetary damages for the tort of conversion, can seek replevin. Replevin is an order requiring the defendant to deliver the property back to the plaintiff, or a judgment decreeing that the plaintiff is entitled to possession.

The showing required for replevin is straightforward. The plaintiff must prove a right to possess the item that is superior to any right the defendant has and must prove the defendant is currently in possession of the property.

Characterizing replevin as legal or equitable is more complicated. It is treated as equitable here since that is a more straightforward way to think about it — as an equitable order requiring the defendant to give the property to the plaintiff. But replevin can also be in the nature of a legal remedy: a judgment of possession that is not enforceable *in personam* but rather gives the plaintiff the right to have the property seized through executing the judgment.

Since personal property can be moved or destroyed before a trial can be held, a plaintiff seeking replevin will often request a prejudgment order of replevin. If a court grants that relief, the defendant will be ordered to return the property to the plaintiff before a final determination on the merits. Prejudgment replevin orders raise significant due process issues because property is taken from the defendant before a full adjudication of the case.

To comport with due process, any prejudgment replevin order must provide some protection for the defendant in the event it is ultimately determined that the plaintiff is not entitled to the property. The typical method is to require the plaintiff to post a bond with the court (a sum of money equal to the value of the property that is the subject of the order). If it is ultimately determined the plaintiff has no right to the property, the defendant is entitled to collect the bond.

Introductory Note — *Palmer v. King* and *Doughty v. Sullivan*

When a plaintiff prevails in an action for replevin and the defendant does not voluntarily turn over the property, what then? In *Palmer*, the local law enforcement agency sent an officer to the defendant's home; the officer found an unlocked window and went through it to seize the property. Did the officer exceed his authority? That is the issue decided by the D.C. Court of Appeals.

In *Doughty*, the trial court awarded the plaintiff possession of a boat that had several previous owners and was currently stored in the defendant's yard. In resolving the defendant's appeal, the Maine Supreme Court traces the history of the state's replevin procedure before determining whether that procedure was properly invoked in this case.

THINGS TO THINK ABOUT while reading *Palmer v. King* and *Doughty v. Sullivan*:

1. How is the remedy of replevin enforced?

2. How do the available procedural protections mitigate the due process concerns posed by a prejudgment writ of replevin?

Palmer v. King

District of Columbia Court of Appeals
41 App. D.C. 419 (1914)

Mr. Justice VAN ORSDEL delivered the opinion of the Court:

The sole question presented by the appeal is whether or not the deputy marshal exceeded his authority in forcing an entrance through the open window, in spite of plaintiff's resistance, in order to execute the writ of replevin? That an assault was committed is settled by the verdict of the jury. It must be conceded that the deputy had no right, even in his official capacity, to commit an assault upon plaintiff, unless it appears that he had a legal right to force his way through the open window in disregard of her opposition, when, if she sustained injuries, it would be her misfortune, and not the wrong of the officer. The question presented does not involve the right of an officer to enter a dwelling through an open window where there is no resistance offered, and where the entrance involves no element of force. The suit is not for trespass *quare clausum fregit*, but for trespass upon the person of the plaintiff.

Since we have no statute defining the powers of officers in executing a writ of replevin, the common law furnishes the rule of procedure in this District. At common-law, as to the right of an officer to enter a dwelling in the service of civil process, no distinction seems to exist between entrance by outer windows and outer doors. In other words, it is not important that the entrance here was accomplished through an open window, if, under the same circumstances, it could have been accomplished lawfully through the door.

Counsel for defendants insist that the writ of replevin is an exception to the law generally applicable to the execution of civil process. It is urged that, where a specific chattel is to be recovered, the officer is not obliged to respect the peace and protection which the law secures to the householder. In a few instances, where this distinction has apparently been recognized, writs for the seizure of a specific chattel have been confused with writs of seizin or *habere facias possessionem* for the recovery of specific real property. In *Semayne's Case*, 5 Coke, 91; 1 Smith, Lead. Cas. 238, it is pointed out that, in respect of the execution of such writs against real property, there has been an adjudication adverse to the title of the holder, and the law no longer accords him any special privilege or security in it. "After judgment it is not the house in right and judgment of law of the tenant or defendant."

The authorities generally, with relation to the powers conferred at common law upon an officer in execution of the writ of replevin, go back to the resolutions in *Semayne's Case*. The following quotation from what was there decided is important: "But it was resolved, that it is not lawful for the sheriff (on request made and denial), at the suit of a common person, to break the defendant's house, sc. to execute any process at the suit of any subject; for thence would follow great inconvenience, that men as well in the night as in day should have their houses (which are their castles) broke, by color whereof great damage and mischief might ensue; for by color thereof, on any feigned suit, the house of any man, at any time, might be broke when *** [he] might be arrested elsewhere, and so men would not be in safety or quiet in their own houses. *** 5. It was resolved, that the house of any one is not a castle or privilege but for himself, and shall not extend to protect any person who flies to his house, or the goods of any other which are brought and conveyed into his house to prevent a lawful execution, and to escape the ordinary process of law; for the privilege of his house extends only to him and his family, and to his own proper goods, or to those which are lawfully and without fraud and covin there; and therefore in such cases, after denial or request made, the sheriff may break the house; and that is proved by the statute of Westm. 1, chap. 17, by which it is declared that the sheriff may break a house or castle to make replevin, when the goods of another which he has distrained are by him [*i. e.*, the distrainer] conveyed to his house or castle, to prevent the owner to have a replevin of his goods; which act is but an affirmance of the common law in such points. But it appears there, that before the sheriff in such case breaks the house, he ought to demand the goods to be delivered to him: for the words of the statute are, after that the cattle shall be solemnly demanded by the sheriffs, etc."

This makes no exception of the writ of replevin. It expressly holds that an officer is not justified in breaking into a dwelling to seize the property of the owner upon civil process. The exception pointed out is where the goods of another than the householder are brought into his house to prevent lawful execution and to escape process of the law. In such case the process is not against the owner of the dwelling, and the privilege and security which extend to him and his family are not invaded by the breaking, after a solemn demand for admission has been made by the officer. . . .

The rule of the common law, as deduced from the cases, seems to be that an officer, in executing a writ of replevin, may not break an outer door or window of a dwelling to gain entrance to seize the property of the occupant or of a person rightfully domiciled therein. He may enter either an open outer door or window, provided it can be accomplished without committing a breach of the peace; he may then, after a request and refusal, break open any inner doors belonging to the defendant, in order to take the goods. 3 Bl. Com. 417; *Semayne's Case*, 5 Coke, 91, 1 Smith, Lead Cas. 238. We think a further reasonable rule is deducible from the cases, that when an officer, in the execution of a writ, finds an outer door or window slightly ajar, but not sufficiently so to admit him, he may open the door or window, provided he does not find it obstructed, but if it is fastened or obstructed so as to require force to overcome the obstruction, he may not use such force, for such an entrance would constitute a breaking. . . .

But it is sought by counsel for defendants to make a distinction between breaking and forcible entry. It is urged that, inasmuch as the officer found the window open, and, in order to enter through the open window, only used sufficient force to overcome the resistance of plaintiff, it cannot be denominated a breaking. We are not impressed by this contention. The deputy, in order to enter, was compelled to commit a breach of the peace, and this was forbidden at common law. We are not disposed to make any distinction between a case where an officer finds a door or window slightly ajar, but obstructed; and where he finds it open, but the entrance obstructed by the lawful occupant of the dwelling, or otherwise, so as to require the exercise of force to overcome the obstruction. . . .

The judgment is affirmed, with costs.

* * *

Doughty v. Sullivan

Maine Supreme Court
661 A.2d 1112 (1995)

LIPEZ, Justice.

Ethelyn Sullivan (Ethelyn) appeals from the judgment entered in the Superior Court (Cumberland County, *Brennan, J.*) affirming the judgment entered in the District Court (Portland, *Rogers, J.*) in favor of Cecil Amos Doughty (Amos) on his complaint requesting a writ of replevin and damages for Ethelyn's wrongful conversion of an 18-foot Pointer boat which Amos allegedly purchased from Neil Doughty (Neil). Ethelyn also appeals from a judgment entered in Neil's favor on her third-party complaint alleging that Neil owed her $1,000. We vacate both judgments.

Background

The record reveals that Bernard Doughty loaned his son, Neil, $1,000 to enable Neil to purchase an 18-foot Pointer boat. To evidence the loan, Neil gave his father a signed "receipt" which stated, "Received from Bernard Doughty $1,000 for one 18-foot Pointer and 45 H.P. motor." Neil Doughty signed this receipt. Bernard believed the receipt gave him a security interest in the boat. Neil testified that he did not intend to give his father a security interest in the boat. He simply wanted his father to have the boat if something happened to him while he was at sea.

Neil stored the boat during the winter of 1989–1990 in the yard of John and Ethelyn Sullivan, his sister. Although Neil used the boat a few times, during the summer of 1990, seawater disabled the engine and Neil left the boat on its mooring in Chandler's Cove. According to John Sullivan, he towed the boat from Chandler's Cove to Bennett's Beach in early October 1990 where he left the boat on the beach for a couple of weeks. Bernard testified that he instructed John to haul the boat back to the Sullivans' yard because he was concerned that the boat would be destroyed over the winter unless it was removed from the beach. Sullivan and a friend testified that they hauled the boat to the Sullivan's yard in late October or early November. Bernard believed that he had a right to repossess the boat because Neil had not yet repaid the loan. On November 19, 1990, Bernard signed a document which stated: "As of this date I transfer my ownership and claim to the note for $1000.00 from Neil Doughty, for the boat (18′ Pointer) and 45 HP Chrysler motor as yet unpaid to Ethelyn L. Sullivan." The document was witnessed and signed by a family friend.

During this same time period, Neil accepted an offer by Amos to buy the boat for $500. On November 21, 1990, Amos gave Neil a check for $500 which Neil cashed that same day. Both Neil and Amos testified that, contrary to the Sullivans' contentions, the boat was still lying on the beach when the sale occurred. Neil could not recall how the boat got from the mooring in Chandler's Cove to Bennett's Beach. Amos testified that he had no idea that someone else claimed an interest in the boat. Sometime after Neil sold the boat to Amos, Amos discovered that the boat was in the Sullivans' yard and he asked Ethelyn to return it to him as he was now the owner. Ethelyn refused, asserting that Bernard owned the boat.

In December 1990, Amos decided that he could not engage in commercial lobstering during 1991 because Ethelyn would not return the boat that he had intended to use. Amos did not attempt to replace the boat until 1992, when he purchased another boat for $1,000.

Amos filed a complaint on July 6, 1992 against Ethelyn, alleging that she had wrongfully converted the boat after he purchased the boat from Neil. Amos sought a writ of replevin pursuant to 14 M.R.S.A. §§ 7301–7312 (1980) to obtain possession of the boat and damages for Ethelyn's wrongful conversion. As a part of his damages claim, Amos sought lost profits that he sustained when he was unable to use the boat during the 1991 lobster season. At trial, it was stipulated that Amos earned $3,830 from lobster fishing in 1992. Amos also sought reimbursement for the boat he purchased in 1992 to replace the boat converted by Ethelyn. In total, Amos claimed damages in excess of $8,500. At the time he filed his complaint, Amos did not attach a bond or an affidavit to support his request for a writ of replevin. . . .

Prior to the trial, Ethelyn filed a motion to dismiss Amos's complaint for failure to file the pleadings required by M.R.Civ.P. 64 to obtain a pre-judgment writ of replevin. Ethelyn contended that 14 M.R.S.A. §§ 7301–7312 and M.R.Civ.P. 64 provided a writ of replevin as a pre-judgment remedy only. Amos attempted to cure his failure to conform to M.R.Civ.P. 64 by filing a motion for a writ of replevin and a personal bond for $1,000 and an affidavit before trial.

After a trial, the District Court concluded that it had subject matter jurisdiction pursuant to 14 M.R.S.A. §§ 7301–7312 (1980), and that Amos was entitled to seek a post-judgment writ of replevin without first seeking a pre-judgment writ of replevin. . . .

Jurisdiction to Issue a Post-Judgment Order of Replevin

Ethelyn first contends that because Amos had failed to replevy the boat before the action was tried, the District Court erroneously concluded that it had jurisdiction pursuant to 14 M.R.S.A. §§ 7301–7312 to issue a writ of replevin after a judgment had been entered. According to Ethelyn, the statute provides a pre-judgment remedy only. Ethelyn further contends that even if Amos was permitted to cure his failure to request a pre-judgment writ of replevin, Amos still did not provide a bond "with sufficient sureties." *Ford New Holland, Inc. v. Thompson Machine, Inc.,* 617 A.2d 540 (Me.1992) (holding personal bond insufficient to satisfy statute). Hence, the District Court was without subject matter jurisdiction to hear Amos's action in replevin.

Amos responds that the bond requirement is intended merely to provide security to the defendant in a replevin action when the plaintiff seeks a pre-judgment writ of replevin. Because he was willing to wait until after a judgment was entered before he obtained possession of the boat, Amos argues that requiring him to post a bond is superfluous. According to Amos, the filing of a complaint confers jurisdiction on the District Court to hear an action in replevin pursuant to 14 M.R.S.A. § 7301, rather than the filing of a pre-judgment writ of replevin. After a careful review of the laws of other states and our own statute, we conclude that 14 M.R.S.A. §§ 7301–7312 confers jurisdiction on the District Court to hear an action in replevin only if the plaintiff has already replevied the property through the issuance of a pre-judgment writ of replevin.

Replevin is one of the oldest legal remedies available under the common law. Historically, replevin lay to recover immediate possession of a specific chattel as compared with other common law actions for trespass or conversion which lay to recover damages for the wrongful taking of a chattel. Cobbey, *A Practical Treatise on the Law of Replevin,* § 17 (2d ed. 1900). Replevin sought only to establish the right to possession and not the right to legal title. The common law action of replevin could be commenced only by the issuance of a writ of replevin and seizure of the property which was deemed necessary for the court to obtain jurisdiction over the action. *Hart v. Moulton,* 104 Wis. 349 (1899).

The plaintiff would apply for a writ of replevin from the court by supplying an affidavit alleging the right to immediate possession of the goods currently in the wrongful possession of a third party. If the affidavit satisfied the common law formalities, the court would issue the writ directing the sheriff to seize the chattel and to deliver the same to the plaintiff. Before the sheriff could serve the writ and seize the property, however, he had to obtain a bond from the plaintiff for twice the value of the goods sought to be replevied. Upon receiving possession, the plaintiff would bring the action in replevin seeking a judicial determination of his right to possession and any damages incurred by the defendant's wrongful retention of the chattel. Hence, replevin was a unique common law action that entitled a plaintiff to a pre-judgment seizure of the chattel, leaving the merits of the plaintiff's claim of right to be tried later.

In some states the common law replevin action was eventually subsumed by a broader statutory action, commonly called an action to recover a chattel, in which a writ of replevin is but one remedy available to the plaintiff and not essential to commencing the action. In these states, therefore, replevin is no longer a distinct cause of action and the writ of replevin has become an appendage to another action. . . .

In Maine, replevin has been a statutory remedy at law since the replevin statute was first enacted in 1821 and copied from the Massachusetts replevin statute enacted in 1789. *Seaver v. Dingley,* 4 Me. (Greenl.) 306, 315–16 (1826). 14 M.R.S.A. § 7301 (1980) provides in pertinent part:

> When goods unlawfully taken or detained from the owner or person entitled to the possession thereof, or attached on mesne process, or taken on execution, are claimed by any person other than the defendant in the action in which they are so attached or taken, such owner or person may cause them to be replevied.

Maine's replevin statute further provides that before the officer may serve the writ, the plaintiff must provide a bond "with sufficient sureties" made out to the defendant for twice the value of the goods sought to be replevied. § 7303. If the plaintiff prevails in his action, "the plaintiff shall have judgment for his damages caused thereby and for his costs." § 7308. If the plaintiff does not prevail, section 7304 provides that "the defendant is entitled to a return of the goods, [and] he shall have judgment and a writ of return accordingly, with damages for the taking and costs." If the sheriff is unable to serve the writ of return, the court may grant a writ of reprisal by which the sheriff seizes plaintiff's personal property to cover the non-returned goods until the plaintiff restores the property which he replevied. § 7310. In the alternative, the defendant may resort to the replevin bond supplied by the plaintiff to recover the value of the goods replevied and any damages incurred from the plaintiff's wrongful retention. § 7311. Finally, an action for replevin may be heard in the District Court if the value of the goods does not exceed $30,000. 14 M.R.S.A. § 7302 (1980), 4 M.R.S.A. § 152(2) (1989).

There is no statutory language suggesting that a writ of replevin is merely ancillary to the underlying replevin action. Nor is there any provision that permits the plaintiff to forgo obtaining possession of the chattel until after a judgment on his action. Indeed, all of the provisions presuppose that the property has in fact been replevied before trial. As the Minnesota Supreme Court noted, in interpreting a statutory provision similar to section 7308 in our replevin statute:

> Why only give [the plaintiff] damages for the detention of his goods, unless they were in fact replevied or delivered to him? Surely if they remained at the trial, with the defendant, or if he had destroyed or converted them, the plaintiff would be entitled to the value of the goods, as well as damages for their detention. The statute has, therefore, made no provision for the trial of actions in replevin, before justices, until the property is found and replevied.

St. Martin v. Desnoyer, 1 Minn. (1 Gil.) 25, 29 (1858).

We also note that our civil rules of procedure contemplate that a replevin action be commenced by applying for a writ of replevin. M.R.Civ.P. 64(c) provides that "a replevin action may be commenced *only* by filing a complaint with the court, together with a motion for approval of the writ of replevin and the amount of the replevin bond."

In summary, our replevin statute does not authorize the court to issue a post-judgment writ of replevin. The writ of replevin referred to in 14 M.R.S.A. §§ 7301–7312 and Rule 64 is a pre-judgment remedy only. The replevin statute does not confer jurisdiction on a court to adjudicate a claim of possession pursuant to the replevin statute until the procedural requirements have been satisfied. If, on the other hand, the plaintiff seizes the property pursuant to a writ of replevin and has provided the appropriate bond to the defendant, the court has jurisdiction pursuant to the replevin statute to determine who is the rightful possessor and to award damages resulting from the wrongful detention of the chattel.

Turning to the facts in the present case, Amos did not file a motion for approval of a writ of replevin, nor did he file the required affidavits alleging his immediate right to possession or a bond for twice the value of the boat, at the time he filed his complaint. Without Amos's affidavit or bond, the District Court had no jurisdiction to issue a writ of replevin to restore the boat to Amos's possession as requested in Amos's complaint. Moreover, because no writ was issued and because the boat was not replevied, the court had no jurisdiction to finally adjudicate which party had the right to possess the boat pursuant to 14 M.R.S.A. § 7301.

. . . Accordingly, we vacate the decision of the District Court[.]

* * *

Problem 52

Replevin awards possession of an item to the person with a superior right to possess it. Is the property described below an appropriate target for replevin?

Lawrence dies at 97, with a simple will that leaves all his major assets — house, car, and bank accounts — to his two sons, divided roughly equally. Not listed in the will, however, is Lawrence's prized coin collection. A statute provides that any property not accounted for by the will must be distributed according to the discretion of the executor of the estate appointed by the court. No executor has yet been appointed for Lawrence's estate. The younger son claims the coin collection belongs to him because it is at his house, where Lawrence stored it. The older son believes it belongs to *him*, because Lawrence often told him, "When I die, this collection is yours." One night, the older son sneaks into his brother's basement through an unlocked door and takes the coin collection. The younger son responds by filing an action for replevin.

— unable to show who has superior right to prop.

Ejectment

A plaintiff entitled to possession of real property that is wrongfully occupied by someone else can seek an order of ejectment. It is essentially what it sounds like. It restores exclusive possession of property to the plaintiff by ordering the defendant to leave. The plaintiff need only show a right of possession that is superior to that of the defendant's.

Ejectment might be a logical precursor to an award of damages for the harm resulting from an ongoing trespass.

The common law remedy of ejectment should not be confused with the statutory procedure of unlawful detainer, available in many jurisdictions to evict a tenant no longer entitled to possession. Unlawful detainer is a unique procedure with many of its own statutory requirements.

Introductory Note — *Patel Taherbhai, Inc. v. Broad Street Stockbridge II, LLC*

In *Patel*, the owner of a Taco Bell restaurant made some alterations to an intersection near the parking lot to accommodate its drive through. However, the alterations encroached on an easement that allowed access to the property. The owner of the land benefited by the easement brought an action for ejectment, reasoning that with that remedy the court ought to be able to order the defendant to remove the encroaching alterations. The Georgia Court of Appeals must decide whether that is an appropriate use of ejectment.

THINGS TO THINK ABOUT while reading *Patel Taherbhai, Inc. v. Broad Street Stockbridge II, LLC*:

1. What are the elements of an ejectment cause of action?

2. What, or who, can be ejected?

3. In what kind of situations would ejectment be useful?

Patel Taherbhai, Inc. v. Broad Street Stockbridge II, LLC

Georgia Court of Appeals
352 Ga.App. 113 (2019)

Brown, Judge.

Patel Taherbhai, Inc. ("Patel") appeals from the trial court's denial of its motion for summary judgment and motion to dismiss, and the grant of partial summary judgment to Broad Street Stockbridge II, LLC ("Broad Street"), in Broad Street's suit against Patel for ejectment and injunctive relief. The suit claims that Patel constructed certain encroachments on an access easement granted to Broad Street over Patel's property and that the encroachments are unsafe and diminish the value of Broad Street's property for development.

. . . Broad Street is the owner of a 22.078 acre tract of undeveloped land located in Henry County off of Hudson Bridge Road. Patel is the owner of a 1.261 acre adjacent tract of land on which sits a Taco Bell restaurant. On July 31, 2001, the parties' predecessors-in-interest entered into a Reciprocal Easement Agreement. Baptist Retirement Communities of Georgia, Inc., is the predecessor-in-title to Broad Street, and Kandathil M. Matthew is the predecessor-in-title to Patel. On April 26, 2004, Matthew and Baptist Retirement executed a First Amendment to Reciprocal Easement Agreement, which granted to Baptist the following access easement:

A perpetual, non-exclusive and unobstructed access, ingress and egress easement over, across, upon and through those portions of the Matthew Property delineated as the "Access Easement" on Exhibit "E[,]" for the purpose of vehicular and pedestrian access, ingress and egress to and from Hudson Bridge Road and for the purpose of installing, maintaining, repairing, replacing and utilizing the curb cuts, driveways and related amenities necessary to the improvement and modification of the Access Road shown on Exhibit "E[.]"

The "Access Road" or Hudson Bridge Drive, is a private road, designed and constructed by Baptist Retirement to provide access to its property from Hudson Bridge Road. The road extends across Patel's lot.

After purchasing its property in 2007, Patel completed construction of its Taco Bell restaurant and received a certificate of occupancy from Henry County on January 10, 2008. As part of the construction process, Patel altered the four-way intersection which is situated on the access easement and leads into the Taco Bell and Broad Street's property, so that larger vehicles could enter the Taco Bell parking lot and drive-thru line. Patel also modified the Taco Bell parking lot, including adding five parking spots that extended into the access easement. Two years after the Taco Bell was constructed, Broad Street purchased its tract of land.

Almost five years after it received its certificate of occupancy, Patel's CEO, Munir Taherbhai, received a call from Broad Street's owner, Stephen Rainer, complaining about the parking lot and intersection. According to Taherbhai, he attempted to negotiate amicably with Rainer, but those negotiations fell apart when Rainer proposed certain modifications that Taherbhai believed "create[d] real safety issue[s]." Those modifications included turning the Taco Bell exit into a "right turn" only and narrowing the lane used to exit the Taco Bell. At one point during their discussions, and based upon pictures of the easement shown to him by Rainer, Taherbhai said to Rainer, "'Yes, there are some parking spots that are in the way [of the easement].'"

After the parties were unable to resolve their dispute, Broad Street filed this action on November 25, 2015, claiming that the "encroachments" create a safety hazard, violate the clear terms of the access easement, and diminish the value of its property. Broad Street sought an injunction ordering Patel to remove the encroachments, and ejectment on the ground that Patel "is unlawfully attempting to exercise possession and dominion over [Broad Street's] Property . . . [and] has refused to vacate and surrender possession of [Broad Street's] Property and to remove Encroachments[.]" . . .

In its first enumeration of error, Patel contends that the trial court erred in granting Broad Street's motion for partial summary judgment because an action in ejectment will not lie to recover an easement. We agree.

"An easement has been defined as 'a right in the owner of one parcel of land, by reason of such ownership, to use the land of another for a special purpose not inconsistent with the general property in the owner.'" Daniel F. Hinkel, Pindar's Ga. Real Estate Law and Procedure, § 8-1 (7th ed., updated April 2019). An easement "is an interest in land owned and possessed by another" and "is classified as an incorporeal interest because it carries with it no appreciable degree of dominion over the land itself." Id. at § 8-1. "The land used by or 'serving' the grantee of the easement is known as the servient tenement; the land served by or benefitting from the easement is known as the dominant tenement." Id. at § 8-2. In this case, Patel's land is the servient tenement and Broad Street's land is the dominant tenement.

. . . Our Supreme Court has explained that the purpose of an action for ejectment "is to evict one from realty who wrongfully withholds possession from the person legally entitled thereto [and that] [e]jectment must be commenced against the person in possession." *Douglas v. Vourtsanis*, 203 Ga. 64, 66 (2) (1947). But, in *Stewart v. Garrett*, 119 Ga. 386, 388 (1904), the Supreme Court stated in a burial plot case that an action for ejectment will not lie for "such an easement or license." Id. See *McDonald v. Butler*, 10 Ga. App. 845, 850 (3) (1912). See also *Bale v. Todd*, 123 Ga. 99, 103 (5) (1905) ("[t]he proper remedy for the injury or disturbance of an easement is an action on the case, and not trespass or ejectment") (citation and punctuation omitted); Pindar's at § 23:27 ("[o]wnership of a mere easement in land does not entitle a plaintiff to maintain an ejectment").

What is required to sustain an action for ejectment is well illustrated by the case of *Ezzard v. Findley Gold Mining Co.*, 74 Ga. 520 (1885). In that case, the owner of land had erected a dam across a stream on his own land, causing water to overflow onto an adjoining owner's land. The adjoining owner brought an action for ejectment against the owner of the dam, and the Supreme Court of Georgia held that his remedy was not ejectment, but rather, an action for damages. . . .

[A]n action for ejectment only lies for something tangible, something of which possession may be delivered by the sheriff to the plaintiff. Where a party's enjoyment of its easement is disrupted or obstructed, the remedy is an action for damages or injunction. See *Bale*, 123 Ga. at 103 (5), 50 S.E. 990. [H]ere, an action for ejectment cannot lie because Broad Street is still in exclusive possession of every foot of land that it owns and its possession is not disrupted in the slightest. Indeed, if the sheriff were to go "restore [Broad Street's] possession, he would [find it] already in possession." This conclusion conforms with the rule that an action for ejectment will not lie for a mere easement. It follows, therefore, that the trial court erred in ejecting Patel from encroaching on the access easement, and in granting Broad Street's motion for summary judgment on the ground that it is entitled to the remedy of ejectment. Accordingly, the grant of summary judgment to Broad Street on its claim for ejectment is reversed.

Judgment reversed in part and vacated in part, and case remanded with direction.

* * *

Problem 53

Ejectment removes a trespasser in order to restore exclusive possession of the land to the owner or person with superior right to possess. Is ejectment an appropriate remedy in the following case?

Shannon owns a strip of land on the beach. It has been in her family for generations. The land is barely accessible. The only way to get to it is by helicopter or by hiking 16 miles through lava rock. Because of the access difficulties, Shannon has not been to the property for years. When she finally does make it out one day, she is distressed to find that a squatter has recently taken up residence in the small bungalow there. No one is present when she arrives, but a review of security camera footage shows the trespasser first got there about six months ago; came and went for several weeks; and was last present about two weeks ago. By talking with some locals who live nearby, Shannon finds out the trespasser's name. Wanting to ensure her right to exclusive possession of her property, Shannon files suit against the trespasser and seeks an order of ejectment.

Chapter 11

Equitable Defenses

Equitable remedies, at least traditionally, are available only when a legal remedy would be inadequate. In that way, equitable remedies fill a void that would otherwise impede a court's ability to provide complete justice. Equitable remedies make it easier for the court to do what is fair under the circumstances.

The same is true for equitable defenses. Since by awarding an equitable remedy the court reaches beyond the default legal remedy, it makes sense that the defendant likewise be allowed to rely on defenses that are not necessarily available to a claim for legal relief—defenses designed to promote fairness. Such equitable defenses correspond only to equitable claims for relief raised by the plaintiff; they will not necessarily bar the entire lawsuit. A plaintiff who is prevented from obtaining an equitable remedy because the defendant has successfully raised an equitable defense can still recover on a claim seeking a legal remedy.

Equitable defenses are affirmative defenses. They require that the defendant plead and prove certain elements, much like a plaintiff must plead and prove the elements of a cause of action. For affirmative defenses, the burden of proof shifts to the defendant, who must prove the elements of the defense being asserted in order to bar the plaintiff's equitable claim.

This chapter examines two defenses that can be raised in response to a plaintiff's claim for equitable relief: laches and unclean hands.

Laches

Laches (from the French "laschesse," meaning to be remiss or dilatory) is a time limitation for bringing a lawsuit. It is similar to a statute of limitation, which is a law that imposes a specific amount of time (often two or three years) from the date of an injury for the injured party to file a lawsuit. If suit is filed beyond the time frame allowed by the statute, the plaintiff cannot prevail regardless of the merits of the claim.

Laches differs from statutes of limitation, however, in that it is a defense based not on a predetermined time limit but on fairness. While a statute of limitation defense is concerned solely with how much time has passed since the plaintiff discovered the injury that prompted the lawsuit, laches is concerned with the effect the passage of time has on the defendant.

If an unreasonable amount of time has passed since the infliction of the harm the plaintiff complains of, and the passage of time has prejudiced the defendant — put him or her at a disadvantage in the litigation or created an economic loss — the defendant can successfully assert the affirmative defense of laches. Since the burden of proof for an affirmative defense is with the defendant, the defendant must prove that the plaintiff's delay in filing is unreasonable and that it resulted in prejudice.

Laches is fact intensive. It requires the court to scrutinize the reason for the delay in filing and its effect on the defendant, with an eye toward determining whether fairness dictates that the plaintiff should be barred from pursuing an equitable remedy.

Introductory Note — *Smith v. Caterpillar, Inc.* and *Perry v. Judd*

The lawsuit in *Smith* is an employment dispute. The plaintiff employee did not file suit until about eight years after the alleged misconduct. The employer asserts a laches defense and the trial court — after giving the employer several opportunities to articulate how it was prejudiced — grants a defense summary judgment motion. On the plaintiff's appeal, the appellate court examines the evidence of prejudice being claimed by the defendant to determine if it establishes laches (or, more precisely, whether the trial court abused its discretion in deciding it did).

Perry is an election case, with a familiar cast of political characters. The issue is whether the plaintiffs — candidates for the 2012 Republican presidential nomination — waited too long to file their lawsuit. The plaintiffs seek the equitable relief of a mandatory injunction requiring the state of Virginia to list their names on the ballot. Timing is critical in this kind of case, for a very practical reason: the ballots have to be printed before election day comes.

THINGS TO THINK ABOUT while reading *Smith v. Caterpillar, Inc.* and *Perry v. Judd*:

1. What are the elements of a laches defense?

2. What constitutes "prejudice" for purposes of laches?

3. How was prejudice established in this case?

Smith v. Caterpillar, Inc.

United States Court of Appeals, Seventh Circuit
338 F.3d 730 (2003)

FLAUM, Chief Judge.

In August 1999 Rebecca Smith charged her former employer, Caterpillar, Inc., with gender discrimination and retaliation in violation of Title VII, 42 U.S.C. § 2000e *et seq.* Smith's allegations arise from conduct that occurred in 1991 during her 60-day probationary employment with Caterpillar as a fire inspector trainee. After twice denying Caterpillar's motion for summary judgment, the district court granted its motion for reconsideration, finding that Caterpillar had presented a valid laches defense to Smith's charges. Smith moved for reconsideration, was denied, and now appeals. We affirm.

I. Background

Rebecca Smith began working as a fire inspector at Caterpillar's East Peoria, Illinois, facility on January 6, 1991. Under the applicable collective bargaining agreement, the first 60 days of her employment were probationary. During this time Smith received training and supervision from a number of the company's more experienced fire inspectors. On two different occasions during her probationary period Smith's training coordinator, Gary Shilling, evaluated her performance and reported deficiencies to the department's chief inspector, Ralph Allsop. After 60 days, on March 7, 1991, Allsop fired Smith for unsatisfactory performance. Caterpillar's East Peoria Facility personnel services director, Robert Buchanan, approved Smith's termination.

On March 20, 1991, Smith filed gender discrimination charges with the Illinois Department of Human Rights ("IDHR"), which were cross-filed with the Equal Employment Opportunity Commission ("EEOC"). Instead of seeking a right-to-sue letter from the EEOC, which Smith could have requested from the federal agency 180 days after filing her charges, Smith chose instead to pursue her claims through the Illinois state administrative process. IDHR investigated Smith's charges and twice issued findings of lack of substantial evidence for her gender discrimination and sexual harassment claims. Smith sought review of IDHR's findings with the Illinois Human Rights Commission ("IHRC"), and IDHR ultimately issued findings of substantial evidence for Smith's charges on August 16, 1996. Smith then filed a formal complaint with IHRC and the parties commenced discovery. In January 1998, two days before her scheduled evidentiary hearing with IHRC, Smith moved to dismiss her state claims, stating that she planned to obtain a right-to-sue letter from the EEOC and pursue her claims in federal court.

Though Smith asserts that she requested a right-to-sue letter from the EEOC in January 1998, the EEOC took no action and Smith made no effort to follow-up on her request for more than one year. In May 1999 Smith submitted a second request and the EEOC issued her a right-to-sue letter on May 19, 1999. On August 17, 1999, when her 90-day period for bringing suit had nearly expired, Smith filed a complaint in federal court, charging Caterpillar with gender discrimination and retaliation in violation of Title VII. Caterpillar filed its first motion for summary judgment, raising the defense of laches as a bar to Smith's claims. Caterpillar claimed that it had suffered prejudice from Smith's delay in filing her lawsuit because witnesses' memories had faded, records had been destroyed, and the company had been exposed to disproportionate years of back pay. The district court initially found no material prejudice to Caterpillar, though it found Smith's nearly eight and one-half year delay in bringing suit inexcusable, and gave Caterpillar leave to refile its summary judgment motion upon presentation of new evidence of prejudice.

Caterpillar next filed its second motion for summary judgment, asserting laches as a defense, reiterating its earlier arguments about prejudice, and submitting new evidence that key witnesses had died, retired, or moved out of state. The district court denied this motion as well, telling Caterpillar that it had to show not only that certain witnesses could not be located or were retired from the company, but also that they were unwilling to testify. Caterpillar then filed a motion to reconsider, submitting still more evidence of prejudice, such as affidavits of relevant witnesses verifying their faded memories and out-of-state residency and information concerning the missing or destroyed personnel records. This time, the district court granted Caterpillar's motion to reconsider, holding that the company had established a convincing laches defense which entitled it to summary judgment on Smith's claims.

II. Discussion

The defense of laches bars an action when the plaintiff's delay in filing the claim (1) is unreasonable and inexcusable, and (2) materially prejudices the defendant. *Jeffries v. Chicago Transit Authority,* 770 F.2d 676, 679 (7th Cir.1985); *Cook v. City of Chicago,* 192 F.3d 693, 695 (defining laches as "an unreasonable delay in pressing one's rights that prejudices the defendant"). Essentially the equitable substitute for a statute of limitations, laches serves to protect defendants from prejudice caused by stale evidence, prolonged uncertainty about legal rights and status, and unlimited exposure to liability damages. *See Cook,* 192 F.3d at 696. In this case Smith does not challenge the district court's determination that her eight and one-half year delay in filing her Title VII claim was unreasonable and inexcusable; however, she insists that laches cannot bar her claim because Caterpillar suffered no material prejudice as a result of her delay. . . .

In this case the district court's ultimate decision to credit Caterpillar's laches defense and grant the company's summary judgment motion was not an abuse of discretion. The court cited several reasons for concluding that Caterpillar had been materially prejudiced by Smith's delay, most notably that: (1) the testimony of several pertinent witnesses would be difficult, if not impossible, for Caterpillar to procure; (2) the witnesses' memories have faded over the several years and they would be unable to recollect specific details of Smith's employment with Caterpillar; (3) the inadvertent loss, or even intentional destruction in the course of business,

[handwritten margin note: π argues Δ was materially prejudiced]

of relevant personnel documents relating to Smith's employment would seriously impair Caterpillar's ability to present a defense to Smith's claims; and (4) the exposure of Caterpillar to liability for back pay has accrued steadily during Smith's delay in filing her lawsuit. Before we look more closely at the district court's reasons, we note that in general the decision to apply the doctrine of laches lies on a sliding scale: the longer the plaintiff delays in filing her claim, the less prejudice the defendant must show in order to defend on laches. *Jeffries,* 770 F.2d at 680; *Hot Wax,* 191 F.3d at 822. Here, given Smith's inexcusable eight and one-half year delay, we recognize that Caterpillar need not present a mountain of evidence establishing prejudice in order to succeed on its laches defense. Still, at minimum we require a showing of prejudice that is material, meaning it affects the substantial rights of the defendant to such a degree that it justifies the equitable relief of barring the plaintiff's claims. *See Jeffries,* 770 F.2d at 680 (requiring merely "some prejudicial change in the condition or regulations of the . . . parties" to establish material prejudice in private discrimination suit) (internal quotations omitted). Based on the record before us and in deference to the district court's decision to credit Caterpillar's laches defense, we are convinced that Caterpillar has produced enough evidence of material prejudice to bar Smith's Title VII claims against the company.

First, Caterpillar submits that several key employees—persons who participated directly in the hiring, supervising, training, and firing of Smith—are either deceased, out of the court's jurisdiction, or retired and out of contact with the company. . . .

Second, Caterpillar argues that the memories of its key witnesses have faded so that they can no longer recall the relevant facts of Smith's employment. The company asserts that this loss of memory will significantly detract from their credibility as witnesses for the defense. We have said that in order to show prejudice from failed memories, a defendant must show both that the memories have faded and that the inability to recall information was caused by the plaintiff's delay. *EEOC v. Massey-Ferguson,* 622 F.2d 271, 275 (7th Cir.1980). . . .

Third, Caterpillar admits that relevant performance reviews, as well as attendance records and materials from training seminars on sexual harassment, have been inadvertently lost or intentionally destroyed as part of routine record maintenance. Caterpillar claims that without this evidence its ability to present a defense to Smith's Title VII charges will be seriously compromised. . . .

Finally, Caterpillar asserts that its potential liability for back pay has increased each day as this suit has lingered on. We have recognized that exposure to disproportionately high back pay due to plaintiff's delay is "the kind of palpable prejudice that . . . can justify a finding of laches." *Cook,* 192 F.3d at 696. Smith argues that this factor does not necessarily result in material prejudice because back pay is an equitable remedy within the discretion of the court. The district court acknowledges as much in its decision, stating that while "it would be within the Court's power to fashion some sort of equitable limitation on any back pay award to mitigate the effects of the delay, this possibility does not eliminate the availability of the laches defense." We not only agree with this particular point, but find that the district court's application of the doctrine of laches to this case was in no way an abuse of discretion. Moreover, our conviction is bolstered, not weakened, by the fact that the district court twice denied Caterpillar's motion for summary judgment; to us this shows that the court's ultimate decision to bar Smith's claims on laches grounds was not made without careful and full consideration of the facts and circumstances before the court.

III. Conclusion

Caterpillar established a valid defense of laches by proving it had suffered material prejudice as a result of Smith's unreasonably lengthy delay in filing her Title VII claim against the company. We therefore conclude that Smith's claims are barred by laches and affirm the district court's grant of summary judgment in favor of Caterpillar.

* * *

Perry v. Judd

United States District Court, Eastern District of Virginia
840 F.Supp.2d 945 (2012)

JOHN A. GIBNEY JR., District Judge.

This matter is before the Court on the plaintiff and intervenor-plaintiffs' (collectively, the "plaintiffs") motion for a preliminary injunction. The plaintiffs are candidates seeking the Republican nomination for President of the United States. Under Virginia law, they failed to obtain the required number of petition signatures to place their names on the ballot for the Republican primary election. Now, they ask the Court for a preliminary injunction ordering that they be listed on the ballot. The plaintiffs argue that Virginia's rules limiting who can circulate candidate petitions and requiring 10,000 signatures violate the First and Fourteenth Amendments to the Constitution.

The equitable doctrine of laches bars the plaintiffs' request for a preliminary injunction. They knew the rules in Virginia many months ago; the limitations on circulators affected them as soon as they began to circulate petitions. The plaintiffs could have challenged the Virginia law at that time. Instead, they waited until after the time to gather petitions had ended and they had lost the political battle to be on the ballot; then, on the eve of the printing of absentee ballots, they decided to challenge Virginia's laws. In essence, they played the game, lost, and then complained that the rules were unfair. . . .

I. Parties and Proceedings

The original plaintiff in this case is Rick Perry ("Perry"), a Republican candidate for the presidency. Three other Republican candidates have intervened as plaintiffs — Newt Gingrich ("Gingrich"), Rick Santorum ("Santorum"), and Jon Huntsman, Jr. ("Huntsman").

The defendants are Charles Judd, Kimberly Bowers, and Don Palmer, the members of the Virginia State Board of Elections (collectively, the "Board"). Pat Mullins ("Mullins"), Chairman of the Republican Party of Virginia, is also a defendant.

Perry filed this lawsuit challenging the petition requirements on December 27, 2011. Gingrich, Santorum, and Huntsman intervened on January 4, 2012. The Court ordered expedited briefing, and, on January 13, 2012, held an evidentiary hearing on the motion for preliminary relief.

The plaintiffs raise claims arising under the First and Fourteenth Amendments to the Constitution. They attack Virginia's rule that only people eligible to register to vote may circulate petitions for signatures to place a candidate on the ballot. The plaintiffs contend that the limitation on who may seek signatures restricts their rights of free speech and association, because fewer people can advocate them as candidates.

The plaintiffs also challenge Virginia's statute requiring statewide candidates to obtain 10,000 signatures, including 400 from each congressional district, to secure a place on the ballot. They claim the number of signatures is too burdensome and, therefore, unconstitutional. Finally, the plaintiffs argue that Virginia's election procedures violate the Voting Rights Act.

Law Governing Preliminary Injunctive Relief

The requirements for preliminary injunctive relief are well established. Such relief is appropriate when the plaintiffs establish that (1) they are likely to succeed on the merits; (2) they are likely to suffer irreparable harm in the absence of preliminary relief; (3) the balance of equities tips in the plaintiffs' favor; and (4) an injunction is in the public interest. *Winter v. Natural Res. Def. Council, Inc.*, 555 U.S. 7 (2008).

Laches is an equitable doctrine that precludes relief when a plaintiff has delayed bringing suit to the detriment of the defendant. The doctrine applies with particular force in the context of preliminary injunctions against governmental action, where litigants try to block imminent steps by the government. "Equity demands that those who would challenge the legal sufficiency of administrative decisions concerning time sensitive public . . . projects do so with haste and dispatch." *Quince Orchard Valley Citizens Ass'n v. Hodel*, 872 F.2d 75, 80 (4th Cir.1989); *see Equity in Athletics, Inc. v. Dep't of Educ.*, 504 F.Supp.2d 88, 100–01 (W.D.Va.2007) (delay in bringing suit is a factor to be considered in granting preliminary relief); *Marshall v. Meadows*, 921 F.Supp. 1490, 1494 (E.D.Va.1996) ("The Fourth Circuit is especially mindful of laches in the context of an impending vote."). . . .

II. Discussion

The Court finds that the plaintiffs are not entitled to a preliminary injunction, for the reasons stated below.

Laches

The parties have fully briefed the issue of whether laches bars the requested relief in this case. Undoubtedly, the only adequate remedy in this case is to include any harmed individuals on the ballot for the Virginia Republican primary election. But the plaintiffs have waited too long to request such relief.

Laches is an affirmative defense to claims for equitable relief. *White v. Daniel,* 909 F.2d 99, 102 (4th Cir.1990), *cert. denied,* 501 U.S. 1260, 111 S.Ct. 2916, 115 L.Ed.2d 1079 (1991). In essence, the doctrine "penalizes a litigant for negligent or willful failure to assert his rights." *Valmor Prods. Co. v. Standard Prods. Corp.,* 464 F.2d 200, 204 (1st Cir.1972). Laches can serve as a defense to First Amendment claims.

Laches requires the proof of two elements: (1) lack of diligence by the party against whom the defense is asserted, and (2) prejudice to the party asserting the defense. *Marshall,* 921 F.Supp. at 1493–94. As stated by the Fourth Circuit in *White,* the first element of laches is lack of diligence, when "the plaintiff delayed inexcusably or unreasonably in filing suit." *White,* 909 F.2d at 102 (citing *Nat'l Wildlife Fed'n v. Burford,* 835 F.2d 305, 318 (D.C.Cir.1987). An inexcusable delay can only occur after the plaintiff discovers or should have discovered the facts giving rise to his cause of action. *See Knox v. Milwaukee Cnty. Bd. of Elections Comm'rs,* 581 F.Supp. 399, 402 (E.D.Wis.1984).

The second element is prejudice to the defendant. *See White,* 909 F.2d at 102. The defendant must prove that he has suffered a disadvantage or some other harm caused by reliance on the plaintiff's conduct. *Id.* (citing *Gull Airborne Instruments, Inc. v. Weinberger,* 694 F.2d 838, 844 (D.C.Cir.1982)). Prejudice can be inferred simply from the plaintiff's delay, or from evidence of specific harm. *Id.* The greater the delay, the less the prejudice required to show laches. *Id.*

In this case, the plaintiffs were permitted to collect the requisite signatures for ballot access between July 1, 2011 and December 22, 2011. On December 22nd and 23rd, the plaintiffs were denied positions on the Virginia Republican primary ballot for failure to comply with the signature requirements of Va.Code § 24.2-545(B). On December 27, 2011, this suit commenced. Central to the plaintiffs' argument against laches is their contention that an injury-in-fact did not arise until December 22nd and 23rd, when they were denied a place on the ballot. They argue that they "timely sought relief at a time actual injury occurred" and "[t]o have brought this suit before they were declined a position on the ballot would have only presented the court with a hypothetical issue and subjected the claim to a ripeness defense." (Br. of Intervenors 4.) The Court disagrees.

Here, the plaintiffs claim a loss of their First Amendment rights of free speech and association. Any injury arose when the Commonwealth limited the categories of people who could spread their message, by banning petition circulators from out-of-state. The first day the plaintiffs were unable to communicate their message effectively was the first day they could circulate petitions. As of that date, they could have brought in an army of out-of-state circulators to persuade people to sign petitions and, ultimately, vote for them. Huntsman, Gingrich, and Santorum declared their candidacies before July 1, 2011; thus, the first day they could have used out-of-state circulators was July 1. Perry declared his candidacy on August 13, 2011, and suffered injury from that date forward. Yet, the candidates waited almost half a year before seeking judicial relief. As to the first element of laches, therefore, the Court finds that the plaintiffs displayed an unreasonable and inexcusable lack of diligence.

This lack of diligence has significantly harmed the defendants. The Board established a reasonable, necessary, and comprehensive schedule of tasks leading to the primary election. Among those tasks is the printing of absentee ballots. To comply with federal law, absentee ballots must be distributed on or before January 21, 2012.[7] To meet this deadline, the Board set a timetable for the localities to design ballots, order them from printers, proofread mock-ups, receive them, and mail them out. By January 13, 2011, the date of the preliminary injunction hearing, the local boards should have received absentee ballots, and begun the process of mailing them out. The filing of this suit, however, has changed the Board's careful scheduling into a chaotic attempt to get absentee ballots out on time. This alone amounts to damage that satisfies the laches requirements. *See Marshall*, 921 F.Supp. at 1494 ("The time element is most important. . . . Under the delay/prejudice ratio, prejudice need not be so severe where, as here, delay is conscious and substantial."). Don Palmer, the Secretary of the State Board of Elections, testified without contradiction that printing ballots is complex and requires a number of technical steps to imbed information into the ballots themselves and to program computers to count them. He also testified that, as of this date, absentee ballots cannot be prepared before they must be available.

[handwritten margin note: damages]

But there is another, more fundamental injury caused by the plaintiffs' delay. Virginia insists that candidates secure 10,000 signatures of registered voters. *See* Va .Code § 24.2-545(B). This requirement serves the valid purpose of limiting ballot access to candidates with a modicum of support and a viable chance in the election. Fringe candidates and crackpots have the potential to complicate needlessly both the ballot and the counting of votes. The 10,000 signature requirement is plainly constitutional (as discussed below), and the number of signatures required is not asserted as a ground for preliminary relief.

None of the plaintiffs have secured 10,000 valid signatures. They ask the Court to order their inclusion on the ballot without having secured the requisite number to show they are viable candidates. The Commonwealth has the right to demand a show of legitimate strength among the electorate. Had the plaintiffs brought suit in a timely fashion, the Court could have allowed the use of non-resident circulators, and the plaintiffs might have been able to muster the required show of support. As it stands now, however, the Court can only speculate whether they would have been placed on the ballot. It is too late for the Court to allow them to gather more signatures — the absentee ballots must go out now.

Accordingly, the Court finds that the plaintiffs have slept on their rights to the detriment of the defendants. The motion for a preliminary injunction is barred by laches.

VI. Conclusion

. . . For the reasons stated above, the motion for a preliminary injunction is denied.

* * *

Problem 54

A laches defense will be successful where an unreasonable delay in bringing the suit prejudices the defendant. Is a laches defense likely to be successful in the case below?

An architect draws plans for an 80-unit apartment complex tower. The developer for the project surreptitiously copies the plans without paying the architect for her services. He then informs her that he has changed his mind and is not going forward with the project. Six months later, the architect learns the developer has indeed started building and is using her plans. The architect is not litigious. She has never sued anyone and is hesitant to do so now. She waits three months, then calls a lawyer referred by a friend. The lawyer is in the middle of a long trial, so the first available time he can meet with the architect is not for another two months. When that meeting occurs, the lawyer advises the architect she has a potential claim for breach of contract and copyright infringement and might be able to obtain an injunction to stop the developer from building the apartment complex.

After thinking it over for several weeks, the architect retains the lawyer to file suit. The lawyer is busy with another trial, however, and it takes two months to get the complaint drafted and filed. By this time, the developer has already completed a significant amount of construction on the apartment building, at a cost of over $1 million. The developer answers the complaint and asserts the affirmative defense of laches.

Unclean Hands

The equitable defense of unclean hands (extended in some jurisdictions to include legal claims) is, as the name suggests, a doctrine that prevents a plaintiff who has engaged in wrongdoing from obtaining a remedy from the court. The idea is that the plaintiff, by committing a wrong, has forfeited the privilege of receiving assistance from the court.

As discussed earlier, equitable remedies are available to ensure a plaintiff is not unfairly denied relief. The unclean hands defense applies to situations where, because of the plaintiff's own misconduct, denying relief would not be unfair.

The key point in evaluating an unclean hands defense is that not just any misconduct by the plaintiff will do. Unclean hands only bars a plaintiff's claim if the misconduct asserted as the basis for the defense is directly related to the events that triggered the lawsuit. Further, the plaintiff's misconduct cannot be minor or relatively insignificant compared with what the defendant is alleged to have done. But plaintiffs who have themselves misbehaved in the course of the transaction or events that are the subject of the lawsuit may find they have no remedy in court because of the unclean hands defense.

Introductory Note — *Kendall-Jackson Winery v. Superior Court* and *Wedgewood Community Association v. Nash*

Kendall-Jackson Winery v. Superior Court is the second of two lawsuits between California wineries E&J Gallo and Kendall Jackson. In the first, Kendall-Jackson sued Gallo for trademark infringement — for using a label with a leaf on it that looked similar to Kendall-Jackson's label. The jury in that case rejected Kendall-Jackson's claims. That prompted the second lawsuit: Gallo turned around and sued Kendall-Jackson for malicious prosecution, alleging the trademark infringement suit was filed without probable cause, purely to harass. Kendall-Jackson, now the defendant, asserts the defense of unclean hands. The misconduct it alleges as the basis for the defense is that Gallo engaged in improper strongarm tactics to get premium shelf placement for its wine in stores. The trial court found no evidence of unclean hands. On appeal, the California Supreme Court is left to sort out whether this is all just more mudslinging amongst rivals or a valid unclean hands defense that should bar relief.

Wedgewood Community Association presents an unclean hands defense in a more straightforward context. The plaintiff homeowners' association sues for an order requiring the defendant homeowner to remove a shed in his yard. The shed is not allowed by the complex rules. The homeowner asserts an unclean hands defense, alleging that one of the association's board members was allowed to build the same kind of structure. The trial court agrees that the association should not be allowed to enforce a rule that a board member has not followed, and grants judgment for homeowner. The Indiana Court of Appeal must decide whether the board member's misconduct bars the association lawsuit.

THINGS TO THINK ABOUT while reading *Kendall-Jackson Winery v. Superior Court* and *Wedgewood Community Association v. Nash*:

1. How broad is a court's discretion in deciding whether the misconduct at issue should constitute unclean hands?

2. How related to the conduct alleged in the lawsuit does the plaintiff's misconduct need to be in order to constitute unclean hands?

Kendall-Jackson Winery v. Superior Court

California Court of Appeal
76 Cal.App.4th 970 (1999)

THAXTER, Acting P.J.

The doctrine of unclean hands does not deny relief to a plaintiff guilty of any past misconduct; only misconduct directly related to the matter in which he seeks relief triggers the defense. (11 Witkin, Summary of Cal. Law (9th ed. 1990) Equity, § 10, p. 686.) The trial court found that Kendall-Jackson Winery, Ltd. (Kendall-Jackson), the defendant in a malicious prosecution action, had no relevant evidence that the plaintiff, E. & J. Gallo Winery (Gallo), acted with unclean hands in relation to its claim and ordered summary adjudication for the plaintiff on Kendall-Jackson's unclean hands defense. The novel issue presented is this: When "unclean hands" is raised as an affirmative defense to a malicious prosecution claim, is the relevant misconduct limited to that which affected the defendant's decision to file and pursue the prior lawsuit? We hold it is not; misconduct in the particular transaction or connected to the subject matter of the litigation that affects the equitable relations between the litigants is sufficient to trigger the defense.

Facts and Procedural History

Kendall-Jackson has a reputation for producing high quality, mid-priced varietal wines. In 1994, Kendall-Jackson was selling over $100 million worth of Vintner's Reserve wine a year, and its chardonnay was the number one selling chardonnay in the United States. (*Kendall-Jackson Winery v. E. & J. Gallo Winery* (9th Cir.1998) 150 F.3d 1042, 1045.) Gallo is the largest wine producer in the world. But, unlike Kendall-Jackson, Gallo has a reputation for producing lower-priced, non-premium wines.

During the 1990's, the market for non-premium wines declined rapidly. Gallo researched how best to enter the premium wine market. Much of its research was directed at the success of the market leader — Kendall-Jackson Vintner's Reserve. Gallo learned that consumers associate the name "Gallo" with "jug wine" and that a colorful grape leaf design attracts consumers. In accord with these results, Gallo introduced in the fall of 1995 a line of premium wine, Turning Leaf, that featured a leaf motif and did not use the Gallo name. (*Kendall-Jackson Winery v. E. & J. Gallo Winery, supra,* 150 F.3d at p. 1045.)

In April 1996, Kendall-Jackson sued Gallo for damages and injunctive relief on causes of action for trademark infringement, trade dress violations and unfair business practices. Kendall-Jackson alleged that Gallo's Turning Leaf wine label and overall appearance mimicked its successful Vintner's Reserve wines. While the lawsuit alleged unfair marketing practices in retail displays, the litigation focused on the label and packaging similarities rather than marketing strategies. (*Kendall-Jackson Winery v. E. & J. Gallo Winery, supra,* 150 F.3d 1042.) Gallo denied employing unlawful marketing practices and resisted disclosing material related to its marketing strategies. The court found for Gallo on the trademark infringement and unfair competition claims. After a 12-day trial, a jury found for Gallo on the trade dress infringement and "palming off" claims. Judgment for Gallo was affirmed on appeal.

In September 1997, Gallo filed this action against Kendall-Jackson for malicious prosecution and intentional interference with contract. Gallo alleged that Kendall-Jackson had filed and prosecuted the federal action without probable cause and for the improper purpose of harassing a competitor. In addition, Kendall-Jackson had induced Chris Lynch, Gallo's former director of marketing, to breach his confidentiality agreement with Gallo. Kendall-Jackson used the confidential information obtained "to file a facially plausible, but knowingly false lawsuit against Gallo." Among the defenses raised by Kendall-Jackson's answer was an allegation that Gallo's claims were barred by the doctrine of unclean hands.

[The trial court] found that Kendall-Jackson had no relevant evidence that Gallo acted with unclean hands in relation to its malicious prosecution or inducing breach of contract claims.

Discussion

Gallo Failed to Establish It Was Entitled to Judgment on the Unclean Hands Affirmative Defense

Unclean Hands

The defense of unclean hands arises from the maxim, "He who comes into Equity must come with clean hands." (*Blain v. Doctor's Co.* (1990) 222 Cal.App.3d 1048, 1059 (*Blain*).) The doctrine demands that a plaintiff act fairly in the matter for which he seeks a remedy. He must come into court with clean hands, and keep them clean, or he will be denied relief, regardless of the merits of his claim. (*Precision Co. v. Automotive Co.* (1945) 324 U.S. 806, 814–815.) The defense is available in legal as well as equitable actions. (*Fibreboard Paper Products Corp. v. East Bay Union of Machinists* (1964) 227 Cal.App.2d 675.)

The unclean hands doctrine protects judicial integrity and promotes justice. It protects judicial integrity because allowing a plaintiff with unclean hands to recover in an action creates doubts as to the justice provided by the judicial system. Thus, precluding recovery to the unclean plaintiff protects the court's, rather than the opposing party's, interests. (*Fibreboard, supra,* 227 Cal.App.2d at p. 727.) The doctrine promotes justice by making a plaintiff answer for his own misconduct in the action. It prevents "a wrongdoer from enjoying the fruits of his transgression." (*Precision Co. v. Automotive Co., supra,* 324 U.S. at p. 815.)

Not every wrongful act constitutes unclean hands. But, the misconduct need not be a crime or an actionable tort. Any conduct that violates conscience, or good faith, or other equitable standards of conduct is sufficient cause to invoke the doctrine. (*DeRosa v. Transamerica Title Ins. Co.* (1989) 213 Cal.App.3d 1390, 1395–1396.)

The misconduct that brings the clean hands doctrine into play must relate directly to the cause at issue. Past improper conduct or prior misconduct that only indirectly affects the problem before the court does not suffice. The determination of the unclean hands defense cannot be distorted into a proceeding to try the general morals of the parties. (*Fibreboard, supra,* 227 Cal.App.2d at pp. 728–729.) Courts have expressed this relationship requirement in various ways. The misconduct "must relate directly to the transaction concerning which the complaint is made, i.e., it must pertain to the very subject matter involved and affect the equitable relations between the litigants." (*Id.* at p. 728.) "[T]here must be a direct relationship between the misconduct and the claimed injuries 'so that it would be inequitable to grant [the requested] relief." (*Mattco Forge, Inc. v. Arthur Young & Co.* (1997) 52 Cal.App.4th 820, 846.) "The issue is not that the plaintiff's hands are dirty, but rather 'that the manner of dirtying renders inequitable the assertion of such rights against the defendant.'(*Ibid.*) The misconduct must "prejudicially affect the rights of the person against whom the relief is sought so that it would be inequitable to grant such relief." (*Ibid.*)

. . . Kendall-Jackson's unclean hands defense is based on two types of alleged marketing misconduct: Gallo's undue influence over shelf schematics and other retailer merchandising activity, and Gallo's movement of a competitor's wines to create product adjacencies. . . .

(1) Gallo's undue influence over shelf schematics and other retailer activity

Shelf schematics are product display plans that wine producers prepare and present to a retailer. The plans typically propose the amount of shelf space and location to be given to individual brands. Schematics are intended to assist the retailer to maximize revenues through product placement. Both Kendall-Jackson and Gallo provide shelf schematics to retailers. The practice is legal.

Kendall-Jackson contends that Gallo's use of schematics is illegal or improper because Gallo works too closely with retailers, provides goods or services of value in exchange for the retailer's use of Gallo schematics, and uses its considerable influence in the industry to achieve favorable shelf schematics. Kendall-Jackson's evidence disclosed that a number of Gallo representatives were employed by large supermarket chains, had offices in the chains or were provided with perquisites such as store badges which enabled them to move more freely about the retailer's premises than other wine distributors. In addition, Gallo representatives or employees participated in restocking or stock resets for retailers in violation of Alcoholic Beverage Control regulations.

(2) Gallo's movement of competitor's wines to create product adjacencies

Product adjacencies are a marketing strategy whereby a wine producer attempts to have its brands displayed adjacent to the market leader brand in the relevant price segment. Adjacencies maximize the exposure of the adjacent brand. Product adjacencies are lawful and commonly used.

Kendall-Jackson contends Gallo's use of adjacencies is illegal and improper to the extent Gallo accomplishes adjacencies by physically moving a competitor's product. A wine distributor can ask a retailer to move a competitor's product, but the distributor cannot lawfully move the product. Kendall-Jackson's documents include direct and circumstantial evidence that Gallo distributors or employees moved bottles of Kendall-Jackson or another competitor to create product adjacencies between Kendall-Jackson Vintner's Reserve and Turning Leaf wines.

The nature of the misconduct indicated by Kendall-Jackson's evidence — Gallo's ties with retailers and movement of a competitor's product — violates the letter and the spirit of the Alcoholic Beverage Control Act. Such evidence supports a defense of unclean hands under the second prong of the *Blain* test. (*Hall v. Wright, supra,* 240 F.2d at p. 795 [unclean hands conduct need not constitute unfair competition under California law].) Gallo has not established that the proffered misconduct is insufficient as a matter of law to support an unclean hands affirmative defense.

Relationship of the Misconduct to the Injuries

The misconduct that brings the unclean hands doctrine into play must relate directly to the transaction concerning which the complaint is made. It must infect the cause of action involved and affect the equitable relations between the litigants. (*Pond, supra,* 151 Cal.App.3d at p. 290.) Cases illustrating preclusive unclean hands conduct directly related to the transaction at issue include *Unilogic, Inc. v. Burroughs Corp., supra,* 10 Cal.App.4th 612, 618 (although defendant converted plaintiff's proprietary information during a failed joint project, plaintiff's unclean hands — bribery to obtain the contract, failure to disclose financial difficulties, and its own conversion of defendant's property — during the same joint project precluded relief); *Camp v. Jeffer, Mangels, Butler & Marmaro* (1995) 35 Cal.App.4th 620, 639 (plaintiffs' suit for wrongful termination was barred by evidence they had lied on their job applications); and *Blain, supra,* 222 Cal.App.3d 1048, 1058 (doctrine of unclean hands precluded legal malpractice action based on injuries caused when physician-defendant followed the advice of his attorney to lie at a deposition, physician's emotional distress and inability to work as a physician were attributable to his own misconduct).

. . . Gallo contends that its alleged unclean hands conduct — illegal and improper marketing practices directed at Kendall-Jackson — is unrelated to the injuries it claims from having to defend against Kendall-Jackson's baseless and malicious infringement action. Gallo urges this court to apply a narrow rule in determining whether particular misconduct precludes a malicious prosecution claim. According to Gallo, the gist of a malicious prosecution action is that the prior lawsuit was filed maliciously and without probable cause. Therefore, in order to bear the requisite direct relationship to a malicious prosecution claim, the unclean hands conduct must relate directly to the defendant's decision to file and pursue the prior litigation. Neither analogous case law nor the equitable principles underlying the unclean hands doctrine supports this narrow rule. . . .

[T]he unclean hands doctrine is not a legal or technical defense to be used as a shield against a particular element of a cause of action. Rather, it is an equitable rationale for refusing a plaintiff relief where principles of fairness dictate that the plaintiff should not recover, regardless of the merits of his claim. It is available to protect the court from having its powers used to bring about an inequitable result in the litigation before it. (*Ford v. Buffalo Eagle Colliery Co.* (4th Cir.1941) 122 F.2d 555, 563; 5 McCarthy on Trademarks and Unfair Competition (4th ed.1997) § 31:45.) Thus, any evidence of a plaintiff's unclean hands in relation to the transaction before the court or which affects the equitable relations between the litigants in the matter before the court should be available to enable the court to effect a fair result in the litigation. The equitable principles underlying the doctrine militate against limiting the unclean hands defense in a malicious prosecution claim to misconduct that bears on the defendant's decision to file the prior action.

. . . In the alternative, Gallo contends that even if the unclean hands evidence need not relate to Kendall-Jackson's decision to file the infringement lawsuit, Kendall-Jackson's evidence in this case does not relate directly to or "infect" the underlying infringement action or the malicious prosecution claim, as a matter of law. The contention has two components: (1) Kendall-Jackson's unclean hands defense is based on conduct that occurred long after the prior lawsuit was filed, and (2) the purported improper marketing practices have nothing whatsoever to do with Gallo's malicious prosecution claims or the prior infringement action.

Gallo's first contention fails on the evidence. Haarstad testified that he was aware of Gallo's unclean hands conduct in 1994, and the documents produced reflect or imply ongoing unclean hands conduct since before the infringement action was filed.

Gallo's second contention also fails. Kendall-Jackson's infringement action sought damages and to enjoin Gallo's use of its Turning Leaf label and packaging. The gist of the lawsuit was that Gallo attempted to capitalize on Kendall-Jackson's success as the market leader in premium wine sales by using a variety of unfair marketing strategies — similar label and trade dress, omitting the Gallo name from the bottle, placing Turning Leaf adjacent to Vintner's Reserve wine in store displays, and so forth. The theory of Kendall-Jackson's unclean hands defense is, although Gallo prevailed on the infringement claims, it is unfair to permit Gallo compensation for defending against Kendall-Jackson's claims because Gallo actually engaged in illegal and improper practices directed at Kendall-Jackson with respect to the marketing of Turning Leaf wines.

On the evidence presented, a jury could find that Gallo's unfair marketing strategies that targeted Kendall-Jackson's share of the premium wine market contributed to Kendall-Jackson's pursuit of the infringement action which, in turn, resulted in Gallo having to defend against Kendall-Jackson's unsuccessful allegations. A jury could find that Gallo's inequitable conduct occurred in the transaction related directly to the matter before the court — the marketing of Turning Leaf wine to compete with Vintner's Reserve wine — and affects the equitable relationship between the litigants. . . .

For all of the reasons set forth above, Gallo did not establish that its unclean hands conduct is not directly related to the "'transaction concerning which the complaint is made'" or does not affect the equitable relations between the parties as a matter of law. (*Pond, supra,* 151 Cal.App.3d at p. 290.) Accordingly, Gallo failed to meet its statutory burden of proving its entitlement to judgment as a matter of law and was not entitled to summary adjudication.

Disposition

Let a peremptory writ of mandate issue directing the trial court to vacate its order granting Gallo's motion for summary adjudication of Kendall-Jackson's unclean hands affirmative defense and to enter a new order denying the motion.

* * *

Wedgewood Community Ass'n v. Nash

Indiana Court of Appeals
781 N.E. 2d 1172 (2003)

MATHIAS, Judge.

Wedgewood Community Association, Inc. ("Wedgewood Association") appeals the Allen Superior Court's determination that despite a restrictive covenant violation by Robert O. Nash ("Nash"), he was not required to remove a shed constructed in his yard.

We reverse.

Facts and Procedural History

The facts most favorable to the trial court's determination reveal that throughout this proceeding, Nash resided at 7204 Bay Head Cove, Fort Wayne, Indiana. His residence is one of 161 lots in Wedgewood Place subdivision. Wedgewood Association is a not-for-profit Indiana corporation that governs the homeowners' association of Wedgewood Place subdivision.

The residents in Wedgewood Place are bound by the "Dedications, Protective Restrictions, Covenants, Limitations, Easements and Approvals, Appended to and Made a Part of the Dedication and Plat of Wedgewood Place Subdivision Section I a subdivision in St. Joseph Township, Allen County, Indiana" ("the Restrictive Covenants"), which has been amended several times since it was originally recorded in 1987. In 1997, Nash received a copy of the Restrictive Covenants as an attachment to his Deed.

In pertinent part, the covenants provide:

Article VI

Architectural Control

No building, fence, wall, or other structure shall be commenced, erected, or maintained upon any lot, nor shall any exterior addition to or change or alteration therein be made until the plans and specifications showing the nature, kind, shape, height, materials, and location of the same shall have been submitted to and approved in writing as to harmony of external design and location in relation to surrounding structures and topography by the Board of Directors of the Association, or by the Architectural Control Committee to be composed of three members, the first Committee members to be:.... A majority of the Committee may designate a representative to act for it. In the event of death or resignation of any member of the Committee, the remaining members shall have full authority to designate a successor. In the event said Board, or the Architectural Control Committee, fails to approve or disapprove such design and location within thirty (30) days after said plans and specifications have been submitted to it, this article will be deemed to have been fully complied with.

Article VII

General Provisions

Section 1. No lot shall be used except for residential building purposes. No building shall be erected, altered, placed or permitted to remain on any lot other than one detached single-family dwelling not to exceed two and one-half stories in height. Each house shall include not less than a two-car garage, which shall be built as part of said structure and attached thereto.

. . . .

Section 7(a). No structure of a temporary character, no trailer, boat trailer, camper or camping trailer, no basement, tent, shack, unattached garage, barn or other outbuilding, shall be constructed, erected, located or used on any lot for any purpose, including use as a residence, either temporarily or permanently; provided, however, that basements may be constructed in connection with the construction and use of a residential building. . . .

In February of 2000, Nash erected an eight-foot by ten-foot garden shed in his backyard, without first submitting written plans to the Architectural Committee or receiving written approval from the Wedgewood Board of Directors or the Architectural Control Committee, all required steps pursuant to Article VI of the Wedgewood Place Restrictive Covenants. Wedgewood's Board President Steve McMichael ("McMichael") was immediately notified of the shed by a resident.

Within one day of the erection of the shed, McMichael and Architectural Control Committee Chairperson Michael Tucker ("Tucker") went to the Nash residence to discuss the shed. They knocked at the Nash residence door, but there was no answer. Later that same day, Tucker again went to the Nash residence, and knocked at the door. Again, there was no answer. Attorney Robert E. Doelling, Jr. then sent Nash a letter notifying Nash that he was in violation of a restrictive covenant. . . .

On March 31, 2000, Wedgewood Association filed a complaint against Nash for violating the Restrictive Covenants. Wedgewood Association requested "declaratory and injunctive relief in law and equity for breach of the Restrictive Covenants including but not limited to an Order requiring [Nash] to remove from the Premises said Shed and for judgment against [Nash], . . . , for court costs, attorney fees, and for all other relief as is just and proper in the premises." . . .

Standard of Review

Wedgewood Association's suit requested declaratory and injunctive relief in law and equity. The trial court entered specific findings of facts and conclusions of law. Pursuant to Indiana Trial Rule 52, our court will not set aside a trial court's findings or judgment unless clearly erroneous. Additionally, we must pay heed to the trial court's ability to judge the credibility of the witnesses. . . .

I. Unclean Hands

Wedgewood Association argues that the trial court was clearly erroneous when it determined that even though Nash was in clear violation of the restrictive covenant prohibiting outbuildings, Wedgewood Association was not entitled to relief based upon their own unclean hands. The principle of unclean hands is that "he who comes into equity must come with clean hands." *Keller v. Ind. Dept. of State Revenue,* 530 N.E.2d 787, 788 (Ind. Tax Ct.1988). The doctrine of unclean hands is not favored and must be applied with reluctance and scrutiny. *Shriner v. Sheehan,* 773 N.E.2d 833, 847–48 (Ind.Ct.App.2002) (citation omitted). For the doctrine of unclean hands to apply, the misconduct must be intentional, *id.* (citation omitted), and the wrong that is ordinarily invoked to defeat a claimant by using the unclean hands doctrine must have an "'immediate and necessary relation' to the matter before the court." *Keller,* 530 N.E.2d at 788 (quoting *Keystone Driller Co. v. Gen. Excavator Co.,* 290 U.S. 240 (1933).

Nash argues that Wedgewood Association had unclean hands because one of its Board members, Koenig, was also violating the restrictive covenant prohibiting outbuildings and shacks that Nash himself was violating. Nash argues that "[i]t is clearly inequitable for Wedgewood to bring a suit based on Nash's alleged violation of a restrictive covenant when Wedgewood's board member is in violation." Br. of Appellee at 10. Nash also complains that Wedgewood Association has not actively sought out covenant violations.

Nash relies heavily on *Stewart v. Jackson,* 635 N.E.2d 186 (Ind.Ct.App.1994). *Stewart* involved next-door neighbors, wherein one was trying to enforce a restrictive covenant against the other. The Jacksons were operating a home daycare out of their residence, contrary to the restrictive covenants governing the neighborhood. The Stewarts brought the suit requesting injunctive relief prohibiting the Jacksons from operating the daycare. At trial, the Jacksons presented evidence that several other people in the neighborhood were violating the restrictive covenants. They presented evidence of instances where neighbors worked from their homes: four other daycare homes, a salesman that worked from his home, a woman who taught piano lessons in her home, a woman that sold crafts from her home, and a man who ran a computer consulting business from his home. *Id.* at 188. The Jacksons also presented evidence that the Stewarts themselves had operated as a toy manufacturer and wholesaler from their home, and that Mr. Stewart operated his contracting construction company from his home. *Id.*

A panel of this court concluded that the unclean hands doctrine was one of the theories used by the trial court when it denied the Stewarts' request for injunctive relief. *Id.* at 189. Our court concluded that Indiana recognizes the ability of a party to purge itself of wrongdoing, which restores that party's right to seek equitable relief. *Id.* at 189 (citing *Keller,* 530 N.E.2d at 790). Our court then concluded that because the Stewarts were no longer operating businesses from their home, they had purged themselves of unclean hands, and therefore, their claim against the Jacksons could not be defeated based upon the unclean hands doctrine. *Id.* Additionally, in a footnote, this court found that even though there was evidence that the Stewarts were in violation of other restrictive covenants for fence heights and commercial vehicle parking, such violations did not support an unclean hands finding because the violations were merely incidental to the issues in the case. *Id.* at 190 n. 1 (citing *Keller,* 530 N.E.2d at 788).

We conclude that the *Stewart* case is dissimilar to ours. One very important difference between *Stewart* and our case is that in our case, the plaintiff is Wedgewood Association, not an actual resident of the neighborhood. It was very important to the *Stewart* case decision, and the application and applicability of the unclean hands doctrine, that one neighbor was complaining of another neighbor's covenant violation while at the same time, the complaining neighbor also might have been violating the same covenant.

In our case, however, Wedgewood Association is not and cannot possibly be violating the same restrictive covenant as Nash because Wedgewood Association is not a resident of the neighborhood. Additionally, although Nash complains of the actions of one of the board members, such conduct does not convert Wedgewood Association into a fellow resident. Alleged selective enforcement of restrictive covenants is clearly not a violation of the restrictive covenant forbidding outbuildings and may be remedied by the ballot box of the association officer elections. Therefore, the unclean hands doctrine is not applicable to this case, and the trial court's decision was clearly erroneous. Based upon the trial court's conclusion that Nash's outbuilding was in violation of the restrictive covenant prohibiting such outbuildings, and our conclusion that the doctrine of unclean hands (the only basis for the trial court's decision) is not applicable to the facts of this case, we conclude that Wedgewood Association's injunction should have been granted. . . .

Conclusion

Because the trial court based its decision upon the erroneous application of the unclean hands doctrine to the facts of this case, we reverse the trial court's determination that regardless of Nash's restrictive covenant violation, his shed could remain on his property, and conclude that Nash must remove his shed. . . .

Reversed.

* * *

Problem 55

The doctrine of unclean hands preserves judicial integrity by ensuring that the court does not assist in wrongdoing. Should the unclean hands defense apply in the following scenario?

Al has an illegal drug lab in his house where he manufactures narcotics. He is getting nervous because his neighbor, Sherry, enjoys entertaining friends and has parties in her backyard three times a week. Al is afraid one of her guests will discover his criminal operation and inform the police. Al files a lawsuit against Sherry for nuisance, alleging that her parties are noisy and go into the late hours of the night. He asks for an injunction preventing her from having more than two guests at a time. Sherry — who knows about Al's drug lab but had not to this point said anything — answers the complaint and asserts an unclean hands defense. She alleges that Al's criminal conduct of manufacturing drugs bars him from equitable relief.

Chapter 12

Contempt

Overview of Contempt

Contempt is a court's power to enforce its own orders. Contempt is important in the study of remedies because the contempt power is key to how equitable remedies operate. Equitable remedies are court orders that require a person to do something or not do something. Contempt is what motivates the subject of such an order to follow it. When someone disobeys a court's order, the consequence is that he or she can be found in contempt of court and face a sanction — a monetary penalty, or in some cases, imprisonment.

The contempt power is an important consideration for a plaintiff in deciding which remedies to pursue because enforcement through contempt is possible only for equitable remedies. A defendant cannot be found in contempt for failure to pay a legal judgment. That distinction can make an equitable remedy more effective in certain situations.

Finding a person in contempt for failure to obey a court order requires a showing that the order is clear and understandable and the disobedient party had the ability to comply with the order but did not.

Introductory Note — *Williamson v. Recovery Limited Partnership*

Discovery of sunken treasure in the late 1980s led to protracted litigation, including *Williamson v. Recovery Limited Partnership*. The people who recovered the treasure formed business entities to help market and sell it. Allegations of impropriety in managing the businesses led to a lawsuit, and part of the relief sought in that suit was an equitable order requiring the defendants to turn over certain corporate documents to the plaintiffs. After the order was issued, the plaintiffs moved for a finding of contempt, alleging the defendants had not complied. The district court found the defendants in contempt and issued monetary sanctions. The defendants appealed, requiring the Sixth Circuit to determine whether the district court abused its discretion in deciding the plaintiffs adequately proved contempt.

THINGS TO THINK ABOUT while reading *Williamson v. Recovery Limited Partnership*:

1. What is the standard of proof for a contempt finding?

2. Was the failure to comply with the order in this case intentional, or merely negligent? Does it matter?

Williamson v. Recovery Limited Partnership

United States Court of Appeals, Sixth Circuit
467 Fed.Appx. 382 (2012)

PER CURIAM.

In these consolidated appeals, Defendants appeal the district-court order finding them in contempt and awarding $234,982 in costs and attorney fees against them jointly. . . .

I.

In September 1988, a sunken pre-Civil War steamship, the S.S. *Central America,* was located and recovered in the Atlantic Ocean, having sunk in a hurricane off the coast of South Carolina in 1857. A large commercial shipment of gold was recovered from the wreckage. *See Columbus-America Discovery Grp. v. Atlantic Mut. Ins. Co.,* 56 F.3d 556, 561 (4th Cir.1995). Following several trials and appeals in that *in rem* proceeding in admiralty, the plaintiff salvor, Columbus-America Discovery Group (CADG), was awarded 90% of the recovered treasure, and the insurance companies claiming subrogated interests in the recovered treasure some portion of the remainder.

Defendant Thomas G. Thompson organized RLP in 1985 to finance a search-and-recovery project for the shipwreck of the *S.S. Central America,* and is its general partner as well as chairman of CX. Defendants Gilman D. Kirk, Jr., Michael J. Ford, James F. Turner, and W. Arthur Cullman, Jr., are other directors of CX and managers of RLP (collectively with Thompson, "Defendant Directors").

Plaintiffs Dispatch Printing Company, an Ohio corporation, and Donald C. Fanta (Plaintiffs) are investors in and members of CX, and limited partners of RLP. Dispatch Printing Company invested $1 million in RLP and Fanta invested $500,000 in the project ($250,000 in RLP, and $250,000 in CX's predecessor).

A.

Plaintiffs' complaints alleged that Thompson and Defendant Directors organized RLP in the mid-1980s, and organized CX in 1998 to take over from RLP the recovery, marketing and sale efforts for the treasure. At Defendant Directors' direction, RLP transferred its salvage rights to CX for the treasure already recovered (Up Treasure), more than one ton of gold and silver, and other artifacts, as well as the treasure remaining at the shipwreck (Down Treasure), in exchange for an additional ownership interest in CX for RLP and its partners. Thereafter, at Defendant Directors' direction, CX took over from RLP the management of operations to market the Up Treasure and also the financing, recovery and marketing efforts regarding the Down Treasure.

Plaintiffs' amended complaint alleged that starting in 1999, Defendants began a series of wrongful maneuvers to take control of the companies and treasure to the exclusion of their minority investors, including deliberately abandoning all corporate formalities, refusing to hold annual meetings to elect new directors, refusing to provide investors with financial statements, and wasting millions in assets through self-dealing transactions. . . .

After Defendants removed the action to federal court in April 2006, the parties filed numerous motions, including cross-motions for injunctive relief. Following a settlement conference and 10 1/2 hours of court-led mediation on July 10, 2006, the district court ordered a review of CX's and RLP's financial affairs from 2000 to date by KPMG, a forensic accounting firm Plaintiffs retained.

B.

On July 20, 2006, the district court entered a Consent Order that provided in pertinent part:

> 1. Plaintiffs' claims against Defendants for injunction to compel production of financial and business records of CX and RLP, and for accounting of the companies' financial affairs, are hereby fully and finally resolved and —adjudicated in accordance with the terms and conditions of this Order. . . .
>
> . . . .
>
> 3. Within sixty (60) days after entry of this Order, Defendants shall provide Plaintiffs' accountant [KPMG] (hereafter, the "Accountant") with full access and opportunity to review the documents and materials *regarding the period from January 1, 2000 through the date of entry of this Order, identified in the July 11, 2006 list by Accountant, for the purpose of preparing a report (hereinafter, "Report") of the financial affairs and condition of CX and RLP.*
>
> *Defendants shall make available to the Accountant upon request all documents in response to paragraph 25 of the Accountant's July 11, 2006 letter regardless of their date. The preceding sentence shall not otherwise enlarge or contract the scope of the documents reviewable by the Accountant.*
>
> 4. All documents and materials *identified* in the July 11, 2006 *list by the Accountant* shall be produced by Defendants to Accountant, provided, however, that individual personal information . . . may be redacted . . . Defendants shall make the documents *listed* in the Accountant's July 11, 2006 letter available to the Accountant at CX's Ohio office, or at the Ohio office of CX's accountants. Defendants and their accountants shall provide reasonable cooperation and assistance to the Accountant [KPMG] in connection with its Report. . . .

After entry of the July 20, 2006 Consent Order, Plaintiffs filed five motions for contempt, asserting that Defendants failed to comply with the Consent Order and other orders. Although the district court denied Plaintiffs' motions, it found that Defendant Entities had violated the Consent Order and other orders, and reserved the issue of sanctions. . . .

On October 16, 2007, Plaintiffs moved for damages for violations of the Consent order and other orders, seeking approximately $400,000 in fees for KPMG, and legal fees. The district court found Defendants in contempt and awarded damages against them collectively of $193,892 in accounting fees and $41,090 in attorney fees against them collectively. Both sets of Defendants timely appealed and the appeals were consolidated. . . .

II.

The order from which this appeal was taken resulted from cross-motions — Plaintiffs' Motion for Damages filed on October 16, 2007, which argued that Defendants violated court orders in ten instances. The district court granted Defendants' motion, and granted Plaintiffs' motion in part, finding two instances of willful failure to comply with its orders. The first was Defendant Entities' failure to timely deliver to KPMG documents described in paragraph 3 of the Consent Order [documents and materials regarding the period from January 1, 2000 through July 20, 2006, identified in KPMG's July 11, 2006 list], and the second was Defendant Directors' failure to show that they were unable to comply with the Consent Order.

A.

. . . The movant in a civil contempt proceeding bears the burden of proving by clear and convincing evidence that the respondent "violated a definite and specific order of the court requiring him to perform or refrain from performing a particular act or acts with knowledge of the court's order." *Glover v. Johnson,* 934 F.2d 703, 707 (6th Cir.1991). This Court requires that the prior order be "clear and unambiguous" to support a finding of contempt. *Grace v. Ctr. for Auto Safety,* 72 F.3d 1236, 1241 (6th Cir.1996). Ambiguities must be resolved in favor of the party charged with contempt.

"Once the movant establishes his prima facie case, the burden shifts to the contemnor who may defend by coming forward with evidence showing that he is presently unable to comply with the court's order." *Elec. Workers Pension Trust Fund v. Gary's Electric Serv. Co.,* 340 F.3d 373, 379 (emphasis in original), citing *United States v. Rylander,* 460 U.S. 752, 757 (1983) ("Where compliance is impossible, neither the moving party nor the court has any reason to proceed with the civil contempt action. It is settled, however, that in raising this defense, the defendant has a burden of production.").

. . . .

The Defendant Directors' defiance of a Consent Order issued on July 20, 2006 prompted the district court's contempt finding. The Consent Order — which the

Directors individually endorsed — required the Defendants to account for certain disputed documents: "Within sixty (60) days after the entry of this order, Defendants shall provide Plaintiffs' accountant [KPMG] . . . with full access and opportunity to review [certain specified] documents and materials . . . for the purpose of preparing a report . . . of the financial affairs and condition of" the Entities. The Consent Order further compelled "Defendants and their accountant," Stephen Alexander, to "provide reasonable cooperation and assistance to [KPMG] in connection with its Report."

The Defendants then took nearly two years to finally produce all the required documents. In the interim, the court repeatedly chastised the Defendants for their delays and non-compliance. At one point, the court issued an order finding "a total lack of good faith of at least CX and RLP in compliance with the" order. In the same order, the district court questioned "the claim by Defendants' counsel that CX and RLP could not locate minutes from Board or Member meetings," which the court described as "basic to the performance of the Defendants' legal obligations in terms of organizational management." The district court also noted the Directors' apparent indifference to the order at an in-court hearing held five months after entry of the Consent Order, warning that "a word to the wise would be in order with regard to the individual defendants" going forward.

Ultimately, the district court ordered that the Defendants be held in contempt for refusing to produce the required documents in a timely manner. In its well-reasoned opinion, the court rejected five contempt allegations but agreed with two: failure to produce recovered-treasure inventories and failure to produce certain accounting work papers. Finding that the individual Directors willfully violated the Consent Order, the court first quoted Justice Hughes in *Wilson v. United States*, 221 U.S. 361, 376 (1911):

> A command to the corporation is in effect a command to those who are officially responsible for the conduct of its affairs. If they, apprised of the writ directed to the corporation, prevent compliance or fail to take appropriate action within their power for the performance of the corporate duty, they, no less than the corporation itself, are guilty of disobedience, and may be punished for contempt.

It went on to lay out the basis for its finding of contempt:

> The officers and directors of the entities had a clear obligation to comply with the Consent Order entered in this case. The Plaintiffs have shown a clear violation of the Order; thereafter, the Defendants must show that they were unable to comply with the order by demonstrating the impossibility of compliance. *United States v. Rylander*, 460 U.S. 752, 757 (1983).

> No such showing has been made by the entities nor by the officers and directors. The evidence presented by the officers and directors is minimal at best. The record discloses that no formal meetings were held to establish methods of locating or obtaining documents subject to disclosure by

the Consent Order. No evidence of follow up on the delivery of documents was presented. No documentation of steps taken to comply with the Consent Order was made part of the record in this case. No officers or employee was designated to comply with requests, as far as the record indicates. . . .

The district court thus concluded that the "individual directors and officers" were "in willful contempt of" the court's prior orders because 1) the Directors "had a clear obligation to comply with the Consent Order"; 2) they failed to comply; and 3) the failure resulted from purposeful inaction. Ample evidence in the record supports each element of the district court's reasoning. . . .

The district court's opinion notes that the Directors 1) never formally met to discuss the Consent Order; 2) never designated any directors or officers to oversee compliance with the Consent Order; and 3) never took any other affirmative steps to comply with the Consent Order.

The deposition testimony of the Director Defendants supports the district court's findings. When asked whether the directors "ever set up a policy or procedure by which the company would report back to the directors as to the status of the production of documents under the Consent Order," Director Defendant Gilman Kirk replied, "No." When asked whether the directors "appoint [ed] anyone to be the responsible person for ensuring compliance with the" Consent Order, Director Defendant Michael Ford said, "Not that I know of." When asked whether he ever spoke with Alexander about the Consent Order, Director Defendant Thomas Thompson answered, "No."

That the Directors lacked personal knowledge of the records' whereabouts is no excuse. Though non-compliance can be excused if compliance is impossible and "lack of possession or control of records" can be grounds for impossibility, *see, e.g., United States v. Rylander*, 460 U.S. 752, 757 (1983), the Directors' ultimate control over the disputed documents cannot seriously be questioned. Alexander and Robol may have been the only individuals who directly accessed the records, but the Directors had the ability to, at the very least, monitor Alexander and Robol and ensure that the Entities complied with the district court's order. Indeed, the Directors' fiduciary duties under Delaware law *required* them to oversee the actions of their officers and employees. *See, e.g., In re Citigroup Inc. Shareholder Derivative Litigation*, 964 A.2d 106, 122–23 (Del.Ch.2009).

Our own longstanding precedent confirms that ignorance is no defense to inaction in the face of a court order. More than 75 years ago, we upheld a district court's finding of contempt against corporate directors who failed to ensure their corporation's compliance with a permanent injunction issued against it in a patent infringement case. *Telling v. Bellows-Claude Neon Co.*, 77 F.2d 584, 586–87 (6th Cir.1935). In rejecting the directors' ignorance defense, we held:

That the injunctional order was disobeyed by the corporation, and that it is liable, is not in dispute. That the decree was directed not only to the corporation, but to its officers and agents, and that Telling and Curtis knew its terms, is also not in controversy. It is urged, however, that lack of knowledge on the part of Telling and Curtis that their orders had been disobeyed and their records falsified, and the failure of the evidence to show any willful or contumacious acts upon their part in defiance of the injunction, absolves them from liability. We do not understand, however, that in cases of corporate infringement knowledge of the director or officer charged with infringing that the article manufactured or sold (or leased or serviced) did infringe, is material. Nor is either willfulness or contumaciousness an essential element in civil contempt, however indispensable it may be to a finding of criminal contempt . . .

Parties to an order must take *"all reasonable steps* within their power to comply with the court's order." *Elec. Workers Pension Trust Fund of Local Union 58, IBEW v. Gary's Elec.*, 340 F.3d 373, 379 (6th Cir.2003) (emphasis added). The Directors' failure to take meaningful steps to ensure compliance with the Consent Order solidly underpins the contempt judgment of the district court here.

Supreme Court precedent, Delaware law, CX's charter, and the Directors' endorsement of the Consent Order all compelled the Directors to abide by the order's terms. The district court found that despite this clear obligation, the Directors failed to take even modest steps toward ensuring compliance. Finding no grounds to disturb the district court's well-founded exercise of its broad discretion, we affirm the district court's judgment [.]

* * *

Problem 56

Contempt is the failure to comply with a clear court order despite having the ability to do so. What are the best arguments to be made in defense of the alleged contemnor in the below case?

The divorced parents of a 12-year-old child share physical custody. The parents live in different states, about a thousand miles apart. A court order from the divorce case requires that the child spend six months per year with each parent. At the conclusion of the six-month period, the order directs that the parent with whom the child is residing must arrange for and facilitate travel for the child to the other parent's home.

The child's six months with her father nears its conclusion, and the father books a ticket for her to travel on an airline to the city where the mother lives. When the travel day arrives, the father takes the child to the airport and accompanies her to the gate. But the child refuses to get on the plane, insisting she does not want to go. The father tries to convince her but she is steadfast in her refusal. The plane leaves without her on board. When the child does not arrive as scheduled, the mother files a motion in the court that handled the divorce case, asking that the father be found in contempt for failure to comply with the travel order.

Direct and Indirect Contempt

This chapter has focused so far on contempt for not obeying a court order. A related usage of the term contempt might be more familiar: when a person is found to be in contempt for disrupting court proceedings. That kind of contempt is called direct contempt. Direct contempt refers only to conduct that occurs in the courtroom, in the presence of the judge.

The contempt more relevant to the study of remedies — contempt for failure to obey a court order — is referred to as indirect contempt, or constructive contempt.

Because the conduct alleged to constitute indirect contempt happens outside the courtroom and the judge is not a witness to it, a more involved process is required to prove contempt occurred. The party seeking a contempt finding must present evidence showing the order in question was violated and a hearing must be conducted to allow the alleged contemnor to present a defense.

Introductory Note — *Ex parte Daniels* and *State v. Diaz de la Portilla*

The contemptuous conduct in *Ex parte Daniels* is a litigant arguing with a judge and then refusing to leave the courtroom after being ordered to do so. In *State v. Diaz de la Portilla*, the basis for the contempt is a party's failure to appear at a scheduled hearing. In both cases, the issue on appeal is whether the contempt is direct or indirect.

THINGS TO THINK ABOUT while reading *Ex parte Daniels* and *State v. Diaz de la Portilla*:

1. What is the purpose of allowing a court to summarily find someone in direct contempt?

2. What type of punishment can be imposed for direct contempt? For indirect contempt?

3. What procedure must be followed before punishing someone for direct contempt? For indirect contempt?

Ex parte Daniels
Texas Court of Criminal Appeals
722 S.W.2d 707 (1987)

McCORMICK, Judge.

This is an application for writ of habeas corpus filed pursuant to the provisions of Article 11.06, V.A.C.C.P.

Applicant was held to be in direct criminal contempt of court by the Honorable Max W. Boyer, sitting by assignment in the 308th District Court in Harris County. The contempt order was the result of an incident which occurred on January 22, 1985, while applicant was appearing pro se.

In the course of the proceedings, applicant became involved in an argument with Judge Boyer. The judge ordered applicant to leave the courtroom and to not return until she obtained counsel. When applicant failed to leave the courtroom immediately, the bailiff was ordered to escort her out.

Applicant apparently went peacefully with the bailiff until they reached the doorway of the courtroom. At that point, applicant is alleged to have physically attacked the master of the court. The bailiff then moved to restrain applicant and a general disturbance erupted in which several people were involved.

The record indicates that at some point after this occurrence the trial judge ordered applicant brought before him for a summary contempt proceeding. During the course of this hearing, applicant did not have the benefit of retained counsel but instead continued to act in a pro se capacity. Applicant was found to be in direct criminal contempt and ordered to be confined in jail for a period of thirty days. No fine was imposed. Applicant was ordered to pay thirty-three dollars in court costs. . . .

Contempt power is a necessary and integral component of judicial authority. *Gompers v. Bucks Stove & Range Company,* 221 U.S. 418 (1911). While it is clear the exercise of this authority should be tempered with common sense and sound discretion, contempt power is accorded wide latitude because it is essential to judicial independence and authority. *Ex parte Browne,* 543 S.W.2d 82 (Tex.Cr.App.1976); *Shillitani v. United States,* 384 U.S. 364 (1966).

At the outset of any discussion or judicial determination of the right of due process in a contempt case, it is necessary to distinguish "direct" contempt from "constructive" contempt. Direct contempt is contempt which is committed or occurs in the presence of the court. In direct contempt cases the court has direct knowledge of the facts which constitute contempt. Constructive or indirect contempt involves actions outside of the presence of the court. Constructive contempt refers to acts which require testimony or the production of evidence to establish their existence.

The distinction is important because due process imposes different standards for the proceedings in which the contempt is adjudicated. In cases of constructive contempt in which factual issues relating to activities outside the court's presence must be resolved, due process requires the accused be afforded notice and a hearing. *Ex parte Standard,* 596 S.W.2d 218 (Tex.Cr.App.1980); *Ex parte Mouille,* 572 S.W.2d 60 (Tex.Cr.App.1978). In a situation involving indirect or constructive contempt, the contemner cannot be legally confined without a reasonable opportunity to obtain counsel. *Cooke v. United States,* 267 U.S. 517 (1925); *Ex parte Flournoy,* 312 S.W.2d 488 (Tex.1958), and cases cited therein.

In cases of direct contempt, however, the behavior constituting contempt has occurred in the presence of the court. The judge has personal knowledge of the events in question and the court is allowed to conduct a summary proceeding in which the contemner is not accorded notice nor a hearing in the usual sense of the word. *Ex parte Flournoy,* supra; *Ex parte Norton,* 610 S.W.2d 512 (Tex.Cr.App.1981).

Furthermore, in cases of direct contempt, the accused has no right to counsel. *Cooke v. United States,* supra; *Ex parte Norton,* supra. The right to counsel is, of course, one of the most fundamental protections guaranteed under the United States Constitution. The rationale for this very limited exception to the basic principle of the right to counsel was explained in the case of *Cooke v. United States,* supra:

> "To preserve order in the courtroom for the proper conduct of business, the court must act instantly to suppress disturbance or violence or physical obstruction or disrespect to the court, when occurring in open court. There is no need of evidence or assistance of counsel before punishment, because the court has seen the offense. Such summary vindication of the court's dignity and authority is necessary. It has always been so in the courts of the common law, and the punishment imposed is due process of law. . . ." 267 U.S. at 394.

Applicant has argued that the acts of contempt which she is accused of having committed did not take place in the judge's presence. Applicant states that the judge did not actually see much of the activity which took place at the door of the courtroom. Applicant states that the judge required testimony before he could make a complete determination that contemptuous actions occurred. Therefore, applicant argues her contempt was constructive rather than direct and applicant therefore argues that she was denied due process because she was denied the right of counsel.

The record reflects that the activities which gave rise to applicant's being held in contempt occurred in the 308th District Court while Judge Boyer was present and seated at the bench. Applicant states in effect that due to the rapid and confusing sequence of events the judge did not actually see everything that occurred, but only witnessed a general disturbance. Applicant urges this Court to accept the proposition that this means the actions constituting contempt did not occur in the presence of the court.

Applicant overlooks the fact that "in the presence of the court" does not necessarily mean in the immediate presence of the trial judge. *Ex parte Aldridge,* 169 Tex. Cr.R. 395 (1960). As we stated above, the rationale justifying the harsh remedy of direct contempt adjudications is that the authority and ability of the courts to conduct the peoples' business is compromised by the disruptive actions of the alleged contemner. *Ex parte Harvill,* 415 S.W.2d 174 (Tex.1967). It is for this reason that this Court has held that the court is present whenever any of its constituent parts, the courtroom, the jury and the jury room are engaged in pursuing the work of the court. *Ex parte Aldridge,* supra. It was for this reason that the applicant in *Ex parte Aldridge,* supra, was properly determined to have committed direct contempt when he placed contemptuous publications in the corridors of the courthouse where prospective jurors would necessarily see them. *Ex parte Aldridge* 334 S.W.2d at 169.

In the case before us, it is clear that applicant's behavior was sufficiently "before the court" to justify a determination that she was in direct contempt of the court. Her actions took place in the presence of the trial judge. Even though some details of the disturbance were not noted by the trial judge due to the confusion and rapid sequence of the events does not mean the incident did not occur in the presence of the court. It is undisputed that the judge witnessed what he considered a disturbance and felt compelled to interrupt court business and intervene in the activities which took place at the courtroom entrance. The judge felt it was necessary to further interrupt the court's business by calling a recess.

The bailiff and the master of the court are court officers. The ability of the 308th District Court to conduct its duties was compromised by the direct physical attack on one of its officers in the courtroom and in the physical presence of the trial judge. As such, applicant's actions constitute direct contempt. . . .

The relief prayed for is denied.

* * *

State v. Diaz de la Portilla

Florida Supreme Court
177 So.3d 965 (2015)

LEWIS, J.

This case is before the Court for review of the decision of the First District Court of Appeal in *Diaz de la Portilla v. State,* 142 So.3d 928 (Fla. 1st DCA 2014). In its decision the district court ruled upon the following question, which the court certified to be of great public importance:

> Whether a party who is ordered by a trial court to appear at a scheduled hearing, but fails to do so, may be found in direct criminal contempt under Florida Rule of Criminal Procedure 3.830; or whether such conduct should be addressed as indirect criminal contempt under Florida Rule of Criminal Procedure 3.840?

Both Diaz de la Portilla and the State take the position that the failure to appear pursuant to an order should be treated as *indirect* criminal contempt under rule 3.840. We agree.

Background

This criminal contempt matter arises from the failure of Respondent Alex Diaz de la Portilla to appear pursuant to a court order at a hearing on a motion to hold him in contempt during a dissolution of marriage proceeding. During the dissolution proceeding, Diaz de la Portilla was ordered to deliver one of two dogs owned by the couple into the wife's custody, which he failed to do. As a result, the wife filed a motion for contempt. A hearing on the motion was scheduled, and the trial court issued an order to show cause that directed Diaz de la Portilla to appear.

During the hearing on the motion for contempt, at which Diaz de la Portilla did not appear, the trial court held him in civil contempt for failure to comply with the order to transfer the dog to his wife. The court ordered Diaz de la Portilla to comply with the order or be committed to jail for thirty days. However, Diaz de la Portilla still did not transfer the dog, and another motion for contempt was filed. The motion was served on counsel for Diaz de la Portilla, and at a subsequent hearing on the motion, only counsel for Diaz de la Portilla was present, not Diaz de la Portilla himself. No explanation was provided for his absence.

The trial court verbally held Diaz de la Portilla in civil contempt for failure to comply with the order to appear, as well as the order to transfer the dog. The trial court also held Diaz de la Portilla in criminal contempt, explaining:

> At this juncture in this case it is my opinion that it is no longer practical, no longer possible for me to coerce compliance because your client is not going to do it. He is going to absent himself; he is going to continue to vilify his wife; he is going to continue to thumb his nose at this Court and to challenge my authority to enforce not only my Orders but the Orders of [the

predecessor judge.] . . . Based upon the sworn Motion and the sworn testimony today I find him to be in civil contempt for not appearing today and not giving the dog to [his wife] as per [the predecessor judge's] Order. . . . In addition, based upon the fact that I have ordered him to appear and he has not appeared here today I find him in direct criminal contempt. . . .

Analysis

Direct Criminal Contempt

This Court has previously explained the difference between direct and indirect criminal contempt:

> Where the act constituting the contempt is committed in the immediate presence of the court, this contempt is defined as direct. Where an act is committed out of the presence of the court, the proceeding to punish is for indirect (sometimes called constructive) contempt. A review of the Rules of Criminal Procedure . . . reflects the greater procedural due process safeguards imposed when proceedings are for indirect criminal contempt.

Pugliese v. Pugliese, 347 So.2d 422, 425 (Fla.1977). Direct criminal contempt, also referred to as summary contempt, *see Scott v. Anderson,* 405 So.2d 228, 237 (Fla. 1st DCA 1981), is governed by Florida Rule of Criminal Procedure 3.830, which provides for limited procedural protections:

> A criminal contempt may be punished summarily if the court saw or heard the conduct constituting the contempt committed in the actual presence of the court. The judgment of guilt of contempt shall include a recital of those facts on which the adjudication of guilt is based. Prior to the adjudication of guilt the judge shall inform the defendant of the accusation against the defendant and inquire as to whether the defendant has any cause to show why he or she should not be adjudged guilty of contempt by the court and sentenced therefor. The defendant shall be given the opportunity to present evidence of excusing or mitigating circumstances. The judgment shall be signed by the judge and entered of record. Sentence shall be pronounced in open court.

In contrast, rule 3.840, governing indirect criminal contempt, requires additional procedural protections be provided to the person being held in contempt. *See Pugliese,* 347 So.2d at 425.

The United States Supreme Court explained the purpose and parameters of summary contempt in *Cooke v. United States,* 267 U.S. 517 (1925). In *Cooke,* an attorney wrote a derogatory letter to a trial judge questioning his impartiality and requesting that he recuse himself. After the trial court confirmed that the attorney wrote the letter, it found him to be in contempt without allowing him to present a defense or mitigation. However, the Supreme Court determined that the circumstances did not warrant the use of summary procedures because the defiance did not occur in open court. The Supreme Court explained:

To preserve order in the court room for the proper conduct of business, the court must act instantly to suppress disturbance or violence or physical obstruction or disrespect to the court when occurring in open court. There is no need of evidence or assistance of counsel before punishment, because the court has seen the offense. Such summary vindication of the court's dignity and authority is necessary.

The Supreme Court reasoned that routine due process requirements were not necessary in cases involving conduct in open court viewed by the judge, and the need for immediate vindication of the dignity of the court justified bypassing normal procedural due process requirements. However, the Supreme Court concluded that there would be no justification for a departure from normal procedures when the contempt did not occur in open court. The Supreme Court later commented that where the facts on which the contempt is based are established through testimony, summary contempt, without an opportunity for defense, is not justified. *In re Oliver,* 333 U.S. 257, 275 (1948).

This Court has also discussed the distinctions between direct and indirect criminal contempt. In *Pugliese,* which involved a dissolution of marriage, the judgment of dissolution required the husband to vacate a portion of the marital residence by a certain date. After the judgment was entered in the dissolution proceedings, counsel advised the husband that he was not yet required to vacate the premises because counsel had filed a motion for new trial, stay of execution, and notice of hearing. The wife filed a motion for contempt and notice of hearing, which were served on counsel for the husband only, not the husband. During the contempt hearing, the husband admitted he did not vacate the property and was held in contempt. The order did not specify whether the contempt was civil or criminal, or, if criminal, direct or indirect.

On review, this Court concluded that because the conduct did not occur in the presence of the trial court, it was, at most, indirect criminal contempt. The Court rejected the assertion of the wife that the admission by the husband in open court to the contemptuous conduct (remaining in the residence) supplied a basis for direct criminal contempt. The Court explained that the position advocated by the wife eliminated the distinction between direct and indirect criminal contempt because any time a trial court hears testimony in connection with indirect criminal contempt for conduct that occurred outside its presence, the testimony will nonetheless occur within the presence of the trial court. Additionally, the Court provided the following recommendation with respect to the conversion of civil contempt proceedings into criminal contempt proceedings:

> It is possible to convert civil contempt proceedings to criminal contempt proceedings after a hearing is commenced. Such a conversion would mandate the continuation of the hearing to provide for issuance of an order to show cause that complies with the rule with fair opportunity to the respondent to prepare and be heard. However, such practice flirts with procedural due process flaws. Accordingly, better practice suggests that such situations be anticipated in advance wherever possible so that the full due process safeguards required by Fla. R.Crim. P. 3.840 will be afforded.

Id. at 426–27.

. . . The procedures delineated by rule 3.830 governing direct criminal contempt simply are not suited for application to a failure to appear pursuant to a court order. The order of contempt adjudicates the defendant guilty, and the provisions of rule 3.830 define the essence of due process in direct criminal contempt proceedings. *See Hutcheson v. State,* 903 So.2d 1060, 1062 (Fla. 5th DCA 2005) (citing *Keeton v. Bryant,* 877 So.2d 922, 926 (Fla. 5th DCA 2004); *M.L. v. State,* 819 So.2d 240, 242 (Fla. 2d DCA 2002)). Before a person may be convicted for direct criminal contempt, rule 3.830 requires the trial court to inform the defendant of the basis for the contempt and inquire whether the defendant has any cause to show why he or she should not be adjudicated guilty and sentenced for contempt. Fla. R.Crim. P. 3.830. Additionally, the defendant must be provided with an opportunity to present evidence of excusing or mitigating circumstances. *Id.* When an individual fails to appear, the court is not capable of making the necessary inquiries of the absent individual, and likewise is unable to hear evidence of excusing or mitigating circumstances. The rules of criminal contempt must be strictly followed so as to protect the due process rights of the defendant. *See Pugliese,* 347 So.2d at 426 (holding that due process demands conformity with rule 3.840); *see also Searcy v. State,* 971 So.2d 1008, 1014 (Fla. 3d DCA 2008) (holding that courts must strictly comply with rule 3.830).

Additionally, treating a failure to appear as direct criminal contempt does not fulfill the purpose of this narrow form of contempt, which applies when a contemptuous act occurs in the presence of the court, is an affront to the court, disrupts and frustrates an ongoing proceeding, and requires immediate action to vindicate the authority of the court. *See United States v. Wilson,* 421 U.S. 309, 315–16 (1975). Direct criminal contempt should not be employed where time is not of the essence. Where a contempt is based on an individual's failure to appear, the trial court would still be required to conduct a hearing at a later date, when the alleged contemnor is present, to conform to the due process requirements of rule 3.830. Immediate action to preserve the court's order and authority is simply not possible where the disruptive misconduct is a failure to appear.

Moreover, the trial court may not have personal knowledge with respect to whether an individual knew that his or her presence was required, or whether the individual was somehow unable to appear, and therefore could not know whether the nonappearance was willful. *See United States v. Nunez,* 801 F.2d 1260, 1264 (11th Cir.1986). Intent is an essential element of contempt, *see Woods v. State,* 987 So.2d 669, 676 (Fla. 2d DCA 2007), and to support a conviction for direct criminal contempt, the trial court must have knowledge of each element of the contempt. *See In re Terry,* 128 U.S. 289, 312 (1888) ("The judicial eye witnessed the act and the judicial mind comprehended all the circumstances of aggravation, provocation, or mitigation; and the fact being thus judicially established, it only remained for the judicial arm to inflict proper punishment."). Each act or event associated with a failure to appear that provides the basis for a charge of criminal contempt does not occur in the actual presence of the trial court, and, therefore, cannot constitute direct criminal contempt. Instead, should a failure to appear result in a charge of criminal contempt, a court must follow the procedures delineated by rule 3.840 governing indirect criminal contempt.

Conclusion

We remand this case for proceedings consistent with this opinion.

* * *

Problem 57

Direct contempt is conduct that is witnessed by the judge and can therefore be summarily punished. Indirect contempt is a failure to obey a court order and requires a fact-finding process before punishment can be imposed. Is the conduct of the witness described below contempt? If so, is it direct or indirect?

A witness in a civil lawsuit is subpoenaed for deposition (ordered to appear at the office of the lawyer representing the plaintiff and answer questions under oath). The witness appears at the lawyer's office and answers the first few questions, but then refuses to answer any others. The next day, lawyers for both sides appear in court and explain the situation to the judge presiding over the case. The plaintiff's lawyer submits two exhibits to the court: the validly issued subpoena ordering the witness to testify at deposition; and a transcript of the deposition which shows the questions the witness refused to answer. After reviewing the exhibits, the judge makes a finding that the witness was lawfully subpoenaed and was obligated to answer the questions posed. The plaintiff's lawyer requests that the judge find the witness in contempt.

Civil and Criminal Contempt

The sanction imposed for contempt is either a monetary penalty or imprisonment. Depending on the circumstances, a contempt proceeding can be either civil or criminal. Civil contempt is coercive. It is designed to motivate the subject to comply with an order in the future. Contempt is also considered civil when it is compensatory, a monetary payment intended to reimburse the plaintiff for losses incurred as the result of the contemptuous conduct. Criminal contempt, on the other hand, is entirely punitive. It is intended to punish the subject for past noncompliance.

Contempt proceedings can trigger interesting procedural issues because it can be difficult to tell whether the contempt sanction imposed is civil or criminal, and the answer to that question bears greatly on the procedure the accused contemnor is entitled to. If the contempt is criminal, a higher degree of due process protection — trial by jury, for example — might be required.

Contempt is not criminal solely because imprisonment is involved. The sanction of imprisonment is criminal when it is intended to be punitive. But imprisonment can also be used as a tool of coercion to achieve future compliance with an order. A court might use imprisonment to coerce compliance by requiring that the person who disobeyed an order be jailed until he or she complies with that order. As long as the person has the ability to comply, that kind of contempt sanction is coercive, not punitive, and is therefore considered civil, not criminal.

Introductory Note — *Koninklijke Philips Electronics v. KXD Technology, Inc.* and *Wronke v. Madigan*

Koninklijke Philips Electronics involves a common scenario where contempt is employed as the ultimate remedy in a civil suit: a trademark infringement case where the infringer is ordered to stop selling counterfeit goods but continues to do so. After finding the defendants in contempt, the district court imposed an array of monetary sanctions. The defendants immediately filed an interlocutory appeal (an appeal that comes before the final judgment in a case). That requires the Ninth Circuit to decide whether the contempt sanctions were civil or criminal, because only criminal contempt sanctions are appealable before the final judgment.

In *Wronke v. Madigan*, the contempt sanction is imprisonment. On habeas corpus, the petitioner claims that the imprisonment constitutes criminal contempt and he must be released because he was never provided a jury trial as is constitutionally required before imprisoning someone for a crime. The district court must therefore decide whether the petitioner's ongoing imprisonment is a civil or criminal contempt sanction.

THINGS TO THINK ABOUT while reading *Koninklijke Philips Electronics v. KXD Technology, Inc.*, and *Wronke v. Madigan*:

1. What distinguishes civil contempt from criminal contempt?

2. Why is it necessary to distinguish between civil and criminal contempt?

Koninklijke Phillips Electronics v. KXD Technology, Inc.

United States Court of Appeals, Ninth Circuit
539 F.3d 1039 (2008)

WALKER, Circuit Judge:

Defendants-Appellants KXD Technology, Inc., Astar Electronics, Inc., Shenzen KXD Multimedia, Inc., Shenzhen Kaixinda Electronics Co., Ltd., KXD Digital Entertainment, Ltd., and Jingyi Luo, a/k/a James Luo, appeal from an order of the United States District Court for the District of Nevada imposing monetary sanctions for civil contempt. Because we lack appellate jurisdiction, the appeal is dismissed.

I. Background

Plaintiff-Appellee, Koninklijke Philips Electronics N.V. ("Philips") sued the above-named defendants, alleging that they had infringed Philips's registered trademark and had knowingly offered counterfeited Philips goods for sale in the United States. On January 5, 2006, the district court issued an amended temporary restraining and seizure order that was immediately served on the defendants at the Consumer Electronics Show in Las Vegas, Nevada. The following day, because defendants' principal place of business and warehouse was in California, Philips sought and was granted a temporary restraining and seizure order by the United States District Court for the Central District of California. That order was served at defendants' California warehouse, where the Marshals Service found and confiscated counterfeit products bearing the Philips trademark.

On March 14, 2006, the district court issued a preliminary injunction that principally enjoined defendants from dealing in any product that infringed Philips's trademarks. The district court also ordered defendants to file a report setting forth their inventory of counterfeit Philips products by April 13, 2006 and a report describing in detail their compliance with the preliminary injunction by May 15, 2006. Before these reports were due, on April 10, 2006, the district court issued another seizure order, which resulted in the confiscation of additional counterfeit Philips products at locations controlled by the defendants.

By February of 2007, it became clear to the district court that the defendants had no intention of complying with its orders. The district court noted that there was "abundant evidence of the Defendants' non-compliance and active violations of both the TRO and preliminary injunction." In fact, the defendants had failed to file any reports, required or otherwise, showing that they had complied in any way with the district court's orders. This failure continued even after the plaintiff moved for sanctions on October 11, 2006. At the sanctions hearing, the district court granted plaintiff's motion for civil contempt sanctions, holding the defendants jointly and severally liable to the plaintiff for: (1) $353,611.70 in attorney's fees; (2) $37,098.14 in seizure and storage costs; (3) $1,284,090.00 in lost royalties; and (4) $10,000.00 per day until the reports were filed. In addition, the court ordered defendants to post a $2 million bond.

The defendants now appeal the district court's imposition of sanctions. The plaintiff contends that such an interlocutory appeal is impermissible and that we lack jurisdiction to hear it.

II. Analysis

Civil vs. Criminal Contempt Orders

"The rule is settled in this Court that except in connection with an appeal from a final judgment or decree, a party to a suit may not review upon appeal an order fining or imprisoning him for the commission of a civil contempt." *Fox v. Capital Co.,* 299 U.S. 105 (1936). This court "do[es] have jurisdiction[, however,] to hear appeals from criminal contempt orders because they are appealable when entered." *Bingman,* 100 F.3d at 655.

Thus, to ascertain its jurisdiction, a court of appeals "must decide whether the order before [it] [i]s one for civil contempt or one for criminal contempt." *Id.* As we have noted, the "distinction between the two forms of contempt lies in the intended effect of the punishment imposed. The purpose of civil contempt is coercive or compensatory, whereas the purpose of criminal contempt is punitive." *United States v. Armstrong,* 781 F.2d 700, 703 (9th Cir.1986).

Although this explanation of the "dichotomy between civil and criminal contempt is helpful, it is not quite complete." *Bingman,* 100 F.3d at 655. Often it is necessary to explore other aspects of the contempt order to determine its character. For example, the Supreme Court has found it useful to ascertain to whom the fine is payable, suggesting that a fine "is remedial when it is paid to the complainant, and punitive when it is paid to the court." *Hicks ex rel. Feiock v. Feiock,* 485 U.S. 624, 632 (1988). Also instructive is whether the fine imposed is conditional in nature. In this regard, the Supreme Court has stated that "[a]n unconditional penalty is criminal in nature because it is solely and exclusively punitive in character. . . . A conditional penalty, by contrast, is civil because it is specifically designed to compel the doing of some act." *Hicks,* 485 U.S. at 633.

Taking all of these considerations into account, the Supreme Court has stated that:

> A contempt fine accordingly is considered civil and remedial if it either "coerce[s] the defendant into compliance with the court's order, [or] . . . compensate[s] the complainant for losses sustained." Where a fine is not compensatory, it is civil only if the contemnor is offered an opportunity to purge.

United Mine Workers v. Bagwell, 512 U.S. 821, 829 (1994). Thus, an otherwise criminal contempt order (i.e., an order not intended to be compensatory) will nevertheless be categorized as civil, and thus not appealable on interlocutory review, when the defendant is given an opportunity to comply with the order before payment of the sanction becomes due.

The Instant Contempt Order

The contempt order here is plainly civil under the above test. The attorney's fees, lost royalties, and storage costs were assessed in order to compensate the plaintiff for losses sustained. Furthermore, the per diem fine was not to be assessed until fourteen days after the entry of the order, and the defendants could avoid the fine by complying with the terms of the injunction. Because the per diem fine allowed the defendants the opportunity to purge the contempt before payment became due, it was a civil sanction. We also note that the district court was cognizant of the distinction between the two types of contempts. Although the district court warned the defendants that it "may desire to impose criminal sanctions *next time*," it limited itself "*this time* to civil sanctions." . . .

Finally, to the extent that defendants could face irreparable harm because the contempt order amounts to an executable judgment that the plaintiff could use to levy on defendants' assets, any harm that defendants face is entirely of their own making and does not move us to create a new exception for interlocutory review here. Defendants were afforded the opportunity to immediately appeal the district court's preliminary injunction but declined to do so. Therefore defendants waived any challenge to the sanctions imposed based on the underlying injunction. Furthermore, because the district court's sanction order imposed a bond in an amount approximating that of the sanctions imposed, the plaintiff would have had little reason to execute a judgment based on the sanction order had the defendants actually posted the $2 million bond as ordered. It was the defendants' choice to defy the district court's order, which in turn forced the plaintiff to seek security in other ways.

Additionally, holding that a civil sanction is directly appealable if it is immediately payable risks eviscerating the fundamental rule that compensatory sanctions are civil and not appealable on interlocutory review. Further, we note that defendants will have the opportunity to appeal the sanctions imposed after a final judgment. In sum, we are not persuaded that the defendants face irreparable harm and, in any event, find that, because of defendants' conduct, any risk of harm is appropriately placed upon them.

III. Conclusion

The appeal is dismissed for lack of jurisdiction.

* * *

Wronke v. Madigan

United States District Court, Central District of Illinois
26 F.Supp.2d 1102 (1998)

McCUSKEY, District Judge.

On July 8, 1996, Petitioner, Kenneth L. Wronke, filed his petition under 28 U.S.C. § 2254 for a writ of habeas corpus. Wronke challenges an order entered on October 5, 1995, in the circuit court of Champaign County. The court found Wronke in indirect civil contempt of court and ordered him to be transported to the Champaign County Correctional Center until he purged himself of the contempt. . . . Following careful consideration of the merits of Wronke's claims, the petition for writ of habeas corpus is DENIED.

Facts

On July 12, 1990, Elinor Wronke n/k/a Elinor Canady filed a petition for dissolution of marriage in the circuit court of Champaign County. The case was originally assigned to Judge Harold L. Jensen. A judgment dissolving the marriage of the parties was entered on August 30, 1990. On July 15, 1991, a memorandum order was entered which resolved all remaining issues, including the amount of child support to be paid by Wronke for the two minor children of the parties. On February 6, 1992, Judge Jensen was recused from further proceedings in the case. The case was assigned to Judge Ann A. Einhorn. Wronke was represented by an attorney in the proceedings until his attorney withdrew as counsel on October 15, 1993. From that point on, Wronke appeared pro se. On October 26, 1993, Judge Einhorn ordered that Wronke was to have no visitation with his children and was to have no contact whatsoever with the minor children. On August 31, 1994, Judge Einhorn recused herself from hearing any further matters in the case. On September 6, 1994, the case was reassigned to Judge Jeffrey B. Ford for further proceedings. After Judge Ford ruled on various matters in the case, Wronke filed a motion for substitution of judge on March 21, 1995. Again, on August 25, 1995, Wronke made an oral motion for Judge Ford to recuse himself. The motions were denied.

On October 5, 1995, Judge Ford found Wronke in indirect civil contempt of court and ordered that he was to be transported to the Champaign County Correctional Center until he purged himself of the contempt order. Judge Ford stated that Wronke could purge the contempt by "removing or causing to be removed, the names of his children from the sign along State Route 49 within 14 days of this order" and by "paying the child support arrearage of $44,226.20." . . .

Analysis

"Normally, the federal courts do not become involved in child support disputes, as this is one of the matters most clearly allocated to the state courts in our federal system." *Puchner v. Kruziki,* 111 F.3d 541, 542 (7th Cir.). In this case, as in *Puchner,* Wronke's failure to pay child support became a federal case when he sought a writ of habeas corpus under 28 U.S.C. § 2254 "challenging his incarceration pursuant to a contempt order entered by the state court judge." See *Puchner*, 111 F.3d at 542....

I. Constitutional Claims

Wronke first argues that he is entitled to habeas corpus relief because he was denied his request for a jury trial and has, in fact, spent much more than six months in custody. Wronke also argues that his "incarceration for civil contempt interminably was contrary and repugnant to existing law constitutionally."...

It is true that a criminal contemnor cannot be imprisoned more than a total of six months without a jury trial. *Cheff v. Schnackenberg*, 384 U.S. 373, 380 (1966). However, a jury trial is not required in civil contempt proceedings. *Cheff*, 384 U.S. at 377; see also *Hicks v. Feiock*, 485 U.S. 624 (1988) (it is only when the punishment is criminal in nature that federal constitutional protections must be applied in the contempt proceeding).

Civil and criminal contempt differ in important respects. *Puchner*, 111 F.3d at 544. "If it is for civil contempt the punishment is remedial, and for the benefit of the complainant. But if it is for criminal contempt the sentence is punitive, to vindicate the authority of the court." *Hicks*, 485 U.S. at 631 (1988) (quoting *Gompers v. Buck's Stove & Range Co.*, 221 U.S. 418 (1911)). "[C]ivil contempt is a tool used by courts to compel compliance with their orders. The contemnor 'holds the keys to the jailhouse' in his own hands, and compliance produces an immediate release." *Puchner*, 111 F.3d at 543. In other words, imprisonment for civil contempt is "wholly avoidable." *Puchner*, 111 F.3d at 544. A civil or remedial contempt order is always dischargeable upon full compliance with the court's order.

In this case, the court determined that Wronke was in indirect civil contempt of court because he violated a court order when he put his children's names on a sign and because he failed to pay $44,226.20 in court ordered child support, which the court found he had the ability to pay. Wronke could have avoided the contempt finding by complying with the terms of the circuit court's orders. In addition, Wronke could purge himself of the contempt, and secure his release from the Champaign County Correctional Center, by removing the names from the sign and by paying the overdue child support. Accordingly, Wronke's sanction is clearly civil in nature. See *Hicks*, 485 U.S. at 634–35 n. 7. Therefore, Wronke had no right to a jury trial before being incarcerated for civil contempt.

Wronke's challenge to the indefinite length of his incarceration also fails on the merits. Incarceration for civil contempt may continue indefinitely. *United States ex rel. Thom v. Jenkins*, 760 F.2d 736, 740 (7th Cir.1985). This is because the contemnor has the ability to secure his release by complying with the court's orders. Accordingly, a civil contemnor may be incarcerated until he either complies with the court's order or adduces evidence as to his present inability to comply with that order. See *United States v. Rylander*, 460 U.S. 752 (1983)....

IT IS THEREFORE ORDERED THAT the petition for writ of *habeas corpus* is DENIED.

* * *

Problem 58

Civil contempt is compensatory or coercive. Criminal contempt is punitive. What kind of contempt is described in the following situation?

A manufacturing plant is sued by a county for polluting in violation of environmental regulations. The court issues an injunction requiring that the plaint stop the manufacturing process that is creating the pollution. The plant violates the order by continuing to use the same process and is found in contempt of court.

As a sanction, the court orders: "The defendant shall immediately deposit $10,000 in an escrow account. Upon each further violation of the injunction, $1,000 shall be deducted from the escrow account and paid to the county. After one year, the remaining balance of the account, if any, shall be returned to the defendant."

Chapter 13

Statutory Remedies

A legislature can create a right to bring a lawsuit for a specified wrong by enacting a statute providing for such a right. In many cases, statutes not only create the right to bring a cause of action but also go a step further and provide for a particular remedy.

A common statutory remedy is injunctive relief. An example is the federal Civil Rights Act of 1964, which prohibits racial discrimination in a variety of contexts. Injunctive relief is specifically provided for in the statutory text as a remedy to prevent further discrimination.

A statute might also allow for restitution — the disgorgement of a benefit obtained by the defendant as a result of violating the statute. California's unfair competition law, for instance, prohibits unfair business practices and provides that the court may make such orders as may be necessary to restore to the plaintiff any money or property "acquired by means of such unfair competition." (Cal. Bus. & Prof. Code § 17203.)

Some statutes impose monetary penalties for violations. One such statute is the federal Fair Housing Act, which provides penalties ranging from $10,000 to $50,000 for engaging in discriminatory housing practices. (42 U.S.C. § 3612, subdivision (g).) Statutes sometimes even create their own remedial system that is untethered from traditional common law remedies. State workers' compensation laws are an example. They provide a system of compensation for workers injured on the job, payable over time through mandatory insurance carried by employers.

When a statute specifically mentions a remedy (or remedies), two questions often arise: (1) Is the plaintiff required to prove an entitlement to the remedy, or does it automatically issue upon proof of the merits of the statutory cause of action? (2) Is the statutory remedy the only remedy available to the plaintiff, or are other generally available remedies in play as well?

This chapter examines both of those questions.

Entitlement to Statutory Remedy

A plaintiff typically has the burden to prove entitlement to the remedy requested. To recover damages, the plaintiff must prove, to a reasonable degree of certainty, both that harm has occurred and the amount that will compensate for it. For an injunction, the plaintiff must show an ongoing threat of irreparable harm that damages would not adequately remedy.

But what if the law the plaintiff has sued under provides for a fixed sum the defendant must pay upon proof of a violation of the statute, regardless of the harm the plaintiff actually suffered? Must the plaintiff prove the amount of damages with reasonable certainty in that case? Indeed, does the plaintiff need to prove he or she was harmed at all? The answer is that to bring a lawsuit, the plaintiff will always need to prove some kind of harm or invasion of a legally protected interest occurred because of the defendant's conduct. A person who has experienced no harm has not been aggrieved, and therefore has no standing to be in court. But assuming the plaintiff is aggrieved in some fashion, if the statute clearly provides for a fixed sum payable upon proof of the merits of a claim — referred to as statutory damages — a prevailing plaintiff is automatically entitled to judgment in that amount; there is no need to prove the amount of harm incurred.

For injunctive relief, whether a prevailing plaintiff is automatically entitled to the remedy will again depend on the text of the statute. If the statute clearly indicates an intent that an injunction should issue upon proof of the underlying claim, the plaintiff is entitled to that remedy without a further showing. If the statute merely provides that an injunction is available as a remedy, a court will require a plaintiff to prove entitlement to injunctive relief in the typical fashion, by showing that irreparable harm will occur in the absence of an injunction.

Introductory Note — *Committee to Elect Dan Forest v.*
Employees Political Action Committee
and *Jackson v. Bartec*

Committee to Elect Dan Forest v. Employees Political Action Committee is a statutory damages case. The statute requires certain disclosures by groups that pay for political advertisements. The question before the court is what kind of harm the plaintiff must show was caused by the statutory violation in order to be entitled to the damages the statute provides for.

Jackson v. Bartec is a statutory injunction case. The statute prohibits smoking in public places and allows injunctive relief for a violation. The appellate court confronts two questions: whether a prevailing plaintiff is automatically entitled to an injunction even without showing irreparable harm; and whether the violation in this case constitutes irreparable harm in any event.

THINGS TO THINK ABOUT while reading *Committee to Elect Dan Forest v. Employees Political Action Committee* and *Jackson v. Bartec*:

1. Did the court decide the plaintiff was automatically entitled to the statutory remedy?

2. How did the plaintiff show harm resulting from the statutory violation?

Committee to Elect Dan Forest v. Employees Political Action Committee

North Carolina Court of Appeals
260 N.C.App. 1 (2018)

DILLON, Judge.

During the 2012 election cycle, a political advertisement sponsored by the Employees Political Action Committee ("EMPAC"), the political arm of the State Employees Association of North Carolina ("SEANC"), ran on television supporting Linda Coleman, Democratic candidate for Lieutenant Governor. The Committee to Elect Dan Forest (the "Committee") commenced this action seeking statutory damages, contending that EMPAC's television ad violated the "stand by your ad" law, which was still in effect during the 2012 campaign cycle.

The trial court granted summary judgment for EMPAC, concluding that the law was unconstitutional as applied because Mr. Forest could not forecast any evidence that he suffered any *actual* damages, presumably because Mr. Forest won the election anyway. We reverse the trial court's order granting summary judgment and remand the matter for further proceedings consistent with this opinion.

I. Background

In 1999, the General Assembly enacted a "stand by your ad" law, codified in N.C. Gen. Stat. § 163-278.39A, to regulate political advertisements. The Disclosure Statute required in relevant part that any television ad sponsored by a political action committee contain: (1) a "disclosure statement" identifying the sponsor of the ad spoken by *either* the sponsor's chief executive officer ("CEO") *or* its treasurer; *and* (2) a "full-screen picture containing [this] disclosing individual" featured during the disclosure statement.

The Disclosure Statute creates the right for a candidate to seek statutory damages against an ad sponsor who runs a non-conforming ad in the candidate's race. N.C. Gen. Stat. § 163.278.39A(f).

In 2012, North Carolina's race for Lieutenant Governor featured two candidates: Dan Forest and Linda Coleman. EMPAC ran a television advertisement in support of Ms. Coleman during the 2012 election cycle. There is evidence in the Record that this ad's disclosure statement violated the Disclosure Statute in two different ways: (1) the picture of the disclosing individual was not a "full-screen" picture, but rather was much smaller; and (2) the disclosing individual depicted in the ad was neither EMPAC's CEO nor Treasurer, but was rather Dana Cope, the then-CEO of EMPAC's affiliate entity, SEANC.

Mr. Forest's Committee filed a notice of complaint with the State Board of Elections (the "SBOE"), whereupon EMPAC pulled the offending ad and ran a new ad for the remainder of the 2012 election cycle with a disclosure which complied with the Disclosure Statute. Mr. Forest won the 2012 election for Lieutenant Governor by a narrow margin of 6,858 votes out of over 4 million votes cast. After the election, Mr. Forest's Committee commenced this action seeking statutory damages against EMPAC for its nonconforming ad supporting Ms. Coleman. The trial court granted summary judgment to EMPAC. The Committee timely appealed. . . .

II. Analysis

In this matter, the trial court granted summary judgment in favor of EMPAC on the Committee's claim for statutory damages, concluding that "in the absence of any forecast of actual demonstrable damages [suffered by Mr. Forest], the statute at issue is unconstitutional as applied." In essence, the trial court did not declare the Disclosure Statute unconstitutional *per se*, but rather held that Mr. Forest lacked standing to seek damages under the Statute since he did not suffer any actual damages, apparently because he won the election.

On appeal, the Committee contends that the trial court erred in its ruling. . . .

A. Dan Forest's Committee Has Standing To Seek Damages

The trial court essentially concluded that Dan Forest's Committee lacked standing to bring this suit based on the absence of any evidence that Mr. Forest suffered any actual damage. That is, because Mr. Forest *won* the 2012 election, he had no standing, in the constitutional sense, to seek statutory damages allowed under the Disclosure Statute. However, based on controlling precedent, it is clear that Mr. Forest's Committee does have standing: simply because Mr. Forest won his election does not mean that he did not suffer an injury sufficient in a constitutional sense to confer standing.

. . . According to our Supreme Court, "[t]he North Carolina Constitution confers standing on those who suffer harm[,]"*Mangum v. Raleigh Bd. of Adjustment*, 362 N.C. 640 (2008), and that one must have suffered some "injury in fact" to have standing to sue, *Dunn v. Pate*, 334 N.C. 115, 119 (1993).

Our Supreme Court has held in a variety of contexts that a party has standing to bring suit where a private right has been breached, even where the party has not suffered actual damages beyond that fact that a breach occurred. The breach itself is an "injury in fact." For instance, one has standing to seek nominal damages where some legal right has been invaded but no actual loss or substantial injury has been sustained. Nominal damages are awarded in recognition of the right and of the technical injury resulting from its violation. A party to a contract has standing to bring suit where the other party has breached the contract, even if no actual damage is shown. *Kirby v. Stokes County*, 230 N.C. 619, 627 (1949). An owner of land has the right to exclusive possession of his property and has standing to bring suit against anyone who trespasses, even where the owner suffers no actual damage; the owner's legal right to exclusive enjoyment of his property has been invaded. *Hildebrand v. Southern Bell*, 219 N.C. 402, 408 (1941) (holding that a landowner "is entitled to be protected as to that which is his without regard to its money value").

If EMPAC had *slandered* Mr. Forest in its political ad, Mr. Forest would have had standing to seek at least nominal damages for this tort, even though he won the election. *Wolfe v. Montgomery Ward*, 211 N.C. 295, 296 (1937) (holding that a plaintiff who has been slandered has standing to seek nominal damages even where there is no evidence that he suffered actual damages).

The private right at issue in the present case was not one that existed at common law but rather was one created by our General Assembly in the Disclosure Statute to provide an enforcement mechanism. This private right is a right expressly conferred by our General Assembly on a candidate to participate in an election where sponsors of political ads supporting his or her opponent must make themselves known to the public in their ads. The General Assembly acted within its authority to create a private right not recognized in the common law[.]

Our Court has held that a party has standing to sue for *statutory* damages without having to demonstrate actual damages where the statute at issue creates a private cause of action as a mechanism to enforce the provisions of the statute at issue. *See Addison v. Britt*, 83 N.C. App. 418, 421 (1986).

. . . We are not to be concerned with the "wisdom or expediency" of the Disclosure Statute, but rather we are only concerned with whether the General Assembly had the "power" to enact the law. *In re Denial*, 307 N.C. 52, 57 (1982). We conclude that the General Assembly acted within its authority in 1999 when it enacted the Disclosure Statute to require that political ads disclose their sponsors and to provide the committee of a political candidate running for office with a private cause of action to seek damages against the sponsor of a nonconforming ad, just as we conclude that the General Assembly acted within its authority in 2013 to repeal the law.

B. Dan Forest's Committee May Seek Statutory Damages Without Showing Evidence of Actual Damage

Having concluded that Mr. Forest's Committee has standing to bring this action, we now consider whether the Committee may recover the statutory damages provided under the Disclosure Statute without presenting any evidence that Mr. Forest suffered any actual monetary damages.

The Disclosure Statute provides that a candidate receiving a favorable verdict is entitled to statutory damages equal to the "total dollar amount" spent by the ad sponsor to air the nonconforming ad. In this case, while the exact amount EMPAC spent on the nonconforming ad has yet to be determined, EMPAC argues that *any* amount of statutory damages would be an unconstitutional "windfall" to Mr. Forest's Committee, since Mr. Forest won the election. The Committee, though, argues that the statutory damages imposed by the Disclosure Statute is not unconstitutional "as applied" here *even if* the Committee fails to present evidence of actual quantifiable damages.

We conclude that the General Assembly has the authority to provide for statutory damages and, therefore, that the Committee may seek statutory damages. . . . Furthermore, statutory damages which may exceed a plaintiff's actual damages are not unconstitutional unless the statutory damage award "prescribed is so severe and oppressive as to be wholly disproportionate to the offense and obviously unreasonable." *St. Louis v. Williams*, 251 U.S. 63, 66–67 (1919). . . .

Therefore, we conclude that the Committee need not put forth evidence of actual damages in order to seek statutory damages. Such is not required in other contexts where statutory damages are allowed. However, we recognize that there may be situations where an award of statutory damages might be unconstitutionally excessive and would need to be reduced. For example, if a political action committee spent $1 million running an ad which did not feature the picture of the disclosing individual until a second after the disclosure statement commenced (where the Disclosure Statute requires the picture be displayed "*throughout the duration* of the disclosure statement"), an award of $1 million might be deemed unconstitutionally excessive. Such an award may be viewed as "oppressive" and "wholly disproportionate" to such a minor technical violation, and it might be appropriate to reduce such award.

But, here, it could be argued that EMPAC's violation was more substantial. Specifically, it is possible that having Dana Cope, a then-popular executive director of EMPAC's affiliate entity, SEANC, shown as the disclosing individual may have given the ad a level of gravitas that it would not have enjoyed if an unknown officer of EMPAC had been depicted. We conclude, however, that it is premature to decide whether the statutory damages allowed under the Disclosure Statute would be unconstitutionally excessive in this case, as *the amount* of statutory damages, if any, has yet to be determined. . . .

III. Conclusion

This matter involves the partisan political process. And there is an element of political irony; a Republican invoking a law passed by a Democratic-controlled General Assembly and later repealed by a Republican-controlled General Assembly. However, our job is not to consider the politics of the parties involved. Rather, our job is simply to apply the law, irrespective of politics.

Applying the law, we must conclude that our General Assembly acted within its authority in 1999 when it enacted the Disclosure Statute, creating a private cause of action in favor of political candidates against the sponsors of political ads who fail to properly disclose their identity, just as the General Assembly acted within its authority when it took away this statutory right in 2013. Therefore, we must conclude that the trial court erred in granting summary judgment in favor of EMPAC. We reverse the order of the trial court and remand the matter for further proceedings consistent with this opinion.

REVERSED AND REMANDED.

* * *

Jackson v. Bartec

Ohio Court of Appeals
No. 10AP-173, 2010 WL 4632557 (2010)

BRYANT, J.

Plaintiff-appellant and cross-appellee, Alvin D. Jackson, M.D., Director of Ohio Department of Health ("ODH"), appeals from a judgment of the Franklin County Court of Common Pleas that both denied ODH's request for a permanent injunction and vacated ten existing violations entered against defendants-appellees and cross-appellants, Bartec, Inc., dba Zeno's Victorian Village, and its chief executive officer Richard Allen (collectively "Bartec"), all arising under Ohio's Smoke Free Workplace Act, R.C. Chapter 3794 ("Smoke Free Act"). Because (1) the trial court wrongly vacated Bartec's ten violations of the Smoke Free Act, and (2) ODH is entitled to an injunction against Bartec, we reverse.

I. Facts and Procedural History

On August 13, 2009, ODH filed a complaint in the Franklin County Court of Common Pleas, seeking preliminary and permanent injunctions that order Bartec to comply with R.C. Chapter 3794 and to pay all outstanding fines resulting from past violations of the Smoke Free Act. By the time of trial, Bartec had accumulated fines stemming from ten separate violations of the Smoke Free Act. . . .

In a February 22, 2010 decision and entry, the trial court denied ODH's request for an injunction and vacated as unenforceable the ten existing violations against Bartec under the Smoke Free Act. The trial court determined the violations resulted because Bartec was "being held responsible for the decisions of a third-party that are out of [Bartec's] control," ODH "implemented a policy of strict liability against property owners for violations of the SmokeFree Act," and ODH's enforcement of the Smoke Free Act was "stricter than allowed by R.C. 3794.02."

II. Assignments of Error

On appeal, ODH [contends] the trial court abused its discretion by denying its Complaint for a Statutory Injunction. . . .

III. Overview of Smoke Free Act

The Smoke Free Act, central to the errors the parties assigned on appeal, prohibits smoking in public places or places of employment, with certain exceptions that include private residences, designated smoking rooms in hotels, nursing homes, retail tobacco stores, outdoor patios, and private clubs. R.C. 3794.02 and 3794.03. Pursuant to R.C. 3794.07, ODH promulgated rules for ODH, or its designee, to use in enforcing the statutory provisions of the Smoke Free Act.

Upon receipt of a reported violation, ODH or its designee provides the proprietor of an establishment with a written notice of the reported violation; the proprietor may submit in writing statements or evidence to contest the report. Ohio Adm .Code 3701-52-08(D). ODH reviews the report, the evidence the proprietor submitted to contest the report, as well as other information the investigation yielded, such as interviews and on-site investigations, to determine whether a violation occurred. Ohio Adm.Code 3701-52-08(F)(1)(a). If the violator has no previous violations within the past two years, ODH issues the warning letter contemplated under R.C. 3794.09(A). Ohio Adm.Code 3701-52-08(F)(1)(a). If, however, the alleged violator has a prior violation in the past two years, a fine may issue pursuant to R.C. 3974.09(B) and a more comprehensive administrative review commences, including a hearing that provides the alleged violator with the opportunity to present its case and cross-examine any adverse witnesses. Ohio Adm.Code 3701-52-08(F)(2). . . .

IV. Permanent Injunction

ODH asserts the trial court erred in denying ODH's complaint seeking a statutory injunction against Bartec due to Bartec's repeated violations of the Smoke Free Act. ODH sought injunctive relief pursuant to R.C. 3794.09(D), which states "[t]he director of health may institute an action in the court of common pleas seeking an order in equity against a proprietor or individual that has repeatedly violated the provisions of this chapter or fails to comply with its provisions." ODH urges us to apply *Ackerman v. Tri-City Geriatric & Health Care* (1978), 55 Ohio St.2d 51 to the statutory injunction it seeks and to reject the equitable analysis typically associated with injunctions.

In *Ackerman*, the Supreme Court of Ohio held "that when an injunction is authorized by statute, normal equity considerations do not apply, and a party is entitled to an injunction without proving the ordinary equitable requirements, upon a showing that the party has met the requirements of the statute for issuance of the injunction." *Hydrofarm, Inc. v. Orendorff,* 180 Ohio App.3d 339, 905. Accordingly, this court has recognized "*Ackerman* clearly states that 'statutory injunctions should issue if the statutory requirements are fulfilled.'" *State ex rel. Scadden v. Willhite,* 10th Dist. No. 01AP-800, 2002-Ohio-1352.

ODH characterizes R.C. 3794.09(D) primarily as a tool not to remedy injustice between the parties but to prevent harm to employees and the general public from violations of the Smoke Free Act. See R.C. 3794.04 (stating "it is in the best interests of public health that smoking of tobacco products be prohibited in public places and places of employment and that there be a uniform statewide minimum standard to protect workers and the public from the health hazards associated with exposure to secondhand smoke from tobacco"); see also *State ex rel. Brown v. Chase Foundry & Mfg. Co.* (1982), 8 Ohio App.3d 96 (finding that an injunction prescribed under R.C. 3704.06, through Ohio's implementation of the federal Clean Air Act, does not require a weighing of the equities because the General Assembly had already determined that illegal emissions into the air were worthy of injunctive relief). ODH thus argues it met the requirements of R.C. 3794.09(D) when it demonstrated Bartec incurred ten citations and did not pay any of its accumulated fines. According to ODH, the trial court, when presented with such facts, erred in not issuing the requested statutory injunction.

Not all statutory injunctions fall within the *Ackerman* rule. Rather, the holding in *Ackerman* "is limited to those statutes that contain specific criteria that the court must use in determining entitlement to an injunction." *Stoneham,* supra. If "a statute merely provides that a party is entitled to injunctive relief as well as other types of relief, there is no 'statutory injunction' within the meaning of *Ackerman,* and the party requesting the injunction must use the general equitable principles governing the issuance of injunctive relief." *Id.*

Here, we need not decide whether the injunctive relief contemplated in R.C. 3794.09(D) is a "statutory injunction" within the meaning of *Ackerman* with the evidence presented at the evidentiary hearing the trial court held, ODH demonstrated not only that it met the statutory requirements for an injunction but also that the equities supported the requested injunction. ODH presented the trial court with copies of the ten violations previously found against Bartec, eight of which were intentional. Bartec neither objected to the trial court's admitting the violations into evidence nor presented mitigating evidence suggesting the injunction should not issue. Rather, Bartec attempted to reargue the merits of ten underlying violations that already were final orders.

On this record, the evidence is overwhelming that Bartec repeatedly and intentionally violated the Smoke Free Act, failed to comply with its provisions as R.C. 3794.09(D) requires, and in so doing exposed patrons and employees to the very harm the statute is designed to prevent. Due to the hearing the court conducted and the evidence adduced as a result of the hearing, the trial court could reach no other conclusion than that ODH is entitled to the statutory injunction it requested. We thus sustain ODH's assignment of error and remand with instructions to issue an injunction against Bartec pursuant to R.C. 3794.09(D). . . .

Judgment reversed and case remanded with instructions.

* * *

Problem 59

To obtain statutory damages, a plaintiff need not have suffered cognizable financial harm. But to have standing to bring a lawsuit, a plaintiff must have been harmed in some way. Can the below plaintiff recover statutory damages?

A statute prohibits employers from asking job applicants about criminal convictions for marijuana possession. The statute reads: "In order to reduce the stigma associated with conduct that has now been decriminalized, no employer shall require an applicant to provide any information about previous convictions for possession of marijuana. Applicants harmed by a violation of this section shall be entitled to statutory damages in the amount of $200 per violation."

Deborah applies for a job as a barista at a coffee shop. One of the questions on the application is, "Have you been convicted of any crime in the past 10 years (including marijuana possession)?" Deborah, who has never been convicted of any crime, truthfully answers, "No." She then sues the coffee shop for violation of the marijuana conviction disclosure statute and seeks statutory damages of $200.

Exclusivity

For a plaintiff pursuing a remedy provided by a statute, it is important to know whether the statutory remedy is the only remedy allowed, or if it is in addition to other potentially available remedies.

Two factors influence a court's decision about whether a statutory remedy is exclusive of all others. The first is the statutory language itself. If the text clearly indicates a legislative intent to limit the plaintiff to the remedy provided in the statute, that will be the plaintiff's exclusive remedy. On the other hand, if the text clearly indicates the specified remedy is in addition to other remedies provided for by law, the plaintiff's remedial choices will not be constrained.

Where the statutory text is not clear about whether the specified remedy is exclusive or cumulative, history becomes important. If the statute created a completely new right and corresponding remedy, that suggests the legislature intended the specified remedy to be exclusive. If the statute merely codifies an existing common law cause of action, that suggests the legislature intended the specified remedy to be in addition to the remedies already recognized for that claim.

Introductory Note — *Hodges v. S.C. Toof & Co.* and *Livitsanos v. Superior Court*

Hodges and *Livitsanos* both involve claims for wrongful termination. In one case, the court finds the plaintiff is entitled to common law and statutory remedies. In the other, the court finds the statutory remedy exclusive.

In *Hodges*, a statute prohibiting retaliatory discharge of an employee provided an equitable remedy for affected employees: reinstatement. It also allowed recovery of wages lost in the interim. The plaintiff employee sued under the statute and also brought a cause of action for common law wrongful discharge. He prevailed at trial and the jury awarded compensatory and punitive damages. On appeal, the defendant employer contends the plaintiff was limited to the remedies described by the statute.

Livitsanos involves workers' compensation exclusivity — the issue of whether an employee's claim for damages against an employer is barred because injured employees can only recover under the workers' compensation system. Resolving the issue requires the California Supreme Court to evaluate the scope of the workers' compensation law and decide whether the claim brought by the plaintiff falls within it.

THINGS TO THINK ABOUT while reading *Hodges v. S.C. Toof & Co.* and *Livitsanos v. Superior Court*:

1. Does the court find the statutory remedy is exclusive, or not? What does it rely on in making that decision?

2. Do both decisions use the same reasoning, or does each court take a different path to reach its respective conclusion?

Hodges v. S.C. Toof & Co.

Tennessee Supreme Court
833 S.W.2d 896 (1992)

DROWOTA, Justice.

In this retaliatory discharge action, Plaintiff-Appellant Carl E. Hodges alleges Defendant-Appellee S.C. Toof & Company terminated Plaintiff's employment because of his jury service. At trial, the jury returned a verdict for Plaintiff and awarded him $200,000.00 compensatory and $375,000.00 punitive damages. The Court of Appeals, while upholding the jury's finding of retaliatory discharge, vacated the award of compensatory and punitive damages holding that under T.C.A. § 22-4-108, the exclusive remedy for an employee's discharge because of jury service was reinstatement and lost wages. We granted Plaintiff's application for permission to appeal in order to (1) decide whether the remedy provided by T.C.A. § 22-4-108 is exclusive. . . .

Plaintiff Carl Hodges had been continuously employed by Defendant S.C. Toof & Company for some 19 years prior to his termination in January 1988. At the time of his firing, Plaintiff's position was that of assistant warehouse supervisor in Defendant's printing business. During his tenure, Plaintiff received 20 merit raises and had never been disciplined. In the summer of 1987 Plaintiff was called for jury service and sat as a juror in a three-month trial from mid-September to December 18, 1987. In early January 1988, Plaintiff was fired.

Analysis

In 1986 the Legislature amended T.C.A. § 22-4-108 by adding a new subsection providing:

> (f)(1) No employer shall discharge or in any manner discriminate against an employee for serving on jury duty if such employee, prior to taking time off, gives the required notice pursuant to subsection (a) to the employer that he is required to serve.
>
> (2)(A) Any employee who is discharged, demoted, or suspended because such employee has taken time off to serve on jury duty shall be entitled to reinstatement and reimbursement for lost wages and work benefits caused by such acts of the employer.
>
> (B) Any employer who willfully refuses to rehire, or otherwise restore an employee or former employee shall be guilty of a misdemeanor.

The issue presented is whether the statutory remedy, namely "reinstatement and reimbursement for lost wages and work benefits," is the sole and exclusive relief available to an employee who has been "discharge[d] or in any manner discriminate[d] against . . . for serving on jury duty." Resolution of this matter necessitates an examination of the state of the law on retaliatory discharge at the time the statute was enacted. This is so because if a statute creates a new right and prescribes a remedy for its enforcement, then the prescribed remedy is exclusive. *Turner v. Harris,* 198 Tenn. 654, 664 (1955); *Nashville & C. R.R. v. Sprayberry,* 56 Tenn. 852, 854 (1874). However, where a common law right exists, and a statutory remedy is subsequently created, the statutory remedy is cumulative unless expressly stated otherwise. *See Leach v. Rich,* 138 Tenn. 94, 105 (1917); *State v. Duncan,* 71 Tenn. 679, 684–88 (1879). Further, the Legislature is presumed to know the state of the law on the subject under consideration at the time it enacts legislation. *Jenkins v. Loudon County,* 736 S.W.2d 603, 608 (Tenn.1987).

The doctrine of employment at will, well established in Tennessee, allows either party to terminate the relationship with or without cause. *Payne v. The Western & A. R.R.,* 81 Tenn. 507, 517 (1884). However, in 1984 we recognized an exception to this rule and allowed a plaintiff to pursue an action for retaliatory discharge where she was terminated for exercising her rights under the Tennessee Workers'

Compensation Law. *See Clanton v. Cain-Sloan Co.,* 677 S.W.2d 441 (Tenn.1984). In *Clanton,* we found an action for retaliatory discharge necessary in order to prevent employers from circumventing their statutory obligations. Importantly, *Clanton* is not limited to retaliatory discharge actions arising from an employee's exercise of workers' compensation rights, but rather makes the tort action of retaliatory discharge available to employees discharged as a consequence of an employer's violation of a clearly expressed statutory policy.

Given that our recognition of a common law tort action for retaliatory discharge predated the 1986 amendment to T.C.A. § 22-4-108, that the Legislature is presumed aware of this prior recognition, and that the remedies subsequently provided by the amendment are not expressly stated to be exclusive, then the statutory remedies must be considered cumulative. Plaintiff here was thus free to pursue a common law remedy in damages. Had the Legislature intended to limit relief to the statutory remedies, it could easily have done so. . . .

We therefore reverse the Court of Appeals' judgment insofar as it holds that the statutory remedies provided by T.C.A. § 22-4-108 are exclusive, and reinstate the jury award of compensatory damages.

* * *

Livitsanos v. Superior Court

California Supreme Court
2 Cal.4th 744 (1992)

ARABIAN, J.

We granted review to consider whether the exclusive remedy provisions of the Workers' Compensation Act apply to bar an employee's claims for intentional and negligent infliction of emotional distress, where no physical injury or disability is alleged. We hold that claims for intentional or negligent infliction of emotional distress are preempted by the exclusivity provisions of the workers' compensation law, notwithstanding the absence of any compensable physical disability.

Facts

Plaintiff Apostol Livitsanos began his employment at Continental Culture Specialists, Inc., a yogurt manufacturing company owned by Vasa Cubaleski, in 1976 in the shipping department. Two years later, plaintiff was promoted to supervisor of the department and in 1980 he was made manager, with attendant salary increases. Plaintiff alleges that, as an inducement to remain at Continental, an oral employment agreement with Continental included a provision, repeated by defendant Cubaleski on many occasions to plaintiff and other employees, that "Continental is your future" as long as plaintiff followed proper procedures, and that "if Continental makes money, so will you." Plaintiff believed his employment was of indefinite duration, and would not be terminated without good cause. . . .

Throughout plaintiff's term of employment, defendant Cubaleski praised plaintiff's performance, telling him that he had "saved the company," and that he would "someday own Continental."

In late 1988 or early 1989, for no apparent reason, Cubaleski began a campaign of harassment against plaintiff. This campaign took several forms. Cubaleski falsely accused plaintiff, along with Continental's office manager, of writing fraudulent checks to an outside contractor as part of a scheme to siphon funds away from Continental. Cubaleski communicated this charge to other Continental employees, as well as to an employee of an outside accounting firm. In addition, Cubaleski told Continental employees and others that $800,000 was "missing" from Continental, implying that plaintiff had stolen the money. Cubaleski threatened to have plaintiff "put in jail" because of the "missing" money.

In December 1988, Cubaleski borrowed $100,000 from plaintiff and promised to repay the entire amount by January 9, 1989. By March 15, 1989, Cubaleski still had not repaid plaintiff. When plaintiff asked Cubaleski for the money, Cubaleski became angry. Instead of repaying the loan, Cubaleski falsely told others that plaintiff owed him $24,000. Cubaleski knew there was no such debt owed to him by plaintiff. Cubaleski eventually repaid the $100,000 debt by paying $50,000 to plaintiff and by assuming a $50,000 debt plaintiff owed to Continental.

In or about April 1989, plaintiff took a four-week vacation. While plaintiff was on vacation, Cubaleski told other Continental employees that plaintiff had given himself an unauthorized pay raise, that money was missing from Continental (implying that plaintiff had stolen it), and that plaintiff was trying to sabotage Continental by telling certain employees to decrease the amount of fruit in the yogurt. When plaintiff returned, Cubaleski instructed Andy Stylianou, Continental's sales manager, to telephone plaintiff and accuse him of taking an unauthorized pay raise and sabotaging Continental. . . . Approximately two weeks later, plaintiff was terminated. . . .

Plaintiff filed suit against Continental and Cubaleski for breach of contract, defamation, intentional infliction of emotional distress, negligent infliction of emotional distress, and money lent. He alleged that defendants engaged in a campaign of harassment resulting in the wrongful termination of his employment. Defendants demurred to the causes of action for defamation and negligent and intentional infliction of emotional distress. The trial court sustained Continental's demurrers without leave to amend, apparently on the ground that the employer's conduct was "a normal part of the employment relationship" and therefore barred by the Workers' Compensation Act.

Discussion

Plaintiff contends that because he did not allege any physical injury or disability resulting from defendants' conduct, his cause of action for intentional infliction of emotional distress is outside the scope of the workers' compensation law. . . .

The touchstone of the workers' compensation system is industrial injury which results in *occupational disability* or death. Labor Code section 3208 defines "injury" as "*any* injury or disease arising out of the employment. . . ." (Italics added.) Labor Code section 3208.1 describes "specific" injuries "occurring as the result of one incident or exposure *which causes disability or need for medical treatment*" and "cumulative" injury as "occurring as repetitive mentally or physically traumatic activities extending over a period of time, the combined effect of which *causes any disability or need for medical treatment*." (Italics added.) Thus, . . . a compensable injury is one which causes disability or need for medical treatments.

Moreover, the workers' compensation system is designed to compensate *only* for such disability or need for treatment as is occupationally related. "Temporary disability" benefits are a substitute for lost wages during a period of temporary incapacity from working; "permanent disability" payments are provided for permanent bodily impairment, to indemnify for impaired future earning capacity or decreased ability to compete in an open labor market. The basic purpose of the Workers' Compensation Act is to compensate for the disabled worker's diminished ability to compete in the open labor market, not to compensate every work-related injury.

Thus, compensable injuries may be physical, emotional or both, so long as they are disabling. . . .

Compensation for psychiatric injury is not new; . . . an employee who suffers a disabling emotional injury caused by the employment is entitled, upon appropriate proof, to workers' compensation benefits, including any necessary disability compensation or medical or hospital benefits. . . .

So long as the basic conditions of compensation are otherwise satisfied, and the employer's conduct neither contravenes fundamental public policy nor exceeds the risks inherent in the employment relationship, an employee's emotional distress injuries are subsumed under the exclusive remedy provisions of workers' compensation. . . .

The question remains whether, in light of the foregoing principles, the demurrers to plaintiff's causes of action for intentional and negligent infliction of emotional distress were properly sustained. As discussed above, there is no merit to plaintiff's assertion that purely emotional injuries lie outside the scope of the workers' compensation system. The mere failure to allege physical disability will not entitle the injured employee to a civil action. To this extent, the demurrers were properly sustained. . . .

Disposition

. . . The judgment . . . is reversed, and the case is remanded to . . . consider on the merits the remaining issues identified herein.

* * *

Problem 60

Whether a statutory remedy is exclusive is a question of legislative intent. How should the court rule in the below case regarding the defendant's argument that the plaintiff is limited to the statutory remedy?

Jesse legally parks his car on the street while he does some shopping downtown. When he returns, he finds the car gone. A newly hired local police officer mistakenly believed Jesse's car was parked in a loading zone and impounded it. By the time Jesse sorts out what happened, the car has been sold at auction.

Jesse sues the police department for conversion on the theory that impounding the car was an unauthorized taking of his property. He seeks damages for the fair market value of the car ($50,000). He also alleges a cause of action for wrongful vehicle impoundment under a statute enacted just last year. The statute provides: "No law enforcement officer shall, intentionally or negligently, impound a vehicle without legal cause to do so. The remedy for the wrongful impoundment of a vehicle as described in this section shall be either (1) return of the vehicle; or, (2) statutory damages in the amount of $20,000, plus any incidental expenses associated with the impoundment." The police department argues the statute provides the exclusive remedy for wrongful impoundment of a vehicle.

Presume able to recover damages

Chapter 14

Attorney Fees

Attorney fees are not, strictly speaking, a remedy. They are an award that comes after a plaintiff has prevailed in a lawsuit and obtained a remedy. In some situations, fees can be awarded to a prevailing *defendant*, further differentiating attorney fees from what is usually considered a judicial remedy.

Still, attorney fee awards are an important component of the civil remedial system. Litigation is expensive. The biggest expense — by far — is the cost of an attorney. And litigants in American courts typically pay their own way. The rule that parties to a lawsuit bear their own attorney fees is known as the American Rule. The American Rule is generally thought to encourage access to justice, as compared with other approaches, such as the English Rule, where the losing party pays the attorney fees of the winner. A potential plaintiff will not be discouraged from suing, the thinking goes, by the prospect of having to foot the bill for the defendant's attorney in the event the lawsuit is unsuccessful.

In some circumstances, however, the American Rule can decrease access to justice. If a legally protected right is violated, but the violation either did not result in a great deal of financial loss or in a loss that is readily measurable in monetary terms at all, then a person will be discouraged from filing suit by having to pay attorney fees that may well exceed any potential recovery. Indeed, to file a lawsuit where the costs exceed the potential recovery would not be economically rational.

To alter the dynamic created by the American Rule, attorney fees can be awarded to the prevailing party in litigation in certain circumstances. Generally speaking, attorney fees are awarded to the winner of a suit in two situations: (1) when a statute provides for it; or (2) when the parties have agreed to it in a contract.

When one of those exceptions to the American Rule applies, the prevailing party will be awarded attorney fees on top of any other remedy obtained. Awarding attorney fees requires the court to first determine who the prevailing party is (something that is usually obvious but not always) and then calculate the amount of fees that should be awarded.

Prevailing Party Determination

"Prevailing party" means the party who won the lawsuit. That can be more difficult to ascertain than it sounds. Should the plaintiff be deemed the winner if the jury returns a verdict in the plaintiff's favor on any cause of action alleged in the complaint? What if the complaint alleges a dozen causes of action and the plaintiff loses on all but one? What if the plaintiff asked for damages in the amount of $10 million but is awarded a fraction of that, say, $100,000?

Courts generally define prevailing party as the party who obtained the relief sought; put more plainly, the party that got what it wanted. The trial judge, who is familiar with the claims, evidence, and procedural wrangling in the case, is given broad discretion to decide who truly prevailed in the action for purposes of a fee award. Before awarding fees, the court will ensure that the party claiming to have prevailed has indeed been successful in achieving what it set out to accomplish in the suit.

Introductory Note — *Tobeluk v. Lind* and *Harris v. Rojas*

Tobeluk v. Lind and *Harris v. Rojas* present the two typical mechanisms for attorney fee awards: statute and contract. The fee entitlement in *Tobeluk* is claimed under two different statutes. (Note that Alaska has rejected the American rule and has a statute that generally requires the losing party to pay attorney fees to the winner in all cases.) The fees in *Harris* are claimed under a contractual provision.

In both cases, the court finds that the party claiming entitlement to fees did not prevail in the action. A dissenting opinion in *Tobeluk* takes the contrary position that the plaintiffs accomplished enough through the lawsuit to be the prevailing party.

THINGS TO THINK ABOUT while reading *Tobeluk v. Lind* and *Harris v. Rojas*:

1. What factors did the court consider in order to decide whether the plaintiff prevailed in the action?

2. How does the court determine a plaintiff's litigation objective?

3. Must a party obtain all the relief it sought to be deemed the prevailing party? Most? Some?

4. Why is the trial court the best judge of who prevailed in the action?

Tobeluk v. Lind

Alaska Supreme Court
589 P.2d 873 (1979)

CONNOR, Justice.

After extensive litigation the parties to this case entered into a settlement, pursuant to which a consent decree was entered. The question now presented on appeal is whether the superior court erred in denying appellants an award of attorneys' fee as prevailing parties.

In 1972, a civil action was initiated by Alaska Native children of secondary school age to compel the provision of secondary schools in their communities of residence. Their claims alleged violation of the Alaska Constitution, Art. VII, s 1 for failure to provide the schools, as well as equal protection and racial discrimination claims under the U.S. Constitution, Fourteenth Amendment, 42 U.S.C. ss 1981, 1983, 2000d, and Art. I, s 1 of the Alaska Constitution.

Appellants' claims under Art. VII, s 1 of the Alaska Constitution were dismissed by the trial court and that dismissal was upheld by us on appeal. The equal protection and racial discrimination claims were remanded for trial. Soon afterwards the appellees initiated settlement negotiations. A year of protracted negotiations followed, during which this case was the focus of a good deal of political attention.

. . . In May 1976, the State Board of Education adopted a set of regulations implementing local secondary school programs, which had been drafted by the appellants, negotiated by the parties, and incorporated in the December draft settlement agreement. On several occasions during the negotiations, the appellees submitted proposals to the effect that a provision be added requiring each party to bear its own costs. These were rejected by the appellants. In September 1976, the parties concluded a settlement, consisting of a statement of agreed facts and a consent decree. A final order approving the settlement was entered in October 1976. Both are silent on the issue of costs and attorney's fees. The consent decree requires the state to engage in a $20 million construction program for local secondary schools and to initiate steps to secure funding through bond initiatives for secondary school construction in the 126 villages where the members of the appellants' class reside. . . .

The appellants then filed a notice of taxation of costs with the clerk of trial courts, requesting fees and costs that were incurred between October 1974, when the appellants began discovery related to the prosecution of their equal protection claim, through October 1976, when the settlement was finally approved. The total amount sought is $219,379.32, covering 3,085.75 hours of work by the attorneys and the costs of taking depositions, interviewing witnesses, and conducting the settlement negotiations.

Sustaining the appellees' objection, the clerk deferred to the superior court for a determination of costs, if any, to be awarded. Ten memoranda were submitted by the parties encompassing over 300 pages, and oral argument was held on two occasions, lasting a total of over four hours.

After the second argument, the court ruled from the bench in favor of the appellees. The court concluded that, in the circumstances of the case, the plaintiffs could not appropriately be deemed the prevailing party "without some further indication that had the case gone to trial their legal position, as opposed to the relief they requested, would have been vindicated." In its order of April 22, 1977, the court stated that the plaintiffs' status as "prevailing party" could not be inferred from the settlement because of the political nature of the case. Plaintiffs appeal from the superior court's denial of costs and fees.

The issue presented is whether appellants are entitled to costs and fees under Rule 82 of the Alaska Rules of Civil Procedure or the federal Civil Rights Attorney's Fees Awards Act of 1976.

The Alaska rules and the federal statute are similar in that both provide the court with the discretionary authority to award attorneys' fees to a prevailing party, and both intend fee awards to be compensatory rather than punitive.

Despite the above similarities, the two fee award provisions are based on dissimilar underlying policies. The purpose of Rule 82 is to partially compensate a prevailing party for the expenses incurred in winning his case. It is not intended as a vehicle for accomplishing anything other than providing compensation where it is justified. In comparison, the explicit purpose of the fee shifting provision in the federal statute, 42 U.S.C. s 1988, is to encourage meritorious claims which might not otherwise be brought. We find it convenient, therefore, to discuss the state and federal questions separately.

Alaska Civil Rule 82

Civil Rule 82 provides for the awarding of attorney's fees to the prevailing party. We defined the term "prevailing party" in Buza v. Columbia Lumber Co., 395 P.2d 511, 514 (Alaska 1964):

> . . . (I)t has been established by case law that the prevailing party to a suit is the one who successfully prosecutes the action or successfully defends against it, prevailing on the main issue, even though not to the extent of the original contention. He is the one in whose favor the decision or verdict is rendered and the judgment entered.

Failure to recover the full measure of relief sought or to prevail on all the issues raised does not necessarily preclude that party from "prevailing party" status, provided that he is successful with regard to the "main issue in the action." Cooper v. Carlson, 511 P.2d 1305, 1308 (Alaska 1973). However, there is no "immutable rule that the party who obtains an affirmative recovery must be considered the prevailing party." Owen Jones & Sons, Inc. v. C. R. Lewis Co., 497 P.2d 312, 313–14 (Alaska 1972).

Appellees suggest that where the issues have not been fully litigated, the prevailing party should be determined by considering the likelihood of success on the merits. On several occasions the trial court, expressing its opinion, commented that appellants' equal protection argument was not "as insubstantial as the state would contend" and that appellants had "made a compelling case."

However, ruling from the bench in favor of the appellees after the second argument, the court concluded: "it would not be appropriate to term the plaintiffs in this case, in light of the settlement and all surrounding circumstances, a prevailing party without some further indication that had the case gone to trial their legal position, as opposed to the relief they requested, would have been vindicated."

In its final order the court stated: "The existing record would not support a finding that the plaintiffs were likely to prevail on their State or Federal constitutional arguments."

Appellants submit that the substantial relief they obtained qualifies them as the "prevailing party." A number of facts lend support for their position. The consent decree provides a comprehensive plan for the provision of local secondary schools including $20 million in construction funds for these schools. The regulations drafted by the plaintiffs and voluntarily enacted by the state are incorporated in the decree. The court retains jurisdiction over the case until the program is substantially completed, requiring progress reports every four months. Because the funding to implement the agreement is contingent upon the passage of a bond issue, the consent decree states that if the bond issue should fail, and the decree become void, that the plaintiffs retain their legal remedies. Additionally, the parties stipulated that "the facts set forth in the Statement of Agreed Facts be considered established and the parties shall not relitigate such facts."

To refute appellants' claim of "prevailing party" status, the appellees contend that they have planned to provide local secondary school programs since 1970, and that the settlement of the case is the result of political, rather than legal, considerations and efforts. They maintain that the consent decree was merely a recognition of the termination of the suit.

Although the prevailing party is the party who prevails on the suit as a whole, where each party has prevailed on a main issue the court retains discretion to refrain from characterizing either as the prevailing party, and a denial of attorney costs and fees in such instances is appropriate. The superior court's finding that appellants' status as a prevailing party could not be inferred from the settlement agreement is supported by the record. The consent decree does not operate as either an admission of liability or an adjudication on the merits. No decision or verdict was entered in favor of either party. Given the political nature of the case, it is unclear whether either party won on any of the legal issues.

We have consistently held that both the determination of "prevailing party" status and the award of costs and fees are committed to the broad discretion of the trial court. We will not interfere with the trial court's determination unless it is shown that the court abused its discretion by issuing a decision which is arbitrary, capricious, manifestly unreasonable, or which stems from an improper motive. Clearly it is within the trial court's discretion to deny attorney's fees altogether. Since the superior court has stated the basis for its decision, and we find no evidence of error or abuse of discretion, the denial of attorney's fees under Rule 82 must be upheld.

42 U.S.C. s 1988

Fee awards are authorized by section 1988 to encourage public interest and civil rights litigation by private individuals. Congress did not make fee awards mandatory, but, in order to effectuate a policy of vigorous enforcement, it specified a liberal standard to be used by the court in exercising its discretion.

It is intended that the standards for awarding fees be generally the same as under the fee provisions of the 1964 Civil Rights Act. A party seeking to enforce the rights protected by the statutes covered by section 1988, if successful, 'should ordinarily recover an attorney's fee unless special circumstances would render such an award unjust.' Newman v. Piggie Park Enterprises, Inc., 390 U.S. 400, 402 (1968). . . .

Like Rule 82, the awarding of fees under section 1988 is within the trial court's discretion. But that discretion is narrowly limited to insure the effectiveness of the underlying cause of action. Also, section 1988 is like Rule 82 in requiring a determination of the "prevailing party". It is well established that a party may be considered to have prevailed when he vindicates rights through a consent judgment or without formally obtaining relief. However, this does not imply a requirement that attorney's fees must be awarded in all cases which end in settlement. Whether to award attorney's fees must be determined by a close scrutiny of all of the circumstances surrounding the settlement. In the instant agreement, as in many settlement agreements, the reasons for the settlement are not clear without looking behind the express provisions.

Although the rule under section 1988 is that attorney's fees will be awarded to a prevailing plaintiff almost as a matter of course, the trial court still retains its discretion to determine whether the plaintiff is in fact the "prevailing party". To avoid abuse of fee shifting provisions, various factors have been used by federal courts to make this determination. In addition to inquiring whether a party achieved substantial relief, the courts have considered the merits of the claim, whether the plaintiffs rendered a substantial service or significantly advanced the public interest, the necessity for the action, and whether the suit served as a "catalyst" prompting compliance with the law by the defendant. . . .

Using the federal interpretations as guidelines, we cannot conclude in the case at bar that plaintiffs are the prevailing parties. They lost on the merits of the only issue which was litigated. The likelihood that they would have prevailed on the merits of the other claims if the case had gone to trial is uncertain. Evidence that the state had begun the implementation of a program and policy regarding rural secondary school programs before this lawsuit was initiated creates doubt concerning the importance of the lawsuit in bringing about the result. If the settlement agreement were to be set aside, it appears that the state's actions would remain the same. Likewise, it remains debatable whether constitutional rights have been furthered as a consequence of the settlement.

In the instant case the court was confronted with an unusual agreement and consent decree which required legislative and gubernatorial action. The final result was made contingent upon the passage of a bond issue by the voters, and the appellants reserved their right to return to court if the measure were to fail at the polls. We conclude that the record provides sufficient basis to warrant the trial court's denial of attorney's fees under section 1988.

We hold that in light of the characterization of the settlement agreement as a "political decision" and the indeterminate question of whether plaintiffs qualify as the prevailing party, the denial of attorney's fees was within the allowable discretion of the trial court under both the Alaska rules and section 1988.

AFFIRMED.

RABINOWITZ, Justice, with whom BOOCHEVER, Chief Justice, joins, dissenting, in part.

I am in agreement with the disposition of the Civil Rule 82 facet of this appeal but cannot join in the majority's affirmance of the superior court's refusal to award attorney's fees pursuant to 42 U.S.C. section 1988. Based upon controlling federal criteria governing the award of attorney's fees in civil rights litigation, I am of the view that the superior court abused its discretion by denying any award of attorney's fees to appellants since the consent decree resolved public issues of significant magnitude. I reach this conclusion for the following reasons.

In my view, the extensiveness of the relief awarded appellants providing for the elimination of alleged inequities in secondary education is impressive. Also, I think it clear that the institution of this litigation hastened the provision of local secondary schools in rural Alaska. . . .

Further, I do not believe that the circumstance of implementation of the consent decree being dependent upon passage of appropriate bonding constitutes a "special circumstance" which would justify a denial of attorney's fees. By upholding the denial of attorney's fees on the facts of the present case, the majority, in effect, would impose a requirement that plaintiffs in civil rights cases procure a stipulation in the settlement agreement as to liability of the defendant in order to collect attorney's fees as the "prevailing party." Such a strict interpretation of the term "prevailing party" in 42 U.S.C. section 1988 is inconsistent with express congressional intent that section 1988 be applied to settlement cases, and would substantially reduce the number of such suits which could be satisfactorily concluded by consent degree.

Given the narrow range of discretionary authority for award of attorney's fees under 42 U.S.C. section 1988, as interpreted by the federal courts, I would hold that appellants were the prevailing parties and would remand the matter to the superior court for determination of reasonable attorney's fees under 42 U.S.C. section 1988.

* * *

Harris v. Rojas

California Court of Appeal
66 Cal.App.5th 817 (2021)

WILEY, J.

George Harris leased commercial space from Abel Rojas. This appeal concerns the attorney fee clause in their lease.

Harris sued Rojas; Rojas cross-complained. The litigation continued for nearly three years and culminated in a seven-day jury trial. Jurors heard Harris's and Rojas's mutual recriminations. Harris asked the jury for $200,000. The jury gave him $6,450 on his contract claim, which was 3 percent of his request and which the court offset and reduced in the final judgment. For this, Harris's lawyers demanded a $296,744.68 attorney fee from Rojas. The trial court denied the fee request on the ground there was no prevailing party.

We affirm. When the demand is $200,000 and the verdict is $6,450 or less, the trial judge has discretion to decide the "victory" is pyrrhic and nobody won.

I

. . . .

The dispute between Harris and Rojas arose entirely from their commercial relationship of tenant and landlord. In 2013, the two entered a lease for 1,200 square feet of commercial space. The lease identified the premises, specified the duration and rental rate, and defined rights and duties. For instance, Harris and Rojas agreed to indemnify each other for losses, damages, and expenses resulting from each one's own negligence. In this respect, this contract incorporated tort law, which is significant for reasons we later explain.

The lease contained an attorney fee clause, which made the defaulting or breaching party liable for fees and costs arising "on account of breach or default by either party of any of their obligations hereunder." The clause is mutual in the sense it applies both to Harris and Rojas. The word "either" makes this term reciprocal rather than unilateral.

In the Burbank action, Harris sued Rojas on August 9, 2017. The case concerned Harris's complaints about landlord Rojas. Harris's second amended complaint had his business Tap'd Out as his coplaintiff and included five causes of action: breach of contract, breach of the covenant of good faith, tortious interference, declaratory relief, and negligence-premises liability.

Harris alleged he was one among "myriad" neighboring commercial tenants at this site. Over time, Harris used his leased space for different commercial purposes, including a bicycle repair shop and then a storage area for his restaurant business. Most recently, Harris and a partner ran a studio offering dance lessons. Harris called his studio Tap'd Out Dance Studio.

Harris had complaints about landlord Rojas. Initially there were three main complaints, but apparently Harris later boiled them down to two. First, neighboring tenants protested the loud music from Tap'd Out; Harris contended their protests were unwarranted. Harris's pleading did not explain how unwarranted protests affected or harmed him. Second, unidentified people "unnecessarily badgered" Harris's patrons over parking. The pleading did not link these unidentified people to Rojas. Harris contended Rojas did not resolve these issues, and Rojas's inaction was an unlawful attempt at constructive eviction.

Rojas too had complaints. Rojas filed a cross-complaint against Harris on September 19, 2017 that had three claims: ejectment, breach of contract, and nuisance. Rojas alleged Harris had punched holes in walls, disrupted other tenants with loud music, made unreasonable parking demands, kept premises dirty and unwholesome, and had created "noise, filth, annoyance, and crowding."

On June 22, 2018, Rojas filed a separate unlawful detainer case against Harris, assertedly because Harris had stopped paying rent and would not surrender possession.

Our information about this unlawful detainer case is limited. Harris apparently chose not to appear. On November 13, 2018, the court reportedly entered a judgment against Harris and in Rojas's favor for possession, for $13,014.66 in past rent, and apparently for accruing interest and rent from the date of judgment. Harris reportedly blocked entry to the unit until the sheriff perfected an eviction on March 7, 2019. The four-month delay apparently added rent to Rojas's judgment, bringing the total to over $17,000.

In the Burbank action, a seven-day jury trial began in early January 2020. . . .

Each side won something, but neither side won much. The jury's special verdict awarded Harris *$6,450* in damages for Rojas's breach of contract. Tap'd Out got nothing. Rojas won *$6,450* on a negligence claim against Harris.

We pause to note the identical $6,450 figures. The jury awarded $6,450 *for* Harris and *against* Harris. In his bid to be recognized as the prevailing party, Harris ignores this fact.

The limited record explains neither how nor when Rojas added a negligence claim to this case. Nor do we know its factual basis.

Harris also won $500 on a negligence claim against Rojas. The record does not reveal this claim's basis.

The jury wrote on its verdict form that its multiple awards to Harris were for the "exact same identical harm."

To complete our tour of the verdict form, the jurors assigned responsibility for harm at 15 percent for Harris and 85 percent for Rojas. This reduction meant Rojas's award was $967.50.

The Burbank court offset the adjusted sums and entered a net judgment in Harris's favor for either $5,907.50 or $5,882.50. The judgment's internal discrepancy of $5,907.50 versus $5,882.50 is a difference of $25. Neither Harris nor Rojas seems to have noticed this discrepancy, or if they have noticed it, they have decided against explaining it to us. We pass by this mysterious detail.

After trial, Harris moved for an award under the lease's attorney fee clause. His fee and cost request totaled $296,744.68. The court denied Harris's motion, ruling there was no prevailing party. Harris appeals this order.

II

When a court rules there is no prevailing party, we review the order for an abuse of discretion.

The American rule is each side bears its own attorney fees, but parties can contract out of that rule. When they do, Code of Civil Procedure section 1021 directs courts to enforce their agreement. (*Id.* ["the measure and mode of compensation of attorneys and counselors at law is left to the agreement, express or implied, of the parties"].)

. . . For two independent reasons, we affirm the trial court's ruling Harris was not a prevailing party. First, Harris's recovery was slight compared to his demand, and the skimpy record he provided gives no other basis for assessing his litigation objective. Second, considering the two related matters together, Harris was no winner at all. We explain.

First, recovering five or six thousand dollars on a demand for $200,000 obviously is not a "simple, unqualified" win. A recovery this modest is more nearly the opposite. In this situation, the trial court had discretion to conclude no one won the case because the ostensibly prevailing party received only part of the relief sought.

How does a trial judge evaluate whether there is a prevailing party? The case law directs courts to determine the party's litigation objectives and to see if it achieved them. (*Hsu, supra,* 9 Cal.4th at pp. 876–877; see also *Scott Co. v. Blount, Inc.* (1999) 20 Cal.4th 1103, 1109 [trial court is to compare the relief awarded on the contract claim or claims with the parties' demands on those same claims and their litigation objectives].)

Determining a party's true litigation objective is no mean feat. When the case is strictly about money, the litigation objective is a dollar figure. The true value of a case is a matter of opinion, and parties normally conceal their true opinion on this vital topic. That is why we call that look a poker face. What economists call a reservation price usually is a carefully guarded secret; if the other side perceives this closeted sum, it will offer that amount in settlement negotiations and nothing more. So each side typically bluffs while searching the other side for clues. Successful mediators use sustained efforts in a confidential setting to extract this private information from both sides. By discovering previously hidden common ground, a mediator can settle the case. But this exploration is often difficult, which is why successful mediators can command premium rates.

The difficulties extend beyond secrecy. A party's valuation can change by the minute as developments arise and as parties gain information. And once the dust has settled, pride often leads everyone to claim victory. Public relations professionals are not the only spin doctors. There are many amateurs as well.

Amidst the posturing and revision, determining a litigant's true objective can be a challenge.

Despite the challenge, trial courts are well positioned to evaluate what counts as a win. The trial court gains familiarity with the parties and the attorneys during the case and the trial. Some interactions are on the record; some are not. The trial judge may have overheard or assisted off-the-record settlement efforts. On-the-record episodes may have unreported aspects. (E.g., *Olive v. General Nutrition Centers, Inc.* (2018) 30 Cal.App.5th 804, 823 [when jury announced the verdict, both sides' faces showed transparent dismay; trial court determined no party prevailed].)

Through it all, trial judges gain perspectives and insights an appellate court is wise to respect. . . .

On this minimal record, Harris's litigation objective in the Burbank action was purely quantitative: $200,000. So too was his Burbank jury verdict. The court's task is to compare the sum Harris sought with the sum the jury awarded.

On this comparison, we defer to the trial judge's commonsensical decision. Reaping merely five or six thousand dollars after spending three years pursuing $200,000 drastically falls short of the goal. A slight recovery more resembles a tie than a win.

. . . Litigation is a practical human endeavor, not an entertaining sport where rules can make a one-point margin into total victory. In litigation, spending great effort only to achieve little is not simple and unqualified success. Litigation is not for sport. It is to resolve disputes so everyone can return to productive activity. It always has costs, including opportunity costs.

. . . The trial court said Harris did not prevail. This ruling was well within the court's discretion.

Disposition

We affirm and award costs to Rojas.

* * *

Problem 61

To be the prevailing party in a lawsuit for purposes of an attorney fee award, a party must obtain the relief it asked for. Should the plaintiff in the following case be deemed the prevailing party?

A law requires that animal shelters must allow dogs access to an outdoor area of at least 500 square feet for a minimum of one hour per day. The statute provides for a private right of action and injunctive relief. It also provides for an attorney fee award to a plaintiff who prevails in an action under the statute.

An animal protection organization learns that a shelter has no outdoor area, so the dogs housed there are never allowed outside. The organization files a lawsuit under the outdoor access statute and asks for an injunction ordering the shelter to build a suitable outdoor area for the dogs. Two weeks before the case is scheduled to go to trial, the shelter voluntarily builds an outdoor exercise yard and begins allowing the dogs outdoor time for more than an hour per day. As a result, the court dismisses the lawsuit as moot. The plaintiff, claiming to be the prevailing party, moves for an award of statutory attorney fees.

Calculation

Once the prevailing party has been determined in a case with an entitlement to attorney fees, the court must calculate the correct amount of fees to award.

To understand how courts calculate attorney fee awards, it is helpful to first understand the methods that are not used. An attorney fee award to a prevailing party is not calculated based on the fees actually paid by that party. That would preclude recovery for plaintiffs who pay attorney fees by way of a contingency fee (a percentage of the monetary recovery in the lawsuit, paid only after the case is resolved), which is a common arrangement. It would also preclude awards to plaintiffs whose lawyer has taken the case *pro bono*, undesirably disincentivizing such representation.

Nor are attorney fee awards calculated based solely on the fees billed by the party's attorney, even if not yet paid by the client. That would undesirably incentivize inflated billing.

Instead, the way courts calculate attorney fee awards is to determine the total amount of fees that is reasonable under the circumstances. The amount of reasonable attorney fees is arrived at using what is called the lodestar method. The lodestar method provides a formula to guide the court in deciding on an amount of reasonable fees. (A "lodestar" is a star used to navigate a ship.) The formula is simple multiplication:

[Reasonable Number of Hours to Litigate the Case] ×
[Reasonable Hourly Rate for Services Rendered] = [Reasonable Attorney Fees]

To arrive at the solution to that equation, the court must first determine how much time was reasonably required to litigate the case. The trial judge should be in a good position to do that, as he or she is relatively familiar with the work that has been done over the life of the case. Once the court has determined a reasonable number of hours, the hourly rate must be calculated. Here the court will look to factors such as the attorney's experience, skill level, and the typical rate for attorneys in the relevant geographical area with a comparable level of experience and skill, and it will determine an appropriate hourly rate to multiply by the time spent on the case.

The way this works in practice is that the attorney for the prevailing party submits billing records in support of the request for fees, which reflect the time the lawyer spent on the case and the lawyer's customary hourly rate. The court will then decide whether those baseline numbers are reasonable, or if either or both need to be adjusted downward because they are unreasonably high. The ultimate goal is to award attorney fees to the prevailing party that accurately reflect the work necessary to achieve the result obtained.

Introductory Note — *Pasternack v. McCollough* and *In re Home Depot, Inc.*

In *Pasternack* and *Home Depot*, a party is deemed to have prevailed (the defendant in *Pasternack* and the plaintiffs in *Home Depot*) and is awarded fees. The issue on appeal in both cases is whether the trial court correctly calculated those fees.

Pasternack involves a statute that awards attorney fees to a defendant who prevails in the litigation by way of a particular dispositive motion (an "anti-SLAPP"). The plaintiff contends the trial court was too generous in its fee award but faces a high hurdle on appeal — the standard of review is abuse of discretion, extremely deferential to the trial judge's decision.

Home Depot is a massive class action case that resulted in a massive fee award: $15.3 million. In its comprehensive opinion, the Eleventh Circuit explains why common fund cases (where attorney fees are paid out of the plaintiff's recovery) are not exceptions to the American Rule, and why the district court was ultimately misguided in its lodestar calculation.

THINGS TO THINK ABOUT while reading *Pasternack v. McCollough* and *In re Home Depot, Inc.*:

1. Was the same method of calculation used in both cases? If not, what was different about them?

2. Were the fees awarded by the trial court in each case reasonable? Why or why not?

Pasternack v. McCullough

California Court of Appeal
65 Cal.App.5th 1050 (2021)

BIGELOW, P. J.

Lawrence Pasternack sued Thomas McCullough, Jr. and his law firm (collectively, McCullough) for malicious prosecution. In 2018, we reversed an order denying McCullough's special motion to strike under the anti-strategic lawsuits against public participation (anti-SLAPP) statute. (Code Civ. Proc., § 425.16.) In our disposition, we ordered the trial court to issue a fee award pursuant to section 425.16, subdivision (c)(1), which entitles a prevailing defendant on a special motion to strike to recover his attorney fees and costs. This appeal arises from the resulting attorney fees award of $146,010 to McCullough. Pasternack's primary dispute with the award is that the trial court erroneously ordered him to pay an hourly rate for attorney fees that was greater than what was actually paid for McCullough's defense. We conclude the trial court properly determined the reasonable market value of the attorneys' services and affirm the attorney fees order.

Procedural Background

On remand from our 2018 decision, McCullough moved for entry of judgment and sought attorney fees in the amount of $330,420. Lewis, Brisbois, Bisgaard & Smith LLP (Lewis Brisbois) represents McCullough in these proceedings. The Lewis Brisbois attorneys presented declarations and a time chart showing they expended over 500 hours on the action and attested their market rates ranged from $300 to $600 per hour.

Pasternack opposed McCullough's fee motion, arguing the hours claimed were excessive and disputing the amount of the hourly fees. He submitted a letter from Roy Weatherup, McCullough's lead counsel on appeal. Weatherup explained McCullough's defense was paid by his insurer at a rate of $140 per hour; Pasternack's lawsuit against McCullough was part of a block of hundreds of cases in which Lewis Brisbois gave a volume discount.

Pasternack also submitted an expert declaration from a former Lewis Brisbois partner explaining why insurance defense firms accept lower hourly rates in exchange for large volumes of case assignments from insurance companies. He asserted the agreed-upon rates are not "below market" because they are a product of an arms-length negotiation. These lower rates are profitable for the law firm because there is no measurable risk of nonpayment and such an arrangement serves as a gateway for future business. Insurance clients are courted by defense firms, in part because a defense firm becomes efficient in handling similar cases by building up resources — such as standard briefs — from prior similar cases. In this case, for example, Weatherup had extensive experience in anti-SLAPP matters and the issue raised in the prior appeal.

The trial court granted McCullough's attorney fees motion by order dated August 28, 2019 and awarded McCullough $146,010 in fees using the lodestar method. It struck time that was billed for activity unrelated to the motion to strike and that was "block billed" or failed to specify the tasks accomplished. The court further found "the nature and complexity of the legal issues on appeal [did] not warrant 528.1 hours of work performed by two partners billing at the rate of $600." Thus, the court not only reduced the hours claimed by the attorneys but also reduced the hourly rate requested by one of the partners from $600 to $250 per hour.

The trial court declined to adopt Pasternack's suggested market rate of $140 per hour for each attorney. The court explained, "First, $140 per hour is not the market rate for experienced appellate lawyers in Los Angeles County and the Court exercises its discretion to not so narrowly focus on the 'package rate' agreed to in this matter, especially since the specific rate for handling anti-SLAPP appeals remains unclear; neither [Pasternack's attorney nor the expert presented] sufficient information for the Court to conclude that $140 is the prevailing market rate for anti-SLAPP appeals in the insurance defense setting. Second, the Court finds the reduced amount awarded herein fully compensates Defendants for their work in this matter in light of Defendants' extensive prior experience handling appeals involving the 'interim adverse judgment rule.'" . . .

Discussion

The primary issue on appeal is whether the trial court erred when it applied hourly rates to its lodestar analysis that exceeded the hourly rate actually paid by McCullough's insurer for his defense. Relying on cases not involving attorney fees, Pasternack contends prevailing parties may not recover more than the actual fees they paid under a "paid in full" or "make whole" rule. We are not persuaded.

We review a trial court's fee award using an abuse of discretion standard. We conclude the trial court did not abuse its discretion in this case. It is well established that an attorney who accepts a reduced rate from a client is not precluded from seeking a reasonable hourly rate pursuant to the lodestar method. . . . A trial court has discretion to award an hourly rate under the lodestar method that exceeds the rate that was actually incurred or paid. . . . Here, the trial court properly determined the market rate for experienced appellate lawyers in Los Angeles County and "exercise[d] its discretion to not so narrowly focus on the 'package rate' agreed to in this matter."

We now turn to decide whether the trial court nevertheless abused its discretion because the amount it awarded shocked the conscience. Pasternack argues the lodestar amount calculated by the trial court was unreasonable and should be reversed. Not so.

The record shows Lewis Brisbois submitted evidence regarding the hours expended and reasonable rates for the work done. The trial court was entitled to rely on Lewis Brisbois's declarations to determine the reasonable rates for experienced attorneys in Los Angeles County. "[T]he trial court is in the best position to value the services rendered by the attorneys in his or her courtroom." (*Syers, supra,* 226 Cal.App.4th at p. 702.)

The trial court thoroughly examined the record and reduced both the time claimed and the hourly rate for one of the partners. Indeed, "[t]he award granted was significantly reduced from the original request as a result of the trial court's indication that it did not look favorably on the full request. Thus, it clearly appears that the trial court exercised its discretion. In these circumstances, we cannot conclude that the award of attorney fees shocks the conscience or suggests that passion and prejudice had a part in it. As such, we conclude that the trial court did not abuse its discretion in awarding the attorney fees that it did." (*Akins v. Enterprise Rent-A-Car Co.* (2000) 79 Cal.App.4th 1127, 1134.)

Disposition

The attorney fees award is affirmed. McCullough to recover his costs on appeal.

* * *

In re Home Depot, Inc.
United States Court of Appeals, Eleventh Circuit
931 F.3d 1065 (2019)

TJOFLAT, Circuit Judge:

Following a data breach at Home Depot, the information for tens of millions of credit cards was stolen, and a class of banks who issued the cards sued Home Depot to recover their resulting losses. Home Depot eventually settled with the class. As part of the settlement, Home Depot agreed to pay the reasonable attorney's fees of Class Counsel. The agreement specified that the attorney's fees would be paid separate from and in addition to the class fund, but the parties left the amount of those fees undetermined.

The District Court awarded Class Counsel $15.3 million in fees. It reached this award using the lodestar method, finding Class Counsel's hours to be reasonable and applying a multiplier of 1.3 to account for the risk the case presented. The Court also used the percentage method as a cross-check to ensure the amount of fees was reasonable. . . .

The main issue underlying the appeal is whether the fee arrangement outlined in the settlement should be characterized as a constructive common fund or as a fee-shifting contract. We hold that this is a contractual fee-shifting case, and the constructive common-fund doctrine does not apply. . . . We affirm the District Court's decision in all respects except one: it was an abuse of discretion to use a multiplier to account for risk in a fee-shifting case.

I.

In 2014, Home Depot experienced a massive data breach. It started when hackers installed malware on Home Depot's self-checkout kiosks. The malware would siphon off the personal financial information of customers who paid at the kiosks using a credit or debit card. The hackers then made this information, including names, card numbers, expiration dates, and security codes, available for sale on a black-market website. Approximately fifty-six million cards were compromised. It did not take long for a large number of fraudulent transactions to occur using the stolen information.

A flood of lawsuits followed. Consumers whose personal information was stolen and banks that issued the compromised cards filed over 50 class actions. . . .

The parties participated in three rounds of mediation, resulting in a preliminary settlement agreement that the parties presented to the District Court for approval.

The settlement agreement defined the class as follows:

> All banks, credit unions, financial institutions, and other entities in the United States . . . that issued Alerted-on Payment Cards. Excluded from this class are entities that have released all of their claims against Home Depot, but not excluded from the class are independent sponsored entities whose claims were released in connection with [the release offers] made by Mastercard. . . .

In exchange for settling the case, Home Depot agreed to provide the following relief. First, Home Depot agreed to pay $25 million into a settlement fund. The fund would be used to pay any taxes due and to pay any service awards to class representatives that the District Court approved. The remainder of the fund would be distributed to class members who had not released their claims. No money in the fund would revert to Home Depot. Second, Home Depot agreed to pay up to $2.25 million to some of the smaller banks (the "independent sponsored entities"). To be eligible, these banks must certify that they did not have sufficient time or information to appropriately consider the release offers — i.e., that they were misled and/or coerced. Home Depot did not create a fund for these payments; if less than $2.25 million was claimed, Home Depot would pay only the amount claimed.

Finally, Home Depot agreed to adopt security measures to protect its data. These measures include developing a "risk exception" process to identify risks in its data security; designing safeguards to manage any risks identified; monitoring its service providers and vendors to ensure compliance with those safeguards; and implementing an industry recognized security control framework.

On the matter of attorney's fees, the settlement agreement provided that Home Depot would pay the "reasonable attorneys' fees, costs and expenses" of Class Counsel. But the agreement left the amount of fees undetermined. Pursuant to the agreement, Class Counsel would submit to the District Court a requested amount in fees and expenses, to which Home Depot was free to object. While each party reserved its right to appeal the District Court's decision on attorney's fees, the amount awarded — no matter how large or how small — would not affect the "finality or effectiveness" of the settlement. Notably, the agreement stated that Home Depot's payment of attorney's fees would be "separate from and in addition to" the settlement fund. In other words, payment would not come from the $25 million set aside for class members.

The District Court approved the settlement agreement, noting that the issue of attorney's fees would be decided separately.

After the terms of the settlement were approved, the dispute over attorney's fees began.

Courts calculate attorney's fees using one of two methods: the percentage method or the lodestar method. Under the percentage method, courts award counsel a percentage of the class benefit. *See* The class benefit generally includes any benefits resulting from the litigation that go to the class. In this Circuit, courts typically award between 20–30%, known as the benchmark range.

Under the lodestar method, courts determine attorney's fees based on the product of the reasonable hours spent on the case and a reasonable hourly rate. The product is known as the lodestar. Sometimes courts apply to the lodestar a multiplier, also known as an enhancement or an upward adjustment, to reward counsel on top of their hourly rates.

Class Counsel advised the District Court that it had discretion to choose either the lodestar or the percentage method. Under either approach, Class Counsel requested $18 million in fees. In contrast, Home Depot argued that the District Court had to use the lodestar method, and based on its calculations, a reasonable fee would be about $5.6 million.

After entertaining a hearing on the motion for attorney's fees and reviewing the parties' briefings, the District Court issued a five-page decision. Following Home Depot's recommendation, the District Court adopted the lodestar approach. The District Court accepted the lodestar proposed by Class Counsel — about $11.7 million — as "an appropriate measure of the time expended by the plaintiffs in this case." Next, it applied the same multiplier used in the consumer-track settlement, 1.3, to arrive at a reasonable fee of $15.3 million. . . .

While the District Court agreed with Home Depot on using the lodestar method, it declined to adopt the lodestar proposed by Home Depot: about $5.6 million. . . . The District Court employed the percentage method as a cross-check on the lodestar. The parties agreed that the class benefit should include the $25 million settlement fund, the $2.25 million Home Depot agreed to pay to some smaller banks (the sponsored entities), and $710,000 in expenses. . . .

In sum, the District Court ordered Home Depot to pay Class Counsel $15.3 million in fees. It reached this award using the lodestar method, under which it accepted the lodestar proposed by Class Counsel and applied a multiplier of 1.3 to account for risk. The Court also used a percentage cross-check, which, after including the $14.5 million premiums in the class benefit and excluding any attorney's fees, showed that the fee award was slightly more than a third of the class benefit, which the Court found to be reasonable.

Home Depot appeals the award of attorney's fees. . . .

II.

We review a district court's award of attorney's fees for abuse of discretion. An abuse of discretion occurs if the judge fails to apply the proper legal standard or to follow proper procedures in making the determination, or bases an award upon findings of fact that are clearly erroneous. Under this standard, district courts have great latitude in setting fee awards in class action cases.

A.

. . . .

1.

In the American legal system, each party is traditionally responsible for its own attorney's fees. *Hardt v. Reliance Standard Life Ins. Co.*, 560 U.S. 242, 253 (2010) ("Each litigant pays his own attorney's fees, win or lose, unless a statute or contract provides otherwise."); *see also Alyeska Pipeline Serv. Co. v. Wilderness Soc'y*, 421 U.S. 240, 247 (1975) ("In the United States, the prevailing litigant is ordinarily not entitled to collect a reasonable attorneys' fee from the loser."). This principle is known as the American Rule.

There are three exceptions to the American Rule: (1) when a statute grants courts the authority to direct the losing party to pay attorney's fees; (2) when the parties agree in a contract that one party will pay attorney's fees; and (3) when a court orders one party to pay attorney's fees for acting in bad faith. These exceptions — when one party pays for the other's attorney's fees — describe fee-shifting cases.

Some courts, including this one, have described common-fund cases as an exception to the American Rule. That is incorrect. And it is important to understand why.

A common-fund case is when a lawyer who recovers a common fund for the benefit of persons other than himself or his client is entitled to a reasonable attorney's fee from the fund as a whole. This is typical in class actions, where the class might receive a large payout, from which the attorney derives his fees. Common-fund cases are consistent with the American Rule, because the attorney's fees come from the fund, which belongs to the class. In this way, the client, not the losing party, pays the attorney's fees. . . .

Thus, the key distinction between common-fund and fee-shifting cases is whether the attorney's fees are paid by the client (as in common-fund cases) or by the other party (as in fee-shifting cases).

2.

Applying this understanding of attorney's fees, we are convinced that this is a fee-shifting case.

On its face, the settlement agreement provides that Home Depot will pay the attorney's fees. The agreement states that "Home Depot agrees to pay the reasonable attorneys' fees, costs and expenses of counsel for the Financial Institution Plaintiffs." Even more explicit, the agreement goes on to state that "[a]ny award of attorneys' fees, costs, and expenses shall be paid separate from and in addition to the Settlement Fund." That sounds like fee shifting. Indeed, it is hard to imagine how the settlement agreement could be any clearer that Home Depot will pay the attorney's fees, and that payment will not come out of the class fund. . . .

Still, Class Counsel insists that we should treat this arrangement as a constructive common fund. Where class action settlements are concerned, courts will often classify the fee arrangement as a "constructive common fund" that is governed by common-fund principles even when the agreement states that fees will be paid separately.

The rationale for the constructive common fund is that the defendant negotiated the payment to the class and the payment to counsel as a "package deal." The defendant is concerned, first and foremost, with its total liability. Thus, courts have recognized that, as a practical matter, defendants undoubtedly take into account the amount of attorney's fees when they agree on an amount to pay the class. . . .

But this package-deal reasoning does not apply here. Put simply, there was no package: Home Depot did not negotiate the attorney's fees simultaneously with the settlement fund. The fees were left entirely to the District Court's discretion. The parties did not even agree to a cap, often referred to as a "clear-sailing agreement." So it cannot be said that Home Depot took into account the amount of attorney's fees when it negotiated the size of the class award, because the amount of attorney's fees was completely undetermined. . . .

Admittedly, a defendant could (and probably does) make an educated guess concerning the amount of attorney's fees, even when the amount is left undetermined. But if this were enough to create a constructive common fund, it would be virtually impossible to contract for fee-shifting. The purported rule would be that any class settlement — no matter whether the fees are paid by the defendant or out of the class award, or whether the fees are negotiated separately or as part of the settlement — should be treated as a common fund. As a result, construing the agreement here as a constructive common fund would effectively eliminate the ability to contract for fee-shifting absent perhaps some magic-word requirement.

In sum, we hold that the constructive common fund does not apply when the agreement provides that attorney's fees will be paid by the defendant separately from the settlement fund, and the amount of those fees is left completely undetermined. We construe the settlement agreement here as a fee-shifting arrangement.

3.

Ordinarily, after classifying the fee arrangement, the next question would be which method the court should use to calculate the attorney's fees. In common-fund cases, we have directed courts to use the percentage method. This case, however, is a contractual fee-shifting case, and the appropriate method for such a case is not clearly governed by any binding precedent.

But the parties do not challenge the District Court's selection of the lodestar method. Even though Class Counsel believes this is a common-fund case, they say the District Court had discretion to choose either the percentage or the lodestar method because several of the claims raised in the complaint were under state statutes with fee-shifting provisions. Class Counsel may be right that the District Court had discretion to choose, but the proper method here has nothing to do with the state statutes. The District Court awarded the attorney's fees pursuant to a contract — the settlement agreement — not pursuant to a statute. Nevertheless, because the parties do not challenge the District Court's use of the lodestar method, we do not question it. . . .

Home Depot argues that the District Court abused its discretion by applying a multiplier to Class Counsel's lodestar. Home Depot bases its argument on Supreme Court precedent outlining the use of multipliers in statutory fee-shifting cases. Although we are not bound in a contractual fee-shifting case by statutory fee-shifting cases, we agree that it was error for the District Court to enhance Class Counsel's lodestar based on risk.

1.

We begin by summarizing the Supreme Court's precedent on statutory fee-shifting cases. Fee-shifting statutes allow counsel for the prevailing party to recover a reasonable fee. *Perdue v. Kenny A. ex rel. Winn*, 559 U.S. 542, 550 (2010). A reasonable fee is one sufficient to attract competent counsel to represent the case, but not one that provides a windfall for attorneys. There is a strong presumption that the lodestar yields a reasonable fee for this purpose. Because the lodestar is presumed to be sufficient, a multiplier will be appropriate only in "rare and exceptional" cases. *Id.* To warrant a multiplier, the fee applicant must produce "specific evidence" that an enhancement is necessary to provide a reasonable fee. An enhancement may be necessary if the lodestar does not reflect the true value of counsel's work.

The question becomes, what specific evidence would satisfy this standard. The Supreme Court has made it plain that "most, if not all," of the factors used to determine a reasonable fee are already subsumed in the lodestar, and it is not permissible to enhance a fee based on a factor that is subsumed. That would be "double counting" — i.e., a windfall.

For example, the novelty and complexity of the issues are reflected in the number of hours spent on the case, as complicated litigation will demand more time. Similarly, the skill and experience of the attorneys will be reflected in the hourly rates. Thus, courts should not use these factors to justify a multiplier.

As for the results obtained, this factor should be folded into the quality-of-representation factor. *Perdue*, 559 U.S. at 554. This is so because the results obtained are relevant to attorney's fees only if those results are attributable to counsel's performance, rather than, say, the other side dropping the ball. And the quality of representation should be used to enhance the fee only in the rare cases where the fee applicant demonstrates that the "superior attorney performance is not adequately taken into account in the lodestar calculation."

Finally, the Court determined that risk is not an appropriate basis for a multiplier in statutory fee-shifting cases. The Court explained that the "risk of loss . . . is the product of two [inputs]: (1) the legal and factual merits of the claim, and (2) the difficulty of establishing those merits." *Dague*, 505 U.S. at 562. The second input is subsumed in the lodestar — "either in the higher number of hours expended to overcome the difficulty, or in the higher hourly rate of the attorney skilled and experienced enough to do so." *Id.* While the first input is not reflected in the lodestar, "there are good reasons" not to enhance fees for the risk presented by meritless claims. *Id.* at 563.

. . . If fees are enhanced for contingency fee cases as a class — rather than based on a risk assessment of each case — it would inevitably overcompensate some cases and undercompensate others. Conversely, if fees are enhanced based on the riskiness of each particular case, it would reward lawyers for taking cases with relatively little merit and incentivize bad claims. For this reason, not adjusting fees for risk is consistent with fee-shifting statutes. These statutes limit fees to prevailing parties, and adjusting fees for risk effectively subsidizes the attorney's losing cases — a result at odds with the prevailing party requirement. Plus, enhancing for risk "would make the setting of fees more complex and arbitrary, hence more unpredictable, and hence more litigable." For all of these reasons, the Supreme Court decreed that courts could not use a multiplier in statutory fee-shifting cases to account for risk.

If these precedents apply, it was an abuse of discretion for the District Court to apply a multiplier. The District Court's only stated reason for using a multiplier was the exceptional risk taken by counsel in litigating the case. And risk, according to the Supreme Court, is not an appropriate basis for enhancing an attorney's fee in *statutory* fee-shifting cases. But this is a *contractual* fee-shifting arrangement. As such, we must consider whether and to what extent these precedents apply.

2.

There is no question that the Supreme Court precedents are specific to fee-shifting statutes. . . .

For this reason, we have held that the Supreme Court precedent requiring the use of the lodestar method in statutory fee-shifting cases does not apply to common-fund cases. . . .

But this is a contractual fee-shifting case, not a common-fund case. As such, it is more closely related to the Supreme Court precedent governing fee-shifting statutes. And just because precedent is not technically binding does not mean we should blithely disregard it. To promote consistency in the law, we should adhere to precedent where its reasoning applies. . . .

With that in mind, we consider whether the Supreme Court's reasons for limiting the use of multipliers in statutory fee-shifting cases apply to contractual fee-shifting cases. The Court's reasons largely turn on the point that most of the factors used to justify an enhancement are already subsumed in the lodestar, so it would result in a windfall to count them again with a multiplier. This reasoning makes it just as unreasonable to double-count in a contractual fee-shifting case as it is in a statutory fee-shifting case.

Here, the District Court used a multiplier to account for risk. The Supreme Court forbade adjusting for risk for a number of reasons. To start, the Court said that risk was partly reflected in the lodestar. For the part of risk that is not reflected in the lodestar, the Court gave one reason for not using it to justify an enhancement that is specific to statutes — subsidizing losing claims contrary to the prevailing-party requirement found in most fee-shifting statutes. But the Court gave other reasons that apply equally in contractual fee-shifting settings, such as incentivizing merit-less claims and making fees less predictable. Thus, on the whole, we find that the Court's prohibition on enhancements for risk applies to contractual fee-shifting cases when courts use the lodestar method.

Because it is inappropriate to enhance a lodestar in a fee-shifting case to account for risk, the District Court abused its discretion in applying a multiplier on the basis of the "exceptional litigation risk that class counsel took in litigating this case." . . .

IV.

For the foregoing reasons, we affirm the judgment of the District Court in part, vacate in part, and remand for further proceedings consistent with this opinion.

AFFIRMED in part, VACATED in part, and REMANDED.

* * *

Problem 62

Courts must calculate attorney fees in a way that makes the amount awarded reasonable. The lodestar method is used to generate a presumptively reasonable amount. Did the trial court correctly calculate the attorney fee award in the case below? If not, what should the court have done differently?

A plaintiff prevails in a lawsuit for a statutory violation. The statute provides for reasonable attorney fees to the prevailing party. The plaintiff's counsel moves for an award of an attorney fees, supporting the motion with uncontroverted evidence that the reasonable hourly rate in the geographic area for an attorney with like experience and skill is $500 per hour. The motion is also supported by records reflecting plaintiff's counsel spent a total of 250 hours litigating the case. Based on that evidence, the motion requests an attorney fee award in the amount of $125,000 ($500 × 250).

After reviewing the motion, the trial court rules as follows: "I find the hourly rate to be an accurate reflection of the prevailing rate in this area for an attorney with this experience and skill level. I also find that counsel expended a reasonable number of hours working the case. However, I make the further finding that this case involved very straightforward legal issues and simply was not a difficult one to litigate. For that reason, I am reducing the requested attorney fees by 40 percent. The court will enter a total fee award in favor of the plaintiff in the amount of $75,000."

-abuse of discretion

Chapter 15

Remedies for Civil Rights Violations

Remedies are the tools courts use to resolve individual disputes. The implications of a dispute's resolution usually will not extend beyond the parties to it. But it is important to also recognize that judicial remedies can play a broader and more profound role in society, as an instrument of social justice and change. This chapter explores how remedies for civil rights violations help shape the national culture to better reflect the ideals professed in its founding documents.

Civil rights are fundamental freedoms guaranteed to a country's inhabitants. They protect people from government overreach and prohibit wrongful discrimination. In the United States, the most well-known civil rights were created by the federal Constitution. The Constitution articulates (among others) the right to freely speak and practice religion, the right to equal protection of the law, the right to due process, and the right to be free from unreasonable government searches and seizures. Building on the rights guaranteed in the Constitution, Congress has passed legislation such as the Civil Rights Act of 1964, for example, which prohibits discrimination based on race, color, religion, sex, or national origin. The Voting Rights Act protects free and fair access to the ballot box, a critical component to a functioning democracy. Many states have their own civil rights laws that mirror federal law or provide greater protections.

Creation of a right is merely the first step, however. A right is empty without a mechanism to enforce it. For a right to truly have meaning, there must be a remedy for a violation. Cases involving the enforcement of civil rights have been some of the most noteworthy decisions in history. And remedies for civil rights violations are likely to have a prominent role in the years to come as the United States continues struggling to fulfill promises made in its founding documents so many years ago.

The remedies most commonly used to protect civil rights and that have potential to change behavior in a way that promotes social justice are injunctions, damages, and attorney fee awards.

Injunctions and Structural Injunctions

Injunctions are powerful medicine to enforce civil rights. When a right is violated—if an employer or business engages in prohibited discrimination, for instance—the court can issue an injunction to directly remedy the violation. An injunction will require that the discriminatory practice stop immediately. And it is enforceable by the contempt power, meaning failure to comply could potentially result in imprisonment.

A particular kind of injunction is noteworthy in the civil rights context: the structural injunction. A structural injunction is an order requiring an entire organization or governmental entity to change its policies or practices. The goal is to prompt largescale behavioral change at an institutional level to achieve broad, lasting reform. Structural injunctions are necessary when a civil rights violation is such a widespread practice that piecemeal enforcement would not effectively vindicate the right at issue. Structural injunctions have been used, perhaps most famously, to desegregate schools. (*Brown v. Board of Education of Topeka*, 349 U.S. 294 (1955).) They have been used to require prisons to provide adequate medical care to inmates. (*Coleman v. Wilson*, 912 F.Supp. 1282 (E.D. Cal. 1995).) And they have reformed the tactics of police departments that have engaged in racial profiling. (*Floyd v. City of New York*, 959 F.Supp.2d 540 (S.D.N.Y. 2013).).

Structural injunctions have historically been an important mechanism for civil rights reform and will in all likelihood continue to play an outsize role in that area.

Damages

Damages may not fit as naturally with civil rights enforcement as injunctions but are nonetheless a critical enforcement mechanism. Compensatory damages in civil rights cases provide compensation for harm experienced by the plaintiff and deter future civil rights violations.

Compensation is necessary to recognize that a violation of a person's civil rights does indeed inflict real harm. A civil rights violation does not typically cause financial harm. Nor is there a physical injury in most cases (although there certainly is in some—lawsuits for excessive force by a police officer, for example). Instead, compensatory damages in civil rights cases will usually be for emotional harm—the mental suffering that comes from being oppressed by the government or treated poorly because of one's race or another protected characteristic. The valuation of such emotional harm is left to the discretion of the trier of fact.

In addition to compensatory damages, punitive damages may be available in civil rights lawsuits. Punitive damages promote justice by vindicating society's interest in punishing those who disrespect our fundamental values. They also help deter future civil rights violations, providing an important behavior-shaping component.

Attorney Fee Awards

Civil rights protection statutes often provide that reasonable attorney fees be awarded to a prevailing plaintiff. Potential for an attorney fee award is crucial because civil rights violations may not inflict the kind of harm that is readily measurable in dollars. As discussed above, the harm from a civil rights violation will often be limited to emotional injury, which may or may not be assigned a significant monetary value by a jury.

A person whose rights have been violated might understandably be hesitant to retain an attorney to pursue a case that may result in an injunction and a small amount of monetary compensation, if any. And a person without the financial means to hire an attorney (which, statistically speaking, is nearly everyone) will probably not be able to retain one under an alternative fee arrangement like a contingency fee without the potential for substantial monetary recovery.

Attorney fee awards address both of those problems. They incentivize plaintiffs to pursue civil rights cases that do not involve easily calculable financial damages. And they incentivize attorneys to represent plaintiffs in such cases even when the client cannot afford to pay attorney fees out of pocket. Those incentives allow for more robust civil rights enforcement through the courts.

As litigation becomes progressively more expensive, attorney fee awards will only increase in their importance to civil rights enforcement.

Introductory Note — *Brown v. Board of Education of Topeka* and *B.B. v. County of Los Angeles*

In 1954, the Supreme Court decided in *Brown v. Board of Education* that segregating schools by race violates the Constitution. It left open the question of what to do about it. Reproduced here is the Supreme Court's later opinion in *Brown*, addressing the question of the appropriate remedy. The Court ultimately leaves it for the individual state courts to fashion relief but provides some guidance about what it should look like ("orders and decrees consistent with this opinion as are necessary and proper to admit to public schools on a racially nondiscriminatory basis with all deliberate speed").

B.B. v. County of Los Angeles arose from the tragic but all too common circumstance of a Black man killed by police. The majority opinion decides a discrete question of California law: whether a statute limiting a defendant's tort liability commensurate with percentage of fault applies in the case of an intentional tort. In a powerful concurrence, Justice Goodwin Liu notes that "variants of this fact pattern have occurred with distressing frequency throughout this country." The concurrence explains how — more than six decades after *Brown* — existing civil remedies have fallen short of ensuring the constitutional promise of equal justice under law.

THINGS TO THINK ABOUT while reading *Brown v. Board of Education of Topeka* and *B.B. v. County of Los Angeles*:

1. What is the constitutional violation in each case?

2. Is the relief awarded sufficient to remedy the constitutional violation that occurred? If not, what other relief would help?

Brown v. Board of Education of Topeka

United States Supreme Court
349 U.S. 294 (1955)

Mr. Chief Justice WARREN delivered the opinion of the Court.

These cases were decided on May 17, 1954. The opinions of that date, declaring the fundamental principle that racial discrimination in public education is unconstitutional, are incorporated herein by reference. All provisions of federal, state, or local law requiring or permitting such discrimination must yield to this principle. There remains for consideration the manner in which relief is to be accorded.

Because these cases arose under different local conditions and their disposition will involve a variety of local problems, we requested further argument on the question of relief.... Full implementation of these constitutional principles may require solution of varied local school problems. School authorities have the primary responsibility for elucidating, assessing, and solving these problems; courts will have to consider whether the action of school authorities constitutes good faith implementation of the governing constitutional principles. Because of their proximity to local conditions and the possible need for further hearings, the courts which originally heard these cases can best perform this judicial appraisal. Accordingly, we believe it appropriate to remand the cases to those courts.

In fashioning and effectuating the decrees, the courts will be guided by equitable principles. Traditionally, equity has been characterized by a practical flexibility in shaping its remedies and by a facility for adjusting and reconciling public and private needs. These cases call for the exercise of these traditional attributes of equity power. At stake is the personal interest of the plaintiffs in admission to public schools as soon as practicable on a nondiscriminatory basis. To effectuate this interest may call for elimination of a variety of obstacles in making the transition to school systems operated in accordance with the constitutional principles set forth in our May 17, 1954, decision. Courts of equity may properly take into account the public interest in the elimination of such obstacles in a systematic and effective manner. But it should go without saying that the vitality of these constitutional principles cannot be allowed to yield simply because of disagreement with them.

While giving weight to these public and private considerations, the courts will require that the defendants make a prompt and reasonable start toward full compliance with our May 17, 1954, ruling. Once such a start has been made, the courts may

[handwritten margin notes: Δ's burden — public interest — w/ good faith]

find that additional time is necessary to carry out the ruling in an effective manner. The burden rests upon the defendants to establish that such time is necessary in the public interest and is consistent with good faith compliance at the earliest practicable date. To that end, the courts may consider problems related to administration, arising from the physical condition of the school plant, the school transportation system, personnel, revision of school districts and attendance areas into compact units to achieve a system of determining admission to the public schools on a nonracial basis, and revision of local laws and regulations which may be necessary in solving the foregoing problems. They will also consider the adequacy of any plans the defendants may propose to meet these problems and to effectuate a transition to a racially nondiscriminatory school system. During this period of transition, the courts will retain jurisdiction of these cases.

The judgments below, except that in the Delaware case, are accordingly reversed and the cases are remanded to the District Courts to take such proceedings and enter such orders and decrees consistent with this opinion as are necessary and proper to admit to public schools on a racially nondiscriminatory basis with all deliberate speed the parties to these cases. The judgment in the Delaware case — ordering the immediate admission of the plaintiffs to schools previously attended only by white children — is affirmed on the basis of the principles stated in our May 17, 1954, opinion, but the case is remanded to the Supreme Court of Delaware for such further proceedings as that Court may deem necessary in light of this opinion.

It is so ordered.

* * *

B.B. v. County of Los Angeles

California Supreme Court
10 Cal.5th 1 (2020)

Opinion of the Court by CHIN, J.

In this case, we consider the application of Civil Code section 1431.2 to tortfeasors held liable for injuries based on the commission of an intentional tort. Here, the intentional tort was a battery that, combined with other factors, tragically led to the death of Darren Burley. While attempting to subdue Burley, deputies from the Los Angeles County Sheriff's Department, after getting Burley facedown on pavement, used their knees to pin him to the ground with as much body weight as possible. One of the deputies — defendant David Aviles — pressed one knee into the center of Burley's back and another onto the back of Burley's head, near the neck. Aviles disengaged after Burley's hands were cuffed behind his back and his ankles tightly cinched together with a nylon cord. But when paramedics arrived, they found Burley, still cuffed and facedown on the pavement, with a different deputy pressing a knee into the small of his back and with no pulse. They restored Burley's pulse through resuscitation efforts, but he never regained consciousness and died 10 days later.

A jury found that Aviles had committed battery by using unreasonable force against Burley. The court later entered a judgment against Aviles for the entire amount of the noneconomic damages the jury awarded — $8 million — even though the jury also found that only 20 percent of the responsibility for Burley's death was "attributable to" Aviles's actions. . . .

I. Factual and Procedural History

On the evening of August 3, 2012, the Los Angeles County Sheriff's Department received a report of an ongoing assault in Compton, California. Upon arriving at the scene, Deputies David Aviles and Steve Fernandez observed Darren Burley approach them in slow, stiff, exaggerated robotic movements with his fists clenched at his sides and a blank stare on his face. He was foaming at the mouth and making grunting and growling noises. Based on these observations, the deputies suspected Burley might be under the influence of PCP. The deputies ordered Burley to get on his knees facing away from them. Burley did not respond.

A distraught woman suddenly appeared in the street, pointed at Burley and yelled, "He tried to kill me!" She began to flee, and Burley ran after her. Fernandez, in an effort to stop Burley's pursuit and knock him down, "hockey checked" Burley, ramming a shoulder into Burley's side. Burley lost balance and fell, hitting his head on a parked truck and then landing facedown on the pavement. Aviles attempted to handcuff Burley, but Burley resisted. A struggle ensued, during which Burley punched Aviles — who was wearing a bulletproof vest — in the chest and Aviles punched Burley in the face approximately five times. Fernandez came to Aviles's aid, and the two deputies wrestled Burley to the pavement, facedown. As Burley continued to struggle, Fernandez tried "to get [Burley's lower body] pinned to the ground" by kneeling "with all [his] weight on [Burley's] hamstring area." Meanwhile, Aviles tried "to pin" Burley's upper body to the ground by mounting Burley and pressing one knee into the center of his back, at the top of his diaphragm, and another knee down on the back of his head, near the back of his neck. Aviles, who weighed 200 pounds, used "as much [body] weight [as he] was able to apply." Burley struggled, trying to raise his chest from the ground. According to a witness, one of the deputies — who, from the witness's description, appeared to be Aviles — held Burley in "some type of head-lock" during most of the struggle and was "choking" him.

More deputies arrived on scene and found Burley facedown with Aviles and Fernandez trying to restrain him. Deputy Paul Beserra attempted to restrain Burley's left arm, while Deputy Timothy Lee assisted on the right and Deputy Ernest Celaya held Burley's feet. Celaya "Tasered" Burley multiple times in the calf area, and Lee "Tasered" him once in the rib cage area, all without apparent effect. The deputies eventually maneuvered Burley's hands behind his back and cuffed him. Even though restrained, Burley was still "flinging" and "twisting" his upper body, so Aviles remained on Burley's back, using his "upper body weight" to push down on Burley and "keep him in place." Other deputies applied a "hobble restraint" to Burley's legs by wrapping a nylon cord around his ankles and "cinch[ing] it tight." A witness testified that one of the deputies hit Burley in the head "at least seven to ten times" with a flashlight, and that Burley appeared to be gasping for air.

After Burley was handcuffed and hobbled, all of the deputies disengaged except Beserra, who "took over" from Aviles and "relieve[d]" him of "attempting to control [Burley's] upper body." From that point forward, Beserra was the only deputy to "touch[ ]" Burley. According to Beserra, he continued to keep Burley "restrained" facedown on the ground because Burley, though "handcuffed and hobbled," was "still violently fighting against the restraints" and thus posed "a threat to himself and to" the officers. During this time, Beserra did not use "any more force" or place any of his weight "on top of" Burley. "After about 30 seconds," Beserra "felt that [Burley] was no longer fighting against the restraints," so he "placed [Burley] on his left side in order to put him in a recovery position" and "to facilitate . . . medical monitoring." About 90 seconds later — or "approximately two minutes" after Burley was handcuffed and hobbled — Beserra heard Burley's breathing become labored. Beserra then "motioned" for the other deputies "to bring . . . over" paramedics, who were already on scene and "about 10 to 20 feet away . . . rendering aid to" the woman Burley had earlier chased. The paramedics responded "immediately," but as they were "walking over to render aid," Beserra felt Burley's body "go limp" and "motionless." This occurred "approximately . . . a minute after [Beserra] placed [Burley] on his side and after [Beserra] heard [Burley's] breathing become shallow."

Baserra's account was sharply contradicted at trial by Jason Henderson, Sr., a fire captain and paramedic with the Compton Fire Department. Henderson testified that when he and other paramedics arrived at the scene, they "got out of [their] rigs and then [immediately] started moving towards where [Burley] was." Henderson did not recall any of the deputies calling them over or indicating that Burley needed help, or any medical personnel treating the woman Burley had chased; she was already in one of the deputy's vehicle when they arrived. When they reached Burley, he was not "on his side," but was "face down" on the pavement with his hands cuffed behind his back and a deputy "leaning on" him and applying "weight" with a "knee in the small of [his] back." Burley "appeared to be unresponsive," so Henderson "asked the deputy to get off [Burley] and to unhook him" so Burley could be assessed. After Burley was "uncuffed," the paramedics "rolled him over" and "checked his pulse," but could find none. They restored his pulse after five minutes of resuscitation efforts, but he never regained consciousness and died 10 days later. According to the autopsy report, the cause of death was brain death and swelling from lack of oxygen following a cardiac arrest "due to status post-restraint maneuvers or behavior associated with cocaine, [PCP] and cannabinoids intake."

Burley's children and estranged wife, on behalf of themselves and Burley, sued the County of Los Angeles (County) and the deputies, asserting, as here relevant, claims for battery, negligence, and wrongful death (based on the alleged acts of battery and negligence). Regarding Aviles, the jury found in a special verdict that he had committed battery by using unreasonable force against Burley, and that 20 percent of the responsibility for Burley's death was "attributable to" Aviles's use of unreasonable force. The jury also found that Burley himself had been negligent and that he bore 40 percent of the responsibility for his own death. The jury attributed the remaining 40 percent of the responsibility to the other deputies. Despite this allocation, the trial court entered a judgment against Aviles for 100 percent of the noneconomic damages — set by the jury at $8 million — because his liability was based on commission of an intentional tort: battery.

The Court of Appeal reversed the judgment, holding that section 1431.2 limits the liability for noneconomic damage of *all* defendants — including intentional tortfeasors — to their proportionate share of fault. . . .

II. Discussion

The issue here is the extent of Aviles's liability for "'non-economic damages,'" which, for purposes of applying section 1431.2, are defined as "subjective, nonmonetary losses including, but not limited to, pain, suffering, inconvenience, mental suffering, emotional distress, loss of society and companionship, loss of consortium, injury to reputation and humiliation." (§ 1431.2, subd. (b)(2).) As set forth above, section 1431.2, subdivision (a), provides: "In any action for personal injury, property damage, or wrongful death, based upon principles of comparative fault, the liability of each defendant for non-economic damages shall be several only and shall not be joint. Each defendant shall be liable only for the amount of non-economic damages allocated to that defendant in direct proportion to that defendant's percentage of fault, and a separate judgment shall be rendered against that defendant for that amount." The question before us is how, if at all, this section applies to intentional tortfeasors like Aviles.

. . . We hold that section 1431.2, subdivision (a), does not authorize a reduction in the liability of intentional tortfeasors for noneconomic damages based on the extent to which the negligence of other actors — including the plaintiffs, any codefendants, injured parties, and nonparties — contributed to the injuries in question.

III. Disposition

For the reasons set forth above, we reverse the judgment of the Court of Appeal and remand for further proceedings consistent with this opinion.

Concurring Opinion by Justice Liu

In Compton, on the evening of August 3, 2012, several witnesses called the police after they saw Darren Burley attacking a woman in the street. When police arrived and attempted to stop him, Burley resisted arrest; the police suspected that Burley was under the influence of drugs. Deputy David Aviles then pinned Burley to the ground while other officers beat him with a flashlight and tasered him repeatedly. Deputy Aviles pressed his knees on Burley's neck and back with the full weight of his 200-pound body. A witness saw Burley gasping for air. When Burley lost consciousness, none of the officers rendered aid. Burley never regained consciousness and died 10 days later.

Darren Burley was Black. By happenstance, we heard oral argument in this case one week after another Black man, George Floyd, was killed by a Minneapolis police officer who pressed his knee into Floyd's neck with the full weight of his body for 8 minutes and 46 seconds — an incident that galvanized protests in every state across the country and throughout the world. (Burch et al., *How Black Lives Matter Reached Every Corner of America*, N.Y. Times (June 13, 2020); Bender & Winning, *Antiracism Protests Erupt Around the World in Wake of George Floyd Killing*, Wall Street Journal (June 7, 2020).) In all likelihood, the only reason Darren Burley is not a household name is that his killing was not caught on videotape as Floyd's was.

Sadly, what happened to these men is not happenstance. Variants of this fact pattern have occurred with distressing frequency throughout the country and here in California. (See, e.g., *People v. Mehserle* (2012) 206 Cal.App.4th 1125, 1133 ["[Oscar] Grant protested, 'I can't breathe. Just get off of me. I can't breathe. I quit. I surrender. I quit.'"]; *Garlick v. County of Kern* (E.D.Cal. 2016) 167 F.Supp.3d 1117, 1134 ["[David] Silva was chest-down with weight on his back. . . . [T]hroughout the altercation, Silva was . . . yelling out 'help,' and 'help me.'"]; *Martinez v. City of Pittsburg* (N.D.Cal., Mar. 8, 2019, No. 17-cv-04246-RS) 2019 WL 1102375, p. *3 ["Once [Humberto] Martinez was secured, Elmore . . . continued to apply pressure to the side of Martinez's head and kept his knee on Martinez's upper back for approximately 30 seconds. . . . Eventually, one of the officers noticed that Martinez was turning purple, at which point they rolled him to his side and removed the handcuffs."]; *People v. O'Callaghan* (Mar. 13, 2017, B265928) 2017 WL 958396, p. *1 [nonpub. opn.] ["[Alesia] Thomas remarked, 'I can't move' and 'I can't breathe'" and officer "proceeded to kick Thomas three times in her lower abdomen"]; *C.R. v. City of Antioch* (N.D.Cal., June 25, 2018, No. 16-cv-03742-JST) 2018 WL 3108982, p. *2 [witness "testified that he heard [Rakeem] Rucks say at some point while he was on the ground, 'Get me up out of the dirt. I'm breathing dirt. It's hard to breathe."].)

Today's opinion holds that Civil Code section 1431.2 does not permit an intentional tortfeasor to offset liability for noneconomic damages based on the negligence of other actors. Thus, Burley's family may recover the full amount of their noneconomic damages. But even as the wrongful death judgment here affords a measure of monetary relief to Burley's family, it does not acknowledge the troubling racial dynamics that have resulted in state-sanctioned violence, including lethal violence, against Black people throughout our history to this very day.

Wrongful death statutes trace their origins to the 19th century, when state legislatures, alarmed at the increasing rate of fatal workplace accidents, attempted to force corporations to compensate the family members of accident victims. The elements of a wrongful death action are the underlying tort (in this case, battery), a resulting death, and damages. (Code Civ. Proc., § 377.60.) Although this tort encompasses the wrong inflicted on Burley and provides compensation to his family, it gives no hint that what happened here has a history. And reckoning with that history is necessary if we are to prevent the wrongful deaths of more African Americans in the future.

The Legislature has at times attempted to redress the specific harm of violence against African Americans. Burley's family has also sought relief under the Tom Bane Civil Rights Act (Bane Act), which provides a right of action against a person who, whether or not acting under the color of law, violates "by threat, intimidation, or coercion" another person's federal or state rights. (Civ. Code, § 52.1, subd. (b).) The Bane Act was passed to "'stem a tide of hate crimes'" against minorities in the 1980s. (*Venegas v. County of Los Angeles* (2004) 32 Cal.4th 820, 843.) In addition, the Ralph Civil Rights Act of 1976 (Ralph Act) forbids violence or intimidation "on account of" certain protected characteristics, including race. (Civ. Code, § 51.7, subd. (b).) These laws acknowledge the racial dimensions of acts of violence against African Americans. But in the excessive force context, applying the coercion element of a Bane Act claim has not been straightforward. And although the Ralph Act provides liability for intentional discrimination, one may ask what other measures are necessary given what we know about unconscious bias. (See Banks, Eberhardt & Ross, *Discrimination and Implicit Bias in a Racially Unequal Society* (2006) 94 Calif. L.Rev. 1169, 1182–1189.)

Moreover, the efficacy of these laws has sometimes been undermined by the very racial disparities they were meant to correct. When litigants have recovered damages, verdicts have often reflected racial disparities in income and health outcomes. Until the Legislature prohibited the practice this year, California juries routinely consulted tables estimating earning potential based on race and gender when awarding economic damages to prevailing plaintiffs. (Civ. Code, § 3361, added by Stats. 2019, ch. 136, § 2.) This "perpetuate[d] systemic inequalities" and "disproportionately injure[d] women and minority individuals," who on average earn less than white men. (Stats. 2019, ch. 136, § 1; see Avraham & Yuracko, *Torts and Discrimination* (2017) 78 Ohio St. L.J. 661, 664.)

Nor should we assume that damages are enough to reliably deter police misconduct. Local jurisdictions must indemnify officers for any nonpunitive damages judgments or settlements in suits brought against them (with few exceptions), which effectively means that taxpayers foot the bill. (Gov. Code, §§ 825, subd. (a), 825.2.) And these payouts often come from law enforcement budgets specifically set aside for such purposes or from the local jurisdiction's general funds. (See Schwartz, *How Governments Pay: Lawsuits, Budgets, and Police Reform* (2016) 63 UCLA L.Rev. 1144, 1165; *id.* at p. 1241 [Los Angeles Sheriff's Department budgeted more than $35 million for lawsuit payouts annually between 2012 and 2014].) As a result, officers and their departments are often insulated from the financial consequences of their actions. . . .

With respect to injunctions, high court precedent has constrained substantive review of police misconduct claims. In *City of Los Angeles v. Lyons* (1983) 461 U.S. 95, the high court held that Adolph Lyons, a Black man pulled over and put in a chokehold by Los Angeles police officers, did not have standing to seek an injunction against the use of chokeholds because he could not establish that he would again be subject to the same abuse. Moreover, in order to hold municipalities liable for failure to train or supervise officers (often a necessary component of structural reform), the high court has held that a plaintiff must show that the department's conduct amounted to "deliberate indifference to the rights of persons." (*City of Canton v. Harris* (1989) 489 U.S. 378, 388.) . . .

A wrongful death judgment with substantial damages is one way of affirming the worth and dignity of Darren Burley's life, and I join today's opinion. But the racial dimensions of this case should not escape our notice. How are we to ensure that the promise of equal justice under law is, for all our people, a living truth? Whatever the answer, it must involve acknowledging that Darren Burley's death at the hands of law enforcement is not a singular incident unmoored from our racial history. With that acknowledgment must come a serious effort to rethink what racial discrimination is, how it manifests in law enforcement and the justice system, and how the law can provide effective safeguards and redress for our neighbors, friends, and citizens who continue to bear the cruel weight of racism's stubborn legacy.

I Concur:

CUÉLLAR, J.

* * *

Problem 63

Civil rights remedies exist to compensate for harm incurred by the plaintiff and to prevent future violations. Assuming the court finds for the plaintiffs in the lawsuit described below, what remedies should be awarded?

A lawsuit is filed against a city police department alleging the department has systematically violated the constitutional rights of the city's Black and Hispanic residents by disproportionately detaining and searching them without reasonable suspicion of criminal activity. (Caucasians make up 65 percent of the city's population; Black and Hispanic residents are 15 percent and 10 percent, respectively; yet in 35 percent of all law enforcement detentions the subject is a Black person and in 20 percent the subject is Hispanic.) The lawsuit alleges that race-based detentions are an ongoing practice by the police and are encouraged by department policy.

There are two plaintiffs in the lawsuit: a Black man who has been detained and searched without reasonable suspicion four separate times and a Hispanic man who has been subjected to such treatment three times.

Introductory Note — *Hudson v. Michigan* and *Tanzin v. Tanvir*

Hudson v. Michigan is a criminal case where the defendant moved to suppress evidence obtained in violation of the Fourth Amendment right to be free from unreasonable law enforcement searches and seizures. The issue is whether the exclusionary rule should apply to bar the seized evidence from the criminal trial. In deciding the exclusionary rule dos not apply, the Supreme Court heavily relies on the availability of civil remedies — attorney fee awards in particular — to deter future civil rights violations.

The civil right at issue in *Tanzin v. Tanvir* is religious freedom, as protected by the federal Religious Freedom Restoration Act. That statute allows a plaintiff to seek "all appropriate relief" for a violation. The Supreme Court must therefore determine what remedies are "appropriate relief" in a civil rights case.

THINGS TO THINK ABOUT while reading *Hudson v. Michigan* and *Tanzin v. Tanvir*:

1. Do monetary damages effectively deter civil rights violations?

2. Does the potential for a damages award against an individual defendant (as opposed to a government entity) make a difference on the deterrence issue?

3. Approximately what amount would be an appropriate damages award in each case?

Hudson v. Michigan

United States Supreme Court

547 U.S. 586 (2006)

Justice SCALIA.

We decide whether violation of the "knock-and-announce" rule requires the suppression of all evidence found in the search.

I

Police obtained a warrant authorizing a search for drugs and firearms at the home of petitioner Booker Hudson. They discovered both. Large quantities of drugs were found, including cocaine rocks in Hudson's pocket. A loaded gun was lodged between the cushion and armrest of the chair in which he was sitting. Hudson was charged under Michigan law with unlawful drug and firearm possession.

15 · REMEDIES FOR CIVIL RIGHTS VIOLATIONS

This case is before us only because of the method of entry into the house. When the police arrived to execute the warrant, they announced their presence, but waited only a short time — perhaps "three to five seconds," — before turning the knob of the unlocked front door and entering Hudson's home. Hudson moved to suppress all the inculpatory evidence, arguing that the premature entry violated his Fourth Amendment rights. . . .

II

The common-law principle that law enforcement officers must announce their presence and provide residents an opportunity to open the door is an ancient one. See *Wilson v. Arkansas,* 514 U.S. 927, 931–932 (1995). . . . In *Wilson,* we were asked whether the rule was also a command of the Fourth Amendment. Tracing its origins in our English legal heritage, we concluded that it was.

. . . From the trial level onward, Michigan has conceded that the entry was a knock-and-announce violation. The issue here is remedy.

III

A

In *Weeks v. United States,* 232 U.S. 383 (1914), we adopted the federal exclusionary rule for evidence that was unlawfully seized from a home without a warrant in violation of the Fourth Amendment. . . .

Suppression of evidence, however, has always been our last resort, not our first impulse. The exclusionary rule generates "substantial social costs," *United States v. Leon,* 468 U.S. 897, 907 (1984), which sometimes include setting the guilty free and the dangerous at large. We have therefore been "cautio[us] against expanding" it, *Colorado v. Connelly,* 479 U.S. 157, 166 (1986), and "have repeatedly emphasized that the rule's 'costly toll' upon truth-seeking and law enforcement objectives presents a high obstacle for those urging [its] application," *Pennsylvania Bd. of Probation and Parole v. Scott,* 524 U.S. 357, 364–365 (1998). We have rejected "[i]ndiscriminate application" of the rule, *Leon, supra,* at 908, 104 S.Ct. 3405, and have held it to be applicable only "where its remedial objectives are thought most efficaciously served," *United States v. Calandra,* 414 U.S. 338, 348, (1974) — that is, "where its deterrence benefits outweigh its 'substantial social costs,'" *Scott, supra,* at 363. . . .

What the knock-and-announce rule has never protected, however, is one's interest in preventing the government from seeing or taking evidence described in a warrant. Since the interests that *were* violated in this case have nothing to do with the seizure of the evidence, the exclusionary rule is inapplicable.

B

. . . .

It seems to us not even true, as Hudson contends, that without suppression there will be no deterrence of knock-and-announce violations at all. Of course even if this assertion were accurate, it would not necessarily justify suppression. Assuming (as the assertion must) that civil suit is not an effective deterrent, one can think of many forms of police misconduct that are similarly "undeterred." When, for example, a confessed suspect in the killing of a police officer, arrested (along with incriminating evidence) in a lawful warranted search, is subjected to physical abuse at the station house, would it seriously be suggested that the evidence must be excluded, since that is the only "effective deterrent"? And what, other than civil suit, is the "effective deterrent" of police violation of an already-confessed suspect's Sixth Amendment rights by denying him prompt access to counsel? Many would regard these violated rights as more significant than the right not to be intruded upon in one's nightclothes — and yet nothing but "ineffective" civil suit is available as a deterrent. And the police incentive for those violations is arguably greater than the incentive for disregarding the knock-and-announce rule. . . .

Hudson complains that "it would be very hard to find a lawyer to take a case such as this," Tr. of Oral Arg. 7, but 42 U.S.C. § 1988(b) answers this objection. Since some civil-rights violations would yield damages too small to justify the expense of litigation, Congress has authorized attorney's fees for civil-rights plaintiffs. This remedy was unavailable in the heydays of our exclusionary-rule jurisprudence, because it is tied to the availability of a cause of action. For years, "very few lawyers would even consider representation of persons who had civil rights claims against the police," but now "much has changed. Citizens and lawyers are much more willing to seek relief in the courts for police misconduct." M. Avery, D. Rudovsky, & K. Blum, Police Misconduct: Law and Litigation, p. v (3d ed.2005); see generally N. Aron, Liberty and Justice for All: Public Interest Law in the 1980s and Beyond (1989) (describing the growth of public-interest law). The number of public-interest law firms and lawyers who specialize in civil-rights grievances has greatly expanded.

Hudson points out that few published decisions to date announce huge awards for knock-and-announce violations. But this is an unhelpful statistic. Even if we thought that only large damages would deter police misconduct (and that police somehow are deterred by "damages" but indifferent to the prospect of large § 1988 attorney's fees), we do not know how many claims have been settled, or indeed how many violations have occurred that produced anything more than nominal injury. . . . As far as we know, civil liability is an effective deterrent here, as we have assumed it is in other contexts.

In sum, the social costs of applying the exclusionary rule to knock-and-announce violations are considerable; the incentive to such violations is minimal to begin with, and the extant deterrences against them are substantial[.] Resort to the massive remedy of suppressing evidence of guilt is unjustified.

* * *

For the foregoing reasons we affirm the judgment of the Michigan Court of Appeals.

It is so ordered.

* * *

Tanzin v. Tanvir

United States Supreme Court
141 S.Ct. 486 (2020)

Justice THOMAS delivered the opinion of the Court.

The Religious Freedom Restoration Act of 1993 (RFRA) prohibits the Federal Government from imposing substantial burdens on religious exercise, absent a compelling interest pursued through the least restrictive means. 42 U.S.C. § 2000bb *et seq.* It also gives a person whose religious exercise has been unlawfully burdened the right to seek "appropriate relief." The question here is whether "appropriate relief" includes claims for money damages against Government officials in their individual capacities. We hold that it does.

I

A

RFRA secures Congress' view of the right to free exercise under the First Amendment, and it provides a remedy to redress violations of that right. Congress passed the Act in the wake of this Court's decision in *Employment Div., Dept. of Human Resources of Ore. v. Smith*, 494 U.S. 872, 885–890 (1990), which held that the First Amendment tolerates neutral, generally applicable laws that burden or prohibit religious acts even when the laws are unsupported by a narrowly tailored, compelling governmental interest. RFRA sought to counter the effect of that holding and restore the pre-*Smith* "compelling interest test" by "provid[ing] a claim . . . to persons whose religious exercise is substantially burdened by government." §§ 2000bb(b)(1)–(2). That right of action enables a person to "obtain appropriate relief against a government." § 2000bb-1(c). A "'government'" is defined to include "a branch, department, agency, instrumentality, and official (or other person acting under color of law) of the United States." § 2000bb-2(1).

B

Respondents Muhammad Tanvir, Jameel Algibhah, and Naveed Shinwari are practicing Muslims who claim that Federal Bureau of Investigation agents placed them on the No Fly List in retaliation for their refusal to act as informants against their religious communities. Respondents sued various agents in their official capacities, seeking removal from the No Fly List. They also sued the agents in their individual capacities for money damages. According to respondents, the retaliation cost them substantial sums of money: airline tickets wasted and income from job opportunities lost.

More than a year after respondents sued, the Department of Homeland Security informed them that they could now fly, thus mooting the claims for injunctive relief. The District Court then dismissed the individual-capacity claims for money damages, ruling that RFRA does not permit monetary relief.

The Second Circuit reversed. 894 F.3d 449 (2018). It determined that RFRA's express remedies provision, combined with the statutory definition of "Government," authorizes claims against federal officials in their individual capacities. Relying on our precedent and RFRA's broad protections for religious liberty, the court concluded that the open-ended phrase "appropriate relief" encompasses money damages against officials. We granted certiorari, and now affirm.

II

As usual, we start with the statutory text. A person whose exercise of religion has been unlawfully burdened may "obtain appropriate relief against a government." 42 U.S.C. § 2000bb-1(c). . . .

The question then becomes what "appropriate relief" entails. Without a statutory definition, we turn to the phrase's plain meaning at the time of enactment. "Appropriate" means "[s]pecially fitted or suitable, proper." 1 Oxford English Dictionary, at 586; see also Merriam-Webster's Collegiate Dictionary 57 (10th ed. 1996) ("especially suitable or compatible"). Because this language is "open-ended" on its face, what relief is "'appropriate'" is "inherently context dependent." *Sossamon v. Texas*, 563 U.S. 277, 286 (2011) (interpreting identical language).

In the context of suits against Government officials, damages have long been awarded as appropriate relief. In the early Republic, "an array of writs . . . allowed individuals to test the legality of government conduct by filing suit against government officials" for money damages "payable by the officer." Pfander & Hunt, Public Wrongs and Private Bills: Indemnification and Govt Accountability in the Early Republic, 85 N. Y. U. L. Rev. 1862, 1871–1875 (2010); see *id.*, at 1875, n. 52 (collecting cases). These common-law causes of action remained available through the 19th century and into the 20th. See, *e.g., Philadelphia Co. v. Stimson*, 223 U.S. 605, 619–620, 32 S.Ct. 340, 56 L.Ed. 570 (1912) ("The exemption of the United States from suit does not protect its officers from personal liability to persons whose rights of property they have wrongfully invaded").

Though more limited, damages against federal officials remain an appropriate form of relief today. . . . Damages are also commonly available against state and local government officials. In 1871, for example, Congress passed the precursor to § 1983, imposing liability on any person who, under color of state law, deprived another of a constitutional right. By the time Congress enacted RFRA, this Court had interpreted the modern version of § 1983 to permit monetary recovery against officials who violated "clearly established" federal law. *E.g., Procunier v. Navarette*, 434 U.S. 555, 561–562 (1978); *Siegert v. Gilley*, 500 U.S. 226, 231 (1991). . . .

A damages remedy is not just "appropriate" relief as viewed through the lens of suits against Government employees. It is also the *only* form of relief that can remedy some RFRA violations. For certain injuries, such as respondents' wasted plane tickets, effective relief consists of damages, not an injunction. Given the textual cues just noted, it would be odd to construe RFRA in a manner that prevents courts from awarding such relief. Had Congress wished to limit the remedy to that degree, it knew how to do so. See, *e.g.*, 29 U.S.C. § 1132(a)(3) (providing for "appropriate equitable relief "); 42 U.S.C. § 2000e-5(g)(1) (providing for "equitable relief as the court deems appropriate"); 15 U.S.C. § 78u(d)(5) (providing for "any equitable relief that may be appropriate or necessary"). . . .

The Government also posits that we should be wary of damages against government officials because these awards could raise separation-of-powers concerns. But this exact remedy has coexisted with our constitutional system since the dawn of the Republic. To be sure, there may be policy reasons why Congress may wish to shield Government employees from personal liability, and Congress is free to do so. But there are no constitutional reasons why we must do so in its stead. . . .

* * *

We conclude that RFRA's express remedies provision permits litigants, when appropriate, to obtain money damages against federal officials in their individual capacities. The judgment of the United States Court of Appeals for the Second Circuit is affirmed.

It is so ordered.

Justice BARRETT took no part in the consideration or decision of this case.

* * *

Problem 64

Deterrence of civil rights violations can be accomplished through both injunctions and monetary damages. Which of those remedies would most effectively deter future violations in the following case?

A quadriplegic woman is unable to enter a coffee shop because the doorway is too narrow to accommodate a wheelchair. She sues the coffee shop under the Americans With Disabilities Act, a federal law that requires businesses to be physically accessible to everyone, including the disabled. The case goes to trial and the court finds in favor of the plaintiff. By that time, the coffee shop has constructed a new entrance wide enough for wheelchair access.

The trial judge indicates she will either issue an injunction requiring the coffee shop to fully comply with all requirements of the Americans with Disabilities Act; or will enter a judgment for monetary damages against the coffee shop in the amount of $15,000.

Chapter 16

Selecting Remedies

The study of remedies is about understanding the different options available to judicially resolve a dispute. When there are options, there are choices. Litigation often involves making choices from among several different remedies.

When more than one remedy is applicable, the plaintiff can choose which remedy (or remedies) it wants upon proving the case on the merits. Fairly obviously, the plaintiff will want to choose the remedy that is most beneficial—the one that achieves the best possible outcome.

What constitutes the best possible outcome for the plaintiff depends on the circumstances. But the decision about which remedy to pursue must always be made in the context of two truths: (1) The plaintiff's ability to choose among remedies is not unfettered. In some cases, the pursuit of one remedy may preclude the plaintiff from choosing another. (2) The choice of remedy can have significant procedural consequences for how the dispute is resolved. Selecting a particular remedy may give the plaintiff a right to have a jury trial, while selecting another may not.

This chapter first discusses the rule that a plaintiff cannot obtain inconsistent remedies and then examines the procedural consequences that flow from selecting certain remedies.

Electing Between Inconsistent Remedies

Some remedies are cumulative; they address different problems and can therefore be awarded to a plaintiff concurrently. An example is damages and an injunction: damages to compensate for harm that has already occurred and an injunction to prevent more harm from occurring in the future.

But some remedies are inconsistent, meaning that if both were awarded to a plaintiff, the result would be a double recovery—recovering two remedies for the same harm. An example is damages and restitution. A plaintiff cannot recover damages to compensate for a loss caused by the defendant and at the same time recover restitution for the gain the defendant realized from inflicting the harm. An embezzlement case makes it easy to see why: a business owner who has lost $100,000 because it was embezzled by an employee cannot recover $100,000 in damages (representing the business owner's loss) and $100,000 in restitution (representing the employee's gain). The remedies are inconsistent; the plaintiff must select one or the other.

Remedies are inconsistent when they provide relief based on different legal theories. Another example is rescission of a contract versus expectation damages for breach of contract. Rescission provides relief based on the theory that the contract should not be enforced and puts the plaintiff in the same position as if the contract never existed. Expectation damages, on the other hand, provide relief based on the theory that the contract should be enforced, and puts the plaintiff in the same position as if it had been fully performed. The theories are fundamentally inconsistent, so a plaintiff in a contract case must choose between rescission and damages. The plaintiff cannot pursue both.

In evaluating whether remedies are inconsistent, a court must determine whether multiple remedies are necessary to completely fix the harm incurred by the plaintiff or whether they would result in an unfair double recovery.

Introductory Note — *Teutscher v. Woodson*

Teutscher is an employment case involving wrongful termination. The plaintiff alleged he was unlawfully fired and prevailed at trial. He was awarded economic damages including compensation for future wage loss. And the employer was ordered to rehire him, an equitable remedy available under federal law. The Ninth Circuit has to decide whether the plaintiff should get all the relief awarded in the trial court or must elect between inconsistent remedies.

THINGS TO THINK ABOUT while reading *Teutscher v. Woodson:*

1. Was the plaintiff unjustly enriched by the remedies awarded? If so, how?

2. Could the plaintiff have obtained both legal and equitable remedies by using a different litigation strategy?

Teutscher v. Woodson

United States Court of Appeals, Ninth Circuit
835 F.3d 936 (2016)

FRIEDLAND, Circuit Judge:

This appeal requires us to examine the limits on a district court's authority to award front pay and reinstatement as equitable remedies for a retaliatory discharge after a plaintiff has already sought and been awarded by a jury front pay damages to compensate for the same harm. Plaintiff-Appellee Scott Teutscher went to trial against his former employer, Riverside Sheriffs' Association ("RSA"), on retaliatory discharge claims under both state law and the Employee Retirement Income Security Act, 29 U.S.C. §§ 1001–1461 ("ERISA"). A jury awarded him lump-sum damages on his state law claims, and the district court then entered judgment in his favor on his ERISA claim. Even though, at Teutscher's request, the jury had been instructed to include front pay in its damages award, the district court granted Teutscher additional equitable remedies consisting of reinstatement as well as front pay until reinstatement occurred. RSA appeals these equitable remedies, arguing that they improperly duplicate Teutscher's recovery from the jury.

... We hold that ... the reinstatement remedy is improper because Teutscher waived that relief when he elected to seek the duplicative front pay remedy from the jury. We accordingly reverse the district court's equitable awards.

I.

Defendant-Appellant RSA is an organization that represents law enforcement employees in Riverside County, California for collective bargaining purposes. RSA also administers the RSA Legal Defense Trust (the "Trust"), an ERISA-governed plan. The Trust provides legal defense services to RSA members in civil and criminal actions arising from incidents in the course of their employment. From 2002 until his termination in 2005, Plaintiff-Appellee Scott Teutscher worked on an at-will basis for RSA as the Trust's Legal Operations Manager. . . .

During Teutscher's tenure as Legal Operations Manager, the Trust began covering legal expenses for Deputy Sheriff Duane Winchell's defense in criminal and civil proceedings unrelated to Winchell's employment. Teutscher eventually started expressing concerns that the Trust's coverage of Winchell's defense costs was unlawful because it was disallowed by the Trust's governing plan documents. Teutscher later met with an officer in the Riverside Sheriff's Department and accused RSA's president and its executive director of improper coverage approvals. Shortly after Teutscher revealed that he had contacted law enforcement about the coverage issues, RSA's executive director terminated Teutscher's employment.

Teutscher filed the instant lawsuit alleging that RSA terminated him in retaliation for reporting his suspicions that the Trust's coverage of Winchell was illegal. In the operative complaint, Teutscher asserted claims against RSA under federal and California law arising out of his termination, including retaliatory discharge in violation of section 510 of ERISA, 29 U.S.C. § 1140; wrongful discharge in violation of public policy under California common law; and retaliatory discharge in violation of California Labor Code §§ 98.6 and 1102.5. After this court partially reversed an earlier grant of summary judgment in favor of RSA, the case proceeded to a jury trial on the three state law claims pursuant to Teutscher's timely jury demand, and to a simultaneous bench trial on his ERISA claim.

During trial, Teutscher presented evidence that RSA's executives threatened to terminate him if he "didn't keep [his] mouth shut" about the Winchell coverage issues. He argued to the jury that the executives acted on that threat by firing him after he reported to outside authorities his suspicions that the coverage was illegal. RSA in turn presented evidence that Teutscher had made repeated mistakes in his job, which had led the Trust's Board to assign RSA's executive director to supervise Teutscher's work. RSA also introduced evidence that Teutscher had been investigated and disciplined for failing to follow Trust policy in responding to an officer-involved shooting incident, and that he was placed on administrative leave shortly before his termination for, among other things, angrily throwing a work file. Teutscher argued that these performance-related grievances were merely pretext for retaliation, and that they were belied by his consistently satisfactory job performance ratings and by a raise he received shortly before his termination.

Teutscher also put on testimony about wages he had lost since his termination and wages he would have earned for the remainder of his anticipated working life at RSA. Teutscher testified that, at the time of his termination, he had been earning an $86,000 annual salary plus annual bonuses and the value of a company car. During closing arguments, his counsel placed the total value of compensation at $98,236 per year. Teutscher, who was 55 years old at the time of trial, testified that had he not been wrongfully terminated, he would have continued working at RSA until his Social Security "would kick in, probably 65, 67." Teutscher testified that he was instead forced to look elsewhere for work. After about six months, he found his first replacement job working at an auto business, earning roughly $8,000 per year in 2006 and 2007. In 2008, Teutscher began working at the San Bernardino County Sheriff's Department for an annual salary of roughly $42,000, which had increased to $52,000 by 2012.

The district court adopted Teutscher's proposed jury instruction on damages, and, without objection, instructed the jury on how to calculate Teutscher's damages should it find that he was wrongfully discharged. . . .

Following deliberations, the jury returned a verdict in favor of Teutscher on his state law claims for wrongful and retaliatory discharge. Using a general verdict form to which neither party had objected, the jury awarded Teutscher lump-sum damages of $457,250 and separately awarded punitive damages of $357,500.

Based on the evidence presented at trial, the district court adjudicated Teutscher's ERISA claim, holding RSA liable for retaliating against Teutscher in violation of section 510. The district court then heard argument on an appropriate ERISA remedy. Teutscher asked that his ERISA remedy include back pay and reinstatement. RSA objected that back pay was unavailable under ERISA as a form of compensatory relief. RSA also objected that reinstatement would conflict with the jury's award of lost future earnings and would constitute impermissible double recovery because Teutscher was already made whole by the remedy he elected to pursue from the jury. RSA further contended that reinstatement was impossible because of continuing acrimony between the parties.

The court issued a ruling denying back pay but ordering RSA to reinstate Teutscher and to provide him interim front pay at the rate of $98,235 per year until such reinstatement occurred. RSA filed objections to the court's ruling, protesting that it would be impossible to reinstate Teutscher because his position had by then been eliminated, and again arguing that the equitable front pay and reinstatement awards duplicated the relief Teutscher had obtained from the jury and that Teutscher waived his right to those equitable awards when he elected a make-whole remedy on his legal claims. The district court nevertheless entered judgment in accordance with its earlier ruling.

II.

. . . The question here is whether Teutscher was unjustly enriched by being granted reinstatement and compensatory damages as relief for the same retaliatory discharge. To the extent that the damages award included a front pay component covering the same period during which Teutscher would be reinstated, he clearly was.

Reinstatement and front pay are alternative remedies, which cannot be awarded for the same period of time. This is because front pay is the monetary equivalent of reinstatement. A reinstated individual will earn the salary associated with the job in question, so a plaintiff granted both front pay (calculated based on the job's salary) and reinstatement for the same time period would essentially obtain his salary twice over, earning an undue windfall.

Duplicative recovery is easily avoided when only equitable relief is at issue — the district court may craft an award comprising exclusively reinstatement, exclusively front pay, or interim front pay until reinstatement occurs. The same avoidance must be achieved when, as in this case, front pay is submitted to the jury to determine.

Teutscher argues that there was no overlap in this case because it is clear from the size of the jury's verdict that it did not grant him any front pay. Thus, in his view, the district court could order reinstatement without duplicating his recovery. But Teutscher ignores the problem created by his failure to object to the lump-sum verdict form used by the jury, which prevents us from parsing the award. As explained above, we have no way of knowing that Teutscher is correct in assuming the jury awarded zero front pay, and there are many possible explanations of the jury verdict that would contain a front pay component. For example, the jury may well have decided that, with reasonable effort, Teutscher should have been able to find more remunerative work than his two-year stint at an auto business, and it may have declined to award him a substantial portion of his back pay request, instead apportioning damages across both back and front pay. Simply stated, nothing about the jury instructions or the evidence presented at trial permits us to conclude that the jury's damages award and the court's reinstatement award do not overlap.

The question remains what to do about this potential overlap. Faced with a similar problem of potentially duplicative legal and equitable awards, the Third and Eighth Circuits decided to remand for a new determination of remedies. *See Squires*, 54 F.3d at 176–77 & n.16 (vacating the jury's award in favor of a new trial on compensatory damages with more precise instructions); *Savarese v. Agriss*, 883 F.2d 1194, 1205–06 (3d Cir. 1989) (vacating potentially overlapping compensatory damages award and equitable back pay award and remanding for a new trial and recalculation of back pay by the district judge); *Greminger v. Seaborne*, 584 F.2d 275, 278–79 (8th Cir. 1978) (vacating the jury's monetary judgment and remanding for the district court to determine an award of back pay and out-of-pocket expenses that would not conflict with its equitable reinstatement remedy). We think the better course on this record is to simply reverse the equitable reinstatement award and permit Teutscher to keep the full amount of damages he obtained from the jury.

Teutscher's own litigation choices are what lead us to this conclusion. On the record before us, it is evident that Teutscher waived his right to a reinstatement award when he affirmatively elected to seek front pay from the jury. The election-of-remedies doctrine, which refers to situations where an individual pursues remedies that are legally or factually inconsistent, operates to prevent a party from obtaining double redress for a single wrong. A party is bound by his election of remedies if three conditions are met: (1) two or more remedies existed at the time of the election, (2) these remedies are repugnant and inconsistent with each other, and (3) the party to be bound affirmatively chose, or elected, between the available remedies.

Each of these conditions is met here. As explained above, reinstatement and front pay are alternative remedies for retaliatory discharge, which cannot both be awarded for the same period of time. Teutscher proposed the damages instruction that required the jury to determine the amount of compensation he would have earned for the remainder of his working life at RSA, and he did not object when the jury was charged to include front pay damages in its lump-sum verdict. Teutscher therefore elected to seek a make-whole remedy from the jury, which necessarily included a front pay award for the entire period covered by any potential reinstatement award.

In sum, having submitted front pay to the jury in the manner that he did, Teutscher could not then take a second bite at the apple by seeking a duplicative reinstatement award from the court. We therefore conclude that Teutscher is entitled to keep the full amount of compensatory (and punitive) damages the jury awarded, but that the district court's equitable reinstatement award must be set aside.

As a final note, we emphasize that our holding that the jury's monetary award precluded the district court's equitable award in this case turns on the particular way in which Teutscher chose to pursue his claims. As the "master of his complaint," Teutscher was entitled to decide what law to rely on and what remedies to pursue. *Ultramar Am. Ltd. v. Dwelle*, 900 F.2d 1412, 1414 (9th Cir. 1990). There are several ways in which Teutscher likely could have pursued legal and equitable relief at the same time. Among them, he could have pursued only back pay from the jury and sought a forward-looking remedy only from the court in equity. Alternatively, Teutscher could have requested that the jury be instructed to award only that prospective compensatory relief that did not overlap with an equitable reinstatement or front pay remedy. . . .

The legal and equitable awards in this case, however, . . . were designed to remedy precisely the same loss. . . . Given the potential for a windfall and in light of

Teutscher's affirmative election to seek front pay from the jury, the court's reinstatement award must be set aside as well.

We therefore REVERSE the district court's equitable awards of reinstatement and front pay.

* * *

Problem 65

A plaintiff must elect between remedies when doing so is necessary to prevent a double recovery. Which categories of damages in the below case would constitute a double recovery? Or can all the damages permissibly be awarded?

Gerald is surprised to get a call from his friend Frank, whom he has not seen since high school. Frank says he is calling because he is starting a business and looking for financing. He asks Gerald to loan him $50,000 and Gerald agrees. They sign a contract requiring repayment of the money, with interest, within one year. A few weeks later, Gerald finds out Frank is not starting a business—he is actually a compulsive gambler and has taken Gerald's $50,000 and gambled it away. A year comes and goes, and Frank does not repay the loan.

Gerald sues for fraud and breach of contract. The jury finds that Frank breached the contract by not repaying the money and also committed fraud because he falsely represented he was starting a business to induce Gerald to make the loan. The jury awards damages in the amount of $55,000 as expectation damages for breach of contract (the loan principal plus interest owed under the terms of the contract) and $255,000 for fraud ($55,000 in future economic damages, $100,000 for emotional distress, and $100,000 in punitive damages).

Overlapping

Introductory Note—*Helf v. Chevron USA, Inc.*

Helf involves an employee injured on the job. She pursued a claim for workers' compensation benefits, which state law provides is the exclusive remedy for *accidental* workplace injuries. She then sued her employer for *intentionally* causing her injuries. Summary judgment was granted for the employer on the merits of the tort claim and on the alternative ground that the plaintiff was required to, but did not, elect between inconsistent remedies.

The Utah Supreme Court says that summary judgment was improperly granted on the merits. It must then decide whether the employee's pursuit of the workers' compensation remedy bars her pursuit of tort damages because those are legally inconsistent theories of recovery.

THINGS TO THINK ABOUT while reading *Helf v. Chevron USA, Inc.*

1. Is workers' compensation legally inconsistent with recovery of damages for an intentional tort?

2. Did the court decide the plaintiff must elect between workers' compensation and damages? If so, when would that election have to occur?

3. Which has the better argument — the majority opinion or the dissent?

Helf v. Chevron USA, Inc.

Utah Supreme Court 361 P.3d 63 (2015)

Justice DURHAM, opinion of the Court:

Introduction

Jenna Helf worked at an oil refinery operated by Chevron U.S.A. Inc. Her supervisor instructed her to add sulfuric acid to an open-air pit containing waste products from the refinery and she was injured by a poisonous gas produced by the resulting chemical reaction. Ms. Helf obtained workers' compensation benefits for her injuries. She then sued Chevron, alleging it was liable for an intentional tort because her supervisors knew that she would be injured when her immediate supervisor instructed her to add sulfuric acid to the pit.

Chevron moved for summary judgment, arguing that (1) Ms. Helf had not produced evidence that Chevron's managers knew or expected that Helf would be injured when her supervisor told her to add sulfuric acid to the pit and (2) Ms. Helf could not prevail as a matter of law because her election to obtain workers' compensation benefits for her injury barred her from seeking a tort remedy. The district court concluded that the election of remedies doctrine did not bar her suit. But the court agreed with Chevron that Ms. Helf failed to produce evidence that would support a conclusion that one of Chevron's managers had the requisite knowledge or intent to support an intentional tort claim. The district court therefore granted summary judgment.

Ms. Helf now appeals, arguing that summary judgment was not appropriate.

We hold that the district court erred by granting summary judgment. Ms. Helf produced evidence that when a worker added sulfuric acid to the pit earlier that same day, a chemical reaction produced a poisonous gas that triggered emergency alarms located 150 feet from the pit and made workers in other areas of the refinery sick. There is a dispute of material fact precluding summary judgment because a reasonable jury could conclude that at least one of Chevron's managers knew that Ms. Helf would be injured when her supervisor instructed her to initiate this same process.

We also hold that the district court correctly ruled that the election of remedies doctrine does not bar her lawsuit. We agree with other courts that have held that workers are not required to choose between accepting workers' compensation benefits and an intentional tort claim.

We therefore reverse the district court's summary judgment ruling and remand for further proceedings consistent with this opinion. . . .

Analysis

I. Summary Judgment

Workers may not sue their employers for injuries caused by on-the-job accidents. The exclusive remedy for work-related accidents is the workers' compensation scheme, which was created by the legislature to distribute benefits to injured workers. UTAH CODE § 34A-2-105(1). A worker, however, may sue an employer for injuries caused by an intentional tort.

In order to prevail in a civil lawsuit, therefore, a worker must prove that an agent of the employer intentionally caused the worker's injury. In other words, the worker must show that the employer's agent had "a specific mental state in which the [agent] knew or expected that injury would be the consequence of his action." This mental state can be proven either (1) with evidence that the agent "desired the consequences of his actions" or (2) with evidence that the agent acted with the knowledge that "the consequences were virtually certain to result."

Ms. Helf does not allege that anyone at Chevron maliciously desired to injure her. Instead, she alleges that her supervisors knew that an injury was virtually certain to occur when they either directed or allowed her to neutralize the contents of the open-air pit. Chevron asserted in its motion for summary judgment that Ms. Helf had not produced evidence creating a dispute of fact as to whether a Chevron manager acted with this knowledge.

. . . Taken in the light most favorable to Ms. Helf, the evidence and all reasonable inferences drawn from it would support a jury conclusion that the night-shift supervisor knew that adding sulfuric acid to the pit would release dangerous quantities of hydrogen sulfide gas. He was told that during the day shift the neutralization process had triggered sensors designed to detect dangerous levels of hydrogen sulfide gas that were located 150 feet from the pit and that emergency alarms had sounded. He was also told that hydrogen sulfide gas from the neutralization process caused workers in other areas of the refinery to become ill. The day-shift supervisor expressed his concern about adding sulfuric acid to the pit to the night-shift supervisor. The day-shift supervisor further testified that the hydrogen sulfide release was a dangerous event and that the night-shift supervisor "should have had a clear expectation not to continue" the neutralization process.

Given this evidence of the night-shift supervisor's knowledge, a reasonable jury could infer that he also knew or expected that an injury would occur when he told Ms. Helf to neutralize the pit. . . . We therefore conclude that summary judgment was inappropriate. There is a dispute of material fact as to whether the night-shift supervisor knew that Ms. Helf would be injured. . . .

II. Election of Remedies

Chevron argues in the alternative that even if Ms. Helf produced sufficient evidence to survive summary judgment, it was nevertheless entitled to judgment as a matter of law because Ms. Helf was bound by her election to receive the remedy of workers' compensation benefits for her injury. . . .

1. The Election of Remedies Doctrine

In its most basic terms, the election of remedies doctrine "prevent [s] double redress for a single wrong." *Angelos v. First Interstate Bank of Utah,* 671 P.2d 772, 778 (Utah 1983). If a defendant wrongfully retains possession of a plaintiff's cow, for example, the plaintiff may not recover both the cow *and* the reasonable value of the cow. The plaintiff must elect one of these two remedies.

The election of remedies doctrine also refers to a plaintiff's choice between legally or factually inconsistent theories of recovery for a single wrong. One common example of the application of this rule occurs when a plaintiff is not paid for services rendered to a defendant. The plaintiff may either recover damages for breach of contract or, if no valid contract governs the services provided, the plaintiff may recover the reasonable value of the services under a quantum meruit claim. Because a breach of contract remedy requires a valid, enforceable contract, while a quantum meruit remedy presupposes that no contract governs the services provided, a plaintiff may recover only one of these two inconsistent remedies. *Reilly v. Natwest Markets Grp. Inc.,* 181 F.3d 253, 263–64 (2d Cir.1999).

Thus, at its core, the election of remedies stands for the rather straight-forward principle that a plaintiff may not obtain either (1) a double recovery or (2) legally or factually inconsistent recoveries for the same wrong. The more difficult question is when a plaintiff should be deemed to have made an irrevocable election between available remedies or theories of recovery.

Where a plaintiff must choose between alternative remedies for a single theory of liability, an election is not final until a judgment is fully satisfied. Courts treat this type of election as a choice between consistent remedies because the remedies do not rest upon irreconcilable factual or legal theories. Thus if a plaintiff obtains a judgment authorizing a writ of replevin for the return of a cow wrongfully obtained by a defendant, the election is not final until the cow is returned. If the plaintiff later discovers that the cow had died while in the defendant's possession, the plaintiff may still pursue a claim for payment of the reasonable value of the cow. *See Largilliere Co., Bankers, v. Kunz,* 41 Idaho 767, 244 P. 404, 404–05, 406 (1925) (permitting a plaintiff to simultaneously pursue both a claim for damages for the conversion of a flock of sheep and a writ of replevin for the return of the sheep "until a satisfaction of its demand is obtained" because these two remedies are consistent).

... Thus unless another doctrine, such as estoppel, dictates that a plaintiff's election among inconsistent remedies is final at an earlier stage of the litigation, an election is not binding until one remedy is pursued to a determinative conclusion.

2. Application of the Election of Remedies Doctrine Where a Worker Brings Both a Workers' Compensation Claim and an Intentional Tort Claim

In applying these general principles to this case, we must examine the remedies available to an injured worker. A worker injured on the job may potentially recover either worker's compensation benefits or intentional tort damages. These two remedies are inconsistent. Workers' compensation benefits are paid to workers injured by an "accident arising out of and in the course of the employee's employment." UTAH CODE § 34A-2-401(1). These benefits are the exclusive remedy for work-related accidents. *Id.* § 34A-2-105(1). In order to recover tort damages for an injury, on the other hand, a worker must prove that an injury was caused by an intentional tort rather than an accident. The question before this court, therefore, is when does an injured worker make a binding election between these two inconsistent remedies? ...

If these two remedies could be pursued in a single forum, the answer would be simple. The worker could plead in the alternative that the injury was caused by either an accident or an intentional tort, and after the fact-finder made a final determination regarding the nature of the injury, the worker would elect the remedy available under the facts found by the jury or administrative body. The problem, of course, is that a worker may not pursue these two remedies in a single forum. The labor commission has exclusive jurisdiction to award workers' compensation benefits for accidents, while the district court has exclusive jurisdiction to award damages for an intentional tort.

Because these remedies must be adjudicated in separate forums, a strict application of the election of remedies doctrine presents injured workers with a cruel dilemma. If a worker choses to apply for and receives workers' compensation benefits, the worker may be deemed to have made a binding election of this remedy because the worker pursued it to a determinative conclusion. By accepting workers' compensation benefits for urgent financial needs, such as medical expenses or living expenses if the worker becomes disabled, a worker who may have been injured by an intentional tort would be barred from asserting a tort claim. If the worker instead elects to forego workers compensation benefits and gambles on an intentional tort claim, the worker would have to survive without any benefits, and the burden of sustaining potentially protracted litigation, until the completion of the trial and inevitable appeal or appeals. This hardship would in most cases be extreme because any worker contemplating a lawsuit would likely be severely injured in order to justify the expense and stress of a lawsuit against a well-funded employer.

. . . This interpretation of the election of remedies doctrine, similar to the much-criticized application of the doctrine in the early twentieth century, effectively requires an injured worker to choose at peril between inconsistent remedies at an unreasonably early stage in the litigation. Forcing this choice is especially harsh because of the difficulty of predicting the outcome of an intentional tort suit. Because the line between an accident and an intentional tort is based upon the subjective knowledge and intent of the worker's supervisors, which most often must be inferred from the surrounding circumstances, the worker is in a poor position to evaluate the odds of success before a jury resolves this factual dispute.

. . . The election of remedies doctrine is a rule of "procedure or judicial administration." 25 AM.JUR.2D *Election of Remedies* § 2 (2014). It is equitable in nature and is invoked "to the end that justice may be served." 28A C.J.S. *Election of Remedies* § 1 (2008). As an equitable judicial principle, the election of remedies doctrine should be applied to produce fair outcomes for litigants. It certainly applies to prevent the worker from obtaining a double recovery or recovering two inconsistent remedies. But it should not be applied to force the worker to make a binding election before knowing how a jury will resolve an intentional tort claim.

The district court, therefore, correctly ruled that the election of remedies doctrine does not bar Ms. Helf's lawsuit against Chevron. To avoid a double recovery, however, if Ms. Helf eventually prevails, she may not retain the inconsistent remedies of workers' compensation benefits and an award for tort damages. In order to prevent an inconsistent recovery, a worker "who recovers civilly against his employer" may no longer receive workers' compensation benefits and must "reimburse the workers' compensation carrier to the extent the carrier paid workers' compensation benefits, or by permitting the carrier to become subrogated to the claimant's civil claim to the extent of benefits paid."

Conclusion

We reverse the summary judgment in favor of Chevron and remand for further proceedings consistent with this opinion.

Associate Chief Justice LEE, dissenting:

The Utah Workers Compensation Act provides that "[t]he right to recover compensation" in an administrative proceeding under the statute "is the *exclusive* remedy against the employer" for "any accident or injury or death, in any way contracted, sustained, aggravated, or incurred by the employee in the course of or because of or arising out of the employee's employment." UTAH CODE § 34A-2-105(1) (emphasis added). A statutory claim is "in place of *any* and *all* other civil liability whatsoever, at common law or otherwise." *Id.* (emphasis added).

This exclusive remedy provision is the heart of the Workers Compensation Act. It preserves the essential bargain of workers compensation established almost a century ago in Utah. Under this bargain, workers give up their right to sue their employers in tort for workplace injuries. In return, workers are granted the right to statutory remedies that are afforded without regard to proof of fault.

... I would affirm on the ground that Jenna Helf voluntarily opted for the remedies available to her in workers compensation, in a manner foreclosing her right to sue in intentional tort. ...

The doctrine of election of remedies is longstanding and well-settled. One branch of the doctrine is a bar on double recovery. But there is more to the doctrine than that. As the majority acknowledges, the doctrine of election of remedies also precludes a plaintiff from advancing "legally or factually inconsistent recoveries for the same wrong." Under this branch of the doctrine, a plaintiff's election of a remedy is final once a "judgment is fully satisfied." Satisfaction of the judgment, moreover, precludes more than just double recovery; it bars the plaintiff from asserting a new claim that is legally or factually incompatible with the already-satisfied claim.

This principle is both simple and well-settled. It holds the plaintiff to its initial election once a judgment is final and satisfied by the defendant. And it precludes subsequent litigation on an inconsistent theory of liability — not just because double recovery is prohibited, but because it is unfair to subject the defendant to a subsequent round of litigation on a new, inconsistent theory of liability. *See, e.g., F.T.C. v. Leshin,* 719 F.3d 1227, 1232 (11th Cir.2013) (The doctrine of election of remedies. ... "limits a party with the choice of two remedies that are inconsistent with each other from obtaining both remedies or from obtaining first the one remedy and then, at a later date, an alternative one."). That principle should apply here. Ms. Helf filed a workers compensation claim and was awarded compensation on the basis of an allegation that her injuries resulted from a workplace *accident.* Under the doctrine of election of remedies, Helf should now be barred from advancing the inconsistent theory that her injuries were the result of an *intentional tort.* ...

* * *

Problem 66

A plaintiff cannot obtain multiple remedies if that would result in recovering twice for a single wrong or if the remedies are legally inconsistent. Should the plaintiff in the below case be required to elect a remedy, or can he permissibly be awarded both remedies? Why?

A builder contracts with a homeowner to design and build an addition to her house. The contract calls for the homeowner to pay the builder $100,000. Relying on the contract, the builder pays an architect $25,000 to draw plans for the addition. The homeowner then breaches the contract by telling the builder she has decided to move and no longer wants to go through with the project.

The builder sues for breach of contract and seeks two remedies: expectation damages in the amount of $75,000 and reliance damages in the amount of $25,000.

Procedural Consequences

Selecting remedies can have procedural consequences, meaning the remedy chosen can affect the way the dispute is resolved. The distinction with the greatest procedural impact is the distinction between legal and equitable remedies.

Enforcement — how plaintiffs ultimately get what was awarded by the court — is very different depending on whether the remedy awarded is legal or equitable. Legal judgments are enforced *in rem*. There are a variety of ways for a plaintiff to execute a legal judgment; all essentially result in forcing a sale of the defendant's property or seizing it to satisfy the judgment. Equitable orders are enforced *in personam*; the defendant must comply with the order or face a sanction for contempt of court.

Aside from enforcement, the most important procedural consequence that comes from deciding between a legal and equitable remedy is who will determine whether the plaintiff is entitled to the remedy. There are two options, a judge or a jury.

Whether there is a right to have a jury decide the dispute depends on the nature of the relief the plaintiff asks for. For federal cases, the Seventh Amendment to the United States Constitution provides a right to a jury trial for "Suits at common law, where the value in controversy shall exceed twenty dollars." Most state constitutions contain a similar provision. The effect is that if the plaintiff seeks damages — a legal remedy — the action is considered a "suit at common law" and the Seventh Amendment right to jury trial applies. If, on the other hand, the plaintiff seeks an equitable remedy, there is no right to a jury trial and a judge will decide the dispute.

That is straightforward enough. The difficulty comes when a plaintiff seeks multiple remedies, some legal and some equitable. In that situation, the court must determine what the true nature of the action is — whether the ultimate relief the plaintiff is seeking is legal or equitable.

Introductory Note — *Nationwide Biweekly Administration, Inc. v. Superior Court* and *Dairy Queen, Inc. v. Wood*

Nationwide Biweekly Administration involves two causes of action created by statute: California's unfair competition law and false advertising law. California courts typically look to history to determine whether a claim is legal (and therefore requires a jury trial) or equitable (and therefore does not). But here history is of little help because the claims at issue were relatively recently created by statute. The California Supreme Court must use a different approach to determine whether there is a right to jury trial.

Dairy Queen explains how to decide if there must be a jury trial when the plaintiff's claims can be construed as either legal or equitable. The plaintiff sued for breach of contract (which is remedied through the legal relief of damages) but asked for relief in the form of an accounting (an equitable remedy where the defendant is ordered to provide financial records). The United States Supreme Court provides guidance to federal trial courts regarding how to construe such mixed claims for purposes of the right to a jury trial.

THINGS TO THINK ABOUT while reading *Nationwide Biweekly Administration, Inc. v. Superior Court* and *Dairy Queen, Inc. v. Wood*:

1. How does a court determine if a plaintiff's claims are legal or equitable?

2. What standard is used to decide if there is a right to jury trial when the plaintiff seeks both legal and equitable remedies?

3. Why not allow a jury trial, if the plaintiff wants one, for any kind of claim?

Nationwide Biweekly Administration, Inc. v. Superior Court

California Supreme Court
9 Cal.5th 279 (2020)

Opinion of the Court by CANTIL-SAKAUYE, C. J.

Under two of California's most prominent consumer protection statutes — the unfair competition law (UCL) and the false advertising law (FAL) — the Attorney General or local prosecuting authorities may bring a civil action against a business that has allegedly engaged in an unfair, unlawful or deceptive business act or practice or false or misleading advertising and may obtain civil penalties as well as injunctive relief and restitution in such an action. In this case we must decide whether, when the government seeks civil penalties as well an injunction or other equitable remedies under those statutes, the causes of action are to be tried by the court (that is, the trial judge) or, instead, by a jury....

For the reasons discussed hereafter, we conclude that the causes of action established by the UCL and FAL at issue here are equitable in nature and are properly tried by the court rather than a jury....

I. Facts and Proceedings Below

Petitioners Nationwide Biweekly Administration, Inc., Loan Payment Administration LLC, and Daniel S. Lipsky, the alleged alter ego, principal and sole shareholder of both entities (hereafter collectively referred to as Nationwide) operated a debt payment service in California and other states. Nationwide's program claimed to save debtors money through a process in which the debtor would reduce the amount of interest owed over the life of a loan by having the debtor accelerate the repayment of the debt through an extra monthly payment each year. Under the program, a debtor would pay to Nationwide one-half the debtor's ordinary monthly loan payment every two weeks (biweekly) rather than one full payment once a month, resulting in an extra month's payment each year (26 half-payments equal 13 full payments), and Nationwide would in turn pay those amounts to the debtor's lender. Nationwide advertised its services statewide, mostly through direct mailers to consumers with outstanding residential mortgages, and through follow-up telephone conversations with consumers who responded to the mailers.

In May 2015, the district attorneys of four counties, acting on behalf of the People, filed a civil complaint alleging that Nationwide had violated the UCL and FAL by, among other things, employing business practices that: (1) misleadingly implied that Nationwide was affiliated with the consumer's lender; (2) disguised the amount that Nationwide's services actually cost by failing to fully and adequately disclose the amount, payment schedule, and effect of Nationwide's fees; and (3) overstated the amount of savings a consumer could reasonably expect to receive through Nationwide's services. The complaint also stated that Nationwide's practices have been the subject of numerous consumer complaints and regulatory and law enforcement activities around the country, including an action brought by the federal Consumer Financial Protection Bureau (CFPB).

The complaint's prayer for relief requested that the court (1) issue an injunction prohibiting the business practices found to violate the provisions of the UCL or FAL, (2) order restitution of all money wrongfully acquired by Nationwide from California consumers in violation of the UCL and FAL, and (3) impose civil penalties up to $2,500 for each violation of the UCL or FAL found by the court. . . .

We granted the People's petition for review to determine whether there is a right to a jury trial in a UCL or FAL action brought by the government when the government seeks civil penalties as well as injunctive relief and restitution. . . .

Under the California Constitution, is there a *Constitutional* Right to Jury Trial in a UCL or Fal Action When the People Seek Both Injunctive Relief And Civil Penalties?

. . . .

A. General California Constitutional Jury Trial Principles

Article I, section 16 of the California Constitution — the jury trial provision — states in relevant part that "[t]rial by jury is an inviolate right and shall be secured to all. . . ." From the outset of our state's history, our courts have explained that this provision was intended *to preserve* the right to a civil jury as it existed at common law in 1850 when the jury trial provision was first incorporated into the California Constitution. As this court observed in *People v. One 1941 Chevrolet Coupe* (1951) 37 Cal.2d 283 (*One 1941 Chevrolet Coupe*): "The right to trial by jury guaranteed by the Constitution is the right as it existed at common law at the time the Constitution was adopted. . . . It is the right to trial by jury as it existed at common law which is preserved; and what that right is, is a purely historical question, a fact which is to be ascertained like any other social, political or legal fact. The right is the historical right enjoyed at the time it was guaranteed by the Constitution." (*Id.* at pp. 286–287.) "Our state Constitution essentially *preserves* the right to a jury in those actions in which there was a right to a jury trial at common law at the time the Constitution was first adopted." (*Crouchman v. Superior Court* (1988) 45 Cal.3d 1167, 1175 (*Crouchman*).)

Pursuant to this historical approach, as a general matter the California Constitution affords a right to a jury trial in common law actions at law that were triable by a jury in 1850, but not in suits in equity that were not triable by a jury in 1850. (*C & K Engineering Contractors v. Amber Steel Co.* (1978) 23 Cal.3d 1, 8–9 (*C & K Engineering*).) In applying this test, our cases have explained that the *form* or *title* of a statutory cause of action is not controlling and that if the *substance* of the cause of action is one that would have been triable by a jury at common law, there is a right to a jury trial even if the statute's designation might suggest that it is an equitable proceeding. (See, e.g., *One 1941 Chevrolet Coupe, supra,* 37 Cal.2d at p. 299.) "'In determining whether the action was one triable by a jury at common law, the court is not bound by the form of the action but rather by the nature of the rights involved and the facts of the particular case — the gist of the action. A jury trial must be granted where the gist of the action is legal, where the action is in reality cognizable at law.'" (*Ibid.*) In the *One 1941 Chevrolet Coupe* decision, for example, the court held that the gist of the action at issue in that case — a civil lawsuit by the government seeking forfeiture of an automobile that was allegedly used to illegally transport a prohibited drug — was legal because at common law a similar cause of action for forfeiture of otherwise lawful property that was allegedly used for unlawful purposes was triable by a jury in a court of law. The court ruled that the fact that the statutory provision authorizing the cause of action designated the forfeiture action as a "'special proceeding'" did not change the legal nature of the action.

... In a case like *One 1941 Chevrolet Coupe* that involves a single cause of action that at common law in 1850 was triable only by a jury, or conversely a case involving a single cause of action that at common law was triable only by the court (see, e.g., *People v. Englebrecht* (2001) 88 Cal.App.4th 1236, 1245 [action for injunctive relief to abate a nuisance]), the determination whether the gist of the action in question is legal or equitable is relatively straightforward. When a case involves multiple causes of action or multiple issues, some of which are legal in nature and would have been triable by a jury at common law and some of which are equitable in nature and would have been triable by the court at common law, the analysis is somewhat more complex.

B. Cases Involving Severable Legal and Equitable Issues

When the legal and equitable causes of action or issues presented in a case are severable, past California decisions establish that a party retains the right to a jury trial of the severable legal issues and a court trial of the severable equitable issues. ...

At the same time, California decisions have also repeatedly held that when severable legal and equitable causes of action or issues are present in a single proceeding, the trial court generally has authority to determine in what order the matters should be heard, and if the equitable issue is tried by the court first and if the court's resolution of that issue determines a matter that would otherwise be resolved by a jury with regard to the legal claim or issue, the court's resolution of the matter will generally be binding and may leave nothing for a jury to resolve. (See, e.g., *Raedeke v. Gibraltar Sav. & Loan Assn.* (1974) 10 Cal.3d 665, 671 (*Raedeke*) ["It is well established that, in a case involving both legal and equitable issues, the trial court may proceed to try the equitable issues first, without a jury . . . , and that if the court's determination of those issues is also dispositive of the legal issues, nothing further remains to be tried by a jury"].) And although a trial court retains discretion regarding the order in which the issues should be tried, the governing California cases express a preference that the equitable issues be tried first. This general "equity first preference" is a long standing feature of California law and has always been viewed as fully compatible with the right to jury trial embodied in the California Constitution.

C. Cases Involving Nonseverable Legal and Equitable Issues

Unlike proceedings in which multiple legal and equitable causes or issues are severable, when a cause of action involves legal and equitable aspects that are not severable California decisions have relied upon "the gist of the action" standard in determining whether the action should be considered legal or equitable for purposes of the constitutional jury trial issue. (See, e.g., *C & K Engineering, supra,* 23 Cal.3d 1, 9–11 [in action seeking damages for breach of contract ("in form an action at law") but relying solely on "the equitable doctrine of promissory estoppel," court concluded "[t]he 'gist' of such an action is equitable"]; *Central Laborers' Pension Fund v. McAfee, Inc.* (2017) 17 Cal.App.5th 292, 344–350 [in action by shareholders seeking money damages for breach of corporate directors' and officers' breach of fiduciary duty, court concluded that the gist of the action was equitable]. In our decision in *C & K Engineering,* we noted that "[a]lthough we have said that 'the legal or equitable nature of a cause of action ordinarily is determined by the mode of relief to be afforded . . . ,' the prayer for relief in a particular case is not conclusive" and "'[t]he fact that damages is one of a full range of possible remedies does not guarantee . . . the right to a jury.'" (*C & K Engineering,* at p. 9.) . . .

D. Application of Constitutional Principles to UCL and FAL Actions

As we shall explain, in light of the particular nature of the civil causes of action authorized by the UCL and FAL, we conclude that the gist of a civil action under the UCL and FAL is equitable rather than legal in nature. Such causes of action are equitable either when brought by a private party seeking only an injunction, restitution, or other equitable relief or when brought by the Attorney General, a district attorney, or other governmental official seeking not only injunctive relief and restitution but also civil penalties. Accordingly, we conclude that there is no right to a jury trial in such actions under the California Constitution.

To begin with, the statutory causes of action established by the UCL and FAL are clearly not of like nature or of the same class as any common law right of action. . . . The UCL and FAL were enacted for the specific purpose of creating new rights and remedies that were not available at common law. The statutes deliberately broaden the types of business practices that can properly be found to constitute unfair competition, and eliminate a number of elements that were required in common law actions for fraud. The statutes explicitly authorize government officials and injured private individuals to obtain injunctive relief to prevent a business from continuing to use the practice to the detriment of other consumers and to obtain restitution and other clearly equitable relief. (Bus & Prof. Code, §§ 17203, 17204.) Such causes of action for unfair competition that authorize injunctive relief against unfair or deceptive business practices had no close or analogous counterpart at common law. . . .

Accordingly, in the absence of a comparable common law counterpart, in deciding whether there is a right to a jury trial under the California Constitution, we must look to the statutory scheme as a whole to determine whether the gist of a cause of action under the UCL or the FAL seeking both injunctive relief and civil penalties is legal or equitable. . . .

With respect to the application of the gist of the action standard, our independent analysis of the UCL and FAL causes of action as a whole convinces us that the gist of the civil causes of action authorized by the UCL and FAL must properly be considered equitable, rather than legal, in nature.

To begin with, the bulk of the remedies provided for in the statutes — injunctive relief, restitution, and other clearly equitable remedies such as the appointment of a receiver (see Bus. & Prof. Code, §§ 17203, 17535) — are clearly equitable in nature. As the legislative history of both the UCL and FAL make clear, the primary objective of both statutes is preventive, authorizing the exercise of broad equitable authority to protect consumers from unfair or deceptive business practices and advertising.

Second, although the statutes also authorize in actions brought by the Attorney General, a district attorney, or other government officials (but not private parties), the imposition of civil penalties — a type of remedy that in some contexts is properly considered legal in nature — the UCL and FAL statutes specify that in assessing the amount of the civil penalty to be imposed under these statutes, the court is afforded broad discretion to consider a nonexclusive list of factors that include the relative seriousness of the defendant's conduct and the potential deterrent effect of such penalties, the type of qualitative evaluation and weighing of a variety of factors that is typically undertaken by a court and not a jury. (Bus. & Prof. Code, §§ 17206, 17536.) Notably, the civil penalties that may be awarded under the UCL and FAL, unlike the classic legal remedy of damages, are noncompensatory in nature; they require no showing of actual harm to consumers and are not based on the amount of losses incurred by the targets of unfair practices or misleading advertising. . . .

Finally, as discussed above, the expansive and broadly worded substantive standards that are to be applied in determining whether a challenged business practice or advertising is properly considered violative of the UCL or FAL call for the exercise of the flexibility and judicial expertise and experience that was traditionally applied by a court of equity. Particularly in light of the equitable nature of the substantive standards that apply in UCL and FAL actions — both in actions brought by private parties and by government officials — we conclude that the gist of the civil causes of action authorized by the UCL and FAL must properly be considered equitable in nature. Accordingly, we conclude that under the California Constitution, there is no right to a jury trial in a cause of action under the UCL and FAL, including when the action is brought by a government official and seeks both injunctive relief and civil penalties. . . .

V. Conclusion

For the reasons set forth above, we conclude that in causes of action under the UCL or FAL seeking injunctive relief and civil penalties, the gist of the actions is equitable, and there is no right to a jury trial in such actions under California law either as a statutory or constitutional matter. Given the specific attributes of the UCL and FAL discussed above, we have no occasion to determine whether there is a right to a jury trial in other settings in which the government seeks injunctive relief and civil penalties under other statutes authorizing those remedies.

The judgment of the Court of Appeal, holding that Nationwide has a right to a jury trial under the California Constitution in such actions, is reversed and the matter is remanded to the Court of Appeal for further proceedings consistent with this opinion.

* * *

Dairy Queen, Inc. v. Wood
United States Supreme Court
369 U.S. 469 (1962)

Mr. Justice BLACK delivered the opinion of the Court.

The United States District Court for the Eastern District of Pennsylvania granted a motion to strike petitioner's demand for a trial by jury in an action now pending before it on the alternative grounds that either the action was 'purely equitable' or, if not purely equitable, whatever legal issues that were raised were 'incidental' to equitable issues, and, in either case, no right to trial by jury existed. The petitioner then sought mandamus in the Court of Appeals for the Third Circuit to compel the district judge to vacate this order. When that court denied this request without opinion, we granted certiorari because the action of the Court of Appeals seemed inconsistent with protections already clearly recognized for the important constitutional right to trial by jury in our previous decisions.

At the outset, we may dispose of one of the grounds upon which the trial court acted in striking the demand for trial by jury — that based upon the view that the right to trial by jury may be lost as to legal issues where those issues are characterized as 'incidental' to equitable issues — for our previous decisions make it plain that no such rule may be applied in the federal courts. In *Scott v. Neely*, decided in 1891, this Court held that a court of equity could not even take jurisdiction of a suit 'in which a claim properly cognizable only at law is united in the same pleadings with a claim for equitable relief.' That holding, which was based upon both the historical separation between law and equity and the duty of the Court to insure 'that the right to a trial by a jury in the legal action may be preserved intact,' created considerable inconvenience in that it necessitated two separate trials in the same case whenever that case contained both legal and equitable claims.

Consequently, when the procedure in the federal courts was modernized by the adoption of the Federal Rules of Civil Procedure in 1938, 28 U.S.C.A., it was deemed advisable to abandon that part of the holding of *Scott v. Neely* which rested upon the separation of law and equity and to permit the joinder of legal and equitable claims in a single action. Thus Rule 18(a) provides that a plaintiff 'may join either as independent or as alternate claims as many claims either legal or equitable or both as he may have against an opposing party.' And Rule 18(b) provides: 'Whenever a claim is one heretofore cognizable only after another claim has been prosecuted to a conclusion, the two claims may be joined in a single action; but the court shall grant relief in that action only in accordance with the relative substantive rights of the parties. In particular, a plaintiff may state a claim for money and a claim to have set aside a conveyance fraudulent as to him, without first having obtained a judgment establishing the claim for money.'

The Federal Rules did not, however, purport to change the basic holding of *Scott v. Neely* that the right to trial by jury of legal claims must be preserved. Quite the contrary, Rule 38(a) expressly reaffirms that constitutional principle, declaring: 'The right of trial by jury as declared by the Seventh Amendment to the Constitution or as given by a statute of the United States shall be preserved to the parties inviolate.' Nonetheless, after the adoption of the Federal Rules, attempts were made indirectly to undercut that right by having federal courts in which cases involving both legal and equitable claims were filed decide the equitable claim first. The result of this procedure in those cases in which it was followed was that any issue common to both the legal and equitable claims was finally determined by the court and the party seeking trial by jury on the legal claim was deprived of that right as to these common issues. This procedure finally came before us in *Beacon Theatres, Inc. v. Westover*, a case which, like this one, arose from the denial of a petition for mandamus to compel a district judge to vacate his order striking a demand for trial by jury.

Our decision reversing that case not only emphasizes the responsibility of the Federal Courts of Appeals to grant mandamus where necessary to protect the constitutional right to trial by jury but also limits the issues open for determination here by defining the protection to which that right is entitled in cases involving both legal and equitable claims. The holding in *Beacon Theatres* was that where both legal and equitable issues are presented in a single case, 'only under the most imperative circumstances, circumstances which in view of the flexible procedures of the Federal Rules we cannot now anticipate, can the right to a jury trial of legal issues be lost through prior determination of equitable claims.' That holding, of course, applies whether the trial judge chooses to characterize the legal issues presented as 'incidental' to equitable issues or not. Consequently, in a case such as this where there cannot even be a contention of such 'imperative circumstances,' Beacon Theatres requires that any legal issues for which a trial by jury is timely and properly demanded be submitted to a jury. There being no question of the timeliness or correctness of the demand involved here, the sole question which we must decide is whether the action now pending before the District Court contains legal issues.

The District Court proceeding arises out of a controversy between petitioner and the respondent owners of the trademark 'DAIRY QUEEN' with regard to a written licensing contract made by them in December 1949, under which petitioner agreed to pay some $150,000 for the exclusive right to use that trademark in certain portions of Pennsylvania. The terms of the contract provided for a small initial payment with the remaining payments to be made at the rate of 50% of all amounts received by petitioner on sales and franchises to deal with the trademark and, in order to make certain that the $150,000 payment would be completed within a specified period of time, further provided for minimum annual payments regardless of petitioner's receipts. In August 1960, the respondents wrote petitioner a letter in which they claimed that petitioner had committed 'a material breach of that contract' by defaulting on the contract's payment provisions and notified petitioner of the termination of the contract and the cancellation of petitioner's right to use the trademark unless this claimed default was remedied immediately. When petitioner continued to deal with the trademark despite the notice of termination, the respondents brought an action based upon their view that a material breach of contract had occurred.

The complaint filed in the District Court alleged, among other things, that petitioner had 'ceased paying as required in the contract;' that the default 'under the said contract (was) in excess of $60,000.000;' that this default constituted a 'material breach' of that contract; that petitioner had been notified by letter that its failure to pay as alleged made it guilty of a material breach of contract which if not 'cured' would result in an immediate cancellation of the contract; that the breach had not been cured but that petitioner was contesting the cancellation and continuing to conduct business as an authorized dealer; that to continue such business after the cancellation of the contract constituted an infringement of the respondents' trademark; that petitioner's financial condition was unstable; and that because of the foregoing allegations, respondents were threatened with irreparable injury for which they had no adequate remedy at law. The complaint then prayed for both temporary and permanent relief, including: (1) temporary and permanent injunctions to restrain petitioner from any future use of or dealing in the franchise and the trademark; (2) an accounting to determine the exact amount of money owing by petitioner and a judgment for that amount; and (3) an injunction pending accounting to prevent petitioner from collecting any money from 'Dairy Queen' stores in the territory. . . .

Petitioner's contention, as set forth in its petition for mandamus to the Court of Appeals and reiterated in its briefs before this Court, is that insofar as the complaint requests a money judgment it presents a claim which is unquestionably legal. We agree with that contention. The most natural construction of the respondents' claim for a money judgment would seem to be that it is a claim that they are entitled to recover whatever was owed them under the contract as of the date of its purported termination plus damages for infringement of their trademark since that date. Alternatively, the complaint could be construed to set forth a full claim based upon both of these theories — that is, a claim that the respondents were entitled to recover both the debt due under the contract and damages for trademark infringement for the entire period of the alleged breach including that before the termination of the contract. Or it might possibly be construed to set forth a claim for recovery based completely on either one of these two theories — that is, a claim based solely upon the contract for the entire period both before and after the attempted termination on the theory that the termination, having been ignored, was of no consequence, or a claim based solely upon the charge of infringement on the theory that the contract, having been breached, could not be used as a defense to an infringement action even for the period prior to its termination. We find it unnecessary to resolve this ambiguity in the respondents' complaint because we think it plain that their claim for a money judgment is a claim wholly legal in its nature however the complaint is construed. As an action on a debt allegedly due under a contract, it would be difficult to conceive of an action of a more traditionally legal character. And as an action for damages based upon a charge of trademark infringement, it would be no less subject to cognizance by a court of law.

The respondents' contention that this money claim is 'purely equitable' is based primarily upon the fact that their complaint is cast in terms of an 'accounting,' rather than in terms of an action for 'debt' or 'damages.' But the constitutional right to trial by jury cannot be made to depend upon the choice of words used in the pleadings. The necessary prerequisite to the right to maintain a suit for an equitable accounting, like all other equitable remedies, is, as we pointed out in Beacon Theatres, the absence of an adequate remedy at law. Consequently, in order to maintain such a suit on a cause of action cognizable at law, as this one is, the plaintiff must be able to show that the 'accounts between the parties' are of such a 'complicated nature' that only a court of equity can satisfactorily unravel them. In view of the powers given to District Courts by Federal Rule of Civil Procedure 53(b) to appoint masters to assist the jury in those exceptional cases where the legal issues are too complicated for the jury adequately to handle alone, the burden of such a showing is considerably increased and it will indeed be a rare case in which it can be met. But be that as it may, this is certainly not such a case. A jury, under proper instructions from the court, could readily determine the recovery, if any, to be had here, whether the theory finally settled upon is that of breach of contract, that of trademark infringement, or any combination of the two. The legal remedy cannot be characterized as inadequate merely because the measure of damages may necessitate a look into petitioner's business records.

... We conclude therefore that the district judge erred in refusing to grant petitioner's demand for a trial by jury on the factual issues related to the question of whether there has been a breach of contract. Since these issues are common with those upon which respondents' claim to equitable relief is based, the legal claims involved in the action must be determined prior to any final court determination of respondents' equitable claims. The Court of Appeals should have corrected the error of the district judge by granting the petition for mandamus. The judgment is therefore reversed and the cause remanded for further proceedings consistent with this opinion.

Reversed and remanded.

Mr. Justice HARLAN, whom Mr. Justice DOUGLAS joins, concurring.

I am disposed to accept the view, strongly pressed at the bar, that this complaint seeks an accounting for alleged trademark infringement, rather than contract damages. Even though this leaves the complaint as formally asking only for equitable relief, this does not end the inquiry. The fact that an 'accounting' is sought is not of itself dispositive of the jury trial issue. To render this aspect of the complaint truly 'equitable' it must appear that the substantive claim is one cognizable only in equity or that the 'accounts between the parties' are of such a 'complicated nature' that they can be satisfactorily unraveled only by a court of equity. *Kirby v. Lake Shore & Michigan Southern R. Co.*, 120 U.S. 130, 134. See 5 Moore, Federal Practice (1951), 198–202. It is manifest from the face of the complaint that the 'accounting' sought in this instance is not of either variety. A jury, under proper instructions from the court, could readily calculate the damages flowing from this alleged trademark infringement, just as courts of law often do in copyright and patent cases. Cf., e.g., *Hartell v. Tilghman*, 99 U.S. 547, 555.

Consequently what is involved in this case is nothing more than a joinder in one complaint of prayers for both legal and equitable relief. In such circumstances, under principles long since established, the petitioner cannot be deprived of his constitutional right to a jury trial on the 'legal' claim contained in the complaint.

On this basis I concur in the judgment of the Court.

* * *

Problem 67

In federal cases, there is a constitutional right to a jury trial for claims seeking a legal remedy. There is no right to have a jury determine claims for equitable relief. A case with both kinds of claims can present procedural challenges for the trial court. Did the judge make an appropriate procedural ruling in the trial described below?

A homeowner sues a bank in federal court for wrongful foreclosure, alleging a single cause of action for loan fraud. The foreclosure sale is scheduled to happen within a few months. The homeowner seeks injunctive relief to stop the sale and damages for fraud. Given the time sensitive nature of the case, the trial judge announces the following procedure: "I'm going to fast-track this case so we can find out whether an injunction is warranted before it's too late. I know the plaintiff has requested a jury trial, but there is no right to have a jury decide the equitable claim for an injunction; she only has the right to a jury for the legal claim for damages. So we will bifurcate this trial. We'll have a bench trial where I will decide whether the plaintiff has proven the cause of action for loan fraud. If she has, I'll issue the injunction. And then if and when she's proven the loan fraud claim, we can bring in a jury to decide what damages are appropriate."

The homeowner objects to that procedure and asks for a jury to decide the whole case, but the court overrules the objection and proceeds with a bifurcated trial. After the evidence has been presented in the first phase, the judge concludes the homeowner has not presented sufficient evidence to prove loan fraud and therefore denies the request for an injunction. And since the homeowner has not proven her only cause of action, the court enters judgment for the bank, ending the case.

in federal court

Index